A HISTORY *of* ENGLISH AND IRISH GLASS

by

W. A. THORPE

of The Victoria and Albert Museum

VOLUME ONE

HOLLAND PRESS

This facsimile edition was printed in 1969

C 6069786 5

Printed in Germany

A HISTORY of ENGLISH AND IRISH GLASS

BERNARDO RACKHAM
QVI HVIVS SINGVLA GENERIS COGNOVIT
ET
HERBERTO READ
QVI SVB SPECIE VIDET VNIVERSI
REDDO DENIQVE LIBELLVM

PREFACE

THIS book is designed as a history of fine glass in England and Ireland from the 13th century until the second quarter of the 19th century. At several points the subject impinges on bottle glass and plate glass, but even economically these manufactures are distinct ; moreover, they are work, not art. I hope I am wrong to stop short about the year 1845. The 19th century, which destroyed handicraft, discovered technology, but it did not learn to use it in the service of design. To do so is the business of the age in which we live. By what is called the industrial revolution fine glassmaking has been less affected than most arts. It may call in chemistry to make a good metal, but it remains in essence a handicraft. That is why the present book ends with some illustrations of what modern glassmaking can do if it only gives up the stale repetitions of antiquarian sentiment and shows some sympathy with the will to form of its own time. The limits of the book may seem arbitrary. Neri (1611) used the term " art of glass," and what he meant was a skilful undertaking ; but I think the name may be re-filled by a technique which uses chemistry and manipulation with a view to design. Glass for Neri was " made by art " ; and so are glasses. It is a proud phrase. It implies that we are all of us astonishing creatures ; that the potter, and not the pot, makes the shape of the pot ; and that the works of man, though they may be less important than the works of God, are considerably more interesting. " Made by art " is well thought too, for sculpture or painting as well as for glasses, and a clean take-off for an art criticism that is still encumbered with cheap mysticism or trumpery metaphysics.

Three factors have determined English glass—technique, economy, design. I have tried to show how these factors have operated one upon another, and so to present my subject as the development of an economic style. A historian is at the mercy of his sources. It would be too much to hope that we know most of this or that item because, when it happened, it was most worthy of remembrance ; and there is thus a danger of giving emphasis to matters of which we are most copiously informed. But there is not much use for history which does not try to estimate as well as to record, and I should be glad to think that I had kept the balance. In political history we have at least some guide in contemporary reputation, but when the story of an art is to be pieced together from the most casual allusions the determining forces do not easily appear. The literary sources provide some chronological data, made public by Mr. Buckley, but technique and taxation are the matters of which they speak most freely. And on the whole, I think they are right. For design we must look to the glasses themselves. There, too, the bias of survival has not, I think, been unjust. We should not miss Mansell glasses if we had them ; what matters is the flint baluster.

PREFACE

The illustrations have been selected with no special policy, but for interest: æsthetic, technical, or documentary. Glasses have not been rejected because they have been published before, but the majority of the illustrations now appear for the first time. Neither in the text nor in the illustrations have I given special attention to glasses with engraving of historical interest. They belong to the byways of social history, rather than to the art of glass, and by Sir John Risley, Mr. Grant Francis, and others they have been adequately treated elsewhere. An attempt has been made to give a date to every specimen. From the invention of flint-glass until the end of the 18th century there are a number of landmarks and glasses connected with them : the Ravenscroft specimens (1676–8), the accession of George I (1714), the first Jacobite Rising (1715), the Excise Act, and the second Jacobite Rising (1745), the Seven Years War (1756–63), the beginnings of classicalism (c. 1770), and the Napoleonic wars. On form and technique alone some chronological development can be traced, and if this is spaced out between the fixed points of reference and certain dated glasses or silver analogies which come to our aid, it is, I think, possible to date most glasses within ten years, and a good many as near as five. In calculating the dates of glasses or of items of style, I have considered the vogue of a particular type rather than its range. In the history of taste vogue, not range, is the important thing, and it may be worth remark that the vogue of an item is much nearer in time to its inception than to its disappearance. Vogues are short where they have no other sanction than fashion, and in 18th-century glass I doubt whether they were ever much longer than ten years ; dealers and manufacturers must keep their public lively. Glasses especially are frangible, and Hartshorne was right in his epigraph " tout passe, tout casse." The only exceptions are luxury pieces which cost much and were well treated, and some types made for a special market, e.g. the tall-stemmed glasses made at Newcastle for the Dutch market, which changed little in forty years.

I have to thank the authorities of the British Museum (Department of Ceramics), the Royal Albert Memorial Museum, Exeter, the Guildhall Museum, the London Museum, the Northampton Museum, the Saffron Walden Museum, and the Victoria and Albert Museum (Department of Ceramics) for allowing me to reproduce glasses in their collections. For like permissions I am indebted to the following private owners and collectors, several of whom have kindly allowed me to use their collections for purposes of study: Mrs. Applewhaite Abbott, Mr. Robert Alexander, Mr. John M. Bacon, Mr. George F. Berney, Mr. Joseph Bles, Dr. Tancred Borenius, Mr. Henry Brown, Mr. Wilfred Buckley, C.B.E., Mr. Arthur Churchill, Mr. Hamilton Clements, Mr. A. O. Curle, Mr. Cecil Davis, Lady Davy, Mrs. Dickson, Mr. Robert Frank, Mr. H. Helliwell, Mr. Henry Holford, The Worshipful Company of Ironmongers, Mr. H. R. P. Lomas, Mrs. Hamish Miles,

PREFACE

Col. R. F. Ratcliff, C.M.G., Sir John S. Risley, K.C.M.G., C.B., K.C., Mr. William Roscoe, Mr. M. S. Dudley Westropp, Mr. S. D. Winkworth, Mr. W. W. Winkworth. Messrs. J. and L. Lobmeyr of Vienna and the Orrefors Glass Company of Stockholm were good enough to supply me with photographs of glasses made by them, which I wished to illustrate. Lastly, I would mention the late C. Kirkby Mason, who always showed me great kindness, and whose glass I often visited. His collection, which was without rival for the 17th century, has now been dispersed, but the specimens which I illustrate from it may stand more appropriately in his name ; and I would therefore ask the indulgence of any who have subsequently purchased them.

My best thanks are due to Mr. M. S. Dudley Westropp of Dublin for allowing me to examine the Gatchell Papers in his possession, and to The Worshipful Company of Glass Sellers of London, through their Clerk, Mr. G. J. Leckie, for leaving me in their offices in the evening to take notes from their Court Minutes and their legal documents. Mrs. H. C. Halahan of Chiddingfold kindly helped me with information of Sussex glassmaking. Mr. John M. Bacon, Mr. A. J. Kiddell, and Mr. W. W. Winkworth have communicated facts to me. Several correspondents who have helped me are recorded in the proper places. The drawings of cut-glass design are by Mr. J. Gower Parks; for some other of the drawings I am indebted to my brother, Mr. J. K. Thorpe. I have a great obligation to Mr. Francis Buckley for notes he has sent me, and especially for his invaluable researches in 18th-century newspapers without which this book could not have been written. The bibliography will show my debt. Finally, I would express my most grateful thanks to my colleagues Mr. Bernard Rackham and Mr. Herbert Read for all that I have learnt from their example. Their book on *English Pottery* is the happiest union of aposteriori and apriori methods and a notable contribution to art history. I do not know of a better model, and to them I inscribe this platonic copy.

May, 1929.

W. A. THORPE.

CONTENTS

[xi]

CONTENTS

CONTENTS

CONTENTS

LIST OF ILLUSTRATIONS TO VOLUME ONE

COLOUR PLATE

FIGURES IN THE TEXT

CHAPTER I

The Principles of Technique

But when I pry'd into the Materials and observed the Furnaces, the Transmutations, the Liquefactions, the Transubstantiations that are incident to this art, my Thoughts were raised to a higher Speculation.

JAMES HOWELL, *Familiar Letters* (1650).

§1. THE EXCELLENCE OF A GLASS VESSEL

PURE art is sensitive without being anxious ; it feels but it does not care, and it therefore moves towards a condition which may be described as decoration. Poet and painter work in images, and the image is beset on two sides. It has contact on one side with an actual experience of the artist ; for the artist, being sensitive to life as well as sensitive in the use of his medium, cannot have experiences which are not part of himself. The nature of his experience, and therefore the nature of his image, will depend on his own disposition, beliefs, feelings. His experience is always an *interested* experience, and the interest is apt to pass over from his having of the experience to his handling of the images which accrue from it. The artist is pure artist in so far as he keeps his interest out of his art, but so far also is he mere artist. The image is beset on the later side by the material which the artist happens to employ, words, colour, clay, metal, and in being translated into concreteness it will suffer change. Thus images, which are the medium of all artists, are liable to modification both by the experience in which they begin and the material in which they have issue. These three stages, experience, image, and what we may call contact, enter into one another and in the artistic act become one. The pure artist differs from the assertive artist in that he deals serenely with his images as items for his construction. He handles them from a position of neutrality, and shuts off the interested experience in which they have their start.

The glassmaker, who is a type of the useful artist, also works with images, but what precedes them is not an interested experience but an intention or programme which orders that his viscous manipulations, his images of what may be done with glass, shall occur within the limits of a serviceable form. His image, therefore, is only related on one side : it may be changed by contact with a material, but it does not arise in a human experience, and it is in no sense a symbol referring to something other than and prior to itself. The glassmaker, therefore, has no literary means of revealing sentiment or stating a belief, but that does not mean that his art is inarticulate. The mere forms which he creates are more reserved in their communications than the hewn declaration of a statue or the bright myths of painting, and since he works in a very private tradition the themes and motives of the other arts seldom intrude upon him. Yet the glassmaker has his own language of form and its grammar of technique, and by it he may confess himself, his country, his epoch, with scarcely less precision than the painter or the poet. For he is colloquial in his utterance as well as reticent, and the idioms of his thinking most directly become the idioms of his glass. Idioms of form and treatment in glass are sentiment expressing itself without the aid of representation and in defiance of a programme, and glasses differ as much in idiom as a Gothic sculpture of the 14th century differs in "feeling" from a statue of the Renaissance. In idioms the glassmaker goes outside his formal duty and contributes from feeling or fancy some symptom of his character, or his epoch or his race.

The Venetian tradition was to European glassmaking what Latin was to European speech. It provided most nations, and even those with an independent tradition like Germany, with a common basis for the art of glass. The nations of Europe made their own languages of form, which were as distinct from Venetian as French and Italian were distinct from Latin ; but it is worth notice that the Teutonic nations were those who owed least both to Rome for their language and to Venice for their glass. English flint-glass considered as a language of form occupies a position midway between "teutonic" and "romance."

But a vessel has substance as well as form, and in the species of vessel with which we are concerned that substance is perhaps more delightful to the eye than any material compounded by man. Most glasses belong to the category of useful vessels, and if we are enquiring in what their excellence resides, we must consider the form of a glass as a vessel, and its character as a material. Each we shall find is modified by the other. Excellence of form in a glass vessel is determined by two conditions, fitness and beauty. If a glass is to be regarded as a vessel at all it must be convenient to some purpose of man. Just as a man may be so arrayed in garments that he is no longer a man but a clothes peg, so a vessel of glass if too delicately fashioned and tricked out in fineries passes from one category into another. It becomes not a vessel but an ornament. That is not necessarily a disparagement, for the glassmaker like any other artist may use his technique in a purely decorative convention. But glassmaking is primarily a useful art, and when the programme of the glassmaker is utilitarian any departure from it will mean a loss of effectiveness in his finished work ; for the usefulness of his work is one of the conditions of its *artistic* beauty.

Besides fitness there is also beauty of design ; and here perhaps we may find a true analogy in the representational arts, in which also design is the supreme condition of excellence. If we imagine a painter who, possessing all the apparatus of his art, yet had no world and no experience, his picture would be a simple coherence of forms or system of relations, and abstract in the sense that a figure in Euclid is abstract. He would indeed have full freedom of constructive design, but we could find no standard for judging his work except its internal coherence. But in life and fact this freedom is restricted by the existence of a world which must enter into the artist's experience and so into his painting. When this happens his picture takes content from life, and becomes in one degree or another representational. Thus we have at one end of the scale the painting of fidelity which, attempting to be more precise than experience, defeats its own end ; and at the other the painting of abstraction which will have no limitation and tries to dispense with experience altogether.

The arts of service to which the art of making vessels belongs, enjoy a like restriction on the impulse of creative design. It is imposed not by the irksome necessities of verisimilitude but by the dictate of fitness. As painting must make some compromise between design and the world, so in the vessel arts beauty and fitness discipline one another. When a jar, or a jug or bowl, seeks to transcend this limitation as painting seeks sometimes to transcend representation, it either falls into its own depravity or ceases to be itself. It either becomes a decoration or becomes a different art.

Yet within the terms of service there are many beautiful forms. The names we give to the vessels of common use are of functions rather than of shapes, and those functions are determined by climate or custom as they control the dietetic habits of man. But adequate to every function there is an infinity of shapes, and therefore this art of making a vessel will proceed by limitation and selection, and it will have issue in the seizure of a right possibility. Such a selective art gives a formal rhythm which surpasses the conditions of mere fitness, and by compelling the attention of taste establishes its claim to be beautiful. The taste of those who enjoy it is correlative to the mood in which the artist makes his selection. An equilibrium of interests is the condition under which he is able to capture his single possibility ; its occurrence gives him the temper of artist and makes the formal beauty of his vessel. On the other side his completed work focuses the interests of its respondents and becomes the occasion of an equilibrium which the artist had to discover for himself. The shape of a vessel is beautiful as other works of art are beautiful when it establishes such a harmony of interests in those who use or survey it.

But the artist of a vessel does not choose his possibility entirely in a void. His selection is aided by predispositions which give a direction to his research and make his vessel not merely an absolute rhythm but a revelation of himself. The evidence of such predispositions is plainest perhaps in the assertive arts, for these proceed from the more conscious processes of the mind ; but they do not cease to control the forms of serviceable rhythm or pure pattern, because those forms are not arranged as an experience. An artist's predispositions may have their roots in the character of a race, a nation, or a family, in a faith, a school, or even a fashion, but their appearance in art does not belong to any one faculty or function of the man's integrity. They are the whole man and often the forgotten man, and their declaration is a latent will by which the rhythms or characteristic movements of a mind are directly imparted to a given material. In the arts of service, therefore, or in non-representational decoration, there is a necessary correspondence between the chosen created form and the idiosyncrasies of thought. A psychology of art is likely some day to distinguish the types of cultural or racial consciousness and classify the *mere* forms in which they have their artistic expression ; but the fact which it will explore is already familiar. The formal rhythms of vessels are men's gestures concluded in a material, and they speak to familiars in the same way as shrugging shoulders or the wave of a hand. Gesticulation makes man aware of what is taking place in the mind of his fellow and enriches or eliminates the spoken word. In human intercourse we read such movements and infer the character of a person or a people. But the study of the vessels is a harder task, for here the gesture is divorced from its author and frozen into permanence for our observation. The most difficult task of connoisseurship is thus the interpretation of form, and the endeavour to return with it to the true source.

The excellence which we have been considering is the excellence of vessels as such, and we must now pass from the general to the particular, and consider vessels of glass ; for the material itself will contribute something to our canon. It is a substance of such beauty that ever since the Arabian shipwreck[1] it has had more eulogy than evaluation. The most solemn historians have been compelled to take notice of it ; its own Neri had a fine string of epithets and qualities, and even the laborious Johnson wove a period to record his admiration. It has had, too, many variations which have affected the excellence of the vessels for which they were used. It is manifest that the glass of the Egyptians, the glass of Venice, the glass of China, is capable of different beauties ; and we shall not attempt a common denominator, but proceed rather to the English variant, which is glass of lead ; and any conclusion we may reach will therefore be limited in its application to our present subject.

Glass of lead has aptitudes and propensities, but they do not become values or enter our canon until they have been brought into harmony

[1] Fama est appulsa nave mercatorum nitri cum sparsi per litus epulas pararent nec esset cortinis attolendis lapidum occasio glebas nitri e nave subdidisse. Quibus accensis permixta arena litoris translucentes novi liquoris fluxisse rivos et hanc fuisse originem vitri.—Pliny, *Hist. Nat.*, XXXVI. 65.

[4]

with one another and with the particular work that the artist has in hand. It is often said that the good artist exploits, and that an artist therefore *should* exploit, the capacities of his medium ; and the notion is sufficiently true to be a dangerous falsehood. It is of course obvious and fundamental that the medium makes one half of the character of its art. It does not make the whole ; and the theory that mediums should be given way to is a technical materialism, an artistic *laissez-faire.* The aptitudes of a medium are only *conditions* of an art, and it is a week-kneed and decrepit art that converts them into *forces,* and accepts their domination.

The aptitudes, therefore, of English metal must not be too liberally enumerated or unduly exalted ; and there are only three which may be described as values. English lead glass is *heavier* than that used in any other technique, and this character makes it more viscous in its plastic and heated state, thicker and stronger when it is grown cold. Thus it modified the frail and slender forms of Venice to which Englishmen had formerly adhered and became the chief determinant in the growth of English design. The artistic importance of early English glass lies in the absolute appropriateness of medium to design and of design to medium.

The second value of glass of lead is its *softness;* and this explains the second great age of English glass (*v.* Chap. VI), just as weight goes some way to explain the first. When the glyptic processes of Germany invaded this country in the first half of the 18th century the softness of the English metal had two contrary effects. Cutting and engraving were distinguished not in their technique but in their purpose, and the lead glasses prohibited the precision and finesse for which the harder soda glass of Germany had been appropriate ; at the same time it was favourable to heavy decorative cutting. Thus it happened that while English engraving had no serious artistic achievement, the cut-glass of the Anglo-Irish period became the envy of Europe.

The third value of the English glass, its capacity for holding the light, was enhanced by the first and supported the second. Glass, like water, has no colour but that of the light which plays upon it or the background in which it stands. The older techniques had aimed at complete transparency, and their glass is often blown so thin that it seems only a bodiless transmitter of the light. English glass, being thicker and sometimes less transparent, *retained* the light instead of transmitting it, and in virtue of this capacity it has a brilliance not matched in any other technique. It is only an æsthetic delight, but it supports so admirably the sobriety and grace of the design that it may be readily claimed as an artistic value. In glass of the early 18th century this aptitude of the metal is still kept in a decent restraint. Vessels are not made to exhibit their brilliance. They are made simply to be good vessels, and a due harmony of the art and its

[5]

medium is still maintained. Sixty years afterwards the cutting of Anglo-Irish glass becomes the final exploitation of this same aptitude, and in some sense the beginning of an artistic decline. Anglo-Irish cut-glass, like baroque architecture or Hellenistic sculpture, had its own genius, but it was, in fact, a decadence. Glassmakers had become so obsessed with the aptitudes of the lead metal that they ceased to be conditions of their art but forces which sought to control it. The art now became the slave of its medium, and vessels were made to exhibit those flashes and rever-berations of light which were fostered by elaborate cutting. Anglo-Irish glass is decadent not because it is cut, but in so far as the cutting seeks to exploit the medium rather than to enhance the vessel. The word decadence, moreover, is a description and not an impeachment. It indicates merely the closing of an evolutionary process which deprived the art of one set of values but put another set in its place. The second set were the values of sculpture. Strictly speaking a sculptured vessel is one in which the vessel is entirely hewn, and shape and decoration are not thought apart, but in the Anglo-Irish period there was the same co-ordination between glass-makers and glass-cutters that there was in the 17th century between the German glassmakers and the decorators whom they supplied. In the best cut-glass of the Anglo-Irish period the hyphen well indicates the complete unison of two arts, the making of a vessel and a species of glyptic. In the jug illustrated on Plate CXLII the cutting is not evidently adventitious, for the vessel's form is partly determined by it. A cutting in itself elaborate is there used to admirable effect without infringing either the design of the vessel or its utility. The wafer-seal on Plate CXXXVIII. 1 is of the same type, but here the artist was less limited by the exigencies of useful form, and his work, in so far as it is free from this interest, becomes an instance of " pure art " in glassmaking. At this period, too, the art of glass turned to those services in which the mere play of light became a utilitarian sanction—to chandeliers and girandoles and table ornaments. In this mode it supplied material for inde-pendent designers who built up many architectural pieces of great beauty (Plates CXXXVIII. 2, CXL, CXLI, CXLVII).

It is odd to find that Ruskin, who in modern times has some claim to be considered the founder of concrete æsthetics, entirely misunderstood the character of glass and succeeded in condemning Irish glass. He committed himself to a *laissez-faire* theory of art, and declared that " all cut-glass was barbarous " because it was a violation of the true character of the material : glass is by nature ductile, cutting does not exploit its ductility, and therefore glass treated in any other way than by blowing must offend every canon of art. It would be difficult to find any passage in which there are more false assumptions and more false logic. Ruskin did not realize first of all that glass has not one, but two, characters, and

neither is more " real " or more " natural " than the other ; it is soft in
its molten state and hard when it has been annealed. In the first state
it is susceptible to one set of processes : blowing, drawing, tooling and
the like, which we call plastic. In its hard state it can only be treated by
a second set of processes: cutting, engraving, stippling, scratching, etching,
which may be called collectively glyptic. If Ruskin had desired a warrant
for this second mode of treatment, he need only have made the most
elementary enquiry into the history of glassmaking from Roman times
until his own ; glyptic work in glass would hardly have persisted for two
thousand years if it had been foreign to the true nature of the material.
Ruskin, no doubt, was trying to say that in a vessel the important thing
is the design, and that a vessel of glass receives its design mainly from the
glass-blower with his pipe and his other tools. So far his argument was
sensible enough ; and we may even agree that a design strikes hardest
and stays longest when it is not interrupted by ornament. But Ruskin
made no distinction between the bad ornament which interrupts design
and the good ornament which supports it. He just disliked cutting, and
in attempting to justify his own taste on technical grounds he fell into the
error of inventing bad reasons for a simple preference which required no
explanation.

§2. MATERIALS

We may begin our account of technique with the substance which
becomes the glass artist's medium. The ingredients of the metal are of
three kinds: the body, the flux, and the auxiliaries used to clear or
colour the matter resulting from the fusion under heat of the first two.
The term glass in a general sense is applied to a hard or soft, brittle or
glutinous, transparent or opaque substance which results from the fusion
of a siliceous body with an active mineral solvent such as the alkalis,
earthy bases or metallic oxides.

A. SILICATE BODY

Silica is a stony substance found in a natural state in the form of flints,
pebbles, quartz, or sand, and when it is brought to a fluid state by combination with an alkali or an oxide under great heat, the molten metal
which results may be drawn, blown, moulded into hollow vessels ; and
these can be re-heated and adapted without losing their original shape.
Silica is abundantly distributed throughout the mineral world, and was
obtained by the Murano glassmakers in the form of small pebbles which
were brought for their use from the river valleys of Alpine Italy, especially
from the river bed of the Ticino, where they were found in great plenty
and purity. These stones are not apt for compounding with an alkali
until they have been reduced by repeated heating to a pulverine material

called frit. This process, which was known as calcination, and necessarily preceded the manufacture of the glass itself, is described with some nicety in Neri, Merret, Haudicquer de Blancourt, and the later English treatises of the 18th century which were derived from them ; for upon the fineness of the frit and its freedom from alien or impure matter the success of the manufacture largely depended. For a time flints were the English counterpart of the white quartz of the Venetians, and they continued in use until at the beginning of the 18th century they were quite superseded by a very superior white sand. Since they were found in most districts they were very cheap, and the expense of calcination did not enhance the cost beyond what the prevailing markets could bear. The glassmen selected flints for their clear black lustre, avoiding those where a yellowish appearance gave suspicion of iron, which might endanger the transparency of the metal. Appropriate flints being selected, it was necessary that they should undergo calcination. For this they were first dipped in water, and then placed in a furnace of moderate heat, where they remained till they were white through and through. The operator watched them as a cook watches cakes, and the length of the baking varied according to the heat of the furnace and the size of the stones. When they were done they were immediately plunged into water and so left till they were cold. By the time they were withdrawn from the water they were cracked and shivered in flakes and fragments and might easily be reduced to powder, but at times it was necessary to give the more obdurate pieces a second calcination. When the whole baking had been reduced by pounding to a fine sandy powder, it was ready to become an ingredient.

It is evident that the preparation of an artificial frit of this kind must have been inconvenient, and wherever the practice persisted in England during the 18th century there is reason to suppose that the frit[1] was purchased ready for use from persons who made the preparation of it their sole employment. But even before the end of the 17th century the calcination of flints had been superseded for the finer sorts of glass by the use of natural sand, which in certain districts was found in a state of refinement and required no further preliminary than simple rinsing and sifting. It afforded the glassmakers a ready-made frit. Dossie, writing in 1758, has an interesting passage which may with advantage be quoted here : " Flint glass is of the same general kind with what is in other places called crystal glass. It had this name from being originally made from calcined flints before the use of the white sand was understood, and though no flints are now used in its composition, it retains still the name. This kind differs, however, from the German and other crystal glass in being partly formed of lead, whereas the fluxing

---

[1] " Pulvereen " is mentioned in one of the petitions against the Excise Act of 1695, and was then imported. *Tracts Relating to Trade.* B.M. 816: M.: 12–136.

bodies employed for the others are only salts or arsenic, and in having a white sand (which, as is said before, appears to be fragments of crystal) for its body. Instead of which calcined flints, or the white river pebbles, are used for the crystal glass in other places; there being no sand of this kind of equal goodness out of England, as far as is hitherto known."[1] Some allowance must no doubt be made for our author's patriotic ignorance, for we know that even during the 18th century sand was employed by the French plate glass manufacturers of St. Gobain[2], and that at the present day perfectly good sand is obtained not merely at Fontainebleau, which has for some time been famous for it, but in Holland and Belgium also.[3] But as evidence for practice in fine glassmaking his verdict must stand.

It is important in glassmaking that the frit should be pure, and although theoretically it does not matter from what materials it is prepared, the chances of a good clear metal are greatest where the least elimination of impurities is required. We know how important the pure white quartz of the Alpine valleys was to the Venetians, and Dossie was probably right in thinking that English glass in fact owed something of its peculiar quality to the sand no less than to the lead of which it was composed. In the technical manuals which were published at intervals during the 18th century, the mention of names either of places or of people is sufficiently rare; but throughout them all there is a constant emphasis upon the sand found at Maidstone, Woolwich, Alum Bay in the Isle of Wight, and most important of all, at King's Lynn in Norfolk, and from those centres distributed to the glasshouses throughout the country. It is true enough that at only one of these places (Lynn) did a glasshouse exist; but if we remember how often in the early history of English glassmaking the locality of glasshouses was determined by the neighbourhood of some convenient material such as the woods of Chiddingfold, or Buckholt, or Drumfenning, or the clays of Stourbridge, the fact is itself sufficient proof that the distribution of the English glassmakers was already fixed long before sand superseded flint in their technique. The presence of only one glasshouse on a sandbed is not therefore surprising. But in the middle of the 18th century, when transport was neither easy nor rapid, and the temptation to fall back upon local material the greater in consequence, it cannot have been without very good reason that Lynn sand found its way all over England and even to Ireland.[4]

---

[1] Dossie (R.), *Handmaid to the Arts* (1758) *s.v.* glass; *cf. infra*, p. 148, for possible continental attempts to imitate English *flint*-glass.

[2] Chambers (E.), *Cyclopedia*, ed. 1788, *s.v.* glass.

[3] Marson (P.), *Glass and Glass Manufacture* (1918), p. 5.

[4] There are frequent notices of Lynn sand being imported in the old Waterford newspapers. Westropp (M.S.W.), *Irish Glass*, 1920, pp. 168-9.

B. FLUXES

To fluxes, or solvents, we now pass. Ever since glass was first manufactured the archetype has always been the native rock crystal which is pure silica. The alchemy of glass sought to discover how the imperfect silica of flint or sand might be so transmuted as to resemble the natural crystal, and yet might be susceptible of fusion and pass during cooling through a viscous state in which it could be plastically treated so as to become a vessel. In that process the blow-pipe does for the molten metal what the potter's wheel does for his clay. The alkalis used in making glass are the carbonates of soda or of potash, and during the progress of fusion the carbonic acid of these salts is dissipated, and the alkali unites with the silica. It is the use of one or other of these alkalis that determines the two great technical traditions which before the invention of glass of lead divided European glass between them.

In the passage of history they appear to belong respectively to the Eastern and to the Western elements in European culture, but they really proceed from geographical rather than from cultural influences. The first, or soda tradition, belongs to the sea and to the south ; that is, it makes its first appearance round the Mediterranean sea-board, where soda in one form or another is readily obtainable. It includes the glass of Phœnicia, Syria, Arabia, most of the glass made in Roman times, and finally the technique which Venice herself derived from the near East and reluctantly disseminated through northern and western Europe. It is difficult for us who have lost the wonder of little things, with whom glass has passed into a flat familiarity, to recover for ourselves the ancient joy of so strange and beautiful a substance, or the reverence accorded to those who had the secret of its manufacture. That the eyes of antiquity, no less than the eyes of the Middle Ages, could not contemplate glass without excitement is sufficiently evident from the fact that a story was invented to explain how it, like fire or trouble, came into the world. The legend transmitted to us by the elder Pliny[1], with which all children are familiar, has none of the magic of myth, and although its setting—a desert place by the sea—is good enough for anything, its Prometheus is only a band of shipwrecked merchants. But of its analytical, as distinct from its historical, truth there can be little doubt, and it may be taken as proof that the soda flux employed in antiquity by glassmakers of what one may call by a Venetian analogy, *façon de Tyr*, was derived from the natron deposits of Egypt, Syria, Tripoli, and Arabia, rather than from the lixiviated ashes which were known to the trade of later times as *barilla* and *rochetta*. But when in the 11th and 12th centuries Venice brought back from the East the sovereign mantle which had slipped from Tyrian shoulders

---

[1] Pliny, *Hist. Nat.*, XXXVI. 65 ; *cf.* XXXVI, 43–47, and Dillon, *Glass*, p. 76 *sq.*

it was probably from vegetable ashes rather than from natron that her soda was extracted. The maritime plants providing the ashes grew in salt marshes by the sea, and include various species of Salsola, Chenopodium, Salicarnia, of the general order of Chenopodiaceæ, which were vaguely called *kali* by Neri.[1] These ashes had the name *rochetta* when they were brought from the Levant, but the purest kind was produced in Spain, plant and ashes being called indifferently *barilla*. Both were in the 16th century used by the Venetians, and the introduction of barilla into England about 1621 was, coal fuel excepted, the chief innovation that the English technique owed to Sir Robert Mansell. His traveller, James Howell, writing to him from Spain in 1621, describes its preparation in a passage which will bear quoting again : " I am now (thanks be to God) come to Alicant, the chief rendezvous I aymed at in Spain, for I am to send hence a commodity called Barilla to Sir Robert Mansell, for making of Crystall-Glasse, and I have treated with Signor Andriotti, a Genoa merchant, for a good round parcell of it, to the value of 2000 pound, by letters of credit from Master Richant and upon his credit I might have taken many thousand pounds more, he is so well known in the kingdom of Valencia. This Barilla is a strange kind of vegetable, and it grows nowhere upon the surface of the Earth, in that perfection as here. The Venetians have it hence, and it is a commodity whereby this Maritime Town doth partly subsist, for it is an ingredient that goes to the making of the best Castile Soap. It grows thus : 'tis a round thick Earthy shrub that bears berries like Barbaries, but 'twixt blue and green, it lies close to the ground and when it is ripe they dig it up by the roots, and put it together in Cocks, wher they leave it dry many days like Hey, then they make a pit of a fathom deep in the earth and with an instrument like one of our prongs they take the Tuffs and put fire to them and when the flame comes to the berries they melt and come into an Azure Liquor and fall down into the pit till it be full, then they dam it up, and some days after they open it and find this Barilla-juice turned to a blew stone so hard that it is scarcely malleable. It is sold at an hundred crowns a Tun but I had it for lesse ; there is also a spurious Flower called Gazull that grows here, but the glass that's made of it is not so resplendent and clear."[2] Barilla was imported into England throughout the 18th century and was used as a subsidiary flux with lead oxide.[3]

The second or *potash tradition* depends upon an inland technique, and

---

[1] *L'arte vetraria*. Florence, 1612. I am indebted to the authorities of the Royal Botanical Gardens, Kew, for some notes on this point.

[2] *Fam. Letters*, ed. 1650, p. 40.

[3] B. M. *Tracts*, 816, M. 12, mention " Borillo." It was used at Stourbridge in the second half of the 18th century, and in 1777 attempts were being made to produce it in England. See a paper in the Transactions of the Society of Arts for that year.

belongs to the mountainous and wooded districts of France, Germany, and Central Europe. It would be too much to assert that the glassmakers who took their living from the woodlands of the north may claim a direct descent from the *façon de Tyr* which the Romans propagated throughout the provinces of their empire, and history has been content to describe as Roman glass ; but it is certain that it was from the Phœnico-Roman craft that the barbarian peoples of the North first acquired the art of making glass. At first no doubt the pupils obtained their materials from the same source as their masters, but as time passed and the Roman organization began to disintegrate, we may surmise that Northern glassmakers were compelled to adapt the traditional technique to the materials which they found ready to their hands. And it thus came to pass that the glass industry fastened itself upon regions of mountain or of forest where there was not only an abundance of fuel for the furnaces but vegetable products whence an alkaline flux might be procured in place of the natural soda of the Mediterranean. To some such origin may be attributed the *Waldglas* manufactured from the ashes of beechwood in the districts of southern Germany, once the marches between Bohemia on the south and Bavaria, Saxony, and Silesia on the north. *Waldglas* continued in vogue long after Germany had felt the impact of Venice (16th century), and the *Roemers* made of it in the 17th century are among the most characteristic and most beautiful of the German glasses.

In France during roughly the same period the alkali of the potash technique was derived from bracken, and the glass resulting was called *verre de fougère*. This type is represented in England by the Anglo-French glass made at Chiddingfold between the 14th and the beginning of the 17th centuries, and by the Lorraine glassmakers who came to England in the middle of the 16th century, and after some wandering and persecution took up their abode at Stourbridge, where their tradition has continued until the present day.[1]

The third great technical tradition is *glass of lead*, and it may be justly claimed as *tota nostra*. We shall have something to say later of its inventor, Ravenscroft, but here we would only point out a most misleading and unsupported theory of its origin which was given currency as recently as 1923 by the late H. J. Powell. The theory runs thus : The transition from wood fuel to coal fuel which took place about 1610–15 caused a much dirtier combustion, and it therefore became necessary to close the glass-pots in order to protect the metal from impurities. The result was a loss of heat which made the fusion of silica and salts much more difficult, and to remedy this a second flux—oxide of lead—was *eventually* introduced. To this we would reply thus : (1) No existing piece of English lead glass can be dated before the last quarter of the 17th century. (2) The loss of

[1] Stourbridge adopted lead glass at the end of the 17th century.

heat might be equally well remedied by increasing the temperature of the furnace. (3) At least fifty years elapse between the covering of the pots and the invention of lead glass, and if these two events are cause and effect it is impossible to explain so long an interval between them. (4) Finally, the theory is based upon suggestions which were made to explain the origin of English lead glass long before the significance of Ravenscroft was established, or indeed his name even known to historians of glass. Powell's book was written at a time when Hartshorne's great work had already been published more than twenty years, and when many of the researches of Mr. Francis Buckley were already available ; and it is therefore unfortunate that Powell, in his discussion of this problem, should have uttered suggestions which had been for many years obsolete as if they proceeded from his own technical knowledge. In almost exactly the same form as it is stated by Powell, the theory of the covered crucible appears in several French handbooks of the 19th century, from one of which we quote[1]. It is entitled *Les Merveilles de l'Industrie*, published in Paris in 1873, and the names of Mansell, Buckingham, and Ravenscroft are not even mentioned :

Le verre avait toujours été fabrique avec du bois comme combustible lorsque en 1635 (*sic*) on commença dans certaines verreries anglaises à fondre le verre avec la houille. On se servait d'abord de creusets decouverts ; mais on ne tarda pas à les surmonter d'un dome et le creuset presenta la forme de celui que nous avons representé dans les premières pages de cette notice. On s'était aperçu en effect, que les vapeurs provenant de la houille colorait le verre et lui donnait une teinte brune. On evita cette alteration en couvrant le creuset. Mais avec cette forme des creusets le verre fondu était moins chaud, de sort qu'il fallait augmenter la quantité de combustible. Pour user moins de houille on força la dose du fondant, c'est-à-dire du charbonate de soude. Mais on obtenait ainsi du verre de moindre qualité et qui était toujours coloré. C'est alors que vint l'idée d'employer au lieu d'un fondant alcalin le minium (oxide de plomb) qui rend infiniment plus fusible le mélange vitrifiable.

The facts there is every reason to accept. The inferences are entirely false. The difficulty of the covered crucible might, as we have seen, be solved either by additional heat or by a stronger flux, and in the absence of any evidence whatever for the production of lead glass before the decade 1670–80 there seems no choice but to conclude that the first of the two solutions was adopted, probably by Percivall himself[2], and remained in vogue till the awakening of chemical experiment in the reign of Charles II led to the Ravenscroft revolution. We get a much closer approximation to the truth (in spite of obvious inaccuracies) in an encyclopædic work[3] which ran through several editions during the 18th century, and kept fairly closely in touch with developments in the manufacture of glass ;

---

[1] Figuier (L.), *Merveilles de l'Industrie* (Paris, 1873), p. 78.
[2] *v. infra*, p. 90 *sq.*   [3] Chambers, *loc. cit.*

it is from this that Pellatt's[1] statement is derived. Chambers says, the italics being ours :

> This manufacture appears to have been much improved in 1635, when it was carried on with sea coal or pit coal instead of wood, and a monopoly granted to Sir Robert Mansell, who was allowed to import the fine Venetian glass for drinking, *which was not brought to perfection before the reign of William III.*

The chronology of the Ravenscroft revolution will be briefly treated in a later place, but some notice of the quality of the new metal may here be relevant. In its first or soft state it was a close, heavy, glutinous substance which may be compared for consistency to golden syrup in cold weather, and contrasts very strongly with the metal of *façon de Venise*, which resembles the same confiture in summer time. The Venetian metal, being very thin, cools quickly, and by reason of its fluidity it is difficult to handle ; but in the hands of a practised operator it may be blown to a very thin film, and in drawing, trailing, twisting, and pincering admits of much gesture and finesse. It is interesting to observe how the character of the Venetian art has been determined by the difficult medium. Venice, except for a very brief period, has always been preoccupied with technique, and the play of her own conquest. She begins with an imperfect material and devotes her whole endeavour to compelling its reluctance and exploring its aptitudes ; but when she has at length acquired mastery of the one and knowledge of the other, comes a delighted pride in her facility in which she sometimes forgets the discipline of design and makes play with her metal according to precedent or fancy. The influence of Venetian technique (as distinct from Venetian forms) in other countries is chiefly evident in the way glass is used to decorate glass.

The English metal on the other hand was much closer and heavier. Its weight and consistency made it more difficult to blow, and easier to treat with tools, than the Venetian metal ; and for that reason those parts of the technique which were performed at the chair by various methods of tooling, became in the English glasshouses at least as important as the blowing, drawing, trailing, and moulding on which the older technique had largely depended. The syrup of Venice had become, in a much truer sense, a molten *metal ;* and that it was quite as much *forged* as blown is fairly evident if we compare the illustrations to a work dealing with the " flint glass " technique, *The Manufacture of Glass,* published in London in 1845, in which the work done at the chair is given prominence, with a book like Haudicquer de Blancourt's *Art of Glass* (English edition, 1699), in which blowing is the only operation which appears, and work at the chair is not represented at all. In its second or

---

[1] Pellatt (A.), *Memoir on the Manufacture of Glass* (London, 1821).

hard state also glass of lead had its peculiar virtue. The Venetians themselves had observed the peculiar capacity of fluid lead for holding the light, and used it in making a vitreous glaze or paste known as " glass of lead," which was apt to receive any colour of the spectrum, and thus very serviceable for the imitation of natural gems. When the English came to employ lead for the manufacture of ordinary white transparent glass this character of the flux gave a massive splendour to vessels made in the new material and determined the English repertory of forms.

The kind of decoration developed in England is also to be attributed to the nature of the metal. It is softer than the " crystal " of Germany and the Netherlands, and therefore less suitable for fine engraving ; and this is at least one reason why the English engravers never attained to the same delicacy and precision as their German masters. On the other hand, from its capacity for holding the light, it gained more by cutting than the duller glass of Germany, and when economic conditions in the last quarter of the 18th century permitted the free development of that art, the result was a cut-glass which had no rival on the continent. This result of the lead flux is admirably stated by Dossie as early as 1758 :

> The admission of lead into glass renders such glass less hard and transparent than that made of salts only. But there is in glass of lead a power of reflecting the rays of light of the same nature with that of diamonds, and gives a lustre and brilliant appearance to vessels of round figure not found in the mere glass of salts, where the too great transparency and want of play occasion a deadness of look when seen by the other. For polygonal vessels, however, or those cut with flat sides, or such as are decorated with flowers or other ornaments cut in them or with gilding the glass of salts is preferable, as may be observed in the instance of those brought from Germany. This must not, however, be extended to such pieces as are cut with a great number of angles for the parts of chandeliers or other purposes where the play of light is wanted.[1]

This passage makes it easy to see what were the respective points of English and German glass. It explains also why, even at the end of the 18th century, little glass of lead seems to have been made on the continent. If Dutch or French glassmakers could copy lead glass it was equally possible for those of Germany and Bohemia. But in Germany the decoration was at least as important as the glass, and the Germans therefore had no desire to imitate. Their own hard metal was appropriate to the fine detail of their engraving which was their chief distinction ; for the German engravers to essay the flabbiness of the English metal would have been the repudiation of their whole tradition, and the

---

[1] Cf. with this Marson (P.), *Glass*, p. 111 : " Soda lime glasses are found to be hard to cut and do not give such brilliant and prismatic effects as the glass made from lead compositions."

glasshouses which supplied them were bound to respect the decorator's convenience.[1]

C. AUXILIARIES

Having now considered the three chief technical traditions in modern European glass, and seen how each owes its distinctive character to the type of flux employed, we pass to the third kind of ingredient, the auxiliary substances used chiefly to clarify or colour the glass. The need for a clarificant arises either from the latent presence of impurities in the material or from their production by the chemical processes which take place in the "founding" of the metal. Nitre was sometimes inserted as a subsidiary flux, but its more general function was to purge the strong tinge of yellow left from the phlogiston of the lead. Its use was thus indispensable to the English technique of the 18th century, and it was frequently included also among the ingredients of potash glass. It may be noticed that in the specimen recipes we have quoted the percentage of nitre in English glass is nearly 9, while in German it is about 5.

The other important purgative used to render the glass colourless was black oxide of manganese, erroneously described as magnesia[2]. This substance is very generally distributed in most countries, but that employed by the English lead glassmakers was obtained largely from the Mendip Hills[3] or imported from Piedmont.[4] The best kind was found

---

[1] It may be of interest to quote two of Dossie's prescriptions for glass made in England and in Germany in the middle of the 18th century.

English flint glass.

White sand	120 lb.
Red lead	50 lb.
Pearl ashes	40 lb.
Nitre	20 lb.
Magnesia (*i.e.* manganese)	5 oz.

German glass.

Calcined flints or white sand	120 lb.
Pearl ashes	70 lb.
Nitre	10 lb.
Arsenic	10 lb.
Magnesia (*i.e.* manganese)	5 oz.

The last prescription is interesting in connection with the continental attempts to imitate English *flint*-glass, long after the English were making "*flint*-glass" with sand. *Cf. infra.*, p. 148.

[2] *Cf.* Pomet (P.), *History of Drugs* (1712). I. 103 : "The last ingredient of cristalline glass is manganese." Plot (R.), *Oxfordshire* (1676) : "Magnesia in the glasshouses called manganese."

[3] Dossie, *op. cit.*, II, 248.

[4] *Dictionarium Polygraphicum* (1735), *s.v.* glass.

in beds of lead ore, and in its natural state is of a brownish black colour, but before use in the glasshouse it was reduced by calcination to a fine powder. When fused with glass it vitrifies very readily, and tinges the metal a dull blue-black colour, and for that reason it was very generally employed to remove the greenish tint in the metal which frequently resulted from the presence of iron in the silica. Its action is thus described by Dossie : " The three primitive colours of yellow, red, and blue when mixed in due proportion destroy each other, and produce the effect of grey in the case of opaque bodies and of black in such as are transparent. Now the tinge of magnesia in glass being purple, which is a compound of blue and red, and being added to the greenish or yellowish tinge of the glass consequently destroys the appearance of it, especially the greenish, as the proportion of red in it is greater than that of the blue ; but a proportion of black being produced the glass is obscured in the same degree." In the use of black manganese there were two difficulties ; the power of imparting colour was very great, and the proportion of manganese to the other ingredients in a pot of metal required a very nice adjustment, the result of even the slightest excess being to stain the whole pot of metal black. Moreover, even when the mixer was successful in this the black manganese was apt to settle to the bottom of the pot, so that the lower metal from which " tale glass " was made, was of darker hue than the rest.[1] There was a partial remedy for this. If white arsenic (more generally used for a milk-white opaque glass), charcoal or other carbonaceous material were added, an effervescence took place and all colour gradually disappeared ; and this explains why a small quantity of arsenic was sometimes included even in the formulæ for transparent glass[2]. So much superstition is current concerning the metal of glass that connoisseurship may take from chemistry both a general criterion and a warning. Throughout the 18th century the constant *aim* of the glassmakers was to produce a perfectly clear and transparent metal, except when the metal was deliberately coloured, and any tinting is both a defect and an accident, in some cases an accident of time. Because it is a defect it is no more deserving of artistic esteem than, *e.g.* the iridescence of Roman glass ; and because it is an accident we cannot treat it as evidence of either date or origin. During the period of the Ravenscroft revolution (*c.* 1673–85) it is not so ; for then we are concerned with a period of transition from one type to another, and it is legitimate to speak of " early metal."

But when the technique of lead glass was established there was great diversity in the colour of the metal, not merely at different periods and in different glasshouses, but in the same glasshouse and even in the same pot. A dark tint in the metal is vulgarly supposed to be not only a guarantee of

[1] *The Manufacture of Glass* (London, 1845), p. 10.
[2] Dossie, *op. cit.*, II, 263-4 ; Marson (P.), *op. cit.*, p. 34.

antiquity, but even a monopoly of the Waterford factory, and glass with the " beautiful blue tint " is so plentiful that very little discernment is needed to explain the advantages of such a notion. But there seems to be no ground whatever to account for its origin ; if marked pieces of beautiful glass were occasionally found in the dark metal, we might explain the Waterford myth as arising in a simple logical error. Some blue-black glass is Waterford ; this is blue-black, therefore. . . . But Mr. Dudley Westropp, of the National Museum of Ireland, who in a long devotion to the study of Irish glass has examined many hundreds of pieces, has never encountered a single specimen of marked Waterford glass in the so-called bluish black metal. On the contrary, he possesses documentary evidence[1] that the management of the Waterford factory, in contrast with their brethren of Cork, were at particular pains to secure a clear and transparent metal. It is not, of course, possible to aver that Waterford never produced a " blue " piece, for even in the best regulated factories accidents are possible. If any particular factory is to be held responsible for the blue metal (and such an attribution seems on the whole undesirable, for it is beyond doubt that the blue metal occurred everywhere), we may regard the Cork factories as having been especially careless in clarifying their metal ; there are in the Dublin Museum, and in Mr. Westropp's own collection, a series of marked Cork decanters which do exhibit this peculiarity, but even from these no general inference can be drawn. In spite of the fact that late in the 18th and early in the 19th century the Irish factories, and indeed the English also, copied one another's designs in the most bewildering and inconsiderate manner, any hope of classification must turn towards form and embellishment rather than to metal ; of which we shall speak later.

Besides the clear glass purged with manganese many types of *coloured glass*, as distinct from coloured glass pastes, were produced in England during the 18th century, and the oxides employed were largely the same as those in use at the present day. Many of these varieties do not seem to have been made in very great quantity, and in consequence are rare at the present time ; and the following list is all the account of them required here :

> Ruby glass : Calx casii, *i.e.* gold prepared by precipitation with tin, and copper oxide.
> Yellow glass : Red tartar and magnesium (i.e. manganese).
> Emerald glass : Copper oxide.
> Purple glass : Magnesia (*i.e.* manganese) and zaffer (oxide of cobalt).
> Green glass : Oxides of iron and cobalt.
> Dark blue glass : Oxide of cobalt.

And several other varieties. In the *Dictionarium Polygraphicum* (1735) only

[1] *Gatchell Papers*, in the possession of Mr. Dudley Westropp.

five species of coloured glass are described, one of them being milk-white glass[1] ; in the second edition of the *Handmaid* (1764) there are as many as fourteen different species. Between these two dates we may infer a considerable progress in the making of the coloured glass ; and this was no doubt due to the development in decoration by which the glassmen, as Mr. Buckley has shown, endeavoured to compensate for the loss of form which had followed the Excise legislation of 1745–6. The most important of the coloured types, at least from a collector's point of view, are the blue and the opaque white, but the earliest reference to the former dates from 1762, when Michael Edkins[2] was painting blue glass for the Bristol glasshouses ; and there is enamel painting on some existing pieces (*e.g.* Plate CXXXV. *b.* 2) which, as we shall see later, may well be specimens of his work. The ordinary substance used for imparting the blue colour was zaffer[3] (oxide of cobalt), which had been known to the Venetians[4] ; but the earliest reference to its application to the dyeing of English glass seems to occur in a paper read to the Royal Society, in 1745.[5] In the *Dictionarium Polygraphicum* (1735) it is compounded with other chemicals to make a blue paint, but does not appear to have been used for dyeing the metal, although several other varieties of coloured metal are there discussed. We may infer that the blue glass of the type made at Bristol in the 'sixties first became general in England during the decade 1735-45. Whether any existing pieces can be ascribed to so early a date is a matter of some doubt, most specimens being restricted to the second half of the century on the score of decoration or shape.

We pass next to opaque white glass which was in origin the glassmaker's attempt to simulate porcelain[6]. Porcelain is a middle nature, between the two extremes of earthenware and glass, and the search for the porcellanous mean was the great quest of industrial alchemy in the 17th and early 18th centuries. The winner of this research was the German chemist Böttger. The losers were Daniel Krafft, the great Kunckel, and the French chemist Ferchault de Réaumur. At the time when Germany was experimenting with clays and furnaces, Réaumur, observing the affinity of glass and

---

[1] There is evidence that coloured glass was made in England before the end of the 17th century ; dyed green glass was common *c.* 1720-30. There was a regular trade in smalts in 1696 ; *cf.* p. 157.

[2] Owen (H.), *Two Centuries of Ceramic Art in Bristol* (1873) ; chapter on Bristol glass, pp. 384 *sq.*

[3] Dossie, *op. cit.*, II., p. 302.

[4] Merret's Neri, c. xii.

[5] *Phil. Trans.* XLIII, 497 : " Zaffre is used by the glassmakers and enamellers and is made of cobalt calcined after the subliming of flowers."

[6] The first attempts to simulate porcelain were made at Venice about 1470 by Maestro Antonio. Hannover (E.), *Pottery and Porcelain* (English ed., London, 1925), Vol. III, p. 7.

porcelain, attempted to make porcelain not by synthesis but by conversion, that is to say, by reducing glass rather than by refining earthenware. Subsequent research showed that the secret of porcelain lay in a combination of earths, and that it could not be discovered, as Tschirnhausen[1] tried to discover it, by prestidigitation in a glass furnace. But at the stage of industrial experiment of which we are speaking, namely, the last quarter of the 17th century, it was no rash notion of alchemy to suppose that it was through glass, not through earthenware, that the right approach to porcelain lay ; and Tschirnhausen may at least command our sympathy, because it was his failure that showed Böttger the true approach to porcelain, and because Tschirnhausen himself died on the eve of his pupil's triumph.

Opacity in glass is a state of imperfect vitrification,[2] and a chemical attempt to arrive at this condition may begin either at the end or at the beginning of the vitreous process. The earlier and the normal method was to begin at the beginning by including in the initial composition or frit some substance to prevent the total vitrification which was the glass-maker's usual aim. Occasionally an opaque condition might result from some indissoluble matter accidentally present in the silica, but this was only a failure in the making of clear glass, and normally it was necessary to use a special material ; of this we shall have something to say in a moment. The other and more interesting method was to begin with the final (annealed) state of clear glass, and to try to restore it to the intermediate stage of opacity through which it had already passed. This process is called devitrification, and it is surprising that we find no hint of the experiment in the greatest glassmaker of modern times, Johann Kunckel (b. 1630, d. 1703), whose researches in a different field led to the invention of a peculiar type of ruby glass.[3] The possibility of such a change seems to have been first noted by the German chemist Neumann,[4] who in distilling milk in a glass retort observed that the bottom of the vessel acquired the appearance of porcelain ; but for the pioneer of devitrification we must turn to a French alchemical scientist who devoted much of his time to ornithology and won popular fame as the inventor of the thermometer.

René Antoine Ferchault de Réaumur was born at La Rochelle in 1683 (four years after Kunckel had published his *Ars Vitraria Experimentalis*) and received his early education in that place. He appears to have been an infant prodigy, and at the age of sixteen he was teaching philosophy,

[1] Hannover (E.), *op. cit.*, p. 34.
[2] Powell (H. J.), *Principles of Glassmaking* (London, 1883), p. 20.
[3] *I.e.* glass made with purple of cassius instead of the copper which had been used by medieval glassmakers for ruby glass for windows. For Kunckel see Schmidt, *Das Glas*, p. 308 *sq.*
[4] *Chemical Works*, ed. William Lewis, M.D., 1759.

THE PRINCIPLES OF TECHNIQUE

i.e. physics, chemistry, and "natural history," as well as metaphysics in the Jesuits' College at Poitiers. In 1699 he went to Bourges to study mathematics and civil law. His reputation as a scientist was made early, and in 1708, at the age of twenty-five, he was elected a member of the *Académie des Sciences.* Like several Englishmen, notably Dr. Merret, Dr. Plot, and Mr. Houghton, to whom reference will be made later, he was never an academic scientist given to curious researches, but studied as the 17th century always studied, in order to further the "happiness of man and the material interests of civilization"[1]; and on this account he was appointed (1710) to the Directorship of Louis XIV's *Description* of the arts and manufactures of France. At that time Kunckel's experiments were already awakening interest and the greater nations of Europe had entered the last lap of the race for porcelain. Réaumur cannot have been unaffected by the prevailing excitement in the industrial world. Böttger's stoneware was already in being at the time of his appointment ; and in the exercise of his office he must have come into close contact with the factories at Rouen and St. Cloud, where a soft porcelain was already being made. Réaumur's own interests readily responded, and Réaumur's porcelain was the eventual result. His experiments seem to have been protracted over some years, but they were at last published in 1739 in a paper which he read before the *Académie des Sciences* on the method of converting glass into a semi-porcelain. Even England was alive to the general impulse. The Chelsea factory was only a few years short of its foundation, and Réaumur had his counterpart in an English Fellow of the Royal Society, William Lewis, through whom his glass-porcelain was made known in England.[2] Lewis was a man of much the same type as Christopher Merret. He was born in 1714, matriculated at Christ Church in 1730 and took his degree in 1734. After taking medical degrees—M.B. in 1741 and M.D. in 1745, he practised for a while in Dover Street, but his interests lay chiefly in the direction of experimental chemistry and industrial research, and after a short time he abandoned the practice of medicine and withdrew to Kingston-on-Thames in order to have greater leisure to pursue his studies. The same year he was elected a Fellow of the Royal Society and soon afterwards he was instrumental in founding the "Society for the Improvement of the Arts and Manufactures" ("The Society of Arts") which sought to place the discoveries of academic science at the disposal of working industrialists. The title of his famous book, the *Commercium Philosophico-technicum* (1763), is sufficient indication of his purpose ; it was in fact a handbook of the latest scientific knowledge for manufacturers and others who were limited to the traditional lore of their

[1] Buckle (H. T.), *Civilization in England*, Vol. I, p. 300.
[2] Lewis (William), M.D., *Commercium Philosophico-technicum* (London, 1763), pp. 230 *et seq.*

art. In the particular field of glassmaking their work was an odd but not unhappy blend of casual empiricism with a superstitious reverence for prevailing " mixtures," and there was ample reason why a book like the *Commercium* should have much greater significance in England than upon the Continent. For upon the Continent the more delicate industries like glass and porcelain were fostered by a high patronage which spared no pains for the success of its enterprise and kept a body of tame alchemists perpetually in its service. There was thus an effective link between scientific theory and industrial practice which had been generally lacking in this country. It is true that George II made a half-hearted attempt to extend the practice of the German potentates,[1] but in England the workshop entered the laboratory even less frequently than the laboratory descended into the workshop.

Dr. Lewis had first become interested in the problems of devitrification when Réaumur published his paper in 1739, and he had himself made successful experiments of the same kind. They are of considerable interest to students of glass, and I therefore subjoin his lucid account.[2]

The mixing of glass reduced to powder with other less easily vitrifiable substances for the forming of a paste to be afterwards formed into a sort of porcelain has been a contrivance long practised but it is very troublesome and the result subject to many faults ; but this new ware is made of glass alone and that with much less trouble and without reducing it to powder. By this art vessels of glass are changed into vessels of a sort of porcelain without altering their form, and the meanest glass serves as well as the best for the purpose. Our common, coarse green glass bottles used for covering melons being by this means changed into a beautiful white sort of porcelain. . . . And for this reason the vessels of this sort of ware are very cheap.

It is very certain that all porcelain ware is a substance in the state of semi-vitrification and in order to bring glass which is wholly vitrified into the condition of porcelain requires no more than to reduce it to a less properly vitrified state. The question which would naturally be started on this occasion is whether it be possible to reduce glass to a less vitrified state, it having already undergone what is esteemed the last change by fire. But when we consider that the glass of antimony, the vitrifications of many of the metals, as glass of lead,[3] and the counterfeit gems coloured by metals are more or less easily reduced by chymistry to metals, etc., the reducing (of) sand flints, etc. after they are vitrified at least a little way back towards their native or pristine state may appear not wholly impracticable, and the attempts which Mr. Réaumur made on this occasion were what gave him the first hints of glass porcelain.

The method of making it is this. The glass vessels to be converted into porcelain are to be put into a large earthen vessel such as the common fine earth dishes are baked in or into sufficiently large crucibles ; the vessels are to be filled with a mixture of fine white sand and of gypsum or plaister-stone burnt into what is called plaster of Paris, and all the

---

[1] *Cf.* Buckley (F.), *History of Old English Glass* (London, 1925), pp. 35–36, based on *Daily Courant*, 22 Feb., 1707, and 8 Sept., 1720.

[2] *Comm. Phil. Techn.*, p. 230 *et seq.*

[3] This, of course, is not the lead-glass which is usually called " flint-glass " or by the French " cristal," but the vitreous matter described by Neri (Merret's ed., 1662, p. 105 *sq.*).

interstices[1] are to be filled up with the same powder so that the glass vessels may nowhere touch each other nor the sides of the vessel they are baked in. The vessel is to be then covered down and luted and the fire does the rest of the work, for this is only to be put into a common potter's furnace and when it has stood there the usual time of the baking of the other vessels it is to be taken out and the whole contents will be found no longer glass but a very elegant porcelain and has almost the properties of that of China.

Dr. Lewis adds the following notes of his observations during experiment. Bottle glass devitrified with white sand received no change; in a strong red heat the change proceeded very slowly; but when the fire was raised to a strong white heat the thicker pieces required about three hours to become white through and through.

The glass became at first blue and its transparency diminished and when held to the eye in the light had a yellowish hue; afterwards it was changed a little way on both sides into a white substance. Externally still bluish; and as this change advanced still further through the glass the colour of the vitreous part in the middle turned nearer to yellow; the white coat was of a fine fibrous texture, and the fibres were disposed nearly parallel to one another and transverse to the thickness of the piece: by degrees the glass became throughout white and fibrous, the external blueness at the same time going off and being succeeded by a dull whitish or dun colour; by a still longer continuance in the fire the fibres were changed gradually from the external to the internal part and converted into grains and the texture was then not unlike porcelain.

We shall return to that in a moment; in the meantime it is important to notice that both Réaumur and Dr. Lewis misconceived the nature of their process and the cause of opacity. Réaumur had undertaken his research with a view to its commercial possibilities, but he thought it a condition of success that the glasses to be converted should be set in a refractory medium such as sand or plaster of Paris which would not adhere to them during the process; and in his view, which still persists in his disciple Lewis, the cause of the ultimate opacity lay not in the glass itself but in the medium in which, in Réaumur's own phrase, it was *cemented*. The French glassmaker d'Artigues was the first to demonstrate his error, and subsequent research by Dumas, Bontemps, Hall, Peligot, and others showed that devitrification itself was only half the battle; its complete success depended upon the presence of a favourable element in the glass itself. This substance was some form of lime.[2]

[1] *i.e.* The spaces between the vessels as they stand in the pot or crucible. The "cementation" in sand or plaster of Paris was intended to secure uniformity of heating, and so in the end uniformity of colour. What Réaumur was really discovering in this experiment was crystal-formation in glass. Devitrification is crystallization. Its cause was a loss of heat, not in the temperature of the furnace, but in the molten metal itself, analogous to what is called in the smelting of steel the arrest point.

[2] See Bontemps (G.), *Guide du verrier* (Paris, 1868), pp. 197 and 203; and *cf.* Peligot (E.) *Le verre* (Paris, 1877), pp. 424 *sq.* Bontemps gives an excellent account of devitrification based on the experiments of Réaumur, d'Artigues, Hall, Faraday, Dumas, and others, and on his own long experience.

Bearing these two facts in mind, let us turn for a moment to the actual specimens of opaque white glass which survive from the middle and latter part of the 18th century. There are few departments of glass in which questions of attribution are more difficult. We know a number of places where white opaque glass was made, that it was made at Venice, in Bohemia, and the South of Germany, in Spain at La Granja de San Ildefonso, in the British Isles at Bristol and Stourbridge and Waterford, and probably also in the Netherlands ; there are moreover a few inscribed specimens which, in view of distant orders and migrant craftsmen, serve only to add to our confusion. But if we waive for a moment all questions of provenance it is possible in the whole corpus of specimens to distinguish two main technical families. There is in the first place a number of pieces which are close and smooth in texture and of a thick firm white colour. They came notably from Bristol, and they have the quality of a true white enamel because they are all made with an oxide of tin as the determining ingredient (Plates CXXXV, CXXXVI, and Frontispiece) ; some specimens of Venetian, Spanish and German origin appear to be of the same composition. We shall come to these in a moment. There is a second class of white opaque wares called *Milchglas* by the Germans and *pâte de riz* or *verre d'albâtre* by the French, of a much coarser texture and a much more watery complexion. Both the opacity and the coloration are very irregular ; sometimes they are semi-transparent and sometimes almost as close as a true enamel glass. Their specific gravity is very low, in which they offer a marked contrast to true enamel, and both the metal and the workmanship are rough. In consequence of this the painting which they often bear is usually poor, and here again they are greatly inferior to true enamel glass, which admits of as much delicacy in painting as porcelain itself. Finally many specimens of this *Milchglas* exhibit a curious degradation in colour. A vessel which in some parts is quite white and very nearly opaque verges in other parts into a very pale blue, or opalescent, or sickly yellow hue, presents in fact similar graduations of colour to those which Dr. Lewis had noticed during the devitrification of bottle glass. There are specimens also in which parts of the glass, usually the pontil-mark, have no coloration whatever, but retain the transparency of ordinary glass. These characteristics are chiefly apparent in two families of white glass, of which one is certainly of Bohemian or South German provenance, while the other has been ascribed[1] to the Spanish factory at La Granja de San Ildefonso. There is, however, no doubt that glass of this type was extensively made in Bohemia, the Tyrol, Switzerland, the Netherlands, and France, and there is extremely little evidence for distinguishing one country from

---

[1] Riano (J. F.), *Spanish Arts* (London, 1879), p. 244 *sq.* This Spanish collector seems to have had good authority for asserting that La Granja did make white opal glass.

another. Dossie gives a formula for a white enamel made with bone-ash, and since phosphate of lime was certainly used in England during the 19th century, bone-ash glass was probably being made here at the time he wrote. Specimens of the milk-and-water glass which are certainly English are found not infrequently, and were probably made in this way.

Before we pass to tin enamel glass there is a minor type of white opaque glass which was certainly made in England. Arsenic would not make a true enamel glass, but it gave quite a satisfactory opaque white for ordinary vessel glass. Neri makes no mention of its use for milk-white glass[1] and there seems to be no evidence that it was used for that purpose at Venice or in glasshouses which worked in a Venetian tradition. It was, however, part of the normal chemical repertory of Silesian and Bohemian glassmakers in the early part of the 18th century[2]; and since a very small quantity was commonly employed as a clarificant for ordinary transparent glass, the use of a larger percentage to procure opacity would not be a matter of much difficulty. The *Dictionarium Polygraphicum* (1735) makes no reference to opaque white glass made with arsenic, but roughly reproduces the traditional Venetian prescription for tin enamel glass, and gives a percentage of tin (on the batch) of 7·1 which may be compared with Neri's percentage of 11·75. The first notice of white opaque arsenic glass which I have found in the records of English glassmaking comes from Dossie.[3] In 1758 he gives three prescriptions for a semi-transparent white glass which he describes as " much the same as the German glass brought here in porringers, cream-pots and vinegar cruets, of which we frequently meet with the remains." The first of these is clearly of German origin and an English version of the *Bein-oder Opal-glas* to which we have referred ; its percentage of bone-ash is 5 and may be compared with the 9·1 per cent of Krafft and Kunckel.[4] Dossie's third recipe is for a true tin enamel glass of the Venetian type ; but his second, with which we are here concerned, is for arsenic glass. He gives 1 lb. of white arsenic to 10 lb. of ordinary flint glass frit, *i.e.* 9·1 per cent of arsenic in the batch, and the same percentage as that of bone-ash in the Krafft–Kunckel formula. The smallness of the batch in this pre-scription seems to indicate that Dossie only intended it as a surface enamel or a body for small vessels and not as the material of large vessels. He makes this clear when he adds that " this was made in a considerable

---

[1] *Op. cit.*, caps. 54–5.   [2] Von Czihak, *Schlesische Gläser*, p. 59.
[3] *Handmaid of the Arts* (1 ed., London, 1758), Vol. II, p. 312.
[4] Krafft and Kunckel give :

Sand	60 lb.
Pure Potash	40 lb.
Bone-ash	10 lb.

Kunckel's notes on Neri, Chap. XXXVI, French ed. of the *Ars. Vitrar. Exper.*, Paris, 1752, p. 102. Kunckel says that Krafft was the " inventor " of this porcelain glass, a statement which in his mouth is probably true.

manufactory[1] near London and was used as a white ground for enamel
(*sc.* colour-painting) in dial plates, snuff-boxes, and other pieces which
have occasion to go to the fire several times to be finished." If glass of this
type first appears about 1758 and is not mentioned in 1735, it seems likely
that it was introduced from Germany during the infiltration of German
glassmakers and glass-decorators which may be said to begin about 1713.
We may find a parallel in Meyer Oppenheim, a German glassmaker who
worked at the Snow Hill Glasshouse, Birmingham, and took out a patent
for ruby glass in 1755. Pococke, who visited Stourbridge in 1751, observes
that glass was then being made there in all the capital colours. There
is good reason to suppose that arsenic enamel was made at both Bristol
and Stourbridge. Anthony Amatt, the Bristol potter, long after the
Bristol tin enamel glass had become famous, still adhered to his old recipes
for white enamel ; and the prescription which is preserved among his
notebooks was for a white enamel glass determined by a 10·71 percentage
of arsenic.[2] Moreover we know that the technique of the Waterford
factory was derived from Stourbridge through the notebooks which John
Hill bequeathed to Jonathan Gatchell[3] ; and among the Gatchell papers
there is preserved a prescription for enamel glass which contains 4 per cent
of arsenic and no tin at all. The great quantity of material in the batch
makes it certain that it was used as the body of large vessels and not, like
Dossie's arsenic composition, as a " white ground for dial plates, snuff-
boxes, etc."

We must turn finally to the third type of opaque white glass—the
true enamel glass made with an oxide of tin. From the earliest times white
vitreous enamel determined by tin was commonly made in the Venetian
glasshouses. At first, however, it was chiefly manufactured as a paste for
decorative purposes as in *latticinio* glass, or for combination with other glass
pastes in a vessel of variegated hue. Neri in 1612 gives the following
formula[4] :

[1] Probably the Battersea factory.
[2] Owen (H.), *Two Centuries of Ceramic Art in Bristol* (London and Bristol, 1873), p. 385.
Amatt was born at Derby (Jewitt (L.), *Ceramic Arts*, I, 396), and Pountney (*loc. cit.*)
suspects that he could not have been apprenticed at Bristol. In later life he returned for
a time to the Midlands (Stoke-on-Trent is mentioned, Owen, *op. cit.*, p. 291), and also
went to Scotland.
Amatt's formula is :

Flint glass	16 lb.
Lead	5 lb.
Arsenic	3 lb.
Nitre	3 lb.
Borax	1 lb.

the nitre and borax forming an auxiliary flux to the lead. Owen, *loc. cit.*
[3] Westropp (M. S. D.), *Old Irish Glass* (London, 1920), pp. 173-4.
[4] *L'arte vetraria* (Florence, 1612), cap. 55.

Crystal frit	448
Calcined tin	60
Manganese	2½

i.e. an 11·75 percentage of oxide of tin, and it is clear from the size of Neri's batch that entire vessels of this material were being made in the Venetian glasshouses in Antwerp at the time when Neri was preparing his book. The technique was generally known in Italy, Germany, France, and England during the 17th century. Among surviving pieces the Venetian is of a close, firm, delicate texture ; the tin glass of other countries resembling rather a heavy and rather coarse enamel. Both types may be seen in the Victoria and Albert Museum. But in the middle of the 18th century England had her own metal, which was quite different from either potash glass or soda glass. If she wished to experiment in coloured glass she must discover some means of colouring which was suitable to it. Bone-ash (phosphate of lime) was suitable to give opacity to potash glass, but the Bristol glassmakers were not acquainted with the devitrificatory technique which it involved ; moreover English flint-glass was *rebelle à dévitrification.*[1] The Bristol glassmakers, therefore, had to choose between the heavy tin glass of the Venetian tradition and an arsenic enamel. Their success was due to an exceedingly skilful modification of Venetian practice ; for they reduced the amount of tin-oxide to the minimum required to render their glass opaque. In this way they avoided the ponderous[2] enamel which would result from a high (*e.g.* 10 per cent) percentage of tin, and while ensuring opacity allowed their material to retain the full character of glass. Their proportion of tin-oxide was only ·86 per cent in the following batch[3] :

Oxide of lead	43.71
Binoxide of tin	.86
Alumina	·33
Lime	.14
Potash	6.39
Soda	.82
Silica and loss	47·75
	100.00

The glasses which we illustrate in Plate CXXXV are neither pure enamel nor pure glass, but combine the qualities of both. No one can claim

[1] Peligot, *loc. cit.*
[2] The specific gravity of tin is 7·29, of lead 11·35.
[3] Analysis by the late Prof. Church and cited in Owen, *loc. cit.* It will be seen from a comparison of this analysis with the prescriptions given by Dossie, *loc. cit.*, that we have here an ordinary specimen of flint glass, with a very small percentage of tin. Compare the latter with Neri's 11·75 per cent, Dossie's 13 per cent of tin-oxide and 9 per cent of arsenic (*op. cit.*, p. 312–3), the 7·1 per cent of the *Polygraphicum*, and the extremely high percentage of tin (28·1) given by Loysel (J. B.), *Essai sur l'art de la verrerie* (Paris, 1799–1800), p. 168.

that they have any great artistic merit, but they are at least an adequate consolation prize in the race for porcelain, and in technical history an excellent instance of the mere curiosity. They are remarkable perhaps more for their decoration than for their form and for the fact that they were painted by artists who were chiefly employed in the painting of enamelled earthenware (delft); but of the technical excellence of their surface we require no further assurance than the way in which the rough brushwork of the delft painters was modified by the more delicate surface of enamel glass.

We have now surveyed in a brief way the chemistry and composition of English glass and shown how it differed from that of the Continent. It was to the chemistry rather than to the processes or apparatus of glass-making that the variations of different countries and of different factories in the same country were chiefly due. Even in the 18th century the glassmakers had never entirely thrown off the joint heritage of close craftsmanship and alchemical lore which had descended to them from medieval times; and as their art became catholic in Europe their traditional reticence was increased by the desire to specialize in a particular ware or win a particular market. Even in the middle of the 18th century the English glassmakers were still very jealous of their arcane practices, as we may observe from a broadsheet which, though it refers to plate glass and not to glass of lead, is a good illustration of their general attitude. This undated and anonymous pamphlet,[1] which is entitled " The Case of the Plate Glassmakers of Vauxhall," is a protest against a duty of " one penny in a pound on the metal or metallic preparations," and clearly refers to the glass Excise Act (9 Geo. II, c. 12) of 1745, which provided that " after the 25th day of March 1746 " this sum " shall be raised, levied, collected . . . upon all the Materials or Metal or other Preparations whatsoever which shall hereafter be made use of in the making of all crown Plate, Flint Glass, and all white Glass."[2] Its date is therefore fixed to 1746 or soon afterwards :

This duty then, as it is easy to imagine, must necessarily enhance the price which was overloaded before. And in the next place as to the Secret (which is in truth the property of those who now possess it) it is further provided by the said Act that the Exciseman appointed to take the weight of the materials shall have admittance at what hour he thinks fit. So that in a course of visits it will become his as much as theirs and he may communicate to as many more as he pleases. . . . Villars [sic] Duke of Buckingham thus became Master of it through the over-complaisance of the Venetians; and England stands indebted to his address for the use of it. And after his Example the Ministers of several Foreign Powers have frequently endeavoured to extort the same indiscreet compliment from the Manufacturers above quoted, though hitherto without effect.

[1] B.M., 1890. c. 1.
[2] Buckley (F.), *History of Old English Glass* (1925), pp. 146–7.

THE PRINCIPLES OF TECHNIQUE

We have here the same desire for secrecy which led the astute Ravenscroft to deceive those who, like Dr. Plot, visited his glasshouse, and to encourage the general use of the term flint glass; which merely explained what everyone knew and left his secret intact (*infra*, p. 123).

§3. FABRICATION

With method and apparatus it was a different matter. The nature of the furnaces, the blow-pipes, and the other instruments, and the order of operations vary very little in both the English and the continental techniques; and although the early technical treatises, especially Haudicquer de Blancourt (*Art of Glass*, English edition, 1699), derive their accounts mainly from Neri and therefore from the Venetian technique, there are very few divagations from them in later English works which had definitely taken cognizance of the lead flux, such as the *Dictionarium Polygraphicum* (1735), Dossie's *Handmaid* (1758), the later editions of Chambers (*e.g.* 1788), Porter's *Treatise on the origin, progressive improvement and present state of the manufacture of Porcelain and Glass* (1832), the brochure on the *Manufacture of Glass* (1845) already cited (*supra* p. 17), which was based almost entirely on the methods in use at the factory of Apsley Pellatt, and lastly in a modern technical handbook like Marson's (1918). There is further evidence for this identity of process in the fact that the technical terminology current among workmen, at the present day no less than in the 18th century, is largely a corruption of Italian words or their French equivalents. The calcination furnace is caulker (*calcaria*), the stoke-hole is the tease-hole (*tizzonaio*), the iron rod is puntee (*ponteglo*); and we owe it to the French that glass is still " founded " (*fondre*) in the " siege " (*siège*).[1] To these processes we now come in the second stage of the technique, namely, in the formation of the glass vessel.

Three different kinds of furnaces were employed in the manufacture. The first of these, known as the calcar or caulker, was used for the preliminary calcination of the materials which was necessary before they could be completely vitrified. The objects of this process were in the main three. In the first place it expelled all moisture that might be present in the ingredients, and later prove injurious to the crucibles during vitrification. It had the further advantage of destroying any carbon in the materials, which was apt to cloud or colour the resulting metal; but the most important object was to ensure a chemical union of the silica, alkali, and metallic oxide at a moderate temperature; for otherwise when the

---

[1] For terminology *v.* Powell (H. J.), *Glassmaking in England*, pp. 41–6; and *infra*.

materials reached the glass-furnace proper the great heat would fuse the alkali, which would at once rise to the surface, leaving the other ingredients to subside on the bottom of the crucible. The uncombined alkali would in this way be dissipated in vapour, and a part of the silica would never be vitrified at all. In the fritting furnace the heat emanated from the top of the furnace, and was gradually increased over a period of three or four days until the materials were reduced to a paste ; they were then withdrawn, and while still hot were cut into cakes and stacked for future use. But where there was use of a lead flux as in English "flint glass," this process was greatly simplified; the ingredients being on that account much more readily fusible, the calcination was employed for the silica alone, or sometimes was altogether omitted.

FIG. I.
General view of a glasshouse,
early 19th century.
(*After Pellatt.*)

The second furnace in which the "founding" or vitrification of the materials took place, was generally known in England as the " working furnace "—as the author of the *Polygraphicum* observes, "that where the workmen work." It was a structure of brick or clay, oval outside and round outside, having a domed roof which terminated in a chimney, and six apertures. The largest of the latter was called the great bocca, and through it the crucible and the fuel were introduced. Two smaller holes or *bocellas*, more generally called nose-holes, served for taking out the molten metal at the end of the blow-pipe or the puntee ; there were three other openings. This arrangement of the furnace, which was the ordinary type while the Venetian influence still lasted, seems to have been modified in the later and larger furnaces, which had six boccas. The number of the crucibles in each furnace varied from six to twelve according to the size of the furnace. The crucibles and pots, large vessels capable sometimes of holding a ton of molten metal, had a domed top and a single opening in the side nearest to the wall of the furnace. The difficulty in making the crucibles was always to find a material which would withstand the intense heat of the furnace without cracking and permitting any of the metal to escape, and at the same time resist the corrosion of the raw materials, the breaking of a crucible being one of the greatest disasters that can happen in a glasshouse. The clays of Stourbridge in Worcestershire are particularly well adapted for this purpose, and have been for three centuries in very general use throughout Great Britain. It was their excellence which first attracted the itinerant glassmen from Lorraine and explains why Stourbridge is, London excepted, the only centre of glassmaking which has had a continuous tradition from the 16th century until the present day.

FIG. 2.
Glasshouse Pots.

The fashioning of a crucible is an ancillary technique which it would be hardly relevant to describe here[1]; it requires not so much a profound knowledge of clay as great art in the treatment of it; and it is a branch of glassmaking in which the advent of chemical knowledge and mechanical processes has failed to effect any notable alteration. Chemistry can analyse the Stourbridge clay, but it cannot improve upon it nor discover a quick device to supersede the slow and simple methods by which it was built into crucibles in the 18th century.

The crucibles, being set in the furnace and brought to a white heat, were filled with the frit, which was shovelled through the boccas. At the first they are fully charged, but the bulk of the material decreases during the time of vitrification, so that it becomes necessary from time to time to add a fresh portion of frit; and this is continued till the pots are filled with the molten metal; whereupon the bocca is partly closed with wet clay, leaving an aperture just sufficient for the removal of impurities or the withdrawal of a sample of metal for inspection. The materials, under the effect of the heat, do not at once lose their opacity, but give off by degrees a white porous scum called sandiver or glass-gall which lies heavily on the surface of the metal and is skimmed off and sold for other purposes. The sandiver consists of alkaline impurities which have no aptitude for uniting with the silica, and being lighter than the fused metal, rise to the surface. It is very necessary that they be removed at once, for not only do they corrode the top of the crucible, but discolour the glass. When this has been done, and the pure metal brought to a fluid state, the heat of the furnace is abated in order that the metal may cool somewhat and gain the consistency necessary for handling it. When it has been cooled to the heat most suitable for working, the material, especially glass of lead,

[1] Marson (P.), *op. cit.*, chap. IX, has an admirable account of glasshouse pots.

has lost its fluid character, and becomes a tenacious mass, soft enough to register any touch of a tool, but capable of being bent without cracking, or drawn out into a long fine wire without ever parting by reason of its tenuity. It is then ready to be informed by the glass-blower.

The glassmaker's implements are simple and few, and it is just that fact which gives them their significance. They are simple and few because of all the arts glassmaking is most subject to its medium, and it must observe therefore a most restricted technique. The glass-blower controls the most extraordinary material ever treated by an artist or borrowed from Nature by the ingenuity of man. Molten glass is not so much a substance as a moment in a chemical change, unique in the same sense that fire is unique. There is nothing else like it, and the artist who would work with it must wait for its sympathy. That is why his implements have remained always simple and few, and why also in the history of glassmaking there have been singularly few revolutions.

The first of the glassman's implements, both in use and in importance, is the blow-pipe. It is a hollow iron rod or tube varying in length from two and a half feet (1735) to five feet (early 19th century). This the glass-blower inserts through one of the apertures in the wall of the furnace and dips into the pot of metal, twirling it round several times, and so collecting upon the end a sufficient quantity to form the article which he intends. If the vessel is to be of any great size the rod is removed for a moment and exposed to the air, so that the surface of the glass already gathered is sufficiently cooled for a fresh portion to be added. When this has been

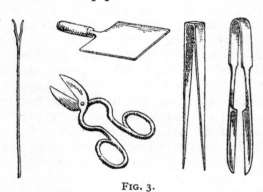

FIG. 3.

Glassmakers' tools other than the blow-pipe and the pontil.

done often enough the blow-pipe is held for a few moments in a vertical position so that the mass may be elongated by its own weight beyond the length of the rod. The glass is then rolled on the flat surface of a polished iron plate called the marver (French, *marbre*, see Fig. 1) until it assumes a cylindroid shape called the *paraison*. The operator then applies his lips to the other end of the blow-pipe and blows strongly and steadily till the molten mass is gradually distended into a hollow pear-shaped globe ; but after each bout of blowing he quickly removes the end of the pipe from his lips, lest he draw the flame into his mouth. The blowing has often to be repeated several times before the requisite size and thickness are attained.

THE PRINCIPLES OF TECHNIQUE

If an elongated shape is desired the glass-blower swings the rod and its molten vessel with a regular motion like a pendulum, or sometimes whirls it in a circle above his head. In this way he produces the most elementary glass form, from which all glass vessels are derived by one modification or another. It is a simple bottle with a globular body, of a type very common in the green wine bottles of the 17th and 18th centuries, and is attached to the blowing iron by a long neck; but having a round bottom, it will not stand, and it requires to be flattened at the end farthest from the blowing iron; or more frequently it is hollowed concavely at that end sometimes to half the depth of the globe, as in the squat green wine bottles of the 17th century. But let us suppose that the glass-blower is making a decanter of one of the types illustrated in Plates CXXV *et seq.* The vesicle of glass on the pipe may receive its shape by being blown into a mould (Figs. 5, 6). It may also be modified by being rolled and pressed on the marver, until it takes *e.g.* a squat round shape like the jug in Plate LXI. 2 (*c.* 1725 and earlier), a shouldered form like the decanter in Plate CXXV. 2, a taper form like Plate CXXVIII. The earlier and simpler decanters and bottles, *i.e.* of the middle of the 18th century, were marvered,[1] while as early as *c.* 1760 we have evidence that the glassmakers used a battledore, or palette (Fig. 3), a flat piece of wood with a handle for flattening the bottoms of decanters and jugs. Decanters made in this way which on other considerations must be dated about 1760 have no pontil-mark (*v. infra*) but a smooth bottom slightly concave. The typical Anglo-Irish decanter with its maker's name on the

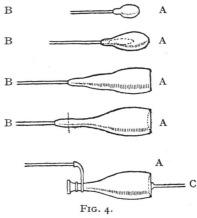

FIG. 4.

Putting rings round the neck of a decanter.

A. The paraison.
B. The blow-pipe.
C. The pontil or iron.

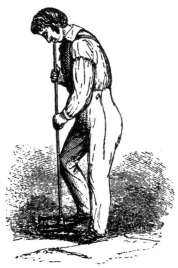

FIG. 5.
Blowing into a Mould.
D

[1] The asymmetry of many 18th century vessels, and the fact that couples are seldom an exact pair make it probable that moulds were not in general use for the formation of plain vessels. But they must have been used for specimens with certain kinds of surface ornament (Fig. 7). For moulding early in the 19th century see Figs. 5 and 6.

[33]

FIG. 6.

A Mould.

bottom was blown into mould, and this was the only regular method of signing a piece. When it has taken its rough delineation it is necessary to detach it from the blowing iron, and for this purpose a second instrument called by the Italians *ponteglo*, and by the English pontil or puntee, is brought into use. This puntee is a solid iron rod similar to the blowing pipe, but lighter, shorter, and more within the control of the operator. On one end of it an assistant collects a small quantity of molten metal from the pot, and then applies it to the embryo decanter on the side opposite the pipe. The two molten substances unite, and the vessel is then detached from the blow-pipe near the point of contact by touching the neck with a drop of water (early 18th century) or a wet iron (early 19th century) which cracks the hot glass, a slight tap then communicating the fracture all round the neck.

The shivered fragments which fall to the ground are called cullet (French, *collet*). The cullet, which accumulates very rapidly, is diligently collected and stored for future use, because it is a very necessary ingredient of every pot of metal, assisting the fusion of the raw materials and smoothing out the striations and stringy appearance to which most metals are otherwise liable. The general practice was to use cullet of the same mixture as the fresh batch of metal; but cullet was scarce in the 18th century and many glasshouses which did not produce or conserve a sufficient quantity were obliged to collect broken glass from other sources. Thus there

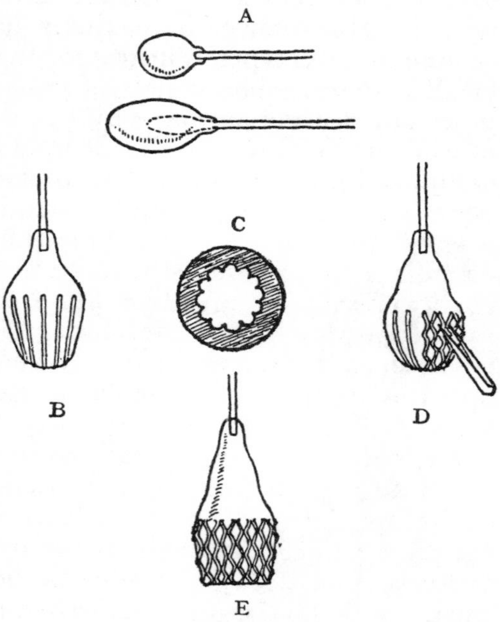

A

C

B

D

E

FIG. 7.

Technique of ornament "nipt diamond waies."

A. The paraison.
B. The paraison with the canes picked up out of.
C. The mould, in ground plan.
D. Nipping.
E. The result.

appears to have been a regular commerce in broken fragments of glass,[1] and in factories where " foreign " cullet was used the quality of their own mixture was necessarily affected ; and it is this practice which makes the quality of the metal an uncertain guide to origins. There is no type of 18th-century metal either in England or Ireland which can be ascribed to any particular glasshouse. (But *cf. supra*, p. 18.)

The " collet " being broken, the operator receives the pontil, with the vessel attached, from his assistant, and gives it another heating in the furnace. He then takes his seat at the glassmaker's chair. This is a hard board bench with two flat horizontal arms extending some distance towards the front ; the operator sits between the arms with the iron laid in front of him, rolling it rapidly to and fro with his left hand, and with his right working the glass vessel with the various tools that hang on the chair by his side (Fig. 8). The rotatory motion thus imparted to the vessel keeps the molten metal in a constant shape while other operations are in progress.

The vessel may now be cut with shears, opened out or " branched " with a tool resembling a pair of sugar-tongs called procellas (*hodie, pucellas*) or crimpled with crimpling irons not dissimilar from those used in the waving of hair. A pair of callipers and a pair of compasses were also required when a vessel was being made to a given design. At this stage also fine threads of glass, previously prepared by an assistant, may be applied to the vessel in a decorative sense. If the operator is engaged upon a decanter little will remain to be done at the chair, beyond widening the neck a

FIG. 8.

Work at the chair

little, turning the edge outwards to form a horizontal rim, and perhaps encircling the neck with the two or three rings of glass which became common on English and Irish decanters towards the end of the 18th century (Fig. 4). But for other vessels, bowls, dishes, plates, the chair work is more elaborate. The operator starts as before with a hollow globe with a " collet " and then proceeds to cut away with his shears the upper parts, leaving the part attached to the pontil in the shape he desires. By repeatedly heating the vessel and then twirling with his left hand and

---

[1] At least as early as 1697. " Many hundreds of poor families keep themselves from the Parish by picking up broken glass of all sorts to sell to the Maker." *Tracts relating to Trade*, Brit. Mus., 816, M. 12/136.

tooling with his right, he may reduce the globe to an open bowl and the open bowl to the almost flat disc required for plates or salvers. If on the other hand a jug or vase is wanted the original globe will be pinced and pressed with tweezers until it accords with the pattern from which he is working. The glassman, therefore, has within his competence all shapes, from a closed and indented vessel to a perfectly flat disc; but all alike are derived from the original pear-shaped globule transferred from the blow-pipe to the pontil.

The making of stemmed vessels, of which the goblet or wine-glass may be taken as the type, is peculiar, and requires separate description. A wine-glass has three parts, bowl, stem, and foot, and requires three men to make it, a " footmaker," a " servitor," and a " boy." The footmaker begins by gathering sufficient metal for the bowl on his blowing iron and shapes it by blowing and marvering in the manner already described. The servitor then receives it and drops a small quantity of hot metal on the end (*i.e.* base) of the bowl and by a reheating makes the join perfect. He then draws out the stem from the blob of metal on the base of the bowl, leaving a small knob at the end of the stem. Finally he dips the end of the stem into the pot of molten metal and collects another blob of glass which he squeezes with a pair of clappers and spreads out to form the foot. The wine-glass is then transferred from the blow-pipe to the iron and the upper part of the bowl is reheated and trimmed with shears, and by " branching " adjusted to the requisite size. The numerous varieties of knop and baluster in early 18th-century glasses were all executed by tool work at the chair.

Such was the general theme, but there were variations. In the case of drawn-stemmed glasses (Plates XLV, XLVI, etc.) the stem was not applied to the bowl, but drawn out from it by working the glass downwards to a knob at the base. The "servitor" pulls this out and at the same time the footmaker who has been preparing the foot applies it hot to the end of the drawn stem. The air-bubbles or tears frequent in the bases of bowls and in the stems of 18th-century wine-glasses were fortuitous in origin, but about 1700–1710 began the practice of pricking the blob of metal in a regular way, so as to make small bubbles of air, and then covering it with a fresh coat of metal. By accident also the tears gradually trailed downwards, forming irregular streaks of air inside the stem; and this gave rise to one of the few decorative devices which are organic to the material, the air twist. This type of decoration was produced by pricking the blob of metal so as to make a number of regular bubbles : and as the blob was drawn out to form the stem and at the same time twisted, the bubbles became a set of regular spiral threads of air inside the stem. These air twists are often extremely bright, and on this account they have been called mercurial twists. This name, even if used metaphorically, is most misleading. We have it on the authority of a practising glassmaker that the inclusion of mercury within the molten metal is a technical impossibility.

Two other modes of decoration require notice. From about 1740 spiral twists of white and coloured enamels were frequently enclosed in the stems of wine-glasses, the filigree process being as follows. The glass-maker used a small cylindrical mould a few inches high and fluted on the

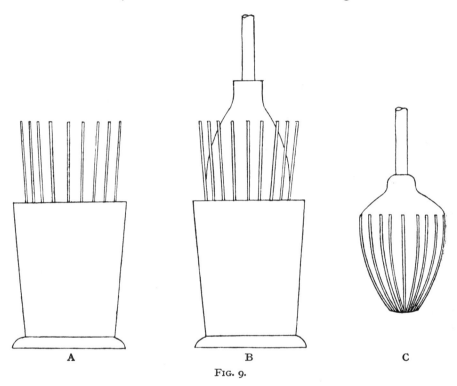

A   B   C

FIG. 9.

Method of making filigree stems.

A. The mould with canes of enamel erect round the inside.
B. The paraison inserted.
C. The paraison withdrawn; it was subsequently dipped in metal, marvered and drawn with a twisting motion into a long fine column.

inside. He took a number of fine canes of enamel, white or coloured, and set them upright in the flutes round the inner side of the mould, thus forming a breastwork of canes projecting above the top. Taking a blob of molten metal on the end of his blow-pipe he thrust it into the mould, whereupon the canes of enamel adhered to the surface. When the glass was withdrawn from the mould it formed a short thick column with the enamel canes on the surface. This mass or paraison was then marvered until the canes were firmly embedded in it. Then a second man seized the end of the paraison, and slowly drew it out into a long rope of glass of the requisite thickness, twisting it as he pulled. In this process the canes of enamel in the glass became tenuous spiral threads, and by a practised workman they could be regulated with great precision. When the rope was several yards in length it was beginning to cool off, and it was then broken into short sections a few inches in length, which were subsequently attached to a bowl and became the stem of a wine-glass, a " colour twist " or " white-twist " stem. The arrangement of the spiral threads inside the stem was determined by the order and shape of the canes when they were first planted in the mould. By a repetition of the process it was possible to obtain a stem with two or more spirals inside one another (*v.* Fig. 9).

Stems of English wine-glasses were sometimes made in which the spiral threads were not of enamel but of coloured *glass*. In this case the glassmaker first dipped his pipe in a special pot of coloured glass and obtained a blob at the end of it. This blob he then dipped in a pot of ordinary white glass to give the coloured glass a casing of white. The paraison so formed was drawn out and twisted in the manner already described. Threads of coloured glass and threads of coloured enamel can be readily distinguished. The enamel spirals are precise in outline, while the coloured glass threads tend to fuse with the clear metal in which they are enclosed.

Latticinio work of the Venetian type was made with these canes of coloured glass and of white glass, and was used for the fabrication of entire vessels. The glassmaker employs a cylindrical mould of stoneware or metal and arranges his canes in the desired order and combinations of colour round the inner side in an upright position. Then having heated the canes so that they will easily weld on to the other glass, he gathers a ball of white glass on his blow-pipe and thrusts it into the mould. He blows till all the rods of glass have adhered to the white glass, and then withdraws the whole matter from the mould. The rods are then bound on to the core by another workman using a rope of molten glass. The paraison thus formed is heated and marvered into a homogeneous mass, and the glassmaker then cuts it with shears at the bottom, so that all the canes of glass are gathered together in a point. When the mass of glass is blown into all manner of vessels the original canes have become a series of fine coloured stripes lying a little below the surface of the glass.

The threads or stripes of milk-white enamel were made with an oxide of tin,[1] and usually set very close together. *Latticinio* glass was only made in England very rarely ; a pair of flint-glass candlesticks in the Victoria and Albert Museum (Bles Loan), which date from the first half of the 18th century, have feet with narrow panels of *latticinio* glass radiating from the

[1] Garzoni (Tomaso), *La piazza universale* (Venice 1589), p. 541.

centre. Coloured filigree work is represented in English glass by the white and coloured stems which were popular for wine-glasses *c.* 1740–80. For the most part these technical dexterities, which at Venice were used with a fine sense of their artistic value, were beyond the competence of English glassmaking and foreign alike to the material with which it worked and the taste it served. From an æsthetic point of view the lead metal gave English glassmakers a set of new opportunities. They seized these opportunities, refusing to train themselves too long in another tradition ; and to that fact we must attribute their success.

When the glass vessel " is brought into the form that the workman had first designed in his mind,"[1] it is detached from the pontil to which it has all along been fastened in the same way that it was parted from the blowing tube, by wetting it at the point of contact and then gently tapping it. By this abrupt separation a rough mark known as the puntee-mark or pontil-mark is left on the underside of the vessel. In the 18th century this roughness was left in its original state. Many pontil-marks were so sharp as to imperil the fingers of maid-servants who washed the glasses, and in the latter part of the 18th century the practice began of smoothing and polishing the pontil-mark. Knowledge of this fact is often of assistance in dating glasses, but it has to be remembered that the rough pontil-marks on old glasses were often polished at a later date, and also that even in the 19th century all pontil-marks were not polished.

From the pontil the vessel was caught on a wooden fork and conveyed to the third of the three furnaces, the annealing oven or leer (*lier, lehr*). Earthenware is but a partial transmutation, a very incomplete chemistry. It is soft and stiff in the hands of the potter, and when he turns from his wheel to his oven he has only to drive it up the slope of solidity and dismiss it, firm and final, at the top. But the glassmaker has a further task. Between the dust of his frit and his tempered work is the flux of his material and the swift epoch of his art. He must therefore take his stuff upon a double journey, conducting it first right out of the realm of solids, and then by the coaxing of his leer restoring it to solidity.

For it is a property of glass to be a bad conductor of heat. If the glass is cooled too rapidly there is a disparity of tension, the outer parts being violently contracted while the inner substance remains expanded and soft ; and glass left in this condition is liable to fracture from accidental friction, rough handling, or even from sudden changes in the atmosphere. It is therefore necessary that the very great heat at which the metal is worked shall be reduced by a slow and equable degradation ; and this process requires great nicety. The later type of leer or annealing oven is a long, low, rectangular tunnel fitted with a number of shallow trays (leer-pans or fraiches) which carry the vessels and can be pushed

[1] *Dictionarium Polygraphicum* (1735).

[39]

easily along the bottom of the chamber. The heat is at one end of the tunnel and the leer-pans are pushed forward in the oven so that they follow one another in single file, beginning at the end where the heat is greatest and proceeding through lesser degrees of heat till they emerge very little warmer than the temperature of the atmosphere.

This type of leer was invented about 1780 by the famous Huguenot glassmaker George Ensell (Hennezel), one of the partners in the Wordsley flint glasshouse near Stourbridge. There is a pleasant story that he travelled Bohemia in the guise of a fiddler, and having won favour with the glassmakers by his play-ing and gained access to the glasshouses, he was at length given employment as a *tiseur* and had opportunity for study-ing Bohemian practice. This account is doubtless an etiological myth, but it shows that several improvements, and among them the tunnel-leer for which George Ensell was responsible, were borrowed in the first instance from German glassmaking. Be-

FIG. 10.

Annealing in Ensell's leer.

fore the introduction of the tunnel-leer with its gradations of heat and travelling pans English glass seems to have been annealed in the topmost compartment or "tower" of an ordinary furnace in a rather haphazard manner. The glassmakers were aware that the glass must cool gradually, but they had no scientific apparatus for the purpose. According to *Glass Manufactures of Birmingham and Stourbridge* (1851) glasses were formerly annealed simply by setting them on the top of the furnace : this probably refers to the upper compartment of an ordinary furnace which was called a leer but did not differ in shape from the other furnaces. The *Dictionarium Polygraphicum* (1735) speaks of the tower of the leer as the place where glasses were allowed to anneal and harden, and it illustrates a leer of this kind.[1] In some of the larger factories there was probably a special furnace for the annealing,[2] but both the sources cited imply that in early times the annealing was done in the upper part of the furnace in which "founding" was actually taking place (Fig. 11) ; and in the smaller glasshouses this was no doubt literally true. Evidence of faulty

[1] *Dict. Polygr. s.v. Furnace* and *Glass.* Dossie gives no account of the furnaces as being "too well known."

[2] The term leer itself seems to imply a distinct furnace.

annealing may sometimes be noticed in 18th-century glass, for example, in the bowl in Plate LXXXIV. *a.* 2, where the curved surface is slightly crackled.

FIG. 11.

The 18th century furnace.

(From the *Dictionarium Polygraphicum*, 1735.)

The heat passed from the lower vault or furnace (A) into B the upper vault, reverberating from the roof upon the glass-pots (E). C C C are the boccas or work-holes and D the tower or annealing oven. In some furnaces the tower was partitioned, one part being used for annealing, the other for preparing the tinctures used in coloured glass.

§4.   DECORATION

The vessel of glass has now received its form, and we have described several kinds of ornament which it may receive during the actual process of fabrication. We pass next to the several methods of decorating glass after it has been annealed ; these will be of two kinds, intrinsic decoration which involves some modification of the glass itself, and adventitious decoration in which some additional matter is applied upon its surface.

A. INTRINSIC ORNAMENT

The intrinsic decoration of the hard glass depends on processes which are alike in being glyptic and differ only in the purposes for which they were used. The first of these is line-engraving with a diamond-point, the sole method practised in this country until the early years of the 18th century. Of all kinds of engraving practised in modern Europe it has the simplest equipment and the longest history. The Venetians were the first to engrave their glass with the diamond, and there are many examples of their work dating from the 16th and 17th centuries. In the earlier examples the ornament is in the form of arabesque leaves, scrolls, and flowers drawn in outline and hatched crosswise ; they are often combined with gilding or painting in colours ; during the 17th century there is a tendency to greater naturalism and the drawing is less exact. From Venice the technique passed to Hall in the Tyrol and to the South of Germany. Luther's friend Mathesius in his *Sermons to Glassmakers*[1] says that "nowadays all sorts of beautiful lines and festoons are drawn with the diamond on beautiful bright Venetian glasses." Until the methods of gem-cutting were adapted to glass by Kaspar Lehmann of Nuremberg it was the only glyptic process applied to glass. The Altarist glassmakers who settled at Liège introduced it to the Netherlands, and during the 17th century, when commerce flourished in Holland, it had a great vogue there not only among professional glassmakers, but as a diversion for amateurs and young ladies. Röemer Visscher, a rich merchant of Amsterdam who was the centre of a cultured circle at Minden early in the 17th century, had three daughters who were celebrated for their skill in engraving with the diamond, and several fine examples of their work are preserved in the Rijksmuseum at Amsterdam and elsewhere on the Continent. During the latter part of the 17th century there was an important school of diamond-engraving in the Netherlands, many of whose works have been preserved.[2]

English glass of the 16th and the first half of the 17th century is so scarce that it is difficult to say to what extent the diamond was used here. The Verzelini group of glasses (Plates I, II), to which we shall refer later, were probably engraved by a foreigner working in this country, and during the monopoly of Mansell England was so closely in touch with Netherlandish glassmakers that there were probably numerous immigrants. The Buck-

[1] *Die xv Predigt vom Glaszmachen*, Nürnberg, 1562.
[2] For a full account of this school see Hudig (F. W.), *Diamond Engraving*, in Buckley (W.), *European Glass* (London, 1926), pp. xiv–xxxiv.

ingham glass (Plate VII. 2) was probably engraved by an artist of this kind. There are, moreover, a number of glasses made *à la façon de Venise* which bear a rather inferior diamond-engraving (*e.g.* Plate V. 1). These glasses and their engraving were probably executed in England, the Netherlands, and at Hall in the Tyrol, but there is no sufficient reason for attributing them to one country rather than another. The glass illustrated on Plate V. 1 is not impossibly English, but even if it is not it illustrates the type of diamond-engraving which was no doubt being practised here.

In the 18th century specimens of diamond-engraved glass are more frequent and were probably executed by Englishmen as well as Italians. The surviving specimens show no influence of the Netherlandish school, and there are several glasses of which the engraving is undoubtedly by an English hand. The goblet on Plate CI. 1 is an exceedingly interesting specimen of this type. The subject, Adam and Eve, resembles in treatment the painting on Bristol enamelled dishes of the second half of the 17th century, and as the figures of the date 1714 are also similar to those found on Bristol " delft," it seems likely that the glass was made and engraved at Bristol. It is difficult to suppose that work so characteristically English can be done by any but an English hand. The author at any rate must have been a professional engraver, not an amateur, and well acquainted with Bristol work. A glass with similar engraving but about thirty years earlier in date appears in Plate XXXVII. There was probably no regular trade in diamond-engraved glasses, and most of the surviving specimens which are not obviously amateur work must have been done to a special order (*e.g.* Plate XCII. 1, Buckley, F. Plates XVIII and XIX). The most numerous 18th-century glasses of this type are crudely engraved by persons under the influence of wine or love or political infatuation, but as these pieces often carry a date they are very valuable for chronological purposes. Diamond-engraving never attained much vogue in England ; most of the professional work was probably done by silversmiths to a special order. Mr. Bles illustrates several very good examples. The technique was primarily suited to the thin metal of Venetian glass, but in heavy flint glass the fine lines of the diamond lost their effect ; the wheel-engraver could do much better.

The second kind of glyptic process which we find in English glasses is pointillé. This is a process of stippling or dotting with a fine diamond needle and may be used with such delicacy that you would think the design had been breathed upon the glass. Superficially it resembles ordinary stipple-engraving, but in the glass technique the lights are rendered by the small punctures and the shadows by the untouched ground. As far as we know it was never practised in England, but in the Netherlands it attracted several artists of distinction. The first of these was Frans Greenwood (b. 1680, d. 1761–2), who was described by one of his contemporaries as the inventor of the technique. He was a dilettante of wide interests, a poet and a collector, and during the latter part of his life he held a civil post at Dordrecht and devoted his leisure to literature and the arts. There are in existence at least nineteen glasses which illustrate his work; they show a preference for figure subjects, sometimes of classical divinities, sometimes in the genre manner of Dutch painting at that period. A pupil of his who signed his work D. Wolff attained an equal reputation, but differed considerably in style from his master. Whereas the mood of Greenwood's work is of the 17th rather than the 18th century, Wolff's glasses usually show groups of children drawn with the fancy of the 18th century. Wolff's style has in it much more of the rococo period; one of his favourite subjects is two boys with a dog, drawn in a manner which suggests the arcadian convention of Watteau and Boucher. Of his life very little is known. He was born at Utrecht, but most of his work seems to have been done at the Hague, where he was employed as a coach painter. The date of his birth is not known, but he was married in 1787 and died before 1808. The six glasses which are signed by him bear dates between 1784 and 1796. These and other stippled glasses which can be attributed to Wolff, as well as the work of other Dutch artists who used the same technique, are fully discussed by Dr. Hudig, and both Wolff's work and Greenwood's properly belong to Netherlandish rather than to English art. What makes it interesting for our present purpose is that both Greenwood and Wolff frequently used English glasses (Plate XCIII; cf. Plate CI. 2); probably because lead glasses, on account of their softness, were more easily stippled than the hard soda glass, and being much stronger than Dutch glass, were not likely to crack under the little taps of the hammer with which the stipplers struck their needle.[1]

Last come the most familiar ornaments of all, wheel-engraving and cutting. We shall allude in a later place to the date of their introduction, and mention only the process here. It is important to remember that the technical method was in principle the same. There was only this difference; engraving treated the glass simply as a *field* just as the etcher treats his copper or the K'ang Hsi painter his porcelain, and his work was mainly representational design or elaborate formal decoration. Cutting was a less delicate business and sought to exploit the chief aptitude of the metal—its capacity for light; only rarely has cut ornament an independent value as design.

For cutting and for the deeper kinds of engraving it is necessary that the glass should be made heavy and strong, lest the cutting pass right through the vessel. The glass-cutter worked in front of a frame in which there was a rotating iron disc. This was operated by an assistant who turned by hand a large fly-wheel connected with it by a belt. The disc

[1] It is recorded that Wolff used a hammer to make his dots. Hudig, p. xxvi.

had a bevelled edge and a fine thread of sand and water fell upon it from a receptacle which hung above. The actual cutting was performed by the abrasive action of the sand, and the workman held the vessel very gently against the edge of the wheel, following the design in diagonal lines across it. When the whole pattern had been worked out in the rough, the glass was taken to another frame for smoothing. Here the wheel was of stone and the abrasive medium much finer. The supreme polish was given on a wooden wheel and by rotating brushes with polishing powders.

FIG. 12.

Cutting glass with steam-power.

(From Pellatt's *Curiosities of Glass*, 1849.)

In Silesia and Bohemia water-power was used during the 18th century for turning the wheels of the cutter and the engraver, but I am not aware of any evidence that it was used in England. At some time during the Anglo-Irish period steam-power was introduced in England for this purpose, but it is difficult to determine the exact date. Cutting wheels driven by steam are mentioned at Bristol in 1810 and 1815[1] and in Ireland in 1818, but there is reason to suppose that steam-power and the machinery it involved were first introduced at Stourbridge. The essay we have already cited, *Glass Manufactures of Birmingham and Stourbridge*, stated that the invention was due to Dovey of Stourbridge and Benson of Dudley. John Benson of Dudley is not mentioned in Stourbridge Directories after 1800 and the name of James Dovey of Stourbridge occurs during exactly the same span of years, 1790–1800. This perhaps indicates that the two men were partners, or at any rate that they collaborated. Mr. Buckley has recently found a reference to Dovey as early as 1772, but one is inclined to think that the invention for which the two men were responsible, perhaps jointly, belongs to the last ten years of the 18th century. There is no doubt, however, that the older method of turning the wheel by hand continued in use long afterwards; hand-power was still being used at Dublin in 1821.[2] It is a nice question how far the greater ease and smoothness of steam-driven cutting wheels contributed to the decline of the art, how far

[1] The later date is derived from the *Bristol Guide* published in that year. I owe the earlier date to Mr. Francis Buckley.

[2] Westropp, p. 197.

these new facilities were the perfection of technique in which art becomes deft and placid. The cut-glass which claims most serious attention certainly belongs to a period before steam-power was used at all, and it is evident that as steam-power became more general at the beginning of the 19th century there was a loss of design as well as a failure in restraint. But some hesitation is required before we make a scapegoat of machinery. Mr. Westropp has pointed out that the earlier cut-glass is unevenly and often carelessly cut, and he attributes these irregularities to the clumsiness of the hand-wheel and a failure in co-ordination between the man who worked the wheel and the man who cut the glass. That may be true enough, but a failure of that kind can scarcely be claimed as a mark of primitive vigour or in itself as an artistic merit. Uneven cutting is an accident which has nothing to do with the artist ; the art is not concerned with the way a wheel rotates but with the sensitive eyes and fingers that apply the vessel to it. The glass-cutter's tools are hand and eye, and the wheel is only a condition of their use, and it seems to us irrelevant to attribute the later failure of cutting to a mere condition. There may have been a "perfection of technique," but it was a spiritual and not a technical perfection. The later glass-cutters failed because they had forgotten the sense of endeavour, because they had learned by too long familiarity with their art to be contemptuously lavish of their own skill. To attribute the loss of economy in the later cut-glass design to the facilities of steam-power is like blaming your engine because you are arrested for driving recklessly. The water-power of the early Bohemian glassmakers provided them with an automatic set of cutting wheels, but it did not destroy either their design or its execution.

Engraving is the same in principle as cutting, but it required to be done much more delicately, and employed a wider range of tools. The frames are much the same as for cutting, but the abrasion was performed by a series of small fine copper wheels of different sizes, ranging from a quarter of an inch to an inch in diameter, somewhat similar to the wheels used by a dentist ; and the great skill of the German engravers, which the Englishmen never attained, lay not merely in the use of the copper wheel, but in knowing which graduation of wheel to select for a particular type of work or a particular stage in it. It is important to notice that wheel-engraving on glass was only a particular application of a technique used for engraving crystal and other natural stones.[1] The following account, taken from the *Dictionary of Arts and Sciences* (London, 1754), dates from a time when wheel-engraving on glass was becoming common in England, and it shows quite clearly what the method was : " To fashion and engrave vases of agate, crystal, lapis lazuli they make use of a kind of lathe like that used by pewterers to hold the vessels which

---

[1] Lehmann himself was a gem-cutter.

[46]

are to be wrought with proper tools ; that of the engraver generally holds the tools which are turned by a wheel and the vessel is held to them to be cut and engraved either in relievo (*i.e. hochschnitt*) or otherwise ; the tools being moistened from time to time with diamond-dust and oil ; or at least emery and water. To engrave figures on any of these stones when polished such as medals, seals, etc., they use a little iron wheel the ends of whose axis are received within two pieces of iron placed upright as in the turner's lathe, and to be brought closer or set further apart at pleasure : at one end of the axis are fitted the proper tools, being kept tight by a screw. Lastly the wheel is turned by the foot and the stone applied by hand to the tool and is shifted and conducted as occasion requires." The technique of glass-engraving was an adaptation of this process : it is evident from this account and from Fig. 13 that the engraving wheels were turned by a treadle machinery worked by the engraver himself. There was no need of the fly-wheel and the assistant required to rotate the much larger wheels of the cutter (*cf.* Figs. 12, 13). English engraving such as we find on Jacobite glasses was generally left rough, but in Germany the engraved work often received a high polish. Engraving partly polished is found on English glasses which date from 1750–60, and it became more frequent towards the end of the century. Good engraving requires great art, for it is performed on the under-side of the wheel, and the operator in pressing his glass against it has no view of the surface on which

FIG. 13.

Engraving glass on the wheel with treadle power and a jet of sand.

(From Pellatt's *Curiosities of Glass,* 1849.)

he is working, because it is hidden by the thread of sand dripping from above. He has thus to depend on a fine touch and a sense of direction.[1]

The etching of glass by hydrofluoric acid has been always very rare and might be ignored but for the mistaken notion that the stippled glasses were etched by this process. Some early experiments were made by A. S. Marggraf (1709–82) and by Priestley (1733–1804), but the credit for a thorough investigation of this method is due to a French scientist, Marcassus de Puymaurin, who in 1788 published a paper on the subject.[2] The glass to be etched was covered in a thin layer of varnish through which

[1] Von Czihak (E.), *Schlesische Gläser*, pp. 136–139. Dillon, *op. cit.*, pp. 283–284. Marson, *op. cit.*, pp. 109–112.
[2] *V.* Amoretti (C.) and Soave (F.), *Scelti opuscoli sulle Scienze* (Milan, 1778–1803), Vol. XI (1788), pp. 420 *et sq.*, for Marcassus de Puymaurin's paper. I have not seen the original copy in French and therefore cite from the Italian version. J. P. C. de Marcassus de Puymaurin was born in 1757 and died in 1841.

the design was incised, and it was then set in a bath of hydrofluoric acid. Marcassus de Puymaurin found that English flint glass was much better adapted to this process by reason of the high percentage of lead which it contained : " Il vetro inglese ov' entra molta calce di piombo è facilmente intaccato dall' acido." On the other hand Bohemian glass " non è d'una qualità tutta equale. Le materie ond 'e composta non hanno subito una fusione bastante per essere mescolate fra loro esattamente. L'acido fluorico agisce Sorr' esso disuqualmente i patto ch' egli v' imprime sono scabri e non fanno un effetto piacevole." Even in England, however, this technique was rarely practised, and certainly it was not used before the 19th century. The difficulties of the process were admitted by Pellatt as late as 1849 : " etching by fluoric acid has been introduced but its bite is not sufficiently rough and is not found effective for general purposes."[1]

B. ADVENTITIOUS ORNAMENT

We pass finally to the adventitious types of ornament. A form of ornament common in the middle of the 18th century was *enamel painting*,[2] of which several specimens appear in Plates CXXX–CXXXII and CXXXIV–CXXXVI. This mode of ornament was of course borrowed from the Germans and the Dutch, with whom the process had attained the status of an independent art, and reached England about the middle of the 18th century.[3] In Germany the art had been practised since the 16th century, but great secrecy was observed in the preparation of the colours, the fluxes, and the grounds, and even when Dossie wrote "a very small share in the preparation of the colours and yet less in that of the grounds and fluxes is hitherto gained by the artists of this country" (1758). The common materials of all enamels were lead and tin, and equal quantities of each, together with a colorificant, were calcined together in a kiln till they were reduced to powder ; sifted, rinsed, and dried by evaporation. Soft and easily fused enamels were used for painting, a strong active flux being added in order that they might melt at a low temperature. The fine enamel powder was mixed with an oil medium in order to give it cohesion and was then painted on the vessel. The painted glass was next heated in an enamelling furnace of low temperature until the painted designs were melted and fused upon the glass. Finally the glass was reannealed by a gradual cooling of the enamelling furnace or muffle (Fig. 14).

This art never reached the same technical accomplishment or artistic excellence in England that we may admire in the great enamelled *Humpen* and other painted glasses of Germany, and the cause does not lie entirely

---

[1] *Curiosities of Glassmaking*, p. 127.
[2] Glass painting in this account means the painting of glass vessels.
[3] Dossie, *op. cit.*, 1 ed., 1758.

in the incapacity of English artists. Clean and solid enamel painting required a hard refractory glass which would not melt too easily in the heat of the muffle and so flood the application of colour.[1] English metal, on the contrary, contained about 40 per cent of lead and was comparatively soft. The excellence of German glass had chiefly consisted in the absolute harmony of the vessel and its ornament; the metal and the modes of ornament grew up together and each supported and developed the other. It happened with enamelled painting as it happened with engraving; both techniques when they crossed the water discovered in England an alien metal which had a different set of values and was not really appropriate to either of them. But enamel painting of such artists as Michael Edkins and the Beilby family is interesting because it connects the art of glass with the general stylistic development of the period. Glass is by nature a detached art and only in its ornament can it use the same terms as the other arts of its period or its fashion, but in its enamel painting it pays an occasional tribute to the decorative modes of the 18th century—rococo, chinoiserie, and classicalism.

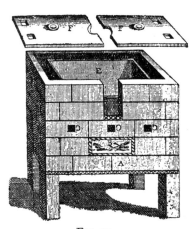

FIG. 14.

The Muffle.

A, ash-hole; B, fireplace; C, bars supporting the pan on which the vessels stand; E, earthenware pan; F, earthenware lids.

(After the *Dictionarium Polygraphicum*, 1735.)

Cold painting in oil-colours was also used in England for decorating glass, but is very rare[2] before the latter part of the 18th century. Newcastle-on-Tyne was perhaps the chief centre; it issued numerous cheap glasses such as mugs and love-tokens in the form of rolling-pins, painted by this method with flowers, sentiments, and doggerel, and sometimes in the case of the love-tokens with a ship at sea.

The *gilding* of glass was in England as in Germany a necessary appendage to the art of painting in enamel colours and was imported from Germany about the same time. In the decade 1750–60[3] there was already a considerable demand in England for German wine-glasses with gilt edges. In the German and Dutch techniques the gilding was not applied by firing but by the aid of a special cement. This material was a compound of gold, size made with oil, and a strong resinous varnish, and its chief virtue was that it resisted the action of water and could only be dissolved

[1] *Cf.* the citation from Dossie, *infra*, p. 203, n. 1, and Marson, *op. cit.*, p. 115.
[2] For an early specimen *v.* Plate XXXVIII. *b.* 2.
[3] Dossie, *op. cit.*, 1 ed. (1758).

E

by spirits of wine or turpentine. Here also the English imitated the Germans, but until late in the century they did not discover the correct process of oil-gilding, but made shift with gum or size, which readily dissolved in water. Thus their ornament soon perished, and there is evidence of their failure in the numerous English wine-glasses which were formerly gilded *over* decorative engraving, but now betray the fact only by a slight darkening of the metal. In Dutch and German glasses the gilding is much better preserved and often shows little sign of age ; in cases of disputed nationality the state of the gilding or the traces of it must always be taken into account. English oil-gilding does not occur on English glasses before *c.* 1740–50, but probably it was first brought hither by German artists about twenty years earlier. It was practised by a German John Grahl, who came from Saxony and in 1785 exhibited some specimens of glass " curiously gilt " before the Dublin Society to support his petition for financial aid. The next year he had taken a pupil, Richard Hand, to whom he disclosed " all the secrets for gilding glass " excepting the nature of the wine spirit varnish which he used. This probably means that he taught Hand the method but kept a reserve on the chemistry, but he received a premium of thirty-five guineas for doing so from the Dublin Society. The notice of him shows very well how the decorative techniques were absorbed from German artists, and how a remote city like Dublin was compelled to use bribery in order to secure their services (*cf. infra,* pp. 283 and 234).

About 1770 a new method of gilding was introduced which gave much more durable results than the cold process. This was burnished gilding, the gold being painted on the glass like ordinary enamel colours and then fired in a muffle. Mr. Buckley considers that " gilt glasses " advertised by Haedy in 1766 were executed by this method.

CHAPTER II

The Age of Adoption (13th century—1592)

L'art de la verrerie est noble et ceux qui y besognent sont nobles.

BERNARD PALISSY.

§1. SUSSEX : THE FRENCH TRADESMEN

THE two earlier currents of European glassmaking to which we have alluded are all evident in England, but only the scantiest relics of them have survived. The lead glass of the 17th and 18th centuries has received of late its due appreciation, but there is for that reason a danger of neglecting the two traditions which preceded it. English glassmaking was derived in the first instance from the potash glass of France and the soda glass of the Venetians, which was introduced by migrant craftsmen. The scarcity of their work does not in the least diminish their historical importance. Arts, like peoples, are given to migration, and that is especially true of artists who can carry their tools upon their backs and find their materials ready to their hands in the country of their adoption. Thus the glassmakers from Venice and Altare had their fortune at their fingers' ends and moved easily to and fro among the princes and peoples of Europe. Their skill in so strange an art ensured them a welcome and a livelihood in most places, but they were aware that for an itinerant craftsman his craft must take the place of his country, and that nationality was chiefly valuable as a ready-made reputation. During the 15th and 16th centuries it was by denationalized craftsmen of this kind that the art of glass was disseminated throughout the North of Europe. The Venetians and Altarists came by families or individuals chiefly to France, the Netherlands, and England, and at a later point we shall allude to the records of their work and their wanderings, in considering the Venetians who came to England.

But three hundred years before there had been another set of immigrant glassmakers of quite a different sort. The Frenchmen who first settled in Sussex in the 13th century did not provide much glass for the windows of English churches, for in the 13th and 14th centuries most of this window glass was imported from abroad. But they came of a tradition which in France did its more important work in the service of the Church, and after their settlement in England they achieved in due course the same dignity. In the making of glass vessels they had not much attainment, and were content with providing a few vessels of common utility, but in their limitations as much as in their strength, they belong to Gothic art in the same sense that Venetian glass belongs to the Renaissance. The Venetians of the 16th century, both at home and in exile, were artists contributing to a pagan culture. The French " verrers " were humbly the servants of a

[51]

religious art, and this contrast between their window glass and the glass vessels of Venice illustrates very exactly the difference between two cultures. The impersonal art of Gothic was the work of a system and a service, demanding a full subordination from its workmen and focussing the collective energy upon a single idea ; the actual glassmakers—such as the Schurterres of Chiddingfold or the various " verrers " of York—were no more than the tradesmen who obeyed orders. The Renaissance artists, on the contrary, worked for the pride and pleasure of individual men, and the Venetian glassmakers, becoming likewise superb, gave attention to beauties which would adorn a great house. Venetian glass was thus palatial[1] rather than domestic, and the Venetian tradition only became domestic when it found a footing in the Netherlands and in England.

At the end of the 13th century we hear of " verrers " who were making window glass at Colchester, and Hartshorne[2] thought it "inconceivable that they did not constantly turn their hands to the fashioning, if not of decorated, at least of simple vessels." The same is probably true of the York glassmakers such as William de Auckland (c. 1351) who is described as a " verrour." Be that as it may, vessels of glass which must be of indigenous manufacture begin to appear early in the 13th century. The Peterborough[3] cup, found within a monastic precinct in one of the earliest graves in a piece of land which became a cemetery between 1214 and 1222, is the most notable example. Edward I's second son Henry (1268–74) had purchased a cup of glass for $2\frac{1}{2}$d., and Edward I had " duo urinalia vitrea."[4] A number of other glasses have been discovered which are dated between the 12th and the 15th centuries.[5] But apart from these isolated specimens and a number of drawings of glasses of the same period[6] we have only one continuous and certain record of vessel glassmaking in England during the Middle Ages.

In the Medici Palace at Florence there is a 16th-century map of England which marks two places only in the county of Surrey ; one is Guildford, the other Chiddingfold. The latter is now a scattered parish

---

[1] This art in exile was chiefly practised under privileges from the local princes, and the Berovieros, when they first invented crystal glass in 1463, exhibited it in different courts in Europe. This happened in the early stages of the Renaissance and led to a partial abandonment of the traditional Gothic vessel-forms. In Italy of the 15th century as in England of the 17th, the style and the metal, the will and the medium, created one another. *Cf.* Labarte, *Hist. des Arts industriels*, IV, 572.

[2] Hartshorne, pp. 131–2.

[3] *Op. cit.*, p. 132, note 2. Irvine (J. T.) in *Proc. Soc. Ant. Scot.*, N.S., x, 149.

[4] S. K. Catalogue, p. lxxii.

[5] P.S.A., 2 S., iv. 284 and v. 114, 132 (South Kilworth), vi. 390 (Anstey), v. 135 (St. Phillack).

[6] Bodleian MSS., *Douce* 180 and 219, the latter illus., in Hartshorne, Figs. 151 and 152.

and lies on the borders of Surrey and Sussex, in country that is still thickly wooded and was formerly dense forest. Its important position in the Florence map is certainly due to its extensive glass manufacture. The Weald was easy of access to immigrants from France, and provided ample fuel for the furnaces, and vegetable ashes as the fluxing material. The glassmaking which was established at Chiddingfold[1] was of the same potash tradition which had grown up in the wooded regions of Northern Europe and was later called *verre de fougère* in France and *Waldglas* in Southern Germany. It was brought across the water by French families from Normandy. The earliest mention of this industry occurs in 1220, when Laurence Vitrearius received a grant of twenty acres of land at Dyers Cross, Pickhurst,[2] for which he paid a yearly rent of forty pence and one pound of wax at the Feast of the Purification. Whether he came by invitation or on his own initiative we have no means of determining, but he must soon have won a considerable reputation, for in 1240 he was employed by Henry III to make window glass, both plain and coloured, for the Abbey at Westminster, which was then in course of completion. He was succeeded by his two sons, William le Verrir and Richard de Dunkshurst, who had an equal share in the tenure of Dunkshurstlande ; it was the former who carried on the industry. Richard was apparently a man of some substance, and owned the moiety of the manors of Prestwick and Okelands in Chiddingfold. The first mention of him dates from 1279, but in 1307 he is described as Richard de Dunkshurst in the deeds of the Abbey of Port Royal des Champs, and it is probable that early in the 14th century he returned to his own country, leaving the glasshouses to his brother " le verir." The last mention of the family appears to be in 1301, when a son of " le verir " is mentioned in connection with a remission of rent[3] ; but thereafter we hear nothing of the Laurence family, and they seem to have been superseded by the later immigration of French glass-making families.

Shortly before 1343 the most important of these families, the Schurterres, arrived in Chiddingfold and acquired some land in the south of the parish at a place called Schurterrehurst (now Surreylands), where they had a glass-furnace and a dwelling-house. The head of the family, John Schurterre, seems to have prospered exceedingly, and in 1368 he purchased a holding at a place called Fromes previously occupied by a glassmaker and dealer, John le Alemayne, who, as his name indicates, probably came from Lorraine and not from Normandy. Alemayne belonged to a body of glassmakers who made Chiddingfold their head-

[1] Dawson (C.), *Sussex glass*, in *The Antiquary*, 1905.
[2] Halahan (Mrs. H. C.) in a paper read before the Newcomen Society, 21 April, 1925, and based on researches by her father, the Rev. T. S. Cooper of Chiddingfold.
[3] Hartshorne, p. 132.

quarters and wandered about the country hawking their stock of " urynells, bottles, bowles, cuppis to drinck and such lyke."[1]

John Schurterre appears to have controlled a good part of the manu-facture in these parts, and we may find evidence for his being the most important glassmaker of England in the 14th century. Alemayne suc-cumbed to his competition ; and besides his furnaces in Chiddingfold itself he had a furnace at Stroudwickswode in the neighbouring parish of Kirdfold, where a certain William Pikebossche was working a furnace with him and for him. When he died in 1379, leaving a young son, his widow Joan found the business so enhanced that she was obliged to take a managing partner, an Englishman from Staffordshire named Glazewryth, to superintend the Kirdfold branch during the six years of her son's minority. The agreement was signed at Plastowe in 1380, and provided that Glazewryth should work the Stroudwickswode kiln, and receive " for each shev of brodglas 20d and for a hundred of vessel glass 6d." But the most convincing evidence of John Schurterre's importance is his custom. When William of Wykeham was building his colleges at Winchester and at Oxford in the second half of the 14th century, he employed two agents named Dedyngton to buy window glass for him. They are described as " of Chiddingfold," but Mr. T. S. Cooper could find no allusion to them in medieval records of Chiddingfold and Godalming. It is probable that they were successful members of the peddling class to which Alemayne had belonged, and that they purchased their glass at the Schurterre glasshouse, just as Alemayne had purchased glass at Chiddingfold in 1352–6 for St. Stephen's Chapel, Westminster, and St. George's Chapel, Windsor, and Richard Holmere for the Chapter House at Westminster in 1352. At any rate there is no doubt that at that time Schurterre was the most considerable glassmaker in Sussex, and therefore in England. Agents employed on so important a commission would naturally have recourse to him ; and the glass in the old windows of New College Ante-Chapel can be matched by fragments from the Fromes furnace.[2] After the death of its founder the fortunes of the Schurterre dynasty cannot be very precisely determined. On the site of their furnace at Fromes a great quantity of 15th-century flashed glass has been found. It is distinguished from the other finds (*e.g.* at Roaring Pond Copse) by a thin flash of white glass outside the ruby flash ; and it is likely that they did not give up glass-making much before the beginning of the 16th century. But if we cannot fix a moment for their final disappearance from glassmaking, we can at least date the beginning of the decline.

In the year 1435 a third family of French metics settled in Chidding-fold and began to make glass. They were called Peytowe (Peto), a name

---

[1] *Cf.* Dillon, p. 492, who cites a medieval document from Beckley (Sussex).
[2] Mrs. H. C. Halahan, *op. cit.*

which sufficiently proclaims their origin (Poitou), and during the remainder of the 15th century they prospered and multiplied, gradually becoming the protagonists of English glass, and winning to themselves the position that the Schurterres had formerly held. Unless the Schurterres were still working at Fromes in the 16th century, which seems unlikely, we hear of only one other family, the Ropleys of West End, who were making glass at that time. The other furnaces were probably worked by various branches of the Peytowe family; and we may see an allusion to one of them in a poem which was published in 1557[1] :

> As for glassmakers they be scant in the land
> But one there is as I do understand
> And in Sussex is now his habitacion,
> At Chiddingfold he works of his occupacion,
> To go to him it is necessary and meete
> Or sende a servante that is discreete,
> And desire him in most humble wise
> To blow thee a glasse after thy devise :
> It were worth many an Arme or a Legge
> He could shape it like to an Egge ;
> To open and close as a haire,
> If thou have such a one thou needst not feare.

There are two entries in the parish registers of Chiddingfold which record the death in 1611 of two members of the Peytowe family, and since the prohibition of wood fuel for glass-furnaces came only four years later, they may be taken as significant of the dissolution of the glass industry in Sussex.

The causes of their failure are not far to seek. The conditions in which Chiddingfold and the Weald of Sussex selected themselves as the original home of English glassmaking contributed also to its decline. The abundance of timber which had made possible the Sussex glass served another industry which was more necessary to society and more lucrative to those who practised it ; and throughout the reign of Queen Elizabeth, we gather a tale of jealousy and indignation among the landowners and ironworkers of Sussex against these " strangers and outlandish men " who consumed the woods for fuel. Outside the law there were burnings and robberies and within it a long series of irate petitions which culminated in 1584-5, when eleven glasshouses in or near Chiddingfold were suppressed by Act of Parliament. The workings of glass and iron in Sussex " as they bring greate gaine to their possessors so do they impoverish the country of woods . . . the glasshouses remove and follow the woods with small charge which the ironworkers cannot easily do." In this sentence Speed lays his finger on the malady which ruined the Sussex industry, and

[1] Charnock (T.), *Breviary of Philosophy*, 1557.

gives a clue to its later history in other parts of England. Indeed, of the poor state of Chiddingfold late in the 16th century we require no other evidence than the course taken by the Lorrainers who came from

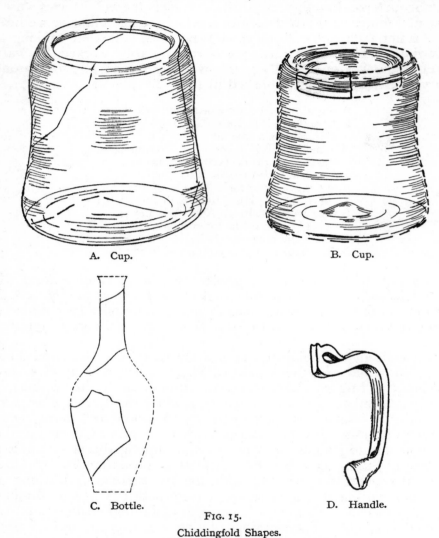

A. Cup.

B. Cup.

C. Bottle.

FIG. 15.

D. Handle.

Chiddingfold Shapes.

Reconstructions from fragments of Sussex glass, 15th–16th centuries.

France in 1567, and at first supplemented and later superseded it. The potash glassmaking in Sussex at that time was a static industry that had maintained a fixed domicile for upwards of three hundred years, but the

Lorrainers imported by Carré could stay there but a little while, and when they left they founded an itinerant craft which for half a century had its brief habitations in woody places (such as Buckholt in Hampshire and Newent in the Forest of Dean), and then as the use of coal became general in the furnaces and Mansell stretched his monopoly the length of England, found a lasting settlement at Stourbridge and on the Tyne.

The vessels of potash glass or *verre de fougère* of Sussex, though wholesome in design, were of a rude fabric, and they evoked but little admiration by comparison with the fine fabrics which Venice was sending to England in the middle of the 16th century. "Neither want here glasshouses," says Camden,[1] "but the glass there made by reason of the manner of the making, I wot not whether, is likewise nothing so pure and cleare, and therefore used of the common sort only." "Neither," says another writer, "can we match the purity of the Venice glasses, and yet many green ones are blown in Sussex profitable to the makers and convenient to the users thereof."[2] It is uncertain when the making of glass in Sussex finally ceased. In the 16th and early part of the 17th century Sussex glass became a household word, and is still spoken of in a familiar way in an edition of Sir Hugh Platt's *Jewel House of Art and Nature*,[3] published in 1653 (p. 36), where the author requires a "dish of the clearest glass that is to be bought ; yet I have seen our Sussex glass serve sufficiently." Our knowledge of the forms and metal of Sussex glass is derived mainly from the fragments which have been found during excavations by the Rev. T. S. Cooper, formerly Vicar of the parish of Chiddingfold, and his daughter, Mrs. H. C. Halahan. There are two main types of fabric; one is pale green in colour and rough in texture, and is probably the earlier in date, but there is no means of attributing it to a particular family or even to a particular century. The other type, which shows a more accomplished workmanship and can scarcely be earlier than the 16th century, is of a deep semi-opaque blue-green colour, and has a very smooth surface. It is usually found in the form of necks of bottles which sometimes have spiral ribbings and are sometimes plain. In the matter of form the fragments of vessel glass, though not numerous, are sufficient for us to reconstruct some of the vessels. The shapes which we illustrate in Fig. 15 have been found on the site of John Schurterre's glasshouse at Fromes, and it seems fairly certain that vessels of this kind were made continuously, though in small quantities, from the 14th to the 16th centuries. The shapes themselves show little trace of development, and though we may incline to call a particular piece 14th century or 16th century according to the

[1] Camden (W.), *Britannia*, trans. Philemon Holland (London, 1611), p. 306. *Cf.* Harrison, *Description of England*, Bk. ii, chap. 6, cited *infra*.
[2] Cited by Blaauw (W. H.) in *Sussex Archæol. Coll.*, i.
[3] First ed., London, 1594.

[57]

quality of the metal, no exact chronology is possible. On the evidence of the passage in Charnock's *Breviary* already quoted, the thinner pieces may be given the later date.

§2. THE NOBLE VAGABONDS

Between the wares of Sussex and the fine art of Venice the Lorraine "Pilgrims" mark an intermediate stage alike in their status, their accomplishment and their historical position. Whereas the Schurterres and the Peytowes were working tradesmen, the Lorrainers had attained in their own country definite rank as "gentilshommes verriers," and we may see in the phrase a desire to connect themselves with the Venetian prestige and dissociate their work from crude *verre de fougère*. Schuermans[1] has inaccurately defined them in saying that where the Venetians were noblemen *because* they were glassmakers, the French families from Lorraine were gentlemen *in spite* of being glassmakers. They belonged rather, as their title implies, to a minor aristocracy who were all the more jealous of their privileges because they were vested in a profession as well as in a pedigree. The *gentilshommes verriers* are a rare instance in history of a technique winning the social prestige usually reserved for blood or acres. Kings coveted the rare substance that many admired and so few understood, and those who had knowledge of the useful and beautiful alchemy[2] might claim a worldly recognition which was equally denied to the detached experimentalist and to the vulgar[3] craftsman. "Tous les rois desiraient cette science," said a 17th-century writer,[4] and if we would seek an explanation for this peculiar dignity of glassmaking in the Middle Ages

[1] Schuermans (H.), *Verres à la Venetienne fabriqués aux Pays Bas*, Lettre III, p. 23, in the Belgian *Bulletin des Commissions Royales sur l'art et l'archéologie*, Brussels, 1883–91.

[2] De Lannoy "abuseth many in promising to convert any metal into gold." For the connection with alchemy *cf.* Hartshorne's note (p. 151) on Cornelius de Lannoy; Neri's preface to the *Art of Glass*; and especially a passage in one of James Howell's letters to Mansell: "The art of glassmaking is here (Venice) very highly valued, for whosoever be of that profession are gentlemen *ipso facto*, and it is not without reason, it being a rare kind of knowledge and chymistry to transmute dust and sand (for they are the only main ingredients) to such a diaphanous pellucid dainty body as you see a Crystal-Glass is. . . . But when I pried into the materials and observed the Furnaces and Calcinations, the transubstantions, the liquefactions that are incident to this art, my thoughts were raised to a higher speculation." (*Familiar Letters*, I, i., xxix.) *Cf.* also such works as Heraclius, *De artibus et coloribus Romanorum*, Theophilus, *Diversarum Artium Schedula*, which well illustrate the character of the art in medieval times; for a modern work see Berthelot (M. P. E.), *Les origines de l'alchimie* (Paris, 1885).

[3] *Cf.* Hallen (A. W. C.), *Glassmaking in Sussex, Newcastle and Scotland*, in *The Scottish Antiquary*, 1893, p. 145.

[4] Cited in Houdoy (J.), *Verrerie à la façon de Venise*, Document xi. (11 January, 1623), Paris, 1873.

we must find it in the combination of an interest in usefulness with a reverence for knowledge. " L'art de la verrerie," said Bernard Palissy, " est noble et ceux qui y besognent sont nobles," and in France it was only this status which saved it from the stigma of vulgarity which the French, like the Greeks, attached to the practice of the useful arts.

In 1448, one hundred and twenty years before their arrival in England, the Lorrainers had received their famous charter from Jean de Calabria, son of King René, with full recognition of " plusieurs beaux droits libertez, franchises et prérogatives, et dont eulx et leurs prédécesseurs ayant joui et usé de tous temps passés et este tenus et reputez en telle franchise comme chevaliers estimez et gens nobles du dit duchié de Lorraine."[1]

The four chief families who held this unique position in Lorraine were de Hennezel, de Thiétry, du Thisac, and du Houx.[2] Chenaye des Bois, writing in 1750,[3] speaks of them as a " noblesse originaire," and derives them from Bohemia. The former phrase is doubtless a concession to the snobbery of a French noble family which would hate to be reminded of their connection with trade, but their place of origin is interesting, for it gives us a connecting link between the two great centres of potash glass in medieval Europe, Bohemia and Lorraine. When these men in 1567 migrated to England they were something better than poor exiles looking for a home. They came with a decent dignity to a country where they might pursue their art and maintain their Protestant faith with a freedom that their own country now denied them. France had been none too kind as a mother of the arts ; at the time of their departure they had perhaps lost something of the prestige which they had enjoyed in the time of King René and his son. France, in the 16th century, laughed at the pretensions of these decayed aristocrats with nothing but their craft to recommend them, as the Wessex of Hardy's novel laughed at John Durbeyfield :

> Votre noblesse est mince
> Car ce n'est pas d'un prince
> Daphnis, que vous sortez
> Gentilhomme de verre
> Si vous tombez à terre
> Adieu vos qualités.[4]

And Corneille (1625–1709) echoes the sentiment and the rhyme :

[1] Cited by Dillon, p. 230.
[2] Grazebrook (H. S.), *Collections for a Genealogy of the Noble Families of de Hennezel*, etc., Stourbridge, 1877. This book is very scarce. The B.M. has no copy, and I am indebted to Mr. Arthur Cochrane, Norroy King of Arms, for the loan of one. Hartshorne, *op. cit.*, p. 169.
[3] Aubert de la Chenaye des Bois (F. A.), *Dictionnaire de la noblesse* (2 ed., Paris, 1770–86).
[4] François Maynard (1582–1646), *Œuvres poétiques*, Ed. G. Garrison, Vol. II, p. 220.

Toute votre felicité
Sujette à l'instabilité
En moins de rien tombe par terre
Et comme elle a l'éclat du verre
Elle en a la fragilité.

When they reached England there may well have been a certain *hauteur* in their demeanour which was obnoxious to those glassmakers who were already long established in the Sussex Weald, and contributed to the ill-feeling caused by their consumption of the woods.

It is a difficult question to what extent the Lorraine immigrants and the Normandy men who came with them were acquainted with the technical processes and formulæ of Italian and especially Altarist glassmaking. Schuermans[1] has shown that glassmakers licensed by the consuls at Altare were settled extensively in France generally and in particular in Normandy and Lorraine ; and when it is remembered that both the Massari in Lorraine and the Bormioli in Normandy, like the four families to which we have already referred, had been long admitted to the nobility of France,[2] that the Altarist family of the Ferri were working for King René, from whom the Lorrainers had received their title, as early as 1442, and that even after the migration to England several Lorraine glassmakers are found in contact, and even in collaboration, with Italians,[3] it is difficult to believe that the Lorrainers' glass, at any rate at the time of their arrival, showed no traces of Italian influence, that it was simply a crude *verre de fougère*. We know that barilla, the soda plant from Spain, was in general use in France in the middle of the 16th century,[4] and jealous as the Altarists were of their private formulæ,[5] its use must surely have been extended to the French glassmakers proper as well as among the Italians. There are no existing specimens which can be proved to be the work of the Lorrainers, but in their absence Dillon makes a good suggestion which goes some way to explain what was the character of Lorraine glass and how it differed both from Venice and from *verre de fougère*. Good glass requires a certain admixture of lime.[6] In *verre de*

[1] *Op. cit., Lettre* XI—X, pp. 131–42. The earliest glassmaking at Altare, near Genoa, seems to have been in the potash tradition and brought thither in the 11th century by glassmakers from Normandy and Brittany, but at the time of the Altarist emigrations (16th cent.) the art probably differed little from that of Venice. Venetians had arrived in Altare early in the 14th century. Hartshorne, p. 31, note 2.

[2] Dillon, *op. cit.*, p. 227.

[3] For example, at Beckley in 1579 several Lorrainers are found in collaboration with a Venetian named Sebastian Orlanden with whom they made " bugles, amells and glass in collers." *v.* Dawson (C.), *Sussex Glass* in *The Antiquary*, 1905.

[4] Dillon, *ibid.*

[5] Glassmaking at Altare in the 15th century was under the control of special consuls who exercised a similar dominion to the Council of Ten at Venice.

[6] Dillon, *ibid.*

fougère and *Waldglas* the lime was provided by the impurities of the rough potash, but the finer soda from Spain (*barilla*) or the Levant (*rocchetta*) was lacking in this respect, so that it became necessary to add a small quantity of lime to each pot of metal. The omission of this was just the mistake liable to be made by men who imitated without understanding a superior technique. Be that as it may, it was perhaps a difference in metal resulting from some such imperfect imitation, together with the lack of hereditary experience in *fine* glassmaking, that made Lorraine glass generally inferior to *façon de Venise*.

The French immigrants in England, like the early glassmakers in South Germany, stand for a fusion of two traditions, the potash tradition of the north and the soda tradition of the south. After the Lorrainers began to carry their nomadic craft among the byways of England, we may surmise that they lost touch with the main current of development, and lacking the incentive which comes from contact with others, the security afforded by a settled abode and the materials which had come to them from the Mediterranean, fell back into the rougher forest glass until they came under Mansell's monopoly and eventually at the end of the 17th century assumed an important place in the history of English glassmaking (*cf. infra*).

The circumstances of their entry into England are sufficient proof of their ability. Religious intolerance may have been a strong motive for their quitting France, but it was under the ægis of an Antwerp business man, Jean Carré, that they were able to obtain a sanction and a custom in this country. Antwerp at this time (second half of the 16th century) was, with the sole exception of Venice, the most important centre of glassmaking in Europe; it was there that the Altarists and Venetians chiefly established themselves, that Verzelini practised his Venetian art and married his Dutch wife before he came to England,[1] and it was in Antwerp and not at Venice that Antonio Neri gathered the knowledge which enabled him to write his classic textbook (*L'arte vetraria*, 1612). Carré's policy is easy to discern. Until the time of which we are speaking (1567) there had been only two, and those abortive, attempts to establish Continental glassmakers in England. In 1549 eight Venetian glassmen who had been compelled by the length of the " close season " to seek their livelihood abroad, quitted Venice[2] and after a brief sojourn in Antwerp were induced by the offers of Edward VI, and through the management of an Antwerp business man, Delame, to establish themselves in London,

---

[1] Sepulchral inscription at Downe, Kent; Hallen, *loc. cit.* note; Hartshorne, p. 158, note 2.

[2] Schuermans, *op. cit.*, Lettre X (*Bulletin*, XXIX, 117). Their names were Josepo Casselari, Marco Terribile, Piero Terribile, Craxioxo, Battista da Chiari, Alvixo di Albertino, Heremia Pixani, Sebastiano Zanon.

probably at the Hall of the Crutched Friars. Soon afterwards a peremptory edict (18 September, 1549) by the Council at Venice recalled all truant craftsmen to their own city ; and seven of the English immigrants, preferring the indignation of their disappointed patrons to the wrath of the dreaded Council, and a brief incarceration in the Tower to permanent outlawry, made terms with the English nobility and returned to Murano less than three years after their arrival. During the fifteen years following their departure (1551) there appear to have been only two Italian glassmen in London, Josepo Casselari, the last of the eight Venetians, and a partner, Thomaso Cavato of Antwerp, who continued working together in London until the former left England to join the rising industry at Liège (1569).

The episode which ended in this way was a failure for the English Government no less than for the promoters at Antwerp, and the anxiety of the former to develop the glass industry again becomes effective in 1564, when a Netherlandish alchemist, Cornelius de Lannoy, came over with a three years' contract and a grant from the English Government, in order to carry out a series of experiments and give instruction to the English glassmen in London, who had been left to their own incompetence. But this second venture was no more successful than the first,[1] de Lannoy being dissatisfied with both his pupils and his " provisyons." The years 1551–67 are therefore a period in which the process of adoption was in suspense, and it was precisely in this stagnation that the astute Antwerp promoter saw his opportunity. There was already evidence that the taste for fine glass was fixed in England ; and Jean Carré, who must have been aware of the failure of his fellow-citizen Delame in a like enterprise and the more recent difficulties of de Lannoy, saw in this barbarous island a virgin market waiting for anyone with enough diplomacy to capture it. It was no less evident that the service of Venetians was inclined to be capricious ; but the " gentilshommes verriers " of Normandy and Lorraine, who had become under Altarist influence fairly proficient in the art, and at the same time were exposed in their own country to ridicule of their pretensions or intolerance of their faith, would be very ready for migration if custom and security were assured them ; and we may surmise that it was through these men, the de Hennezels, du Thisacs, and the rest, that Carré designed to bestow upon England the benefit of glass and on himself a proper share of the emoluments. From what we know[2] of the activities of Carré and his partner Pierre Briet[3] it is probable that they aspired to control the English glass industry as Sir Robert Mansell did half a century

[1] *Cf.* a letter from Armigell Waade to Cecil. *State Papers Domestic* for 1565 cited in Hartshorne, *op. cit.* Appendix, p. 393.
[2] Hartshorne, p. 154.
[3] *State Papers Domestic*, 1567. Hartshorne, p. 153.

later. This enterprise found a ready instrument in the French glassmakers who were already (August 1567) at work in the Weald of Surrey.

In the negotiations which then began Carré encountered three forces, the Queen, the French glassmakers, and a rival promoter from Antwerp, Anthony Becku (also called Dolyn[1]), and his strategy was the attempt to make them all sing to one tune, his own. His gambit was good. He obtained a letter of recommendation from the Bishop of Chartres and wrote to Lord Cecil asking for a licence of twenty-one years to set up a crystal glasshouse in London to make soda-glass drinking vessels by an " art as famous as that of Venice or Antwerp,"[2] and at the same time he forwarded a petition from the Normandy men in Sussex for a monopoly of the window-glass manufacture. Shortly afterwards he received a favourable reply from the Queen, and two glasshouses were erected, one in London for crystal glass and one at " Fernefol "[3] in Sussex, but worked respectively by the Lorrainers and the Normans.[4] Two points are important in this scheme. He had decided to abandon the square furnace of the Normandy men for the round furnace of the Venetians, and he proposed to buy proper soda, that is to say, *rocchetta* from the Levant or *barilla* from Spain, from an Italian merchant, Jean Suigo[5]; this seems to be the earliest indication as far as England is concerned of a trade in the soda requisite for *façon de Venise* glass.

Meanwhile the third party, Becku, made his appearance, and Carré, fearing that he also might obtain a concession, decided to risk the dangers of a triple alliance, and invited the rival to become his partner. Accordingly on 8 September Carré and Becku obtained a patent for twenty-one

---

[1] Anthonye Dowlyn is described as a glassmaker in 1571. He was a " free denizen," and at that date had been resident in England for 12 years (*Hug. Soc. Publ.*, X (1) p. 440). Naturalization required the passage of a bill through Parliament and was retrospective in effect. Denization was by grant from the Crown and was not retrospective, an important difference. Without denization a resident alien could not own land (see Page's Introduction to *Hug. Soc. Publ.*, Vol. X).

[2] Hartshorne, p. 153, based on *State Papers Domestic*, 1567, Patent Roll of Elizabeth, 8 Sept., 1567. *De concessio pro J. Carr et aliis* cited in full by Hartshorne, pp. 393-6.

[3] Fernfold Wood.

[4] Hartshorne (p. 154) assumes that both " Frenchmen and Lorrainers " worked in both glasshouses, but his meaning is not clear. In Sussex there were (1) the old glassmakers of the Chiddingfold region (*supra*, p. 51 *sq.*) and (2) more recently arrived glassmakers from Normandy. Both these were concerned with sheet-glass, and Carré can hardly have expected to use them at any rate at first for crystal; for they were rough workers and had no understanding of soda metal. The crystal glasshouse in London must have been manned by the Lorrainers whom Carré had specially brought over " at great cost " to himself. But his hope was to capture the sheet-glass industry and initiate crystal glassmaking under his own control.

[5] Hulme (E. W.) in the *Antiquary*, xxxiv, 142. Lansdowne MS. No. 76, 17th April, 1568, Contract between Thomas and Balthazar de Hennezel, John Chevalier, and John Carré, cited Hartshorne, p. 398.

[63]

years, which might have become a monopoly of the English glass industry. They undertook to practise the " arte feate and mysterie of glas for glazinge such as is made in Ffrannce, Lorrayne and Burgundy," to supply the realm generally and " to teache Englishe men oure subjectes the same scyence or arte." At the same time Carré seems to have introduced a fourth party, Jean Chevalier, as make-weight against Becku.[1] Becku certainly had little intention of becoming the sleeping partner, and the licence had no sooner been put in order than he wrote to Cecil protesting that since half of the glassworkers had contracted with Carré and the other half with Jean Chevalier, he, Becku, was left with no power in the business. In this difficulty he foolishly confided in Briet, whom he had to a great extent superseded ; but the latter, apparently wearied by Carré's manœuvrings, got quit of the whole matter and set up an independent glasshouse at Boulogne with the avowed intention of cutting out his late partners from a convenient place where no privilege was required. Becku meanwhile had found a second support in Ferdinand Poyntz, who probably came from Sussex, and together they obtained permission to hew wood in Windsor Great Park, not, surely, as Hartshorne suggests, for the furnace established by Carré, but more probably for one of their own which Becku hoped to man with German workmen.[2] Finally Briet, doubtless perceiving that Becku was established independently, returned to partnership with Carré.

That seems to be the last recorded event in this tale of commercial intrigue, but the dispute dragged on for two years, and in 1569 was referred to arbitration.[3] What the verdict was or whether there was a verdict we do not know, but it is extremely unlikely that it was encouraging to Lorraine glassmaking in Sussex. On the Venetian side Carré was more successful. In 1571 he brought over six Venetians whose names are given as Domenyck Cassiler (Cassilari), Lawrence Farlonger, Vincent Giulio, Frauncis Gilio, Biasio Bradarmin, and John Morato. Verzelini came to England the same year[4] and no doubt for the same enterprise. With these men Carré succeeded in starting a Venetian glass manufactory in London, almost certainly at the Crutched Friars. But he did not live to enjoy the fruits of it and when he died, in 1572, it was not long before Verzelini revealed himself as the ablest man on Carré's staff and his natural successor. Carré was buried at Alfold under the description

---

[1] Lansdowne MS., *u.s.*

[2] He sent his son to Germany for the purpose of engaging Germans, and he was preparing " a commodious place against their coming." Lansdowne MS., 76.

[3] The arbitrators, Richard Onslow and William More, examined Becku, Carré, Briet and a Normandy glassmaker, Jean Bongar, probably an ancestor of Isaac Bongar (for whom *v. infra*, p. 94). Hartshorne, p. 155.

[4] *Hug. Soc. Publ.*, Vol. X (2), p. 40.

THE AGE OF ADOPTION

THE AGE OF ADOPTION

"John Garry Mr. of the Glasshouse," and when in 1576 Briet and one Pierre Appell,[1] who had succeeded to his patent, applied for a renewal of the licence,[2] Verzelini had finally established Venetian glassmaking in London with the complete monopoly (1575) of English glass to which Carré had unsuccessfully aspired. Their petition was refused and thereafter the Low Country promoters disappear from history, and the French glassmen, escaping from the manœuvres of their masters and the hostility of Sussex, began the long vagrancy which has left its scattered tokens in the parish registers of England and a permanent memorial in the Stourbridge glasshouses of our own time.

Before we proceed to the main English tradition which starts with Verzelini it will be convenient to follow the side-issue until it rejoins the main stream more than a century later. The date of the departure of the Lorrainers from Sussex and Surrey can be fixed with some precision.[3] In 1574, two years after Carré's death and seven or eight after the first arrival of the Lorrainers, the Bishop of Chichester wrote to Lord Burghley to give notice of a plot at Petworth to rob and murder the Frenchmen and to burn their houses ; it had lately been frustrated by the authorities. Less than two years later, 7 October, 1576, the names of Du Thisac, Hennezel, and Du Houx begin to occur in the parish registers of a Hampshire church. The publication of the evidence derived from this source and the earlier excavations[4] at Buckholt are sufficient indication of the first stage in their journeyings. Their original contract with Carré for seven years was due to expire on 22 April, 1577, but as Carré himself had died nearly five years before that date, it is probable that they left Sussex about the time that the petition of Briet and Appell was rejected (1576), and established a furnace at Buckholt, which lay remotely in the forest between Winchester and Salisbury. The site of the glasshouse was excavated in 1860, and Syer Cuming,[5] who made an exhaustive analysis of the remains, was of opinion that though certain fragments were clearly of Roman or Venetian origin, the majority of the glass and the glasshouse itself dated from the second half of the 16th century. This conclusion was substantially confirmed thirty years later by the discovery of several of the most important names of the Lorraine glassmaking families in the registers at the Walloon

---

[1] Possibly identical with a James Apple who in 1571 was described as a servant of Carré and " borne in Dowchlande." He had then been in England 9 years but is not called a glassmaker (*Hug. Soc. Publ.*, X (1), p. 440).

[2] Hulme (E. W.) in the *Antiquary*, December, 1894, citing Lansdowne MSS., 22.

[3] *State Papers Domestic*, 1574. Hartshorne, p. 156. *Huguenot Soc. Publications*, Vol. IV, Registre de l'Eglise Wallonne à Southampton.

[4] *Journal of the British Archæological Assoc.*, XVII, p. 57.

[5] *J.B.A.A.*, *loc. cit.* The window glass found there was not *cast* but *blown* and still retained a thick hem.

F

Church at Southampton in which Jan du Tisac, Pierre Vaillant,[1] Claude Potier are described as " ouvriers de verre à la Verriere de Boute haut " (7 October, 1576) ; " Monsieur Hennezé et s.f. Louis de Hennezee, Arnoul Bisson, Jan Perne," as " tous de bocquehaut " (6 October, 1577) ; and Jan Buré J. F. (7 October, 1577), and Monsr. du Hou Vierrieren " a bouque haut " (4 January, 1579).

It is probable that at Buckholt the window glass which had originally been the speciality of the Hennezels was gradually superseded by vessel glass, which found a readier market through the peddling dealers, who seem to have been an extensive class and received certain rights under the Statute of Vagabonds (1597). But the sojourn of the Lorrainers in this place endured no longer than their fuel, and less than twelve years afterwards they had advanced another stage, following the woodlands, as their craft required, to the Forest of Dean, where several notices of them occur in the parish registers of Newent[2] between the years 1599 and 1601. One of these is the baptism of Abraham Tyzack, " sonne of a Frenchman at the glasshouse," and an indeterminate mention of " Margaret daughter of Anthony Voydyn, glass-founder." Little more than fifteen years elapsed before the next migration, but during that period personal enterprise and public enactments had destroyed the main motive for their wanderings, and in the long run changed the character of their industry. During the first decade of the 17th century there were experiments in the use of coal for glass furnaces, and in 1610 Sir William Slingsby at the head of a combine of four obtained a special licence[3] for twenty-one years by which " the furnaces works and devises by them newly found out " may be applied " for the boiling of beer and ale and for the melting of glass, ordinance, bell metal, lattyn, copper, brass, tin, lead, and other metal. . . ." Five years later (1615) the use of wood fuel was prohibited by Royal Proclamation.[4] The use of coal thus began to supersede the use of wood, and the effects of the change are precisely stated by Plot[5] : " The goodness of the clay and the cheapness of the coal thereabouts (near Stourbridge) no doubt has drawn the glasshouses, both for vessels and broad glass into these parts, there being divers set up in different furnaces here at Amblecote, Oldswinford, Holloway's End, and Cobourne-brook." The chief cause of their wanderings now disappears.

It is the peculiarity of the Stourbridge clay that when fashioned into

---

[1] The Vaillant family were a well-known dynasty of glassmakers in Normandy : v. Le Vaillant de la Fieffe, *Les verreries de la Normandy.*

[2] Hallam in *Scottish Antiquary,* 1893, p. 149.

[3] Abstract of Patent Roll, 8 Jas. I. Licence to William Slingesby Knight and others dated 28th July, 1610, in Hartshorne, p. 409.

[4] *A Proclamation touching glasses. S.P.D.,* 23 May, 1615.

[5] Plot (Robert), *Natural History of Staffordshire* (1686), *s.v.* Amblecote.

glasspots it is better able than any other to withstand the intense heat of the glass furnace[1]—a fact which had been noted as early as 1566, when a lease was granted for digging clay for glasspots in that neighbourhood. Until recent years it has been almost the only clay used for the purpose in this island, being distributed throughout the country and exported abroad ; and it was probably during their stay in the Forest of Dean that the Lorrainers first heard of its advantages. It was thus for a double benefit of clay and afterwards of coal that the Hennezels, Tyzacks, Titterys, and Du Houx, who seem to have been intermarrying branches of the same stock and distinguished originally by territorial designations, established a dynastic craftsmanship in the Stourbridge area. The Hennezels (or Henzys), Tyzacks, and Titterys were able to start work simultaneously in Worcestershire and on the Tyne, but the Du Houx seem to have remained a short time only. About 1616–21 Isaac du Houx had established a glass-house at Hyde (Cheshire),[2] and in 1636–7 Jacob du Houx, who had married Ann Tyzack in 1625 and had three children by her before leaving Stourbridge, was working at London in the parish of All Hallows.[3] There is evidence also of the Du Houx at Bristol before the end of the 16th century.[4] But the other three families made Newcastle and Stourbridge their preserve, and continuing to intermarry, moved to and fro between the two places with a frequency which is surprising when we consider how much greater the distance was at that time. The first notice of their presence[5] in the region of Stourbridge occurs in 1612, when a son of Paul and Bridget Tyzack was baptized at Kingswinford. Between 1615 and 1630 at least seven members of the Henzey family had children in Olds-winford and Kingswinford ; and some of the family are also found at Amblecote. The Titterys also were making glass at Oldswinford, but the mentions of them are meagre ; they seem to have been less vigorous and prolific than the others, and after the 17th century notices of them are not very frequent. They were quite extinct in 1789.[6] Certainly the Henzeys and the Tyzacks were chiefly responsible for maintaining the tradition both at Stourbridge and Newcastle, and although in 1615 Edward Hensey (*sic*) was " servant to Sir Robert Mansfield " (*i.e.* Mansell) at Newcastle, and the Lorrainers at both places probably resigned their independence when Mansell's monopoly became generally effective, they lost neither

[1] For the chemical qualities of Stourbridge clay *v.* Marson (P.), *op. cit.*, chap. IX.
[2] Earwaker (J. P.), *East Cheshire*, I, 405–8.
[3] Called " Hoe, a Frenchman " (*V. C. H. Glos*, II, p. 213).
[4] *V. C. H. Glos*, II, 213.
[5] It is significant that at Oldswinford the number of burials increased from twenty-five in 1611 to forty-nine in 1612, so that even allowing for a heavy year in deaths the influx must have been considerable. Taylor (M. V.) in *V. C. H. Worcester*, II, 279 n., citing a MS. in the Soc. Art. Library.
[6] Brand (J.), *Hist. of Northumberland* (London, 1789), II, 40.

their individuality nor their enterprise in later times, and established their art in both Ireland and Scotland.[1]

After the Restoration and the revival in glassmaking which came with it, an Irish nobleman, Viscount Conway and Killulta, was planning to set up a glass manufactory on his estate, and a friend, Sir George Ramsden, to whom he wrote for advice on the matter, was much exercised in mind between the rude competence of Stourbridge and the more expensive elegance of a "Sennior Mallyo," a Venetian who probably came to England in the early 'sixties with the influx of Italian artists which is represented by the Duke of Buckingham's manager Rosetti. "But if," says Ramsden, "any will upon their own account come over and make their own work from Stourbridge or any other place where ordinary glass for bottles, window-glass, etc. is made and give some small rent for wood-leave, etc., I think that may be far more advisable than to run the adventure of a quarter of that charge Sennior Mallyo expects."[2] Difficulties of timber, transport and expense seem to have arisen in this case, and it is not certain whether the project ever came to an issue. But less than five years later (early in 1670) Ananias Henzey of Stourbridge had established a glasshouse at Portarlington (Queen's County). We hear that in November, 1670, "he is at present at a stop by occasion of some disappointment in the melting of his metal." In this anxiety he wrote to one Robert Leigh asking him to intercede on his behalf with Secretary Arlington for leniency in the matter of rent. "I have used," he says, "all the best ways and means hitherto to make glass but cannot as yet do it. This is a great damage to me. . . . I have sent to Dublin for things to make a further trial which I hope will do some good and shall not leave off until every experiment has been tried. . . . If the next trial does not succeed I shall have to put out the fire till next summer to get some things

---

[1] In the register of St. Andrew's Episcopal Church, Glasgow, there are numerous entries of glassmakers, some of whom are stated to have come from Newcastle. In 1784 we have an interesting link with Newcastle, Stourbridge, Sussex, and Lorraine in an entry of baptism of a son of William Tweeddal Chrystal glassmaker and Ann Tissaac his wife, v. Hallen, op. cit., p. 156. Mention may be made also of the family of Bigault, which was closely allied with the other Lorraine families. Various glassmakers called Bigo or Bago are mentioned during the 17th century. Jeremy Bago (also called Bagg, in 1642) married a Susanna Henzey at Oldswinford in 1619 (Grazebrook, p. 52) and had a glasshouse at Greenwich. In 1623 Abraham Bigo had glasshouses at Purbeck, I.W. (for the sand), and at Ratcliff, Middlesex. And in the same year Abraham Bigo (presumably a different member of the family) took a lease for glassmaking at Birr, King's County (Westropp, p. 31). Philip Bago, presumably a younger son and "a Frenchman," was naturalized there in 1637. There were Bigos at Bristol in the second half of the 18th century.

[2] Letter from Sir George Ramsden to Viscount Conway and Killulta, dated 4 July, 1665, in the Calendar of State Papers, Ireland, cited in Westropp (M. S. D.), *Irish Glass* (London, 1920), p. 33.

that cannot be had at this time of the year." To this Leigh adds a covering letter : " He has laid out much money on your land and occasioned the coming of several families to dwell there, and if he prove not very unlucky or failing in his art of making glass which he has practised in another place these twenty years past, I do not doubt he will be a great means to plant that part of your Lordship's estate."[1]

This man is probably identical with an Ananias Henzey who had a grant of land in King's County, and if he was forty or so at the time of the Portarlington episode it was probably he who returned to England, and gave evidence in favour of the Glassmakers' Petition in 1697.[2]

The Tyneside settlements, which were more permanent and prosperous, owe their effective foundation to Peregrine Henzey of Oldswinford, who seems to have migrated to the North soon after 1620, perhaps accompanied by his nephew and niece, Edward and Jane[3] ; and during the next century Peregrine is a regular patronymic in the northern branches of the family. Between Edward Henzey (1617) and Peregrine came the Tyzacks, one of whom, " Tymothie Teswick, glassmaker, a Frenchman," had a son, John, baptized at All Saints, Newcastle, in November 1619. Finally some of the Titterys arrived in the district about the same time.[4] Beyond the bare catalogue of their births, their marriages, and their deaths we have little or no evidence for reconstructing the progress of their art in the middle years of the 17th century : but of their prosperity in business and their fertility in private life there is no more striking proof than the six hundred notices of the three families, Henzey, Tyzack, and Tittery, which have been found between the years 1619 and 1750 in the parish registers of All Saints, Newcastle. By the end of the century the Henzeys and Tyzacks of Newcastle had consolidated themselves into a northern group of glassmakers which was only second in importance to the London group represented by Francis Jackson, John Bowles, and John Gutheridge.[5] The Newcastle group had in the last quarter of the century extended their trade far beyond their locality, and even outside England, and they seem to have had a leader in John Tyzack. He had travelled considerably in America and the West Indies, and it was his practice regularly to visit London, where he had a warehouse " near Old Swan Stairs " and an office at the Barbadoes Coffee House in Exchange Alley. He seems to have been the agent and foreign correspondent of his working kinsmen.

[1] Letter from Robert Leigh to Arlington, dated 14 November, 1670. *State Papers, Ireland*, cited in Westropp, *op. cit.*, pp. 33–5.
[2] *Journals of House of Commons*, XI, 707–10, cited by Buckley (F.). *The Glass Trade in England in the seventeenth century* (London, privately printed, 1914), p. 53.
[3] Hartshorne, *op. cit.*, p. 178.
[4] Hartshorne, *ibid.*
[5] *State Papers Domestic*, Car. II, 383, No. 8, cited in Buckley (F.). *Glass Trade*, p. 37.

It was John Tyzack and his followers, Peregrine Henzell, John Henzell, Jacob Henzell, and Peregrine Tyzack, who came into the politics of their trade in 1695-6 and were responsible for the protests and petitions. It was the occasion when William III's Government, with the frank intention of raising money for the French war, levied a tax of 20 per cent on fine glass, on bottles at a much higher rate, and on several of the commodities, of which the most important was coal, required for its manufacture. John Tyzack, in the petition which he presented to the House of Commons, is not the spokesman of a local grievance, but the delegate of a national industry. In the North the names of the three families are found until the middle of the 18th century, and in Worcestershire they intermarried with a number of local and other families, Pidcock, Rogers (whence Samuel Rogers the poet, b. 1763), Croker, Dixon, Weston, Grazebrook, Batchelor, and Brettell, who were the successors of their art and their prosperity. Names of the original families are still mentioned in the last quarter of the century, but in the heyday of Stourbridge glass the industry seems to have passed entirely into English hands, the Hawkes, Honeybournes, Graze-brooks, Pidcocks, Brettells, and others ; at the present day the glass quarter at Stourbridge is still called Brettle Lane.[1]

The natural benefits of Stourbridge and the prosperity of the inhabitants attracted new glassmakers to that region, or enlisted the local families in the trade ; and being so many men of the same trade in the same place, and finding their market more restricted than their output, the less successful among them were reduced to insolvency or emigration. Four bankrupts are recorded, one being a Tyzack, between 1713 and 1743, and throughout the 18th century there were a number of glasshouses in other parts which owed their origin or their advancement to the enterprising failures of their metropolis. The glasshouses at Bolsterstone, Dudley, Whittington (near Chesterfield), Catcliffe, Rothwell, Ferrybridge in Yorkshire,[2] Broseley (Shropshire),[3] and (in a sense which will appear later) Waterford and Cork are all derivatives of the Anglo-French glassmanship of Stourbridge. The cause of all this was " market-hunger " ; and we may find a true analogy in the " land-hunger " to which the early Greek colonies owed their

[1] The Brettells themselves were of French origin (Breteuils), and like the Dixons and the Pidcocks, represent the Henzeys (Hennezels, Ensells) in the female line. The arms of Hennezel and Brettell are the same except in tincture. The connection with the Rogerses was established by the marriage of Thomas Rogers with Anne de Thiétry about the middle of the 17th century.

[2] For all these factories cf. Buckley (F.), *History*, pp. 3–4 and p. 14 ; Hartshorne, *op. cit.*, pp. 176 and 470 ; Kenworthy (J.), *The Bolsterstone glasshouse* (Deepcar, 1914).

[3] For Broseley cf. Buckley (F.), *op. cit.*, p. 14. The Broseley glasshouse was founded in 1732 by Benjamin Batchelor, who is certainly a relative, perhaps a son of the Elisha Batchelor who with Ananias Henzey presented a petition for the repeal of the Excise, 17 Feb., 1697, v. *Journals H. of Commons*, XI, 707–10, cited in Buckley (F.), *Glass trade*, p. 53.

foundation. At Stourbridge during the late 17th and first half of the 18th century we can only judge of the vigour of the parent by the number of her offspring and observe how the florescence of Stourbridge glass late in the 18th century and early in the 19th century was the result of a period of evacuation in which the city sent out colonies to purge herself of intestine idlers, and thereby effected that adjustment of her manufacture and her market which was requisite for prosperity.[1]

There is not much glass that can be certainly assigned to the Anglo-French tradition. A good deal of the work of the Lorrainers and their successors in both the 17th and the 18th centuries was concerned with the making of plate or crown glass for windows, and it was chiefly for this that Newcastle earned so enduring a reputation. But besides this it is probable that rough vessels of various kinds were made for domestic purposes during the 17th century and even later : and certain that some at least of the Anglo-French factories learned to make glass of lead (" flint glass "). In 1696 five out of seventeen glasshouses at Stourbridge were making " flint glass " (i.e. glass of lead), and even in London the proportion was only nine out of twenty-four.[2] From the extensive amalgamation at Stourbridge between French and local English families and the fact that Stourbridge glass was not known in London as late as 1703[3] we may infer that Stourbridge was out of touch with new developments, and did not readily assimilate her wares to those being made at London and other places in the south of England. In the North it was much the same. The Lorrainers at Newcastle, in spite of their London agents,[4] worked in comparative isolation, and being thus thrown back much more upon their own tradition, fell into a conservative habit which remained with them throughout the following century. In 1696 only one of the eleven Tyneside factories was making flint glass,[5] and eighty years afterwards, when the main types of glass were more or less uniform throughout England, there were still only two flint-glass houses out of sixteen large glassworks on the Tyne.[6] This

[1] Taylor (M. V.) in *V. C. H. Worcester*, II, 278 (1906). This brief article is a model of exact scholarship and quite the best account of Stourbridge glassmaking that has appeared. The Stourbridge glasshouses seem to have served only an inland market, v. Neve, cited below.

[2] Houghton (J.), *Letters for the Improvement of Commerce and Trade*, No. 198, 15 May, 1696. List of glasshouses in England and Wales.

[3] Neve (R.), *Builders' Dictionary* (1703), p. 149, says that " Staffordshire " glass was seldom used in London and " he could never learn any account of it."

[4] John Tyzack already referred to ; and Defoe, *Moll Flanders* (Bohn ed.), p. 196, mentions a " Mr. Henzill's glasshouse, that was lately come from Newcastle-on-Tyne." *Moll Flanders* was written 1722, but the fictional date is 1683.

[5] Houghton, *ibid.*

[6] Brand (J.), *Newcastle* (1789) ; Hutchinson (W.), *Northumberland* (Newcastle, 1789), II, 473. Buckley (F.), *History*, p. 6.

fact is important and has an interesting corollary. Most collectors of glass are familiar with a distinctive and not infrequent type of glass, mainly small bowls and jugs, which is usually assigned to Yorkshire or the Tyneside glasshouses. They are in some cases glass of lead, but always of a rough and imperfectly fused material, sometimes white or greenish in colour, but frequently some shade of blue, or blackish blue. The lead specimens seem to be the earliest experiments in flint glass of provincial glasshouses which normally made potash glass. Such pieces are most often found in the north of England before they reach the London market, and they are not sufficiently expensive or elaborate to have travelled far from their place of origin. They are generally assigned to the latter part of the 18th century, but we have no means of dating them exactly, and in form there is no reason why they should not be placed at least half a century earlier. The poverty of their metal makes little appeal to collectors, but their naive design and outspoken technique make them not less attractive than many more imposing pieces in lead glass ; and we may see in them genuine tokens of the Lorraine tradition.[1]

§3. THE CAPTURE OF VERZELINI

If the first glasshouses in the provinces were established by Frenchmen the tradition of London glassmaking was mainly Italian for at least a century after the first of the Venetians came to England, and it was chiefly the London glasshouses that evolved a specifically English glass with a metal and a manner of its own. The influence of Venice is thus the most important antecedent with which we have to deal.

Venice had brought back the art of glass from Syria as early as the 11th century, but the history of Venetian glass considered as an art of the Renaissance really begins in 1463 with the invention of the metal *cristallo* by the Berovieri, one of the most eminent families of glassmakers then working at Venice. It is difficult to regard this event as a mere contingency, for it occurred at a moment in European history when a fresh thought, a fresh will, a fresh taste were first beginning to assert themselves. A new will to form required expression in glassmaking, in pottery, and in the useful arts generally, as much as in painting and literature. The *cristallo* of the Berovieri became thus a fresh medium in the art of glass, and maintained itself throughout the whole of the later Renaissance. Style and metal, form and substance, determined one another.

[1] A few glasses of this type are in the Victoria and Albert Museum : and a small but highly interesting collection mainly of blue pieces was sold at Sotheby's, 2 December, 1926.

THE AGE OF ADOPTION

The style in glassmaking that was born thus only escaped from Venice with the greatest difficulty. In Venice itself the secrets of the art had been jealously guarded from the earliest times and the glassmakers themselves were subject to a very exact control, at first apparently by the guilds into which they formed themselves, and later by the omnipotent Council of Ten. As early as 1224 there was a guild of glass-blowers which fined twenty-nine members of the *ars friolaria* for breaking the rules of their trade. In the 15th century the glassmakers were divided into guilds or *arti*, *e.g.* the *fialai, cristallai, perlai,* and *conterie* (bead-makers), according to the branch of the art which they followed. These divisions were encouraged by the Republic, for every workman was thus dependent on his fellow, and it was difficult for rebels to quit the city and start a glasshouse in foreign countries. Indeed, before the end of the 14th century the Government had stated its intention " ut ars tam nobilis semper stet et permaneat in loco Muriani." Glass and glassmakers were regarded as a State monopoly, and the Council of Ten prohibited both the export of raw materials and the emigration of the glassmakers themselves. But the system of control was not infallible. In the 13th century, before the monopoly was properly established, glasshouses were founded at Treviso, Ferrara, Padua, Bologna, and other places in Italy; but the more rigid supervision of the 15th century did not prevent the Berovieri communicating the method of making their *cristallo* to the city of Altare. Moreover, the tyranny which guarded the art did much to drive it into exile. The princes and the " gentilitie " of Europe were eager to add glassmaking to the arts of their own countries, and they could offer freedom and dignity to any truant who entered their service. There were also opportunities of private enterprise which the more adventurous sort preferred to the cramped security of their own city. It thus happened that not individuals only but whole dynasties of artists—*e.g.* the Ferri of Provence, the Massari of Lorraine, the Saroldi in Poitou, the Bormioli in Normandy, the Castelli in the Netherlands, settled themselves in foreign parts and carried a version of the Venetian art into most regions of Europe. The Council of Ten did all it could to check the egress. Its diplomats in the several courts of Europe were enjoined to seek out the truants, and by threats or promises induce them to return, and at the same time it was made known that their secession would be visited upon the families they had left behind. The subsequent history of glass in Europe is the chief witness to the failure of this policy, but it remains true[1] that glass in the full sense Venetian was never made anywhere but in Venice. The art in exile preserved the technique and to some extent the style of Murano, but it lost, and never attained independently, the splendour and the delicacy of its metropolis.

[1] *Cf.* James Howell, *infra*, p. 81.

These were the conditions in which Giacomo Verzelini came to England ; but his version of " Venice glasses " was twice, not once, removed from truth. It is beyond the scope of this book to follow the distribution of Venetian artists in the Netherlands. It will be sufficient to remark here that in the second half of the 16th century the glasshouses of Antwerp had attained an importance only second to Venice itself. Verzelini was born at Venice in 1522, and doubtless left the city for the same reasons as the eight Murano glassmakers we have already mentioned. He first found employment at Antwerp, and had probably worked there for some years before he came to England ; and in 1555 he married a Dutch woman of good family, Elizabeth, " born in Antwerp, of the ancient house of Van-buren and Mace," by whom he had six sons and three daughters. He arrived in London in 1571[1] with a company of six Venetians whom Carré had brought over from the Netherlands not long before he died (1572). Josepo Casselari, the last of the immigrants of 1549, had returned to Liège before 1569,[2] and it was probably due to his influence that the six Venetians were led to accept Carré's invitation ; for their leader was a certain Domenico Casselari who came of the same family as Josepo and was probably his brother. It is likely that Verzelini himself in the first instance was the servant of the promoter Carré. When Carré died in 1572 Verzelini was apparently left in sole charge of the workmen at the Crutched Friars and the control[3] of the business seems to have devolved upon him, for three years later Domenico Casselari was in his service, and we may infer that the other Venetians were likewise,[4] since

[1] Verzelini must be identified with " one Joseph a Venetian and a glassmaker," who in 1571 was living in the parish of St. Benet Fink in the same house as another " glass-maker born in Venice," Quiobyn Littery and his wife Lucy ; Joseph in 1571 had been here four months (*Hug. Soc. Publ.*, X (2), 41). Schuermans (*Bulletin*, XXIX, 121) quotes Stow that Verzelini arrived in London in 1557 or 1558 ; this statement may refer to a previous visit of Verzelini to this country, but I doubt whether he was permanently settled here before 1571. He almost certainly was brought over by Carré with the other Venetians from the Netherlands. Six of them, Dominych Cassiler (Cassilari), Lawrence Farlonger, Vincent Gilio, Frauncis Gilio, Biasio Bradarmin and John Morato came over in June, 1571, and were registered as Carré's (John Carr's) servants (*Hug. Soc Publ.*, X (2), 40). Another glassmaker, Ombien Lalere, was sojourning with Carré in 1571 and was probably his servant. It is likely that Littery also was employed by Carré.

[2] Schuermans, *Bulletin*, XXIX, p. 118 note.

[3] Not ownership. Verzelini could not in law hold land until he had taken out letters of denization. This he did not do till 26 November, 1576, *i.e.* after his monopoly had been granted.

[4] In 1581 " Versalyn " is described as " Keeper of the glasshouse," and he, his workmen and servants were " of no church " (*Hug. Soc. Publ.*, X (2), 304). In the same year Domenico Cassilari, Vincencius Filiolo, Domenico de Marato, and Marcus Guado, all glassmakers, were living in the parish of St. Olaves in Hart Street (*Hug. Soc. Publ.*, X (2), 221). They are not described as Verzelini's servants, but in view of the notice of Verzelini himself it seems certain that they were.

Casselari was the chief among them.[1] On the 4th of September, 1575, the glasshouse at the Crutched Friars was destroyed by a great fire, so that all the utensils were burnt and only the stone walls were left standing. Thereafter Verzelini removed to a site in Broad Street[2] where he continued working from the date of his monopoly (15 December, 1575) until his retirement in 1592. It would appear that some attempt was made to reconstruct the demolished glassworks at the Crutched Friars. Domenico Casselari was still working there after the fire in the service of Verzelini, and as far as is known at present 1581 is the date when his name is last mentioned. But as late as 1589 "Jacob the stranger," who must surely be identified with Verzelini, is described as making glass at the Crutched Friars. In view of this conflict of evidence we must, I think, assume that after 1575 Verzelini was in control of two glasshouses in London. The new glasshouse in Broad Street was taken over, or more probably built, when Verzelini assumed his monopoly, but so soon as the necessary repairs could be made good the glassworks at the Crutched Friars were reopened with Domenico Casselari as manager under the general direction of Verzelini. Such a supposition is required to give coherence to the four statements (1) that after 1575 Casselari was the servant of Verzelini, (2) that after 1575 Casselari was working at the Crutched Friars, (3) that after the fire Verzelini opened a new glasshouse in Broad Street, and (4) that in 1589 Jacob the stranger was dwelling in the Crutched Friars[3]. There is no room for the suggestion that Casselari set up in independent business ; for quite apart from the contrary statement which we have cited it is highly unlikely that Verzelini's monopoly, whether or not it was rigidly exclusive in the more remote regions of England, would have tolerated a rival maker of Venetian drinking glasses in London and under the eyes and attention of the monopolist himself.

There were two significant facts about him and his relations with the English Government. He was the first Italian and the first glassmaker who was able not only to obtain an official sanction, but also establish a permanent and prosperous glass business in this country ; and in the history of English glassmaking, his is the first effective instance of the monopoly system under which the infant industry grew and prospered. England received the benefit of glass from two sides, from " labour " in the persons of the capricious Venetians or the poor proud vagabonds from France, and from " capital " in the persons of the rich English who used the monopoly system to win the art of glass from the Italian. Verzelini was the only monopolist who was also a professional glassmaker, and the

[1] F. Buckley in *Glass*, V, 103–4. Page states (*Huguenot Soc. Publ.*, VIII, p. xlvi.) that Verzelini had " a large number " of foreign workmen under him.
[2] Powell, p. 29.
[3] Hartshorne, p. 157, based on Lansdowne MS., 59.

privilege which conferred such distinction and prosperity was granted him in order that Englishmen might appropriate the craft that would normally have descended to his sons. There is reason to believe[1] that some at least of his children continued in London after his death, but none of them, as far as we know, practised the art of glass. That brings us to the second fact. "Tous les rois désiraient cette science," but it is clear from the instance of the eight Venetians and the Dutch alchemist De Lannoy that the English Government did not want merely a tame glass-maker to supply the new fashions of the nobility. When they offered Verzelini his monopoly they purposed a serious industrial enterprise.[2] England was already a market which Englishmen had the ambition but not the skill to supply. The eight Venetians of 1549 had known the bread and water of their indignation[3]; Cornelius de Lannoy, the charlatan chemist, in spite of his reputation and his subsidy, came to no permanence because he searched the Continent for clay when he might have found it at Stourbridge[4]; and now (autumn, 1575) in the Venetian who for three years already had made London acquainted with his skill, the English Government saw their man.

His furnace at the Crutched Friars had lately been destroyed,[5] and we may reasonably suspect that there was malice in it. Already in 1573 we hear of a considerable body of Glaziers or glass merchants whose business was to import Venice glasses and place them on the London market. At some date during the reign of Queen Elizabeth they formed themselves into a Glaziers' Company, and arms were granted to them in 1588. Up to the Restoration they were a vigorous corporation, and had a good deal to say during Mansell's tenure of the monopoly. They had a Hall of their own, but it was destroyed during the Great Fire of London, and the Company never seems to have re-established itself afterwards, its place being taken by the new Company of Glass Sellers. In 1575 these men were fifty households strong, and they felt themselves much aggrieved by the proposal to grant Verzelini a monopoly to manufacture Venice

[1] Hallen (A. W. C.), *op. cit.*, p. 148, note 1.
[2] *Cf.* a very definite clause in Verzelini's patent, " for as much as oure intente and meanynge is that the said arte . . . or makyng the said drynkyng glasses shall remayne and have contynuance within oure Realmes of England and Ireland. . . ." cited Hartshorne, p. 400. The same reason in Bowes' patent, Hartshorne, p. 405.
[3] Literally : Hartshorne, p. 149, based on Venetian State Papers, 1549–50.
[4] He could not discover a clay for glasspots which would stand a high temperature (*cf.* Hartshorne, p. 393. Letter from Armigill Waade to Cecil), and this was the chief cause of his failure. Stourbridge clay was first used in glassmaking in 1565 ; Hulme (E. W.) in *Antiquary*, 1894 ; Harrison (G.) in Timmins (S.), *Resources . . . of Birmingham* (Birmingham, 1866).
[5] 4 September, 1575, *v.* Stow's *London* (ed. of 1603), p. 150. The monopoly was granted 15 December, 1575.

glasses. When Verzelini's application was being considered they formally protested to the Privy Council; such a privilege, they said, would mean the "overthrow of fifty households using only the trade of selling of glasses, besides the hindrance of the merchant adventurers bringing trade into this realm." It was a very reasonable jealousy, and like the ironworkers of Sussex, they were not content with the machinery of a legal protest; pillage and burning were more emphatic. There seems to be no definite statement that the glasshouse at the Crutched Friars was deliberately burned, but the coincidence of that event with Verzelini's monopoly and the parallel of the Lorrainers in Sussex do not leave much doubt upon the point. During the two or three years that he had been working unprivileged in London Verzelini, it may be suggested, had encountered a growing hostility from the merchants of glass, which culminated early in the year 1575 in the loss of his glasshouse (4 September, 1575); and when he applied to the Privy Council he was seeking royal protection as much as a royal privilege (15 September, 1575). Arson having failed,[1] the Glaziers took an official course, but Verzelini's later career is a proof of their failure.[2] But at that time the loss of his furnace was a grave disaster for Verzelini. He had only opened his business a few years before; he was at this time fifty-three years of age with a wife and nine children under the age of eighteen; and now he had suddenly lost his livelihood.[3] The English Government, firm set on the acquisition of glassmaking, saw in his misfortune their own opportunity; and the impoverished artist, bribed by the prospect of royal patronage which to a denizen glassmaker meant so much, and the assurance of the entire English market, bound himself to communicate to "Englishmen our natural subjects . . . the arte feate and mystery "[4] which he and his countrymen had always guarded so jealously. On 15 December, 1575, the monopoly was signed for a period of twenty-one years, and soon afterwards Verzelini started work in his new glasshouse in Broad Street. The Italian had sold his heritage, and the English Government, after twenty-five years of failure, had succeeded at last in buying a trainer.[5]

[1] See Strype's edition of Stow's *Survey of London* (5 ed., 1755), Vol. II, p. 327, and Seymour's *Survey of London* (1735), Bk. IV, p. 396.

[2] There seems to be no evidence of a formal protest by the Glaziers till after the destruction of the plant at the Hall of Crutched Friars, but it probably precedes the monopoly itself (15 December).

[3] Verzelini was born in 1522, and married his wife Elizabeth in 1556 about nineteen years before his patent; *cf.* the inscription on his tomb at Downe, Kent. Hartshorne, p. 158, note 2. For his children *cf.* Hallen, *loc. cit.*

[4] *Ministerium*, of course, not *mysterium*. Prof. Ernest Weekley believes the word to be derived from *magister* (mastery).

[5] This is made quite clear in *The Reasons against Sir Robert Mansell's Patent*, S. 13, cited by Hartshorne, p. 424.

There are at present four glasses known which have been, or might be, attributed to Verzelini, and for establishing this group two provisions in the Patent have been considered of importance. The Patent forbade under the penalty of ten shillings (a large sum) per glass, any other manufacture whatever in Great Britain and Ireland of " drynkinge glasses such as be accustomablie made in the towne of Morano," and secondly it prohibited the importation of any such glasses from abroad.[1] Now these four glasses which we annotate in detail in the list of plates, are all goblets with diamond-scratched decoration, and are all dated during the period of Verzelini's monopoly—1580 (W. Buckley Collection), 1581 (W. Buckley Collection, formerly in the possession of Horace Walpole), 1583 (Hamilton Clements Collection), and 1586 (British Museum). Two of them bear the English motto, " In God is al mi trust." One of them, diamond-engraved with a hunting scene, has English names—$\frac{\text{JOHN}}{\text{JONE}}$ DIER and is probably a betrothal or marriage glass. The fourth glass has the initials A F and is similar in the style of the decoration and the lettering to the other three. Finally, the lettering and figuring are of Elizabethan type.[2]

It is clear from these facts, first, that three of these glasses, and probably the fourth also, were made to English orders during the period of Verzelini's monopoly (1575–92), and secondly that, since all of them were made for a definite order, the engraving is contemporary with the glasses. We have to enquire, therefore, in what circumstances these orders could have been executed. If they were executed out of England we have to assume that Verzelini's monopoly was not absolute, or that these glasses were illicitly and surreptitiously imported from abroad. If, again, they were executed in England but not in Verzelini's glasshouse, we have to assume that a glasshouse or glasshouses existed at the same time which were capable of a high quality of *façon de Venise*. Let us deal with these two hypotheses.

Now it is evident from Verzelini's Patent that prior to 1575 it was a common custom to import drinking glasses from Venice, and it is by reference to these that Verzelini's own glasses are described " as good cheape or rather better cheape than the drynkyng glasses comonlye boughte from the Cittie of Murano, and other partes of beyond the seas." We may further admit that at short notice it would not be easy to inhibit a general import trade of this kind. But it is also certain, not merely from the policy of the English Government during the previous twenty-five years to which we have already alluded, but also from a very specific utterance in the deed itself,[3] that the Government purposed the creation

[1] Patent Roll, 17 Eliz., p. 13, cited in full by Hartshorne, pp. 399–401.
[2] Rackham (B.) in *Burl. Mag.*, XXV (1914) and October, 1925.
[3] Patent in Hartshorne, p. 400, lines 34–36.

of an English glass trade, and adopted strong protectionist measures with that intention. Even the patentee himself, unlike his successor Sir Jerome Bowes, who had a monopoly of importation as well as a monopoly of manufacture,[1] had no permit for bringing glasses from Venice. Verzelini's patent was an act of acquisition on the part of England, and the monopoly, it might be argued, must be absolutely rigid just because it was the first. Furthermore, when it is remembered that " Venice glasses " are very tender in transport, and the caution requisite for safety is apt also to incur suspicion : that two of the four glasses bear the motto of a Livery Company of the City of London ; and that the other two both appear to have been made for special occasions ; it becomes exceedingly unlikely that any or all of them are smuggled goods.

There remains the possibility that they were illicitly manufactured in this country, and this in itself is intrinsically less probable than the former supposition. For we are confronted with the question who there was in England at that time capable of uttering such glasses. Certainly there were in 1589[2] fifteen glasshouses in England, but in view of the influx of Lorrainers and Normans after 1567, it is probable that most of these were in the hands of Frenchmen who were largely concerned with " glas for glasynge." Fine glasses of the type we are considering were beyond their competence ; and between the years 1575 and 1592, I have only been able to find one mention of an independent glassmaker in England, a Sebastian Orlanden, who in 1579 was working with a French glassmaker, Godfrey de la Hay, at Beckley in Sussex, and producing " bugles, amells and glas in collers."[3] Moreover, when George Longe, almost the earliest practical English glassmaker we know, petitioned[4] for a licence to make (window) glass in Ireland, he gives a brief review of English glassmaking in which the whole emphasis is upon the Frenchmen, and neither Verzelini nor any other Italian is even mentioned. That is a line of argument which might be pursued by anyone who accepted the two clauses in Verzelini's licence which we have quoted, and believed in the absolute exclusiveness of his monopoly. But here a difficulty arises. We have already seen that at this

---

[1] Patent of Sir Jerome Bowes, 34 Eliz., c. 15 in Hartshorne, p. 407, lines 31–33.

[2] See George Longe's letter, *infra*, note.

[3] Dawson (C.), *loc. cit.* There may have been stray Flemish glassmakers in the provinces, *e.g.* those who were working at Houghton, Cheshire, before the end of the 16th century, or the " Dionise " of Stockport mentioned in 1605 (*V. C. H. Lancs*, II, 404), and they may well have made *façon de Venise ;* but the quality and workmanship of the quartette in question make it unlikely that they were executed in a small provincial glasshouse. But it has been shown above that probably all the Italian glassmakers in London between 1575 and 1592 were employed in one or other of Verzelini's glasshouses.

[4] Petition of George Longe to Burghley, Lansdowne MSS., No. 59, Art. 75, 3 Oct., 1589, and letter of George Longe to Burghley, *ibid.*, Art. 72, both cited in Hartshorne, pp. 401–4.

time there was a regular trade in imported Venice glasses, and this is confirmed by Harrison in a passage which must be dated between 1577 and 1586 (*i.e.* during Verzelini's tenure of the monopoly) ; he writes as follows[1] :

> It is a world to see in these our dais, wherein gold and silver most aboundeth, how that our gentilitie as lothing those metals (because of the plentie) do now generally choose rather the Venise glasses both for our wine and our beere than any of those metals or stone wherein before time we have beene accustomed to drink ; . . . but such is the estimation of this stuffe that mannie because rich onelie with their view, send unto Murana (a towne neere to Venice situate on the Adriatic sea), from whence the verie best are daily to be had, and such as for beautie do well neer match the christall. . . . And as this is seen in the gentilitie so in the wealthie communaltie the like desire of glass is not neglected whereby the gain gotten by their purchase is yet more increased to the benefit of the merchant. . . . The poorest also will have glass if they may ; but sith the Venetian is somewhat to deere for them they content themselves with such as are made at home of ferne and burned stone.[2]

Now unless this passage refers back to conditions *before* 1575, which seems unlikely, we have a statement directly contrary to the terms of Verzelini's patent.   Certainly it was a common custom for household ladies to send a private commission to Murano for a " cupboard of Venice glasses," and if Harrison did not imply a regular trade in imported Venetian glass, we might agree that most of the Venetian glasses used by the nobility were privately imported in this way.   But this, on the evidence before us, is not possible.   It must be concluded, therefore, that until we come to examine the glasses themselves, there is no historical reason why this family of goblets should not have been ordered from Venice and owe their indisputable similarity to emanation from a single Venetian glasshouse ; and that, although this does not affect the purpose for which the English Government granted the Patent, the monopoly was not *in effect* exclusive of imported glasses.

Let us now turn from the circumstances in which these glasses were made to the glasses themselves.   All four are *façon de Venise*, showing some degree of accomplishment, and since outside these four we have no standard of English-made glass at that time to which we can refer them, our method must be one of elimination.   Now at the time of Verzelini's patent four countries in Europe were making *façon de Venise*, viz. Venice herself, the Netherlands, Germany, and Spain.   The last two can be dismissed at once, and we are left with Venice and the Netherlands.   It is certainly true that at this time, as we have seen already, the art of glass *à la façon de Venise* and *à la façon d'Altare* was flourishing exceedingly at Antwerp and to a

---

[1] *Description of England*, Bk. II., vi, p. 147 (ed. of New Shaks. Soc., 1877).   The passage quoted occurs in the second edition of this work (1586), but not in the first edition (1577).

[2] *i.e.* flints.

less degree at Liège, but there is no reason to suppose that one pupil of Murano was any more proficient than another ; and in England a proud parent or a triumphant suitor who wanted a very special glass for a very special occasion, and could afford to despise all home-made " counterfeits," would normally and naturally send his order to the one original Venice and not to inferior Netherlandish imitators no better than " Jacob the stranger." These four goblets, which all bear dates and initials, and in two cases a motto, are clearly occasional glasses for baptisms, betrothals or marriages, and if they were not made in England we may take it as certain that they came from Venice. Our final question, therefore, is whether among authentic Venetian glasses of this period we can find any pieces to match them either in form or fabric ; and here we have a very strong piece of negative evidence in favour of the Verzelini attribution. James Howell was struck by the fact that even the most accomplished Muranese could only produce their best work in their own city : " They say here that though one should transplant a Glasse-Furnace from Murano to Venice itself or to any other of the little assembley of islands about her, or to any part of the Earth besides, and use the same materials, the same workmen, the same fuell, the self same ingredients in every way, yet they cannot make Crystall-Glasse in that perfection for beauty and lustre, as in Murano."[1] The metal is thick and coarse by the side of Venetian drinking glasses, and in one case (No. 3) it has not the purity of colour or rather colourlessness, which we look for in the more accomplished and ceremonial of Venice glasses. Nor can the shapes, especially those of Nos. 1, 2, and 3, be matched in Venetian glass.[2] There is in fact no proof that any or all of them are Venetian work, and until such is forthcoming or until the matter is clinched by the discovery of dated and inscribed pieces as unquestionably similar to these in detail and in decoration as they are Venetian in origin, it is fair to suggest that the present family was made in England and in Verzelini's glasshouse.

Whether they were engraved in the glasshouse is more doubtful. It may well be that Verzelini had in his employ an artist capable of such work, and the correlation of form and ornament in the British Museum goblet is perhaps an argument in favour of that supposition. But an outside engraver, as much as an engraver in the glasshouse, must observe the conditions imposed upon him by the form of a vessel which he is asked to decorate, and the division of the ornament into three zones is evident in the three glasses when such an arrangement is *not* determined by applied bands encircling the bowl. Moreover the details of the work not only of the goblets with the motto IN GOD IS AL MI TRUST, but also of the A.F. glass and the glass with a hunting-scene are so similar that the same artist seems to have been responsible for them all. Diamond-engraving

[1] *Familiar Letters*, I. 1, xxviii.   [2] Rackham, *loc. cit.*

G

was, moreover, an art distinct from the fashioning of glasses. The engraving was the important thing. Decorative artists at any rate in the 17th century were not particular about the material on which they worked, and it is, I think, very doubtful whether the demand for occasional glasses was sufficient to make it worth while for Verzelini to keep a professional engraver permanently in his service. If he did not, then glasses made at Broad Street must have been engraved elsewhere and almost certainly elsewhere in London ; and in the period of Verzelini's monopoly the name of only one promiscuous decorator has been preserved. He was a Frenchman by name Anthony de Lysle, and in 1585 he was working in the Liberty of St. Martin le Grand at his profession of engraving on pewter and glass.[1] At that time an artist who engraved on glass only may well have found himself short of a living, but pewter was still in more general use and there was no doubt ample room for a man who was proficient in both techniques. On that account it is, I think, probable that English glasses of *façon de Venise* were engraved by an artist of this type, and as De Lysle is the only name which has been preserved there is some warrant for suggesting that the engraving of the Verzelini group was due to him. It may be proper in this connection to refer to a glass in the Musée de Cluny which was noticed by Mr. Wilfred Buckley and is strikingly similar in respect of its engraving to the Verzelini group. The decoration is diamond-engraved and as in the Verzelini group is divided into three zones. The upper zone shows hounds pursuing a unicorn, each beast being separated from the next by a tree, as in the Dier glass. Below this is a zone of foliated ornament broken, as in the Dier glass, by three panels ; and these contain respectively the date 1578, three fleurs-de-lys, and the
initials · M · M ·. $\cdot \overset{\displaystyle \cdot A \cdot}{\underset{\displaystyle \cdot D \cdot C \cdot I \cdot}{}}$ The lettering and especially the figuring are strikingly
similar to those of the Verzelini group. The lower zone contains simply a circuit of gadroons. The bowl of the glass is wide and shallow and on that account the engraving is executed on the inside, and not on the outside as in the Verzelini group (Pl. III).

The attribution of the engraving on the Verzelini group to Anthony de Lysle perhaps gains point from the Cluny glass. The three fleurs-de-lys suggest that the decoration was done in France, and since De Lysle was

---

[1] *Publications of the Huguenot Society*, Vol. VIII, p. xlvi. Preface to Letters of Denization. He came " from the dominion of the King of France " and " useth his trade without licence from the Pewterers Company " (*ibid.*, p. 71). Vol. X of the *Hug. Soc. Publ.* (returns of aliens dwelling in the city and suburbs of London from the reign of Henry VIII to that of James I) agrees (Pt. 2, p. 350) with Vol. VIII (Letters of denization and acts of naturalization for aliens in England 1509–1603) as to the date of De Lysle's denization papers (19 March, 1582), but spells the name Anthony de Lisley. I prefer the official spelling of legal process to the haphazard anglicizations taken from parish records.

a French immigrant it may well be that the Cluny glass was engraved by him before he left his own country. The Dier glass which it resembles is the earliest but one of the four dated glasses and is only three years distant from the Cluny glass (1578–81) ; and with the three other glasses attributed to Verzelini may be his later work after he had settled in England. In any case the misspelling of names on the Dier glass (Jone for Joan, and Dier for Dyer) seems to indicate an engraver who was not well acquainted with the English language. It is probable that De Lysle came to England between 1578 and 1580. He took out letters of denization on 19 March, 1582, but there is no warrant for assuming with Mr. Francis Buckley[1] that he came to England in that year, for an immigrant craftsman is not likely to become naturalized in a strange country until he finds himself assured of a living, and De Lysle had probably spent two or three years building up his business before he took that step. Moreover, if we attribute the engraving of any one of the Verzelini glasses to his hand, for example, the British Museum goblet which is dated 1586, or the goblet dated 1583, then we must similarly attribute the engraving of them all ; and since one of these bears the date 1580[2] we must, if we follow our hypothesis, conclude that De Lysle was already in London in that year. On the other hand, if the Cluny glass, which bears the date 1578 and seems to have been engraved in France for a Frenchman, was also engraved by De Lysle then De Lysle must have been still in France in that year. If, therefore, De Lysle is the author of the engraving of the Verzelini quartette he must have come to England between 1578 and 1580.

Very full records have been preserved of London metics at this time, and since no other name occurs of an artist who engraved glass the hypothesis, though not proven, can scarcely be regarded as exorbitant. And if it is accepted it greatly strengthens the attribution to Verzelini of the four goblets whose engraving has been discussed. How long De Lysle continued to work in London is not known, but there is some reason for thinking that he was still working here in 1602 and was the engraver of the Barbara Potter glass at South Kensington (Pl. IV. 2). The engraving is similar to that of the Verzelini quartette and though the correspondence is perhaps not so close as with them, the sixteen years which elapsed between 1586 and 1602 are themselves sufficient to account for the divergence.

[1] In *Glass*, Vol. V, p. 103, *sq.*
[2] The A.F. glass dated 1580 has a pedigree which goes back to Horace Walpole, and it is, I think, fairly certain that it was made and engraved in England. The engraving is certainly by the artist whom I have identified with De Lysle, and it is extravagant to suppose that De Lysle either brought with him French glasses which he had engraved in France or naked French glasses which he subsequently engraved in England.

CHAPTER III

The Age of Assimilation (1592–1673)

The commodity is first imported from abroad to our great discontent. . . . Afterwards the art itself is gradually imported to our visible advantage : yet we continue still to repine that our neighbours should possess any art, industry and invention ; forgetting that had they not first instructed us we should have been at present barbarians ; and did they not still continue their instructions the arts must fall into a state of languor and lose that emulation and novelty which contribute so much to their advancement.

DAVID HUME, *Of the Jealousy of Trade* (1742).

§1. THE PIRATE PATENTEES

VERZELINI did not enjoy the full period of his licence. He had been well past fifty when he assumed it, and after nearly seventeen years of what must have been a highly lucrative practice, he waived the remainder of his privilege (1592) and went into retirement at Downe near Orpington in Kent. He died fourteen years later (1606) at the age of eighty-four, his wife Elizabeth surviving him by ten months. They are commemorated in the chancel of Downe Church (Kent) by a pair of monumental brasses which depict the glassmaker and his wife in civil attire, with the following inscription :

HERE LYETH BVRIED JACOB VERZELINI ESQVIRE BORNE IN THE CITTIE OF VENICE, AND ELIZABETH HIS WIFE BORNE IN ANDWERPE OF THE ANCIENT HOVSES OF VANBVREN AND MACE WHO HAVING LIVED TOGETHER IN HOLYE STATE OF MATRIMONY FORTIE NYNE YEARS AND FOWER MONTHS DEPARTED THIS MORTAL LYFE THE SAID JACOB THE TWENTYE DAY OF JANUARYE, AN° DÑI 1606 AGED LXXXIIII YEARES, AND THE SAID ELIZABETH THE XXVI DAYE OF OCTOBER AN° DNI 1607 AGED LXXIII YEARES AND REST IN HOPE OF RESVRREXION TO LYFE ETERNALL.[1]

Below the inscription are two brass plates containing respectively the figures of three daughters and six sons, by whom the monument was probably erected.

After their father's death the family seem to have fallen into discord, and in 1621 the eldest son and heir, Francis, was plaintiff in a Chancery suit brought against his brother Jacob and a number of other defendants. But apart from this we hear no more of the sons of Verzelini, and when we remember to what extent the art of glass was, at this time, an hereditary profession, and turn for contrast to the Lorrainers in whom fecundity was

---

[1] Verzelini himself was " of no church," but his wife was a member of the Church of England (*Hug. Soc. Publ.*, X (2), 304).

a professional duty, the closure of the family tradition is very significant. The goodwill of a business of seventeen years' standing was not a thing to be rejected with temerity. But during that time Verzelini had done just what the English Government had intended that he should ; he had definitely established fine glassmaking in London, and the Broad Street glasshouse, in which Englishmen and Italians were beginning to work side by side, was the only glass business you could call a going concern.[1] It was clearly absurd that a foreigner should grow rich on English trade, and now that Verzelini was nearing the age of repose, it was time to lay hold of the fruit of his labours, and to take very good care for the exclusion of his sons.

Sir Jerome Bowes became in 1592 the agent of this appropriation, and thereafter the metics give place to the monopolists. Glassmaking hitherto had been an itinerant craft in the hands of the French, and a fine art in the hands of the Italians in London. Each of these had retained a measure of independence in the control of their own work and the ownership of their plant ; but with the retirement of Verzelini and the instalment of Sir Jerome, the schemes of the Government were at last complete. Glassmaking had been a nuisance to landowners ; at its best it only supplied new beauties to "nobilitie and gentilitie" who were still very naive in their refinement. But the supply of glass vessels and glass windows had increased the demand, and glassmaking was now to become an industrial enterprise in which English capitalists found it worth while to invest their money. It was only when Englishmen like Bowes and his successors gave the new art an economic basis, and realized that Italian skill could only be exploited with English money, that glassmaking was finally established in England. It is difficult to know to whom we may assign the credit for the slow capture, or the skill with which a sequence of monopolies was used to effect it, but some enlightenment may be found in the series of contemporary sources brought together by Hartshorne. The great bulk of our knowledge of this period is derived from documents issued under the seal of the Privy Council, or from letters written to or by its members. Several Privy Councillors—e.g. Cecil and Burghley—were at pains to collect information concerning the state of glass in England, and the various licences have a certain similarity of form and wording, and in several cases contain specific statements of policy, which cannot be mere legal formulæ. It is difficult to resist the conclusion that England *took* glass as much as she *received* it, and that her acquisition of the industry was chiefly due to a deliberate and consistent policy maintained by the Privy Councils of Mary, Elizabeth, James I, and Charles I, over a period of nearly a hundred years. Certainly the monopoly was the prize for which Verzelini

[1] With the profits of his business Verzelini bought an estate in Kent (*Proc. Hug. Soc.*, VIII, 247), apparently when he retired.

sold his craft, and under the protection which it afforded, the Government were able to enlist the private enterprise of Englishmen in the service of the new industry.

It is an unhappy accident that only one glass now exists which can certainly be referred to the period of monopolies, but we must not on that account underestimate the great importance of the system, or the signal services to English glass of the early holders of privilege. They were rough soldiers, roystering courtiers, speculative noblemen, quite undistinguished for refinement of taste or disinterested ambition. They were not enterprising bourgeois merchants like Isaac Bongar or Tilson or John Greene ; and the notion of a patronage of the arts would have seemed to them absurd. On the contrary, in both their aims and their status they belonged to the same fellowship of barbarous adventurers as Drake and Grenville and the later company promoters of Central America and the Spanish Main. Their activities extended, of course, to other industries than glass. Some had a sanction for piracy on the high seas, which required more valour and less intelligence than making money out of stolen inventions[1] ; but whether their licence was for piracy or for profiteering, whether their field of exploitation was a new country like the Indies, or a new industry like glass, they acted from a simple and straightforward desire to get something for nothing. It is interesting to find that one of the glass monopolists, Sir Edward Zouche, was a member of the New England Council and held office in 1618 as Knight Marshal of the Household. Mansell, on the other hand, who had won his knighthood by an exploit, was a pirate by instinct, and both his difficulties and his success in business are explained by the fact that he conducted his monopoly as a military despotism. These men made glassmaking an industry as well as an art, and they did so by giving it the satisfactory economic foundation that is essential to artistic achievement. The small group of men, beginning with Bowes and ending with Mansell, who held licences in the first quarter of the 17th century were the nurses of the English art of glass. When it grew up in both an artistic and an economic sense, as it did later in the 17th century, it got rid of its nurses and learned to support itself. It disembarrassed itself of decayed gentility, capricious patronage and military martinets, and became a plain industrial art, with a middle-class tradition and a world market ; and in these conditions it came to its greatest achievement.

---

[1] The credit for perfecting the process of smelting with pit-coal, and its application to glass furnaces is due to men like Simon Sturtevant and John Rovenzon, and not (as Dillon and Hartshorne suggest) to Percival, or still less to Mansell. For this see Sturtevant (S.), *Metallica* (1611), Rovenzon (J.), *Metallica* (1613), and Dudley (D.), *Metallum Martis*, published 1665, but based on experiments contemporary with Sturtevant and Rovenzon (reprinted by the Patent Office, 1858). Sturtevant applied for a patent for his process in 1612, but soon afterwards, for reasons which do not appear, left England.

[86]

THE AGE OF ASSIMILATION

The first of the English monopolists, Sir Jerome Bowes, was a man of the court circle who had already considerable influence in matters of international trade. Nine years before (1583) he had been engaged on behalf of Her Majesty in a commercial parley with the Emperor of Russia. However lacking in courtesy and grace, he was at least a " sturdy goer and strong abider " and Pepys has a story of his rude diplomacy which illustrates very well the type of man into whose hands the control of English glassmaking was beginning to pass :

And among other discourse some was on Sir Jerome Bowes, Embassador from Queene Elizabeth to the Emperor of Russia ; who because some of the noblemen there would go upstairs to the Emperor before him, he would not go up till the Emperor had ordered those two men to be dragged downstairs, with their heads knocking upon every stair till they were killed. And when he was come up they demanded his sword of him before he entered the room. He told them if they would have his sword they should have his boots too. And so caused his boots to be pulled off, and his nightgown and nightcap and slippers to be sent for, and made the Emperor stay till he could go in his nightdress, since he might not go as a soldier. And lastly, when the Emperor in contempt, to show his commanding of his subjects, did command one to leap from the window down and broke his neck in the sight of our Embassador, he replied that his mistress did set more by, and did make better use of the necks of her subjects : but said that to show what her subjects could do for her he would, and did, fling down his gantlett before the Emperor : and challenged all the nobility there to take it up, in defiance of the Emperor against his Queene ; for which, at this very day, the name of Sir Jerome Bowes is famous and honoured there.

Of such metal was Sir Jerome, who on 5 February, 1591–2 received a special licence for a period of twelve years at an annual rent of one hundred marks, to make drinking glasses " like unto such as be most used or wroughte in the said towne of Morano." The import and the terms of this Patent are so similar to Verzelini's that there is no need to repeat them here, but in view of the one existing glass which has been attributed to Sir Jerome, it is important to draw attention to two clauses in the deed. The first of these repeals the previous licence and refers to " drynkynge glasses commonly brought from the Citty of Morano." Now such a clause is easily explicable in the first patent when there had hitherto been no prohibition of imported Venetian glass ; but when Verzelini's patent had already been in force for seventeen years, this clause surely implies that Venice glasses *were* regularly and legitimately imported during Verzelini's monopoly ; unless we are to suppose that the words are simply a repetition of the earlier patent. The second clause provides that Sir Jerome shall " finde furnishe and provide to and for the noblemen within her Majesties Realm . . . to drynke in good and sufficient store and quantitie of faire, perfect good and well fashioned drinking glasses made or to be made in the Citties or townes of Venice or Morano, commonly called Venice glasses." There is no clause parallel to this in Verzelini's patent, and its insertion here implies that Bowes, unlike his predecessor, was allowed to import as well as to manufacture " Venice glasses." It therefore becomes increasingly difficult to say whether glasses issuing from Bowes' factory (almost certainly the Broad Street glasshouse which he took over from Verzelini when he succeeded to the Patent) were actually made in England or brought from Venice. A goblet, probably a christening glass, recently discovered by Mr. Rackham in the collection of Mr. and Mrs. Rees Price, belongs to the period of Sir Jerome's monopoly and was almost certainly uttered by him ; it bears the owner's name BARBARA POTTERS and the date 1602 engraved in diamond point (Plate IV. 2). The shape of the bowl is not usual in Venetian glass, but the upper part of the stem resembles, in both form and metal, a Venetian tazza in the Salting Collection and another tazza, also Venetian, lately in the possession of Mr. C. Kirkby Mason. Whether the glass was imported by Bowes or made by his Venetian workmen in London is not a question which can be definitely settled,[1] but in either case the glass must be described as uttered by him. The engraving is a more certain matter. It must be closely contemporary with the manufacture,[2] but there is no evidence that Bowes employed a diamond-engraver in his own factory or accepted orders for engraved glasses. The engraving may well be by Anthony de Lysle who as we have seen was working in London some years before 1602 and may still have been at work in that year. If the engraving is by De Lysle then we must assume that the glass was purchased naked from Bowes and afterwards privately engraved by De Lysle ; for De Lysle, we know, was an independent tradesman. If it be assumed, further, that glass and engraving are contemporary then the attribution[3] of the former to Bowes and the latter to De Lysle stand or fall together ; and on the whole the two claims seem to strengthen one another.

Before the introduction of coal fuel instead of wood, only two more licences were granted. The first of these was assumed by Sir Percival Hart, a man in favour at the Court and described in the deed as " Our well beloved Sir Percival Hart Knight," and a partner, who was probably subordinate—Edward Forsett. The licence was similar to that of Bowes, but it was to endure for twenty-one years, and the licence to *import* drinking glasses " for nobelmen of Our Realme " does not appear to have been renewed.

The only other licence known to us which preceded the application of Sturtevant's invention was issued in 1608 and permitted Edward Salter to make " all manner of drinking glasses and other glasses and glasse works not prohibited by the former Letters Patent."[4] I can get no further

[1] Modifications of Venetian form might be due as much to an English order as to English manufacture ; *cf.* pp. 111 *sq.* below, for Greene's forms.
[2] A glass engraved for occasional purposes was almost certainly a new glass.
[3] In the sense indicated above.
[4] Referred to in Mansell's Specification, cited in Hartshorne, pp. 416–7.

information of this man, but his endeavour is clear enough. The privileges of Bowes, Hart, Forsett, and of some of the later monopolists had been confined to drinking glasses in the Venetian manner, which were only a small fraction of the vessels which were, or might be, made of glass ; and this privilege of Salter's was, I think, an attempt to extend the licensing system to glass-ware generally. For " other glasses and glassworkes " England had hitherto depended upon the unregulated output of the French vagabonds, and there was an ample market for a serious enterprise of this kind. But only seven years were to elapse before wood fuel became illegal, and doubtless Salter failed because he had not acquired the coal-fuel process. We thus have to wait till Mansell before we find the two types of glass, drinking glasses in the Venetian manner, and all other sorts of glassware, controlled by a single authority.

The sanction under which coal fuel was introduced into glassmaking had only an incidental reference to that art, and was much wider in its scope than the Patents to which we have alluded. The decimation of English woodland, not merely in the manufacture of glass but in other and more important of the industrial arts (of which iron was the most notable instance), had long ceased to be a local grievance as in the time of the Lorraine immigration, and was rapidly becoming a national question which only legislation could solve. An alternative to wood and charcoal for all kinds of smelting purposes was necessary in the interests of wood cultivation and the ships which it supplied,[1] and necessary also for the free development of industrial projects. It is not possible to state when the first experiments were made, but soon after 1600 a series of practical investigations had begun which had issue in Sturtevant's patent of 1603[2] and were eventually recorded in such works as his *Metallica* (1612). The credit was due to private experimentalists like Sturtevant and John Rovenzon, but they appear to have lacked either the capital or the personal influence necessary to make the new system of furnaces a commercial success. Of Rovenzon we have very little knowledge beyond what is contained in his book, and Sturtevant's Patent became entirely sterile a few years after he obtained it, and he disappeared into a mysterious exile. Puissant persons were ready to turn this abortive ingenuity to their own advantage. On 28 July, 1610, a combine of four men headed by Sir William Slingsby obtained a special licence of twenty-one years for the erection of furnaces, ovens, and engines for brewing, dyeing, baking, roasting, brick- and pot-making and also for melting

---

[1] *Cf.* Mansell's Specification *init.*, cited in Hartshorne, p. 416.

[2] Hartshorne states that he " had a patent " in 1611 (p. 182) and elsewhere refers to the " patent of 1603 " (p. 487), but I cannot find the source of his information. There is no trace of this patent in the Calendar of State Papers, but Sturtevant was applying for another privilege, not connected with coal furnaces, in 1603.

glass, ordnance, bell-metal, etc. and other kinds of foundry work with sea-coal, *i.e.* with coal imported by sea from Scotland. The licensees were, like Bowes and Hart, men of the court circle, Slingsby himself being " one of the Carvers of the most excellent Princess Queen Anne," and Andrew Palmer a " Lay Master of His Majesty's Mint." The latter, who had doubtless some technical knowledge of furnaces, was clearly the brains of the company, and Slingsby an illiterate[1] but influential nobleman.

Even before the Patent was actually granted Slingsby was complaining that the business " made as yet but slow progression." It is not difficult to discern the reasons for his failure. The Patent was in effect an attempt to impose a general innovation on at least a dozen distinct industries of which each had its own technique and its own traditions. The combine in its headlong opportunism failed to understand that there is no large manner of imposing improvements ; every industry, by feeling its needs and answering them, grows its own innovations. If Slingsby had been content to confine himself to one industry—to glass as well as to any other—he might have succeeded ; he failed because he tried to encompass all.

But the Slingsby combine was at least valuable in two ways. It called the attention of the glass monopolists proper to the possibilities of the coal furnace : and it made room for a much more powerful and effective combination which survived several changes in its own personnel and in royal policy, and was only superseded by the monopoly of one of its own members. Between 1611 and 1615 three patents were granted, but throughout them all there was an absolute continuity of control.

Sir Edward Zouche already had his eye on the coal furnace while Slingsby was still busy throwing away his chances. Slingsby scented the danger, but could not avert it. On 25 March, 1611, Zouche had collected three partners, Bevis Thelwall (also Louis, or more probably Lewis, Thelwall or Theloall), Thomas Percivall, and Thomas Mefflyn, and obtained a Patent for making " all manner of glasses "[2] for a period of twenty-one years. This combination is of considerable importance, both for its personnel and for its effects. The leading members were Zouche himself and Bevis Thelwall, the latter probably a relative of Dr. Thelwall (or Theloall) with whom James Howell used to correspond. The other partners are described as their servants, a word which, though only indicating a disparity in social status, implies their general subordination to the other two. Thomas Mefflyn was a " glasier," *i.e.* not

[1] See his letter to Salisbury, 26 February, 1610, in which he observes that Zouche is a dangerous competitor and he wants to get his patent settled first. Judged even by Elizabethan standards the letter is grossly ill-spelt. Hartshorne, p. 411.
[2] Not " drinking glasses " as Hartshorne, p. 181. *Cf.* Abstract of Patent, Hartshorne, p. 412.

an artist or manufacturer, but a *dealer* in glass,[1] and he was probably included in the combine as a link between the manufacturers and their market ; the favour of the Glaziers Company was necessary for success. The technician was Thomas Percivall, and in Mansell's specification he is even described as the " Inventor " of the new coal furnace ; but as we have seen already, a knowledge of the coal process was common property by this time, and it required only audacity to lay claim to its invention. Slingsby also had called himself the " Inventor," and in the present context the word means only that Percivall had given some attention to the study of coal furnaces and wished to be regarded as an expert. The magnitude of the new venture is apparent when we consider that the partners spent the large sum of £5000 (perhaps £100,000 on a present valuation) in the perfection of glass furnaces which burnt coal.

The effects of the new combination were of no less importance. Zouche's Patent was likely to infringe several licences for glassmaking that were already in force, and a special reservation was made to protect Sir Jerome Bowes, the Slingsby combine, and (according to Hartshorne[2]) Edward Salter also, from the effects of the new privilege. We cannot regard the immunity as anything more than a legal fiction. Slingsby, even before his patent was granted, had written of his prospects in a mood of depression. After 1610 he and his colleagues pass into a significant silence, and even if they felt that their rights in the matter of glass furnaces were being infringed by Zouche's Patent, they had started so many fine schemes that it was scarcely worth protesting because one of them was filched away. As for the other patentees, they all had received their licences under the old system of wood fuel, and the Zouche combination was well within its rights in making any kind of glass whatsoever, provided it employed a coal process. Thus the effect of the Zouche Patent was virtually to invalidate all licences which had not acquired coal furnaces, and naturally it provoked a considerable opposition. The glasshouse of the Zouche combine which was started at Lambeth was the scene of much indignation and violence, and attempts were made to put a stop to the work. In 1613 two commissioners were appointed by the Government to enquire into the matter, and there is a clause in their report which gives a forecast of the way in which the problem was eventually solved. " Unlawful practices have been used to overthrow the work against which it were good some speedy course were taken that the same may better proceed."[3] The Government, for excellent reasons that will appear in a moment, took

[1] For this meaning of " glasier " see a letter from Sir George More and Sir Edmund Bowyer to James I, 18 July, 1613, cited in Hartshorne, p. 185.
[2] Hartshorne states this categorically in his text (p. 182) but I can find no evidence for it in any of his published sources.
[3] *Cf.* Report of More and Bowyer to James I. Cited in Hartshorne, p. 185.

its stand by Zouche and the coal furnace, and in 1615 made a clean sweep of its injustices by a general prohibition of wood fuel.

Meanwhile Zouche's enterprise had prospered exceedingly, and the Government were waiting an opportunity to enjoy a greater share in its emoluments. The rent of the privilege when first it was granted amounted to only £30 a year, and when Mefflyn died (late in 1613) and a new Patent was issued to include his successor Robert Kellaway, the tribute was instantly raised to £1000 a year. There is no hint of protest in any of the documents that have been made available to us ; a protest would have been both imprudent and indecent. The business was now so lucrative as to be attractive to men of substance and position, and on 19 January, 1614–5, the Patent was again revised to admit the Earl of Montgomery, Viscount Andever, Sir Thomas Haward, Sir Thomas Tracy, Thomas Hayes, and Sir Robert Mansell. The new licence created an oligarchy of ten members and invested them with absolute powers in the field of English glassmaking. It had the sole right to make all kinds of glass whatsoever within the borders of England and Wales, and the sole right also to import glasses from abroad. Certainly it might burn no wood, but its only restriction was its most effective guarantee. Its constitution had scarcely been determined when the Government at last set the seal on a fluctuating policy of fifty years and issued its sagacious " Proclamation touching Glasses " (1615),[1] the order for compulsory coal, without which glassmaking could never have attained an industrial establishment in England. The Zouche oligarchy had the good fortune to be in power at the time, and its monopoly thus differed fundamentally from any that had preceded it ; it was not based, as Verzelini's had been based, on artistic skill, nor like the Patents of Bowes and his successors on ownership, but on a complete identity of the monopolist's interests with the policy of the Government. A private recipe had become the law ; and that was why the regime that followed was as universal, and in some ways as sterile, as a nationalization of glassmaking. The oligarchy of ten did not last long. The original nucleus of members had some practical knowledge[2] (though not, of course, skill in glassmaking) which at first made their position secure, but they soon found themselves overwhelmed by their later acquisitions, and especially by one who had a longer pocket and a more combative personality than any of his colleagues. The injured and elderly Bowes had been placated with an annuity a year before his death (1615), and Mansell, perhaps finding that his partners disliked his domineering ways, adopted the same plan and ousted them from any control of the business with an annual payment of £1800. As he was thus paying a further £1000 in rent to the Government, we can form some estimate of his annual income. At

[1] *S.P. Dom.* Royal Proclamations, No. 42, 23 May, 1615 ; transcribed by Hartshorne, p. 413.　　[2] Hartshorne, p. 184.

what date or dates the seven partners took their leave we do not know, but by the end of 1618 Mansell had succeeded to the single control of the English glass industry, a dominion which he exercised with unabated vigour for nearly forty years.

§2. THE TYRANNY OF MANSELL

Sir Robert Mansell is perhaps hardly so important as the records of his feuds and exploits would lead us to suppose, and in order that we may give him his proper significance in the history of English glassmaking, it is as necessary to explain his failure as to estimate his success. At the time when this masterful veteran waived his colleagues and swept into the sovereignty (1615–8) glassmaking had broken down its last barrier—the difficulty of fuel—and entered itself on the English repertory of industrial arts. But its position was still one of dependence ; it must be stabilized before it could become autonomous, and autonomy was necessary for any serious artistic achievement. The conditions requisite for the birth of an art, though strictly relevant to the present subject, are too large a matter for discussion here. The grandiose schemes of the Egyptian Pharaohs, the licensed robbery that made possible the Parthenon, the temporal possessions which complemented the spiritual vigour of the medieval Church, the exploitations of the Dutch East India Company—all these were substitutes for the economic autonomy of the arts which fed upon them ; and the trivial beauties of English glassmaking at least obeyed the same law. If they rejected a patronage they must organize their output and command their market. English glass, being already an industrial art, had three aspects or characters of which each was related to the other two ; it was an industry, an art, and a business. On the first count its welfare depended on such things as coal, clay, furnaces, sand, soda, and other industrial *conditions* of the actual art of glassmaking. Its function on the other hand was to manufacture useful and beautiful vessels, and here there was need for a degree of chemical lore, great manual dexterity, and above all a sense of design ; but these were unpurchasable capacities which could only be inherited from a tradition or acquired during the training of a lifetime. Finally, glassmaking was a business proposition, subject to the same economic laws and requiring the same organization as any other business enterprise ; and this last condition was particularly urgent where the whole art of the country was being officially fostered and concentrated under a single control. It is evident in the history not only of glassmaking but of other industrial arts also that, an adequate market being assured, a concert of these three forces working in vigorous harmony is the first condition of such a florison as we find in English domestic glass at the beginning of the 18th century. Sir Robert Mansell made some useful contributions to glassmaking in each of our three categories, but it is on his work as an administrator that our estimate of him must finally rest. In spite of feuds and interruptions, his organization imparted to the new industry a formal unity in which we may find at once the strength and the weakness of his regime. It is true that his administrative fabric collapsed during the Civil Wars, but *manet post funera virtus*. If there had been no Mansell English glassmaking might well have waited another half-century for the intrinsic unity, which was the lead metal invented by Ravenscroft.

Let us now consider in due order and in greater detail what Mansell did to improve the industry, the art, and the business of glassmaking. Mansell's most important subsidiary project was to establish a regular sea-borne coal trade between the Scottish coalfields and his London furnaces. In all our documentary sources of this period there is a distinction between sea-coal and pit-coal. The former clearly refers to the Scottish importations, and until the year 1620–1 or thereabouts, this was the only coal used in the London glass trade. It is difficult to say to what pit-coal refers. One would naturally expect it to refer to land-borne coal, but when the sea passage was available Mansell was unlikely to undertake the great labour and expense of bringing coal over land from South Wales or the Midlands. We do know, however, that among his provincial connections there were glasshouses at Stourbridge, on the Trent, and in South Wales, and it may be that " pit-coal " refers to the local coal used in those parts. Mansell's regime did a great deal also to develop the export trade from the Tyne coalfields, but the credit for this scheme is entirely due to his wife Dame Mansell, an astute and capable woman. In 1621, when the feud with the truculent Bongar and other disappointed glassworkers was at its height, Mansell was placed in command of a naval expedition to Spain and Algiers ; and during his absence on this service, the Scottish shipmasters, probably seduced by the Bongar confederacy which was then using every artifice to impede the business of Mansell and so to procure the repeal of his privilege, with no warning whatever raised their charges from fourteen shillings to twenty-four shillings per ton. The increase appears to have been quite prohibitive, and Mansell's London works came to a standstill. But in this grave predicament Lady Mansell, who was in control of the business during her husband's absence, showed great firmness and enterprise. The use of Newcastle coal was a thing never previously attempted or even thought possible in London. The richness of the Tyne coalfields was not widely known at this time, and its use was probably limited to local workers, such as the Lorraine glassmakers who were beginning to establish their furnaces in that region. Through the person of Edward Henzey[1] Mansell had already succeeded a few years previously in establishing his control in the north. Lady Mansell must have been aware of this, and must have known also that it was the presence of coal which had

---

[1] Hartshorne, p. 178.

attracted the Frenchmen to the Tyne, and that on coal depended all her husband's schemes for making Newcastle a provincial outpost of his monopoly. In the present emergency Lady Mansell was led to the notion of making Newcastle coalfields supply the glasshouses of London as well as those of the Tyne. Negotiations were at once opened, and the plan was so successful that three years later[1] (about 1624) the importation of Scottish coal seems to have entirely ceased, and a fleet of forty vessels was regularly employed in bringing coal, saltpetre, and finished plate glass from Newcastle to London. It is extremely likely that Mansell acquired a controlling interest in a pit or pits on the Tyne, which would make him independent of middlemen and shipmasters : and as he himself claims, quite apart from his glassmaking he did an important service to the coal trade.

In the provision of other essential commodities, he showed the same energy. He employed a young Welshman from Oxford, James Howell, who afterwards became celebrated as the author of an intimate but highly sophisticated correspondence, to make a tour of Europe and study the methods of continental glassmaking. His observations were of great value to his master. In a famous passage he described the harvesting of the Spanish soda-plant barilla on which the fine quality of Venetian glass largely depended. Rough soda can be found in nature or prepared from plants in many regions of Europe, but the qualities of barilla were such that a trade in it seems to have grown up in most countries where glass was manufactured *à la façon de Venise.* There is, however, no evidence that it was used by Verzelini and Bowes,[2] and the large contract for £2000 which Mansell placed with a Genoese merchant is the first instance of an extensive or regular use in this country.

We have already seen how important was the clay of which the glass pots were made. Mansell provided that Stourbridge clay, which surpassed all others for this purpose, should be conveyed from Worcestershire to Newcastle and doubtless to London, a practice that does not appear to have been general before Mansell's time. But here he again came into conflict with the malicious practices of Bongar and other jealous persons ; they corrupted the clay, probably before it left Stourbridge, so that the pots cracked and the metal was lost. Partly on this account, and partly from difficulties of transport, Mansell was led to procure clay by sea from various places on the Continent, notably Spa, Paris, and Rouen ; and for the Newcastle glasshouses a satisfactory clay was discovered locally.

The artistic quality of his glasses on the other hand was a thing that no business enterprise could improve. It was not from want of trying that

[1] Defence of Sir R. Mansell's Patent, *State Papers Dom.,* Jas. I, Vol. 162, No. 63, Hartshorne, p. 430.

[2] The soda which Jean Suigo proposed to supply to Carré was probably *barilla ; v. supra,* p. 63.

Mansell failed to do what Ravenscroft succeeded in doing. Through the agency of James Howell he obtained the services of one of the ablest and most accomplished Muranese glassmakers, Antonio Miotti, as in later times the Penroses of Waterford procured the best-known glassmaker at Stourbridge. Miotti belonged to a famous family of Murano that had a tradition of three centuries in glassmaking, and he brought over three other experts. But the wandering Italian glassmakers, as Schuermans has shown, were of a restless habit, and Miotti only held his appointment under Mansell for four years, and then (1623) left for Brussels, where he hoped to establish the first Italian glasshouse and even to rival the Gridolphi at Antwerp. After his departure Mansell's Italian managers, on whom depended the artistic value of his glasses, seem to have changed fairly frequently. Some time before 1627 (though the date cannot be fixed with certainty) two of his workmen, Giovanni dell 'Acqua and Bernard Tamurlayne, disagreed with him on a matter of wages and seceded to Lord George Hay, the holder of the Scottish monopoly which Mansell did not purchase till 1627. During the first ten years of the business there were several complaints, by Inigo Jones and others, of the poor quality of his glass, and although in 1621 he got the Glaziers to certify that his glass was of good quality and superior to Scottish glass—a sad compliment indeed[1]—he himself admitted some years later (1634-5) that his glass was poor stuff until he took the expense of bringing over an entire company of glassmakers from Mantua. Even so we may detect a lack of continuity on the artistic side of Mansell's work which goes some way to explain why he never created a national style such as we find about the same time in Germany and the Netherlands. Moreover, although he could fairly claim to have introduced the making of mirrors (shortly before 1624) there were other opportunities that he missed. He would appear to have been unsympathetic towards the very fine glass forms that were being developed in Northern Europe, some at least independently of Venetian traditions. Peter Horegill and John Greene, father of the Greene whose designs have been preserved to us, lay five years in prison because they attempted to import them. Again in 1619 he was violently hostile to a Flemish metic, Paul Vinion, who tried to manufacture the green-glass forms of Germany and the Netherlands. Hartshorne well suggests that this was an attempt to introduce the *Roemer*, a vessel of very great beauty. If that was so Mansell showed a singular but characteristic stupidity in rejecting a good idea because it occurred to his enemy first.[2] The reasons for Mansell's artistic

[1] Hartshorne, p. 193.
[2] The *Roemer* must have been introduced about this time, but not I think under Mansell's auspices, *cf.* Gayton, *Pleasant Notes* (1654), IV, 234, " a lusty rummer of Rhenish," and Dryden, *Amboyna* I, 1 (1673). " Whilst in full rummers we our friendship crown." In the 1670's the rummer was one of the forms which were supplied to English designs in

failure and possibly for the absence of authentic specimens at the present day are not far to seek. He claimed, justly enough, that in 1624 about four thousand persons found their livelihood in his business, a number which probably includes none of the suzerain glasshouses of the provinces except those of the Tyne; but among so many he himself protests, as though it were a source of great pride, that he had " trayned up severall Natives to make Glasse." Yet the chief emphasis in our sources is always upon the " workmen " or " strangers " procured from abroad. In the Venetian, or at least Italian bias we may find the secret of his artistic failure. The real strength of the Venetian swarm was in the heart of it; the outer members and stray solitary parasites, often detached from their tradition and lacking the stimulus which might come from a personal enterprise and the competition of their peers were, as James Howell understood, creatures of indifferent virtue even in their own art; and it was Mansell's only timidity to cling to this alien and anæmic tradition rather than try what skill there might be in Englishmen.

In organization he had better success. He had the strong hand wherever glass was made in England; from 1615 onwards he had furnaces in London, Greenwich, Purbeck Island, Milford Haven, Newcastle-on-Tyne, the Isle of Wight, the Trent Valley, and the region of Stourbridge, and after his purchase of the Scottish Patent from Thomas Robinson for £250 in 1627,[1] at Wemyss in Fifeshire, at Glasgow and probably at other places in Scotland. The subsidiary services which we have mentioned were at his beck or even under his direction. There were agents to explore the Continent for any men or material he might require, and to suppress with greater effectiveness than equity any who sought to infringe his privilege. The identity of his own interest with governmental policy, his close friendship with members of the Privy Council, and his high favour with two monarchs, gave a sanction to his tyranny which was impervious alike to malice[2] and defiance[3] and just indignation.[4] The Government,

white Venetian metal (Hartshorne, p. 188 and Plate 30). The double-ogee bowl is its metamorphosis in a tall-stemmed wine-glass; and so also (contrary to current opinion) is the familiar rummer of the late 18th and early 19th century.

[1] It had been transferred from Lord George Hay to Robinson, who seems to have parted with it at once.

[2] E.g. the suborning of the shipmasters, supra, p. 94, and the spoiling of his clay cargoes, p. 95; Hartshorne, chap. VIII, p. 196.

[3] E.g. the cases of Peter Horegill and John Greene (1615), Paul Vinion (1618), Sir Ralph and Dame Bingley (1620), Ralph Colborne (1620), Isaac Bongar, John Worrall, and John Dynes (Mansell's perpetual enemies), William Clavell (1634-5), Richard Batson (1641), Jeremy Bago, Greenwich, who was a Lorrainer (Bago=Bigault=Bigo), and had married Suzanna Henzey of Stourbridge, with his partner, Francis Bristow (1641).

[4] Cf. the petitions and protests cited by Hartshorne and the various questions in the House of Commons, or appeals to the Committee of Grievances. Hartshorne, chap. VIII.

H

indeed, had been obliged to repudiate the principle of Mansell long before his practice ceased, and in 1624 an Act of Parliament abolished *in law* the oppressive monopoly and introduced in its place the grant of Letters Patent. Mansell's was the last of the old despotisms, and if not benevolent, it was certainly beneficial. It combined every type of glassmaking then practised in England—window glass, medical and scientific glass, the rough peasant glass made in *Vitrariæ officinæ permultæ*,[1] mirror glass, and lastly the common and finer sorts of domestic glass, under a single control and imposed a general discipline on the wayward and individual glass-makers who were working " of their occupacion " in various parts of England, and but for the Mansell enlightenment, might never have gone beyond their rude peasantries.

But the promise of this period (*c.* 1615–50) lies less in the monopoly of Mansell, than in the nature of the opposition to it ; for it was out of that opposition that the real English tradition and the English national metal eventually grew. Hartshorne, who has the credit of collecting the sources, gives a very imperfect history of Mansell's vicissitudes in the exercise of his monopoly and of his feud with the rival glassmakers and the tireless rebel who led them. The subject is not sufficiently interesting in itself or important enough for the history of glassmaking to warrant a second redaction of the sources. What is important is the *fact* of opposition and the *type* of men who supported it. Bongar's enmity was a declaration of independence, the indiscipline of an adolescent industry, to which magisterial Patentees no longer seemed necessary. Glassmaking had become a general and familiar thing, as attractive to the " small " middle-class merchant as to aristocratic pro-moters like Slingsby, Zouche, and Mansell. Bongar, Paul Vinion, John Greene the Elder, John Worrall, Ralph Colborne, Peter Horegill, Sir William Clavell, John Dynes, Richard Batson, and lastly Jeremy Bago, and other " denobilized " Lorrainers thought the industry sufficiently prosperous to wish (as the Government also wished) to participate in it ; and they had a healthy loathing for Mansel. They were bourgeois merchants and artificers of the same type as those who founded the Glass-sellers Company in 1662, as the men who signed Ravenscroft's certificate in 1676, of the same type as Ravenscroft and Bishop themselves and the other makers of the lead technique. Their successors were the Brettells, Dixons and Grazebrooks of Stourbridge, John Hill who founded " Irish " glass, the Hennezels and Tyzacks of Newcastle, the Ricketts' and Stevens' and Jacobs' of Bristol, the Gatchells of Waterford, the Pughs of Dublin, the Edwards' of Belfast, and the Powells of our own day. These men are the English tradition ; their medium was the Ravenscroft metal, and their highest attainment was reached at the extreme ends of the 18th century.

[1] Paul Hentzer, *Travels in England* (1598), p. 87.

THE AGE OF ASSIMILATION

The epoch of their manufacture cannot be extended to much more than a hundred and fifty years, but during that period, in spite of mischievous legislation and disconcerting influences, they provided one of the most beautiful furnitures of modern times.

The survival values of English glass are three in number and easily detected. If we except heirlooms and other accidents, a glass may survive because it is so beautiful in itself or of such surpassing workmanship that it is cherished as a treasure and becomes immune from the hazards of daily use. It may, secondly, be of a sturdy fabric that will withstand these hazards until its antiquity is recognized. Or, thirdly, it may have received some inscription of an historical or a sentimental kind which causes it to be kept for association's sake. It is thus easy to see why Mansell's glass has left so few traces. Even when it was made *façon de Venise* it was not good enough to be kept for its own sake as the fine glasses of Venice were preserved. And secondly, though it was much less beautiful it was quite as fragile as Venetian glass, and therefore unless it was deliberately preserved, it was not likely to survive at all. It thus fell between the Venetian glasses which have been preserved for their beauty and the English lead glasses which generally speaking have survived on account of their sturdiness. Though the argument from silence is always a dangerous one perhaps the absence of inscribed and dated glasses (of the " occasional " sort) belonging to the Mansell period is a point against the English origin of the Verzelini family.

There are, however, a very few glasses which may perhaps be called English of pre-Restoration date. Mr. Mason had a lacemakers' lamp (Plate VIII. 2) which he found in Sussex, of a type originally French, which may well have been made by French immigrants during the 17th century. There are besides this two glasses almost exactly similar in shape and size, one in Mr. Mason's collection (Plate VIII. 1) and the other in the Victoria and Albert Museum. Both of these are of rough metal and unlikely to be Venetian ; but more important than that, both have a straight-sided, bucket-shaped bowl with a rounded and gadrooned base. They appear to represent an intermediate stage between the egg-shaped bowls of *e.g.* the B. M. " Verzelini " goblet and the rectangular bowl of the Buckingham goblet.[1] Mr. Mason, moreover, has a series of English wooden bowls of late 16th and early 17th century which seem to show the same development. There is also, in the Victoria and Albert Museum, a wine-glass with spiked gadrooning (Plate IV. 3) which appears to be a rude forerunner of some rather simpler goblets which are definitely English lead glass dating perhaps from 1685 (*e.g.* Plates XXVI. 1 and XXXII. 1). The stem of the Museum glass is similar in shape to fragmentary stems which have been dug up on the site of the Broad Street glasshouse, and to stems of two glasses in

[1] *Cf.* Read (H.) in *Burl. Mag.*, XLIII, 247.

the Verzelini group. The spiked gadrooning and the form of the bowl can also be watched on a fragmentary wine-glass in the same Museum which proves to be lead glass. The Museum fragment is not the stem, but its stem is still hollow, and if glasses with the same bowl and the same spiked gadrooning were being made in lead glass about 1680 there is some warrant for supposing that they were made here in soda glass earlier in the century. Two other glasses appear in Plates IV. 1 and V. 1 which must be described as *façon de Venise*, but of a poor sort that might well have been made in England before 1675. It must, however, be quite frankly admitted that the Mansell period is one of the greatest uncertainty. The specimens mentioned were probably made in England, and they seem to indicate the general character of the *façon de Venise* which flourished under Mansell; for Mansell was a system, not a glassmaker.

§3. THE RESTORATION REVIVAL

The barren period of the civil wars and the Puritan domination which followed them came to an end in 1660 with the accession of Charles II ; it is not often that a dynastic event coincides so exactly with the birth of a cultural epoch. The type of English civilization which is usually designated the 18th century has its beginning in the great revival which followed the Stuart Restoration, and the beginning of its end in the French Revolution, *Lyrical Ballads*, and the rest of the Romantic Movement ; and there is a very real connection between the integrity of this epoch and the florescence of English glassmaking which almost exactly coincided with it. It may be possible some day to formulate some kind of law for the periodicity of culture, but even while we only detect the unity of a movement, we can still postulate a general correlation between the forms of art and the forms of thought. The shapes of a Chippendale chair or Queen Anne wine-glass, the toys of Chelsea and Bow, personalities like Lady Mary Wortley Montagu, Horace Walpole or Lord Chesterfield, Wedgwood or Wesley, the empiricism of Newton and Boyle and Hume, the poetry of Pope and the prose of Berkeley, policies, philosophies, fashions are at once the symptoms and the substance of a cultural movement, and possess a thread of common character. As modes of expression they are members of a hierarchy, and it is one of the functions of historical criticism to establish the connection of one member with another and of each member with the whole. A goblet and a genius may, like the mouse and the mammoth in the museum, stand side by side for our inspection.

The great revival of glassmaking between 1660 and 1676 out of which the English tradition grew, was parallel with the general impetus of culture, and to some extent it may be explained by the two principles, Science and Fashion, in which that culture was beginning to express itself. Let us take Fashion as the lesser power first. The intense sociability which is evident in Restoration Comedy, and in the formality of 18th-century society, was in essence an interest in the behaviour of people, a psychological empiricism which is parallel to the philosophical empiricism of Hume and Berkeley and the earlier scientific empiricism of Newton and Boyle. The principle behind it, a vigorous relish for all kinds of experience, was evident also in the cultivation of taste and the childish delight in glass and porcelain and every agreeable domestic toy.

When the Duke of Buckingham entered the field of glassmaking he did so in the service of Fashion. Charles II himself was " graciously enclined to encourage the discovery of new arts and inventions."[1] But the patronage of the Court and the nobility must proceed more discreetly than in the days of Bowes and Mansell. The tyrannous system of monopolies was now dead and in its place there was an independent body of artisans who had a thorough knowledge of the art of glass and no notion of parting with their independence. Such men were Colenet, Vinion, Greene, Holden, Clifford, Powlden, Ward, Tilson, Leigh, Hare, and others.[2] The Duke of Buckingham came as near as the law permitted him to a revival of Mansell's system, partly by importing Venetian workmen and partly by obtaining patents in the name of his agents or servants. It will appear that the Duke had a hand in all patents granted between the accession of Charles II in 1660 and the patent granted to Ravenscroft in 1674. During that period he was at pains to compromise with the independent glassmakers, and the period of his control must therefore be regarded as intermediate between the absolute domination of Mansell and the independence of the glass industry from 1674 onwards.

We may begin with the manufacture of crystal glass by a company of Venetians brought over by Buckingham and working in his glasshouse at Greenwich. On 10 June, 1673 Evelyn visited " the Italian glasshouse at Greenwich where glasse was blown of finer metall than that of Murano at Venice." This glasshouse is known to have belonged to the Duke of Buckingham,[3] and we have to enquire, therefore, when the Venetians were brought over to England and when the patent for crystal glass was granted. Now on the thirtieth of June, 1663 the Duke of Buckingham, in applying to the King for a Clause permitting him the sole manufacture of mirror glass asked that " Your Petitioners Patent for making of Christall may be renewed."[4] " Christall," in this connection, must mean glass for drinking vessels and other domestic wares, and it follows that the original patent to the Duke was granted between Charles II's return to England

---

[1] Petition of the Duke of Buckingham, *S.P. Dom.*, 30 June, 1663 ; Hartshorne, p. 437.
[2] *Ibid.*, pp. 220 *seq.*
[3] Hartshorne, p. 225.
[4] *S.P. Dom.*, 30 June, 1663, Petition of the Duke of Buckingham ; Hartshorne, p. 437.

(early in 1660) and 1663. It will be shown in a moment that between 1661 and 1674 Buckingham had a hand in the only two patents granted, and both these were for a term of fourteen years. We may, therefore, presume that the Duke's first patent was likewise for fourteen years, and this is consistent with the date of Ravenscroft's patent, in which the Duke had no part, fourteen years after the Restoration (16 May, 1674). If Ravenscroft's patent was not granted until the Duke's original patent had expired then the latter must have been granted in 1660 very shortly after the King's return to England ; and we may venture to conclude that the arrival of the Venetian company was nearly coincident with it.

We may now proceed to the two other applications to make crystal glass, (1) Martin Clifford and Thomas Powlden[1] and (2) Thomas Tilson. After the Restoration the revival of glassmaking at first took two courses. Buckingham being merely a rich promoter without practical knowledge introduced Venetian glassmakers ; the practical glassmakers of the merchant class began to experiment for themselves in the composition of crystal, and they were thus the natural rivals of Buckingham. Clifford, Powlden, and Tilson belonged to this class, and I suggest that they were men of practical knowledge but comparatively small capital. Both applications, that of Clifford and Powlden and that of Tilson, refer to their " new invention of making christall glasses," and this phrase suggests that they intended to make glass more or less independently of Venice and quite possibly with English workmen. Clifford and Powlden received a special licence for crystal glassmaking on 10 November, 1661[2] ; it should be noted that this licence was not a patent, for that would have infringed the patent which, as we have shown, the Duke of Buckingham already held. The licence was not ratified as a patent until nearly a year later, October, 1662,[3] and then it was granted to the Duke of Buckingham in the name of his agents or servants.[4] In this lapse of a year we may see how Buckingham followed, in a more discreet and gentlemanly fashion, the example of his predecessor Mansell. The licence to Clifford and Powlden of 10 November, 1661, would be a warning to Buckingham that there were rivals in the field and the surest counter was to enlist them in his service. No doubt Buckingham feared that on technical[5] grounds the King's advisers might see fit to grant a second patent which would seriously damage his own, and during the interval November, 1661 to October, 1662, he probably made representations to the new licensees ; that their licence could never become a patent while his own patent endured, and that if they wished to prosper by their new metal he (the Duke) must have the

[1] The original spelling is retained. Mr. Francis Buckley spells the name Paulden.
[2] *S.P. Dom.*, 10 November, 1661.   [3] *S.P. Dom.*, October, 1662.
[4] See Mr. Buckley's notes to the Bellingham Bill (*infra*).
[5] The technique of glass, not the technique of law.

controlling interest, and they (Clifford and Powlden) must enter his service before their application for a patent went through. In support of this explanation I must refer here to a parallel case which has recently been brought to light by Mr. Francis Buckley.[1] A certain John Bellingham of Lambeth had learnt some process for the manufacture of looking-glass plates for which he held the secret ; and in 1671 Buckingham, apparently fearing that he might apply on technical grounds for an independent patent, offered him the managership of his Vauxhall plate glassworks at the very good salary of £300 per annum—a two-thousand-a-year job instead of the uncertainties of private enterprise. Bellingham not unnaturally accepted[2] and it seems highly probable that the Duke adopted some such manœuvre in dealing with Clifford and Powlden in 1661–2. In this way they gained a rich backing but lost their independence.

The second application was that of Tilson. The licence was issued on 19 October, 1662,[3] but the patent in this case also was not granted until nearly a year later (4 September, 1663),[4] and we may reasonably suspect that the Duke adopted the same policy as before ; Tilson's patent was granted to the Duke of Buckingham in the name of his agents or servants. Tilson's application differed from that of Clifford and Powlden in that it covered mirror glass as well as crystal. Now between Tilson's licence (19 October, 1662) and the Tilson-Buckingham patent (4 September, 1663) the Duke had obtained (20 July, 1663)[5] the sole privilege for making looking-glass plates, and therefore the part of Tilson's application which had reference to mirror glass could not be granted after that date unless it was incorporated in Buckingham's mirror-glass patent, that is to say, unless Tilson were content to submit himself to the Duke and receive the patent on his behalf. This was what actually happened[6] ;

[1] See *John Bellingham's Bill in Chancery against the Duke of Buckingham*, an MS. document dated 1676, discovered by Mr. Francis Buckley, annotated by him and given to the Library of the Victoria and Albert Museum.

[2] Bellingham in 1676 claimed £394 on account of salary and in solution the Duke offered him a lease of the Vauxhall works at a rent of £400 p.a. The Duke was to maintain the patent (originally granted 1663, for fourteen years) and to keep the works in repair. Bellingham complained that the Duke did not do this and that the pots were deliberately damaged by the Duke's agents, and that Ravenscroft and Henry Baker had been allowed to set up glasshouses for fine sorts of glass. For this Bellingham claimed a further £400. Buckingham retaliated by saying the £394 had been paid and by suing Bellingham for the rent of £400. The Bill asks that Buckingham disclose his full agreement with Bellingham.

[3] *S.P. Dom.*, 19 October, 1662.

[4] *S.P. Dom.*, 4 September, 1663 ; Hartshorne, p. 439.

[5] *S.P. Dom.*, 20 July, 1663, minute by Sir G. Palmer ; Hartshorne, p. 437.

[6] As far as crystal was concerned the Tilson-Buckingham patent superseded the Clifford-Powlden-Buckingham patent. The latter was surrendered, *S.P. Dom.*, 4 August, 1663 ; Hartshorne, p. 438.

for a year later when the Company of Glass Sellers and Looking Glass Makers received their Charter of incorporation (25 July, 1664) special provision was made " for saving the rights and privileges of one Thomas Tilson, Merchant and Maker of Christall glasses who holds Letters Patents of the King."[1]

Thus the Duke of Buckingham arrived by four stages, his own patent for crystal (1660), the Clifford-Powlden-Buckingham patent for a new invention of crystal (1662), his own privilege for mirror glass (1663), and finally the Tilson-Buckingham patent (1663), at a control of English glassmaking which nominally at any rate left little chance to outsiders. We need not suppose that the volatile Duke was very rigid in supervising his patents. He had wide and various interests and his glassmaking was only one of them. For long periods he paid no attention to his factories ; in 1667 he incurred the royal displeasure and spent a year in the Tower, and the Bellingham Bill shows that when he had a capable manager he went away and left him, forgetting both the glasshouse and the manager's salary. It is thus not Buckingham but the Glass-sellers Company and the bourgeois manufacturers who really determined the development of glassmaking between the Restoration and the invention of lead glass (1660–76).

Buckingham's patents, however, remained valid. In 1663 (21 August) four glassmakers, Bryan Leigh, Adam Hare, William Broughes, and Ralph Outlye, petitioned for a permit to make both crystal glasses and mirror-glass plates from flints. This application was adversely minuted by one of the King's secretaries with the remark that such a patent was already held by the Duke of Buckingham (not, it may be noted, by Clifford and Powlden). It was referred to the Attorney-General's Department and its rejection may be regarded as certain. It is of interest to note that Bryan Leigh and Company intended to use flints,[2] and I am inclined to think that the " new inventions " claimed by Clifford and Powlden and by Tilson were for making glass with flints which were thought to be a better substitute than sand for imported *tarso*.[3]

Both Buckingham's patents, for crystal and for looking-glass plates,

[1] The document is in the possession of the Glass-sellers Company ; for abstract see Young, pp. 13–15.

[2] Merret writing a year earlier had said that flints were " not further used." I think he meant, not used except for crystal, which he had just been discussing. If he meant " no longer used " at all the documents relating to Leigh & Co. prove him wrong. Plot in 1676 implied that flints were the normal ingredient. See p. 122.

[3] Compare the phrase " new invention of making christall glasses " with Ravenscroft's " particuler sort of Christalline Glass resembling Rock Crystal." Ravenscroft, it would appear, began (1673) in the usual way with flints, but was persuaded by Da Costa to try *tarso*. When lead glass became general the silicate was of less importance and so sand took the place of both imported *tarso* and native flints.

[104]

seem to have run their full course of fourteen years. The Greenwich furnace was still working when Evelyn visited it in 1673[1] and noted how fine was the metal, and in 1676[2] he visited the Duke's Vauxhall glassworks " where they made huge vases of metal as clear ponderous and thick as crystal."[3] The Bellingham Bill of the same year suggests that the expiry of the patent the following year was in Bellingham's mind when he stipulated that the patent should be maintained, *i.e.* renewed. Hartshorne,[4] who at this point seriously misconstrued the sources, states erroneously that Buckingham lost his mirror-glass patent ; this was because he failed to realize that Tilson's name was only a cover for Buckingham's, and thought that the former's patent cancelled the Duke's.

Several inscribed glasses, among them the celebrated Royal Oak goblet, survive from this period, and if they were made in England it is almost certain that they are the work of Buckingham's company of Venetians. We may therefore set forth briefly the arguments in favour of an English attribution. All the three glasses illustrated (Plates VI, VII) are engraved with a diamond and bear inscriptions in the English language ; and in two instances they bear also a portrait of the English King. The Royal Oak goblet was certainly made for the marriage of Charles II in 1663 and the Exeter flute was probably made shortly after his accession. It is highly unlikely that patriotic glasses of this kind would have been imported from abroad, more especially as there were Venetian glassmakers in London who were quite capable of such work. Apart from the engraving, which supports an English origin, there is nothing against it in the form and metal of the glasses themselves. The metal of the Royal Oak goblet is blown very thin, but its quality is not of the first rank and suggests that in any case it was made derivatively *à la façon de Venise*. Its form, moreover, is entirely un-Venetian and on that score alone it must be either Netherlandish or English. We have to ask, therefore, whether a private person or a glass dealer would send to the Netherlands for a glass to celebrate the marriage of the English King. If such an order, for a glass of the first quality, were placed abroad at all it would have been placed almost certainly at Venice itself ; and the points of this glass are against a Venetian origin. The important thing for a glass of this kind was that it should be made by Venetians, and there were, as we have seen, Venetians in London, inferior in skill to Murano, but certainly not inferior to the Venetian metics in the Netherlands. Moreover, two years after the marriage England went to war with Holland and for some time before there had been strained relations between the two countries ; which did not interfere with trade generally, but make it unlikely that the King's health would

[1] *Diary*, 10 June, 1673. [2] *Diary*, September, 1676.
[3] Vases = cylinders of plate glass before they were unrolled. Crystal here = rock crystal. [4] Pp. 224–5.

be drunk in a Dutch glass. Finally the Duke of Buckingham who controlled the Venetian glassmakers in London was a favourite at Court and received royal patronage of his enterprise.[1] These considerations offer a strong probability that the Royal Oak goblet was made and engraved in London ; and they may be applied with slight modifications to the other two glasses. The flute at Exeter (Plate VI) is not in origin an English form, but the flute in some variant or another was the common property of *façon de Venise* at this time,[2] and the same is true of the *Roemer* form (engraved with the Seasons, British Museum, Plate VII. 1). Hartshorne called the latter glass Dutch in spite of the English inscription, because the *Roemer* was primarily a German and Dutch shape. But the repertory of forms was international in all the derivative *façon de Venise* and both the flute and the *Roemer* were probably made in England at this time. English glass made by Venetians in the employ of Buckingham would be simply one location of *façon de Venise*, and a *façon de Venise* which had adopted both the flute and the *Roemer*. In the several locations of *façon de Venise* both form and metal can often be distinguished from Venice itself ; the metal is apt to be coarser than that of Venice and the shapes show some divergence from the Venetian paradigm. But where a glass bears an inscription in English or other ornament of English reference[3] the evidence of form and metal in one location of *façon de Venise* as against another, is not sufficiently definite to upset the evidence of the engraving and the natural conclusion that the glasses themselves were made in England. Nor need that conclusion be overturned by the very strong probability that both the subject of the British Museum *Roemer* and the portrait of the Exeter flute were actually engraved by foreigners.

To Buckingham's Venetians we must ascribe the origin of the "parallel Italian tradition" which is later represented by the Altarist Da Costa and by a whole series of early 18th-century glasses ; it even continues to influence the style of English glassmaking as late as the middle of the 18th century.

The second important influence of this period may be loosely labelled science, but by that word we must understand the inquisitive and experimental spirit which had been formulated by Descartes as a methodic doubt. Words like *sceptical* and *enquiry*, which occur for example in Boyle's book *The Sceptical Chymist*, Locke's *Enquiry Concerning Human Understanding*, and many other titles, possessed a vigour and pregnancy now lost to them. Even during the Civil War there had been a stirring of the new spirit

---

[1] He was official glassmaker to Charles II. Hartshorne, p. 225.

[2] The poet Lovelace in 1649 speaks of " Elles of beer, Flutes of Canary."

[3] I allude to the initials $\begin{smallmatrix} & H & \\ W & & E \end{smallmatrix}$ of the B.M. *Roemer*. This mode of inscribing the initials of the parties to a marriage is very common in English pottery and glass.

when Sir Thomas Browne, declaring that the " two great pillars of truth were experience and solid reason," published his famous *Inquiry into Vulgar and Common Errors* (1646) : and now that wars were done and thought had leisure to pursue its own ways, the impulse of research became a grave and measured scepticism. Thus began the tradition of natural science in England which determined much of the character of 18th-century civilization and, in its gradual application to the happiness of man, created an industrial technology and had issue in the society of our own time. The clues to its significance were the ideas of abstraction and mensuration, Newton and " the cautious and doubting Mr. Boyle " were its pioneers, and it obtained a national sanction in 1662, when it received its great charter from Charles II and became organized as the Royal Society. The object of this body was declared as the " extension of natural knowledge," and that phrase applies to the period generally. The ardour and the methods of investigation were not closed within libraries and laboratories ; the Royal Society was never an institution of academic spirit, and between it and the theologians there was a perpetual antagonism. Enquiry was in the air at this time, just as " duty " or " propriety " or " business " have been the psychological vogue at other periods of our history ; and in the present context—the history of the art of glass—it is to be observed that the flourishing of glassmaking which began with Ravenscroft was only a corollary to the general revival of cultural interests. The invention of glass of lead[1] was a symptom as well as a cause of the regeneration of the art after the Restoration, and that regeneration itself was only one vibration of a much wider dynamic which affected the whole of subsequent history. It is true that the symptom, as is the way with evolutions, became in its own turn a cause and that the nature of the lead metal determined the whole of the later development of English glass, but the origin is still to be found in the first ten years of Charles II's reign.

We have already seen how in the " noble " age of glassmaking the art had something of the character of an alchemy ; and there is sufficient reason to suppose that in the time of Charles II glassmaking was instructed, or at least influenced, by the new chemistry. The connecting link may be found in the person of Dr. Christopher Merret. He was both a practical glassmaker well acquainted with the trade, and a learned member of the Royal Society, and it was he who, seeking a systematic guide for English glassmakers, was led to make an English translation of Antonio Neri's great textbook *L'Arte Vetraria*.[2] The mere event is significant. Neri's book

---

[1] Buckley (F.), *Glassmaking in England in the 17th century*, p. 7. " The great factor which produced a revival in the making of fine glass in England was undoubtedly the invention of glass of lead."

[2] Neri (Antonio), *L'Arte Vetraria*, Florence, 1612. Translation by Dr. Christopher Merret, *The Art of Glass*, London, 1662.

had been published in Italian as early as 1612, and although it was the only serious practical textbook then existing, there had been no call for an English edition for fifty years. Mansell's stupidity never wanted a more striking proof than this omission. But there was now an eagerness for clear knowledge that had not formerly existed. Just as the impulse of science expressed itself in the organization of the Royal Society, so in 1664 a Glass-Sellers Company was inaugurated on the model of the old City Corporations. Glass was declaring its vitality and insisting on recognition. Merret's edition of the *Art of Glass*, published two years earlier, was neither a servile transcript nor a piece of aimless scholarship. He prefaced the work with independent criticisms of his author and the notes and observations he had made in his experience of English glasshouses ; and in his *Advertisement to the Ingenuous Reader* he declared pretty clearly the aims of his undertaking : " Our own workmen in this Art will be much advantaged by this publication, who have within these twenty years last past much improved themselves (to their own great reputation and credit of our nation) insomuch that few foreigners are now left amongst us. And this I rather say because an eminent workman, now a Master, told me most of the skill he had gained was from this true and excellent book (they were his words). And therefore I doubt not 'twill give some light and advantage to our countrymen of that profession, which was my principal aim." It may be noted that two of these statements are encouraging fictions. Certainly there may have been improvement between Mansell's introduction of the Mantua glassmakers (*c.* 1634–5) and the year 1640 when from military causes glassmaking, on the Tyne at least, seems to have come to a standstill.[1] But the Civil Wars and the period of the Commonwealth (*i.e.* the twenty years preceding 1662) were, as Mr. Buckley has shown, a very lean period for glassmaking.[2] In 1642[3] English glassmaking under Mansell's influence had attained an export trade, but in 1657[4] it had entirely disappeared. The fact that in 1660[5] there was again an export trade indicates a recovery, but only a recovery of quite recent date. Moreover, at the end of the Commonwealth period there was still a good number of foreign glassmakers in England. Dr. Merret realized the recent improvement, and his lavish praise is an exhortation disguised as a statement of fact.

There is another thing to notice about Merret's *Art of Glass*. He dedicated it to his friend Robert Boyle, the greatest English chemist of

[1] Hartshorne, p. 200.
[2] Buckley (F.), *Glassmaking in England in the 17th century*, p. 7, and documents quoted pp. 15–20.
[3] *Ibid.*, p. 17.
[4] *Ibid.*, pp. 17–18. Cromwell had no rates for exported glass.
[5] *Ibid.*, p. 20.

that day, and we know that Boyle himself had become interested in the composition of glass, devoted one or two essays to various aspects of the subject, and was intimate with " an ingenious Master of a glasshouse " with whom he was accustomed to make a practical study of the art. The Royal Society itself officially discussed the manufacture of glass and criticized an Italian who had made an unsuccessful attempt to substitute flints for *tarso* and so given the glass a tendency to splinter.[1] The suggestion I would make, therefore, is that by some avenue of this kind a knowledge of experimental chemistry, as distinct from craftsmen's lore, became current among the glassmakers, and available for the experiments by the artists of the Glass-sellers Company which ultimately led to Ravenscroft's invention. For many years past it had been the custom among the Venetians to make a heavy vitreous paste[2] for the imitation of gems and for fancy wares. Its chief ingredient was lead, its chief virtue the capacity to take colour, but as a *metal* it was too " brittle " for everyday use. Merret in his translation of Neri applauded this substance, calling it " glass of lead " and observing that it was not then (1662) being made in England ; and it was perhaps from Merret's description of it that the English glassmakers first got the idea of using an oxide of lead as a flux for a white metal rather than as an ingredient in a coloured vitreous *paste*.[3] If that is so, it may be that some of the experiments[4] made between 1662 and 1676 were an attempt to adjust the other ingredients to this additional flux. Ravenscroft seems to have been the first person to realize that the *proportion* of salts that had hitherto been the only flux might be reduced simply by the

[1] Birch, *History of the Royal Society*, IV, 276.

[2] Pure glass of lead was distinguished from flint glass by Dossie (1758).

[3] Hartshorne's discussion (1897) of this period is entirely vitiated because he failed to realize the difference between the glass *paste* described by Neri and Merret under the title " glass of lead " and the ordinary lead *metal* of " flint glass." Although he knew none of the sealed Ravenscroft specimens since discovered, his antedating of the invention of the lead metal (flint glass) was largely due to this confusion.

[4] These experiments were :

1661.—Thomas Clifford and Thomas Powlsden. Hartshorne, p. 221.

1663.—Thomas Tilson, *ibid.*, p. 222 and p. 224 where the Charter of the Glass-sellers Company is cited with a special reference to Tilson.

1663.—Bryan Leigh and three others. *Ibid.*, p. 222.

1664.—References in Charles II's Proclamation (*ibid.*, p. 439) which though concerning plate and mirror glass and not vessels, is at least a proof of the general experimental activity.

1670.—Ananias Henzey at Portarlington. He had only come from England that year and in spite of many years' experience was in great difficulty experimenting with his metal. *V. supra*, p. 68, and Westropp, *Irish Glass*, p. 33.

1674.—George Ravenscroft. He had *already* been experimenting *before* he first received his patent ; and that was two years before he eventually perfected glass of lead (1676).

addition of an oxide of lead[1] ; but as long as crizzling occurred this adjustment had not been entirely effected.

For fashion and chemistry so much.

There is a further factor to be considered in the bourgeois merchants into whose hands the greatest part of the English trade had passed. Even now it was not the working artist who controlled his art. The management had devolved upon the merchants whose business was to sell, not to make, glass ; and it was men of this kind who focussed the control in a Glass-sellers Company, who promoted such enterprises as the Savoy glasshouse, encouraged experiment and employed Ravenscroft.[2] There had been a loosely-knit body of Glaziers in Mansell's time, but they disappeared during the Civil Wars, and the Glass-sellers Company of 1664 seems to have been an organized revival. Certainly there had been no previous authority that was empowered to publish statutes and decrees, and to punish " abuses and deceits " in the City of London and within a radius of seven miles. The best-known glassmen, manufacturers as well as merchants, were members of it, and subordinated their enterprises to the central control—Tilson, Greene, Moore, Bishopp, and the rest of the signatories to the certificate of improvement[3] in which Ravenscroft obtained from the Company the official recognition of his invention. They found it within their competence to take measures for protecting the industry from foreign competition ; to regulate the glass-pedlars who toured the countryside, and since their immunity under the Statute of Vagabonds (39 Eliz. Cap. 4) had grown so vociferous and overweening as to endanger the business of true licensed tradesmen[4] ; they issued their gracious consent that Mr. Ravenscroft transport so much of his glasses to Ireland, and within this date and that[5] ; they prescribed the sizes and fashions of the glasses he manufactured[6] ; they standardized the designs of glasses already in vogue, and even so far as Venice commanded their execution. In fact they extended to the whole art the virtue of autonomy.

---

[1] *Cf.* also p. 123 *infra*. Plot discerned this at the time and refers to nitre tartar and borax. Nitre (saltpetre) had hitherto been the chief salt (flux) used in England. Mansell had a large control of the market in saltpetre (Hartshorne, p. 434. Letter to Nicholas). Its importation was heavily taxed side by side with various kinds of glass by both Charles I and Cromwell. *V.* Buckley, *Glass Trade, loc. cit.*

[2] Sloane MSS. 857, Papers relating to the Glass Sellers, No. 2.

[3] Cited in full, with all the signatures in Buckley (F.), *Glass Trade*, p. 37, from *State Papers Dom.*, Car. II, 383, No. 8.

The certificate was several times inserted in the *London Gazette*. Other members, devoted to mirrors, were Boulter, Todners, Burroughs, and Hudgeabout. Sloane MS. 867. Hartshorne, p. 449.

[4] Papers relating to the Glass Sellers, No. 12.

[5] *Ibid.*, No. 3.

[6] *Ibid.*, No. 2.

THE AGE OF ASSIMILATION

English glass in its best age had two values—its design and its metal. Both are English, and it was under the auspices of the Glass-sellers Company that they came to their maturity. Even before Ravenscroft's invention there are sufficient indications that England was beginning to develop an independent design. Greene's patterns[1] (Fig. 16) which date from *c.* 1670 illustrate very well how the English glassmen had begun to stabilize and to simplify the current Venetian forms even while their metal was still the same. This independence is evident in two ways. Greene *selects* always from the designs already in vogue at Venice, avoiding for example the very tall goblets with serpentine stems and the more impressive *verres de parade.* He also modifies the actual shape of Venetian glasses ; giving for example a greater compactness to the sweeping curves of the V-shaped bowls. These designs are definitely for domestic glass, and if we can argue from Greene to the general tendency at the time, it would seem that England, by practising only a few strokes of the Venetian repertory, was already moving towards a style of her own.[2] What made that style possible was Ravenscroft's glass of lead ; the style was in a sense derivative, but one is inclined to think that the germs of an individual design were there first. We shall see in a moment how several of the best shapes of early 18th-century glass are a direct development of the official (1672) patterns which the London Glass Sellers required of their artists and imposed upon their customers. There remains the metal. At this period (1660–76) English glass had won economic independence and a middle-class custom, and if it was to maintain the one it must extend the other. *Verres de parade* and cupboards of fine pieces were not enough. The Company therefore must create a ware that besides being beautiful was useful enough to find a general acceptance and sturdy enough to survive its own utility. Such a fabric was glass of lead. It would perhaps be fanciful to suggest that in the slow development from 1660 to 1676, the Company

---

[1] John Greene's famous forms, *v.* Hartshorne, Plate 30, Buckley (F.), *Old London Drinking Glasses,* and Fig. 16 in this book. The designs were English modifications of the traditional Venetian types and they were carried out in Venice by the firm of Allesio Morelli. For the business correspondence *v.* Hartshorne, p. 441, who has extracted it from Sloane MS. 857. The letters fall between 1667 and 1672. Simplification and solidification are very noticeable in several fragments which are proved to contain no lead and immediately precede the invention of Ravenscroft ; this modification is most evident in the Northampton fragment.

[2] *Cf.* Greene's requisition for " Thick beer " and " Thick Claret," which I take to be a stouter and cheaper version of " Beer " and " Claret " glasses, probably for tavern use (Sloane MS. 857, Letter dated 18 January, 1671). In the same letter Greene asks for " flintt sack." I see no reason to doubt the reading, and suggest that he used the term flint to indicate second-quality wares, like those which were then being made in England *really* with flints, and were in the dealer's esteem much inferior to " Venice glasses " proper. Before Ravenscroft " flint " is a disparagement ; Ravenscroft turned it into a compliment.

of Glass Sellers was deliberately seeking a fabric of this kind ; but the hardiness of lead glass explains not only why it prospered in its own time, but why so many specimens have survived into ours.

Before we pass to the main threads of development from the time of William III we must briefly allude to the circumstances in which this " flint glass " or " glass of lead " first made its appearance.

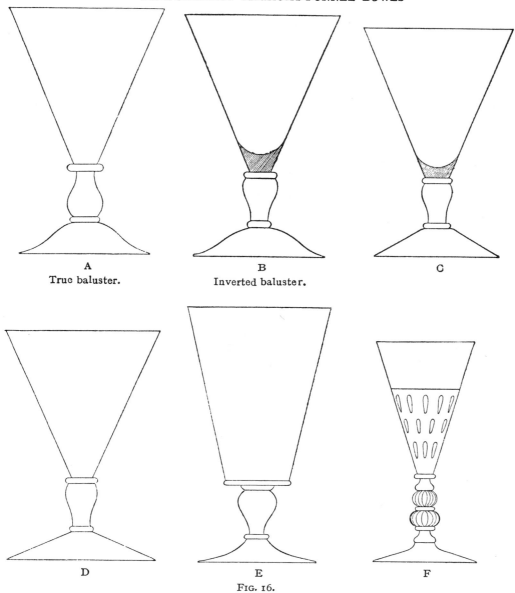

A
True baluster.

B
Inverted baluster.

C

D

E

F

FIG. 16.

The beginnings of English design.

Specifications for glasses ordered from Morelli of Murano by John Greene, Glass Seller of London, 1667–72. Conventional elevations after sketches in the British Museum, partly in perspective. (Sloane MS. 857, Papers relating to the Glass Sellers). For Greene's list of types transcribed from the MS. see Hartshorne, pp. 440–9; but in only one or two cases can these be identified with the sketches.

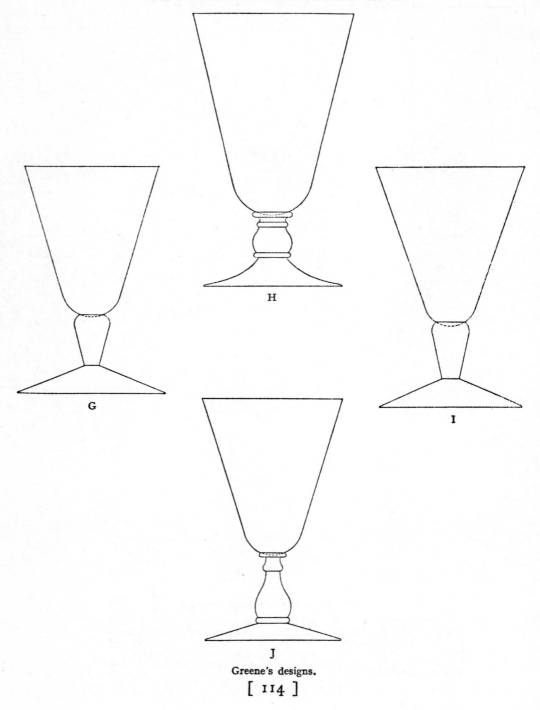

G

H

I

J

Greene's designs.

Greene's designs.

L is the Rummer (Merret's " Romer ") and probably the type called by Greene Rhenish wine glasses ("rñish wine glasses," MS. 10 Feb. 1670).

M is one of the " brandj tumblers " (*ibid*.).   O is the flute; whence ' aleglass.'

CHAPTER IV

The Ravenscroft Revolution

Nothing beyond what is self-developed in the brain of a race is permanently gained or will survive the changes of time.

FLINDERS PETRIE.

BETWEEN 1683 and 1696 we encounter in John Houghton almost as interesting and important a figure as Dr. Merret. For some years he gave particular study to the general state of English industries at that time, and among them to the art of glass, in which he seems to have taken especial interest. Like Merret and Plot he was a member of the Royal Society, and he is another instance of the sceptical and acquisitive temper which was the chief intellectual character of his age. He was also one of the earliest Englishmen to apply to what is now called economics the scientific methods which Boyle used in his chemistry and Sir Hans Sloane in the field of natural history.[1] His work, like Merret's, was definitely undertaken for the advancement of trade, and where Merret had confined himself to technical and chemical matters Houghton was more concerned with analysing the economic basis of the several industries that came under his notice. His investigations were not buried for ever in a treatise, but issued from time to time as a " Journal of Economic Studies " to which he gave the name *Letters for the Improvement of Commerce and Trade*. He was thus a person well acquainted with the commercial developments of his time, and though he probably had not the intimate knowledge of glass technique which we can ascribe to Boyle, Merret, and Plot, his authority is of the highest importance. In his one hundred and ninety-eighth *Letter*, dated 15 May, 1696, he definitely attributes to Ravenscroft the invention of the " Flint glass " of his own time : " I remember the time when the Duke of Buckingham first encouraged glass plates and Mr. Ravenscroft first made the flint glasses." There can be no doubt that when Houghton wrote, flint glass generally meant, and in London certainly meant, glass of lead. Few perhaps outside the profession of glassmaking were then aware of its nature, and the good qualities which were so admired were commonly attributed to the use of flints in its composition. The use of lead is evident from a document which we cite below[2]—a commercial pamphlet

---

[1] *Cf.* Edwards, *Lives of the Founders of the British Museum*, 2 vols., London, 1877.

[2] This passage was as follows, the italics being ours :—

" *Merch.* . . . . But at present till great quantities of oar shall be raised, we do for the most part sell our lead in a sort of Powder, called Lytharge.

LD. B. I have seen that which they call Lytharge of Gold and Lytharge of silver, and as I remember it comes from Poland, or some of those foreign parts. Is yours like that ?

Merch. O, my Lord, much beyond it ; there's none will buy Foreign Lytharge since this was made.

dating from 1700—which proves that lytharge (an oxide of lead) was then used by fine glassmakers in considerable quantities : there is an emphasis

LD. B. Why ? Is this a new thing ?

Merch. Yes, my Lord, good Lytharge was never made a Merchantable Commodity in England, till Mr. Robert Lydall, Chief Operator to the Company, made the Discovery, for which he hath a patent from his present Majesty.

LD. B. All Refiners will tell you that they ever made Lytharge in their common way of Refining.

Merch. True, my Lord, but never a Merchantable Commodity to Profit or Sale in quantities ; all the Drugsters, Apothecaries, Potters and Glassmakers about Town can testify this truth, for it was so bad and mixed with their Wood-ashes and Dust that it was not fit for their use, and therefore Refiners were necessitated to reduce it into Lead again with great waste ; but this Lytharge is made another way, never known in England before, and is so clean and free from all mixture, that it far exceeds all Foreign Lytharge and even Red lead itself. And wherever this Lytharge is known in England, or in any Foreign Parts, they will not buy any other Lytharge, as I am informed.

LD. A. Pray, Sir, what is the use of the Lytharge ?

Merch. My Lord, it is bought by the Drugsters, and used by the Apothecaries, Surgeons and Painters ; but the great use of it is by the Potters in glazing Earthen Ware, *and by the Glassmakers in making fine glass.*

LD. B. Do these Persons lathe off any great quantities ?

Merch. I leave it to your Lordship to judge ; every Traveller knows that there is Earthen Ware used all over the World, and that all the Earthen Ware must be glazed, or else it is so apt to gather dust and filth, that it is not fit for use ; and all this glazing is with Lead Calcined and made into Powder.

LD. A. Earthen Ware was made long before your Invention and therefore the Potters can stand in no need thereof.

Merch. True, My Lord ; the Potters finding no sort of Lytharge made firm and clean enough for their purpose were forced with great Care, Trouble, and Charge to Calcine the Lead themselves, or by continual stirring in an Iron Kettle, to make it into a Course Powder, which they ground fine at the Mill, and so mixed it with other proper Ingredients, and made it fit for the Glazing Trade. But, my Lord, in this way of making, the Fumes are very unhealthy to the Men, and the operation chargeable to the Master ; so our Lytharge is not only much finer and better for their use, but cheaper also.

LD. A. Nay then you will be sure to have all their Custom. But how do the Glass-makers use it, for that is a general Commodity too.

Merch. They use it instead of Red Lead, which is one ingredient in their best Glasses ; it is of such an *Oily, Transparent* and yet *Binding Nature, that it is of singular use to them.*

Lord B. But if Red-lead serve their turn, why will they use Lytharge ?

Merch. For the same Reasons as the Potters, because it is better and cheaper.

LD. A. How is it better ?

Merch. Red-lead is frequently mixed with Dust and Ashes, and often adulterated with Red-oaker or a Brick-dust ; but this Lytharge is always made pure, without either Dust or Ashes mixed with it. And it is observed that the Glass made with this Lytharge is much finer, more white and clear ; and which another great advantage, is not so apt to crack when cold as Glass made with Red-lead is, which is more burnt in the fire than Lytharge, and so more short and brittle in its Nature and Use.

LD. A. Then it is much better indeed. But how is it cheaper ?

Merch. Because Lytharge goes further than Red-lead, which is a compound and has Water, etc., mixed with it, and all that is added to the Lead itself, is useless to the Glass-on the inclusion of lytharge in the batch which seems to show that it was very highly esteemed by the glassmakers and was still enough of a novelty to excite comment. The glassmakers of later times, *e.g.* Apsley Pellatt, ascribed the great improvement in English glassmaking, by which they meant lead glass, to the reign of William III. The Glass Sellers, moreover, had declared as early as 1676 (3 June) that a new type of glass recently invented by one George Ravenscroft could be distinguished from the former glass by a " distinction of sound discernible by any person whatsoever."[1] Seven of the eight glasses which bear Ravenscroft's mark are lead glass, and there are besides a few lead glasses which can be dated before the death of William III (1701) by *other* evidence than their style or workmanship. Finally Ravenscroft's own glasses, which we know by chemical test to contain lead, were described by the Glass Sellers as " Crystalline or flint glasses."[2]

From these considerations it may be taken as proven fact that Houghton when he wrote "flint glasses" meant glasses fused with an oxide of lead. Houghton himself was well acquainted with the glass trade, and it would require the most perverse sceptic to doubt his categorical statement that the new glasses were first made by Ravenscroft. At this point, therefore, it will be in order to assemble the facts concerning him.

He came from an old county family, the Ravenscrofts of Bretten, but the branch to which George Ravenscroft belonged had its home at Hawarden in the county of Flint. He was the second son of George

---

makers, and either consumes, or evaporates in the fire, so that Twenty hundred of this fine Lytharge will make near Two and Twenty hundred of Red-lead ; and as has been observed Lytharge not being so much burnt in the fire, *but being of a much softer nature than Redlead, sooner and at less charge melteth again in the fire and mixeth better with the Sand and Ashes, used by the Glass-makers to their great Advantage.*

LD. B. Then indeed if you sell the Lytharge at the price of Red-lead it has an apparent Advantage.

Merch. My Lord, this Lytharge formerly was sold at above Twenty pounds per Tun, but now the Company, being willing to make it a Universal Commodity over all the World for those Uses are content to sell it near the price of Red-lead, which is the reason that I asserted it was cheaper, as well as better for the use of the Glass-makers."

This document is an advertisement of Lydall's patent (1697) for desilverizing lead and making lead oxide in a reverberatory furnace with " sea-coal." Trade pamphlets of this kind (some of which anticipate the modern dialogue advertisement) were commonly used for boosting new inventions from the time of Sturtevant and Rovenzon downwards. Compare an advertisement in the *Flying Post*, 27 January, 1699–1700, which states that lytharge made under Lydall's patent " is of such a soft oily nature that it . . . is of singular use for all makers of fine glass and hath been approved by the most eminent glassmakers about London who now use the same in place of lead calcined, red lead and lead ashes to their great advantage in many respects." It would appear that red-lead was the form of lead first used in English glassmaking, and so probably by Ravenscroft and Bishopp.

[1] Declaration by the Glass Sellers. *S.P. Dom.*, Car. II, 381, No. 244.
[2] *S.P. Dom.*, Car. II, 381, Nos. 244 and 249, and 383, No. 7.

THE RAVENSCROFT REVOLUTION

Ravenscroft of Sholton in the parish of Hawarden and was born there in 1618. The mark which he put upon his glasses was derived from the arms of the Ravenscrofts of Hawarden (Argent, a chevron between three Ravens' heads erased, sa). His eldest brother John Ravenscroft died without issue, and his younger brother Thomas was at one time a member of the Privy Council and died childless in 1683. George Ravenscroft was thus fifty-six years of age at the time he received his patent. Some branches of the family had settled in Oxfordshire and in Buckinghamshire, and a near relative of his, the Rev. Henry Ravenscroft, married a wife from Henley-on-Thames. Since the glassmaker and most of his ancestors are described as " Gent " or " Esq." and the family were certainly of good position and in comfortable circumstances, it is proper to regard George Ravenscroft as a man of leisure and culture comparable with the potter Dwight, whose interest in glassmaking was not primarily commercial. He seems to have been acquainted with men of science like Plot and Ludwell and doubtless with other members of the Royal Society, whose studies did not cease to be utilitarian in their aim because the method which directed them was chiefly academic. If his discovery of lead glass was due to his own scientific knowledge, he becomes an important instance of the work done by the scientists of that time, and notably by the Royal Society for the " improvement " of English arts and manufactures. Dwight and Ravenscroft, no less than Plot and Houghton, maintained in both theory and practice that the proper end of their philosophy was the " alleviation of human inconvenience." But they did not forget, in adhering to this principle, to pay a very careful attention to business ; Ravenscroft himself, in obtaining a monopoly, took good care that his experiments should not be disinterested, and nearly two years after he ceased to supply the London Glass-sellers, and only a few weeks before his death, we find him bringing a lawsuit against one of their number (Joseph Franklin) who stood in his debt. Ravenscroft died early in May, 1681, at the age of sixty-three, and on the 8th of the month was appropriately buried in the Savoy Chapel. His wife Elizabeth, whose maiden name has not been ascertained, survived him by two years, and was buried in the same place, 12 July, 1683. They left no children.[1]

Ravenscroft set up a glasshouse in the Savoy in July, 1673,[2] and seems to have spent at least a year in preliminary experimental work, having no patent and being probably independent of the Glass-sellers Company. He had been engaged for some time in the general Venetian trade, and soon after he set up his glasshouse he obtained the assistance of two

[1] I would acknowledge my obligations to the Rev. R. B. Ravenscroft for some of this information concerning his family.
[2] Buckley, *History*, p. 25, and *Glass Trade*, p. 35, Extract 17. Ravenscroft had been working for eight months before his petition of March, 1673-4.

Italians, Vicenzo and Rossetto[1] (the latter a Muranese), and an Altarist, Da Costa.[2] In these attempts he had considerable success and claimed to have perfected "a particuler sort of Christalline Glass resembling Rock Crystall, not formerly exercised or used in this our Kingdome." We have no means of determining the nature of this early material[3] or whether at this time he had begun to experiment with the lead flux the use of which he brought to perfection two years later. But whatever these early experiments may have been Ravenscroft was satisfied with them for the time being, or at least thought them likely to satisfy the public ; and in this state of mind he took two important steps. On 27 April, 1674[4] he laid his "particuler sort of Christalline Glass" before the Company of Glasssellers ; and the officers appear to have been so pleased with it that they not only offered him[5] a glasshouse at Henley-on-Thames, where he might pursue his manufacture in comparative seclusion, but undertook to find a market for the whole of his output ; provided only that he were willing to make his glasses according to the shapes and sizes supplied to him from time to time by the Company's Clerk Mr. Samuel Moore who "knowes what is fitter to be made for the Trade both as to ffashion and Size."[6] Such an offer meant that his business was made, and it was naturally accepted with alacrity. Meanwhile, however, Ravenscroft had taken the other step necessary to secure his position. In March, 1673–4, a month before his agreement with the Company, he petitioned the King for a patent for making a "sort of crystalline glass resembling rock crystal." The Attorney-General, Sir F. North, commenting on the application, described it as "glass of a fine sort, as made of different ingredients from those used in any other English glasshouse and as likely to be of considerable public advantage."[7]

[1] Schuermans, in *Bulletin* XXX, 74 ; the date mentioned is 15 June, 1674, but one Italian at least must have been with him the previous year. Rossetto may be identical with a Rosetti who had been manager for Buckingham at the Vauxhall plate glassworks.
[2] Mentioned by Plot, *Nat. His. Oxfordshire* (1676), p. 253.
[3] A pair of decanter bottles shown in Plate IX were probably made by Ravenscroft at this period. They are "crizzled" like several of the marked Ravenscroft pieces, but to a much greater degree ; they have the decoration which Ravenscroft described as "nip't diamond waies" (*cf.* Plate X) ; and one of them is *not* glass of lead. The description of Ravenscroft's glass in 1674 "resembling rock crystall" implies a metal quite different from the Venetian ; the sort that Greene would have liked for his "Thick beer."
[4] This date is referred to in the later Agreement of 5 September, 1674 (Glass-sellers Company MS.).
[5] There is no mention of this arrangement in the Court Minutes of the Glass-sellers Company, which deal almost entirely with formal business.
[6] Sloane MS. 857, Papers relating to the Glass Sellers, No. 2, cited in Hartshorne, p. 451.
[7] "Different ingredients" does not mean lead, which was not disclosed in Ludwell's analysis of 1676 (*infra*, p. 122). The phrase almost certainly implies that Ravenscroft had given up using flints during the first eight months and was now using Italian quartz

THE RAVENSCROFT REVOLUTION

On 16 May, 1674,[1] he received his privilege to make the " particuler sort of Christalline Glass " for the space of seven years.[2] Thus doubly secured Ravenscroft retired to Henley, and there removed from prying eyes continued his manufacture and his experiments. We have to leave him to his secrecy for two years, but during that time we must suppose that his difficulties came gradually to their solution.

In April, 1676 Ravenscroft is again discovered. Dr. Robert Plot, a scientist, a Fellow of the Royal Society and an Oxford don, had been pursuing an enquiry into the general history and topography of Oxfordshire ; and in the course of his tour he visited Henley-on-Thames and closely examined the glasshouse of Ravenscroft. The passage in which he records his interview, with his observations of the process, shows considerable insight and is so important as to be quoted in full.[3]

under the influence of Da Costa. R. had been in trade with Venice, and flints seem to have been normal in England at this time. See p. 104 *supra*.

[1] The O.S. year ended on 24 March, the new year beginning on 25 March. In the documents belonging to the Glass-sellers Company and in those cited by Hartshorne the dates given are, of course, O.S. ; in the Calendar of State Papers the documents are arranged in chronological order N.S. In order to get the chronology of these events clear and in the correct order, it is necessary to work in O.S. and adapt N.S. dates accordingly ; it is evident that O.S. May (for example) is earlier than O.S. January or February of the same year. The order of events may be set out thus :

1. End of February or beginning of March, 1673, Ravenscroft sent in his petition for a patent.
2. On the 8th of this same March the petition was minuted to the Attorney-General (*S.P. Dom.*, Car. II, 360, No. 222 Calendar, Vol. 1673–5, p. 194).
3. On 9 March (the following day) the petition was favourably minuted by the Attorney-General Sir F. North " that the glass is of a finer sort and made of other ingredients than any other glasshouses in England have used, and that the invention may be of considerable public advantage as the glasses thereby made equalize, if not excel, those imported from Venice and France " (*ibid.*, No. 223).
4. On 19 March (*i.e.* five days before the end of the O.S. year 1673) the petition was again minuted and spoken of as a " grant to George Ravenscroft of the benefit of his invention of crystalline glass for seven years " (*S.P. Dom. Entry Book*, 40, p. 172 ; Calendar, Vol. 1673–5, p. 206).
5. Between 19 March, 1673 and the May immediately following (May, 1674, both O.S. and N.S.) the petition went through, and the actual patent was granted on 16 May, 1674, and bore that date. See the document reprinted by Hartshorne, p. 454, which gives the full text of the patent.

Mr. Francis Buckley (*History*, p. 25) has not transferred his dates consistently to O.S., and this renders his chronology obscure. His statement (*ibid.*) that in May, 1673 Ravenscroft obtained his patent for seven years, is palpably false. In March, 1673, the petition was in Civil Service trays ; it became a patent on 16 May following (16 May, 1674).

[2] This is noted as an exception to the usual term of fourteen years ; Ravenscroft was not a professional glassmaker.

[3] Plot (R.), *Natural History of Oxfordshire* (1676), p. 293. The italics are mine.

" To which may be added the invention of making glasses of *stones or other materials at* Henley-on-Thames *lately brought into England* by Seignior da Costa a Montferratees (*sic*) and carried on by one Mr. Ravenscroft who has a patent for the sole making of them ; and lately by one Mr. Bishop. *The materials they used formerly were the blackest flints calcined* and a white Christalline sand adding to each pound of these, as it was found by the solution of these by the ingenious Dr. Ludwell Fellow of Wadham College, about two ounces of Nitre, Tartar and Borax.[1] But the glasses made of these being subject to that unpardonable fault called *crizelling caused by the two great quantities of the Salts in the mixture*, which either by the adventitious Niter of the Air from without or warm liquors put in them would be either increased or dissolved ; and thereby induce a Scabrities or dull roughness irrecoverably clouding the transparency of the glass ; they have chosen rather since to make their glasses of a great sort of white pebbles which as I am informed they have from the river Po in Italy ; to which adding the aforementioned salts but *abating in the proportions* they now make a sort of pebble glass which are hard durable and whiter than any from Venice and will not Crizel, but under the severest trials whatever, to be known from the former by a Seal set purposely on them.

And yet I guess that the difference in respect of Crizeling, between the present glass and the former lies not so much in the calx, the pebbles being Pyrites (none but such I presume being fit for vitrification) as well as flints ; but rather *wholly in the abatement of the salts*, for there are *some of the flint glasses strictly so called whereof I have one by me* that has endured all trials as well as these last. But if it be found otherwise that white pebbles are really fitter for their turns than black Flints, I think they have little need to fetch them from Italy there being enough in England of the same kind, not only to supply this but perhaps foreign nations."

The information contained in this account must have been derived from two sources, first from a piece of the old imperfect glass which Dr. Plot took away with him and submitted for a chemical analysis (" the solution of these ") to his friend the ingenious Dr. Ludwell, and secondly from information supplied by Ravenscroft when he was showing Dr. Plot over the glassworks. Ludwell's analysis explained the failure of the old glass, but Dr. Plot had only Ravenscroft's own word to account for the success of the new ; and between these two sources of information there was, as Dr. Plot himself discerned (" . . . And yet I guess," etc.), a glaring discrepancy. Ludwell had declared that the crizzling was due to an excessive quantity of strong salt fluxes which under the influence of the atmosphere or of a hot liquid produced the " Scabrities." But when Dr. Plot enquired how the improvement had been effected Ravenscroft had answered (the words " they have chosen rather " and " as I am informed," indicating the *oratio obliqua*) that it was due to the substitution of pebbles from the Po Valley for " the blackest flints calcined and white Christalline sand." Dr. Plot saw through this official explanation, and when he had received Ludwell's verdict and came to write up his account he added his own view of the cause in the sentence " to which adding the aforementioned salts but abating the proportions . . .," and a final paragraph (" And yet I guess," etc.) in which he gave his reasons for it.[2]

[1] Had Ludwell's analysis given lead it would certainly have been mentioned here.
[2] The " excessive salts " theory must, I think, have come from Ludwell, not from

THE RAVENSCROFT REVOLUTION

This seems to me the only interpretation which will give coherence to Dr. Plot's account. A patent-holder and one who has greatly improved his wares only a short time before is not likely to betray the secrets of his mixing room to a casual academic visitor. Ravenscroft had already begun to make glasses with a lead flux—a seal bearing the Raven's Head was soon to proclaim it,[1] and he would have been a fool to give the show away. The motive for the falsehood being thus clear the question remains whether Dr. Plot's explanation was correct.

The excess of salts might be reduced in two ways, either by diminishing the proportion of salts or by increasing the rest of the ingredients in a given quantity of materials ; Ravenscroft introduced lead oxide in addition to the salts, and that was the real explanation. Ludwell's conclusion was perfectly sound as far as it went : the crizzling in the specimen which he examined was in fact due to the excess of salts. The error lay with Dr. Plot, who inferred that an improvement must be due to reduction of the one part when it might equally well arise from an increase in the other. The evidence of later developments seems to be conclusive on this point. English flint glass even in the heavy days of Queen Anne was never a pure glass of lead, but was a compound of two fluxes, salts and lead, with the silicate base. The exact ratio of salts to lead varied at different periods and for different purposes ; Dossie,[2] writing in 1758, notices that the quantity of lead had been

Ravenscroft. The passage with such phrases as " Scabrities " and the " adventitious Niter of the air " reads like the reminiscence of the report of a 17th-century alchemist rather than of a chat with a glassmaker.

It is highly probable from Plot's account that imported Po pebbles had been the technical ground for Ravenscroft's original patent. When he was asked the cause of his more recent improvement Ravenscroft repeated this and thus avoided giving the true cause.

[1] (a) The Certificate of improvement was issued first two months after Plot's visit, 3 June, 1676, and published in the *London Gazette* three times the same autumn, 5 October, 2 November, 8 November. The Seal which marked the improved glass is mentioned in the *Gazette*, and is later described specifically as a Raven's Head. *London Gazette*, 25 October, 1 November, 19 November, 1677. *V.* Buckley, *Glass Trade*, pp. 36-48. For the seal see W. Buckley, Pl. 84.

(b) Seven of the existing specimens which bear the Raven's Head seal are lead glass. There is an eighth example, the stem of a wine-glass, in the London Museum (Fig. 20). It has been tested and is not lead glass, but thick and fairly heavy. The seal is badly chipped on one side and Mr. Francis Buckley thought (*History*, p. 29) the figure was that of a female shooting with a bow, the device of Bowles and Lillington. The seal has been examined under a microscope by Mr. Herbert Read and myself and there is no doubt that it represents a bird's head ; but it is out of a different mould from the Ravenscroft seals on the British Museum and South Kensington glasses. The glass may have been " old stock," sufficiently near to the lead glasses to be worth sealing to get it sold ; the glass was dug up and it is impossible to say whether it was crizzled.

[2] Dossie (R.), *Handmaid to the Arts* (1758), *s.v.* Glassmaking. He gives some highly interesting notes and formulæ, and distinguishes pure glass of lead, by which he no doubt meant the same as Merret (a paste or enamel), from the *metal* of lead glass.

[123]

much greater some time ago but had recently been decreased. In the first quarter of the century, and even until *c.* 1746, there had been a great quantity of lead used, and glasses were soft and solid and shining, but the Excise of 1746 reduced the proportion of lead ; and the salt flux, coming into its own again, gave a harder and firmer texture. Now as we know from the sealed specimens, none of which are of great specific gravity, Ravenscroft in 1676 was using only a small proportion of lead oxide with his salts ; and that was why Dr. Plot described even the new sealed glasses as " hard and durable " instead of by some epithet such as " soft " or " brilliant " which we should apply to the great balusters.[1]

The question now arises whether the particular sort of crystalline glass was already made with lead in March, 1673–4. We have shown that the remedy for the crizzling was a decrease in the proportion of salts as the proportion of lead increased, and it is clear from Dr. Plot's account that when Ravenscroft was beginning glassmaking under the guidance of Da Costa (1673–4) his glasses were subject to crizzling. We should therefore expect that in 1674 the glasses contained little or no lead, and this view is supported by two decanters which seem to be "early Ravenscroft," one of which is not lead glass (Plate IX). Had the improvement due to the use of a large proportion of lead been effected in March, 1673–4 when Ravenscroft applied for his patent ? And was the presence of lead the differentia of the " particuler sort of Christalline Glass " ? The phrase " resembling rock crystall " is certainly an argument that it was glass of lead, but in that case it is impossible to account for the silence of the Glass Sellers. Their contract with Ravenscroft being already made, why did they not advertise the improvement at once in the summer of 1674 instead of waiting until the summer of 1676 ? Their silence seems a fairly conclusive proof that the improvement was effected between March, 1673–4 and the spring of 1675–6. In that case the improvement was recent in a measure of months when Plot went to Henley, April, 1676, and we must place the invention of lead glass in the latter part of the year (1675) which ended in the preceding March.

There remains the problem why the strange misnomer " flint glass " clung for more than a hundred and fifty years to a metal which was

---

[1] We may note here that the ratio of salts to silica in Ravenscroft's older glass was 1 : 8 ; it is interesting to compare this with Professor Church's analysis of Bristol opaque white flint glass of date about 1760 (Owen (H.), *Two Centuries of Ceramic Art in Bristol*, pp. 378–87). In the Bristol glass the ratio of salts to silica is 7·21 : 47·75, and thus differs only slightly from the ratio given by Plot (1 : 8). But in the Bristol glass *besides the salts* (and a little tin, etc., required for the opacity) *there is a high percentage of lead* (43·71 per cent of the whole batch). This means that in comparison with Ravenscroft the *percentage* of salts in the whole batch has been *reduced* by the *addition* of another material—lead.

primarily distinguished not by its silica but by its lead flux, and during the greater part of that time was made with sand and not with flints. Let us see how the term came into use in England. The Venetians in preparing their frit had not employed flints, but a hard white translucent quartz (*tarso*) which was found abundantly on the Ticino, the Po, and the Arno, in Tuscany, at Pisa and elsewhere in the north of Italy. There were several qualities of *tarso* and there were besides hard " glass stones " called *quocoli*. These materials were all marble, not flints, and their advantage lay in their purity ; a perfectly *clean* frit which was the first requisite for Venetian crystal could be readily prepared from them. That was the Venetian speciality. The materials, however, did not matter as long as the *frit was pure*. In other countries, and in England, there were no pebbles of marble and the glassmakers were thrown back at first on the nearest substitute—flints, which could be obtained almost anywhere. These, however, were not found in the same pure state as the Venetian pebbles, but mixed often enough with metallic ores which stained the metal, and the glassmakers therefore had the alternative of risking a discoloured glass or undertaking a highly elaborate and costly expurgation.[1] In spite of this English flints (" the blackest flints calcined ") became during the middle of the 17th century the usual source of the silica and gave their name to English glass as distinct from glass made with common sand (*verre de fougère*) and from crystal made with Italian pebbles. During the reign of Charles II, however, the fine crystalline sands of Lynn, Woolwich, and the Isle of Wight came into general use[2] and in the last quarter of the century " powdered flints " were gradually superseded ; for the nature of the silicate mattered less when the quality of the metal was determined by the lead flux. Thus the phrase " flint glass " had its origin.

Why did it persist? After the invention the Company of Glass-sellers, for whom Ravenscroft was working, were putting a new commodity on the market ; and we must remember that it is the salesman, not the customer, who labels the goods, who in fact coins " trade names." Flint glass in the original sense was still quite a new thing and flints differentiated the English from the foreign technique ; and the phrase " glass of lead " was already appropriated to the glass paste or glaze which the English certainly were not making in Charles II's time.[3] There was thus great advantage from a commercial point of view in adhering to the term already in vogue, just because it would be a label and not a description ; and as such it persisted long after the use of a lead flux had passed out of the close

[1] Merret's *Art of Glass*, pp. 7, 258. This was a preliminary calcination in the fritting furnace.
[2] Houghton, *Letter* 198 (1696). *Cf.* with it Plot, *Oxfordshire, u.s.*
[3] Merret's *Art of Glass*, p. 315.

control of the Company, and long after the use of flints had almost entirely ceased.[1]

We must now return to Ravenscroft, whom we have left in conversation with Dr. Plot. Some time before April, 1676 Ravenscroft had acquired a skilled artificer in Da Costa, who had " lately " arrived in England, bringing with him the use of the quartz pebbles which his countrymen of Altare were in the habit of obtaining from the Po. We do not know the date of his coming, but it may be suggested that he was first employed by Ravenscroft when he opened his glasshouse in the Savoy (July, 1673). At his suggestion Ravenscroft began to import pebbles from the Po in place of native flints, and being able in consequence to make a purer metal, petitioned for a patent for " a particuler sort of Christalline Glass resembling Rock Chrystall." Da Costa is the only Altarist glassmaker known to have worked in England at this time, and his innovation was quite sufficient to warrant the application for a patent. There is also Mr. Bishopp. At some time between spring, 1674 and April, 1676 he had joined Ravenscroft at Henley, either as a partner, as Plot suggests, or more likely as an agent or supervisor sent down by the Company of Glass-sellers, of which Bishopp was an important member. Two months after Plot's visit, on 3 June, 1676, the Company issued the following document, which was not only a certificate of merit to Ravenscroft, but an advertisement of their own wares :

Wee under written doe certify and attest that the defect of the flint glasses (which were formerly observed to crissel and decay) hath been redressed severall months agoe and the glasses since made have all proved durable and lasting as any glasses whatsoever. Moreover that the usual tryalls wherewith the essay of glasses are made have bene often reitterated on these new flint glasses with entire success and easy to be done againe by any body, which proofs the former glass would not undergoe, besides ye distinction of sound discernible by any person whatsoever. London, the 3 June 1676.[2]

This document was signed by the Company's Clerk, Samuell Moore and by Hawly Bishopp himself, who had been at Henley and was acquainted with the improvement. The substance of this certificate was frequently printed in the *London Gazette*,[3] and in several of these issues a " Seal or Mark " is mentioned which is later described as a Raven's Head—a punning allusion to the inventor which identifies the surviving specimens. Less than two years after the invention had been perfected glass of lead was being made both at Henley and in Ravenscroft's original glasshouse in the Savoy. Glasses made of the new metal were generally on sale in the shops of the London glass merchants, and the Company had issued a guarantee with

[1] For the materials used see Dossie, *Handmaid, u.s.* White sand is the basis of all his English formulæ irrespective of " quality " of the ware.
[2] Buckley (F.), *Glass Trade*, p. 36 ; *State Papers Domestic*, Car. II, 381, No. 244.
[3] *London Gazette*, Nos. 1136, 1144, 1146, 5 October, 2 November, and 9 December, 1676.

all sealed " Raven's Head " pieces to the effect of " no crizzling or money returned."[1]   The notice ends with the clause . . . " if they shall have been sent into the country or beyond seas to any remoter parts of the world " and we may infer that this implies a provincial and foreign trade in the new wares.[2]

It may be of interest to cite here Ravenscroft's Price List, which has been preserved among the records of the Glass-sellers Company.[3]   Its date is 29 May, 1677, and the sums mentioned are of course the amounts charged to the Glass Sellers and not the retail prices.

Beer glasses ribbed and plain	7 oz.	..	1s. 6d.
Clarrett wine glasses of the same	5 oz.	..	1s. 0d.
Sacke glasses of the same	4 oz.	..	10d.
Castors of the same	3 oz.	..	8d.
Brandy glasses of the same	2 oz.	..	6d.
Beer glasses nipt diamond waies	8 oz.	..	1s. 8d.
Clarrett glasses of the same	5½ oz.	..	1s. 3d.
Sacke glasses of the same	4 oz.	..	1s. 0d.
Purlee glasses at the same prices as the above.			
Diamond Crewitts of a pint, ribbed and plain with stoppers to them	9 oz.	..	2s. 0d.
¾ pint Crewitts of the same sort with stoppers to them	7 oz.	..	1s. 6d.
½ pint crewitts of the same sort with stoppers to them	5 oz.	..	1s. 0d.
Quart ribbed bottles	16 oz.	..	3s. 0d.
Pint bottles of the same	10 oz.	..	2s. 0d.
½ pint bottles of the same	8 oz.	..	1s. 6d.
¼ pint bottles of the same	5 oz.	..	1s. 0d.
Quart bottles all over nipt diamond waies	16 oz.	..	4s. 0d.
Pint bottles of the same sort	10 oz.	..	2s. 6d.
½ pint bottles of the same sort	7 oz.	..	1s. 6d.
Quarterne bottles of the same sort	6 oz.	..	1s. 3d.

Moreover all covers for drinking or " sullibub " glasses ribbed and plain shall be delivered at 3s. per lb., diamond or purled all over at 4s. per lb. and extraordinary work or ornament at 5s. per lb. All purled glasses bottles crewitts are to be at the same rates as if they were diamond.

Several glasses which bear Ravenscroft's mark are closely in accord with these specifications. The beer tankard at South Kensington (Plate XIV. 1) weighs 6½ oz. and the British Museum decanter " nipt diamond waies " holds ·9 of a pint and weighs 11 oz. One or two other pieces approximate to Ravenscroft's measurements ; for example, a brandy tumbler in Mr. Mason's collection (Plate XXV. 1) weighs 2¼ oz. Four types of decoration are mentioned, " diamond " (" nipt diamond waies "), purlee, ribbing, and " extraordinary work or ornament," but

[1] *Ibid.*, Nos. 1246, 1248, 1253, 25 October, 1 November, and 19 November, 1677.
[2] Buckley (F.), *Glass Trade*, p. 38.
[3] The list is given in the last agreement between Ravenscroft and the Glass Sellers, dated 29 May, 1677.

these are not very easy to identify on the existing glasses. Quite clearly " diamond " or " nipt diamond waies " refers to the decoration evident in the British Museum decanter (Plate X. 1), on a pair of decanters (one not lead glass) in Mr. Mason's collection which are, I think, Ravenscroft's work, and on other glasses of this period, notably a goblet in the British Museum which contains a coin of 1687 and may well be Bishopp's work (Buckley, Plate VI) ; the diamonds are not entirely moulded, but formed by pinching up the surface of moulded ribs, as Ravenscroft's own word implies (see Fig. 7).

There are two kinds of decoration on the existing glasses which might have been described as ribbing, (a) the gadrooned moulding round the bases of the South Kensington tankard and several of the bowls marked by Ravenscroft or unmarked and attributed to Bishopp, and (b) the much less noticeable vertical ribs which run the whole height of Mr. Wilfred Buckley's rummer and Mr. Kirkby Mason's jug (Plate X. 2). Since the price list mentions ribbed beer glasses, since the South Kensington tankard, clearly a beer glass, has ribbing of the first type, and since the rummer with ribbing of the second type was used for wine (" a rummer of Rhenish "[1]), I am inclined to identify Ravenscroft's ribbing with the basic gadrooning (a) evident in the marked pieces and common in late 17th-century glasses (e.g. Plates XVII, XXI, XXII, XXIII).

Purlee is more difficult. The word itself may either mean " purled " or it may be a spelling of " pearled " not uncommon in the 17th century. In the latter case it might refer to a dimpled surface (e.g. W. Buckley, Plate 92A shows a later glass with this ornament), and this reference of the word is supported by the phrase " purled *all over* "[2] which seems to imply ornament covering the entire surface. The objection to this view is that none of the Ravenscroft glasses can be described as pearled all over, and most glasses decorated in this way seem to be of later (early 18th century) date. The word purl, on the other hand, is a textile word, and was used in the 17th century of sewing and in extension of loops or inter-laced threads. The word purl means to embroider with gold or silver thread, and the past participle was used as early as Cotgrave (1611) in reference to a border of twisted loops. In this sense purlee might well refer to the threads of trailed glass applied on the surface which are evident in several marked Ravenscroft glasses and other pieces of the period. The difficulty here is the phrase " all over," which must then be taken to mean only a complete circuit of the glass by the threads. On the whole, the reference of " purlee " to trailed threads seems to me the more probable. " Extraordinary work " probably refers to special orders or types of

[1] Gayton, *Pleasant Notes*, iv, 234 (1654), " a lusty rummer of Rhenish."
[2] This important phrase occurs in the original agreement now in possession of the Glass-sellers Company, but was omitted in the abstract made by Young (p. 69).

decoration which did not come within Ravenscroft's normal repertory. Perhaps we may find a type of extraordinary work in a small series of tall goblets with straight-side bowls ribbed round the base and long bulbous stems; several contain a coin of Charles II or William III (Plates XXIX, LXXVII).

The first " Mark or Seal " set on the glasses in October, 1676 does not appear to have borne a Raven's Head, but during the next year a number of imitations of the seal glasses were put upon the market[1] by persons who had no privilege, and in order to distinguish the authentic

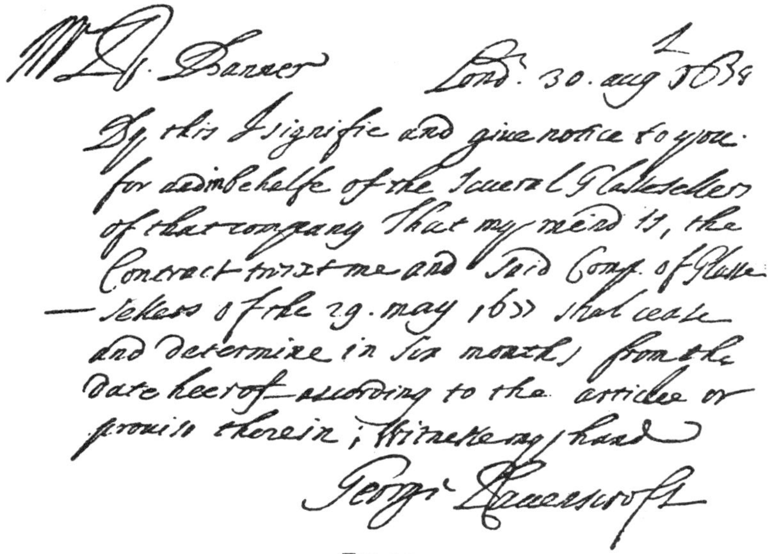
Lond: 30. aug 1678

By this I signifie and give notice to you for and in behalfe of the severall Glassesellers of that company That my mind is, the Contract twixt me and said Comp. of Glasse-sellers of the 29. may 1677 shall cease and determine in six months from the date hereof according to the articles or provisio therein; Witnesse my hand

George Ravenscroft

FIG. 17.

Ravenscroft's letter, dated 30 Aug. 1678, giving six months' notice to terminate his agreement with the Glass-sellers Company (*i.e.* on or about 28 Feb. 1678–9).

(*By courtesy of the Worshipful Company of Glass Sellers*).

wares Ravenscroft, in renewing his agreement with the Company for a further three years (29 May, 1677) and recording a further improvement in his wares, added that in future the seal would bear a Raven's Head, to put their genuineness beyond all question.[2] About this time the practice of sealing glasses became general among the London flint glasshouses. The goblet in Plate XXIII though of rather later date (probably about 1680) is one of these imitations and bears a rough seal, and the Victoria and Albert Museum has lately acquired part of a quatrefoil stem with a

[1] Buckley (F.), *Glass Trade*, p. 38. *Cf.* Plate XXI. 3.

[2] Buckley (F.), *History*, p. 26. Young (S.), *History of the Glass-sellers Company* (1913), p. 69.

seal bearing the letter S, probably the mark of a glasshouse then working at Salisbury Court. But only three months after the new agreement Ravenscroft wrote to the Clerk of the Glass Sellers (30 August, 1678) giving six months' notice to terminate his agreement, but with no hint of his reasons for doing so. It is not easy to understand why he should have broken the connection so abruptly when his agreement had only lately been renewed and there were three years of a lucrative patent still to run. It may have been a quarrel, but the letter to Banner, though formal, is quite friendly. More probably it was advancing years, for Ravenscroft was nearly sixty and died two years later. But I do not think it likely that he was induced to break his agreement to enter the service of some one London glasshouse and so communicate glass of lead to others. His obligation to supply the Glass Sellers ended on 28 February, 1678–9 ; the patent which gave him the sole right to make the " particuler sort of Christalline Glass," of which lead glass was the final form, expired on 16 May, 1681.

Now at the Savoy Ravenscroft had only one furnace and three " chairs " with one master glassmaker and probably one servitor to each " chair "[1]; but since the value of his work depended on the secrets of his mixing-room, it is, I think, highly improbable that they were communicated to these men ; for the glassmakers and the servitors might leave his service and impart their knowledge to other glasshouses in London, to the makers of " counterfeits."[2] Da Costa was probably one of these master glass-makers, a man who manipulated the glass but as far as we know did not compound it. But Hawly Bishopp must, I think, have been in the secret ; he had worked with Ravenscroft, he signed the certificate of improvement as a representative of the Glass Sellers, and after Ravenscroft's death he was employed by them to carry on Ravenscroft's work at the Savoy[3] ; and since it was the lead oxide which redeemed the glass from crizzling, there would have been no point in employing him if he were not acquainted with its use.[4] Here, moreover, we must notice an important fact. Three years elapsed between the date when Ravenscroft ceased to supply the Glass Sellers with glass (28 February, 1678–9) and the date when the Glass Sellers signed the agreement with Bishopp for the continuance of the work (22 February, 1681–2) ; and it is very pertinent to enquire the

[1] There were two " chairs " in 1674, both at Henley and at the Savoy, three chairs at the Savoy in 1678 : *Glass-sellers' MSS.*

[2] *Cf.* Plate XXI. 3 for one of these counterfeit glasses made in imitation of Ravenscroft ; it had a fake seal and is not glass of lead (tested).

[3] See the indenture between Bishopp and the Glass Sellers, 22 February, 1681–2, in the possession of the Glass-sellers Company.

[4] The Glass Sellers state in the agreement of 22 February, 1681–2 that they have " great trust and confidence " in Hawly Bishopp ; this was certainly due to his experience with Ravenscroft.

reason for this interval. Ravenscroft's lead glass was, the Company knew well enough, a very promising manufacture, but they took no steps to secure the lease of the Savoy premises[1] or the services of Bishopp *until Ravenscroft's patent had expired.* This appears to me a strong argument for supposing that Ravenscroft's patent remained absolutely valid during the whole term, and that after Ravenscroft himself ceased work (28 February, 1678–9) no lead glass was made until Bishopp started work again at the Savoy.[2] On the evidence available we are, I think, entitled to regard Ravenscroft as a country gentleman of scientific pursuits whose interest in glassmaking was academic rather than professional, ready though he may have been to benefit by his experiments. The question is, what did he do after 28 February, 1678–9? There seem to be only three possibilities. He might have ceased work at the Savoy and have gone to work for one of the other glasshouses in London; in that case his patent would have been abandoned and the making of lead glass would have become an open competition among any who knew how to make it. But if that is so, it is difficult to understand why the Glass Sellers did not make use of Bishopp's knowledge and start their new venture at once. It is *a priori* unlikely that a man of Ravenscroft's position, who had been master in his own glasshouse, would enter another's service as a subordinate. It is possible, secondly, that Ravenscroft, though his agreement with the Glass Sellers was at an end, still continued working at the Savoy until he died in May, 1681, and his patent expired a few days later. The agreement of 22 February, 1681, between Bishopp and the Glass Sellers speaks of the Savoy works as " late in the possession of George Ravenscroft," but the phrase itself gives no indication of when he ceased work; it might refer to the end of 1678 (February and March) quite as well as to the previous May, 1681. It is conceivable that Ravenscroft, encouraged by his success, no longer thought it necessary to supply the Glass Sellers. But in view of the power of the Company at that time it is difficult to know where Ravens-

---

[1] The lease under which Bishopp worked was Christmas, 1681—Christmas, 1702, but I can find no allusion to Bishopp himself later than 1688 (Sloane MS. 857, a protest against the sale in London of glasses made in the provinces, 28 April, 1688).

[2] There seems to have been only one attempt to rival Ravenscroft. In May, 1675, Sir Philip Lloyd, Richard Hunt, who seem to have had capital, and an Italian Odacio Formica, who had practical knowledge, applied for a fourteen years' patent in Ireland " for their new invention of manufacturing a particular sorte of chrystalline glasses resembling rock crystall, which has never been exercised by any *in that Kingdom.*" The wording is almost exactly the same as Ravenscroft's, but this application is prior to Ravenscroft's perfection of lead glass and probably is based, like R.'s original patent, on imported Italian quartz. In England the Lloyd trio could do nothing without infringing Ravenscroft's patent and they therefore tried Ireland, which was a clear field outside Ravenscroft's privilege. The King gave a warrant for granting this patent to the Lord Lieutenant of Ireland, but I cannot find whether Lloyd actually started work. *S.P. Dom.*, 29 May, 1675. This incident seems to show that Ravenscroft's patent was respected.

croft could have found an adequate market except through the Company which controlled the London market. Moreover, Ravenscroft's agreement with the Company does not provide that he shall sell his glasses *only* to its members ; it provided that he *should* sell them to its members. That being so, there would have been no point in terminating the agreement if he intended to continue work, merely supplying the Glass Sellers or anyone else according to his pleasure or profit. It may be added that on 1 April, 1678, *i.e.* the April preceding the termination of the agreement with Ravenscroft, the Glass Sellers had made an agreement with two other London houses, those of Michael Rackett and the partners Bowles and Lillington, for a regular supply of "white glasses" and incidentally for

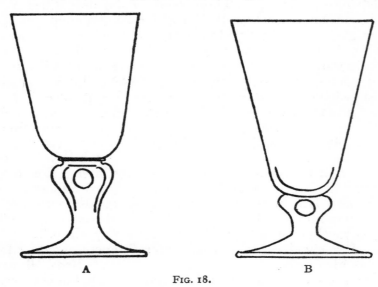

A   B

FIG. 18.

    A. Wine-glass bearing the seal of the London Glassmakers Bowles and Lillington (a female figure shooting with a bow). Not lead glass. Dug up at Northampton and now in the Museum there. H. 5½" (Mr. Buckley's reconstruction). See p. 140.
    B. Sealed wine-glass in the Ashmolean Museum. H. 5½" (Mr. Buckley's reconstruction). *Cf.* Plate XXXVI. *a.* 4, 5.

bottle glass ; the phrase "white glasses," rather than "crystalline glass" or "flint glass," implies that the glass of these manufacturers was a different type from Ravenscroft's. The latter's patent was still running, and a fragment in the Northampton Museum which bears the mark of Bowles and Lillington is not lead glass (Buckley, pp. 28–9). We are, therefore, forced reluctantly to the conclusion that when the notice to terminate the agreement expired on 28 February, 1678–9 Ravenscroft gave up the Savoy glassworks and ceased to make glass. As his patent covered lead glass (which had been evolved from " a particuler sort of Christalline Glass ") and as the Glass Sellers, though they had the opportunity for piracy, yet respected the patent, we must conclude in the second place that lead glass was not made again until Bishopp began work at the end of 1681 (which year ended on 24 March) or early in 1682.[1]

The glasses bearing Ravenscroft's seal which have hitherto come to light are as follows :

1. Large ewer (Plate X. 2) of heavy metal, but much crizzled. Probably one of Ravenscroft's earlier pieces. The type is not mentioned in the price list. *The late C. Kirkby Mason.*
2. Decanter bottle (Plate X. 1), one of the " pint bottles all over nipt diamond waies " sold by Ravenscroft for the large sum of four shillings. Whitish and bubbly metal badly crizzled. *British Museum.*
3. Rummer (Plate XVI. 1) probably sold for " Rhenish," not mentioned in the price list. This is the first known English adaptation of the German *Roemer.* The form, Hartshorne thought,[2] was introduced into England by the Netherlandish glassmaker Paul Vinion about 1620, and it was one of the shapes ordered by the Glass Sellers from Venice in 1672 in white metal (Hartshorne, Plate 30). Passages from Gayton (1654) and Dryden (1673) and a mention of " Romers " in Merret show that in the middle of the 17th century the German *Roemer* was a familiar form in England. The name had already been anglicized as rummer and the phrase " a rummer of Rhenish " seems to show that the German drinking-glass was used for Rhine wines. There were numerous adaptations and imitations of the *Roemer,* especially in green flint glass made in resemblance of the green *Waldglas* of which the German *Roemers* were originally made. The true German *Roemer* consisted of two parts, a rounded upper bowl and a narrow cylindrical bucket which served as a stout handle and was covered with prunts for improving the grip. If the Ravenscroft rummer is compared with a similar glass of green flint metal lately in Mr. Wilfred Buckley's collection (Plate LXII), we may observe the tendency of the bucket to get thinner. It is still hollow, but it approximates a *stem,* and when it ceases (at the beginning of the 18th century) to be hollow, it becomes a stem proper, supporting the rounded bowl of the old *Roemer.* Later still we find the round curved bowl deserted by its straight stem and attached to the balustroid stem of an absolutely different tradition (Plate XLI). In this adaptation we may find the origin of the almost spherical bowl with convex

[1] The agreement is dated 22 February, 1681, O.S. (=22 February, 1682, N.S.). This was after the expiry of Ravenscroft's patent and his own death the previous May, 1681, O.S. [2] P. 188.

sides which was common in flint glass throughout the 18th century. It may be worth adding that *Roemers* of the true German type were being made as hock-glasses early in the 19th century by Fords of Edinburgh. *Mr. Wilfred Buckley.*

4. A large bowl with ornament of trailed threads (? purlee). The crizzling is less apparent than in the previous three glasses. (Plate XII.) *Mr. Wilfred Buckley.*

5. A beer tankard called by Ravenscroft a " beer glass ribbed " ; weight 6½ oz. The specification in Ravenscroft's list was for 8-oz. beer glasses. The degree of crizzling is comparable with No. 4. (Plate XIV. 1.) *Victoria and Albert Museum.*

6. A bowl rather smaller than Mr. Buckley's. It has clearer and better metal than any other Ravenscroft piece and seems to be later than the rest, presumably dating from the end of 1678 (O.S.). (Plate XI. 1.) *The late C. Kirkby Mason.*

7. A highly interesting fragment now in the Guildhall Museum and reconstructed in Fig. 19 bears the same seal as the others and proves after a chemical test to be glass of lead. It has the square funnel bowl similar to Fig. 16, E, but tapering much more sharply towards the bottom. The bowl is let into the stem as in another sealed fragment (Fig. 20) ; and it is evident from this that the inset bowls which are found on balusters must indicate a very early date (soon after 1681). The stem itself is a simple inverted baluster with the quatrefoil divisions (as also in Fig. 20), and gives a standard for dating the quatrefoil stems occasionally found in balusters. The bowl is very long in proportion to the stem and the foot very wide.

8. Quatrefoil stem of a wine-glass, not lead metal, in the London Museum. Dug up in London. See Fig. 20 and p. 123 note.

A pair of decanter bottles in Mr. Mason's collection, though they have no seal, can be assigned without much doubt to Ravenscroft. They are " nipt diamond waies," they are far more highly crizzled than any other glasses of this period, and one does not contain lead ; they are nevertheless of thick metal which might be seasonably described as " resembling rock crystal." These reasons incline one to regard them as specimens of the " particuler sort of Christalline Glass " which was made by Ravenscroft both at the Savoy and at Henley during the experimental period 1673–6 (Plate IX).

Now for *Hawly Bishopp.* He had been trained by Ravenscroft, and as we have seen, he must have understood how to make glass of lead. We may therefore expect to find that his wares are similar in style and body to Ravenscroft's, but that they are more developed, for Bishopp worked later. And by " developed " we are to understand that they contain more lead and are specifically heavier glasses, but that they may still be liable to the old fault of crizzling; for it is to be expected that the errors as well as the virtues of a master will be evident in his pupil. In style, moreover, we must expect them to move away from Venetian influence towards simplicity, but yet to exhibit traces of the Ravenscroft style. Finally, we have no evidence that Bishopp, working independently, ever used a seal. There is no specification for any mark in his agreement with the Glass Sellers of 22 February, 1681–2, and since most of the white glasshouses in London were then sealing their glasses, the omission seems to show that on Bishopp's work no hall-mark was required, or at least that that was Bishopp's opinion. I would even suggest that Bishopp was the only London glassmaker who in 1681 did not mark his wares. There are a number of unsealed glasses so similar in metal and in several items of style to the Ravenscroft group that they might be reasonably attributed to him if we knew nothing whatever of Bishopp. (*e.g.* Plates XI. 2, XIII, XIV, XV, XXIII. *b.* 1.) But it is difficult to ascribe them to the very short interval, of weeks rather than months, which must have elapsed between Ravenscroft's satisfaction with his lead metal and his adoption of the seal mark. If they were made before 1676 they would not be glasses of lead, and if they were made between April, 1676 and Ravenscroft's retirement we should expect them to have borne seals. They must in any case have been made after Ravenscroft's retirement, and when it is remembered that Bishopp took over his partner's plant and probably his staff, there seems good ground

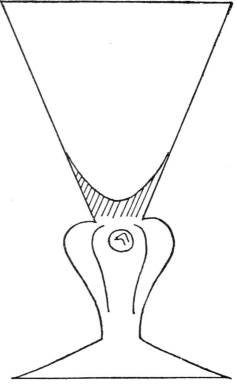

FIG. 19.

Reconstruction of a lead-glass fragment in the Guildhall Museum, bearing Ravencroft's seal. 1676–8. No. 7 on p. 134.

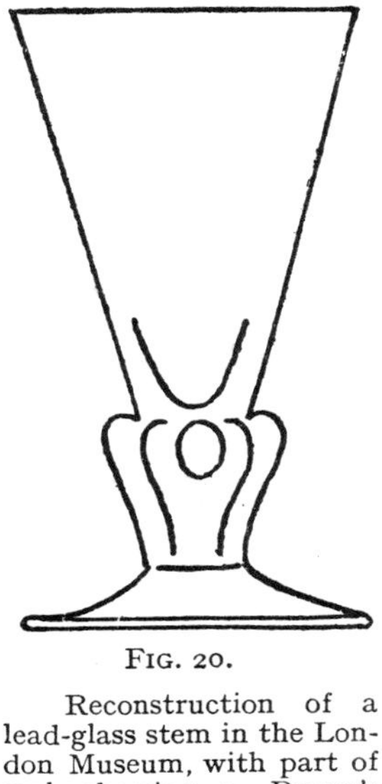

FIG. 20.

Reconstruction of a lead-glass stem in the London Museum, with part of seal showing a Raven's Head. No. 8 on p. 134.

(*Mr. Buckley's reconstruction.*)

for supposing that the glasses in question were made by Bishopp rather than by any of the several other flint glasshouses in London which adopted lead glass after the expiry of Ravenscroft's patent (May, 1681).

Of the Bishopp family of glasses we may refer to the following, all of which are lead glass.

1. A thick heavy bowl in Mr. Mason's collection which in shape is almost a replica of the same collector's sealed bowl. It has the same trailed ornament (? "purlee") and gadrooned base ("ribbed"), but it is much thicker, much heavier, and much more heavily leaded. The metal, in fact, is one of the best existing specimens of early glass of lead. (Plate XIII.)

2. A larger bowl in the same collection as the above. It has a wide flaring rim. The metal is thinner in mass and less developed in quality than No. 1, but in both form and metal compels comparison with Mr. Wilfred Buckley's sealed bowl to which it seems to be related as the unsealed bowl is related to the sealed bowl in the Mason collection. (Plate XI. 2.)

3. A large ewer or jug, heavy lead glass, but apparently crizzled, which has lately come to light and is now in Mr. Wilfred Buckley's collection. It strongly resembles Mr. Mason's sealed jug. (Plate XV.)

4. A beer tankard almost a duplicate of the South Kensington tankard, but a fraction of an inch taller. The metal is thinner and rather less crizzled. (Plate XIV. 2.)

5. A rummer in the possession of Mr. A. O. Curle which generally resembles Mr. Buckley's sealed rummer but differs from it in one or two details, notably in the absence of a wavy collar and in the way in which the bowl slopes into the bucket-stem. (Plate XVI. 2.)

6. A small sweetmeat bowl in Mr. Mason's collection, which is an interesting link between (1) the Ravenscroft and Bishopp bowls and (2) a group of stemmed sweetmeat bowls some of which are illustrated in Plates XXII and XXIII. *a.* It is a small edition of No. 2 above (the Bishopp bowl) but if mounted on a wrythen stem it would not be distinguishable from several of the sweetmeat glasses referred to. These sweetmeat bowls with wrythen knop-and-baluster stem were made at a rather later date, but of the specimen illustrated several at least are so close to the link glass as to leave small doubt of their origin. (Plate XXIII. *b.* 1.)

It is uncertain when Hawly Bishopp ceased to direct the Savoy glasshouse. The lease under which he assumed control in February, 1681–2 did not expire till 1702, but I can find no reference to Bishopp himself later than April, 1688.[1] He must have been one of the most eminent

[1] Sloane MS., *cit. supra.*

glassmakers at that time, but during the last decade of the 17th century there is no mention of him in several sources in which we might expect to find his name had he been still at work. In 1691 several London glassmakers put in a petition to be incorporated as a joint-stock company, and these included two of the Bowles' and Michael Rackett, the maker of " white glasses."[1] A little later, in February, 1692-3, a much more numerous and powerful body made a similar application, but here again the name of Hawly Bishopp does not occur.[2] Finally the proceedings of the Glass-sellers Company contain no reference to Bishopp later than the indenture of 1681, nor is his name mentioned in the literature of protest against the War Tax of 1696.

There was, we know, one other glasshouse in the Savoy at this period. The owner was Henry Holden, and his glasshouse is described as " The glasshouse in the Savoy " in distinction from the glasshouse worked by Bishopp, which was more precisely " in the Savoy at the Riverside." He had had a long experience of glassmaking, and at the end of 1682 or early in 1683 he received an appointment as glassmaker to the King and authority to put the royal arms, no doubt by means of a seal, on all glasses made by royal orders.[3] It is very doubtful whether at this time he made lead glass. His wares are not described as crystalline or even as flint glasses, and when he advises his customers that he uses no " noxious ingredients " he is, I think, tilting at his neighbour's lead glass[4] and pointing out that his own glasses are of a different sort. His own enterprise depended upon

[1] *S.P. Dom. Petition Entry Book I*, p. 200 (Calendar, 5 October, 1691) ; the names are Christopher Dodsworth, John Bowles, Michael Rackett, Phineas Bowles, William Thompson, John Blunt, Robert Hooker, and there are others not mentioned by name.

[2] *S.P. Dom. Petition Entry Book I*, p. 442 (Calendar, 2 February, 1692-3). The names are Sir Thomas Escourt, Sir Rowland Ainsworth, Sir James Etheridge, Sir Henry Marwood, William Monson, Robert Hookes, Thomas Wearge, James Sotheby, Arthur Champney, George Carter, Frederick Herne, John Lethuiller, Robert Winnington, Andrew Phillips, John Jeffereys, Paul Jodderell, John Bowles, Phineas Bowles, Richard Onslow, Nathaniel Herne, Francis Gosfright, Henry Cornish, Charles Sweeting, Nathaniel Molyneux, John Devincke. A hundred and twenty other London glassmakers signed the petition, but their names are not preserved.

[3] Holden advertised his award in the *London Gazette*, 16 April, 1683 : " His Majesty being well satisfied of the knowledge and skill of Henry Holden Esq. in the compounding and mixing of metal without any noxious ingredients for the making of all sorts of glass has been pleased to cause him to be sworn his servant in Ordinary with leave to put his imperial arms on all such glasses as shall be made by his orders. These are therefore to give notice that the said Mr. Holden is now making his glasses at his glasshouse in the Savoy." It is not known when Holden built his glasshouse, but it was probably new in 1683. As far as I am aware no sealed fragments of his work have come to light.

[4] Lead might well be regarded at this date as a " noxious ingredient." *Cf.* the *Discourse or Dialogue concerning the Mining Adventure, supra*, p. 116, note 2. If it was thought noxious to workmen, then *a fortiori* it was dangerous in drinking glasses, at any rate if you wanted to crab someone else's wares.

distinguished patronage and private custom, and he might well despise a gang of tradesmen. He was, moreover, well on in years and had been making soda glass, doubtless of the Netherlandish-Venetian type, fifteen years before lead glass was invented[1] ; and when we remember that Venetian glasses were "preferred of the nobility," the mere fact of royal patronage makes it likely that Holden adhered fairly closely to the derivative Venetian type. He may, I think, be regarded as the elder Tory protesting, a little nobly and peevishly, against a new "poisonous" invention. If ever the triumphant career of lead glass broke his resolution we may expect that his glasses conformed to the style which Mr. Buckley has described as the "parallel Venetian tradition." But he only worked for six years. In 1689 he was succeeded in the office of King's glassmaker by Phillip Dallow,[2] and it is likely that he died in that year.

After the expiry of Ravenscroft's patent in 1681 the technique of lead glass spread rapidly to other glasshouses in London, and four years later Bishopp himself had been outdistanced. In 1685 some of the other glasshouses were making lead glasses very cheaply and selling them at eighteen to the dozen, and Bishopp, who hitherto had only sold fifteen to the dozen, received orders from the Glass Sellers to raise this quota to sixteen. The document in which this demand is made is the most important evidence we have for the extension of lead glassmaking in London, and makes it possible to date it between 1681 and 1685.[3] It may be possible some day to assign London glasses of the 17th century to their proper origins, and it will therefore be convenient to add here a list of the very few London glasshouses which are known to have been making lead glass at this period.

1. *The Salisbury Court Company.* There had been a glasshouse in Salisbury Court, Fleet Street, some years before, but it had fallen into disuse and was reopened in 1684 by a company of partners, whose names are not known, for the making of flint glasses.[4] In the Victoria and Albert Museum there is a fragment of a quatrefoil stem similar to the London Museum fragment. A chemical test proves it to be lead glass, and it bears a seal with the letter S which Mr. Buckley is undoubtedly right in referring to this glasshouse. S might also refer to

[1] He was a partner with John Colenet, the Netherlandish glassmaker, in 1662. *S.P. Dom. Docquet book*, 119 (1662).

[2] *S.P. Dom. Warrant Book*, 35 (160, 162).

[3] Sloane MS. 857, Memorandum dated 3 June, 1685. " We the major part (*sc.* of the Glass Sellers) here considering that other glasshouses do sell 18 to ye dozen of their glasses called flint-glasses to the great prejudice of us partners in this glasshouse we having yet sold but 15 to ye doz, it is now agreed and ordered that Mr. Hawly Bishopp do deliver to all us partners concerned or any other shopkeepers concerned sixteen to the dozen of all sorts of glasses that are sold by dozen and all sorts sold by weight this to be . . ." The document is incomplete and very illiterate ; the spelling has been emended.

[4] *London Gazette*, 11 September, 1684.

John Straw or the two Savoy glasshouses, but these can be eliminated on other considerations. Straw was only Jackson's partner. Holden, as we have seen, did not make flint glass and when he sealed his glasses he used the royal arms ; and there is no evidence that Bishopp ever used a seal except when he worked with Ravenscroft and used his.

2. *The Duke of York* (afterwards James II) had a glasshouse in Wapping, probably the glasshouse in Redmead's Lane which was certainly " near the Hermitage stairs." Flint glasses were being made there in 1684, and the glasses were then marked with a Lion and Coronet " to prevent counterfeits."[1] The ownership of " His Royal Highness " probably ended in 1685 and must have ended in 1688, but the glasshouse may have been taken over by somebody else. We are still waiting for the discovery in London excavations of a glass with the Lion and Coronet.

Between 1684 and 1693 no other glasshouse is known to have been making flint glasses in London, and since in 1696 the London flint glass-houses were only nine in number and that was twelve progressive years after the Duke of York and the Salisbury Court Company are mentioned, it seems likely that in 1684 Bishopp, the Salisbury Court Company, and the Duke of York were the only flint glassmakers in London.[2]

3. *The Falcon Glasshouses.* In 1693 Francis Jackson and John Straw had " glasshouses " for making " the best and finest drinking-glasses and curious glasses for ornament and likewise all sorts of glass bottles." " The best and finest drinking-glasses " must at this date imply lead metal and " all sorts of glass bottles " probably includes flint-glass bottles as well as green-glass bottles. The plural " glasshouses " probably means at this date two glasshouses, one for green bottle glass and one for flint glass.[3] Jackson and Straw were a firm of some importance and enterprise. They had a branch at King's Lynn, no doubt because they were using Lynn sand and found it cheaper to make some glasses on the spot[4] ; their Lynn glasshouse is one of the earliest instances of flint glass being made in the provinces. The firm had another glasshouse near St. Mary Overies Church,[5] and the senior partner Jackson gave evidence to support the petition of the

[1] *London Gazette*, 4 December, 1684.
[2] Bowles and Lillington are not described as making *flint glasses* in 1678, only " white glasses " ; but they may have begun to do so in 1681.
[3] In 1720 there were three glasshouses near the Falcon Stairs (Strype's edition of Stow's *Survey*, 1720, IV, 27), but twenty-seven years earlier it may be doubted whether the plural implies more than two.
[4] It seems fair to argue from this that Lynn sand was then (1693) being used in London for what was still called " flint glass."
[5] *V. infra*, p. 141, note 2.

glassmakers against the war tax of 1695. He was evidently an authority on the economics of glassmaking.

4. *Goodman's Yard Glasshouse.* Drinking-glasses, almost certainly of flint glass, were being made in 1699 at a glasshouse in Goodman's Yard near the Minories. This glasshouse already had an interesting history and was one of the oldest in London at that time. More than half a century before it had been in the possession of Sir Bevis Thelwall. In 1651 two men of the merchant class, Richard Batson[1] and Edmond Lewin, obtained a lease of it for twenty-five and a half years, and later sublet the place to practical glassmakers. In 1677 Batson had dropped out of the partnership, and a year later Lewin was succeeded by Michael Rackett, who, as we have seen, made white glasses and bottles. He worked there alone for thirteen years, but in 1691 took part in promoting a joint-stock company which then took over the glasshouse and was still making drinking-glasses and all other sorts of glasses in 1699–1700.[2] The Goodman's Yard glasshouse was not of course making lead glass in 1678 when Rackett made his agreement with the Glass Sellers, but it must, I think, have begun to do so before 1685.

5. *Bowles and Lillington.* John Bowles was the founder of one of the most famous industrial houses of the 18th century. The Bowles dynasty was chiefly concerned with the manufacture of plate and crown glass at its Vauxhall and Ratcliff factories, and its history is therefore beyond the scope of the present work. But there is sufficient reason[3] for thinking that the first John Bowles made vessel glass as well as other kinds of glass and his position in the industry is so important that no account of the art would be complete without him. He came of an ancient family in Lincolnshire and was born 27 February, 1640–1 at Chatham. His father, Charles Bowles, had great possessions also in Kent and Suffolk, and he had held high office under the Commonwealth. When he died he left a large fortune to be divided among his four sons. One of them, Phineas, was in the King's service and became secretary to Charles II's Navy, and through his offices John obtained a patent for supplying the King's ships.[4] Like the adventurers of the 16th and early 17th

[1] He had been a vigorous opponent of Mansell in 1641 ; Hartshorne, p. 200.

[2] *Flying Post*, 16 March, 1699–1700.

[3] The mention of " white glasses " in the agreement between Bowles and Lillington and the Glass Sellers, 1 April, 1678. This is confirmed by Mr. Francis Buckley's brilliant explanation of the Northampton sealed fragment which shows a female (Lily) shooting with a bow (*History*, p. 29). Ravenscroft's own seal and his family coat-of-arms were a similar pun. One of Bowles' glasshouses was described as a flint glasshouse in 1717 ; see p. 141, note 4.

[4] Not, of course, with glass ; John Bowles was a general merchant.

centuries, John Bowles had no scruple about engaging in commerce, and when in 1665 he came, at the age of twenty-four, into full control of his inheritance, he at once went into business in the City and used his large capital in the flourishing trade with the Levant and in the development of glass manufactures in England. He must have embarked on this latter enterprise fairly early, for he acquired a plate glasshouse at Vauxhall which had passed from the Duke of Buckingham to his apprentice John Dawson, probably during the Duke's incarceration in the Tower (1667–9).[1] About 1670 Dawson and John Bowles were in joint control of this glasshouse, and between that year and 1684 Bowles acquired at least four other glasshouses on the Surrey side. Two of these were already in Bowles' possession in 1678, and it is evident from the business which they undertook that they must have been already working for several years. One of these factories was the Stony Street Glasshouse, while the other is probably to be identified with one of the glasshouses near the Falcon stairs. Six years later (1684) Bowles was in the sole ownership of two other factories in Southwark, the Bear Garden Glasshouse and the St. Mary Overies Glasshouse. In 1684 both these factories were making green (*i.e.* bottle) glass exclusively,[2] and for Bowles' drinking-glasses we must look elsewhere. In 1678 John Bowles also had a factory in Southwark in a thoroughfare called Stony Street which ran from the riverside through the Borough,[3] and in 1717 this glasshouse consisted of two buildings which were then known as " the Flint Glass house " and the " Little Glasshouse."[4] The Bowles business was mainly for plate glass ; even under John Bowles I " the emoluments were prodigious."[5] Among the material brought together by Mr. W. H. Bowles there is no other evidence that flint glass was made in the early

[1] For this see Mr. W. H. Bowles' monograph (1926). The Bill in Chancery of *Bellingham v. Buckingham* proves that the Duke was still owner of a glasshouse at Vauxhall for mirror glass, March, 1671–April, 1674, and is in apparent contradiction to Mr. Bowles. But it is, I think, evident that the Duke had two plate glasshouses at Vauxhall, one for glass plates for windows which passed to Dawson when the Duke was in the Tower (1667–9), the other for mirror-glass plates which Bellingham was managing for the Duke in 1671–4. The Duke's original patent had been revoked five years after it was granted (1668) because his statements in petition were false (Bowles, p. 7) ; for Dawson see Nichols, *History of Lambeth* (1786), pp. 120 *sq.*

[2] Quinquepartite Indenture dated 1 September, 1684, in the possession of the Glass-sellers Company, where John Bowles of the second part is described as " Master of several glasshouses at St. Mary Overye's and the Bear Garden in Southwark for making of Green glass." St. Mary Overies = St. Saviour's, Southwark.

[3] Bowles, p. 13.

[4] Fire Insurance policies (Nos. 33691–5) of date 1717 in possession of the Hand in Hand Branch of the Commercial Union Insurance Company ; Bowles, pp. 61 and 13.

[5] Nichols, *History of Lambeth* (1786), p. 123.

days of the dynasty, and the flint glasshouse in Stony Street, South-wark, must therefore be identified with the glasshouse " in Southwark " where in 1678 John Bowles and William Lillington were making " white glasses." When the white glasses became lead glasses cannot be determined exactly, but it was probably about 1681–5. The Northampton fragment was probably made at Stony Street between 1678 and 1681.

Houghton, writing in 1696, said that there were nine flint glasshouses then at work in London,[1] and if we accept the principle that a flint glass-house of one owner made flint glass under his successor, it may be suggested that the nine were as follows : (1) the glasshouse worked by Bishopp in the Savoy, (2) the other Savoy Glasshouse which probably adopted flint glass when Holden ceased work in 1689, (3) the glasshouse at Wapping formerly owned by the Duke of York, (4) the Salisbury Court Glasshouse, (5) the Goodman's Yard Glasshouse, (6) the St. Mary Overies Glasshouse (Jackson and Straw), (7) the Stony Street Glasshouse (Bowles) and (8–9) two glasshouses near the Falcon Stairs.

It would not be pertinent or indeed possible to give a chronicle and still less a history of the numerous glasshouses which flourished in the provinces during the century which followed. In some few instances the tale of a particular house has been rescued by the industry of its descendants, and Mr. Francis Buckley's invaluable prosopographies have at least made it possible to trace the process of colonization by which the art of glass was disseminated. At the best we have a bare record of birth and marriage, lease and partnership and insolvency, and only in the rarest instances can we identify the work of a particular house. But in the childhood of flint glass a mere catalogue of houses shows the distribution and prosperity of the art at that period. Houghton, whose evidence we must regard as that of an expert, gave in 1696 a full list, with numbers but no names, of the flint glasshouses then at work, and we may try to cover Houghton's skeleton with a little of Mr. Buckley's flesh.

The flint glasshouses known to have been working before 1700 may be grouped thus :

Bristol area. Houghton mentioned four in 1696, and during the next two years a fifth flint glasshouse was established, but it is not known which sites in Bristol they occupied or who were their owners. John Williams and Edward Dagnia, an Italian who later migrated to the Tyne, had a glass-house there in 1651 ; the Dixons were working there in 1698 and may have made flint glass. The flint glasshouse of Cooks in Temple Street had been working for many years in 1741 and was probably in existence when Houghton wrote. To Bristol we must probably affiliate Renell's glass-

[1] *Letters*, No. 198.

house at Topsham near Exeter, which was making flint glass in 1702 and must be identified with a glasshouse mentioned by Houghton in 1696.

Stourbridge area. The difficulty here, as at Bristol, is to distinguish between broad- and bottle-glassmakers and flint glassmakers. In the 18th-century notices "glassmaker" seems to imply that the man made all sorts, "white glassmaker" that he made only domestic glass, and "broad glassmaker" that he made broad glass only. Houghton mentions five flint glasshouses, and two other flint glasshouses were working before the end of the century. Their number had only increased to "about ten" in 1766. In 1760 there are eight makers definitely stated to have been divided among the following families :

Grazebrook	Audnam Glasshouse
Bradley	Brettle Lane or Wordsley
Rogers	Amblecote
Honeybourne	Brierly Hill
Barrar	Amblecote
Denham's	Possibly Brettle Lane
Russell's	? Amblecote
Little	Site uncertain

There were thus eight flint glasshouses in 1760 and five in 1696, but notices of bankruptcy are so common that it would, I think, be unsafe to argue back from the distribution in 1760 to the distribution at the end of the 17th century. What is important to notice is that between 1698 and 1760 the number of flint glasshouses was only increased by one. That does not mean that the industry was less prosperous there than elsewhere ; it means simply that it was established early and served an unvarying inland market.[1] The bankruptcies which are evident about 1730 seem to show that Stourbridge glassmaking was trying to expand. but failing because its market was limited and would not stand more than a limited quota of glassmakers.[2] In this fact we may see the necessity which drove Stourbridge men to Yorkshire, Bristol, and elsewhere. It is significant that the Stourbridge "colonies" (*e.g.* at Whittington, Ferrybridge, Brosely, Bolsterstone) were not founded until early in the 18th century, when the industry had been long enough established in the "metropolis" to outgrow its market. The Worcester glasshouse must be connected with Stourbridge. Only one glasshouse is ever mentioned in that city ; its owner, Edward Dixon, belonged to a family which several times intermarried with the Lorrainers, and is discovered at Whittington and at Bristol. Edward Dixon was in prison for debt in 1727, but as there was no other glasshouse at Worcester, Houghton must have referred to his glasshouse.

[1] This is evident from Neve (R.), *The Builders Dictionary* (London, 1703).
[2] For this *cf.* John Williams' migration to Newcastle-on-Tyne in 1730, p. 146 *infra*.

Newcastle-on-Tyne.   We have noticed already that the early industry on the Tyne was chiefly concerned with bottle glass and more especially with sheet glass of various kinds,[1] and there is no reason to doubt Houghton's assertion that there was only one flint glasshouse working there in 1696.   It is, moreover, certain that the manufacture of flint glass in this district was not due in the first instance to the Lorrainers, but to an Italian family whose names first occur in the middle of the 17th century.   This family was the Dagnia family.   Edward Dagnia, the first of whom we have any record, was working at Bristol in 1651, and seems to have been employed by an Englishman (or Welshman), John Williams.[2]

At some later date, probably in 1684 or a little earlier, the family seem to have migrated to the Tyne.   Edward Dagnia I is not mentioned in Newcastle records and it may be that he died before the sons left Bristol. At any rate in 1684 the three brothers Onesiphorus Dagnia I, Edward Dagnia II, and John Dagnia I were all established in business in Newcastle, and there is not, I think, much doubt they were the first to introduce lead glassmaking on the Tyne.[3]   The dynasty reigned for nearly half a century, but about 1731 seems to have given place to the Williams'.   There were four Dagnia glasshouses all situated near the Closegate ; and of these two are specified as making " white glass," *i.e.* glass vessels other than (green) bottles.[4]   The earliest of these was founded in 1684 when John and Onesiphorus Dagnia with Benezar Durant, J. Wall, and other partners obtained a lease of a messuage near Closegate for 999 years and erected a glasshouse thereon.   This glasshouse must be identified with " a bottle and flint glasshouse with a complete set of tools and workmen for each house " which in 1743 was offered on lease by two later representatives of the family, John and Christopher Dagnia ; for none of the other glasshouses known to have been in the possession of the Dagnias are described as making both bottles and white glass or flint glass.   It would appear that from the beginning there were two furnace houses at this glasshouse, one for white or flint glass and the other for (green) glass bottles, in which Onesiphorus

[1] For the export of sheet glass " of a kind of ash colour " by sea to London, and an interesting description of the method of packing it to avoid breakage in a heavy sea, *v.* Neve, *op. cit.*, p. 149 (1703).

[2] Dudley (D.), *Metallum Martis* (1665), p. 22.   For another family of glassmakers perhaps descended from this John Williams, *v. infra*, p. 283.

[3] For this family see Welford (A. R.), *Local Muniments*, in *Arch. Ael.*, 2 Ser., XXIV, pp. 147–55 ; Adamson (C. E.), *John Dagnia of South Shields* in *P.S.A. Newc.*, VI, 163 ; Wood (H. M.), *The family of Dagnia of Newcastle* in *Arch. Ael.*, 3 Ser., XVII, 229–43 ; Hodgson (J. C.), *P.S.A. Newc.*, 3 Ser., VII, 207, and 3 Ser., IV, 98 ; Buckley (F.), *Glasshouses on the Tyne* in *Trans. Soc. Glass Techn.*, X, 26.

[4] " White or Flint glass " ; Hutton's *Plan of Newcastle* (1772), cited by Buckley, *ibid.*, p. 46.

THE DYNASTY OF DAGNIA

Edward Dagnia I, of Bristol, "Master Edward Dagney of Bristow, an ingenious glassmaker"
(D. Dudley, *Metallum Martis*, p. 22), about 1651

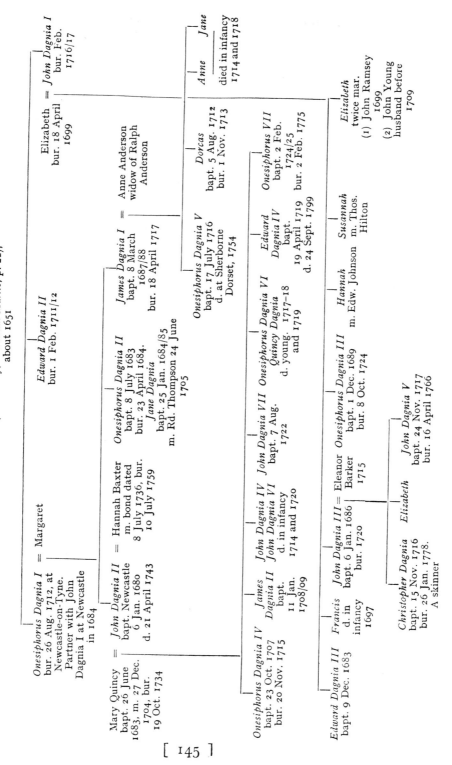

L

[145]

Dagnia did a large trade.[1]   The Closegate white glasshouse was started at a time when lead glass had been " free " for about three years, and its manufacture was spreading very rapidly, and it is not, I think, too much to suppose that lead glass was being made there from the start.   It must certainly be identified with the one flint glasshouse at Newcastle mentioned by Houghton in 1696.   Three other glasshouses at Newcastle distinct from the earliest foundation were in the possession of the Dagnias during the early part of the 18th century.   One of these three is described as a white glasshouse and may be presumed to have made flint glass.   It appears to have been started by Edward Dagnia II, the third of the three brothers, but the date of its foundation is not known.   In 1710 it was transferred by Edward Dagnia to his brother John, presumably because Edward was then in failing health and had no children ; he died the following year and there is no evidence that he had either wife or children.[2]

Of the two other glasshouses one was taken by John and Onesiphorus Dagnia in 1701 in conjunction with a certain John Harrop.   The other glasshouse was " near the Forth Bank " and held under lease by Onesiphorus Dagnia III, son of John Dagnia I.   But in neither case is there any evidence that white glass or flint glass was made.

The last of the three brothers (John) died in 1716–17 and thereafter the family glasshouses split into two groups.   The flint-glass group was held jointly by the sons of John and Onesiphorus Dagnia, but from 1731 onwards the actual manufacture passed into the control of a Stourbridge glassmaker, John Williams, who arrived in Newcastle in 1730 and the next year married the widow of Onesiphorus Dagnia III, son of John Dagnia I.   The bottle-glass group known as the " Bottle-house without Closegate " passed to John and Christopher Dagnia, sons of John Dagnia III and grandsons of John Dagnia I.   In 1743 it was leased to John Williams, whose wife Margery had a life interest in the business, and on Williams' death in 1763 it was worked by the celebrated firm of John Cookson and Co. until 1775.[3]

During the first half of the 18th century the Dagnias in the west end of Newcastle were the protagonists of flint glass just as the Lorraine families in the east were the protagonists of plate glass and crown glass.   During the greater part of the 18th century there were only two flint glasshouses in Newcastle.   Two only are mentioned in 1772 and of these one must be identified with the Dagnia flint glasshouse at Closegate.   The other appears to have been founded in 1728 when Joseph Airey converted an old

---

[1] In 1697 Onesiphorus Dagnia was fined £200 for concealing 2679 dozen of glass bottles. *Treasury Papers*, 4 November, 1697, cited by Buckley, *u.s.*, p. 40.

[2] There seems to be no record of Edward Dagnia II's white glasshouse after this. It was probably included with " Flint Glasshouse without Closegate " just as the " Bottle house without Closegate " included two of the earlier Dagnia bottle glasshouses.

[3] John Cookson was the son of Isaac Cookson ; see below.

dissenters' meeting-house at the Close into a flint glasshouse. Isaac Cookson was at the back of this enterprise. His son John was apprenticed to Airey in 1728, and the firm was called Airey Cookson and Co. for the rest of the 18th century.

Thus until 1728 the Dagnias had a monopoly of the flint glass manufacture in Newcastle; after that date they and their representative John Williams shared the trade with Airey Cookson and Co. Several types of glass can be identified as of Newcastle origin and the earlier of these were probably made by the Dagnias. The tall knopped glasses with short flaring bowls (*e.g.* Plate CXV) had been evolved before 1730 and may be assigned to the Dagnias rather than to Airey Cookson and Co. Mr. Wilfred Buckley has a specimen of this type signed by the Dutch stippler Greenwood and dated 1728,[1] and in the same collection are three glasses of the same type with heraldic engraving executed in the Netherlands.[2] One of these has the arms of William IV of Orange, another the arms of his wife, Anne, daughter of George II of England; while the third has the arms of both; all three can be dated about 1734. Again, between 1760 and 1780, the tall Newcastle type was being used for enamel painting by the Beilbys of that city, and in the last decade of the century by the Dutch stippler Wolff. These dates make it tolerably certain that the type in question was evolved at Closegate while the Dagnias were still in active control, and that as a factory type it remained constant throughout the 18th century and outside the evolutionary changes which came over the baluster and its descendants.

It is, moreover, fairly certain that all the types painted by the Beilbys were made either by the Dagnia glasshouse under the direction of John Williams or by Airey Cookson and Company. The tall knopped glasses had been evolved before the latter firm had been long at work and they may be assigned therefore to the Closegate glasshouses. But the other glasses painted by the Beilbys cannot be ascribed to one glasshouse rather than to the other. Some glasses used by Dutch engravers, *e.g.* the very large goblets with Greenwood's work (*e.g.* Plate XCIII. 1), and the facet-stem glasses with Wolff's, have been very reasonably assigned to Newcastle, which is known to have had a considerable export trade to the Netherlands. Of these the large goblets are rather too early in date for an attribution to Airey Cookson and Co. to be very likely; they must be ascribed to the Dagnias. The facet-stems may have been made in either of the Newcastle flint glasshouses.

It will be convenient at the end of this section to draw attention to the difficult question whether the lead metal was or was not confined

---

[1] *European Glass*, Plate 68.   [2] *Ibid.*, Plate 74.

to England. Three kinds of evidence have to be considered ; documents, silence, and the glasses themselves. We hear of no imitation of English glass on the Continent until 1680 when the Bonhommes, the great house of glassmakers at Liège, engaged workmen to produce *verres à l'Angleterre*. Everything turns on the implications of this phrase. It cannot well refer to form, since English glass hitherto had been an amalgam of other styles and there was not much in England worth imitation by a Netherlandish glasshouse. If the phrase refers, as I think it must, to the metal of English glass, it is not inconceivable that the Bonhommes were anxious to copy, not lead glass, but the earlier "flint glass proper." For their finer types of glass the Liège glassmakers probably imported *tarso* from Italy just as Ravenscroft had done, and the name flint glass, which was already applied to English glass before lead glass was invented, may have suggested to them the use of flints instead of quartz. In that case we must suppose that the Bonhommes were looking for a cheap silicate ; for even though flints required a preliminary calcination they could be found almost anywhere and must have been cheaper than imported *tarso*. Moreover, the Bonhommes at this time were beginning to fear the competition of the German glasshouses, and it seems that they tried to meet it by domesticating glass, *i.e.* by enlarging its sphere of usefulness and so engaging a wider market. Stouter vessels were wanted for this purpose than the frailties of *façon de Venise*, and after the Restoration English glassmaking also had been moving towards a sturdier fabric.[1] Certainly Liège glass early in the 18th century was much more " domestic " than either Venetian or German, and *verres à l'Angleterre* may have been simply a step in that direction ; English glass which was becoming " useful " was made, and was known to be made, with flints.

While that explanation cannot be excluded, it is more natural to suppose that in 1680 the Bonhommes had become aware of the Ravenscroft revolution and were so impressed with the new metal that they wished to copy it. Even after the seal had been placed upon them Ravenscroft's glasses were not quite immune from crizzling, but when they were *new* this may have been less marked ; and there is some evidence[2] that in the latter part of 1677 Ravenscroft was sending his glasses abroad. In that way they probably became known at Liège. The workmen mentioned in Schuermans' document[3] were almost certainly imported from England,

[1] The Northampton fragment, a fragment in the London Museum, and one of Mr. Mason's pair of decanters (Plate IX) may be cited as instances. All appear to date between 1660 and 1676.

[2] See p. 127 *supra*.

[3] *Bulletin*, XXVI, p. 329. Throughout Schuermans appears to refer to MS. sources but does not state what they were ; presumably account books, etc., of the factories concerned.

and I would suggest that they had previously been in Ravenscroft's employ and went to the Netherlands when they were thrown out of work by Ravenscroft's retirement (February, 1678–9). If I have taken a correct view of the period 1673–81 workmen acquainted with the lead-glass process could not have been obtained from any other English glasshouse, and more than two years elapsed between the date when Ravenscroft ceased to make lead glass (February, 1678–9) and the date when Bishopp began to make it again (soon after February, 1681–2). The Bon hommes, it would appear, stepped very acutely into this hiatus and carried off two or three of Ravenscroft's unemployed.

There is no evidence that lead glass was actually made at Liège until late in the 18th century, and if the workmen engaged in 1680 did communicate the process to the Bonhommes it is highly unlikely that lead glass was made there after their death or departure. Until the last thirty years of the 18th century no lead glasses are known which can be assigned to any but an English origin, and even if lead glass was made at Liège for a few years at the end of the 17th century the output cannot have been large. Throughout the 18th century repeated attempts were made to copy English glass, which must refer to metal and not to form. The repetition of them is an argument for failure rather than an argument for success, and all were experiments by continental glassmakers and not attempts to procure English workmen.[1]

In 1710 François de Colnet, a member of a famous family of Flemish glassmakers, established a glasshouse at Ghent for making " cristal anglais "[2] and the following year he was making bottles and glasses *more anglicano* and for six years distributed them all over Flanders.[3] If this was an attempt to copy lead glass it is odd that bottles should be mentioned. Decanter bottles of lead glass had been made in England before that date, but the word " bottles " at that time normally implies a greenish potash glass. Again, some time before 1740, a certain Nizet at Liège had been making experiments in the manufacture of " des verres fins ou cristaux aussi blanc et aussi beaux que ceux d'Angleterre."[4] In 1750 a Namur glassmaker advertised " cristal aussi bon que l'anglais et à meilleur marché qu'à Londres."[5] In France in 1729 a French glassmaker of Saint Paul-lez-Rouen was trying to imitate English flint glass, and in France no previous attempts have been recorded.[6] This tale of isolated endeavours itself shows that continental glassmakers had great difficulty in imitating flint glass ; had flint glass ever become general in continental glasshouses we should surely hear less of the attempts to copy it. It may be that some

---

[1] Oppenheim and Ensell were independent owners ; see p. 150 *infra*.
[2] Hartshorne, p. 41 ; he and Schuermans clearly refer to the same enterprise.
[3] Schuermans, *loc. cit.*   [4] Schuermans, *ibid.*   [5] Schuermans, *ibid.*
[6] Schuermans, *Bulletin*, XXX, 797 ; Hartshorne, p. 102.

small quantity of lead glass was produced by the several glassmakers that have been mentioned, but the large amount of English glass which was being exported in the middle of the 18th century gave these poor imitations no chance of commercial success. In 1760 the French philosopher and glass-maker, Bosc d'Antic, who had studied the industry in England, Germany, and the Netherlands, as well as in his own country, stated that four-fifths of the English output was being sent abroad and that the whole of France was supplied from this country[1]; and Schuermans appears to have found independent evidence that " des cristaux taillés continuaient à arriver chez nous en abondance."[2]

The first attempt which came near reproducing English crystal (*i.e.* lead glass) was that of Libaude, a Frenchman, who in 1772 was awarded a national prize of twelve hundred livres for discovering the "secret" of English crystal.[3] Thereafter it would seem that lead glass became fairly common on the Continent. About this time one of the Ensells of Stourbridge (Ensell=Hennezel) appears to have been driven abroad by the burden of the Excise, and founded a "cristaillerie anglaise" near Vilvorde in Belgium.[4] Again, when Mayer Oppenheim left Birmingham he went to Normandy, and in 1783 he settled at Petit Quévilly (Seine Inférieure) and founded a " manufacture royale de cristaux " which was exclusively occupied with the manufacture of English flint glass.[5] Finally the German glasshouse of Lauwenstein is known to have been making lead glass at the end of the 18th century.[6]

From the foregoing evidence it must be concluded that lead glass was not made in continental glasshouses, or only made very rarely, until the last thirty years of the 18th century. The surviving specimens of con-tinental glass dating from the earlier and middle years of the 18th century are overwhelmingly in support of this conclusion. The normal fabric in German, Venetian, Netherlandish, and French glass is a soda or potash metal; I am not aware of any specimen proven to belong to these countries, and earlier in date than *c.* 1770, which has also been proven to contain lead. Dr. Hudig of Amsterdam has made an exhaustive examination of the documents relating to the Netherlandish glasshouses, but he has found no evidence that lead oxide was ever included in their batch. There is, lastly, the evidence of Bosc d'Antic, the most authoritative contemporary writer on 18th-century glassmaking, and a man who had studied the

[1] *Mémoire sur les verreries; Œuvres*, Vol. I.
[2] *Bulletin*, XXVI, 329.
[3] Hartshorne, p. 102.
[4] Schuermans, *Bulletin*, XXVI, 329.
[5] Le Vaillant de la Fieffe, pp. 300 and 521.
[6] This is one of the few glasshouses which marked their wares. The mark is a lion engraved on the pontil-mark ; see an article by Christian Scherer in *Der Cicerone*, 1913. A marked piece of this factory has been tested.

industry with an international outlook and in the spirit of a scientist. His verdict (1780) on this vexed question does not permit of any reasonable retort: "Quoique quelques compagnies savants aient consommé des mémoires sur la fabrication du flint glass il ne paroit pas moins certain il n'y a encore que l'Angleterre qui fabrique du vrai flint glass. C'est que tout l'art ne consiste uniquement à faire entrer dans cette espèce de verre la plus grande quantité possible de chaux de plomb."[1] It remains true that the standard metal of continental glass was made with salts, the standard metal of England with lead; and though it cannot be asserted that even in the early years of the 18th or the later years of the 17th century lead was never used in continental glass, the presence of lead in a glass until *c.* 1770 provides a very strong probability that it was made in England or Ireland.[2]

There are, lastly, four main types of lead glass of which the origin has been until recently in dispute.

(a) Tall glasses with short flaring bowls and long knopped stems. The bowls often bear Dutch wheel-engraving. The glasses themselves date from about 1740–70. A specimen bearing the signature of a family of enamel-painters who worked at Newcastle-on-Tyne about 1760–80 has recently come to light, and this makes it fairly certain that the glasses of this shape are a factory type of one of the Newcastle glasshouses[3] (Plate CXXXI. 1–3).

(b) Glasses with ogee or straight-sided bowls and stems cut in facets. These sometimes bear stipple engravings by D. Wolff and others, but the lead metal is of such fine quality that it is difficult to give them a continental origin, even though some of them must be dated to the end of the 18th century (Plate CI. 2).

(c) Glasses with bell bowls and knopped stems (2, 3, or 4 knops) containing twists of white or coloured enamel. Non-lead glasses of this type were certainly made in the Netherlands. Similar specimens of lead metal are of poor quality in respect of their metal, and whatever their origin date from the last quarter of the 18th century. It is

[1] Bosc d'Antic (Paul). *Notes* (1780) *sur un mémoire* (1760) *sur les verreries. Œuvres*, Vol. I, p. 160.

[2] The test for lead is as follows: Dip a clean stick in a bottle of hydrofluoric acid and let a drop of the acid fall on the glass, preferably the underside of the foot, or some inconspicuous part. Dip another clean stick in a bottle of sulphide of ammonium and allow a drop to fall on the place previously touched with hydrofluoric acid. If the acid turns black there is lead in the glass; if it sizzles and remains white the glass contains no lead. When the operation is over the spot should be immediately washed or wiped with blotting-paper. If this is done no harm to the glass will result. The hydrofluoric acid should be kept in a rubber bottle.

[3] See "The Beilby Glasses," *Connoisseur*, May, 1928, and Buckley (W.) in *Old Furniture*, August, 1928; see p. 147 *supra*.

possible that they were made in the Netherlands, but there is no definite evidence that this is so, and in its absence they may be regarded as a cheap and inferior English fabric ; for their quality is indeed very poor.

(*d*) Glasses which show strong evidence of Venetian influence, and date from the first half of the 18th century. Two glasses in Plate XXX may be taken as representative of this type. The decoration is very elaborate (*e.g.* the knob in the form of a bird in Plate XXX. 2), but it only implies *façon de Venise*, not necessarily Netherlandish *façon de Venise;* and there is ample evidence that elaborate glasses of this type were made in England. One of the glasses in question (Plate XXX. 1) has a Dutch engraving of a ship and a long inscription in Dutch, but these may well have been added after the glass had left England. For the reasons already adduced in regard to the imitation of English flint glass, I am disposed to agree with Mr. Herbert Read[1] that both these glasses are of English manufacture.

[1] *Burl. Mag.*, XLVIII, 277.

CHAPTER V

The Age of Design (1676–1746)

Something of the severe hath always been appertaining to order and to grace ; and the beauty that is not too liberal is sought the most ardently and loved the longest.

W. S. Landor, *Barrow and Newton*.

§1. General Character

THE study of English glass must always be an attempt to correlate the two sets of facts, upon which our whole knowledge of the subject depends. There is first of all a great quantity of information mainly derived from literary sources, concerning the circumstances and the personalities of the art. The rise of glassmaking, its prime and its slow degradation have their origin in economic conditions and in men ; and a connoisseurship which neglects either of these becomes a mere feast of the eye, an acquisitive triumph or the formal logic of classification. We have, secondly, a great many miscellaneous specimens scattered among public and private collections which exist for different purposes and follow different methods. In the period with which we have hitherto been dealing the amount of information makes a consequential history possible, and our endeavour is to find a context in this development for the few pieces which still survive. In the age which follows the conditions of study are reversed, and we are still seeking a history for the great number of our specimens. Ravenscroft is the link between these two divisions, and it is largely due to Mr. Francis Buckley that the period in which he flourished, the short episode of the seal glasses, permits a more exact correlation of our two sets of facts than any period which followed or preceded it. After Ravenscroft we can still trace one or two main movements, such as the decorative immigration from Germany which began with the accession of the House of Hanover, and the influx of glassmen into Ireland (*c.* 1780–90), but an historical method is not really possible. We know a good deal about the stylistic development and a good deal about the various glasshouses in which it took place, but still we cannot connect the one with the other. The programme of future study of the subject can only be an endeavour to effect this correlation, and in order to do this it will be necessary to go beyond research and beyond observation to a new method, the method of chemical analysis. It is the only means by which the study of glass can attain the exactitude of attribution which the study of porcelain is already beginning to enjoy. There are many varieties of metal : " blue metal," " dark metal," " green metal," a whole spectrum of metals, in which superstition and caprice now make play for the entertainment of collectors. All this error and uncertainty is an abortive science which would find an order in the chaos ; and one would like to believe the manifold variations are not fortuitous, that they may some day be assigned to the factories which caused them. The keenest eye and the longest experience are liable to be deceived, and hope or pride will twist the most disinterested judgment ; chemistry cannot lie. But at present chemistry cannot even speak ; glasses are held too precious for sacrifice, too precious even for the slightest mutilation. It is not permitted to the public collections to chip their specimens, and that restriction is the private collector's opportunity. A systematic analysis of a hundred pieces selected at random or of half a dozen representative types might reveal more than hours of literary research or knowing disputation. Perhaps one may express the hope that collectors may soon prefer a chipped glass whose composition is known to a beautiful and unexamined perfection. A glass with its analysis should be like a dog with a pedigree and easily first in the auction room.[1]

The æsthetic and artistic values of English glass to which we have referred are the values of the period which immediately followed Ravenscroft and may be said, rather arbitrarily, to end in 1746. It is the most classical because it is the most English epoch of the art. The sense of design and the medium which it used grew side by side, and the result was absolute harmony such as outside of England only Venice has attained, and England herself never attained again. The period falls into two parts which are divided by the Treaty of Utrecht and the accession of the House of Hanover to the throne of England. That event encouraged the gradual infiltration of German artists into England, who contributed one or two forms to the English repertory and began to apply the glyptic and other ornament of Germany to English metal. This movement will be considered in the next chapter, to which it properly belongs ; it is sufficient here to note that in the strictest sense the apogee of the English art has a span of less than thirty years. The approximate dates are 1685–1710. During these years English glassmaking did two things. It became so prosperous in an economic sense that new factories began to be founded all over

---

[1] The use of alien cullet makes the method difficult, but the attribution of glasses to their provenance cannot even begin until, for example, we have the analysis of a sufficient number of glasses known (*e.g.* by their engraving) to have been made at Bristol or Dublin to judge what the standard mixture was, or whether there was a standard mixture. Even with the eye it is possible sometimes to detect two glasses which came from the same pot of metal, but until some knowledge has been obtained of the consistencies and the variations of the metal of a given centre of glassmaking there is no means of turning these similarities to account. Besides this, chemical analysis is necessary for determining the important question of the exact proportion of lead at certain periods and for distinguishing arsenic glass from bone-ash glass. The presence of an ingredient merely due to the alien cullet could be readily detected by comparing the proportion with the amount of that ingredient used in other glasses of the same series.

England ; and it collected its items of style from other countries and with astonishing rapidity transformed them into an idiom. England proceeded from one flint glasshouse in 1678 to sixty-one in 1696, and the individuation of style was just as swift.

§2. ECONOMY

Between 1695 and 1699 English glassmaking declared its independence by fighting and winning a war with the Exchequer. There had been taxation before that date. During the Commonwealth period glassmaking had been made the victim of a tax and contributed to the Grand Excise and New Impost which Cromwell had levied to supply his government with money. That he should have noticed the glassmakers at all was in itself a compliment to the rising industry, and the quota which he demanded was so small (5 per cent) that no umbrage was taken. But the glassmakers during that period suffered less from tyranny than from neglect, and at Cromwell's death the art was chiefly in the hands of foreigners and the commerce was fallen into a very low state. The Restoration of Charles II and a renewed interest in the industrial arts released the enterprise which had been slighted or repressed, and during the next twenty-five years glassmaking had attained a far greater prosperity than it had ever known before. In 1695 English flint glass had established itself all over England ; it had captured the trade of the Italian metics and employed as servants those who had formerly been rivals ; it had even made its name known on the Continent, and was attaining[1] an extensive foreign and colonial market. But it was in the nature of things that flint glass, which was still a luxury,[2] should be asked to pay for its prosperity. For three years the King's armies had been fighting the French in Flanders, and in 1695 the Exchequer, being much exercised for money to support the tedious war, put together a scheme for wholesale taxation of the free industries. Besides earthenware and stoneware and tobacco-pipes and plate glass and glass bottles, the Exchequer turned its acquisitive eye upon the flint-glass manufactures, and concluded without much forethought[3] that the emoluments to be derived from an Excise would be worth the cost and labour of collecting it. Accordingly in May, 1695 the Government passed the Excise Act (6 and 7 William and Mary, c. 18), by which it was enacted that all green glass bottles should

[1] English glass was still undersold on the Continent by German and other glass ; this was largely due to the import duties on barilla, saltpetre, and other materials procured from abroad. *Tracts*, No. 121.

[2] Glass-wares, which seem to imply flint glasses, were described as " more for Fancy than Necessity " (*Tracts*, No. 135), and this was used as an argument both for the tax and against it.

[3] The entire proceeds from the Glass Duty, Michaelmas, 1695—November, 1696, were less than £10,000. *Tracts*, No. 117.

contribute a shilling a dozen, and all flint glass and glass plates of all kinds at a general rate of 20 per cent. This Act became effective on 29 September, 1695, and was specifically valid for a term of five years. The next year a further Act was passed, confirming its predecessor and making its effects perpetual. So exorbitant a duty provoked the greatest anger and apprehension, and both before and after the Act came into operation (29 September, 1695), Parliament was beset with petitions by the several classes of persons who took their livelihood from glass. These were the London glassmakers, the Glass-sellers Company, the foreign glassmakers employed by Englishmen, called the Artist Glassmakers, the plate glassmakers, represented by the celebrated John Tyzack, the English workmen, and others. The several sets of petitioners trained their guns on the anonymous " Projector " of the scheme and made frequent use of the pathetic argument ; the poor glassmakers, they said, would be thrown out of work and their wives and children left in destitution. They revealed their natural hatred of the joint-stock companies, for only a combine with large capital and influence would be likely to survive the new tax, and they hinted that the tax was a put-up job by persons who had an interest in the collection of the dues.[1]

There were open hints of corrupt practice and a fair interchange of malice and hyperbole. But the petitioners and the counter-petitioners were so engrossed in the intrigues of the glass world that they forgot to blame, perhaps were too circumspect to blame, the French war and the makeshift Government ; and towards the honourable House of Commons remained without exception self-righteous and respectful. But there were prudent and reasonable voices in the outcry. The London glassmakers at least, to whom several of the more important petitions must be ascribed, gave a plain statement of the economy of glass which the slightest investigation would have revealed to the Exchequer itself. For that reason the petition literature is a source of considerable value. It makes clear the two real objections to the tax. It was in the first place not worth while from the Government point of view. The entire output of English glass amounted only to £63,000[2] (including £30,000 worth of flint

---

[1] *E.g.* John Bowles was interested in several of the joint-stock companies and was also one of the Commissioners of Excise, and Philip Allen, one of the Glass Sellers, was accused of duplicity.

[2] *Tracts*, B.M., 816 : M. 12, 129, a petition made before the Act came into force, states the gross value of *all* glass manufactures at £63,000 p.a. and estimates the net profit from the tax at £11,600. These figures are confirmed by Tract No. 117 which gives details of the Excise Commissioners' Accounts between Michaelmas, 1695, and November, 1696 ; the gross produce of the tax, £17,642 1s. 5d., less colliery charges of £7769 13s. 1d., gave a net profit of less than £10,000. It is interesting to compare these figures with the annual value of the glass trade in 1783. The sum was then £630,000, and was growing rapidly (Macpherson, *Annals of Commerce*, Vol. IV, p. 15).

glass[1]), and the net profit to the Exchequer when the Act was in force was less than £10,000 per annum. And secondly, such a paltry benefit, even in war-time, was not worth the inevitable damage to a rising industry and to the subsidiary trades which served it. The glass manufactures had been lately brought " to so great perfection "[2] and it was a very near-sighted policy to cripple the youngest of the nation's industries for the sake of a few thousands. The consequences perhaps would not be so black as some of the petitioners painted them, but they were certainly right in maintaining that the industry was not yet strong enough to stand a perpetual imposition of £20 in every £100. One petition at least had a lively premonition of the tyrannous invigilation of the glasshouses by the Excise officers of later times, and the actual conditions at the end of the 18th century showed that their fears were just. A 5 per cent duty would have provided a very small income, but it would have fairly measured the strength of the industry; the Excise of 1695 failed because it was much too high.

It may be worth while to give in parenthesis some notes of the state of flint glass in 1695 as revealed in the petition literature.

(a) Materials produced at home : clay (sc. from Stourbridge), sand (sc. from Lynn), ashes, kelp (sodiferous ash produced by the calcination of seaweed, mainly prepared in Scotland), manganese (from the Mendip Hills), coal, wood, white lead (litharge), and red lead (minium).

Materials imported : barilla (from Spain), pulverine frit, saltpetre (nitre), and smalts. These last were brought from Saxony. (E. Darwin, *Botanical Garden*, I, Note 52, states that hitherto (1791) smalts were imported " almost exclusively " from Saxony and used for colouring glass blue (cf. N. Grew's *Musæum Regulæ Societatis*, IV, iii, 376 (1683), " a piece of smalt-glass ").

(b) There was a regular business of collecting broken glass (cullet) for sale to the glasshouses (cf. p. 34).

(c) Workmen were engaged for a term of three to seven years and guaranteed forty weeks' work a year.

(d) In London there was a body of foreign " Artist Glassmakers," mainly from Italy and the Netherlands, distinct from the English workmen. The former were probably well paid ; the latter complained of their low wages " considering the heat and slavery of their work " compared with " cooler trades."

(e) There were about eight hundred persons employed in the glass trade, divided among sixty-one or sixty-two glasshouses.

(f) Two-thirds of the total English output was made in London.

(g) Glasses were sold to the public either by weight or by number.

The short history of the tax proved its folly. Towards the end of 1697 a Committee of the House of Commons was appointed to consider the complaints of the glassmakers and to report upon them. It examined both owners and workmen from the chief centres of the manufacture ; from London an old workman, John Judges, Captain Gutheridge, William Hull, and the clerk of the Gutheridge glassworks, William Buck, but the most important witness was William Jackson, one of the largest owners in

---

[1] *Tracts*, No. 114.   [2] John Cary's phrase (1695).

London and leader of one of the joint-stock companies. He testified that the tax had lessened the output of glass, and that in consequence he and his partners had been obliged to abandon their flint glasshouse at King's Lynn. This evidence was supported by the owner of the St. Mary Overies glasshouse, a certain Jones, and by representatives from Stourbridge (Ananias Henzey and Elisha Batchelour), from the Gloucester area, which was then a centre of bottle-making (Baldwyn), and from the North Country (Broome and Middleton). There was a general unanimity that the glass manufactures had been seriously interrupted by the tax, and the Committee gave its verdict that the industry was in danger and the duty of small profit to the King. On 1 August, 1698, only three years after the imposition, the amount of the duty was reduced by one-half. By that time the French war had ended with the Peace of Ryswick (1697), and the preamble to the repeal (9 William III, c. 45) sheepishly admitted the glassmakers' main point, that the rates were exorbitant and that the petitioners themselves were " discouraged " by them. A year later, by the Act of 4 May, 1699, the entire duty was withdrawn (1 August, 1699). Thereafter the flint-glass industry suffered no impediment for forty-seven years, and prospered

> durus ut ilex tonsa bipennibus
> nigræ feraci frondis in Algido
> per damna per caedes ab ipso
> ducit opes animumque ferro.

Eighty years later the French chemist Paul Bosc d'Antic gives an admirable account of the causes of its success. He wrote with detachment, and as we might expect, condemns English glass as " beaucoup trop lourd "; any fool, he implies, can overcharge his metal with lead oxide. Some of the conditions to which he refers date only from the middle of the 18th century, but much of what he says explains the growth and vitality of the art which was now born :

Les verreries angloises ont une grande reputation. Elles ne sont pas fort anciennes.[1] Leurs progrès rapides sont dû à l'attention singulière du gouvernement de ne pas leur donner des entraves, à ne pas confondre l'interêt du public avec celui du particulier. Les glaces, le crystal, le verre blanc et commun, forment aujóurd'hui une branche consider-able du commerce de la Grande Bretaigne. L'étranger consomme les quatre-cinquièmes des glaces angloises. Il n'est point de pays où les Anglois ne trouvent moyen d'intro-duire leurs ouvrages de crystal et de verre. Autrefois ils tiroient de France presque tout le verre dont ils avoient besoin ; aujourd'hui ils nous fournissent des lustres, des lanternes, de verres à boire, etc. . . . Quelque florissantes que soient leurs verreries les Anglois ne doivent se flatter avec John Cary[2] qu'elles soient portées à la plus haute perfection. Leur crystal n'est pas d'une belle couleur ; il tire sur le jaune ou sur le brun pour peu que la couleur rouge de la manganese domine. Il est si mal cuit qu'il ressue le sel, se crassit, se rouille promptement, est remplit des points nebuleux. (1760.)

[1] The allusion here is to a period of about eighty years, short time by comparison with the antiquity of the art in Venice, Germany, and even in France.
[2] *Essay on Trade*, 1695.

THE AGE OF DESIGN

La découverte du flint glass est entièrement due à la grande Bretagne. Celui qui s'y fabrique presentement (1780) est fort éloigné de la perfection dont je le crois susceptible ; on pourroit même dire que les anglois ont presque perdu tous les fruits de la découverte. . . . Il est très rare de trouver chez eux du flint glass que ne soit infecté de graisse, de points blancs, de fils, et qui ne soit neigeux. . . .[1] (1780.)

Il est aisé de prévoir que l'art de la verrerie fera en Angleterre des progrès plus rapides que dans aucune partie du monde. La richesse de ces insulaires, la patriotisme qu'ils portent jusqu'à l'enthousiasme, la bonne qualité et l'abondance de leur chaux de plomb, de leur potasse et de leur charbon de terre ; la facilité des transports par les canaux qu'ils ont si fort multipliés et par les rivières qu'ils ont rendues presque toutes navigables et surtout la société des arts, établissement fort au dessus de tous nos éloges, association vraiment digne de la Grande Bretagne, sans cesse occupé de la perfection des arts utiles, et qui dépense chaque année pour leur encouragement 100,000 livres de notre monnaie ; tous ces avantages inestimables ne nous permettent pas de douter que cet art important ne soit promptement porté par les Anglois au plus haut point de perfection.[2]

§ 3. THE DETERMINATION OF STYLE

Let us turn now from the economy of the art to the art itself and examine the factors which determined so individual a style. They are three in number, the teachers, the material, and the pupils themselves. Venice at home, and still more Venice in exile, taught the English the *technique* of glassmaking ; and by that word we may understand not primarily the chemical conditions of glass, not the nature of this ingredient or that and the results of their intermixture, but the technique of *manipulation.* Mansell proved that the composition of glass was not a difficult task, still less the grave secret which Venice had tried so long to keep to herself : only enterprise and capital were required to bring the best materials together. The harder thing was to teach strange hands the art of handling a material whose sympathy was so elusive, whose moments of aptitude were so brief. The use of a few simple tools and their application to the molten metal was the most important lesson that England learned from her Venetian immigrants. In Venetian glass manipulation was everything. The thin, emulsive metal demanded a nimble hand and an ingenious brain ; and conversely the brain and the hand learnt to delight in their own triumphs of ingenuity. Venetian glass has its own formal endeavour independent of mere technique and related generally to the disposition of the Renaissance, but throughout that endeavour it remained always an art of dexterity ; cleverness was what chiefly determined its style. But the English were not clever, and they steadfastly refused to assimilate Venetian manners ; instead they made a style to suit their own technical capacity, which was not artistically inferior because it happened to be less accomplished and less elaborate. It is true that late in the 17th century and for

[1] This description of 18th-century metal is singularly accurate ; *cf.* App. I.
[2] *Œuvres*, Vol. I, pp. 161–2. The memoir on glassmaking dates from 1760, the supplementary notes from 1780. For other criticisms by this writer see pp. 150–1 and Plate CXL.

some time afterwards the English glassmakers largely depended on Venetian shapes and Venetian modes of ornament, but it was fortunate for the later development of flint glass that they never did more than imitate them, that they never made them their own or mastered the intricacies of *latticinio* and *millifiori*. In that case there would have been no English glass, but only another tedious version of *façon de Venise*. The presence of Venetian traits in the earliest flint glass is perhaps the most conspicuous fact about it, but they are nevertheless apt to be deceptive. They have nothing to do with English style, for they are only pupillary exploits, the fussy penmanship which a child writes in his copy-book before he develops a hand of his own. The Venetians were good masters not because they taught England how to write, but because England learnt from them how to hold the pen.

The second factor which formed the English style was the lead metal. Its discovery by Ravenscroft is of just the same importance for the art in England as the perfection of *cristallo* by the Berovieri in the decade 1450–60, and it is equally difficult in each case to say whether the new medium ordered a revolution in style or responded to it. The stiff and ponderous lead metal was not apt to be treated delicately and this quality suited the prentice hands of the English glassmakers as well as the more austere taste of their customers. But there is sufficient evidence to show that the lead metal was not solely responsible for the change in style. Before ever it was invented it was the custom of the London Glass Sellers to send to Venice for the finest glasses in their stock, but they did not choose to acquiesce in the Venetian repertory of shapes and styles. They sent their own specifications to Venice, and a set of these drawings which has been preserved shows the way in which English taste was beginning to modify the traditional shapes of Venice even before the nature of the lead metal had begun to assert itself. These designs were ordered from a Venetian firm, that of Antonio Morelli between 1668 and 1672, by one of the most important London glass merchants, John Greene.[1] The modification in style was due partly to selection, and in some few instances to actual simplification of a familiar type. Greene chose the simpler and more distinctly useful shapes among the types then current in Venetian glass and in *façon de Venise*. He avoided, for example, the larger and more impressive goblets, covered glasses with elaborate " bird-

---

[1] His name occurs in the minute books of the Glass-sellers Company from 1664, the year of its foundation, until 1702. He was Renter Warden in 1671 and 1672, Upper Warden in 1673, and Master in 1679. The designs are preserved in the British Museum, and though they are in places badly drawn, one over another, they show very clearly the state of glass design in England at that time. Some of them were published by Hartshorne, but the best selection is given in Percival (M.), *Old Glass and How to Collect it*.

For some of the most important types, prospectively considered, see Fig. 16 and *cf.* Plates XLIII, XLV. The correspondence between Greene and Morelli is preserved in Sloane MS. 857 and was abstracted by Hartshorne, pp. 440 *et seq.*

knobs " and glasses with extravagant serpent stems of filigree twist; and even in the plainer wine-glasses his tendency was to omit rings and rims and put his faith in a purely linear design (*cf*. Fig. 16). As far as our evidence goes this disposition was even more apparent in the glasses made in England before the coming of the lead flux; a few fragmentary English glasses[1] which do not contain lead, but must be dated about 1675, show in most marked degree the tendency to simplify the design and fill out the body of the glass. Greene and his contemporaries in fact domesticated the design of " state " glasses. The prudence which led them to do so was part of their taste, for frangible pieces would have left them æsthetically unhappy; and such a taste was already formed, already evident, before the lead metal provided its opportunity. Thirty years later, in the hey-day of the art, the very brilliance of the metal made for simplicity; for the great balusters were self-sufficient in their splendour, and only a fussy vitality could wish to spoil their surface with ornament. That was one of the reasons why English glassmaking waited so long for cutting, the final exploitation of the lead metal.

And thus the third factor in the determination of flint glass was English taste. This sense of agreeable form does not mean that there was any transcendental affinity between the working of the minds of Englishmen and the particular curves or contrasts or proportions in which they found delight. It means simply that their character was necessarily evident in their works. Flint glass, for all its catalogue of factories and glassmen, was always an anonymous expression, an art without artists; that was its virtue and its limitation. The public which consumed the flint glasses made the chief contribution to its style, and being thus determined by an unspoken agreement between the makers and the users, it may claim to represent the character of the English and the spirit of its age more vividly and more truthfully than arts of higher station which are vested in the endeavours of a school or the idiosyncrasies of individual men. The names of glassmakers may be sought and found in dead records, but the discovery is not relevant to the art because the art is itself unsigned. It is well that it should be. For a work that is signed or which signs itself stands for one man and not for all. On occasion it may rise beyond collective endeavour, but it is apt to fall into a narrower grade.

At the time when flint glass was " brought to perfection " England had been not long released from an exacting morality which was hostile to the arts because, like the baited bear, they afforded pleasure. There is a danger of neglecting the influence of Puritanism in the livelier culture which succeeded it. For Puritanism implied much more than a

---

[1] *E.g.* the Northampton fragment (Fig. 18, A), the Oxford fragment (Fig. 18, B), one fragment in the London Museum, and one of the decanter bottles in Mr. C. Kirkby Mason's collection (Plate IX).

frigid pedantry of conduct or a body of fanatical dogma. By the Roundhead excesses is Puritanism chiefly remembered, but they were the excesses not of a religious complexion but of the blood which fed it. Puritanism was less a faith than a disposition, carried into religious courses by the strength of the Protestant reaction. It was the English representation of a gothic spirit which had slumbered fitfully in Northern Europe throughout the hard gaiety of the Renaissance. For a time it set itself in a political framework, but when the Commonwealth collapsed and royalty sat again upon the throne, the prudence and reason of Puritanism, baulked of their expression in morality and custom, found vent in the æsthetic responses of a culture which seemed to have forgotten it. English sensibility had been quickened by contact with the energetic art of the later Renaissance, and it was now to be joined with the sobriety of a Puritan æsthetic. Puritanism was not submerged by the arts and manners which came into their own at the Restoration ; still less did it impose upon them like a tyrant. It expressed itself through the arts, and especially through the useful arts, as it had formerly expressed itself in a republican politic or a regulative morality. The prudence of affairs, the duty of morality, the reason of science gained an æsthetic connotation in architecture and furniture, and extended the field of taste beyond the terms of mere sensibility. The eye could only find delight where restraint was unbroken and reason satisfied ; and it was due to this demand that a temperate and intelligible design remains the chief character of 18th-century art. Puritanism thus broadened the basis of taste, and in doing so gave to English design an exquisite moderation which preserved the useful arts from the more reckless manifestations of the baroque and the rococo in other European countries. That quality, and not the dregs of the Renaissance, entitles the arts of the 18th century to be called classical. They lost in splendour and ingenious energy : they gained in dignity and grace. Flint-glass design was a notable example of this influence. The age, which produced it was acutely sensitive to the visual world and had a mind that was always vigorous in design, but both for the makers and the users the prudence of a glass was a condition of its being beautiful. To be well made, to be serviceable, to be sightly—those were the requirements of the useful arts ; sightliness took its place among the other values, and by so doing it became the greatest of them all. For sightliness meant beauty of material, a substance that was physically agreeable to the eye, but beyond that it needed a design neither palpable nor obscure which quickened the intellect but left it serene. Flint glass was above all a " good " glass, and that epithet implies an æsthetic in which there was no partition of prudence and fancy, of sensibility and sense. Such an integrity of experience, more evident perhaps in the arts of the 18th century than in its life, is what assimilates that epoch to the spirit of the Middle Ages.

THE AGE OF DESIGN

Having seen how English glassmaking was an economy, and how also it was an art with a spirit of its own, we may now turn to the anatomy of its style. The explanation must be in terms of origin and sequence. The art cannot be understood if we neglect the items of style from which it was construed, and chronology is only an attempt to state the evolution of its style.

§ 4. THE ANATOMY OF STYLE

It is perhaps unfortunate that wine-glasses, because most numerous in survival, have so often been considered the sole product of the art. A wine-glass is certainly an æsthetic unit, but it is not a stylistic unit. The art is not the art of making wine-glasses, not even the art of making *stemmed vessels* to which category wine-glasses, salvers, middle-stands, candlesticks, sweetmeat glasses, and some jelly glasses belong, nor again the art of making vessels such as bowls, plates, tumblers, and others which stand on a low foot or their own bottom. The art of glass and the style of that art extend to all these nominal types; and if we trace the evolution of style in any one of them, *i.e.*, as is usually done, in wine-glasses, there is a danger not only of restricting our analysis, but of treating the utilitarian shape as if it were a stylistic unit. A stemmed vessel may be combined of several stylistic units or features, of which one is pure Venetian, another pure German, another some private idiom of England; if it were, for example, a sweetmeat glass it might conceivably have a double-ogee bowl with Venetian threads round its middle and a gadrooned Venetian base, a mixed baluster and Silesian stem with an air twist, and a domed foot with arched cutting. Such a glass is of course an impossibility, but it illustrates the principles of any chronological verdict. If it came before us we should have to consider not the position of the sweetmeat glass in the history of glass-style (which is often impossible in far less extreme cases), but the chronological limits of its several stylistic features; and only by comparing these *termini ad quem* and *termini a quo* would it be possible to find a range of years for the glass itself. Again we might compare that stylistic dating with what we know of the sweetmeat glass as a utilitarian shape, the date, *e.g.*, when sweetmeats were eaten, or the date when glasses were first used to hold them. Finally, if we were very bold we might consider how the quality of the metal affected our judgment.

Such being the method of dating a specimen, it follows that we must first consider *features*, their exits and their entrances, as far as they can be ascertained. We have therefore tried to draw up·a list of those which seem to have a place in stylistic history, eschewing such capricious variations as " double-glasses " or " ear-rings." Stemmed vessels have been taken as the norm because there is little in bowls and such-like pieces which cannot be found in the bowls of goblets or sweetmeats. The list is

[163]

arranged according to the nationalities from which the features were derived, and according to the three parts of a stemmed vessel—stem, bowl, and foot.

A. VENETIAN ITEMS

The Venetian influence on English style was of two kinds, decorative and formal. At the time of Ravenscroft's invention there were a number of Venetians and other Italian glassmakers established in England, of whom the Dagnia family of Bristol and Newcastle-on-Tyne and Ravenscroft's assistant Da Costa are among the best known. These men formed a distinct body among the London glassmakers and were known as the " foreign Artist Glassmakers." As such they were a superior race to the poor workmen who complained of the heat and poverty of their trade, and they no doubt commanded a higher wage. In the provinces, if we may go by the history of the Dagnia brothers, some of these men must have set up glasshouses of their own, and as their wares were not at first flint glass there may be some few of them who were not counted by John Houghton in 1696. But in London, where the glasshouses at the end of the 17th century can be fairly exactly accounted for, the Venetian metics must have worked in the service of English owners ; for in the list of glasshouses already given there are no Italian names. These Venetians, therefore, did not work by themselves, but in the constant company of Englishmen. In each glasshouse there seem to have been two or three chairs,[1] and at the end of the 17th century it is likely that one of these was controlled by a Venetian " Artist " with an English servitor and foot-maker, while the two or more remaining chairs were entirely staffed by Englishmen.[2] In the average glasshouse at the end of the 17th century we must therefore conceive of one or two Italian " artists " at the same furnace, working with Englishmen, and teaching Englishmen the art of manipulation ; but the master adhered to his own style while the pupils developed theirs. So much preface is necessary for understanding the distinctive manner which Mr. Francis Buckley has aptly termed the " parallel Venetian tradition."

[1] In 1674 Ravenscroft had two chairs in his Savoy glasshouse each controlled by a master glassmaker. The number had increased to three in 1677. See the first (surviving) *Agreement* with the Glass Sellers, 5 September, 1674, and the renewed *Agreement* dated 29 May, 1677.
[2] There can scarcely have been more than one Venetian chair in each factory. For if we assume, as I think we may, a proportional survival, the output of " Venetian " flint glass must have been much less than a third of the whole. Two of Ravenscroft's three chairs must have been run by Italians, for in 1673-4 he is known to have had two Italian assistants (Da Costa and Vicenzo), but this was probably exceptional even as early as 1675, and the distribution of flint glass dating from *c.* 1700 between the two styles makes it probable that English master glassmakers were then in a majority. For Da Costa see Plot, *u.s.*, and for Vicenzo, Schuermans, *Bulletin*, XXX, 75.

For in a strict sense it was a parallel and not an *isolated* tradition ; " Venetian " flint glass and " English " flint glass proceeded from neighbouring chairs fed by the same furnace, and the Venetian master at his chair produced the style to which he had been accustomed as nearly as the lead metal would permit. The covered goblet illustrated in Plate XXX. 2 shows how nearly he succeeded and disposes of the theory that the English style was solely determined by the lead metal. There was no conflict between the two manners, the one sanctioned by a superb tradition, the other radical and utilitarian, for they had their counterparts in the public taste. " Venice glasses " had long ago won themselves a regular demand, and if they could be well made at home they were still fit for ceremonies. Likewise the " English " flint glasses, being so well-wearing and strong, must soon be assured of a general market.

The parallel Venetian tradition is most evident at the beginning of the 18th century, but it continued at least as late as 1750, as long, that is to say, as there were still Venetians left in the English glasshouses. We hear very little of Venetian immigrants in the middle of the century. And their style disappeared with them. There is this difference between the " parallel Venetian tradition " in England and the Venetian influence in English glass. The former made use of all the devices by which glass could be used to decorate itself ; the latter was chiefly evident in pure design. The modification of Venetian form will be treated in a moment ; we shall refer here to the Venetian features which are for the most part features of decoration, and though some one or other of them is often found in " English " flint glass, they proceed as a whole from the Venetian " Artists."

1. *Gadrooning.*

(*a*) *Spiked gadrooning* (Plates XVIII, XXXVI. *b*). This mode of ornament was proper to a fine, thin metal and does not occur in English glass after the 17th century. It is more common in *façon de Venise* than in Venetian glass, and probably came to England by way of the Netherlands (*cf*. W. Buckley, Plate 55A). There is reason to suppose that it was in vogue in English *façon de Venise* before the advent of lead glass,[1] but being a trick only suited to an emulsive metal, it did not long survive in lead glass. Even before 1700 it is not common, and generally occurs as a border round the lower half of a wine-glass bowl. It is most familiar in a distinct series of wine-glasses with a winged or very occasionally a wrythen stem (Plates XXVI. 1, XXXVI. *b*. 2).

[1] This feature is found in one of Greene's designs (Fig. 16, F) and in two early glasses at South Kensington : (*a*) a wine-glass (*c*. 1685) of lead metal with a hollow stem, lacking the upper part of the bowl, and (*b*) a wine-glass of rough soda metal with an urn stem (middle of 17th century). The former certainly dates from *c*. 1685 and the other glass seems to be an earlier version of the same device. The shape of the bowl is similar in both glasses.

(*b*) *Rounded gadrooning* (Plate XI. 1 and many later examples) is full and massive even in Venetian metal and was one of the Venetian devices which developed well in glass of lead. It is probably the type of ornament which Ravenscroft described as " ribbed " in his specifications to the Glass Sellers and it is found in several of his marked glasses. An early instance in which the gadroons approximate a Venetian type may be seen in the jug in the Rees Price collection (Plate XX. 2). Rounded gadroons were executed by blowing into a shallow mould fluted for the purpose, and usually occur round the lower part of a wine-glass, bowl, or other vessel ; they are found also on covers (Plate XIX) and on feet. They grew bigger and fuller as the lead metal developed and became in due course an entirely English feature, being found in all the better kinds of glass from the 17th century until the end of the 18th century. In wine-glasses gadrooning is usually a mark of very early date ; tankards are the vessels in which it occurs most frequently in the middle and latter part of the century.

(*c*) *Wrythen gadroons*, by which are to be understood a series of spiral twists on the body of a glass, are common in several types of small wine-glasses until about 1750 (Plate XXXV. 1). The wrything was done by twisting the paraison while it was being blown[1] and is characteristically exhibited in certain families of ale-glasses (*cf*. Plate LXV) ; in some of these it extends, like spiked gadrooning, about half-way up the bowl and ends on the upper side in wings or in flammiform projections (Plate LXV. 3). *Cf*. p. 169. Wrythen work of a rather similar sort was much in vogue in the Netherlands and especially at Liège ; the English covered bowl seen in Plate LXXIV shows how beautiful it might be when it was extended to the entire surface of a vessel. A wrythen flute (" ale-glass ") in the Guild-hall Museum which must be dated soon after 1681 is perhaps the earliest extant specimen of this ornament in lead glass (Plate XXXV. 1). This ornament at least in its early manifestation is so closely connected with *façon de Venise* that it has been included here among the Venetian items rather than under the influence of the Netherlands to which it more properly belongs.

2. *Ornament " nipt diamond waies "* was a development of gadrooning and, as will be evident from Fig. 7, was executed by pinching together the moulded gadroons into diamond-shaped compartments, this process in-volving a re-heating of the vessel (Plates X. 1, XXXI. 1, XXXIV, etc.). Like the last feature it came to England from the Netherlands (Plate IX is a Netherlandish shape), but in effect it belongs to " Venetian " style in flint glass, and as such is included here. Ravenscroft very aptly gave it a name and it appears in one of his marked glasses, the bottle at the British Museum (Plate X. 1). It is especially common in the first twenty or thirty years of flint glass, but disappears about the middle of the 18th century.

[1] I am not prepared to say that wrything was never moulded.

3. *Pearl ornament* is rather similar in appearance to the last, but differs from it in being produced entirely by blowing into a mould without the aid of subsequent " nipping." The compartments formed are usually much smaller than the nipped diamonds and may be round or oval in shape (Plate LXVII. *b.* 2). It is perhaps the kind of decoration which Ravenscroft called " purlee," but as it does not occur in any of Ravenscroft's glass, I have tentatively suggested another reference for that word (p. 128). Not only bowls, but covers, feet, and in one instance that has come to my notice even a stem, were treated in this manner. Where the design of a vessel is good its beauty is greatly enhanced by " pearls " (Plate LXXV. 1), and before flint glass was cut it was perhaps the most effective mode of " displaying " the metal. Some indeed of the motives in cutting, notably flat diamond facets (Plate CXXVIII), seem to be taken from the moulded pearl ornament which preceded them. Mr. Clements has a goblet (*c.* 1720) in which the moulded diamond compartments are quite flat and smooth, and strongly resemble the diamond facets of cut-glass. Glasses decorated with " pearls " were called *verres fresés*, or pock-marked glasses, in the Netherlands and were extensively made at Liège early in the 18th century. In England pearled glasses like those in Plate LXX. 2 belong to the first quarter of the 18th century ; but there is a series of small wine-glasses with pearled bowls and thin stems, *e.g.* in Mr. Bacon's collection, which may well be twenty years later in date.

4. *Trailing* is the term usually applied to looped threads of glass carried round the body of a vessel in a horizontal sense, and less frequently round the cover or the foot (Plates XVIII, XX, XXII). It occurs in the Ravenscroft-Bishopp family (Plate XIII) and the term " purlee " in the price list perhaps refers to it. The 17th-century use of that word (given on p. 128) fits it exactly ; and as none of the existing Ravenscroft pieces have *pearled* ornament I am inclined to prefer the interpretation of the word as a metaphor from needlework rather than as a spelling of *pearled*. The motive was best suited to a thin metal and went out of general use early in the 18th century, but in tankards and in some ceremonial glasses of the " parallel Italian tradition " it is still found as late as the middle of the century, and in illustrations of earlier types it may occur as late as 1800. In the late 17th century it is often associated with gadrooned or " nipt diamond waies " borders.

5. *Simple threading* is perhaps the oldest and easiest ornament in the whole history of glassmaking. Almost every technique has made use of it, but in England it is chiefly associated with the Venetian influence. It is commonest in the first half of the 18th century, and was especially used as a border round the rim of a tankard (Plate LXXVIII), in which context it continues until about 1760. The small mug illustrated in Plate LXXX. 1 shows its happy effects in a more elaborate use, but such a repeating series

of threads is due to the Netherlands rather than to Venice; similar elaborate threading is frequently found in Netherlandish glasses.

6. *Prunts* are one of the few features which Venice seems to have borrowed from Germany. They are round applied buttons, often with the surface moulded strawberry fashion, and were originally a utilitarian device for improving the grip of a stem. They appear in English glass in two distinct uses. Before the expansion of German glassmaking and its influence in England they had already appeared in English modifications of the Netherlandish-German *Roemer*. Greene ordered this ornament from Venice (Fig. 16, L) and they are not infrequent in English rummers of late 17th-century date (Plate XXXIX. 2), but they tend to disappear as the bucket-stem of the *Roemer* became a knopped stem solid all through (Plate XXXIX. 1). In green flint glass, made in imitation of the *Roemer*, they continue until perhaps 1730. Mr. Berney has an interesting document (Plate C. *a*. 4) in which a prunted rummer stem is combined with an enamel twist, but this must be regarded as something of a freak.

7. *Serpent formation* is highly characteristic of Venetian glass of the 17th century, and was very freely used in Dutch and German *façon de Venise*. In all these techniques the twisted ropes of glass which composed it were sometimes of plain glass and sometimes of white and coloured filigree. The extreme rarity of this feature in English flint glass is a fact of considerable importance as far as its style is concerned. It was used both for stems (Plate XXVIII) and very occasionally for the handle of a covered vessel, as in Mr. Bles's large covered punch-bowl (Plate XXXIV). It was inevitable that a formation so characteristic of Venice should be attempted wherever Venetian artists were at work, but it was much too elaborate either for English skill or English metal, and it may be doubted whether any instances of it were actually made by English hands. The serpent glasses illustrated in Plates XIX, XXVIII, XXX, XXXIV are all lead glass and show how the delicacy of the Venetian stems was modified by the thicker material, but they are perhaps not less satisfactory from an æsthetic standpoint. They must be attributed to Venetian master workmen using lead metal in one of the London glasshouses, and they can scarcely be later than the 17th century. In particular, Mr. Bles's covered goblet is of very thin lead glass and probably dates from *c.* 1681. The same collector's large punch-bowl, in which serpentation is used for the handle, exhibits the same essentials of style, but the metal is not only much more bulky, but contains a much greater quantity of lead; for that reason it may be placed about ten years later, 1690–5. Mr. Clements's serpent glass (*E.I.G.*, Fig. 5) has not much lead and is roughly contemporary with Mr. Bles's covered goblet. The British Museum covered goblet is dated much later, but the glass is probably twenty or thirty years earlier than the inscription (Plate XXX. 1).

8. *Wings* seem to be primarily a Netherlandish feature which was used in " Venetian " flint glass. They may occur to the number of four round the upper part of a wine-glass stem, but they are found occasionally in a circuit round the lower part of the bowl. Winged glasses were certainly not made after the 17th century, and are usually rough in quality and workmanship. The wing itself is not difficult to do, being executed simply by drawing out the hot metal with pincers. On that account I incline to regard them as early attempts at elaboration by English workmen. The Venetian master workmen would have done much better both in idea and execution. Plates XXVI. 1, XXVII. 1, 2.

9. *Folded rims.* See p. 209 below.

The disappearance of these features was the negative determination of style in flint glass. Venice had a fine emulsive metal capable of every finesse, England a heavy treacle. The Venetian influence in England was therefore a survival of the fittest, the retention of those elements in Venetian glass, for example bowl-forms, which went well with the new metal and the gradual elimination of ornaments and devices which were unsuited to the quality of her metal, the skill of her glassmakers, or the taste of the English public.

B. GERMAN INFLUENCE

It was perhaps due to natural antipathy that Germany showed greater independence of Venice than any other European country, and if we postpone for a moment the ancillary art of engraving, the three important features which she contributed to English glass were entirely her own invention.

1. The *Roemer* form (Plate XVI) was an indigenous product of the *Waldglas* manufacture in Southern Germany (p. 12). It was very frequently adapted in the Netherlands, in Scandinavia and even at Venice, and *Roemers* were among the shapes ordered from Morelli by John Greene (Fig. 16, L). Its progeny in England may be divided into two main types.

(*a*) Large goblets of white flint glass sometimes ten or twelve inches in height with a big round bowl gadrooned about the base. In this type we may notice the following stages in the modification of the form.

1. Hollow stems have prunts in the outside and open into the bowl as the bucket-stem opened into the bowl of the original *Roemer*.

2. The stems still hollow and prunted but divided from the upper bowl (Plate XXXIX. 2).

3. Hollow stems, divided from the upper bowl, *without* prunts, thus forming a straight hollow cylinder of glass.

4. The prunted " bucket " of the *Roemer* is now reduced to a *solid* stem ; Plate LV. *a.* 2 has only a slight air cavity.

5. The big spherical bowl then forsakes its rather dull companion No. 4 and is combined with stem types which were not of German origin at all (Plates XXXIX. 1, XL. 1), but had been developed in great variety by England under the influence of Venice ; such were the inverted baluster, the knop-and-baluster (plain or wrythen), and several of the later and degenerate balustroid types common about 1730.

The general effect of this evolution was that the spheroid bowl survived as an independent item, which in the middle of the 18th century was combined with any of the stem-forms then in vogue. *Large* goblets which declare their *Roemer* ancestry usually belong to the late 17th and early 18th century. For the later descendants of the *Roemer* we must turn to

(*b*) Smaller wine-glasses usually six or seven inches in height and made either in green flint glass, which seems to be a direct imitation of the naturally green *Waldglas* of the archetype, or in ordinary white flint glass. As far as form is concerned the stages of departure from the original are much the same as in the big goblets, but straight or balustroid stems wrythen spirally seem to be confined to the smaller glasses. The colour of the green imitations varies from a pale hue little deeper than the original *Waldglas* green to the rich, pure colouring seen in green Bristol flint glass dating from the second half of the century (Plate C ; *cf.* p. 215).

The origin of these features belongs essentially to the 17th century and is distinct from the influence of German forms which found their way into Western Europe with the expansion of the Bohemian glass industry at the beginning of the 18th century.[1] Their arrival in England cannot usually be dated before the accession of George I in 1714, but there is evidence to show that not only were several kinds of German glasses being imported before that date, but that German glassworkers had taken up a livelihood in England. In 1709 a great quantity of very fine German cut and carved glasses, including jellies, wine and water tumblers, beer- and wine-glasses with covers, and several other kinds, had lately been imported and were put up for sale in London.[2] But the Glass Sellers were naturally indignant, and they made a disturbance at the auction, so that the sale could not be completed and the goods were sold off to the public

---

[1] Hartshorne, p. 40. I am inclined to think that the Hanoverian accession has been rather over-estimated as an explanation of the Teutonism in English glass. The funda- mental causes were : (*a*) the great prosperity of the South German and Bohemian glass- making at the end of the 17th century and the export of its products into Western Europe led to its style being copied in the Netherlands, France, and England ; and (*b*) German and Bohemian glassmakers left home in considerable numbers and settled in those countries. For this point *cf. Tracts*, No. 121 (*c.* 1696) : "As there are continually new manufactures of glass setting up in the northern parts of Europe, particularly Muscovy, Hamburgh, Prussia, etc., it is necessary also to regulate the duties in foreign glass imported so that foreigners may not be enabled to undersell us both at home and abroad."

[2] *London Gazette*, 1 October, 1709.

at very low rates.[1] The trade can scarcely have been of very recent growth, for in 1701 the Government placed a duty of £20 a hundredweight on imported glass[2] and thus made some restitution to the Glass Sellers for its meddling conduct in 1695–9. Moreover, as early as 1706 a German glassmaker, a certain T. Meyer, had established himself at the Bird Cage in Long Acre and was making " new fashion crystall Bird Glasses "[3] and in the first decade of the century we have notices of several artists who made animals, birds, and other figures on glasses and are as likely to be German as Venetian. It is probable therefore that the German influence had begun to assert itself in the style of flint glass several years at least before the accession of the House of Hanover to the English throne. It is chiefly evident at this period in stem formation and bowl formation.

2. *German stem formation.* The shouldered stem is commonly known as " Silesian," but it is certainly not exclusive to that part of Germany. It was a column of glass with a projecting shoulder at the top and reeded sides tapering towards the base. Its ground plan was roughly a polygon of from four to eight sides ; the corners at the top were sometimes plain but more usually surmounted by a small boss of varying design. When the sides were four the shoulder often took the form of four arches supporting a plain dome ; glasses of this type had a rounded funnel bowl, a straight funnel bowl or a thistle bowl (*i.e.* a bowl in which the hollow part was set upon a solid sphere of glass). The lower part of the shouldered stem usually tapered into the foot without interruption, but glasses are occasionally found in which the shouldered stem passes into a small knop just above the foot (*c.* 1715) or is encircled at that point by double or treble rings. The German stem had a good many variants and it was used for all kinds of stemmed vessels, not wine-glasses only, but goblets open and covered, sweetmeat glasses, candlesticks, salvers, middle-stands, fruit-dishes, and the like. Very occasionally we find an inverted German stem, and tall pieces often have a double stem, the shouldered half being inversely superimposed upon the other, either directly or by the interception of a knop. It is commonest in the second and third decades of the century.

[1] *Ibid.*, 18 October, 1709.
[2] The *Mercator*, No. 13 (1713) referring to the date 1701.
[3] *Post Man*, 12 February, 1706–7. The bird-glasses can be identified with a number of fragments in the Guildhall Museum and elsewhere. They consisted of a trough for the bird-seed projecting from the base of a pedestal. The latter was surmounted by a portrait head in a " hat that was shaped of the Ramillie Cock " (see Plate LXXXII). The specimen there illustrated and several other fragments are known to be lead glass. A portrait head similar to those of the bird-glasses is found on one or two covered goblets of this period, *e.g.* a glass illustrated in Buckley, Plate VII, which cannot be later than 1714 (by reason of a coin in the stem) and probably belongs to that year. The portraits are not very precise, but represent several different persons both male and female. The portrait on the glass illustrated by Mr. Buckley appears to be that of the first Duke of Marlborough.

It was eclipsed at the height of the decorative period (*c.* 1750) when stems were made very light and thin, but it flourished again very effectively towards the end of the century. It will be seen later (Plate CV. 1) how it was modified by the use of cutting. No one would deny that it was absorbed by an English style, for it never seems to be a mere imitation ; but its armoured angularity was a bit of Teutonic thinking which would never have occurred in a romance glassmaker, and throughout the 18th century it remains a token of the German kings on the English throne and the German element in English culture.

     3. *German bowl formation.* The bowl form which England adopted and adapted from Venice was an outline of straight sides or a moderate curvature. The German bowls introduced between (say) 1705 and 1715 showed an opposite tendency. The outline was much more frequently concave or incurved, and even where part of the bowl was concave the outline as a whole was broken into curves of different character. Not all the German bowls which came to England were of this sort ; there was, for example, a big ungainly bucket bowl[1] (Plate XLVI. 2) which seemed to be due to German rather than to Venetian influence. But the general tendency to incurve the bowl was certainly due to Germany.[2] Incurvature quite changed the character of the design in glasses in which it was admitted, for it implied a scheme of divergences in place of a scheme of approximations ; incurved bowls were difficult to combine in a harmonious design with the baluster stem, and that fact probably contributed to the disintegration of the simple balusters.[3] The " broken " or incurved bowls evident in the period with which we are now dealing may be analysed thus :

     (*a*) *The large double-ogee.* Some glasses of this type must be dated as early as *c.* 1690, for they are combined with a stem nearly as short in

---

    [1] Square bucket-bowls rounded at the base were in fact made at Venice and even ordered by Greene *c.* 1670, but they were not among the most characteristic Venetian shapes. In England their vogue does not precede the German influence, and their similarity to the large bowls, ogee at the base, which were common *c.* 1760, and their incidence in *covered* goblets makes it probable that they were suggested by imported German glasses (Plates CXVI, CXXIV).

    [2] The only exceptions to this were the glasses with drawn stems which were quite certainly due to Venetian influence (Plate XLV), but here the incurvature of the bowl was almost a technical necessity. Drawn stems, both the thick type (Plate XLVI) and the thin (Plate XLV), precede the German influence ; there is record of a short, thick, drawn stem dated 1696, and the tall, thin specimens were certainly an earlier stage. This adaptation is another instance in which " prudence " and the lead metal caused an alteration in Venetian design (*cf.* p. 161 above).

    [3] The disintegration of the baluster (evident in what Mr. G. R. Francis has called the " light balusters ") preceded the Excise of 1745–6 by at least twenty years and must have been due therefore to stylistic necessities. Those necessities seem to have been, (*a*) the gradual lengthening of stem in proportion to bowl, (*b*) the change in bowl curvature. For (*a*) *v. infra*, p. 204.

proportion to the bowl as the stems in some of Greene's specifications (Plates XXVII. 3, XLVIII. 1 ; *cf.* Plate XLIII. *b.* 2, which is certainly a 17th-century glass). The early development of this very effective bowl form is uncertain, but it seems to be traceable in the first instance to the German *Roemer*. The double-ogee, like the *Roemer*, is divisible into the bowl proper and the lower part, or bucket. There was some uncertainty whether the bucket of the *Roemer* was regarded by its imitators as a stem or as part of the bowl. We have seen how it did become a stem, but in another development it belonged to the bowl. The double-ogee glasses are in effect a *Roemer* bowl-and-bucket erected upon one of the romance stems current from 1685 onwards, *e.g.* a disc-knop (Plate XLIX. *b.* 2), a plain baluster or a drop-knop (Plate XLIX. *b.* 1) ; and a comparison of Plate XXVII. 3, a form certainly suggested by the *Roemer*, with Plate XXVII. 2, will explain how this came to pass.

(*b*) *The thistle bowl* is definitely derived from a German bowl which consisted of a straight-sided funnel with a hollow spheroid at its base, but in the English modification the latter became a solid ball of glass (Plate XLIX. *b.* 3). Thistle bowls were usually partnered by their compatriot the shouldered stem, but they are also found with one of the simpler large-knop stems (*e.g.* the mushroom knop, Buckley, Plate XV) or even with a plain baluster.

(*c*) *The bell bowl.* When the break between the funnel and the ball of the last type is very slight the bowl approximates a bell-shape ; but in many bell bowls there is no trace of the ball. Large bell bowls were most frequently made in the second quarter of the 18th century ; some are certainly as early as 1715, but I am not aware that they can ever be dated in the first decade of the century. The stem accompanying these bowls was usually straight or one of the later balustroid types (*c.* 1730). Plates LIII. *b.* 3, LXXXVIII. 3.

(*d*) *The trumpet bowl* in the first quarter of the century is usually the result of a drawn stem, and though it belongs to the category of incurved bowls its origin, as we have seen, is Venetian rather than German (Plates XXXIII. 2, LIII. *b.* 1, XCII, XCVI. 3, etc.).

(*e*) A fifth and quite distinct family of large bowls have no incurvature but are definitely due to German influence. They are rather difficult to define verbally, but may perhaps be labelled the short bucket family ; for their common character lies in two peculiarities ; (*a*) the inclination of the sides is much nearer to the vertical than in the typical rounded-funnel bowls which we have already noticed as the stock English type in the time of Queen Anne, (*b*) their length is shorter in proportion to their width than in the English funnel bowls aforesaid. These two peculiarities give them a squat and tubby look, and among the more gracious expressions of romance form they appear as an undigested Teutonism (Buckley,

Plates XX and XXIII ; Plate XLVI. 2 of this book) ; but that does not mean that they failed to be beautiful in their own home and to their own people.

    4. *Covered goblets.* Goblets with lids were of course frequently made at Venice, ordered by John Greene, and included in Ravenscroft's stock types (*supra*, p. 127), but in the first quarter of the 18th century the fashion for these vessels was due to Germany, where covered drinking-vessels were more commonly used than elsewhere. Covered wine- and beer-glasses were being imported thence in 1709, and apart from this evidence the style of the lids themselves indicates the origin of this feature (*cf.* the following, Plate LXXI. 2, Buckley, Plate VII). But these glasses were chiefly made for ceremonial use.

C. THE INFLUENCE OF THE LOW COUNTRIES

    The features of Netherlandish glass and their influence in England are much more difficult to define. In the 17th century the Netherlands showed a readier pupillage of Italian art than any other European country. Their success was perhaps due to earnest emulation by a bourgeoisie society rather than to any real affinity between the two peoples ; but in the art of glass, as in the arts of painting and pottery, they succeeded in some degree to the position of Italy in the previous century. Antwerp became a second Venice, and *façon de Venise* there had a greater vogue and a more serious attainment than in either Germany or England. The English glassmakers certainly owed a great deal to Antwerp and Liège, but in certain features which are common to the glass of both countries it is not easy to say how much was directly Venetian and how much was Netherlandish embroidery. But in one direction at least we may detect the accentuation of the Low Countries. In the hollow parts of their glass vessels they seem always to have been *afraid of a plain surface.* No other country has so many technical tricks for varying the monotony. *Verres fresés* are perhaps the most conspicuous instance, and there are many other kinds of surface moulding, diamond pattern, fluting, reeding, ribbing, besides the various types of gadrooning proper to Venice. But the plain surface was varied not by applied ornaments but by a modification of the actual metal. The Ravenscroft bottle at the B.M. with its surface " nipt diamond waies " is a convincing instance of this influence in England ; and the quatrefoil stem, so common in the seal period of English glass, was originally hollow, and seems to be derived from the Low Countries rather than from Venice. Pock-marking on English glass is not uncommon in the middle of the 18th century, and there are a great number of small wine-glasses of the decorated period which have faint fluting round the base of the bowl. Both of these are due to Netherlandish influence. Finally the Netherlandish glassmakers were much given to pincered work and to the ropework seen in English fruit-baskets and stands (Plate XCIX. *b*). The *vermicular collar* carried round the stem of a glass, *e.g.* the Ravenscroft rummer in Plate XVI. 1, seems to be due to Netherlandish influence, but in that form it is always a sign of very early date, and even in the 17th-century flint glass it is very rare. Somewhat similar collars were sometimes added to the air-twist and enamel-twist stems in vogue in England 1730–80.

D. FRANCE

The contribution of France to English glassmaking was in men rather than in style; for if origins count for anything the whole of Stourbridge glass must acknowledge the debt. But in the vessels themselves there are very few features which can be identified as of French extraction. There is reason to suppose that the revocation of the Edict of Nantes in 1685 brought an influx of French glassmakers into England; and although these men were occupied with the several sorts of plate glass, it may be that some features of the Poitou and Normandy vessel glass came with them. An ingenious Mr. Grillet who may have been a Frenchman was working in London in 1696 and made " all sorts works enamelled and of glass, different postures of all kinds, animals, Plants, Trees, Flowers and Fruit, together with all manner of representations to the life."[1]

Lacemakers' lamps of the type shown in Plate VIII. 2 were certainly a French type. They are occasionally found in England and such specimens are so unpretentious that it is difficult to believe that they were imported. It may be suggested that the candlestick illustrated, which came to light in Sussex, was made by Frenchmen, presumably Lorrainers working in this country. The two candlesticks in Plate LIV, though they are proved to contain lead, are unlike any flint-glass form and were probably an experiment by a French immigrant who adhered to the French shapes, but made some attempt to copy the English metal. Again there is a distinct family of lamps dating from late 17th or early 18th century (Plate LX[2]) some of which are a heavy potash glass while others are known to be lead glass; and the former class must be either Netherlandish or French. Finally, on Plate LXVIII we illustrate a sweetmeat glass which seems to be a unique form in flint glass, and one of a small family of multiple-knopped glasses which are certainly in a class by themselves. Gerspach (Figs. 101–4) illustrates several similar glasses and ascribes them to Poitou, and the exceptional shapes of the specimens in lead glass may well be due to their being English copies of French originals.

[1] *Post Man*, 3 December, 1696.
[2] All the lamps illustrated in Plate LX have been tested, and are lead glass.

E. THE ENGLISH STYLE

We have now surveyed the borrowings of flint glass in its early days, and it remains to be seen how the items borrowed from other peoples were so used as to become an individual creation. During the last decade of the 17th century the English glassmakers had made safe their economy, they had mastered their special material, and most of all, they had gained a confidence in their own power of design which made it possible to convert to their own use what they borrowed from others without any suspicion of plagiarism or sense of inferiority. What they had once received they now took with a feeling of mastery. The confidence with which they borrowed made it possible for them in their designs to leave their borrowings behind. The elements with which they began and the elements which they collected were combined in an almost endless permutation ; the development in style was as rapid as the spread of flint glasshouses over England. The variety is evident in all sorts of vessels, in posset pots, candlesticks, lamps, ceremonial goblets, sweetmeat glasses, punch bowls, stands, and above all in wine-glasses. Among them all wine-glasses, being in commonest use and most subject to the fashionable caprice, are the only species in which the variations can be explained as a sequence of evolution. But if you survey a hundred glasses of this early period there will be few arbitrary combinations of feature with feature ; the combination is always a coalescence and the beauty and the individuality of the art lie in the nature of this union. It is essentially a matter of proportion, the proportion of one part of a vessel to another and of each to the whole, and the modification of one item or another to accord with the general plan. The English sense of design becomes effective and the English style appears in the construction, the way that the items are put together and reconstrued. The series of proportions is not a thing which can be analysed. A recent writer attempted to state the Greek sense of proportion by reducing its designs to mathematical terms. Such a method is a curious and not very profitable research, for it only substitutes a difficult description for the immediate certainty ; but without it the design of English glass can only be learnt by acquaintance with the glasses themselves. The English style as an individual thing lies not in the assemblage of alien features, but in that impalpable but unescapable thing, a certain kind of proportion.

The analysis of the English style is therefore limited to a statement of particular characteristics : for the manner in which they were combined in different types of vessel reference must be made to the illustrations.

(i) STEMS

1. The *quatrefoil stem* (Plates X. 2, XV, XXI. 2, XXIV. 3) was a squat baluster divided into four lobes by vertical depressions. There were two

types, the *upright quatrefoil* (Plate XXIV. 3) and the *spiral quatrefoil*. The former had appeared in English glass before the invention of the lead metal, *e.g.* the Northampton fragment and the sealed fragment in the London Museum (Fig. 20), and although it was hollow its sides were even then of considerable thickness. The hollowness continued for a short time even in the lead metal, but about 1685 it became solid. It was not a stem type which could be lengthened, and as the stem grew longer in relation to the bowl (*c.* 1690–1700) it was gradually supplanted by other types. It left behind it the *quatrefoil knop* (Plate XXXII. 2) which was used as an element in more complex stem late in the 17th and early in the 18th century ; like its parent it was sometimes hollow and sometimes solid, but the hollow variety is the earlier. In the *spiral quatrefoil* the depressions were twisted and much shallower (Plate XXXVIII. *b*. 2) ; in some of the later specimens they are scarcely perceptible. The spiral quatrefoil could be effectively used at much greater length and seems to have been a favourite with the earliest appearance of the ale-glass type (Plate XXXV. 1). This stem seems to have lasted rather longer than the upright quatrefoil, and in some of the later specimens the depressions have been entirely omitted, leaving the distinctive stem type seen in Plate XXXVIII. *b*. 2, 3. In both varieties of quatrefoil the bowl is *let into* the stem, and this itself is usually a sign of 17th-century date (*cf.* the Adam and Eve glass, Plate XXXVII). The gradual supersession of the short upright quatrefoil by the longer spiral sort and of this last by a plain stem illustrates two important points, (*a*) the simplification of technique and (*b*) the lengthening of the stem in proportion to the length of the bowl in the first twenty years of flint glass.

2. Another of the short early stems may be called the *pilaster stem*, and this again is not found later than the 17th century (Plate XXXVIII. *b*. 2). In shape it has some affinity with the quatrefoil that has ceased to be quatrefoil, but it is both shorter and thicker, and in some instances it is wrythen. The bowl is not always let into it (Plate XXXVI. *b*. 1), but sometimes set upon it.

3. *The knop-and-baluster* consists of a baluster stem surmounted by a knop and rather oddly appears quite as early as the simplest baluster itself (see below). It is notable both in large goblets (Plate XL. 1) and in the small family of sweetmeats already mentioned (Plate XXII). Although most instances date from the 17th or very early in the 18th century I have occasionally seen it forty or fifty years later. In the earlier examples it is more frequently wrythen than plain.

4. *The true baluster.* The stems just mentioned cannot be traced in Greene's forms nor in Venetian glass. For that reason I am disposed to think they came to England from the Netherlands. The baluster, on the other hand, is definitely Venetian in origin. It derives its shape from the calyx tube of the wild pomegranate (Gr. βαλαύστιον) and was one of the naturalistic motives which came into vogue with Renaissance architecture.

N

Its use was extended thence to all furnitures and its development in English glass may be traced to one of Greene's designs (Fig. 16, A). The earliest examples are very short, but like other stems it grew longer and at the same time thinner, in course of time (Plate LXIV. 1). After the baluster stem has begun to break up (*c.* 1700–10) it is found in combination with various knops or even duplicated (Plate LIII. *b.* 3), and still occurs occasionally in the middle of the 18th century. In its thin and elongated form it is most common about 1710–30 (Plate LXIV. 1).

5. *The inverted baluster* is the most beautiful, the most characteristic, and the most prolific of English stem forms. Like its twin the true baluster, it can be traced back to Greene's designs (*c.* 1670), Fig. 16, B, E, etc. Thereafter it grew longer in proportion to the bowl, and is seen to the greatest advantage about 1700. In the thin Venetian metal it had been hollow and it is still hollow, or at any rate contains a cavity, in some of the earliest lead-glass specimens ; later the hollow becomes a large pear-shaped tear, but most characteristically it is solid throughout. Quite plain inverted balusters by themselves must be rare after *c.* 1710.

6. *Knops and knopped stems.* A knop can only be defined as any protuberance in the stem of a vessel hollow or solid, other than a baluster formation ; elsewhere but in the stem of a vessel a knop is a knob. Knopped stems which cannot be classified exactly had begun to appear while stems were still very short and the simple balusters still in vogue ; and some at least must be dated a little before 1700 (Plate XLIX). But most knop formations succeeded the hey-day of the simple balusters and were due to their failure to keep pace with the lengthening of the stem ; for the baluster was a short stem type and could not well be stretched without loss of proportion. Thus about 1700–5 the baluster began to disintegrate into various kinds of *large heavy* knops or was reinforced by them. The varieties of heavy knopped stems are very numerous and it is only possible to give a list of the more important types. Most of the heavy knop types can be dated about 1700–15, but stems with lighter and smaller knops (which Mr. G. R. Francis rather misleadingly calls " light balusters," for strictly speaking they are not balusters at all) continue until much later, and are even evident in glasses decorated by the Beilby family about 1760–70 (Plate CXXXII. *b.* 3). Perhaps the term balustroid stems is convenient for describing these lighter and later sorts, and serves to distinguish them from the mid-century stems which have one or more knops with some sort of internal twist. In the following list the date indicates when the feature in question was *most frequent :* for a feature, once established, was always liable to be copied in later years.

(*a*) *Acorn knop.* 1700–15 (Plate LIX. *b*). The acorn varied in formation a good deal. One or two specimens are probably earlier than 1700. Inverted acorns are not uncommon, and the acorn was also used as a *knob*

(Plate LXXXV). There were two main types, the rounded (Plate L. 3) and the angular (Plate LII. 3) ; the rounded acorns seem to be slightly the earlier, for they are sometimes little removed from the plain inverted baluster (Plate XLIV. 3).

(*b*) *Drop knop.* 1690–1710. This also can be dated before 1700 in some instances when the bowl is long in proportion to the stem (Plate XLIX. *a*. 3). It is very effective, especially when it is combined with the double-ogee bowl (Plates XLVIII. 3, XLIX. *a*. 3 and *b*. 1, LI. 2). In the earlier specimens there is about half an inch to an inch of straight stem between it and the foot. The larger (and probably later) specimens are severely geometric and shaped as the frustum of an inverted cone.

(*c*) *Mushroom knops* are formed with incurved as well as with funnel bowls, and must usually be dated about 1710–15 (Plate XLIX. *b*. 3 ; *cf.* Plate LI. 3). The mushroom occurs in the upper part of the stem in all instances which have come to my notice, and it is difficult to visualize a decent design where this was not so.

(*d*) *The angular knop* in its larger forms goes back to the short stems of *c.* 1695 which are contemporary with the plain balusters, but a rather smaller angular knop was common for the next twenty years. (Plate XLIX. *b*. 2).

(*e*) *Triple-ring knop.* The larger and thicker sorts go back to *c.* 1700, the lighter and smaller mostly date from 1725, and some instances I have seen are twenty years later still. Here, as in one or two other knop types, the bulk of the knop is the chief guide to its date (Plate LVIII).

(*f*) *Ball knops*, nearly spherical in shape, are often found with a German shouldered stem, and set immediately above it, but they also occur in the later types of heavy stem. Ball knops should not be confused with the smaller bullet knops of the balustroid glasses (Plates LVIII, LXXXV, LXXXVII. 3).

(*g*) *Multiple knops.* Stems of this kind consist of the same knop repeated for the whole or the greater part of the stem, sometimes as many as ten knops composing the stem (Plate LXIII. 3). Stems of this type are probably derived from France. The English multiple knops are solid, but can clearly be connected with the hollow undulating stems seen in the candlesticks of Plates LIV. 1 and LVI. *b*. 2. The pieces there illustrated are proven lead glass, but they show no influence of Venetian art and are quite outside the English development in candlesticks, or indeed in any other vessel. It seems likely, therefore, that the archetype of the candlesticks is a Normandy or Lorraine type which a French emigrant tried to reproduce in a metal which he did not properly understand ; for the metal of the candlesticks, though it has lead, is poor stuff. If the archetype were Netherlandish and the maker Flemish some trace of Venetian influence might be expected ; in its absence the archetype is more likely to be a Normandy glass than anything else. The occurrence of very tall stems in

[179]

Normandy glass is established (Gerspach, Figs. 102 *et seq.*) and on that account the tall multiple-knop stems may be regarded as due to the influence of the French glassmakers working in England. Multiple knops are found in combination with both " Venetian " and " English " features (Plate LXXIV).

In the heavier balustroid glasses the foregoing knops are combined with one another and with both types of baluster, but in the light balusters which begin to appear about 1720 they disappear ; for they were essentially the feature of a heavy stem. In the light baluster glasses both varieties of baluster survive, but always with some support, *e.g.* a piece of straight stem or the smaller bullet knop or the button knop. One of the earliest and most graceful of these combinations is the baluster which supports a drawn stem (Plate LIII. *b.* 1), a type which came into vogue about 1715 and had a much shorter career than some of the light baluster stems.

The stems which followed the disintegration of the true baluster and the heavy knops which succeeded it first became general about 1715–20, and may be divided into three main groups. (*a*) The two original balusters still survive, bu tthey grew longer and thinner and were frequently combined with one or more of the smaller bullet knops. Combinations of this kind are in the main anterior to the air-twist stems, but there are some instances which must be dated at least as late as 1760–70. Some of the tall glasses with short flaring bowls and knopped or balustroid stems (Plate CXV) were still being made at Newcastle-on-Tyne about 1770 ; for about that time they were being decorated in enamel colours by two or three members of the Beilby family (Plate CXXX). Another type of stem with knops and a thin baluster was being made at the time of the Rebellion in 1745 (Plate LXXXVIII. 2) ; the glass cited as an interesting example of the tendency to supersede the plain baluster by a series of bullet knops, may be seen by a comparison of Plate LIII. *b.* 1 with Plate LXXXVIII. 2. In the former the drawn stem and trumpet bowl are used with a baluster (*c.* 1715–30), in the latter the baluster has given place to a series of bullet knops. Strictly speaking the term balustroid or light baluster is only applicable to glasses which have the elongated baluster as well as knops ; Mr. Francis applies the term to several types of glass which have only knops, whence all trace of the baluster has disappeared. (*b*) The second type may be called the small knopped stem. This begins as a plain stem, *i.e.* without internal orna-ment, about 1720 and continued for about twenty years. Several glasses illustrated by Mr. Francis as " light balusters " (*e.g.* Nos. 49, 53, 55, 58, besides several other stems which have lost the character of a baluster) are more properly described as knopped glasses. The arrangement of knops in this type showed considerable variety, but the appearance of the air twist (*c.* 1720) seems to have reduced the formation to two main types (Plate CXII. 3 and the half-way knop) ; these will be considered in a later place. (*c*) And thirdly the reduction of the heavy baluster and balustroid glasses produced a quite plain straight stem, the range of which is about 1715–60. Until the ornate stems appeared the plain straight stems seem to have been used for the better quality of glasses, but when the air twist and the enamel twists became fashionable they lost caste and were more generally made for tavern glasses. The evolutionary context of this type is certainly 1715–30, but plain stems were still made in fair numbers throughout the remainder of the 18th century.

Between the disintegration of the balustroid types and the arrival of the small stems the wine-glass stems were divided among these three classes : (*a*) light balustroid glasses, *i.e.* those which do possess a recognizable baluster, (*b*) light knopped glasses, *i.e.* those which have knops but no sort of baluster, and (*c*) the plain straight stem. The three types are therefore contemporary, and their apogees may be placed between 1715 and 1735 ; but all three types overlap the ornate stems by about thirty years, and the knopped stems were actually merged in them.

(ii) BOWL FORMATION

The English bowls vary on the whole less than the stems, and even the varieties which we do find can be brought within the limits of a few definite bowl types ; within each type there are minor changes, but the types themselves are comparatively few, and apart from the German bowl forms which have already been considered, they are almost without exception a modification of some Venetian or Anglo-Venetian prototype. But the developed shapes are so distinctive that they may be regarded as integral to the English style. Greene's designs (*c.* 1670) are a document of the greatest importance in this connection. Though the glasses were actually made in Venice the designs were by an English hand, and until the incurved bowls appear nearly all the English bowl types can be definitely traced back to them. In 1670 they may be taken as the norm to which all the later modifications may be referred (see Fig. 16).[1] Their design is in almost every case a statement in straight lines (*e.g.* Fig. 16, A–J) or a simple convex curvature ; this character in the English bowls, as distinct from those of German antecedents, is the most important romance element in English design. Throughout the first half of the 18th century the two lines of descent run side by side, and it is only as late as *c.* 1750 that one may remark any signs of amalgamation. Throughout that period also the romance bowls are the more characteristic English type.

1. *The straight-funnel bowl.* Venetian glassmaking had been much given to a sharp V-shaped bowl in which the angle of the sides was very

[1] This does not mean, of course, that Greene was a dictator of style or that his designs were deliberately copied. They merely indicate the state of design in the year 1670.

wide (about forty-five degrees in some instances) and there was no curvature at the base. The principle of this design was adopted by Greene, but the angle of the sides was made more acute in order to give greater stability to the whole glass (Fig. 16, A–D; *cf.* for example Nos. C 143–1923 and 5528–1859 in the Victoria and Albert Museum with Plate XLIII. *a*); for in the more obtuse Venetian bowls the sides converged into a thin neck which was very liable to snap. The tendency to stabilize bowl design in this way is already evident in Greene (Figs. 16, B, C) and it became even more marked in the early flint glasses (*e.g.* Plate XLIII). When this contraction took place the English glassmakers were careful also to avoid the thin neck into which the bowl tapered at its base (Plate XLIII. *a*. 2–3), and this they did by letting the bowl into a wide stem (the *inset bowl*). Mr. Mason's small wine-glass with a quatrefoil stem is an interesting example which shows both tendencies at once (Plate XXIV. 3). The straight-funnel bowl, though never very common, occurs most frequently *c.* 1690–1710 in combination with a short simple baluster (Plate XLIII. *a*) or one of the short heavy-knopped stems (Plate XLIX. *a*. 1). It is also found fairly frequently in the second and third decades with the German shouldered stems, and again in some of the earliest cordial glasses, in the latter case usually mounted on a tall straight stem twice encircled with thin collars (Plate CII); but after 1740 it must be extremely rare.

2. *The rounded-funnel bowl* is again a characteristic Venetian form (Plate XLIV. 1–2) which was adopted by Greene, but with less modification than the straight funnel. Greene has several forms approximating this type; in some the sides are partly straight, in others very slightly curved, but in both varieties the base of the bowl is rounded off either actually (Plate L. 2) or by intention (Plate L. 1, fig. 16, G). The rounded-funnel bowl is by far the commonest and certainly the most characteristic bowl in the early 18th century, but usually it lacks the collar which separated it from the stem in several of the Greene designs (the *merese*). Mr. Henry Brown has a rare glass in which this collar still survives (Plate XLIII. *a*. 1). The earlier types are long in the bowl, but even when the bowl is half the length of the Greene drawings it retains its identity. The "Adam and Eve" glass in Plate XXXVII is a very good example. Of the Venetian shapes it was perhaps the simplest and the most useful. Unlike some other bowl types of Venice, it could be rendered as well in a heavy metal as in thin soda glass, and this fact was no doubt the cause of its great popularity. About 1690 it was let into, or more strictly, welded in, a spiral quatrefoil stem, as in the "Adam and Eve" glass of Mrs. Dickson, or a stem of similar shape from which the spiral depressions had been omitted. But its most satisfactory partner was the inverted baluster, and together they make one of the simplest and most beautiful designs in the whole of English glass (Plate XLIV. 2). As the stems began to grow longer the rounded funnel lost its

depth, but it readily adapted itself to the new set of proportions by reducing its length and extending the angle of its aperture ; that was no doubt the chief cause of its survival. These short-funnel bowls put up a good fight against the waisted German bowls, and in the second and third decades were very happily united with the shouldered stem (Plates LXXXVI. 1 and 4, LXXXVII. 4). Both the long and the short funnel often have a small cyst at the lower apex (Plate L. 3). In a smaller version it was the only one of the early bowl forms which was still in regular use after the Excise Act of 1745-6, and it took its place beside the bell bowls, ogee bowls, and other dwarf types of mid-century date (Plate CVI. 2).

3. *The hemispherical bowl* was another characteristic romance form, but in spite of its grace, it never won a permanent footing in England. It was used both for wine-glasses and for sweetmeats, but it is rarely found after 1730. Its stems are the baluster, the heavy-knopped stem and the shouldered stem. The shape was especially suited to a stemmed sweetmeat glass, but in this use it was rapidly superseded by the open double-ogee bowl, which seems to be the counterpart in a wide bowl of the incurved German bowls and probably had the same origin. Plate CIII shows how the shape of the hemispherical bowl was modified at a later date and made suitable for cut ornament (Plates V. *a*, LXXII. 1, 3).

4. *The flute bowl.* Tall flutes with some sort of adventitious decoration were made both at Venice and in the Netherlands during the latter part of the 17th century (*cf.* Plates IV. *a*, VI), and John Greene, when he adopted the form, simplified it according to his usual custom (Fig. 16, o). Thereafter the form became fairly common, but it may be doubted whether the English flint-glass flutes were specialized for ale at so early a date. There is no evidence that Ravenscroft ever made them, but there are several fragmentary pieces which make quite clear the parentage of the later ale-glass. Greene's flute must have been reduced to a form approximating the later ale-glass about 1685. An interesting glass in the Guildhall Museum with narrow wrythen bowl let into a quatrefoil stem (Plate XXXV. 1) and a fragment in the London Museum (Plate XXXVI. *a*, 3) mark the intermediate stage between the flute proper and the knopped ale-glass of *c*. 1710 (V. and A.M. No. C. 239–1912). It is interesting to find that the tendency to lengthen the stem at the expense of the bowl extends to a type so peculiar as the flute. In Greene's redaction the stem is scarcely more than a knop, but it must have become a baluster by about 1690 (Plate XLIV. 3), and thereafter its length and its variety grew. The flute bowl responded to the German influence of the incurved bowl, but it was a much more individual type, and the waisted flute bowl does not occur before 1730–40. It has been assumed by Mr. Francis that the flute bowl was used for champagne. All that is known is the appearance about 1740 of flute bowls engraved with hops and barley, and it may be fairly inferred that these glasses were specially made and used

for ale. Some of the flute-bowl glasses, being without engraving or engraved with a vine motive and of very good quality, were certainly used for wine, but no satisfactory evidence has ever been adduced that they were special to one sort of wine ; and the same is true of the hemispherical bowl. *Cf.* pp. 314–15 and 321.

(iii) FOOT FORMATION

The feet in glasses of all types vary much less than the other parts, and of necessity they are less subject to decoration. Their ornament is usually of Venetian character, *e.g.* gadrooning or pearl-moulding, but their varieties in shape are singularly few.

1. *The pedestal foot* (*e.g.* Plate XVI. 1) was a romance form which did not long prosper in England. The Venetians had taken it from Renaissance design, and they used it gracefully and very frequently for most kinds of glass vessel, but in England it is only evident while the influence of Venice was still strong, and even then it was generally restricted to goblets and bowls of the more impressive sort. It properly belongs to the end of the 17th century and the beginning of the 18th, but occasionally examples may be found after the classical revival had begun *c.* 1760–70. Other examples of the motive may be seen in Plates XVI. 2 and XXIII. *b.* 2 ; its appearance in the Ravenscroft rummer is interesting, and it shows how a German form was modified by contact with Venice ; for the true *Roemer* foot was of different character (*e.g.* W. Buckley, Plate 33A and c). The stand in Plate XXIII. *b.* 2 is a rare and interesting example of an early English pedestal.

2. *The sloping dome* (Plates XLIX. *b.* 2, LI, LV. *b.* 1–2, LVI. *b.* 3) was a fairly common feature at the end of the 17th and beginning of the 18th century, especially in candlesticks and stemmed bowls, and less frequently in wine-glasses. It comes of the Venetian tradition, being probably an adaptation of the pedestal foot.

3. *The square dome* (Plate LIX. *a.* 2) is not common at the end of the 17th century, usual in the first quarter of the 18th, and it still survives in the dwarf glasses, being found both with air-twist and enamel-twist stems. It was certainly not derived from Venice, for such a shape was alien to the fine metal and blown technique of Venice. It was essentially the feature of a heavy metal, and made by tooling at the chair. While the sloping dome was certainly due to romance influence, the square dome seems to belong to the small group of German features already discussed.

4. *The spreading foot* (Plate XLIV *et passim*) has been at all periods and in all kinds of vessel the most frequent shape. At Venice it had been *a* foot form, in England it became *the* foot form, and in this respect it is the counterpart and companion of the round-funnel bowl. In flint glass, no doubt, it became the stock shape because it could be shaped as easily in a thick

viscous material as in a fine syrup. It was shaped by tooling at the chair, and not, like the pedestal foot, by blowing and drawing. The English glassmakers were fond of it because it was easy, but there is no part of a glass in which " breeding " is so evident. Throughout the first sixty or seventy years of the 18th century the shape, that is to say the angle of aperture, does not vary in any chronological sense, but a high, firm, well-fashioned instep is the first mark of a good glass, and especially of a glass that has been properly annealed ; for a badly made and badly cooled foot was apt to sag while the metal was still soft. Flat feet are the sign of a degenerate, and though degenerates may occur while a house is still noble, they are much more frequent when it has gone to seed.

5. *The terraced foot* (Plate LII). Terraces are entirely an English feature and one of the few attempts of the English glassmakers to make a decorative foot. Most connoisseurs would agree that it was an unqualified success. It was a mode of ornament only possible in a thick metal, and was probably executed at the chair by tooling a rotating disc of glass. Terraced feet usually rise into some sort of a dome in the centre, sometimes a square dome of the usual type (Plate LVI. *b.* 1) ; but the rounded dome rising directly from the rim is a scarcer and more distinctive shape not found without terraces (Plate LVII. 1).

All these foot types are liable to have a folded rim, except the last, which I do not remember to have seen with one. The earliest folds were thin and even hollow, after the Venetian practice, but the lead metal did not allow this to continue much after 1690, and thereafter for about twenty years the folds tend to be very wide and thick, showing the same profusion of the metal that is evident in the heavy knops which accompanied them. The folds became slighter and more discreet as this liberality waned, and the normal fold may be said to begin with the balustroid glasses about 1720. It should be added that very thin folds, sometimes even hollow, are found in the flint-glass primitives, where the metal of the rest of the glass is correspondingly slight.

Such are the features of style which are first remarked in stemmed vessels of the classical period. They are the limbs and organs of style, and not style itself. Style itself lies in the manner of their use, in the co-operation and co-ordination of limb with limb. What effects that co-ordination is a sense of design which finds that certain proportions please, and combines the units at its disposal to effect its peculiar pleasure. It is above all proportion that gives their beauty to the glass as to the furniture of the 18th century, but that proportion is not a thing susceptible of exact definition. If it were it would be no longer the driver, but one member of an unregulated team. Proportion would have been reduced to a diagram and the vitality of the art would have become a convention.

Some other features not proper to stemmed vessels cannot well be set in a schedule, for they belong to nominal types which are not only much scarcer at the present time, but even in their own day did not change so rapidly with fashion. For some of these other glasses the reader may be referred to the fourth appendix and to the illustrations, but since some features of stemmed vessels appear in other types also, stemmed vessels must be taken as a criterion to which glasses of a different sort may be referred. Features may be, as we have seen, the shape of a vessel or a decorative device, but in either case they are in some measure a deliberate thing, and in the present condition of study they are a surer guide to style and to chronology (which is style in evolution) than the mere substance of which they are composed. Certainly there are whims and artists' accidents, but the stylistic context of a glass, which we endeavour to express by giving it a date, is determined by its form rather than by its metal.

§ 5. A NOTE ON METAL

Metal changes, but it also varies, and it is the latter fact which makes the mere judgment of metal so untrustworthy. A chemical prescription is a more fixed and final thing than the formal impulse of an artist. The shape which an artist gives to his work is idea and fulfilment in one, but between the theoretical composition of glass and the metal which results is a great gap in which many accidents may occur. These accidents are responsible for half the varieties of tint and tone and texture which are supposed to enhance the interest of an old glass. So much talk about "early metal" is due to mistaking accidental variants for stages in an evolution that it may be convenient here to trace the technological history of the metal in the one particular where it certainly is possible, namely the lead flux.

1. The first stage is the short period of experiment when the use of lead oxide (lytharge[1]) as a flux was not properly understood. Ravenscroft must have known to what extent lytharge might be used, for there are some two or three glasses with the Raven's Head seal which are specifically heavy and must contain a fair quantity of lead. But when this flux passed to other glasshouses (as has been suggested about 1681) there seems to have been some diffidence in its use. There is a fairly numerous group of glasses (e.g. Plate XXX. 2) which are still very thin and can contain only a small quantity of metal; in one or two instances it is only possible to discover its presence by the use of a chemical test (e.g. Plate LIV). Glasses of this type seem to be the early experiments of factories which adopted the lead metal at the expiry of Ravenscroft's patent, but had still to find

[1] Litharge seems to have been more generally used at the end of the 17th century; see document cited *supra*, p. 116, note 2; but both red lead and white lead are mentioned in the petition literature (*Tracts*, 136).

out by trial the best uses of it. Thus it happens that some glasses later than Ravenscroft yet contain considerably less lead than Ravenscroft's own glasses. A glass which on form is very early and is not heavily leaded can usually be dated to the first three or four years of the general use of lead, say before 1685, but by that year the London metal may be regarded as mature. Apart from Ravenscroft's own glasses the period of the incunabula may be fixed fairly precisely to the years 1681–5, but some later extension of this limit, probably as much as ten years, must be made for provincial glasshouses. During this period the metal is blown very thin as if it were Venetian soda glass, and it is usually rough and of poor quality. The series of glasses with spiked gadrooning and wings in most cases seem to belong to the period of incunabula. Particles of lead appearing as small red or black specks can frequently be discerned in the metal of the glass, the defect being due not so much to an excess of lead as to imperfect fusion. Particles of white silicate also appear in the metal at this time. In a group of glasses which from their similarity to Ravenscroft's work seem to have been made by his partner and successor Bishopp there is still a certain whiteness in the metal and a tendency to devitrification (crizzling) from which Ravenscroft himself had suffered. But it cannot be emphasized too strongly that these peculiarities of the incunabula are defects of quality and texture and not peculiarities of tint.

2. When once the lead flux was understood (say from 1685 in London and from 1695 in the provinces) the metal became not merely mature but exuberant. The glassmakers, having discovered the splendour which the new process gave to the metal, used as much lead as they conveniently could, and the results of their pride appear in three ways. First the actual quality of the metal improved, secondly the quantity of lead was increased, and thirdly the glassmakers became reckless in the amount of metal used for a single glass ; so much so that designs were modified or invented with the sole purpose of displaying the material (*e.g.* stem formation of the heavy-knop glasses and the great thickness of metal at the base of the bowl). Specks of undissolved silicate disappear, and though the particles of lead can still be seen occasionally, the effect of the lead is chiefly remarkable in the oily texture of the glass (*cf. supra*, p. 116, note 2) and in its great brilliancy. The lead flecks were the result of imperfect fusion, and until this had been remedied there was probably some restriction on the amount of lead included in the batch. It follows that flecked glasses are more frequent in the earlier part of the exuberant period ; flecks are less common in the great balusters and the heavy-knopped glasses of 1700–10 when lead was most liberally used, but sometimes they can still be detected in mid-century glasses. The extravagant use of lead seems to have declined about 1720–30, for the balustroid glasses, the knopped glasses, and the straight-stem glasses, quite apart from their smaller size

and bulk, are usually less rich and brilliant in their metal. This tendency, however, was only the toning down of earlier excess. There was no general or conspicuous change in the metal until the Excise Act of 1745–6.

3. The Excise obliged the glassmakers to make a little metal go a long way. The tax was not actually on the weight of finished glasses as they were put upon the market, but its effects were much the same as if it had been. The charge was levied on the weight of raw materials of which the metal was composed—" all the Materials or Metal or other Preparations whatsoever." This does not imply that the several ingredients (*e.g.* sand, lead, potash, nitre, etc.) were taxed as independent commodities, but that the Excise was reckoned on the actual weight of metal in the glass pots. Thus it was expedient for the glassmakers to take as many glasses as they could from a single pot of metal ; they had to conserve *bulk*. And the *bulk* of (say) a ton of metal would be greater if the ingredients which composed it were specifically light. Thus it became necessary to reduce the proportion of lead, which being heavy, reduced the bulk of a given quantity of batch ; and apart from the evidence of the glasses themselves, Dossie's explicit statement is a proof that this was actually done. The results of the Excise appear therefore in two ways, to reduce the amount of glass allotted to each vessel and to reduce the percentage of lead in the actual mixture of the metal. The former consequence itself did something to mitigate the splendour of the glass, but the latter is really responsible for changing the character of the metal. After 1746 it became (1) *paler* in tone, (2) much *less oily*, and (3) much *harder*. How this modified lead glass supported the arts of engraving and enamel-painting will be seen in the next chapter.

When questions of chronology arise it is important to remember the limitations of the metallic criterion. At the best it can only decide within which of three periods a given glass may fall ; but within those periods it tells us nothing.

CHAPTER VI

The Age of Ornament

Ὡς ἐπιγινόμενόν τι τέλος, οἷον τοῖς ἀκμαίοις ἡ ὥρα.

ARISTOTLE, E.N., 1174 b.

§1. THE CHANGE IN STYLE

THE decorated glass of England in the 18th century was a marriage of convenience, of commercial and fashionable convenience between two arts that had grown up separately, came of a different tradition, and at the time of their union were too confirmed in their own characters for mutual adaptation or congenial issue. The first partner was English flint glass. It was still young by the side of its contemporaries, but in the first twenty years of its career it established its own set of values and from the first declared its independence of ornament. Decoration did not enter, and did not need to enter into its æsthetic, for the consonance of metal and design made it an impertinence. It may be accounted a plain homely Puritan art, but that was part of its heritage and it has to be accepted.

There are two sorts of design, the synthetic and the rhythmical, of which the first is spatial in character and the second temporal. Synthetic design has parts which it presents in space, and proceeds to a composition of them in a permuted scheme, a scheme, that is to say, which makes you aware of the formal units which compose it and the relations into which they are brought by the act of composition. Synthetic design is most evident perhaps in the art which is derived directly or indirectly from the Greek paradigm, but it can in no sense be regarded as peculiar to any one type of culture. It is evident, for example, in Islamic architecture, or in many of the painted designs on Persian and Turkish pottery. The shape of the Greek temple or the Greek vase depends almost entirely upon it, and later instances may be found in the art of the Renaissance, not merely in architectural compositions but in the shapes of baroque vessels and the parallel though not always identical forms of Venetian glass. But perhaps the most effective example of synthetic design is presented by baroque painters, of whom Rubens and El Greco may be taken as instances ; for in painting synthetic design is not supported by a conventional symmetry, and the art of construction is therefore the more striking. Design of this kind depends for the tranquillity in which it issues upon a quality which may be called proportion and by that term is to be understood a sense of the comparative values of the formal units which are to be co-ordinated. What is most evident, therefore, in synthetic design is the intellectual power which makes actual a complex of relationships conceived in the

[189]

imagination. The composition may be aided, as in Greek architecture and most kinds of pottery, by the concept of symmetry ; and this may be described as an attempt to cut short one-half of the proportional endeavour and reduce it by inverse repetition to the terms of a programme. But symmetry, though without doubt one of the great discoveries of human reason, is apt to become the crutch which supports a creative diffidence, and the designs which most compel attention for their intellectual power usually achieve their effect without its aid. If we proceed from design in general to the particular design of vessel forms symmetry is so universal that it must be regarded as a condition of their construction ; for it would be difficult to find any vessel in which symmetry of an elementary kind is not observed. But what gives character and beauty to the shape of a vessel is its formal endeavour apart from symmetricality.

While synthetic design presents its effects in space, rhythmical design is a continuous experience and has no parts. Whereas the last effect of synthetic design is a stationary repose, the peace proper to rhythmical design is a sense of agreeable or exciting transit. What sort of transit proves agreeable or exciting cannot be generally defined, for it is an evidence of biology exhibiting the idiosyncrasies of individuals or the disposition prevailing at a given epoch or in a given race. Its pleasure proceeds not from an intellect which judges, but from a taste which prefers.

In the art of painting rhythmic design is evident in the fragments of drawing, synthetic design in their composition. There are, as we have seen, some vessel forms whose total design must be regarded as a proportioned synthesis, but simple vessels, that is to say vessels which have no structure, are a type of art which depends almost entirely on rhythmical or instinctive design. That is why the making of vessels in pottery or metal or glass is to be regarded as a *cultural* art. In bowls or jars which have no structural parts (and we may call a foot or a handle a structural part) the designer's energy cannot well work in any other mode, but must reduce itself to continuous line and curvature. The pottery shapes of the T'ang potters, or of many types in Romano-Syrian glass, are perhaps those which show the greatest power and subtlety in a purely rhythmic design. In many cases such works of art owe nothing to proportion, and symmetry, though it is barely present, is not æsthetically effective, and its existence is apt to pass unnoticed. It is true in a general sense that simple pots are an art of pure rhythm.

In more complex works there is no absolute division between the two types of design, for both may, in fact must, occur in the same creation. Synthetic design in its issue may and frequently does approximate the other sort. On that account a merely synthetic design is to be regarded not as a lower order of achievement, but as a preliminary stage which is only surpassed by some artists and in some works of art. For it would probably be admitted that the more considerable works of art are those which, beginning as synthesis, end in rhythm. Synthesis in painting or furniture or architecture is thus the intermediate stage between fragmentary rhythm and total rhythm.

But even though both kinds of design are allied with one another it is usually possible to say which kind preponderates in a given species of art. In English glass design is usually synthetic, that is to say it consists in the composition of parts, which are themselves well defined, according to a given sense of what is proportionate. That the design was a design for structural vessels no doubt supported this tendency, for had it not been so the design must have been rhythmical merely. The use of synthetic design in English glass is the point in which it may be affiliated to the baroque art of the period which saw its birth. In the 17th century composition was the dominant character of both painting and building, and the vessel arts, as far as in them lay, pursued the same mode. But that point apart English glass had a sequestered course, and in the hey-day of the art, which may be placed about the year 1700, its original work was singularly exempt from the baroque *motives*. In some few manifestations the structural units have passed into a time sequence (Plate LXXIV), but if the art is to be judged by its average it remains true to the synthetic type, with an excellence depending upon the proportion of its parts. The content of its design is never very great ; that is what makes it a minor art. But within the ambit of its endeavour it contrives to be at once solemn and gracious, to show splendour without any loss of discretion ; and these classical values were already fixed in their closed circle when the intrusion of ornament began.

The second partner was the decorative art which had passed from Venice to Germany and from Germany to England. At Venice decoration had been intimate from the first with the art of glass and the pair having grown up together and understanding one another, created an idiomatic and beautiful thing. In the gilt and enamelled glasses of Venice there was a complete harmony of form and ornament, of the decorative technique and the metal which carried it, which is rarely evident in the glass of other countries. But when decoration passed to Germany this balance was disturbed. Germany had original glass forms of great beauty, the *Roemer* and the *Humpen* among them, but they lacked the variety, and their metal the fine quality, of Venice. Germany in the 16th century learned to decorate glass much more readily than she made it, and ornament in consequence was apt to be more considered than form. At Nuremberg, Augsburg, and elsewhere gilding, enamel-painting, and diamond-engraving were practised with great facility and, it must be admitted, with considerable artistic success, but the vessels themselves did not match the decoration which clothed them. The glasses were made in the mountain glasshouses, but the decoration was added in the cities, and the decorators were apt to select for their purpose not the forms which were intrinsically most beautiful such as the *Roemer*, but those which offered the most convenient field for painting or engraving. There was thus a divorce between the highest achievements of pure form and the highest achievement in decoration. At Venice only glasses the most handsome were promoted to further glory, but in Germany technical convenience was the chief consideration. The two arts were therefore parallel but not amalgamated, and Germany is thus more notable for glass decoration than for decorated glass. There were two main causes for this dissociation. Glassmaking had been established in the south of Germany long before painted decoration was acquired from Venice or glyptic ornament was introduced to glass by Caspar Lehmann (1609), and the new techniques never won an equal status in the glasshouses with the actual art of fabrication. They were largely practised in consequence by professional decorators who had no connection with the glasshouses beyond that of purchasing their naked wares. The decorators, painters, cutters, and engravers were unrestricted in their movements and might either travel from one city to another taking work upon commission as it came their way, or establish a decorating business in some one city, where they were assured of a wealthy custom. We find on the one hand established houses of Nuremberg or Augsburg, on the other a body of itinerant decorators who wandered at pleasure all over Germany and needed little inducement to settle in other countries. There is thus a notable contrast with Venice in economy as well as in æsthetics. At Venice the unison of form and ornament was the result of a system which sought to prevent emigration by making every branch of glass work dependent on its fellow. But in Germany the decorative arts were independent of the glasshouses both economically and æsthetically, and on that account Germany and not Venice was mainly responsible for extending decoration in France, the Netherlands, and England.

Germany, in the second place, may claim the invention[1] of two decorative techniques which had not been known to the Venetians at all, wheel-engraving and wheel-cutting, and the process, which was in principle the same, belonged originally to the decorators and not to the glasshouses. Caspar Lehmann, who may partly claim to have invented wheel-engraving on glass, was himself a gem-cutter of distinction and he did no more than adapt gem-cutting to a synthetic material which could be made to resemble a natural stone. It would appear that for the greater part of the 17th century wheel-engraving was still in the hands of outside decorators such as the Swanhardt family, and even in later times a good deal of the engraving in German glass must have been done by artists who had no connection

[1] Of course, in modern times; since glass-cutting had been practised in Roman times and even as late as the 9th century; see Lamm (C. J.), *Das Glas von Samarra* (1927).

with the glasshouses. Engraving, moreover, was frequently required for occasional purposes or at any rate executed to a special order, and until the 18th century it resembled the painted techniques which we find in German tankards, *Humpen*, and other vessels. The *Glasschneider* were a regular professional class who had their schools in the several cities or passed from the service of one potentate to another. Towards the end of the 17th century cutting, which implied a more serious modification of form than engraving, must have been adopted in the glasshouses themselves, especially in Bohemia and Silesia. When this happened we find a definite attempt to adapt form and ornament to one another, but glyptic ornament was a late-comer even in German glass and most of the German shapes, original and otherwise, were well established before it became general in the glasshouses. Engraving, even at the beginning of the 18th century, was an end in itself and not an art subsidiary to the fabrication of form. It was in some sense a national craft and the Germans, loving it even better than they loved glass, used it with very little sense of restraint. It is thus true that early in the 18th century when German influence was being felt in England German decoration was either divorced from form or exalted above it. What came to England through the German immigrants was not a style in glass but several methods of decoration which might be applied to it. The influence of German *form* on English glass preceded the decorative immigration and seems to have been due not to German artists, but to German glasses which were being imported into England during the first ten years of the 18th century. That matter has already been discussed.

Such being the age and character of the two partners it is not surprising that their union was a failure, or their offspring puny and affected. In the middle of the 18th century there are certainly some agreeable instances of engraved and painted glasses, but even these are glasses which have been decorated rather than decorated glass; and it must be granted that England never had a decorated glass in the least comparable to that of Venice or even of Germany. In the second half of the century English glassmaking gradually gave up the attempt and by selecting the one technique—cutting—which suited its metal made a triumphant conclusion to its career; for cutting became as intimate with fabrication as gilding and painting had been at Venice. In order to understand why these other decorations failed we must consider for a moment the nature of a dual art.

The essence of style is coherence. The human mind craves order in the world because order is the cast of the human mind, and the artist's endeavour is to impose it on that bit of the concrete world which he makes his medium. The coherence of his work means the presence of harmony between the masses (of three dimensions in stone, or earthenware, or glass, of two dimensions in paint), the intervals and the outlines which it

o

is his business to arrange. The condition of success is an equilibrium of interests, a poise which permits his formal impulse to escape without bias or impediment ; and his work if it is a success induces in the beholder a like equilibrium, which is the recognition of beauty. The glassmaker, like the painter or the scientist, gives coherence to a fragment of world. The clod on the marver may be reduced to a formula or reduced to a wine-glass, but in either case it is being made intelligible to man. Coherence is easier for the glassmaker when he works alone, for he suffers no intrusion of other interests and requires no alien support. But if he admit the painter or the engraver to a share in his finished work he must open his closed system, reorganize his intervals and his masses and find a context for a border of arabesques or a pretty landscape. The English glassmakers tried to do this, adapting both bowl and stem to the new ornament, and failing because they entered too late upon their task. The beauty of decorated glass required a wider coherence than could be found in makeshift alterations. That coherence depends not merely on a harmony of space and line with the new member ; it demands a complete congruence of two arts, that of the engraver or the painter on the one hand, and that of the glassmaker on the other. It is necessary that the two arts should start their course together, that the needs of the glassmaker should be to the decorator as much a condition of his art as the chemistry of his enamel or the edge of his wheel ; and on the other hand the needs of the decorator must become one of the primary limitations on the work of the designer. At Venice the designer and the decorator did not belong to distinct professions, and having served one another from the first they made a conjoint art in which form and ornament could never be thought apart. That unison was the concreteness of which form and ornament are the critical abstractions. For in a decorated vessel there are not two beauties, of the pot and of the painting, which have been joined by an arbitrary link and may be enjoyed together. The beauty is one beauty and the unity is the higher coherence in which the excellence of decorated glasses must always consist. English decorated glass failed as a composite art because form and ornament were nearly always isolated and nearly always conscious of their isolation. The curves of bowl and stem, the gay trickery of a coloured twist, the neatness of a border or the abandon of a scroll may give us detached and individual pleasures, but it is rare to find, as in a Venetian bowl, that the whole combines and controls the parts. In English decorated glasses the possible unison is denied us by a break in continuity or a change of mood, and when we look we are cheated of our coherence and fall back into littleness and multiplicity.[1]

[1] The set of engraved glasses seen in Plate CXXI may perhaps be regarded as a specimen of the best English attainment in decorated glass ; but even there it will be seen that the glass is treated as a plain tableau rolled into a cylinder and there is no attempt.

THE AGE OF ORNAMENT

A. GERMAN TECHNIQUES

The transition from a glass of design to a glass of ornament was due to two factors which are rather oddly separated by thirty years. The first of these was the dynastic change which in 1714 brought the House of Hanover to England, and thereafter the influence of Italian glassmakers is gradually superseded by the infiltration of German decorators who in some cases made glass, but are important because they decorated it. Mention has already been made of the Altarist Da Costa who was working with Ravenscroft and of the Dagnia family who had a glass manufactory on the Tyne for more than half the 18th century. But after the agitation of 1697 we hear no more of the " Artist Glassmakers " who were employed in the London glasshouses. Italian names are never frequent in the 18th century and in the Excise literature of 1745–6 to which we shall come in a moment there is no mention of the " Artists " as a definite body. Their influence on English style is still apparent in the middle of the 18th century, but these later manifestations of the "parallel Venetian tradition" are much less elaborate, and one is inclined to think that they were due to English workmen who still carried on *façon de Venise* in some sorts of glass, rather than to any remnant of the " Artists " still left in England. Besides the Italians there must have been a few German, or more probably Dutch, engravers working here during the reign of William III and Queen Anne, for there are some few glasses with wheel-engraving which bear dates prior to the time when we first hear of English cutters and engravers.[1] The engraving in these glasses is usually nothing more than an inscription or a coat of arms ; the lettering is of an English type, but even so it is scarcely credible that they were engraved by Englishmen. If they were, we must suppose them to be the work of glass-grinders, since there is some evidence that this technique had been acquired by the English some time before the end of the 17th century. In 1678 John Roberts was granted a patent for fourteen years " for his invention of grinding polishing and diamonding glass plates for looking glasses, etc., by the motion of water and wheels." And although this was a much coarser technique it is conceivable that a man like Roberts or one of the grinders who succeeded him might have undertaken to put a simple inscription on a wine-glass. The absence of any decoration on Sir John Risley's glass[2] is perhaps a

to adapt the composition of the engraved design to the shape of the glass. This is in marked contrast with early cutting, which nearly always follows form. The English painters and engravers worked *on* the glass but they very seldom worked *with* it.

[1] *E.g.* some glasses with engraved matter relating to William III and probably all the glasses referring to Queen Anne. *Cf.* Bles, Plate 44 and Francis, Plate XXXVI for examples. Armorial glasses prior to 1719 are also found, apparently engraved by metics. [2] Bles, Plate 44.

point in favour of this suggestion. But in a general sense it must be true that decorative wheel-engraving was not practised in England before the reign of George I ; alien decoration was not required by an art which was then in the flush of its original development. Decorated glass of great beauty there certainly was, but it was essentially a glassmaker's decoration executed by using glass to decorate itself as the Venetians had done at Venice ; and thus in flint glass of the *façon de Venise* we are conscious of no divorce between the form and the ornament, for both were fashioned together. The German decorators who begin to assert themselves in the reign of George I used a process which was quite outside of fabrication, and the period of original English design falls logically between these two terms, though in point of fact it is overlapped by both.

The arrival of the Germans in England may be said to begin with two events which almost coincide, the Peace of Utrecht (31 March, 1713) and the accession of George I (1 August, 1714). There may have been a stray German or two in England before that date, but as we have seen the earliest influence of German form on English glass was probably due to imported glasses and not to the immigrants themselves, and it must have begun during the latter part of the reign of Queen Anne. The restoration of peace in Europe in 1713 enabled Germany to send out her glassmakers and decorative artists as well as to export her glass. The glasshouses of Bohemia and Silesia at the beginning of the 18th century had the most considerable attainment and certainly the largest custom in Europe, and they were flooding the Netherlands and France and England with their wares. The Low Countries naturally felt the impact first. A great number of merchants, as distinct from manufacturers, established themselves at Middelburg and Antwerp and filled their warehouses with engraved glasses from Bohemia, Silesia, Saxony, and Prussia. The influx continued throughout the long reign of Maria Theresa, and the glass-workers of the Low Countries, finding that their wares could not rival those of Germany, turned in self-defence to England and tried to counter the blow by adopting the English style. Their resource was not of much avail.

German imported glass almost extinguished the art which had flourished in the Netherlands under the Bonhommes, the Colnets, and others during the 17th century. The flooding of western Europe with German glass must have begun some time before 1713, for even in 1697 the English glassmakers were seriously afraid of German competition, but there is no doubt that the Peace of Utrecht gave a great impetus to their export and it must have made it easier for Germans, both glassmakers and decorators, to leave their own country and establish themselves in the West. The train of causes which brought German decoration to England is thus : first the prosperity of glassmaking in Germany at the end of the 17th century ; secondly, a peace which made it easy for individuals to leave Germany, and thirdly the presence of a German monarch on the English throne which gave promise of a favourable reception in England. It is probable, as we shall see in a moment, that the consequences were evident in England before the year 1720. It is true that George I had no particular policy in the matter, but that was because he was not interested in the arts. The fact of his nationality, and that England was now in some sense a German domain, was itself a sufficient encouragement.

George II gave definite support to artists[1] from his own country and imported Germans to improve the manufacture of porcelain. Our knowledge of the first cutting and engraving in England is almost entirely due to the series of contemporary advertisements which have been brought together by Mr. Francis Buckley. Mr. Buckley, coupling the Germanism of George II with the fact that the earliest advertisement of curious cut-glass first occurs in 1727, was formerly led to take that year as an initial date for the introduction of the glyptic techniques into England. But soon after writing he found an advertisement of cut flint glass dating from 1719. This important discovery makes it likely that both cutting and engraving were being practised here by German metics soon after the accession of George I. No cut-glass known to the present writer can certainly be dated earlier than c. 1720, but there is a small group of glasses with engraved borders which may well date from that year or a few years later. Several of these are large heavy glasses with drawn stems and tears, which without engraving at all would certainly be placed in the first quarter of the 18th century. The engraving consists of a formal border round the top of the glass, much superior in workmanship to anything attempted by Englishmen even twenty years later. It consists, moreover, of symmetrical scrollwork in the full baroque manner and in this respect resembles the engraved motives of *Laub-und-Bandelwerck* which are found at this time on German glasses. It would appear that the glasses in question were engraved to English or Irish orders (one of them bears a portrait of William III) by German artists at least as early as 1720.

It is probable that gilding and enamel-painting on drinking-glasses were also brought over by Germans. There are no traces of these modes of decoration in early 18th-century flint glass, and although the Venetian artists probably understood both processes they do not seem to have practised them or taught them to their English pupils. They were part of the Venetian inheritance which England refused, and she was not ready to accept them from another source until the character of English glass was so impoverished that it required some decorative support. Gilding was a process highly characteristic of German glass and was used with much greater profusion in Germany than elsewhere. It was

[1] Buckley, p. 35 ; *cf.* p. 220 *infra*.

frequently associated with engraving and cutting, an engraved design being subsequently gilt, as in some of the Jacobite wine-glasses. On that ground alone there is not much doubt that it was brought to England by the German engravers. It is not advertised until quite late, but if it was being used for the best table-glass in 1745 the date of its introduction may well be placed about twenty years earlier. The early baroque borders to which reference has been made do not seem to have been ever gilt over the engraving. The painting of glasses with coloured enamels was also more characteristic of Germany than of other countries, and as there is good evidence that this technique was being practised in England in 1735,[1] there is not much doubt that it came from Germany between 1713 and that year. At the end of the 17th century it was certainly not practised in the English glasshouses. In 1696 a Frenchman by name Grillet advertised that he could execute all sorts of subjects in painted enamels on glass,[2] but at that period it must have been exceedingly uncommon. The only 17th-century glass with painted decoration known to the writer is painted in oil-colours and not in enamel (Plate XXXVIII. *b*. 2). Enamel-painting was regularly practised at Bristol in the middle of the 18th century, and it is not unreasonable to suppose that enamel-painting was occasionally used twenty or thirty years earlier.

The manufacture of coloured glass seems to have been mainly due to Germany. Green is the earliest colour of which specimens have been preserved and green flint glass seems to have been first made in imitation of German *Roemers* of pale green *Waldglas*. Glass in " all the capital colours " was being made at Stourbridge in 1751, and since the green glasses are the only coloured glasses which seem to have been made in the first quarter of the 18th century it may be concluded that the extension of coloured glass manufacture was likewise due to the German influence. There is lastly filigree work which in England is limited to the stems of glasses. These were called " Bohemian " by English glassmakers early in the 19th century, but there is some reason to doubt their tradition in the matter. Filigree, like most other treatments of glass, had been first practised at Venice. German glassmaking was never very fond of it except in serpentine glasses of Venetian type, and the " enamel twist " and " colour twist," the particular forms which filigree assumed in England, seem to have been copied from the Netherlands rather than from Germany. Colour twists in Germany were certainly made, but they are not in the least like those of the English wine-glass. Liège and other glass centres in the Netherlands were making enamel-twist stems of a type similar to the English at the beginning of the 18th century, and the English

---

[1] The *Dictionarium Polygraphicum* illustrates a muffle for firing painted glasses (" the ware ").
[2] *Post Man*, 3, xii, 1696, cited by Buckley, *History*, p. 142.

enamel twists were not much more than a flagrant copy of them. It is highly probable that they were first made here by Netherlandish workmen. The expansion of the German glass trade seems certainly to have brought some of its victims to England. After the Peace of Utrecht glassmaking in the Netherlands, as Dr. Hudig has shown, entered on a lean period, and it seems probable that the peculiar enamel stems of the Netherlands were introduced into England by Dutch or Flemish workmen who had been driven to England by the poor state of the industry at home.

The coming of ornament, thus detailed, was a slow process and the reception of it slower still. It is not difficult to explain the lapse of thirty years between the years 1713–14 and the full florescence of decorated glass in the middle of the 18th century. By far the greater bulk of decorated glasses belong to the middle and latter part of the century, and because they do not afford much guide to the period of incubation they do not prove that decoration began precipitously in the middle of the century. It is known that air twists were being made in 1716,[1] though the earliest dated wine-glass with an air twist is exactly twenty-one years later, and on that analogy it is probable that of the techniques we have just considered, gilding, enamel-painting, as well as cutting and engraving, were occasionally used twenty years before the initial point which on dated or other evidence has usually been assigned to them. If air twists were made in 1706 there is nothing improbable in the assertion that enamel twists were being made in 1735 or that cutting and engraving were occasionally practised as early as 1715. The absence of early specimens and the lapse of thirty years are due to the fact that English glassmaking in 1715 was still in the fullness of its original design and it offered a stout resistance to alien ornament. Between 1714 and 1745 engraving is rare, twisted stems are rare, cutting is rare, and in surviving specimens gilding and enamel-painting do not occur at all. Even in the 'thirties and 'forties engraving was still " curious." Ornament had not yet created its fashion, captured its market, or entered itself in the repertory of the English flint glasshouses ; both the makers and the users of glass were satisfied with pure form.

B. THE EXCISE ACT OF 1745

What finally broke the English resistance was a useless and ill-judged Excise. Since the question of the Austrian succession had come up for debate Europe had been full of backhand schemes and dynastic intrigue, and England found herself involved in one of the professional wars by which in the 18th century the monarchs of Europe were accustomed to settle their squabbles. With its trivial and complicated history we are not concerned, but

[1] See p. 212 and Plate XCV. 1.

from the present point of view it is important because it created the financial stringency which the Government tried to resolve by taxation. In 1744 Pelham, a timid and shuffling politician, had marshalled his broad-bottomed administration (*hodie* Coalition) and assumed the conduct of the war. He was not an incompetent financier, but he had been ill-nursed under Walpole, of whose Excise (1734) he had been one of the chief supporters, and in his later years he played the rôle and earned the reputation of tax gatherer. He became Chancellor of the Exchequer in 1743, he imposed a duty on spirits in the same year, and in 1744 he tried without success to raise money on the sugar trade. But his favourite theme was a tax on land, and he worked it with such persistence that the wags made a rhyme for his tombstone :

> Lie heavy on him, Land, for he
> Laid many a heavy tax on thee.

When he entered office he did so on the condition of pleasing everybody ; and pleasing Hanover was an expensive business. Pelham therefore, in the straits of a French war, a difficult monarch, and a host of variable politicians, found in taxation a more comfortable path than thwarting the Hanoverian interest and denying it the subsidies which it demanded. His financial difficulties were great ; he had to find the money required to support the main issue against France, and he had almost as heavy a task in continuing the German subsidies to which England had been committed by the presence of a Hanoverian monarch. Some of the Hanoverian troops had been dismissed, but under the new Whig ministry the system of subsidies became more exacting than ever. The money formerly used to pay the Hanoverian troops was now diverted to the Austrian subsidy and further large sums were expended in purchasing the interest of Saxony and of one or two of the inferior German potentates, *e.g.* the Elector of Cologne and the Elector of Mainz. Finally in 1746 a force of 18,000 Hanoverians was once more taken into the English service. In these straits the Government made its own artisans pay the cost of the political game, and among other devices had recourse to a taxation of glass, precisely as William III had tried and failed to do fifty years before for the purposes of his French war.

That was the origin of the Excise Act (9 Geo. II, c. 12) which was passed in 1745 and imposed a payment of nine shillings and fourpence " upon all the Materials or Metal or other preparations whatsoever that shall hereafter be made use of in making of all Crown Plate and Flint glass, and two shillings and fourpence on each hundredweight of materials for green bottle glass." Thus began the oppressive duties which hampered English glassmaking for exactly a century and ended by destroying the art of glass in England. It was just over fifty years since the Exchequer of William III had tried the same source of revenue with no success. The period of greatest attainment in English glassmaking was precisely the period of its freedom from taxation ; in glassmaking, as in any other art, industrial or otherwise, a free economy was the first condition of artistic achievement. The fallacy that " poverty is good for art " never needed a more striking refutation. Bosc d'Antic was studying glass and glassmaking at this time and in his later memoir on the subject (1780) he recognized the Excise of 1746 as the most serious reverse that the art of glass had yet sustained in England. " Quelle est donc," he asks, " la raison du plus haut prix du verre blanc anglois? Ce font les droits enormes dont il est chargé." Doubtless he had in mind the Second Excise of 1777 by which the duty on flint glass was exactly doubled three years before he wrote ; and he was moved to sarcasm : " Les anglois paroissent avoir pour maxime de charger de forts droits tous les ouvrages de l'art dont les hommes peuvent se passer. Il n'y a consequemment que les gens riches qui payent les plus fortes impositions."[1]

C. COMPENSATION BY ORNAMENT

The Act of 1745 came into operation the following year and in spite of considerable outcry at the time, expressed mainly in broadsheets and pamphlets, it was never repealed. There were other clauses of some moment to which we shall have occasion to refer later (p. 214) ; here we need only notice in their cumulative order its three immediate consequences for the English style. These were (1) a reduction in size, (2) a reduction in specific weight, and (3) compensation by ornament. Theoretically scale has nothing to do with design. The " composition " of a glass or of any other work of art is independent of its actual size, for the system of relationships remains the same whatever the size of the units which it binds together. In a strict sense, therefore, there was no reason why the designs of the great baluster glasses should not have been reproduced on a scale convenient to the new stringency. But the reply to theory must be that it was not so, and that probably it was not so because it could not be so. Size as much as colour or texture or form must be a factor in any æsthetic provocation, and it is evident in the history both of pottery and glass that design is rarely conceived without respect to size, just as it is rarely conceived without respect to the material. In Chinese pottery, Greek pottery, " Roman " glass there is one set of shapes for the great vessels and another set for the small, and the two series are not given to exchanges. That is because most vessels have a functional reference by which their form is partly determined, but even when pottery form is used in a decorative or " sculpturesque " sense the larger pieces will seldom submit to a reduction, or the smaller to an extension, without losing their character

[1] Œuvres, u.s., pp. 160–1.

as design. Thus when the Excise Act reduced the size of the wine-glass it meant that the older design of the late 17th century must be abandoned. In glasses of " importance " made for special orders or for a small but wealthy market, cost, of course, need not be considered, for it was the customer and not the glassmaker who paid. Thus in the few types of early glass which were still made after the Excise the glassmaker might be as liberal with his metal as ever before. But these parade glasses are the exception, and for the stock factory models, on which the bulk of the trade depended, the glassmakers were obliged to modify their design to suit a small glass, and at the same time they had to find new forms which would prove suitable to ornament. In some few instances this attempt was a signal success, for example in glasses made for the Jacobite clubs which were usually the best types of which the art was capable at that time (Plate CXII), and again in some of the glasses with facetted stems which were exported to Holland and used by Dutch engravers. But it would probably be admitted that on the whole "small" design in the middle of the 18th century is far less satisfactory than the "large" design of half a century earlier. Until design received a fresh impetus from classicalism about 1770 glass form was apt to be paltry and anæmic.

Besides a decrease in size the Excise was also responsible for a decrease in weight of metal. A given weight of metal, say a ton, must be made to go as far as possible and its bulk, as we have seen, would be greater as the heavy ingredients were reduced. This necessity caused a substantial reduction in the lead flux[1] which fifty years before had given the English metal its splendid corpulence and had partly determined original English design. The loss of lead had two effects. It encouraged small design which was primarily due to a reduction in size ; and both æsthetic- ally and technically it changed the character of the metal. Now that the glasses had lost some of their brilliance of material the glassmakers were compelled to seek some æsthetic value to take its place. They might have found it by paying greater attention to design ; they chose instead the support of ornament and looked for help to the German decorators. It is probable that the technical qualities of the degenerate metal gave this direction to their search, or at least encouraged it. The reduction of lead not only made a paler metal, it also made it harder in texture, for the high percentage of lead had made a soft as well as a brilliant metal. In Germany where no lead was used the resulting glasses had been exceedingly hard and the great delicacy of German engraving seems to have been partly due to the convenience of a material which could be cut sharp and clear. In England the small light glasses which followed the Excise approximated the German type of metal and the development of en- graving in the middle of the 18th century was assisted by this quality.

[1] See Dossie's statement, p. 188 *supra*.

THE AGE OF ORNAMENT

A comparison of the earliest engraved glasses, which are still well leaded, and were engraved by German workmen not lacking in technical skill, with the engraving on a thin decanter dating from *c.* 1760 shows that in the former case the engraved line was a furrow, whereas even English engravers of later date could make it an incision. The engraving of naturalistic flowers (*c.* 1760) sometimes shows a surprising exactitude which can scarcely be due to the greater technical skill of the English engravers over the Germans. Dossie recognized, and it has been admitted by later authorities, that lead glass was better suited for cutting than soda glass. That was because of its sympathy with the process, as well as for its finished effect of light reverberation. But cutting was a much less delicate business than engraving, and if the Germans succeeded with the engraving, and on the whole failed with the cutting, of their hard glass, it is difficult to believe that the material was indifferent to either result. And since in England the quality of the later engraving was improved as the proportion of lead decreased it is difficult to assume that the reduction and the improvement were not in some degree cause and effect.

Moreover, glass which contained a reduced quantity of lead was more favourable to enamel-painting[1] and to a technique like burnished gilding which required the use of a muffle. For lead was a substance which would melt at a low temperature and glasses which contained a high proportion of it were apt to become partly fused in the muffle so that the surface of the glass became liquescent and flooded the enamels which were painted upon it. Where a hard soda glass was used, as in Germany, the enamel was made to adhere without risk of this kind, and the outlines of enamel-painting on German glass are thus firm and clear. In England there are no instances of enamel-painted glasses until after the proportion of lead had been reduced and even in these the outlines which distinguish the applied enamel from the glass " ground " are apt to be vague.

The change in design and the aptitude of the poorer metal lead thus to the third consequence of the Excise, compensation by ornament. Decoration had been present in England for at least a quarter of a century, but it had been in suspense. Decorated glasses had been curiosities[2] before, but they now became a standard manufacture. The decorative techniques thus coming into their own won an economic " place," whereas formerly

[1] " It being requisite that the body painted in enamel should undergo a heat sufficient to melt *soft* glass, the matter of such body can only be . . . *hard* glass. " Dossie (2 ed., 1764), I, 262. The italics are Dossie's. " Soft glass " refers to the vitreous matter used for fluxing the pigment.
[2] " Curious " is the term used in the early advertisements of cut and engraved glasses.

[203]

their existence had depended upon caprice. Decorators were employed not by members of the public merely, but by the glasshouses. Glass-making had at length given an unwilling sanction to ornament.

§ 2. MODIFICATIONS OF FORM

The changes which have been discussed had begun some time, before the Excise Act. The period 1720–45 witnessed a general decrease in the size of glasses, and the beginnings of ornament were contemporaneous with it, but neither small design nor decoration gave character to the glass of these islands until after 1746, and it was the Excise which made them both general. It now becomes necessary to analyse the features of style which are evident in the decorated glasses, and for this purpose the enquiry may be divided into two parts, first the modifications of design caused by the Excise, and secondly the several modes of ornament acquired from the Germans.

A. STEM FORMATION

The most important factor in the change which came over design was the great increase in the length of stem in proportion to the bowl, and a corresponding diminution in the length of the bowl. In 1685 the stem was definitely subordinate to the bowl and it was too short to be complicated in design ; hence came the early vogue of the plain simple balusters, true and inverted. From 1690 onwards the stem began to assert itself, and as it grew longer it necessarily became more elaborate in design, for a simple baluster was not sufficient for a tall stem. The heavy knops detailed above (p. 178) were the means by which the glassmakers maintained the significance of the stem after it had outgrown the simple balusters. The simple balusters always belong to the period when the stem is still æsthetically subordinate to the bowl, that is to say, always before 1700. About 1705–10, that is to say, from five to ten years before the German influence became general, the bowl and the stem attained an equivalent æsthetic value.[1] The *haute époque* of the original English style just precedes this adjustment, and stylistically speaking the apogee of the art may be placed at the point of equivalence. Thereafter the encroachment of the stem upon the bowl was interrupted for about twenty years by the vogue of the shouldered ("Silesian") stems, which were an alien form and served to suspend the evolutionary process on which they had intruded. For about twenty years, therefore (1710–15 to 1730), the Silesian stem remained constant and English stem growth was at a standstill. During this period English design was mainly concerned with adapting the long straight-funnel and rounded-funnel bowls to the shouldered stems, and conversely in

---

[1] Not necessarily the same actual length.

modifying the incurved German bowls, as far as was possible, to the older bowl types which had preceded the German influence. The years 1710–15 to 1730 are thus a makeshift period, but the vitality of English design during that time was such that it produced a very satisfactory series of hybrid forms (Plates LXXXVI, LXXXVII). About 1730—the death of George I in 1727 may be said to mark the change—the Silesian stems begin to lose their hold on English design, and as they withdrew the evolution which had been interrupted since *c.* 1710 was free to continue as before. Stem encroachment begins again at the point where it had left off, that is at the point where the stem was just gaining the ascendancy. It is thus possible to see why we find a whole series of comparatively thin stems (compared with the standard of 1705–10) and small bowls for about fifteen years *preceding* the Excise of 1745. When the English stem resumed its growth about 1727 it was bound to become thinner, and when it was furnished with knops or balustroid curves these were similarly bound to become smaller. For a taller stem, which was at the same time as thick as in 1705, would have meant a very cumbrous limb and a loss of proportion in relation to the whole. Moreover, as the stem grew in importance it was inevitable that the bowl should be curtailed. Thus it happened that between 1730 and 1745 the field is held by a series of glasses with very well-developed stems and stunted bowls, the latter derived either from the original English types or from the German incurved bowls. The result of this development was a net loss in the actual bulk of the glasses, for the size of a glass is determined by the bowl. Thus the reduction in size preceding the Excise has no connection with industrial conditions or taxation, but is the result of natural stylistic development. The Excise assisted and stereotyped a set of designs which had already begun to define themselves. This type of stem preceding the Excise has been described by Mr. Francis as the " light baluster," but that term only refers to one motive in its composition. The components of these stems fall roughly into four groups, (1) a thin elongated baluster usually of the inverted type, which occurs fairly frequently in the ordinary wine-glasses, but is perhaps more common in the peculiar glasses with very tall stems made at Newcastle-on-Tyne[1] ; (2) a round shoulder at the top of the stem (Plate XCVII. 3) ; (3) undulating knops in which the stem swells into a protuberance with a continuous curve ; some of these resemble a baluster which has lost its proper contours[2] ; and (4) the knop

[1] For these glasses see W. Buckley, in *Old Furniture*, July, 1928.

[2] A very frequent stem was composed of a round shoulder at the top and an undulating knop at the half-way point. Glasses with portraits of Charles Edward Stuart frequently have stems of this style, and it is likely that they came into fashion about 1740 (Plate CX). Mention may also be made of a degenerate type of glass with a stem of three or four undulating knops containing a coarse enamel twist. These stems are generally combined with an effete bell bowl, and a rather flat foot, and are anachronisms dating from the last twenty or thirty years of the 18th century.

proper, which breaks the line of the stem. Before the Excise these items are usually found to the number of three or four in the same stem and they are very variously permuted. They are contemporary with the earliest air-twist stems, but for an obvious reason were immune from that ornament; for the air twist before *c.* 1740 was peculiar to the drawn stems in which it had originated. The knopped stems were greatly simplified by the Excise and only two of the four motives continued in the filigree stems of mid-century date, viz. the shoulder at the top of the stem and the undulating knop. The reason for their survival is clear. After 1745 filigree stems either of air or coloured glass or coloured enamel became the normal stem type for wine-glasses and since the filigree technique involved the drawing out of the stem, whether or not it was actually drawn out from the base of the bowl, only those protuberances survived which did not break the stem-line (see for example Plate CX).

2. *The drawn stem.* Glasses with this stem followed their knopped brethren and grew smaller *before* the Excise. This will be evident by a comparison of Plates XLVI, XCII, XCV. 1 and CXIII. 1. The latter glass was probably made at the time of the Stuart rising in 1745 and at that date it is scarcely conceivable that its reduced dimensions were due to the Excise. Drawn stems in the middle of the century usually have their proper ornament—the air twist, and much less frequently a twist in white or coloured enamels. Plain drawn stems are not normal after 1750 and even with a twist in them they disappear quite soon afterwards. For a drawn stem implied a trumpet-shaped bowl whose shape was neither convenient to the engraver nor apt for displaying his work.

3. *The straight stem.* This term is generally applied to a straight stem applied to the bowl, not to the stems drawn out from it. It does not seem to occur at all before about 1720 and from that date until the Excise Act it is usually devoid of ornament. After that date it usually contains filigree work of some kind and it became the normal stem for mid-century glasses. The frequent use of this stem is a very good instance of " compensation by ornament." The glassmakers, partly owing to " les droits énormes " and partly to their own lack of initiative, made no attempt to use stem design as an æsthetic contribution to the excellence of the glass, but found a rather cheap technical substitute in the various kinds of filigree ornament, for which a straight stem was the easiest vehicle. After *c.* 1760, however, the straight stem began again to be æsthetically effective. By that time filigree had begun to be superseded for glasses of first quality by cut ornament, and in the development of cutting the straight stem holds an important place. The earliest experiments in cutting had preceded the Excise and had enjoyed a good thick metal for both bowl and stem, but the reduction in weight and thickness after 1746 drove them to the stem, the only part of the glass which was thick enough for their purpose. With

the early facet cutting and the rather earlier fluting the straight stem rehabilitated itself, and contributed to some of the prettiest glasses made in the third quarter of the century.

4. *The cusped stem.* Among the latest of the knopped stems detailed above (pp. 177 *sq.*) there was one which had a single undulating knop half-way between bowl and foot. Almost always it contained an air twist and not very frequently a twist of white or coloured enamels. This stem was the last vestige of the baluster and was most common between 1750 and 1760. Before it was yet dead as a vehicle for filigree it was adopted by the early cutters. When it was made for their use the twists were naturally omitted[1] and the whole surface so cut with facets that the undulating knop became a pair of cusps (Plate CVI. 3). The stem so formed was extensively used for lighting-pieces and sweetmeat glasses as well as for wine-glasses during the second half of the century, but in the latter class most instances seem to be prior to the straight facetted stem and seem to have been first made about 1755.

The general tendency in stem design may be described as a progress from simplicity to multiplicity (1690–1746) and then from multiplicity towards a second simplicity ; but it is simplicity without strength.

B. BOWL FORMATION

The factors which determined bowl shapes in the period of ornament may be set forth thus. The original English bowls, the rounded-funnel bowl, the straight-funnel bowl, and the large double-ogee offered a less sturdy resistance to German bowl design than the English stems. Both the former were at first (Plates LXXXVI, LXXXVII) admirably adapted to the shouldered stem, but they lost something of their size in the process. The double-ogee bowl (Plate XLIX. *b*, 1, 2) was not, I think, ever combined with the shouldered stem, but it had a continuous, though not a very popular course, until its degenerate descendants are discovered *c.* 1740–50. On the whole the original English bowl succumbed about 1720, and the German types which had come over with the shouldered stem held the field thereafter until about 1750. After the period of English and German amalgamation (1710–15 to 1725–30) already mentioned (*supra*, p. 204) very few traces remained of the original English bowl, and between 1730 and the Excise Act the balustroid and knopped stems (*supra* pp. 177 *sq.*) are usually combined with incurved bowls of German type. The encroachment of the stem, which as we have seen began again about 1730, tended to push the bowl off the stem altogether, and this assertive action on the part of

---

[1] I cannot recall any instance of filigree work enclosed in a facetted stem and the two modes of ornament are so abhorrent that it seems doubtful whether stems of this kind were ever made.

the stem reduced the size of the waisted bowls. But there was no serious decrease in the thickness of their sides (compare the thick-waisted bowl with early cutting in Plate CIV. 1) until after the Excise Act. One consequence of the heavy duties killed another. The waisted bowls were again reduced in size, this time in bulk (Plate CXII) also, and this gives us the small, thick bell bowls, trumpet bowls, and double-ogee bowls which occur immediately after 1746, for example on some of the Jacobite glasses. But the Excise, as we have seen, was also an encouragement to engraving, and an incurved bowl was not well suited either to the technique of engraving or to the display of the finished work. In effect, therefore, the Excise Act first reduced the size of the waisted bowl, and less than ten years later had banished it altogether. Thus the general consequence of the duty was to standardize bowl form just as it standardized the stem. The new bowls are of three main types and all are later in date than the bell bowls, trumpet bowls, bobbin bowls, and other small incurved types which are combined with the filigree stems.

1. *The straight-sided bowl* (*e.g.* Plate CXVIII) was evidently the last descendant of the rounded-funnel bowl. It begins to be common about 1755 and was on the whole the favourite type for engraved and painted ornament.

2. *The ogee bowl* (*e.g.* Plate CXX) was also well adapted to ornament since the narrowing of the sides began only a short distance above the top of the stem, and the upper part offered a clear round surface to the decorator. Larger goblets of this type were being made during the Seven Years War, and are found with " Britannia " subjects, ships at sea, and portraits of Frederick the Great engraved upon them (see Plate CXVI and *E.I.G.*, Fig. 55). Ogee glasses were also frequently used by the Beilbys of Newcastle-on-Tyne for painting in white enamels. Those of better quality usually have engraved ornament (*infra*, pp. 236 *sq.*), and perhaps the most successful in design are the rather thicker glasses made for cutting from about 1760 onwards (Plate CXXI).

3. *The square bucket bowl* similarly offered an easy field for ornament and was already in common use at the time of the Seven Years War (1756–63) both for large goblets and for ordinary wine-glasses. The latter were certainly a favourite Bristol shape at this time, for specimens are found with the image and superscription of several privateers which are known to have been operating from that port about the year 1757 (see Plate CXV. 1). The same shape of bowl was also made at the time of the Excise on cider proposed by Dashwood in 1763, and engraved with an apple tree and a protest from the farmers of Hereford or Devon. Similar glasses were made for the Cycle Club and other Jacobite clubs, and were engraved with their emblems, in the years following the Rising of 1745.

THE AGE OF ORNAMENT

C. FOOT FORMATION

In the classical period there had been three main types of foot, (1) the plain spreading foot, (2) the spreading foot with folded rim, and (3) the domed foot, abrupt or sloping, and usually though not invariably with folded rim. About 1705 the foot with a plain surface, usually the domed foot, begins to be moulded in various ways to match the corresponding ornament of the bowl (Plate LXX). This fashion continued for about twenty years and during the period of German and English amalgamation (*supra*, p. 204) sometimes the foot ribs are drawn up into high bosses round the dome to match a similar exaggeration in the bosses of a shouldered stem, the double feature being an interesting example of one style accentuating itself to suit another. During the same period pearl-moulded feet, usually of the domed variety, may also occur. By the year 1730 foot-moulding has become very infrequent, and both the domed and the folded rim have begun to lose popularity. The domed feet, especially those of the sloping sort, had been an important factor in design during the classical period, and especially so about the year 1700, but for a glassmaker who wished to be careful of his metal a dome was a needless extravagance ; and it may be said to have succumbed to the Excise Act. After 1745 domed feet of a puny sort may sometimes be encountered in association with a filigree stem, but in the middle of the century they were a gratuitous conservatism and very ill-suited to " small " design. Mid-century glasses may be neat at times, but the glasses with domed feet are not among them. Outside the stock types the domed foot is more frequent ; for where the rich customers paid[1] economy of metal need not be considered. In " parade " glasses, therefore, the dome was granted a reprieve.

The folded foot, on the other hand, was not an extravagance but a piece of good sense. The rim is the part of a glass most liable to disaster and even when the foot had been ponderous a folded edge was an insurance against the carelessness of housemaids and the abrasions of time.[2] You could not drink conveniently from a lip that was folded, but feet in glasses have a rougher career ; and so folded feet, which had been normal in the first half of the century, are still fairly frequent in the second. But for the more refined among mid-century glasses—those in which engraved ornament was usual—the fold was felt to be a little coarse, and it is usually abandoned in the better sorts, with which " gentlemen may be supplied." But the real cause of its demise was the advent of cutting. The edge of the foot was a convenient part for the unpractised cutter,[3] and as edge-cutting

---

[1] *Cf.* Bosc d'Antic, cited *supra*, p. 201.
[2] Among 18th-century glasses which are now collected, chipping is in fact common where there is no fold, and very uncommon where there is one.
[3] See p. 247 *infra*.

P

(herein called " scalloping ") became more common the fold naturally disappeared. In the middle of the century, therefore, the plain spreading foot must be considered the normal type.

The advance of cutting was also responsible for a revival of the dome. Cut-glasses in the middle of the century were luxuries, and supplied only to the richer customers who could be made to bear the cost of the Excise which in ordinary " lines " fell on the glassmakers themselves. In glasses intended for cutting the manufacturer could be freer, he was indeed bound to be freer, with his metal ; and when once the cutters had mastered, first sliced geometric patterns, and then relief diamond patterns, the wide surface which the dome offered was too good a field to be neglected. Thus after about 1760 the dome again becomes common, not in wine-glasses, but in cut-glass sweetmeats and candlesticks which were made for a wealthier type of customer (Plates CXLI, CXLII).

D. INTRINSIC ORNAMENT

By this term is to be understood the sort of decoration effected by a modification of the glass itself and not by any applied technique or alien material. The ornament of *façon de Venise* in flint glass had been wholly of this kind, and its success æsthetically had been due to the fact that fabrication and decoration were parts of the same process. But by the year 1745 *façon de Venise* was comparatively rare. At that date glasses which still show Venetian influence were usually made for special occasions[1] or for ceremonial purposes. In the middle of the century " glassmakers' decoration " of the Venetian type had mostly passed out of the English style altogether. The only important exceptions are the rounded gadrooning and nipt work still found as a basic ornament for tankards (Plate LXXVIII) and similar vessels, and simple thread-work (*ibid.*).

But during the first half of the 18th century the Netherlandish glasshouses had evolved an intrinsic ornament which was distinct in character from that of Venice. They do not seem to have understood in what contexts (for glassmaking as for architecture) a plain surface may be æsthetically cogent or æsthetically necessary, and they were not always content to have their surfaces unadorned. This tendency usually took the form of wrything or twisting the walls of a hollow vessel in a spiral sense, or again in beaded or pearled moulding, and in pincer-work. These features, more especially the first two, are occasionally evident in mid-century flint glass and were probably suggested by the Netherlands. It is likely that there were Netherlandish glassmakers at work in this country and certain that " Flanders glasses " were being imported ; for in 1754

[1] For example, glasses of this type were being made for political occasions about 1745–50 and often contain a Stuart coin or a Hanover coin within a prunted bulb.

they paid a considerably higher duty than "Venice glasses."[1]   This influence appears in a very frequent family of small rough drinking-glasses of which a specimen is illustrated in Plate LXVI. 9.   The wrything of these is of the Liège type, and they differ from the earlier wrythen glasses of the "winged" type (Plate LXV) in that the spirals are in very low relief and continue right up to the top of the glass, flattening out sharply, as at Liège, just before they reach the lip.   I have seen one or two flint-glass tumblers with similarly wrythen sides.   Pincered work is not common in England.   At Liège it had been a very favourite device, especially in basket-work vessels such as fruit bowls or dessert plates.   In England it is usually confined to basket-work bowls which were certainly copied from Netherlandish fashion and were obviously suitable to pincered work. These are very scarce at the present time, but their form is so fragile that these may not fairly represent the numbers manufactured.   They are several times mentioned in advertisements from 1725 until 1758.   We may refer lastly to stem-wrything, a type of intrinsic ornament which had been in use from the earliest days of flint glass (*e.g.* Plate XXII).   During the early part of the 18th century it was used sometimes for green-flint drinking-glasses of rummer derivation (Plate C. *a.* 2, 3) and for clear glasses of the same type. It is uncertain when the manufacture of these glasses ceased, but it was probably about 1730.   The stems wrythen had been of rough balustroid or shouldered form, but the same ornament was also used for the straight stems in vogue about 1750 and was associated with one or other of the stunted bowls.

§3.   Modes of Decoration

So far we have considered briefly the modifications of form which overtook glass in the middle of the 18th century ; and for the sake of convenience intrinsic ornament has been placed in that category.   We may now proceed to the second factor, decoration proper, and under that head have been placed the glyptic techniques, filigree work, and dyed metal.   Both colour and filigree strictly belong to the process of fabrication but they have nothing to do with form and in their use and purpose are more akin to ornament.   For that reason we venture to include them here.

[1] The duties on imported glass in 1754 were :—

Balm glasses		2s. 3d. per doz.
Burning glasses		11d. per doz.
Water glasses		3s. 11d. per doz.
Cullet		1d. per 112 lbs.
Coarse drinking-glasses		11d. per doz.
Flanders	ditto	8s. 3d. per 100
French	ditto	10s. 1d. per 100
Venice	ditto	5s. 11d. per 100

Dict. of Arts and Sciences (1754), II, 1446.

A HISTORY OF ENGLISH AND IRISH GLASS

A. FILIGREE ORNAMENT

The principles of filigree have been considered in the technical part of this book (*supra*, pp. 36 *sq.*). At Venice and in some continental glass of *façon de Venise* filigree work had been used both for stems and for the parts of a vessel which were blown as well as drawn. England never mastered, and probably did not try to master, the second and much more difficult of these processes, and filigree work in England is confined to stems, shafts, and handles,[1] that is to say, to the parts of a vessel which were drawn and tooled but not blown, and to toys made on the same method, such as swords and walking-sticks. I venture to take "filigree" as a general term to include all kinds of internal thread-work or cane-work whether of air, coloured glass, white enamel, or coloured enamel.

Air twists.   It is probable that the air twist is fortuitous in origin, and for that reason it cannot be said to be derived from any other country, though other countries, notably the Netherlands, certainly used it. Even if it be not peculiar to English glass it is highly characteristic of it. In the fabrication of glasses air bubbles or tears are apt to gather where the metal is thick enough to hold them, *e.g.* in knobs, in the thick glass at the base of the bowl of a wine-glass and in the stem itself. Lead glass was more prone to tears than other metals, and within ten years of its discovery air bubbles were being regarded as a happy accident.   When this use of the air bubble became deliberate, it took the form of a grouping of small bubbles or of one or two large tears, round or pear-shaped. The smaller bubbles were apt to lose their rotundity after their enclosure in the stem and to dribble downwards so as to leave irregular streaks of air. The air twist as a deliberate ornament seems to have been suggested by this accident.

The advent of the air twist has been considerably post-dated. The earliest date has been hitherto placed about 1735 on the basis of a dated specimen recorded by Mr. Francis Buckley as bearing the date 1737, but there is reason to believe that air twists were made at least twenty years earlier. Mr. Grant Francis has an air-twist stem in a wine-glass with low wide bowl gadrooned at the base, which is almost certainly of 17th-century date[2] and in general design resembles a very early glass of Mr. Bles with a wrythen stem (Plate XXII. 4). Moreover, there is in the British Museum an interesting flint-glass calender with an air-twist shaft and a metal mount engraved with the initials *E. C.* and the date 1716.[3]

[1] *E.g.* the branches of a chandelier, the shaft of a calender, the handle of a mug, as well as the stems of drinking-glasses, bowls, candlesticks, and the like.
[2] *Old English drinking glasses*, Plate II, No. 7.
[3] The base of this calender is also interesting, as an English attempt to reproduce Venetian *millefiori* in flint glass ; it contains sections of coloured cane in a haphazard arrangement, and at this date seems to be unique.

[212]

The air threads in this glass are irregular and fairly wide apart, and in this respect it resembles Mr. Francis's wine-glass. Finally there is a group of drawn-stem glasses of fair size with engraved baroque borders[1] round the bowl which are certainly before 1730 and may be as early as 1715. In these glasses the air twist is usually much less primitive than in the two instances just cited (Plate XCV and F. Buckley, Plate LVIII A). Thus there would seem to be three stages in the evolution of the air twist. (1) Early in the 18th century and probably at the end of the 17th it was an occasional trick, but was in no sense customary. (2) About 1715–20 it was adopted and fairly frequently used for the one type of glass whose form was best suited to it, namely the drawn-stem wine-glass. Early drawn stems (*e.g.* Plate XCII) often have the large pear-shaped tear ; and when the stem was being drawn out from the base of the bowl it was a comparatively simple matter to prick it and pull out the resulting bubbles into a twist. The air twist probably was peculiar to wine-glasses of this type until about 1735. In the knopped or light baluster types (*supra*, p. 178) it was much more difficult to execute and while these were in vogue the air twist could not be extended to other stems than the drawn stem. But as the knops became fewer and simpler (Plate CX) it was so extended even where one or two knops still remained ; for during the interval the glassmakers had become more skilful with the air twist. (3) After about 1735–40 the air twist becomes general in all sorts of stem, more especially in those which were quite straight, and it continued in very general use for about fifteen years ; after which it was gradually superseded by enamel-twist stems and cut stems. In the last forty years of the century air twists may be regarded as exceptional.[2] It may be added that for obvious reasons the air twist was never used in moulded stems (*e.g.* the shouldered stems) or in cut stems.

Enamel twists. Whereas the air twist had been merely encouraged by the Excise Act of 1745 the enamel twist seems to have been indirectly the result of it (*supra*, p. 201). It was copied from Netherlandish glass rather than from Bohemia, and since the earliest-dated specimen is of the year 1747[3] it was probably introduced immediately after the Excise Act. Being thus later in arrival than the *ubiquitous* air twist it is not common in double- or single-knopped stems, which were beginning to disappear before the enamel twist was really established. The normal stem for the enamel twist is the straight stem. Enamelled stems may be divided into three types, (1) white enamel only, (2) white mixed with coloured enamels, and (3) coloured enamels without white, in what seems to be a chrono-

---

[1] Probably by German metics ; *cf.* p. 238.

[2] For a chandelier of cut-glass (English and about 1770 in date) with branches containing air twists, see *Old Furniture*, I, 215 (illus.).

[3] I owe this information to Mr. Francis Buckley.

logical order. The twist may be a strip or a thread of enamel, and frequently a spiral of one kind is enclosed within a spiral of another kind, strip within thread or thread within strip. The coloured twists were mixed in great variety, and there seems to be no need to analyse the combinations used. Enamel twists in general remained in vogue for about thirty-five years, but after 1760 the cut stem was a serious rival, and all but the coloured twists had passed their prime. Enamel twists may occur in all kinds of stemmed glasses, but in sweetmeat glasses and candlesticks they are very rare. Their vogue was ended by the Second Excise Act (1777) which, besides doubling the duty on flint glass, imposed a tax of 18s. 8d. per cwt. on all enamelled glass.[1] Very few enamel twists seem to have been made after that date.

B. COLOURED GLASS

The dyeing of flint glass by the several metallic oxides belongs æsthetically and economically to the tendency which we have described as compensation by ornament. A glass which depended æsthetically on design, as we have seen, must be lavish of metal, where that metal was lead glass, and an artificial dye offered a cheap technical beauty to take its place. Most authorities have confined the manufacture of coloured domestic glass to the second half of the 18th century and with one important exception, which will be mentioned in a moment, that verdict cannot at present be disturbed, provided the initial date be taken as 1745 and not the arbitrary 1750. But even before the Excise Act there is no ground for assuming that the English glassmakers were *incapable* of making coloured metals. With the single exception to be referred to there are no specimens of coloured glass in the style of the classical period nor even specimens which can be dated before 1745 ; and in this respect the surviving glass probably represents fairly accurately the state of the manufacture. But the hiatus was due to taste rather than incapacity. It may well be that the " Artist Glassmakers " were manipulative workers only, not acquainted with the chemistry of coloured glass, but the owners of London glasshouses in the last quarter of the 17th century were men of intelligence[2] and it is inconceivable that they had not studied the standard textbook of Neri, which had been translated for their benefit and contained the fullest notes of the oxides required for colouring. Moreover, a second work, Haudicquer de Blancourt's *Art of Glass*, which likewise gave directions for colouring glass, had been translated only two years after its publication in France (1697), and at a time when the English industry was full of confidence and

---

[1] F. Buckley, *History*, pp. 94 and 151.
[2] *E.g.* Bowles, Jackson, Gutteridge, and of course Ravenscroft himself.
[3] Buckley, p. 145, Westropp, p. 41 (Dublin, 1729).

enterprise (1699).[1] The translation must have answered a demand in the trade. Moreover, the technique of flint glass had been, in John Cary's phrase, " brought to perfection " (1695) ; and here was all the technical information required. Had the London owners decided that public taste would ensure a demand for coloured glass or that they had any hope of creating one, they could easily have found the means to its manufacture. Coloured glass in fact, like filigree and *millefiori* and a too delicate design, was part of the Venetian tradition which the early flint glassmakers rejected because they preferred to do so ; but there would be nothing impossible in the discovery of a coloured glass made in England even so early as 1700.

There is indeed one type of coloured glass—green—which seems to have been made some time before the Excise Act of 1745 and probably before the end of the 17th century. These early green glasses are with few exceptions either a close version of the German *Roemer* (Plate LXII) or of a shape palpably derived from it (*cf.* p. 327). Apart from Merret's mention of " Romers " there is ample literary evidence that Rummers (" of Rhenish ") were being used in England in the 17th century, and on the analogy of the German stoneware bottles copied at Fulham (" greybeards ") it is likely that they were made here. In these glasses a green metal was in some sense " natural," and the earliest existing specimens of coloured flint glass which are a *pale* green in tint seem to be an attempt to copy the metal as well as the form of the German glasses. About 1720 we find one or two instances of green metal used for other forms of drinking-glass ; an interesting glass in the British Museum[2] with a drawn air-twist stem and an engraved baroque border is a good illustration, as is the wine-glass with a shouldered stem figured in Plate C. *b.* 1. But these early green glasses are far from common.

After the Excise Act the manufacture of green glasses rapidly became a regular practice and when Dr. Richard Pococke visited Stourbridge in 1751 glass was being made " in all the capital colours." It is fairly certain that this statement included flint glass for domestic use as well as plate-glass for windows.[3] Only three years later a German glassmaker, Mayer Oppenheim of Birmingham, had taken out a patent for a particular sort of ruby glass, and this was a much more difficult matter than such colours as blue or green. Moreover, Oppenheim's patent was for domestic glass ; for his specification is explicitly called flint glass and includes the

[1] The glassmakers had just won their first conflict with the Exchequer (*supra*, p. 155) and there were big capitalists in the London industry like Bowles and Jackson. The difficulty in this matter was to adapt prescriptions for colouring soda glass of Venetian type to the totally different metal of flint glass. For the solution of this difficulty in one instance by the Bristol glassmakers, see pp. 26 *sq.*

[2] F. Buckley, *History*, Plate LVIIIA.

[3] It should be made clear that plate glass had been made in colours for centuries : the point at issue in this section is the use of colouring matter for flint glass.

normal percentage of lead oxide. His process was doubtless an attempt to imitate the ruby glasses which had been first made by the German chemist Kunckel some years before ; and whereas window glass was coloured with copper, Oppenheim used a mixture of "braunstein" and "Dutch gold."[1] The fact that a difficult colour like ruby was being made for domestic purposes in 1754 makes it highly probable that domestic glass was included in Pococke's remark. It was probably the novelty of coloured *glasses* which attracted his notice, for coloured glass plates were quite familiar and not likely to cause comment. At Bristol the manufacture of coloured glasses seems to have begun a year or two later. The earliest recorded date for the manufacture of coloured glass at Bristol (1762) is provided by the notebooks of a certain Michael Edkins, who was employed to paint blue and opaque white glass by several of the Bristol glasshouses. A grandson of Michael Edkins, William Edkins, had in his possession a number of opaque white glasses which he knew to have been made at Bristol, and to have been painted by his grandfather. These pieces are all of the fine tin glass whose technique has been already mentioned, and by reference to them it has been held that a family of white opaque glasses of similar quality were made at Bristol, and that the peculiar metal constituted by a small percentage of tin was *peculiar* to Bristol glasshouses. There is no evidence that tin was not used for a like purpose in other centres of glassmaking, but beyond the question of composition the quality of the glasses known to have been made at Bristol is so distinctive that there is little danger in the assertion that glasses of the same metal were made in the same place. Among this family there are several glasses which can be dated as early as *c.* 1755 on the analogy of painting which they bear with painting on contemporary English porcelain,[2] and there exists a piece of the same type which actually bears the date 1757.[3] We are therefore entitled to assert that opaque white glass was being made at Bristol during the pentad 1755–60, and the same may be held true of the blue glass also painted by Michael Edkins, and of certain glasses of fine green metal which can be assigned to Bristol.[4] Approximately, therefore, the manufacture of coloured glass at Bristol seems to have begun between 1745 and 1755. The mean date 1750 is probably accurate within a year or two. Of the three main types of coloured glass made in England in the middle of the 18th century opaque white seems to have owed its inception to two causes besides the Excise Act. The first of these was the early

[1] For these substances see Hartshorne, p. 462.
[2] This was kindly pointed out to me by Mr. Bernard Rackham.
[3] Mr. Arthur Churchill kindly reported this glass to me.
[4] Small enamel-painted scent-bottles, sometimes diamond-cut under the enamels, which occur in similar forms in green and blue glass as well as in the distinctive opaque white metal which has been shown to be of Bristol manufacture. For a type of one of these see Plate CXXXIV.

manufacture of porcelain in England which was closely contemporary with the Excise.[1] The German glassmakers persisted in their not elegant *Milchglas* because it resembled porcelain and could no doubt be very cheaply made, and the establishment of porcelain manufacture in England, especially in a centre of glassmaking as Bristol was, may well have turned the minds of English glassmakers to a like proceeding. And secondly, when Dossie wrote the *Handmaid* (1758) cruet bottles and other small pieces of *Milchglas* were being imported into England,[2] and if we may judge by analogy from the gilt glasses which were imported from Germany and then copied in England, German *Milchglas* also must be accounted a cause of the white opaque glass made in England.

It is a difficult matter to gather the frequent coloured glasses of the latter part of the 18th century round the small nucleus which can certainly be assigned to Bristol flint glasshouses.[3] Coloured glasses were made in considerable quantities at London, on the Tyne, and in the region of Birmingham and Stourbridge. The white opaque glass of these places may be distinguished from that of Bristol, since it approximates the quality of German *Milchglas* rather than of a tin enamel, and is on the whole of a much poorer quality than the Bristol fabric. There is some reason to suppose that the Midlands, and presumably the Tyne also, imparted the white opaque colour to their glasses by means of bone-ash or arsenic rather than by the tin used at Bristol, but there is no evidence that tin was not used by them also. If it was we may expect to find their wares of much heavier quality and more replete with tin than those of Bristol, since the fine quality of the latter seems to be due to the very *small* quantity of tin[4] included in a flint-glass batch. But both at Bristol and elsewhere white opaque glass was largely used for vases and decorative pieces rather than for merely useful wares and in spite of its resemblance to porcelain, tea and coffee sets do not appear to have been made very extensively.[6] The decorative pieces (*e.g.* Plates CXXXV, CXXXVI) were painted in colours

[1] *E.g.* Heylyn and Frye's patent, 1744, Chelsea *c.* 1745, Bristol (Lowdin) *c.* 1750; for which see Honey (W. B.), *Old English porcelain* (1928), pp. 54, 17 *sq.*, and 139 *sq.* respectively.

[2] See p. 25 *supra*.

[3] These were
   1. Temple Street glasshouse, 1701–93.
   2. St. Thomas Street, 1701–98 (flint glass made intermittently, otherwise Crown).
   3. Redcliff Backs.

[4] ·86 per cent in Church's analysis of one of William Edkins's glasses. Owen, *loc. cit.;* and see p. 26 *supra*, where this subject is discussed more fully.

[5] As Oppenheim did not leave the Snow Hill glasshouse till 1783 it must be presumed that he carried his patent into effect. None of his ruby glasses has been identified.

[6] Not apparently because of the hostility of hot liquids to glass; teacups and saucers of white opaque glass were made not infrequently at Venice and in Germany, and clear glass was of course used for punch.

(and also adorned with gold) in the modes current among the contemporary painters of porcelain and the excellence of this attainment at Bristol was no doubt due to the fact that the city was a centre for enamelled earthenware and porcelain as well as for glass, and decorative painters were thus available on the spot (see below p. 225). The differentiation of white opaque glass is a problem which can only be solved satisfactorily by a fairly thorough system of chemical analysis, and the difficulties of such a project are not small.

When we turn to glasses of other colours than opaque white it would seem that Bristol has claimed more than her fair share of existing specimens. There is some definite standard of the blue and green glasses made at Bristol,[1] but during the latter part of the 18th century and in the first half of the 19th, Stourbridge and Birmingham were quite as important centres of coloured glassmaking as Bristol, and it is scarcely conceivable that this fabric was in any sense inferior. This is especially true of plentiful green and blue glasses (*e.g.* decanters, rummers, drinking-glasses, finger bowls), which appear to date from the last quarter of the 18th and the early part of the 19th centuries and are conspicuous for their " slickness " of metal and depth of colouring ; and although Bristol seems to have evolved several distinctive forms (*e.g.* the taper decanter, and the decorative vases of Plate CXXXVI), these were probably copied when their reputation was established. Birmingham has no aura of antiquity. It is not creditable to a glass to say that it was made at Birmingham, partly no doubt because Birmingham made glass at the time of the Great Exhibition (1851). This sentiment has no doubt led many to give a Bristol prestige to late 18th-century coloured glasses which may equally well have been made in London, in the Midlands, on the Tyne, at Warrington, or in Ireland. The accident which has preserved some record of a Bristol glass painter is also to blame for the wholesale attribution of coloured glass to Bristol. No doubt if a painter at Dublin or Birmingham had left his notebooks behind him some other name would have been chosen for a portmanteau. Even when we turn to the early period covered by Edkins's accounts (1762–88) there is no ground for the assumption that several types of coloured glass, for example the small coloured scent-bottles of a type shown in Plate CXXXIV, which have been hitherto called Bristol, were in any sense exclusive to that city. As early as 1752 cut smelling-bottles of all colours were being made in London and sold at Birmingham,[2] and

---

[1] *I.e.* glasses which bear the mark of the firm of Jacobs at Bristol.

[2] *Birm. Gazette*, 27, vii, 1752, cited by Buckley, *History*, p. 121. The cutting at this date was probably flat diamonds ; the smelling-bottles may well have been of the " Bristol " form (Plate CXXXIV), but they are not described as gilt, whereas in 1763 toilet bottles at Bristol were described as blue and gold, but not described as cut, *Bristol Journal*, 15, x, 1763, Buckley, p. 103.

there is some reason for thinking that green glass was being made at Birmingham a year earlier. Moreover Mr. Buckley thought it probable that the manufacture of coloured glass was carried to Warrington by Josiah Perrin some time before 1767, to Dublin by the Williams' in 1764, and to Belfast by Benjamin Edwards in 1771[1] ; and no reason has been advanced for a contrary opinion. The firm of Jacobs at their glasshouse at Temple Street, Bristol, were given to signing their blue glasses in gold, notably their decanters with a gilt label and a gilt chain suspending it from the neck, and there is a frequent series of blue decanters with lozenge stoppers, plain except for the label, which resemble the marked specimens and may perhaps have been made at Temple Street. But apart from these and from the opaque white glass considered above there is no group of coloured glasses which on their style can be certainly assigned to Bristol. It can only be said that coloured glasses of good quality were made there.

C. ENAMEL PAINTING

Dossie writes thus of enamel-painting in 1758 : " The practice of enamel-painting is of late introduction amongst us and the manner of conducting it with respect to the preparation and composition of the colours, fluxes, and grounds has been carefully concealed in places abroad, where it has been longer established, a very small share in the preparation of the colours and yet less of that of the grounds is the whole hitherto gained by the artists of this country." This statement makes it highly probable that enamel-painting in England was first practised subsequently to the Excise Act of 1745, and such a date is consistent with what is known of the early history of painting on porcelain and enamel[2] in this country. The application of painted ornament to glass " for compensation " is a corollary to considerable activity on the part of Englishmen to introduce into England numerous chemical modes of decoration practised on the Continent. This movement had been in progress for some few years before Dossie wrote, and it declared itself formal in 1755 by the foundation of a " Society for the Encouragement of the Arts and Manufactures "— the present Society of Arts ; and the progress of decoration in England and in particular the decoration of glass, enamel, porcelain, must be largely attributed to the chemical knowledge which it made available to the public. Dr. Lewis himself was associated with it and he had spent many years in research before he published his exceedingly important book *The*

[1] Buckley, *History*, p. 103.
[2] As at Bilston and Battersea. Both the colours applied and the ground are enamel in character. I use the term enamel-painting in connection with glass to denote painting in white or coloured enamels on a ground which may (as in Bristol opaque white glass) or may not (as in the glasses painted by the Beilbys at Newcastle-on-Tyne) be itself of enamel character.

Philosophical Commerce of Arts in 1763. I have no information of Dossie himself but he inscribed his *Handmaid* to the Society of Arts and in an introductory letter he pointed out " the correspondence betwixt the design of this work and the views of your institution." Progress was very rapid at this time, not progress merely in applying the new knowledge but further progress in the labour of research, and only six years after the publication of the *Handmaid* the author's own investigations had rendered his work obsolete. A new edition, published in 1764, contained much new matter, and the discrepancies between the two editions are the differences between borrowing a process and making it your own. The endeavours of the Society were viewed with favour by the Sovereign, and some of the experiments which Lewis published in the *Commercium* had been performed at Kew by Royal Command.[1] The two books published under its auspices were written by individuals and were not officially published by the Society, but in their matter and their spirit they stood for a corporate enterprise, and in view of the state of the arts at that time they were a very considerable achievement, comparable in their own sphere to the *Philosophical Transactions*. The Society of Arts, like the Royal Society, stood for the application of scientific and especially chemical knowledge to the arts, and their work was as effective in the distribution of knowledge as in the encouragement of enterprise by the premiums they offered.[2]

In the particular field of glassmaking the Society of Arts received a just tribute from Bosc d'Antic,[3] and the age of ornament of which one aspect is discussed in the present section must be explained as much by its appetition as by the decorative influences which came from abroad.

The materials requisite for painting on flint glasses were four in number. (1) Metallic substances used as colours. (2) The glass or vitreous matter mixed with the colour in order to bind it together, that is to say the flux. (3) An oil medium described by Dossie as the secondary vehicle ; this was worked up with the colouring matter and the flux in

[1] *Com. Phil. Tech. init.* The Royal Licence which inaugurates the book is dated 1761, but nearly all the work embodied in it had been done during the previous reign, and the interested monarch was certainly George II.

[2] The tendency of which the Society of Arts formed a part had issue in the industrial arts of the 19th century. It turned technique into technology, and the results are not now highly esteemed. But it seems probable that criticism in the future will be content to regard the 19th century as a period of gestation, not the death of a technique, but the birth of one. The 19th century in discovering technology discovered a new *artistic* technique which the present century is beginning to employ. Many of the cranes, turbines, motor-cars, aeroplanes, and other machines of the present time are things of great beauty, and they may well be regarded as a collective art, cultural and anonymous, like the art of the Middle Ages, beside which the arts of the 18th century will one day be reckoned neat and paltry.

[3] *Supra*, p. 159.

order to give them sufficient fluidity for painting, and it evaporated during the firing of the colours. (4) A white-enamel ground ; in some instances (*e.g.* Plate CXXIII) this was fired on the surface of clear flint glass and the enamel colours were then painted over it, but when the immediate ground was Bristol opaque white glass, this was of course omitted. In other instances white enamel was painted directly on the surface of clear flint glass as in the glasses so decorated by the Beilbys. Dossie complained in 1758 that the English painters on enamel were obliged to prepare a white enamel made at Venice for the ground and " to put up the remains of a kind of glass formerly made there for a flux and to procure the colours." Dossie gave in his second edition the most elaborate instructions for preparing the grounds, fluxes, and colours, and though he refers chiefly to the painting of " pictures " on glass plates there was no essential difference between that technique and painting on drinking-glasses or on white opaque glass vases. He refers to painting on glass vessels as well as on glass plates and for the latter required " crown glass which being a glass of salts is hard and transparent." Flint glass was less suitable because it contained over 40 per cent of lead and was soft ; and that is no doubt responsible for the scarcity of English flint glass painted in enamel colours.

Bristol is the city chiefly associated by tradition with painting on glasses, and here the art seems to have been chiefly confined to coloured glasses of the more delicate kind, though as far as I am aware there is no evidence that clear glasses also were not painted at Bristol. All our positive knowledge of the Bristol painting is derived from some particulars which have been preserved concerning Michael Edkins, a promiscuous decorator who lived at Bristol and was employed by several of the glasshouses to paint glasses. The only sources of this information are (1) a statement written by the painter's grandson, William Edkins, Junior, an eminent citizen of Bristol and a collector of local art, to the dictation of his father, William Edkins, Senior, in or about the year 1840. (2) Certain notebooks and accounts formerly in the possession of Michael Edkins. (3) Information obtained from William Edkins, Junior, by the late Hugh Owen of Bristol and published by him in his *Two Centuries of Ceramic Art at Bristol* (1873), and (4) a collection of glass made by William Edkins, Junior, among which some pieces were stated by him to have been painted by his grandfather. This information was gathered together by Owen, but his book is not now very accessible and it may be convenient to repeat the facts here. Michael Edkins appears to have come from Birmingham[1] to Bristol at the age of about twenty shortly before 1762. The first entry in his ledger, a charge of three guineas to Mr. William Powell " for painting a post chaise with handsome gold ornaments, cyphers, and crests ; carriage and

[1] Several of the Beilby family were also apprenticed at Birmingham, then the chief centre of enamel work.

wheels vermillion," is dated February 1762 and the motto *Veni Vidi Vici* on the cover of the book seems to show that his arrival was recent.[1] The narrative of his life may be continued in the statement of his son[2] :

My father was apprenticed in a manufactory in Birmingham ; his master died before his apprenticeship expired, when he came to Bristol and became acquainted with Mr. Thomas Patience and the Hope family who were delft potters at Mr. Frank's delft pottery on Redcliffe Back ; close to Messrs. Little and Longman's glasshouse now (*c.* 1840) Llewellyn's wharf ; where he became a pot painter—that is, to ornament dishes, Flemish[3] tiles for grates dairies etc., which were all at that time painted by the hand with pencils made by the workmen themselves, of bristles from the noses and eyelids of oxen. He followed the pot painting till the delft pottery declined, when he became a coach and general painter. Was with Mr. Moffat and Mr. Simmons ; both in Bristol. Was Mr. Simmons' right-hand man—assisted him for instance in such works as the bas relief paintings on each side the altar piece in Redcliffe Church which he principally painted, and he wrote the decalogue etc. At length he pitched his tent in Bridge Street where he did the principal part of the decorative work and coach-painting in the city and neighbourhood. He was exceedingly clever at ornamenting enamel and blue glass-ware, then much in vogue, at which he had no equal ; which he principally did for Messrs. Vigor and Stevens, successors to Messrs. Little and Longman. He was a very good musician and charming counter tenor singer, so much so that Mr. Powell (who died in Bristol and was buried in the Cathedral) introduced him on the stage in Bristol and Covent Garden London. He would probably have settled in the latter place but for the dispute between Mr. Powell the proprietor and Messrs. Rutherford Coleman and other proprietors ; but he quitted the theatre in disgust and returned to his business in Bristol. Still when the London Company came down in the summer he and several other tradesmen—viz. Winstone and Richards etc. (which was the custom of the time) played and sang whilst they (the London Company) were here. But he had a stronger inducement than the others, being more connected with the Theatre, as he painted the scenery properties etc. He had a large family—thirty three children.

To this account may be added one or two other facts. In 1859 William Edkins, Junior, showed Owen a set of half a dozen delft plates bearing the initials $\frac{E}{M\ B}$ over the date 1760, which he said had been painted by his grandfather. Owen states, no doubt on the authority of William Edkins, Junior, that the initials stood for Michael Edkins and his wife Betty and were painted by him " as a labour of love " shortly before he left Richard Frank's pottery. Pountney adds that Michael Edkins did a great deal of work for Joseph Flower, who was a friend of his, and shared his interest in music and the theatre, and that Edkins also painted at least one signboard. It would appear from the former statement that Edkins married about the time of his arrival in Bristol, and at a very early age, but there is not as far as I know any evidence to show where his wife came from or where the marriage took place. If Owen's statement concerning the plates is correct—and there is no reason to doubt it—they must have been painted retrospectively some years after the marriage.

Owen, p. 331, note 2.   [2] *Ibid.*, pp. 330–2.
[3] Made at Bristol but called Flemish after the imported wares from the Netherlands.

This vivid creature seems to have fallen out of the Renaissance by mistake. If you put his portrait[1] between the anecdotes of his grandson and the pages of his ledger it is not difficult to see what manner of man he was : sensitive, petulant, prolific, always at work and always short of money, carried away by his tastes and overridden with children, a very fair specimen of temperament in an age when artists were tradesmen and temperaments not encouraged. A perverse fortune might have dropped him in Staffordshire, a gloomy land of prudence and endeavour. There he would have grown a little steadfast and unhappy. But culture was gay at Bristol and rather cosmopolitan, and it was scarcely an accident that having chosen Bristol he found there spirits like his own. He has perhaps no right to a reputation, for Bristol painting was essentially a collective art, signed by the city which produced it[2] with a fancy which Staffordshire was too serious, and porcelain too sophisticated to attain. On the whole it was a reasonable irony which required that Edkins should live life for his hobbies and be remembered for his hackwork. Edkins painted for the following glasshouses at Bristol :

> 1762–1767 Little and Longman, Redcliffe Backs
> 1767–1787 Longman and Vigor   „   „
> 1765   William Dunbar and Co., Bristol and Chepstow
> 1775–1787 Vigor and Stevens, Thomas Street
> 1785–1787 Lazarus Jacobs, Temple Street

and the following extracts from his ledger contain references to glass[3] ; they indicate which among existing objects may possibly have been painted or gilt by him. I have modernized the spelling.

				s.	d.
1762.	Apl. 26.	To five doz. enamel beakers		10	0
	Jan. 19.	To one set of jars and beakers 5 in a set		2	6
	July 19.	To 4 blue jars and beakers with mosaic borders to match a large set for Mr. Wilson		2	0
	26.	To 1 pint blue can ornamented with gold and letters			8
1763.	Aug. 18.	To 6 enamelled pint cans "wrote" *Liberty and no Excise* at 4d.		2	0
	Sept. 30.	To 18 enamel basins		1	6
	Oct. 28.	To 13 cans and milk jugs		1	1
1764.	Oct. 1.	To 4 enamel canisters		1	0
1766.	Aug. 20.	To 6 long doz. fine wine (-glasses) "wrote" *Pitt and Liberty* at 3s.	£1	16	0
1769.	(No date).	To three pr. blue cornucopias ("Cornicopios") ornamented with gold		3	0
1770.	Nov. 6.	To 12 hyacinth glasses, blue gilded		2	0

[1] Engraved by Owen, Fig. 117, after an oil painting formerly in the possession of William Edkins, Junior.

[2] The identification of Bristol delft painters is an amusing game, but I am not sure that it does not in itself imply a misunderstanding of their art. They are not meant to be identified, not even by those who must find an " Artist " in everything.

[3] Owen, pp. 380–1.

A further list seems to refer to a " parcel " of goods exported to Europe or the Colonies[1] and is undated.

A venture delivered to Michael Palmer.

	s.	d.
2 large sets enamel jars and beakers	11	0
3 blue quart cans	9	0
6 ditto pints	9	0
1 small set jars and beakers blue	2	6
12 enamel half pint cans	5	0
12 ditto basins	0	5
1 enamel cream jug	0	5

in a box marked MP *stores.*

A second box contained :

	s.	d.
1 large set blue jars and beakers	7	6
2 pint blue cans	3	0
2 ditto enamel beakers	2	6
12 enamel beakers	5	0
4 ditto basins	1	8
12 blue basins	8	0
12 blue half pint cans	8	0
2 boxes	2	6

Marked No. MP 2
Stores.

All the items in this list must be presumed to have been painted in enamel colours ; where glasses were gilt either without painting in colours or in addition to it this seems to be indicated in the ledger. Enamel in the list refers to white opaque glass, not of course to the colouring matter. Canisters probably refer to tea-caddies of the type shown in the Frontispiece, and basins to finger bowls,[2] and some other items are obvious, but it is not certain to what precise forms " cans," " beakers," and " jars " should be referred. Owen referred to a covered vase (type Plate CXXXV. *b.* 1) as a jar and to an open vase (type Plate CXXXV. *a.* 3) as a beaker.[3]

There remains the difficult problem of identifying Edkins's work. There are two avenues of approach. William Edkins, Junior, was a general collector and he had among other things a number of pieces of Bristol opaque white glass. These included some specimens which William Edkins declared to have been painted by his grandfather, but only one type is specifically mentioned, tea-caddies decorated with birds and flowers and labelled for different kinds of tea—BLACK, GREEN, BOHEA, HYSON. Several of these exist at the present time, and the painting, both birds and flowers, may with reasonable certainty be attributed to Edkins. One of

[1] Owen (p. 382) suggests the Colonies, but Lady Charlotte Schreiber found several pieces of Bristol white opaque glass in the Netherlands, including two candlesticks which will be identified in a moment as painted by Edkins (*Journals*, 1911, Vol. I, Plate facing p. 1, and Vol. II, p. 292).

[2] Buckley (*History*, p. 108) cites an advertisement of " finger basins " (1793).

[3] Owen, pp. 383–4.

these which came originally from William Edkins's collection is in the Victoria and Albert Museum (Frontispiece) and another, formerly the property of Lady Charlotte Schreiber, is now in the same museum (*ibid.*). Both these show on one side a finely painted bird (not the same bird) perched on a branch, and on the other a bouquet of closely painted flowers whereof the brushwork has a rather "swirled" effect. It is conceivable, but not, I think, very likely, that the flowers were added by a painter different from the painter of the birds, and if it be assumed that this was not so we may argue from the flower-painting to the painting on other types of opaque white Bristol glass. Flower-painting of *precisely* the same kind is found on a group of white opaque candlesticks some of which have wrythen stems (Plate CXXXV. *b.* 2). No candlesticks are mentioned in the extracts from Michael Edkins's ledger made by Owen, but the argument from style in this case seems quite convincing. There are several other types of flower-painting on Bristol glass, but they all differ considerably in detail from the neat "swirled" flowers of the candlesticks and the tea-caddies. Among them several distinct types of flower-painting (*e.g.* Plate CXXXV. *b.* 1) can be distinguished, which may be the work of distinct painters. Edkins was, as we have seen, a very versatile artist, and it is conceivable that he had several different flower styles, but at the time he worked there were numerous other decorative painters in Bristol, and on the evidence that has been brought forward hitherto there is no warrant for attributing any or all of them to his hand.

The other avenue of approach lies through the delft earthenware plates with Edkins's and his wife's initials and the date 1760 (p. 222 *supra*). One of these plates is now in the British Museum and another at South Kensington, and both of them show figure and garden subjects in the Chinese style. Chinese subjects not very remote in style from the painting of the delft plates are also found on opaque white Bristol glass, particularly on a series of large vases (*e.g.* Plate CXXXVI). But the Chinese style was a commonplace among the decorative artists who painted Bristol delft and Bristol porcelain in the latter part of the 18th century,[1] and even where the ground of the painting was roughly the same, as in Bristol delft, the differentiation of styles is not easy and their attribution to artists whose names are known very precarious indeed. And this difficulty is further increased when the ground is in one case an ordinary covering enamel, comparatively coarse, and in the other a very fine glass containing less than 1 per cent of tin. Moreover, in one instance, a white opaque vase at South Kensington, where the Chinese painting seems most to resemble the painting of the delft plates, the painting has been dated by Mr. Rackham to about 1755 by analogy with the painting on contemporary porcelain ;

[1] See Pountney (W. J.), *Old Bristol potteries.*

and in 1755 it is not certain that Edkins had yet arrived in Bristol.[1] The glasses and the plates have in fact little in common but the fact that the painted subjects are a Bristol version of the Chinese manner ; and that in itself is no argument for authorship.

That Michael Edkins painted on blue glass is proved by his ledger, but as far as I am aware there is no blue glass of which the painting has been ascribed to Edkins with the same authority as the labelled tea-caddies, nor do there seem to be any blue glasses in existence which can be identified with the descriptions in Edkins's ledger, e.g. "blue jars and beakers with mosaic borders" or blue cans "ornamented with gold and letters" ; and without some such object of reference it is impossible to proceed further. There is a well-known family of small scent-bottles and other trinket glasses cut in diamonds or gilt or painted in enamel colours (Plate CXXXIV), these techniques being employed singly or by twos or even all together. Bristol has long had a reputation for coloured and painted glass of the first quality and these pieces are certainly finely done ; but that again is not proof.

Clear flint glasses were also painted in white and coloured enamels, but apparently not before 1755. A good many of these glasses can be assigned to a family of decorative artists who did glass-painting at New-castle-on-Tyne for about twenty years, c. 1760–80. There were probably decorative artists in many parts of the country who could do work of this kind.[2] Michael Edkins himself may have done it since the "fine wine" glasses in his ledger are not specified as "blue" or "enamell." But since this decoration at Bristol seems to have been confined to coloured or white opaque glasses we may look elsewhere for the painting on clear glass. And since there is no evidence that painters of the latter sort were gathered together in one city or school peculiarities of style will be a surer guide than in the case of Edkins.

The glasses attributable to the Beilbys of Newcastle may be divided into three groups.

A. *The white family.* The wine-glasses are of small size with straight-sided or ogee bowl, and enamel-twist stem, and there are also a number of ale-glasses of the same period. The decoration on all these is in white enamel only and may be divided stylistically into three groups.

---

[1] The first entry in his ledger is dated February, 1762.
[2] "Curious paintings on glass" were advertised at Bristol, probably by a London merchant, in 1755, and almost certainly indicate a novelty (*Bristol Journal*, 28, vi, 55) ; this probably refers, like "engraved glass pictures," to vessels. Enamelled glasses were advertised by Phillips of King's Lynn in 1771 (*Norwich Mercury*, 9, ii, 71) and "newest fashioned wine-glasses . . . enamelled" by this same warehouse in 1758 (*ibid.*, 5, viii, 58) and "enamelled glasses" in 1757 (*Ipswich Journal*, 12, ii, 57). Enamelled decanters were advertised by B. Edwards of the Drumrea Glasshouse in 1772 (Westropp, p. 99).

THE AGE OF ORNAMENT

1. Naturalistic motives copied from wheel engraving, *e.g.* flowers, vine motives, hops, barley heads, floral festoons, and occasionally birds.

2. Rustic subjects of a fanciful and agreeable kind, *e.g.* hunting-scenes, fishing, shooting, skating, and idyllic subjects (Plate CXXXII).

3. Conventional scenes, half fanciful, half decorative, especially landscapes with classical ruins, obelisks and the like, or very occasionally figure subjects in the Chinese style (Plate CXXXI. 1).

Among the white family must be included the painting of several decanters with rococo panels and vine and grape motives (Plates CXXX. 2, CXXXI. 2).

B. Landscapes in colours supported by rococo scrollwork. These are very rare; two specimens only are known to me, one in Mr. Clements's collection (Plate CXXIII. 2) and an inferior painting of the same scene in the Victoria and Albert Museum.

C. Heraldic glasses, the arms painted in colours and white.

1. Goblets with very elaborate heraldic work supported by rococo scrollwork, vine motives, hops, or festoons. The bowls are usually ogee or of square bucket shape (Plate CXXIV) and there is considerable range of colour. Several firing glasses (*e.g.* Plate CXXIII) must also be included in this category, though their decoration is much simpler, and also the decanter in Plate CXXX. 1 which has the same arms as Plate CXXIV and was probably a member of the same set. These glasses are rare.

2. Tall goblets with long-knopped stems and short flaring bowls. The painting on these usually takes the form of fictitious heraldry (Plate CXXXI. 3) or as in Plate CXXXII. *b.* 3, a lover's token. The range of colours is much more restricted than the heraldic glasses proper.

In two of these groups we have specimens which bear a signature. One of these glasses illustrated and described in Plate CXXIV bears the Royal Arms as borne by George II and George III, and can be dated by the style of the glass to about the year 1760; since it bears also the three feathers of the Prince of Wales it seems probable that it was made and decorated to celebrate the birth of George III's eldest son, George Augustus Frederick, afterwards George IV (b. 12 August, 1762). The signature on this glass is *Beilby NCastle invt & pinxt,* and several other heraldic glasses, of which a few bear the royal coat of arms (*e.g.* the decanter in Plate CXXX. 1), though they are not signed, can be certainly attributed to the same hand; it is probable that one or two sets of wine-glasses with the Royal Arms were painted to order about the same time. The other signed glass belongs to group C2 (Plate CXXXI. 1 and 3) and bears the signature *Beilby pinxit;* on one side is a fictitious coat of arms, on the other classical ruins with an obelisk. The latter may be compared with the "classical" glasses in the third division of the "white family," and the treatment of the heraldic side of the glass makes it certain that another group of unsigned glasses conspicuous for amorous or fantastic heraldry were painted by the same hand, or at any rate in the same workshop as the person who signed himself Beilby.

From these two glasses and their immediate camp-followers numerous other glasses in the white family and the not numerous coloured family can be awarded to the same author ; and this on two grounds, first that the white enamel in all three groups (A, B, C) is almost always conspicuous for a faint tincture of blue which seems to have been an accident peculiar to this workshop, and secondly that several items of style which occur on the signed glasses or their immediate fellows can be traced on the other glasses by direct or secondary comparison. A " royal " glass seen by the writer had hops and vine motives besides the coat, and this connects with the decanter on Plate CXXX. 1 and with a fairly numerous group of ale- and wine-glasses where the treatment of these motives is exactly similar. The tall slender leaves of *Beilby pinxit* occur also in Plate CXXXII. *b*. 3 (goblet), and again on a small ale-glass (Plate CXXXII. *a*. 2) ; whence the train of analogies may proceed to glasses which have flower-painting alone, the flower in Plate CXXII. *a*. 2 being established as a Beilby item. Plate CXXX. 2 connects with Plate CXXX. 1, and this with the signed glass, and in Plate CXXIII. 2 both the sentiment and the composition resemble the small " white " glass of Plate CXXXII. *b*. 2. The latter again connects with the small series of sports and pastimes some of which appear in Plate CXXXII. *b*. 1, 5. The very characteristic rococo scrolls of the signed "royal" glass occur in the "white family" as do the festoons of Plate CXXIV and the hatched brushwork of Plate CXXX. 1, the butterfly of Plate CXXX. 2 and several other features more minute. In fact the glasses which can be attributed to this workshop are fairly numerous, but not too numerous to warrant the attribution ; for it will be shown in a moment that at least two painters were engaged on this work and for a period of nearly twenty years.[1]

The engraver Thomas Bewick was an unruly youth, and when he was fourteen years old (1767) and living at Cherryburn in the county of Durham, his parents apprenticed him to a certain Ralph Beilby, an engraver of Newcastle-on-Tyne, who with his brother William had ridden out one day to pay a visit in the neighbouring village of Bywell. Bewick's indentures lasted seven years (1767–74) and after three further years spent in travel and study he was taken into partnership (1777) by his former master, and rapidly became the leading spirit in the new firm. During his apprenticeship Bewick lived with his master's family and in an autobiography written many years afterwards[2] he records some details of Ralph Beilby himself and of his brothers and sisters ; and his evidence makes it certain that

[1] For some other types of white enamelled glasses see *Connoisseur*, LXXXI, 10–23 (1928).
[2] Bewick (T.), *A memoir of Thomas Bewick written by himself*. London and Newcastle-on-Tyne, 1862.

[228]

two of the latter were the painters, and probably the sole painters, of the Beilby glasses. The father of the family, William Beilby, was born at Scarborough, 12 March, 1706, and on 1 September, 1733, he married a Mary Bainbridge at Durham (d. 1778). He was a jeweller and silver-smith by trade and a man of some standing in the city of Durham. He had seven children, John (b. May, 1734, d. July, 1755), Richard (b. May, 1736, d. June, 1766), Elizabeth (b. August, 1738, d. April, 1813), William (b. June, 1740, d. February, 1819), Ralph (b. August, 1743, d. January, 1817), Thomas (b. December, 1747, d. November, 1826), and Mary (b. 1749, d. 1797). The father, William Beilby, had come to grief in business at Durham and about 1760 he and his family migrated to Newcastle-on-Tyne, where he died in 1765,[1] two years before Bewick's connection with the family began. The Beilbys were thus left (1765) in great straits and Mrs. Beilby took employment at a school in Gateshead while her children practised their several arts. The two eldest children had died before Bewick went to Newcastle and are not mentioned by him, nor does he refer to the eldest daughter Elizabeth, who seems to have left home to be married, also before Bewick's arrival. Of the remaining four children, who were all artists, Bewick gives some particulars. Ralph Beilby was junior to William, but a certain firmness of character and greater prosperity in business had established him as the head of the family. He had been apprenticed as a seal-cutter, but appar-ently finding that this business did not meet the needs of the family he had become a general engraver and accepted any kind of engraving that was offered him. " Such was the industry of my master that he refused nothing coarse or fine. He undertook everything which he did in the best way he could. He bitted up and tempered his own tools and adapted them to his own purpose and taught me to do the same. This readiness brought him in an overflow of work and the work-place was filled with the coarsest kind of steel lamps, pipe moulds, bottle moulds, brass clock-faces, door plates, coffin plates, book-binders, letters, and stamps, steel, silver and gold rings, etc. He also undertook the engraving of arms, crests, and cyphers on silver and every kind of silversmith's work, also engraving bills of exchange, bank-notes, invoices, account-heads, and cards."[2] Bewick adds that his master never thought of landscape or historical work,[3] and it is evident that he was primarily an engraver and jeweller. Had he been a painter of glass Bewick in so detailed a description would almost certainly have said so. Thomas again had learnt enamelling from William, but he seems to have been mainly a drawing-master and in 1769–70, in the middle of Bewick's apprenticeship, he was teaching at Grimshaw's Academy, Leeds.[4]

[1] *Archæologia Aeliana*, xi, 70.   [2] Bewick, *Memoir*, pp. 56–7.
[3] He made some attempt to learn landscape-engraving but did not care for it.
[4] This fact was ascertained by Mr. Francis Buckley.

It would appear that he was not permanently at home and his profession together with Bewick's silence make it unlikely that he did glass-painting.[1]

There remain William and Mary, who in 1762 were aged respectively twenty-two and thirteen. About 1767 when Bewick joined the household and the brother and sister were aged twenty-seven and eighteen they had " constant employment of enamel-painting on glass "[2] ; and Bewick does not say that any other member of the household did painting on glass. The glass-painting we have been considering must therefore be attributed either to William or Mary or to both working in collaboration. The Prince of Wales glass (Plate CXXIV) is the earliest evidence of this activity, but in 1762 Mary was only thirteen years old and not likely to have had any hand in it. On that account I would assign the big heraldic glasses (Group C 1) to William Beilby, but the other types appear to be rather later in date, and it would not be proper to distinguish the work of one artist from the other. The signature in all instances known to me is " Beilby " without further name or initial, and it is likely that the young sister followed fairly closely the style of the brother who taught her. The glasses painted by these two are fairly numerous, but this is not surprising, since their work continued for seventeen or eighteen years and Bewick's word " constant " suggests that it was their chief occupation.

The latest date for the glass-painting can be approximately fixed by three considerations. (1) In 1777 Ralph Beilby entered into partnership with his former pupil and thereafter was concerned mainly with engraving copper plates for the numerous books which Bewick illustrated.[3] (2) Old Mrs. Beilby died in June, 1778.[4] (3) The concurrence of these two events probably meant a break-up of the family. Ralph had now other interests than the maintenance of the family, Thomas was an independent unit, and the rest of the family being dead or married, William[5] and Mary had thus lost their home, and having been always a " pair " in the Beilby family seem to have left Newcastle together and went to live in Fifeshire, where Mary died in 1797. Some while before the end (1 October, 1774) of his apprenticeship Bewick had formed a distressing attachment for Mary Beilby (then aged about twenty-three), but shortly before his articles expired she had a paralytic stroke which seems to have made her an invalid.

[1] It is possible that he assisted William with heraldic work, which he understood, but it is doubtful whether this help extended to the actual painting. Ralph Beilby attained some eminence in Newcastle and was a man of wide interests outside his profession.

[2] Bewick, *Memoir*, pp. 56–7.

[3] *British Birds, British Quadrupeds, Gay's Fables and other works*. See B.M. Catalogue, *s.v.*

[4] I am indebted for this fact and other information to a genealogy in the possession of Miss Hannah Bennett, a connection of the Beilby family. *Archæologia Aeliana*, XIV, 112 incorrectly states that Mrs. Beilby was still alive in 1789.

[5] He did not marry until *c.* 1790 ; his eldest child was born in 1794.

Bewick adds[1] that "long after this" she and William went to live in Fifeshire. Bewick, however, was writing a casual memoir many years afterwards and it is probable that their departure followed immediately on Mrs. Beilby's death (1778). The year 1778 may therefore be taken as the last terminus for their glass-painting and it is quite consistent with the existing specimens, none of which can be dated on form to the last twenty years of the 18th century.

D. GILDING

Oil gilding of a type to be described hereafter is occasionally found before the Excise Act of 1745 and its introduction must be ascribed to the decorative immigration from Germany which began early in the reign of George I. After the Excise the practice of gilding gave a good opportunity for "compensation by ornament," but the technical difficulty of a suitable medium was always considerable. The technique was at first ancillary to engraving and enamel-painting. The latter point is explicitly stated by Dossie and the connection with engraving is evident from certain glasses engraved with Jacobite emblems which can be dated before 1750 and show faint traces of gilding over the engraved design.[2] But the regular fashion in gilt glasses seems to have begun between 1745 and 1758 and was certainly due to the importation of gilt glasses from Germany,[3] that is to say from Bohemia and Thuringia.[4] It was the excellence of these glasses that the gold was burnt into the ground and therefore proved durable, but English decorators who tried to imitate them with an oil process seem to have had considerable difficulty at all times in getting a satisfactory result ; the Jacobite glasses just referred to are some of their early failures. In 1758 the situation was thus described by Dossie : "The gilding enamel and glass by vitreous colours and annealing was a necessary appendage to the art of painting in enamel ; but there is yet another criterion which made the communication of the best method of doing this of some importance to the public. It is the great demand now (1758) subsisting for drinking-glasses with gilt edges which are mostly at present either imported from Germany or fraudulently imitated here by gilding with gum-water or sizes that will not bear moisture." Dossie goes on to describe the process of oil gilding and explains why it was generally a failure in England.

Both oil gilding and fired gilding were practised in England when Dossie wrote. The method of oil gilding consisted in cementing gold leaf on the surface of glass by means of an oil or varnish medium and without

---

[1] *Memoir*, p. 79.
[2] The dark colour of the engraved part in some of the Jacobite glasses is referred to here. This is of course due to the oil medium, not to the gold.
[3] Dossie, *op. cit.*, Vol. I, p. 470 (1 ed., 1758).
[4] Lewis, *Com. Phil. Tech.* (1763), p. 614.

subsequent firing in a muffle or coffin. "When drinking-glasses are to be gilt without burning there should either be some gold size formed of oil, or some kind of varnish compounded of the gum resins, that will not dissolve in water but require either spirit of wine or turpentine for their solution. At present, nevertheless, this is not only neglected by those who gild drinking-glasses for sale, but glasses gilded with gum Arabic or the sizes which will dissolve in water are imposed upon the public for the German glasses gilt with annealed gold and sold at a dear rate under that pretence ; though after they have been used for a very short time the gold peels off and rubs off in spots when the glasses are cleaned and renders them very unsightly. As the glasses with gilt edges are at present[1] much in fashion and the true kind are brought from Germany or elsewhere,[2] the incitement of the cultivating this branch of gilding here would not be an unfit object of the premiums of the worthy society[3] for the encouragement of the arts. . . ."[4]

Dossie also describes in both editions of his work (1758 and 1764) the method of gilding enamel and glass " by burning," *i.e.* by firing in a muffle or coffin. The gilding might be done, he says, either by the aid of a flux, for which glass of salts is suggested, or without any flux at all. Similarly the gold itself might be applied either in the form of leaf gold blown upon the surface of the glass, or in the form of gold powder sprinkled upon it. If the leaf gold was to be used without flux a weak solution of gum was required to act as an adhesive on the surface of the glass ; if a flux was used then the flux was treated with the gum adhesive. Dossie states further that for burnt gilding it was better to avoid a flux, as its absence left the surface of the gold more even ; and this was no doubt the usual method in England where glass of salts was not generally[5] made. The mention of glass of salts (borax), indeed, makes it likely that Dossie was simply transcribing a German process. When the gold had been made to adhere to the glass it was fired in a muffle ; when the ground was soft, as in lead glass, only a low temperature was necessary, to prevent the ground flooding the application. The firing process was the conclusion common to all the varieties of burnt gilding described by Dossie and it is this, and not burnishing, which distinguishes the two processes. When the gold had been fired-on the burnishing was done by means of a piece of bone, an iron burnisher, or "a fine agate," but Dossie and Lewis agree that unfired gilding with an oil medium could also be burnished if desired. The term burnished gilding has sometimes been taken as necessarily

[1] Anno 1758.
[2] Bohemia and Thuringia ; see above.
[3] The Society of Arts, founded shortly before this was written.
[4] Dossie, *Handmaid*, 1 ed., I, 372, 2 ed., I, 470.
[5] For domestic purposes ; crown glass was not lead glass.

implying a fire process, and as distinct from "oil gilding." The real distinction is between fired and unfired gilding, and it would appear that when Dossie wrote the former method was chiefly used when a muffle was required for firing on coloured enamels and gilt ornament was fired on at the same time ; as was no doubt done by the manufacturers of coloured glass (*e.g.* Plate CXXXIV) whether at Bristol or elsewhere.[1] In his account of fired or "burnt" gilding Dossie makes no reference to the gilt rims of wine-glasses, and we may conclude that in 1758 at any rate these were always gilt by the unfired process by the aid of one or other of the oil or resinous mediums. Unfired gilding continued to be used until the end of the century, and is found on coloured glasses of a rough sort which were painted in oil-colours and not in coloured enamels (*e.g.* lovers' tokens of blue glass).

Dr. Lewis, like Dossie, remarks on the importation of German gilt-rimmed glasses[2] and, like Dossie, he was much concerned for the improvement of arts and manufactures. His book was, however, due to his own investigations of some years' duration, and is quite independent of his predecessor. He had obtained from a German chemist, Ziegler, an improved method of gilding which he seems to have intended for the rims of wine-glasses. It is intermediate between Dossie's unfired oil process and his fired and burnished gilding. Lewis claimed that by the Ziegler process gilt glasses might be prepared " as durable as those brought from Bohemia and Thuringia." The medium used was amber and oil, strengthened with white lead ; in this respect it differs from any process described by Dossie, the lead being no doubt an adaptation of the varnish to the lead metal of English glass. This substance after standing for some while was applied very thin on the surface of the glass and the gold leaf then blown[3] upon the glass and pressed down by the application of a piece of cotton. Lewis does not leave it at this, nor does he state that the glasses were definitely fired in a muffle. He merely required that they should be " laid in a warm place," until the varnish was properly hardened ; after which the gold was to be burnished, no doubt by the means which Dossie describes.

There are thus four pieces of evidence for the earliest gilt glasses, (1) the Jacobite glasses of *c.* 1745–50 with traces of gilding and some few earlier specimens, (2) Dossie's statement that gilt-rimmed glasses were being

[1] For these details see 1st ed., I, 320–2 ; 2nd ed., I, 374–9. I have not thought it necessary to give any account of gilding with sprinkled gold dust, and suspect that this was the method employed for the German gilt-rimmed wine-glasses which retain their gold so well even after nearly two centuries. The sprinkled gold was of course fired and burnished just as gold leaf.

[2] *Com. Phil. Tech.* (1763), p. 614.

[3] Dossie and Lewis agree on this. I do not think Mr. Buckley can be right in stating that the gold was " painted " on the surface of the glasses (*History*, p. 109).

made in England (1758) and similar implication by Lewis, (3) the evidence of Edkins's ledger that coloured glass was being gilt at Bristol in 1762, and finally (4) the advertisement of " gilt glasses " in 1766 by the unknown German at Bath,[1] and very frequently during the next twenty years. Again, the surviving specimens of gilt glass may be divided into three types, (1) wine-glasses with traces of edges and several other imperfect types which were palpably gilt by an oil medium and not fired, (2) coloured and opaque glass painted in fired colours and gilt also presumably by a fire process, both types being subsequently burnished, and (3) occasional clear glasses where the gilding though fairly well preserved does not appear to have been burnt on in a muffle (*e.g.* Plate CXXII. *b*).

Mr. Francis Buckley suggested that the Bath advertisement of 1766 indicated a new type of gilding, and he thought it marked the introduction of burnished gilding. In that particular case the glasses were no doubt gilt by the firing-and-burnishing method ; for the advertiser was a German. But in view of the evidence from Dossie and Edkins it must be concluded that gilding by fire and burnish was practised in England some years before, and it is extremely likely that the credit is due to the Society of Arts and to its first publicist Dossie. Since Dossie associated the gilding of glass with the gilding of enamel and with the burning-on of coloured enamels, I am inclined to think that gilding by fire and burnish was mainly confined to painted glasses,[2] usually of coloured metal ; and that oil gilding was reserved for glasses which would not otherwise go to the coffin. I am not aware of any English glasses which had their rims gilt by the burnt-in method. Even at the end of the century when muffle gilding was well known the other type of gilding was still common. So late as 1786 even a German, John Grahl of Dublin, was still using a spirit varnish without firing and was awarded a premium by the Dublin Society. And about 1770 oil-gilt rims were still usual even on the very best flint glasses ; Mrs. Dickson's goblet with Beilby painting (Plate CXXXII. *b*. 3) has traces of an oil-gilt rim, even though the colours have been fired. It is probable that the gilding was done after the glass had left the Beilby workshop ; the poor relics of gold are in marked contrast to the coloured glasses of Bristol type which have the gold fired on. Again, the gilding of Mr. Berney's three glasses (Plate CXXII. *b*.), though it is better preserved than any English gilt rim known to me, does not seem to have been fired on. It was perhaps done by an improved oil process like Ziegler's which Lewis (who had no commercial interest in saying so) guaranteed to be as durable as the burnt and burnished gilding of Bohemian and Thuringian glasses.

---

[1] *Bath Chronicle*, 20 November, 1766 ; Buckley, *History*, p. 122.

[2] *E.g.* the blue glasses of fine quality usually ascribed to Bristol. The white opaque Bristol vases which have no other ornament but gilding appear to have been gilt by an oil or varnish method and perhaps placed subsequently " in a warm place."

"A warm place" in Lewis's account can scarcely refer to a muffle. If he had meant muffle he would certainly have used that word or at any rate the word "burnt."

It will, perhaps, be a convenience to collectors to classify 18th-century gilding at the end of this section :

1. Gilding over engraved ornament, *e.g.* on Jacobite glasses, and sometimes on other engraved glasses, *e.g.* the well-known carousal glass in the Rees Price collection (Hartshorne, Plate 46).

2. Gilt rims, especially on clear drinking-glasses ; and always, I think, by an oil process.

3. Decorative gilding on clear flint glass, *e.g.* Plate CXXII. 2.

4. Gilding on coloured glasses without enamel-painting, *e.g.* for the labels of blue decanters.

5. Gilding on white opaque (Bristol) vases without other decoration.

6. Gilding combined with enamel-painting on clear, coloured, and white opaque glasses.

In luxury pieces[1] gilding occasionally showed high accomplishment, for example in toilet sets and inkstands of coloured glass. Mr. S. D. Winkworth has a beautiful "Ladies' Toilet" in which the principle of German *Zwischengoldgläser*[2] is applied to flat-glass panelling (see Plate CXXXIII. *b.*), but I am not aware that this technique was ever used for the decoration of English drinking-glasses. The interest of gilt glasses, and of enamel-painted glasses too, lies in the endeavour rather than in the achievement. The Society of Arts and its two spokesmen, Dossie and Lewis, were desperately anxious to introduce decoration into the English industrial arts, but they were preoccupied with the merely technical interest and they forgot that they were introducing alien values. For them " art " meant decorative chemistry, just as for Wedgwood it meant the classical style, and both were false to the genius of English culture ; neither scientific technique nor classicalism had arisen in the artistic experience of the English people. English glass in particular had been the art of a people in 1700 ; in 1770 it was the art of a period. The Society for the Encouragement of Arts and Manufactures was a worthy body of men, quite sincere and quite disinterested, as worthy in fact as Wedgwood himself. It was also a movement of no little significance which contributed its share to the " industrial revolution " ; and it must share the responsibility for the Great Exhibition.

[1] This term has been used primarily in an economic sense of pieces where the cost of production was not the first consideration (p. 247 *infra*). They have not much reference to economic style ; and English glass is the history of an economic style, *i.e.* an artistic impulse economically conditioned.

[2] Drinking-glasses gilt between two layers of glass ; see Schmidt, *Das Glas.*

E. WHEEL ENGRAVING

The glyptic decoration of glass, like the art of glass itself, came to England by a slow progress. England in the 18th century acquired the arts of engraving and cutting much as she had acquired glassmaking in the 16th century, from foreigners who settled here and slowly communicated their skill to natives who worked under them. The city of Nuremberg, in which engraving had chiefly flourished in the 17th century, was related to the German immigrants as Venice had been related to the Italians in the previous assimilation; and the Netherlands, in which the migrant art first halted, played a similar part in each development. In engraved ornament as in the style of glass itself we have to trace the foreign style which persisted until Englishmen were masters of the art, and then the native idiom which supervened upon it and finally superseded it altogether.

The engraving of English glass falls historically into four phases, (1) heraldic engraving and inscriptions, (2) decorative formalism which was due to German influence, (3) decorative naturalism, which was an original idiom (" flowered glasses "), and (4) designs representing scenes and subjects. Except in the first instance, heraldic engraving, which occurs before any decorative engraving at all, these four phases may be contemporary, but stylistically they can only be arranged in this order, the order that is to say in which they first appear in England. In attempting to trace a chronological development two important reservations have to be made. London was the chief centre of cultured society, in which decorated glass was in greatest demand, and it was also the part to which an immigrant craftsman would first come and the place where he would try first to find work or to establish himself in a business of his own. It thus happens with engraving, as it had happened with glass itself, that the style of London was more sensitive to new influences from abroad or new fashions at home; and throughout the 18th century London is thus considerably in advance of provincial centres like Bristol, Stourbridge, or Dublin.[1] Stylistic priority is therefore not always chronological priority and two specimens of engraving which belong to different stages of the art may in fact be contemporary. For example a piece of crude apprentice work (e.g. Plate XCVI. 2) executed in London[2] may be contemporary with, or even earlier than, a much more accomplished piece of work executed in the provinces where the art had not yet passed to English pupils. And secondly, chronology must be based on the *vogue* of this or that feature, which usually comes quite soon after its introduction; for when once a

---

[1] I call Dublin provincial deliberately; before 1780 it is strictly on a par with the English provincial centres in its relation to London.

[2] I do not, of course, imply that the instance cited was actually engraved in London.

new motive had been used it was liable to be repeated at a later date when it was, stylistically speaking, an anachronism.

HERALDIC AND INSCRIPTIONAL

There is ample evidence that glass was being wheel-engraved in England during the last decade of the 17th century and during the reign of Queen Anne. There is a glass at the British Museum dating certainly from the end of the 17th century and bearing the arms of William III (Plate XXXI. 1). Mr. Francis has a large goblet engraved with the arms of Queen Anne before the Act of Union with Scotland, and therefore to be dated between 1702 and 1707.[1] Mr. Kirkby Mason again had two glasses without arms inscribed respectively *To Ye Glorious & immortal memory of Queen Anne* and *To Ye Pious memory of Queen Anne* which must be dated about 1715, not only on form but by reference to contemporary pamphlet literature in which these toasts are mentioned.[2] Sir John Risley again has a firing glass without arms engraved with the toast SUCCESS TO Wᴹ & MARY[3] which must be referred to the years 1688–1794 on the ground of both its legend and its lettering. There is no evidence that wheel-engraving was practised by Englishmen at this time and we have no choice but to assume that these glasses were executed by German or Dutch metics. It is, moreover, evident that at this early stage engraving of arms or toasts was rare in fact, as it is now rare in survival, and that it was only executed to special orders. Wheel-engraving was in no sense a general practice as is evident from the frequency of diamond-engraved glasses in the early years of the 18th century. The specimens cited make it clear that engraving was entirely complimentary and was not used decoratively at all ; for decoration the diamond was still supreme. And this character of the earliest engraved glasses is confirmed by the first allusions to " crests and cyphers " in advertisements of engraved glasses published by English dealers or artists. These do not occur until a rather later date, but the earliest English engravers known confined themselves to this kind of work and their advertisements are found seven years before the earliest advertisement of flowered glasses (1742).[4] Benjamin Payne of London advertised " several curiosities engraved on glass," and " the Arms of all the Royal Family finely engraved on glasses," both in 1735. At Dublin in the same year Joseph Martin advertised only " arms, crests, words, letters or figures carved on glassware " and declared that he was the only engraver employed by the

[1] Illus. in *Old English drinking glasses*, Plate XXXVI.
[2] See *Apollo III*, 165 *et seq.*, and illus. on p. 169.
[3] Illus. in Bles, Plate 44 and *Apollo III*, 166.
[4] *Daily Journal*, 30 August, 1735, and 12 June, 1735 ; Buckley, *History*, p. 120. But for flowered glasses see p. 241 *infra*.

glasshouse in Fleet Street.[1]   That the earliest engraving was of the complimentary kind is quite consistent with the absence of notices of engraved
glass before 1735.   For the trade in this work cannot have been large
and was probably carried on by persons of no fixed abode or by engravers
of a general sort who had one servant, a German, who was capable of the
art.[2]   Engraving, naturally enough, only got a place in advertisements
when it was practised by or through firms who were well established and
could afford to advertise.   That meant that it had attained an economic
status, and such a regular position was only possible when engraving
became decorative as well as merely complimentary ; for then it could
enlist fashion in its service and no longer depended merely on the caprice
of a family or a club.   For that reason the advertisements of Payne and
Martin must, I think, belong to the *end* of the period when engraving on
glass was primarily heraldic and inscriptional.   If a man could make his
living by engraving " cyphers " on glass the demand must have been
considerable and the art well established ; and in view of the engraved
glasses which can be dated before 1735 we must suppose a long period of
incubation when it was a rare thing to have arms on glasses and the execution was casually done by stray Germans.   No other explanation at any
rate will explain (1) the fact, (2) the purpose, and (3) the style of the
earliest wheel-engraving on flint glass.   After 1735 the engraved glasses
ran parallel with purely decorative engraving, but after decoration was
fairly started they are more frequent ; but not so much more frequent as
one would expect, in view of the great progress in engraving in the middle
of the 18th century.   In a general sense one may venture to assert that
decoration supersedes heraldry.

DECORATIVE FORMALISM

At the beginning of the 18th century the German *Glasschneider*, a body
which included engravers as well as cutters, had developed an elaborate
system of formal ornament which seems to have been architectural in
origin and is based, like most baroque ornament, on the concept of symmetry.   The engravers were not of course original designers and, like other
" small-artists " (*Kleinkunstler*), they took their designs from published
pattern books.   They worked in the modes called *Laub-und-Bandelwerck* and

[1] Westropp, p. 49, citing *Dublin Evening Post*, February, 1735.   Martin did not say he
was the only glass-engraver in Dublin ; the words " the only person . . . employed by
the glasshouse in Fleet Street " almost certainly imply that there were others.

[2] Mr. Buckley found no reference to engraving on glass in advertisements by
engravers of silver (p. 76) ; Mr. Bles (p. 56) has well suggested that the professional
types of diamond-engraving were done by silver-engravers, and in that case it is unlikely
that they would ever have undertaken wheel-engraving, which required a special and
much more elaborate apparatus than the diamond-point.

Groteschgewerk. Several pattern books which seem to have determined the style of German engraving during the first half of the 18th century were published at Nuremberg and Augsburg shortly before and shortly after 1700, and their influence is at once apparent in German engraved glass. The earliest of these pattern books to influence the glass engravers was Agidius Bichel's *Allerhand Inventiones von Frantzöischen Laub-Werckh*, published at Augsburg in 1696, and a little later another Augsburg designer published a *Neues Buch mit französischem Laubwerck und Fruchten.* Both these works were general handbooks of ornamental design, but at the beginning of the 18th century several books of patterns were published which were expressly intended for glass engravers and other *Kleinkunstler.* These naturally came not from Augsburg, a city conspicuous for all manner of ornament and especially for the arts of gold and silver, but from Nuremberg, the birth-place and chief centre of glass-cutting and glass-engraving.—J. C. Reiff's *Zierathen-Buchel vor Glasschneider und Künstler* and Paul Decker's *Neue Croteshgen-Werk vor Goldschmidt, Glasschneider und andere Kunstler.*[1]

Paul Decker was himself an architect and the German pattern books in general are an application of architectural composition to decorative design in two dimensions. Baroque ornament was the dominant mode in German engraving for the first half of the 18th century and in its character as design three tendencies may be observed. It is, first, decorative logic rather than decorative drawing—exact, intricate, rational. The petty absolutes of the German engravers are amazing in their technical dexterity, and their system of relationships is admirably conceived. But the scrolls and bands and arabesques, even when there is moderation in their use, as there is in the earlier glasses (*c.* 1700), cannot be grasped ; they have to be worked out as you work out an engineer's design for a pumping station or a skyscraper. They make you " wonder where you are "; and that is perhaps an emotion which the artist is entitled to exploit. But in these German glasses it is not easy to avoid the impression that baroque engraving is a formula. It has ingenuity but it lacks vitality. In England engraving was gently awakened from its dogmatic slumber by a quality of pleasantness which is made evident in the " flowered glasses."[2] From the rationalism of baroque engraving follow two other tendencies : the economy of motive which is symmetry—the cardinal principle of baroque, and corresponding with it a diffidence in the use of purely natural forms.[3] This mode of

[1] There is a copy of Decker's work in the Victoria and Albert Museum ; for the others see Schmidt, *Das Glas*, p. 275 *et seq.*

[2] See Jerom Johnson's advertisements of these, e.g. *Daily Advertiser*, 21 December, 1742 (Buckley, p. 120). It is, I think, relevant to compare another art which came from Germany to England—porcelain modelling. The figures of Chelsea and Bow are usually inferior in modelling to those of Meissen, but they are more " pleasant." It is a question of an inferior technique finding æsthetic compensation.

[3] The German engravers had of course their own naturalism—fat fruits and comely

ornament declared itself in England between the heraldic period and the "flowered glasses"; not in its full complication, but nevertheless definitely German and definitely baroque. It appears as formal borders of arabesques and scrollwork round the rim or foot of a wine-glass (*e.g.* Plates XCIV–XCVI), occasionally on other kinds of vessel (*e.g.* Plate XCI), and belongs to the period 1720–50. These borders occur, and occur most characteristically, on large and heavy glasses which on form can scarcely be later than 1720 and in one or two cases are of a type commonest before 1710 (Plate XCIV); and the year 1720 is to be regarded as a very conservative date for their inception.[1] The absence of advertisements at this time is no obstacle to this dating; the existing advertisements of later date were issued mainly by well-established firms[2] and in 1720 a German engraver might well have been doing casual work without any Press notice at all. Moreover, Mr. Francis Buckley's discovery that *cut* flint glass was advertised as early as 1719 makes it fairly certain that decorative engraving was already being practised; for the specimens themselves leave no doubt that engraving arrived in England some years before cutting.[3] There is not, I think, much doubt that the heavy glasses with borders were engraved by Germans. The engraving is restricted to a narrow zone below the rim, but technically it is fairly accomplished and as far as it goes it is not very different from some of the styles practised in Germany twenty years before (*c.* 1700). That the ornament was not extended to the whole surface of the bowl, as in the German glasses, seems to be due to public taste rather than to technical incompetence.

The earliest English engravers seem to have adopted the border from the German metics, but they made its composition less formal. The rigid scrolls and arabesques were gradually abandoned and the borders assumed rather the character of a wreath. I have seen glasses of the light baluster type which appear to date from about 1730 and had a naturalized border of this kind, and that may perhaps be taken as an approximate date for the engraving of these borders by Englishmen. I do not think that the later term "flowered glasses" can refer to these borders, naturalized or not. Flowered glasses are not mentioned till 1742 and the borders quite certainly occur for fifteen or twenty years before that date. In 1735 Payne,

flowers corresponding with the "*Deutsche Blumen*" of German porcelain-painting; but it can scarcely be denied that the prevailing tendency in engraving was formal, not naturalistic.

[1] Mr. Buckley insists quite rightly that usually the engraving should be dated by the glass on which it occurs and not the glass by its engraving (p. 77).

[2] *E.g.* Johnson and Haedy.

[3] "Flowered glass buttons" were advertised in 1722 (*Evening Post*, 6 March), but it is difficult to agree with Mr. Buckley's suggestion (p. 76) that these were engraved by a silversmith. Mr. Buckley himself admits (*ibid.*) that silversmiths' advertisements give no indication that they ever engraved on glass.

the earliest *English* engraver in London at present known, advertised heraldic work but no "flowered glasses"; instead he refers to "several curiosities engraved on glass." It may be suggested that this phrase refers to the naturalized baroque borders, and that Payne, an Englishman, called attention to them as "curious" because they had formerly been executed by Germans. The glass illustrated in Plate XCVII. 2 seems to be an early instance of the way in which the German baroque border was naturalized by an Englishman; the glass itself can scarcely be later than 1730. No. 3 in the same Plate is probably a piece of 'prentice work, but there the glass is a few years later in date. It is noticeable that in both these glasses the engraver, though he is less formal, still adheres to the idea of symmetry; they may be contrasted with a later piece of engraving (Plate XCVII. 1) from which all trace of symmetry has vanished. It is evident again from Plate XCVIII. 1 that baroque borders were still being engraved by German metics about 1745 and even at that date had lost little of either their formality or their symmetry.[1] Borders of this kind, whether naturalized or formal, are not common after 1750; by that time they had been superseded generally by the fuller naturalism of "flowered glasses," for which a border was too cramped an arrangement.

DECORATIVE NATURALISM

There was always a streak of natural sentiment in 18th-century convention. Even Pope shows traces of it; and in writers like Collins, Gray, Young, Thomson, Christopher Smart, Mrs. Barbauld, and a painter like Richard Wilson, there is abundant evidence of a sensitive response to green fields and the open sky which was not less authentic because it was sometimes tinged with melancholy or too delicately wrapped in arcadian fancies. And outside the poets, though Nature was the proper adjunct of a country residence, it did not thereby cease to be Nature or cease to be noticed; for even the most urbane must retire sometimes to the country to hunt the fox or be reminded of their constituents. The "flowered glasses" are homage to gardens by the arts and manufactures which were promoted in London, and with their arrival, about the year 1740,[2] pleasantness succeeds a neat sophistication as the normal character of English engraving.

To this phase of the art belong large natural flowers—roses, for example, and daffodils, sunflowers, daisies and carnations; birds, moths, bees, and butterflies; vine branches with their grapes, hops and heads of

---

[1] Jerom Johnson called himself the "maker" of his cut and engraved glasses, but the actual work may well have been done by Germans in his employ. He seems to have had a fairly large business.

[2] Jerom Johnson's advertisement, 21 December, 1742; but even at that date flowered glasses are not described as "curious" or "new-fashioned."

barley. These motives are due to the transition of engraving from German to English hands and they are characteristic of English engraving in the same sense that the rounded-funnel bowl and the simple baluster had been characteristic of English glassmaking forty or fifty years before. Usually the engraving is left rough, but engraving which is partly polished is found as early as 1750, and the tendency to polish was increased as time went on. Flowers, birds, and insects are found on most varieties of glass vessel, but for candlesticks and sweetmeat glasses, which were heavy and expensive, cutting was generally preferred ; I can recall only a very few examples with engraved ornament. Naturalistic engraving of the first quality was in vogue for about twenty years (1740–60) and during that period it would seem to be applied only to the better types of glass. Among these it is found on bowls, decanters, tankards, goblets, and most frequently of all on the small wine-glasses with ogee bowls or straight-sided bowls which succeeded the Excise Act of 1745 (Plate CXXVII). Mention may be made here of the peculiar engraving executed in 1745 and during the years following for supporters of the exiled Stuarts. In these the rose was stylized according to the heraldic convention and furnished with two buds emblematic of " James III " and his two sons, Charles Edward Stuart and Henry, afterwards Cardinal of York. This type of engraving was originally done for Jacobite societies like the Cycle Club, probably before the Rising of 1745, but in later years (no doubt soon after 1750) it was used primarily as decoration by any who had sympathy with the Tory side. On those glasses where the heraldic rose (six to eight petals) and buds occur without further emblem or superscription the political symbolism was probably not very vivid.

As long as the English artists attempted the formal complications of Germany their technical skill usually broke down. Thus the loss of the art was the substitution of a single motive for a considered design in which many motives were brought into coherence. The control of a difficult design and the skill required for its execution went hand in hand, each encouraging the other. In their actual use of the wheel the Englishmen were proficient but never masterly. They turned, therefore, to simple motives in which such skill as they possessed could be used to advantage, and their timid spirit was sanctioned by a simple agricultural taste which found something alien in baroque ornament.

About 1755–60 engraved decoration had become general for all qualities of glass and this extension brought with it a return to formalism, a formalism not vigorous but idle. When once engraving had won place as a regular " line " output as well as quality had to be considered and this led the engravers to abbreviate their effort by adopting devices because they were easy or familiar—festoons, dentil edges, trellised work, crossed hatching, and several varieties of husk pattern and geometrical border

THE AGE OF ORNAMENT

(Plate CXVII. *b.* 2, 3). Stereotyped flowers with disc-like petals and cross-hatched centres superseded the large natural flowers, and at the same time polishing became more and more common, until the entire design was sometimes polished.[1] Formality was further increased by the advent of the classical manner (*c.* 1770). It was the death-blow of the "flowered glasses" and made festoons of various kinds the staple motive of glass-engraving.

SCENES AND SUBJECTS

The earliest subjects of wheel-engraving strictly belong to the heraldic phase and were probably executed by Germans. Before 1745 (the Stuart Rising) subjects usually have some political significance; there is not much doubt that some of the earlier portraits of William III are before that date (*e.g.* Plate XCII. 2), and they are usually combined with a toast or equivalent inscription. Analogous with these are the portraits of Charles Edward Stuart engraved on wine-glasses *c.* 1745–50, and the very few glasses with portraits of the Duke of Cumberland. There is no reason to doubt that all or nearly all these subjects (*c.* 1745) were engraved in England or Ireland by English or Irish engravers.[2] Again during the Seven Years War (1756–63) there are a number of subject glasses made for ships and patriotic societies, to honour the King of Prussia (1756) or to celebrate the Battle of Quiberon Bay (1759). But these, like the earlier political glasses, are clearly special cases and were not made with a decorative intention. Scenes or subjects used as decoration required great skill with the wheel and are a development subsequent to the flowered glasses; they do not become at all general until about 1760. Decorative scenes may have been occasionally engraved by German metics at an earlier date, but a good deal of this type of engraving was probably executed abroad on imported English glass. The Newcastle goblet in Plate CXV. 2 is a good instance of this. The glass is of a type made for the continental market[3] and the engraving is so German in sentiment as well as in actual technique that I do not think it can have been executed in England.

[1] "Best London polish" in Barker's advertisement (*Newcastle Chronicle* 1, iv, 1780, Buckley, pp. 128–9) probably refers to this.
[2] In 1752 the St. Mary's Lane glasshouse at Dublin advertised wine-glasses "with . . . toasts or any flourish whatsoever" (Westropp, p. 43). This almost certainly refers to political engraving for the Williamite festivals then held in Dublin on the anniversaries of the monarch's birthday and his Battle of the Boyne. Mr. Francis has suggested that a certain family of Pretender portraits were engraved out of England after 1752 to the Prince's own order (*Jac. Drinking Glasses*, pp. 25–6). This does not seem very probable and there is certainly nothing in the technique of the facing-right portraits to warrant it.
[3] *Cf.* Plate CXXXI. 1, 3, a Beilby glass which came to light in Holland. Frans Greenwood stippled an English glass of this type in 1722.

A HISTORY OF ENGLISH AND IRISH GLASS

An advertisement by a German in 1766[1] and several later advertisements by Christopher Haedy (1772 and 1778)[2] refer to "glass pictures," an item not advertised by the Ayckboums or any other vendor of engraved glass. These, one might expect, were flat glass plates, not vessels; but none such have ever come to light and Mr. Francis Buckley has suggested[3] that the term refers to glass vessels engraved with "pictures" and not merely "flowered." That may very well be; but in any case the term picture must imply a fairly elaborate composition and suggests that ordinary wine-glasses with a subject were in vogue rather earlier. The glasses engraved for Bristol privateers during the Seven Years War (Plate CXV. 1, c. 1757) show that even so early the art was well enough advanced for any kind of subject or scene. The year 1760 is convenient and probable as an initial date; and scenes and subjects do not occur very frequently after 1780. During that period two important influences assert themselves in engraving; the Chinese manner, which had gained popularity from its vogue in porcelain and enamelled earthenware; and the classical manner due partly to the sentimental baroque settings of French painting and partly to the Adam revival. These being noted the "subject" glasses may be divided into the following main types[4]:

1. Fanciful symbolism and sentimental allegory, e.g. the set of seasons in Plate CXX. b.
2. Naturalistic landscapes, comparable with the painted landscapes of the Beilbys (Plate CXXII. a.).
3. Sporting subjects, especially hunting (Plate CXX. a. 2).
4. Classical ruins.
5. Chinese scenes (Plate CXXI).[5]

Scenes of these kinds can scarcely be called frequent and they were certainly limited to the most expensive grades of glass. Nor are they so characteristic of the English art as the flowered glasses of an earlier date. But subject engravings like the set of Chinese scenes in Plate CXXI all very happily combined with the facetted stem, are among the most charming, as they are certainly the most accomplished, work of the English engravers.

[1] *Bath Chronicle* 20, xi, 1766 (Buckley, *History*, p. 122).
[2] *Bristol Journal*, 11, i, 1772 (Buckley, p. 123).
[3] *History*, p. 77.
[4] I refer only to subjects used decoratively; engraving of ships, inns, coaches, etc. belongs to a different category, for there the intention is not primarily decorative.
[5] I would hazard the suggestion that these glasses were made and engraved at Bristol, where the Chinese style was certainly popular; and that as much for their mood of gaiety as for their technical excellence. *Cf.* pp. 223 and 225 *supra*.

F. CUTTING

Cutting is a much less delicate art than engraving and more intimate with the metal it adorns.   Engraving required only a clear field and its style can be traced independently of the vessels to which it was applied ; that is, indeed, why it never had the success which other kinds of decoration enjoyed at Venice.   Cut-glass, on the other hand, is appropriately spelt with a hyphen ; for cutting is a more serious aggression on the shape of a vessel, and its use varied with the types for which it was employed, and even for parts of the same vessel.   Its style, like every other technical development, proceeds from the simple to the complex, but it cannot be traced as a uniform growth, and when we come to consider its detail it will be necessary to treat first of particular motives in cutting and then of the vessel shapes or vessel parts to which they were applied.

English cut-glass has always enjoyed the envy of other glassmaking countries and it may claim to be the most successful decorated glass produced in England, in fact the only decorated glass which is comparable in point of excellence to the glass which Venice had decorated by other means ; and that for two reasons.   At the period when cutting reached its highest attainment, and before elaboration had set in (c. 1760–90)[1] there was a unison of form and ornament which is not evident in any other decorated glass of England.   Cutting was used to enhance form and not simply as an adventitious ornament (e.g. Plates CXXXIII. a., CXXXIX). And, secondly, cutting was admirably suited to the peculiar metal of English glass both in its technique and in its æsthetic effect.   A metal which contained 40 per cent of lead was exceedingly soft by the side of soda glass, and this was a great advantage to a glyptic technique which depended on the broad statements of geometry and did not aspire to the nicety of engraving. Moreover, the great quantity of lead was what gave the English metal its peculiar brilliancy, and cutting in facets, diamonds, and other motives was the one decorative technique which could exploit this quality to the full. Cutting was a supreme success in England because of all modes of ornament it alone was organic to the material.[2]

There is now positive evidence that cut flint glass was being made in England as early as 1719,[3] and it would therefore appear that the technique

[1] Certainly not later than 1770 for English luxury types (for which see below) ; and 1780–90 for the glasses made in Ireland.

[2] For Ruskin's misunderstanding on this point see above, p. 6.

[3] *Whitehall Evening Post*, 27. x. 1719, cited by Buckley in *Glass*, V, 247 : " John Akerman continues to sell . . . plain and diamond-cut flint glasses." The absence of the words " curious " or " new-fashioned," and the phrase " continues to sell," suggest that the cutting had been going on for some little while, perhaps several years.   John Akerman was a member of the London Glass Sellers, and had premises first in Cornhill and after 1746 in Fenchurch Street.   He did a good deal of business in the provinces.   The name

was introduced from Germany early in the reign of George I. At that time English metal had lost little of its first exuberance and was better suited to cutting than at any later period ; so that it is not easy to explain why cut-glass did not flourish at once. The difficulty of the technique, and perhaps the hostility of public taste, are the only reasons which can be suggested for the delay, but by 1735 cut-glass must have been well known. The earliest Englishman who sold cut-glass was William Watkinson in 1727.[1] He described himself as a " Chinaman,"[2] *i.e.* a dealer, but it may well be that he did the cutting himself on naked glasses which he had purchased, or employed a German to do the work for him. The word " curious " indicates that cut-glass was then something of a novelty. By 1742 at any rate cut-glass must have been generally familiar, for in that year Jerom Johnson was advertising " all cut, scalloped, and flowered glasses " at the end of a long list of specialities, as if they were the most usual things in the world ; in the same year, too, though his lustres were " most curious " and his salts " new-fashioned," his candlesticks were merely diamond-cut and scalloped.[3] That list in itself is sufficient evidence that cut-glass was then well established ; there are even several glasses which on form cannot be dated later than 1725 (Plates CIII, CIV. 2, 3).

What held up further progress was the Excise Act, hostile to cutting because it meant a general reduction in weight and bulk.[4] Thus

Akerman is found in Germany, Bessarabia, Sweden, and (*c.* 1690) among Wiltshire farmers. John Akerman may have been a German who came over about 1714. He is last mentioned about 1785. I do not see why Mr. Buckley claims for him " fame for having introduced into this country the cutting and engraving of fine crystal " ; his is merely the first name yet known connected with cut flint glass. It seems fairly likely from the extent of his business that he had more than one cutter, no doubt Bohemian as Mr. Buckley suggests, but there is surely no ground for suggesting that Akerman employed Mr. Buckley's rather mythical figure, the father of Christopher Haedy. Haedy I is based on an advertisement in the *Bath Chronicle*, 20 November, 1766, of the sale by auction of the " stock in trade of a German " who, so he said, was selling off to meet his creditors. The wording of this advt. is similar to some of Haedy's advts. (*e.g. Bristol Journal*, 11 January, 1772), and the advertiser claimed to be " the first that brought the art of cutting and engraving of glass from Germany." I think the German at Bath may have been connected with Haedy, but his claim to have been " the first " probably means nothing. All the Haedy advertisements suggest that his importance lay in disseminating cutting in the middle and latter part of the 18th century : to connect him with a father (the Bath German), the father with the introduction of cutting, and the introduction with Akerman is a brilliant surmise, but does not leave me quite comfortable.

[1] He is not stated in his advertisement to have been the " Maker " (as Jerom Johnson described himself in 1742). *Daily Post*, 27 October, 1727.

[2] Of course a dealer in china, earthenware and porcelain ; so, in the 18th century, glassman=a dealer in glass.

[3] *Daily Advertiser* 21, xii, 42 (Buckley, p. 120.) The candlesticks must be of the type appearing in Plate CXLIV. *b.* 4.

[4] Affecting both the act of cutting and the æsthetic result.

in the middle of the 18th century, until in fact cutting found freedom in Ireland (from 1780), cut ornament was limited to two fields, (1) those parts of the small Excise glasses which could be cut without danger to the fabric, *i.e.* rims, stem, and base of bowl in wine-glasses, and (2) luxury types (*e.g.* candlesticks, sweetmeats, chandeliers) where cost was no object. The first of these were the more frequent " lines " and that was, I think, the reason why the several varieties of *flat* or *sliced* cutting appeared first ; they did not require as thick a metal as relief-diamonds and other convex types. A theory has been advanced[1] that the Excise Acts were favourable to cutting because cutting was a decorative compensation for loss of bulk. This view seems to me to be based on very superficial economics. It was no doubt true that the taxation of enamel (1777)[2] and the decline in engraving left cutting without a serious rival, but the increase in bulk required for *elaborate* cutting more than counterbalanced the reduction due to the Excise ; and cutting did not become elaborate, *i.e.* have recourse primarily to convex motives until it had found full economic freedom in Ireland. And this is as true of the First Excise as it is of the Second. In luxury types there was in fact very little development in cut style between 1746 and 1780 ; that is precisely why it is so difficult to distinguish a cut-glass candlestick contemporary with Jerom Johnson's advertisement of " diamond-cut and scalloped candlesticks " (1742) with similar glasses made in Ireland soon after 1780. But what is important is the normal commercial repertory, the glassmakers' stock " lines." It is on these that a manufacturer will make his business a failure or a success, for with these his profit depends on output, and on an aggregate cost price. It was the repertory types which were hard hit by the Excise. Moreover, it was in repertory types that style developed ; for, being made in great numbers they gave the cutter more frequent practice in cutting suitable to this or that vessel form, and they were themselves more subject to the vicissitudes of fashion, on which the development of style partly depends.[3]

Thus the development of cutting in England falls into three phases which are both stylistic and economic; first (*c.* 1714–19 to 1745) a period

---

[1] By the late H. J. Powell, article *Glass* in the *Encyclopædia Britannica*, 12 ed.

[2] 27 Geo. III, c. 13. " For every cwt. of materials or metal by what name soever the same are or may be called or known that shall be made use of in Great Britain in the making of Plate, or Flint Glass, or Enamel . . .—£1. 1. 5½."

[3] I would compare the luxury glasses (*e.g.* chandeliers, epergnes, table " branches," cut glass, sweetmeats, and candlesticks) to the fur coat, and repertory wine-glasses to the spring hat. Fur coats are less subject to stylistic change than spring hats, but hats, though a repertory type, may be of as good quality as (*mutatis mutandis*) the sets of " good " but not " luxurious " wine-glasses with which " gentlemen might be supplied." *Cf.* Bosc d'Antic's remark cited above : " Il n'y a consequemment que les gens riches qui payent les plus fortes impositions " (1780) ; *i.e.* it was the rich customer, not the glassmaker, who paid for the extra bulk required for an elaborately cut glass.

of slow but steady progress culminating in the types of cutting described in Jerom Johnson's early advertisements ; secondly, a period of arrest (1745–80[1]) when the development splits into (*a*) luxury types wherein style is more or less stationary, and (*b*) repertory types which are full of stylistic enterprise, but perpetually thwarted by lack of bulk; and thirdly the period of economic freedom and stylistic florison (Ireland, 1780 to 1825[2]). It will now be convenient to analyse the motivation of cutting during these three periods; and three classes of cutting will be considered, (1) sliced cutting where the motive is flat or nearly so, (2) incised cutting, where a channel is formed by two acute slices of opposite sense (*e.g.* sprig ornament), and (3) relief-cutting of the first or second degree ; and these according to the thickness of metal required for their safe practice.

(i) EARLY PROGRESS

The incunabula of cutting, that is to say specimens which can be dated before 1745, exhibit in embryo several of the more important motives which continued in vogue until the later days of Irish glass, not flat or scalloped motives merely, but incised motives and even relief motives ; but since cutting was being practised in England for at least twenty-five years before the Excise Act and there was no restriction on bulk this is not in the least surprising. The attribution of certain cut motives to this period has been based on the following principles. (1) The chronology of form being fairly certain to within ten, and in some cases to within five, years, during the first forty years of the century, cut motives may be given an inceptional date by the glasses in which they occur ; these include large rounded-funnel bowls preponderant over a heavily knopped stem (Plate CIV. 2), the larger and early incurved bowls (Plate CIV. 1), the later and less precise shouldered stem (Plate CIII), the simple baluster (Plate CIV. 1), the triple-ring knop, rib-moulded feet, the double-ogee sweetmeat bowl, the domed foot, and several other early features ; and there is the further fact of cutting on very heavy types which were later reduced by the Excise. (2) Motives in themselves simple, both technically and æsthetically, are early ; but before cutting had suffered any impediment we should expect to find, and do in fact find, some of the convex motives which *c.* 1750–60 are rare except in luxury types. (3) A simple *composition* of motives is also early, but here again we must expect to find that the ground is more crowded before 1745 than it is afterwards. Generally there is the simplicity of experiment (*c.* 1720–30) and then a burst of complication immediately preceding the Excise Act (1745). The early cut motives may be tabulated thus, but the list makes no pretence of

[1] The grant of Free Trade to Ireland.
[2] Irish Excise.

[248]

being exhaustive, nor does it imply that the several motives were not occasionally repeated during the arrest period, even on repertory types.[1]

A.   Flat cutting.[2]

 1.   The small German facet, a motive brought from Germany by the earliest German cutters and specially adapted to a knopped stem (Plate CIV. 2).

 2.   Flat vertical flutes, found on a shouldered stem and combined with ribbed foot-moulding (Plate CV. 1).

 3.   Rounded (bowl) flutes (Plate CIV. 2) of a type which reappears late in the century.

 4.   Triangular facets; a bowl motive (Plate CIV. 3 and Plate CV. 1).

 5.   Large diamonds (bowl motive), *i.e.* flat parallelograms. This motive was especially suited to a thin body and therefore was in considerable vogue for repertory types during the arrest period (*e.g.* Plate CXXV. 3), but there is not much doubt that it appeared during the early progress, and it is probably one of the motives which gave their name to Jerom Johnson's " diamond-cut " glasses (1742).

 6.   Long hexagons (stem motive, Plate CVI. 1) and long diamonds, also a stem motive (Plate CVI. 3), a glass notable for its very German flower-engraving, for which *cf.* p. 239 *n.* 3). Johnson would probably have called both these diamonds. The usual small stem-diamonds, and their numerous variants belong mainly to the next period when cutting was thrown back on to the stem and stem motivation developed accordingly (*cf.* Fig. 25).

 7.   Several types of polygonal foot cutting (*e.g.* Plate CVI. 1). The later fan-panelling of the foot probably appeared before the Excise (for a post-Excise specimen see Plate CXIX. 5).

B.   Incised and sliced motives.

 1.   Zigzag circuits, the angles sometimes capped (Plate CIII. 2, CIV. 1) This motive occurs sporadically during the arrest period (*e.g.* the 1760 decanter of Plate CXXVI. 1) ; and it is occasionally doubled (Plate CV. 3). In Plate CV. 3 it is the basis of diamonds within diamonds in slight tiered relief.

---

[1] On point of going to press I would record a highly interesting glass in the Royal Albert Memorial Museum, Exeter. It is a sweetmeat glass, 7½ ins. high, with large bell-bowl and shouldered stem. The bowl has the familiar vertical ribs commonest about 1720, but the ribs are not left plain. They are lightly snicked with the cutting wheel, and so become vertical chains of snicks. The bowl rim is cut in a timid zigzag less than ¼ in. in depth. The foot rim is cut in plain arc scallops. The glass illustrates the motto of the early cutter—stick to the rims and the thick places. It is the earliest English cut-glass I have seen and the coy origin of Lady Grisell Baillie's " corner'd brim " sweetmeats (1727). H. H. Clarke Bequest, No. 312.

[2] I have ventured to use the term flat to include motives which are very slightly concave, and motives which are at a slight angle to the surface.

2. Lunar slices (Plate CIV. 1), mainly a bowl motive, and frequently composed as a zigzag circuit (Plate CVI. 3, lower part of bowl). For later usage of this motive see Fig. 33.

3. Festoons (Plate CVII. 1).

4. Arches, very frequently doubled (Plate CIII. 1 and Plate CV. 1).

C. *Relief motives.*

1. Relief triangles (Plate CIII. 1).

2. Relief diamonds, the apex sliced off flat (Plate CV. 3).

D. *Edge-cutting or scalloping.*

What is called scalloping in the early advertisements was one of the earliest cut motives. Scalloped dessert-glasses were advertised by Johnson in 1739,[1] and scalloped candlesticks in 1742.[2] After the Excise scalloping was very frequent, no doubt because edge-cutting, like stem-cutting, was an easy way of cheating the Exciseman; but it was naturally confined to other than drinking vessels, even when applied to the foot. It is probable that " scalloping " included all types of rim-cutting and the following varieties may be enumerated.

1. Arch and angle, probably the earliest scalloping of all (Plate CIII. 1 and Plate CV. 1).

2. Regular undulating rims (Plate CV. 3).

3. Zigzag rims (Plates CIV. 3, CVIII. 2). See p. 323.

4. Numerous varieties of foot-rim scalloping. These must have appeared some little while before the Excise. But, edge-cutting not being affected by the reduction in bulk, scalloped motives developed very considerably after the Excise Act, more especially on sweetmeat glasses and candlesticks. The earliest foot cutting is in arcs (Plate CV. 1) or straight lines (Plate CVIII. 2).

(ii) THE ARREST PERIOD (1746–80)

The Excise Act restricted the more elaborate motives already born. At the same time it (1) standardized several of the flat motives which were specially suited to the thin sides of a bowl or other hollow part and (2) developed in much greater variety the motives peculiar to these parts of a vessel, *i.e.* rim and stem, which were not affected by the reduction of bulk or not so seriously affected as to render them an impossible field for cutting.

1. *The large flat diamond* became a very frequent motive for hollow vessels or hollow parts of a vessel, *e.g.* for cruet bottles (Plate CXXXVII. 1, 2), decanters (Plate CXXVIII. 1, 3), wine-glasses (Plate CXXVIII. 2).

2. *Scale-pattern* of numerous varieties was a notable instance of the

---

[1] *Daily Post*, 20 July, 1739, Buckley, p. 120.
[2] *Daily Advertiser*, 21 December, 1742, Buckley, *ibid.*

development of the flat motive. It appears very characteristically on the necks of bottle forms, *e.g.* decanters (Plate CXXVII. *b.* 1) and cruet bottles (Plate CLI. 8) and was also employed for the base of an ogee bowl and for the sockets of candlesticks.

3. *The arch-and-sprig* was one of the motives by which stem-cutting sought to encroach as far as it dare on the lower part of a wine-glass bowl (Plate CXVII. *a.* 3).

4. *Fluting* during this period was of three main kinds. (*a*) Neck flutes used for bridging the neck and body of a shouldered bottle form (Plate CXXV. 3). (*b*) Rounded flutes ("comb fluting") used for the base of a decanter and for other vessels and parts of vessels (Plate CXXVI) ; on decanters it appears first about 1755 and continued in very general use until the end, and it was always liable to become a decoration for other parts of a vessel, *e.g.* bowls and lids. (*c*) Stem fluting sometimes quite plain (Plates CVI. 2, CXIX. 4), sometimes adapted to the cusp (*e.g.* Plate CVII. 2), sometimes again notched at the edges (Plate CV. 2) ; this seems to be the order of development. Fluting was in very frequent use at the end of the 18th century and afterwards, especially (*b*) and (*c*), but these can usually be detected by other features of style found in combination with them.

5. *Stem diamonds.* Under this head may be included the numerous types of stem facet (flat or very slightly concave) which are exceedingly common in mid-century glasses and perhaps the most characteristic cut motive of that period. They vary considerably in actual size, but the normal shape may be taken as a parallelogram with angles of about sixty degrees and one hundred and twenty degrees (Fig. 25). Besides these, very long diamonds (Plate CVI. 3), sometimes hooked (Plate CXXXVIII. 1), and several kinds of polygonal facet, notably long hexagons (Plate CVI. 1) and even the small German polygon, occur not infrequently. These motives are probably all implied in the term " diamond cut " of the mid-century advertisements, and they are a notable instance of one of the few types of cutting encouraged by the Excise.

6. *Sliced motives* are most generally found on the feet of candlesticks and sweetmeat glasses, where they are adapted to the shape of the foot (*e.g.* to the dome) and occur in numerous varieties (Plate CXLIV. *b*).

7. *Incised motives.* The incised zigzag and the lunar slice are also found in mid-century glasses, *e.g.* the decanter of Plate CXXVII. *b.* 1 and on Mr. Winkworth's " Ladies' Toilet " (Plate CXXXIII. *a.*).

8. *Scalloping.* Numerous varieties of edge curvature which are scarcely capable of exact analysis occur in mid-century glasses, most frequently in the nozzles and feet of candlesticks and other lighting pieces, and on the rims and feet of sweetmeat glasses. Curved scalloping is also frequent in the canopies (due to the influence of the Chinese style) which came into general vogue for epergnes, girandoles, and chandeliers about

1770, and are contemporary with, and associated with, the early evidences of "classicalism" (*e.g.* Plate CXLI, the urn motive in chandelier summits). The more daring kinds of scalloping are usually confined to luxury pieces. In wine-glasses edge-cutting is much more restricted and usually takes the form of plain narrow slicing and underslicing ; sometimes the foot both in wine-glasses and in other stemmed vessels is cut round the edges so as to become a regular polygon. Mention may be made lastly of the agreeable edge-slicing applied to the lozenge stoppers of the shouldered decanter and its taper derivatives (*c.* 1755–75, Fig. 35, c and e), a very charming instance of economy in cutting.

9. *The relief diamond* is from an evolutionary standpoint the most important motive evident during the arrest period. We have already seen that it had declared itself before the Excise Act of 1745 ; and on luxury types it is not uncommon during the thirty-five years preceding the Irish florison. By 1750 it was already being double-cut (Fig. 26) and in its most attractive form, a large plain relief diamond, it is quite common in luxury pieces *c.* 1770, *e.g.* the dated bowls on Plate CXXXIX, in the earlier and simpler chandeliers and in girandoles, epergnes, and the larger candlesticks (in the latter mainly applied to the foot) (Plate CXLI, foot). When cutting found full freedom the relief diamond of the English luxury pieces was seized by the cutters in Ireland, and in innumerable variations and adaptations became the staple motive of Irish glass and of the English imitations of it.

10. *Branch-notching*. The cutting of branches (in chandeliers, epergnes, etc.) into notches seems to have begun about 1760–70, and there is definite proof that it went out of fashion in 1788, when plain branches came into vogue.[1]

(iii) THE PERIOD OF ECONOMIC FREEDOM (IRELAND)

The exuberant cutting associated with Irish glass is not a divergence from the English style, but a fulfilment of it in economic conditions which allowed cutting to do as it pleased. The cutters in Ireland adopted almost all the motives which had already declared themselves in England, and

---

[1] See a letter from Messrs. Perry & Parker and Co., lighting outfitters of London, to Sir Roger Newdegate of Arbury Hall, Nuneaton, dated 17 October, 1788 and cited by Powell, *Glassmaking*, p. 150 and by Edwards, *Dict. of Eng. Furniture*, *s.v.* Chandeliers. The firm of Perry was supplying chandeliers from 1756 onwards, and obtained their glass from a glasshouse in Southwark. Their early designs which I have consulted are dated and are of considerable interest. They show (1) that many " Irish " types were being made in England as early as 1790, and (2) that the exuberance of cutting has been considerably post-dated—certainly by twenty to thirty years. " Large " cutting, as distinct from the " miniature " style of the early 19th century, was very well developed in 1790 even in England. I have to acknowledge the courtesy of Messrs. Burt, Escaré & Perry & Co., of Wardour Street, in permitting me to examine their pattern books.

they added to them some fresh motives which were suited to bulky vessels and an elaborate composition. But there is no such thing as an indigenous Irish style. Irish cutting is what would have happened in England if Ireland had never received Free Trade and if England had not been thwarted time after time by an increase in duty. There are some motives, certainly, which do not seem to appear before the Irish Free Trade measure and the subsequent migration of English glassmakers to Ireland, but the Irish style consists for the most part in the *use* and *variation* of motives already familiar. The luxury types of England became the repertory types of Ireland, and the economy of design in cutting which had been the sovereign virtue of cut-glass in 1770 (Plate CXXXIX, Fig. 33) did not long survive the Irish freedom (1780). Exuberant cutting was already well advanced in 1790 and there is very little work of first-class importance after that date. The Irish style has nothing to do with the national distribution of glassmaking ; it is merely the last phase of English glassmaking.

I shall not recapitulate the motives already evident in England which the Irish glass-cutters adopted, but proceed to analyse the principal novelties, both novelties of use and novelties of idea.

1. *Relief diamonds.* The relief diamond, as we have seen, was not used in very great variety in mid-century England, and its composition had usually been a single circuit of diamonds, impinging on one another at their extremes and running round the body of a vessel. The earliest work of the Cork Glass Company (*init.* 1783) shows the adoption of this scheme ; what Mr. Westropp has described as a circuit of " vesica and splits " was simply an adaptation of the diamond circuit and except for the splits is not different from the cutting of English luxury glass of ten to twenty years earlier. The relief diamond may be regarded as the staple motive of Irish glass on two counts. It was the unit of the diamond *fields* or diapers which were used with great profusion by the Irish cutters ; and it was itself varied very considerably in two directions, (1) by keeping it large and then double cutting it so that we have cross-cutting or cutting in depression inside cutting in relief (Fig. 26. 2), and (2) by greatly reducing its size and assembling it in large fields of small but plain diamonds (Fig. 32).[1] The field of large double-cut diamonds is most characteristic of the first ten or fifteen years of Irish cutting and is found on jugs (Plate CXLV), while a field of plain diamonds of small size is mainly a development of the early 19th century (see Plate CLX). The tendency was to reduce the double-cut diamonds (Fig. 32) to smaller plain diamonds (Fig. 34, F) and these smaller diamonds to smaller diamonds still (Fig. 34, B). The very small plain relief diamonds required great technical dexterity, but not a very thick metal, and they were therefore very common (*a*) in England early in the 19th

[1] The terms " large cutting " and " miniature cutting " are convenient labels for these two styles.

century when the Excise had been several times increased and (*b*) in Ireland after the Excise Act of 1825. The last development of the diamond was the strawberry diamond (Plate CLX. *a*. 3 and Fig. 34, A), which is in principle a combination of the double-cut diamond with a field of small relief diamonds, and thus combined in a single motive both the preceding tendencies. It was used by Pellatt in England in 1810 but was probably introduced a little before that time. It is the favourite diamond motive in Pellatt's incrusted work and in the late (1830) Waterford designs. It may be regarded as essentially a Regency feature, and it continued to be common in the degraded glass manufactures of the Victoria era.

2. *Fluting*. The last phase of English glass witnessed also considerable development in the use of the flute. Broad flat flutes were the normal decoration for the lower part of wine-glass bowls of the square bucket-shaped sort with short stems. Slightly concave flutes were normally cut round the bases of decanters and jugs. But by far the most important of the flutes at this period is the *pillared flute*. This is a half-section of a cylindrical column with the rounded surface turned outwards. It naturally required a much thicker metal than flat fluting and did not therefore become common until after 1780 in Ireland. Pillared flutes were not simply used as borders nor for the stems of vessels, but in broad bands similar to the field of relief diamonds. Chronologically they occur between the large double-cut diamonds and the small-diamond field, that is to say, they are most common, *c*. 1790–1800.

3. *Prismatic cutting*. Horizontal prisms (Fig. 34, C) had occasionally occurred during the arrest period, but only in luxury types (*e.g.* the wafer seal of Plate CXXXVIII.). Like the pillar flute they required thick metal and chronologically they belong chiefly to the same decade (1790–1800). They were used with very pleasing effects by the Irish cutters. They responded much more readily than relief diamonds to the form of a vessel, and they are a notable instance of a simple cut motive which was almost always subordinated to the shape of the vessel. This is particularly evident in the dish of Plate CLVI. *b*, where form and cutting cannot be considered apart. In the same way they could be effectively adapted to almost any curved surface, notably to the underside of a flaring lip (as in the jug of Plate CLVIII. *b*. 2) or to the neck of a bottle form. In the latter application they continued in vogue until *c*. 1830 for the later and more elaborately cut decanters. But in jugs, butter dishes, and bowls, I do not think they were at all general after 1800.

4. *Herring-bone fringes* (Fig. 34, E) are almost entirely a 19th-century development, and both æsthetically and chronologically they may be partnered with the strawberry diamond. There were two main varieties, upright and slanting, and in both long and short " bones " were cut in an alternation of crest and trough. Like the strawberry diamonds they

became part of the Victorian jargon, especially at Stourbridge and Birmingham.

5. *Edge-cutting.* Elaborate scalloping still continues and is very evident in the trays of candlesticks and chandelier-lights, and in the canopies of chandeliers. It is also evident on the rims of jugs and other vessels to which it was not inconvenient. But a less deep and daring rim-cutting is still found about 1790 (*e.g.* Plate CLVII. 2, 3) and is on the whole more characteristic of the last phase. Yet reference must be made to an elaborate rim motive, *trefoil scalloping* (Plate CVII. 3), which seems to belong chiefly to the early years of the Irish florison. Early in the 19th century it was superseded by the well-known fan-cut edges which appear in the late Waterford designs published by Mr. Westropp (*cf.* Plate CLX. *b.* 2.).

The period of Irish glass (1780–1825) is so usually connected with developments in cutting, that an important new tendency in form is apt to be neglected. Classicalism in the third quarter of the 18th century provided English glassmaking with a new formal incentive which was much needed at that time. There had been no such invigorating influence since the advent of German form early in the reign of George II, and as we have seen the average mid-century glass is not remarkable for its excellence as a design. The influence of Greek vessel shapes on English pottery and glass may be traced to two sources, the " classical " architecture of the Adams brothers and the publication of Sir William Hamilton's celebrated collection of Greek pots (1766–77).[1] Wedgwood was responsible for popularizing the new shapes and during the next half-century, and even later still, classical form was the most notable characteristic of English pottery. The makers of pottery and porcelain were content to imitate classical shapes, but the reaction on glassmaking was less direct. It was an influence rather than an imitation. In some glasses, *e.g.* pickle jars, the glassmakers do not get much further from the Greek than the porcelain manufacturers, but nearly all the forms most characteristic of Irish glass show some classical influence. Such are the large boat-shaped fruit bowls (Plate CXLIV.*a.*) the round salad bowls with overturned rim (Plate CXLVIII), the boat-shaped salt-cellar (Plate CLII. 5, 7), numerous varieties of urn-shaped cruet bottle (Plate CLIV. 2,3), jugs of the type shown in Plate CXLII, the stems of candlesticks (Plate CXLIII. 1, 4), and the square foot. The Greek vase was, moreover, the parent of an urn motive which is very common in chandeliers and epergnes, both as part of the stem (Plate CXL) and as a decorative summit (Plate CXLI); and in some of the later " fingered " chandeliers the total design itself is suggested by a Greek pottery form (Plate CLXIII). We may add in parenthesis that this classical influence is sometimes associated with features of Chinese origin, for example the canopies of chandeliers

[1] *Antiquités etrusques grecques et romaines.* Ed. D'Hancarville (P. F. Hugues), 4 vols., Naples, 1766–77.

(Plate CXL), while Mr. Westropp illustrates[1] a round salad bowl with over-turned rim which has three legs after the manner of a Chinese tripod. For the makers of pottery classicalism was a matter of the most serious devotion. The Greek forms meant fashion, art, culture, something which carried them beyond their own rude industry, and they were accordingly copied with an untiring conscience. In their wish to be refined they became vulgar and introduced into their art a note of falsity which eventually destroyed English form. But by the glassmakers classicalism was more casually received. They had their own prestige and the tradition of culture which Venice had given them. They had no need to aspire. And so glass treated classicalism with a certain dignity and discretion, allowing itself to be influenced, but seldom deigning to imitation. In this way classicalism was the cause of a restoration in design. That was a very necessary revival at a time when English glass had found its true ornament and Ireland was able to give it free play. For without some force to counter the exuberance of cutting the invalid master which was English design must have succumbed to the attentions of his servant. Classicalism first appears in English glass, both moulded (Plate CXLIII. 1, 4) and cut (Plate CXLI), about ten years before Irish Free Trade (1780) and, with cutting, it may be regarded as the chief determinant of the " Irish " style. But the *classicism* of English glass had then been dead for more than half a century. For classicism is not a style or a mood or a philosophy, still less is it an affinity with ancient Greece ; it is rather a moment in the cultural experience of every people, and in the development of every artistic technique. And however ready we may be to admit that cutting was the appropriate ornament of English glassmaking and cut-glass its natural conclusion, the classicism of the art in England must be placed between the discovery of lead metal and the first coming of an alien influence.

[1] *Irish Glass*, Plate XXXIX, above, No. 2.

FIG. 21.

Early stem cutting; flutes and the German facet. About 1720. *Cf.* Plate CIV. 2 and p. 249.

FIG. 22.

Relief triangles below a double arch (*init. c.* 1730). See Plate CIII. 1 and p. 249.

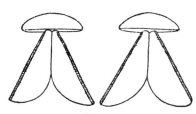

FIG. 23.

Lunar slices in a zigzag (*init.* 1730–40).

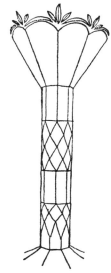

FIG. 25.

FIG. 26.

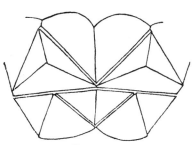

FIG. 24.

Bowl cutting of a sweetmeat glass (pyramids), *init.* 1730–40. See p. 249.

Actual wine-glass showing development of *stem* cutting due to the Excise Act (1745); *c.* 1750–60. See pp. 250–1 and Plate CXIX. 5.

[1. Arch - and - sprig (lower part of bowl).
2. Bowl flutes.
3. Stem flutes alternate with
4. Stem diamonds.
5. Fan panelling (foot)].

Wafer seal, date 1750 (coin). See Plate CXXXVIII.

[1. Prismatic cutting.
2. Circuit of relief diamonds.
3. Hooked diamonds].

S

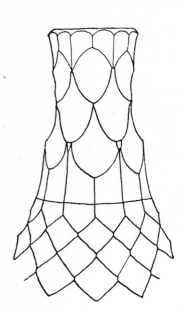

FIG. 27.

Flat cutting suited to hollow
parts. About 1730–80.

1. Scale pattern.
2. Neck fluting (*cf.* Fig. 25, No. 2).
3. Plain flat diamonds.

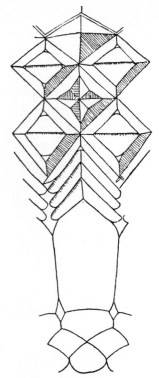

FIG. 28.

Large relief diamonds, double
cut, in a field. About 1780.
See pp. 252–3 and Plate
CXLV.

FIG. 29.

Circuit of double
festoons (cruet-bottle,
Plate CLIV. 1).

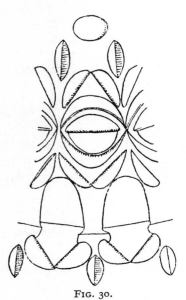

FIG. 30.

Pedestal of Fig. 33. English
luxury cutting; based on the lunar
slice. About 1770.

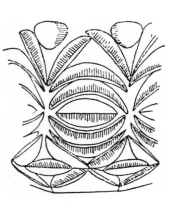

FIG. 31.

Exuberant use of the lunar slice.

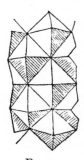

FIG. 32.

Plain relief dia-
monds in a field.
See p. 253. Last
quarter of 18th cen-
tury. *Cf.* Fig. 29.

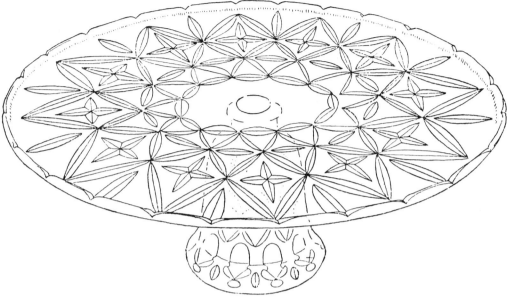

FIG. 33.

Apogee of English cutting in luxury piece (*c.* 1770) preceding the Irish exuberance; discreet use of the lunar slice. For the detail of the pedestal see Fig. 30, and for the style see p. 249. *Cf.* also Fig. 23 and note the absence of a field of diamonds. *S. D. Winkworth, Esq.*

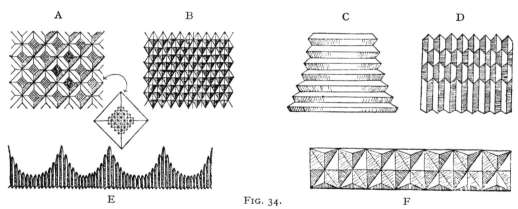

FIG. 34.

Later types of cutting.

A. Field of strawberry diamonds. First half of 19th century.
B. Field of small plain relief diamonds. Late 18th and early 19th century.
C. Horizontal prismatic cutting. See p. 254. About 1790.
D. Alternate prisms. Late 18th and early 19th century.
E. Herring-bone fringe. First half of 19th century.
F. Plain relief diamonds; characteristic before 1800, but occurring later; usually as a border or zone rather than in a field.

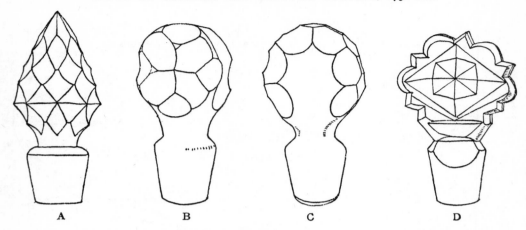

A. Decanter stopper, called "spire stopper" by Thos. Betts (1752). About 1750.

B. Decanter stopper, c. 1760.

C. Decanter stopper, c. 1765.

D. Decanter stopper, convex diamond cutting and scalloped edge, c. 1760–70.

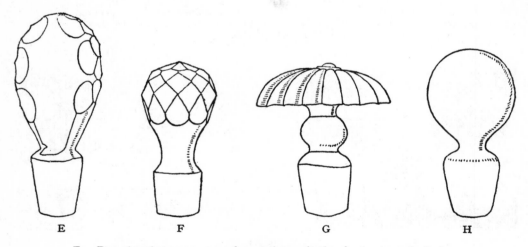

E. Decanter stopper, c. 1770, elongated to suit the slender taper body (as in Plate CXXVIII).

F. Cut stopper of a "square" (i.e. square decanter); Betts in 1758 was selling "Cutt squares stopt." Continued till end of 18th century.

G. Mushroom stopper, mainly Irish. Late 18th and early 19th century.

H. Plain stopper, English and Irish. Early 19th century. Cf. Plate CLIX. 2.

FIG. 35.

CHAPTER VII

The Anglo-Irish Revival : cut-glass

Laissez-faire, morbleu ! Laissez-faire.

MARQUIS D'ARGENSON (1751).

Never forget the material you are working with, and try always to use it for doing what it can do best.

WILLIAM MORRIS.

§1. FREE TRADE AND THE MIGRATIONS

BOTH the delay in the development of cutting and its flourishing during the Anglo-Irish period were primarily due to economic legislation. In the Excise Act of 1745 which came into force the following year there were two significant clauses. The first, as we have seen, placed a duty of 9s. 4d. on every hundredweight of materials used for making glass in Great Britain, *i.e.* in England and Scotland. The second clause prohibited the export of glass from Ireland to any country whatsoever. We have already seen how the first of these provisions, in conjunction with the German immigration, was the chief determinant of the age of ornament; we have now to consider the enactments which affected one country in relation to the development of style in the other. The second clause restricted the *output* of glass in Ireland in precisely the same degree that the first clause limited the English *style*. Before 1746 the glass industry in Ireland was not yet sufficiently advanced to have developed an export trade[1]; and after 1746 she was prevented by the Excise Act from acquiring one. Thus between 1746 and 1780 the few Irish flint glasshouses could only supply the very limited Irish market, and they could not therefore enjoy the wide custom and economic prosperity which were requisite for any artistic achievement. It is significant that in 1746 the St. Mary's Lane Glasshouse at Dublin could claim that it was "the only art and work of its kind carried on in this kingdom."[2]

The prosperity of Irish glassmaking only began with the coincidence of an English event with an Irish event in 1777–9. When England was involved in the War of American Independence and there was considerable pressure on the revenue the glass Excise of 1746 was doubled. It had very serious effects and is chiefly responsible for the decline of English glass

---

[1] On the contrary Ireland could not even supply her own market, but imported considerable quantities of glass from England, *e.g.* from 1719 to 1727 she imported an average of 133,000 drinking-glasses and 35,000 dozen bottles per annum. In 1735–6–7 the imports amounted to over £10,000 per annum. Westropp, p. 142.

[2] *Faulkner's Dublin Journal*, December, 1746, cited by Westropp, p. 42.

towards the end of the century ; moreover, it made a thin metal more necessary than ever and prevented any further elaboration of the simple English cutting which had been developing very slowly during the last fifty or sixty years. The American Civil War contributed also to the Irish event ; it had always been the custom for the English Government and the English people to treat Ireland as a troublesome but profitable preserve which might be bullied, or ignored as convenience might dictate. Her trade as well as her land had always been regulated or neglected in the interests of England, and all her industries, including glass, were sinking in a general depression.[1]

The Irish people, handicapped by their disorderly temperament and preoccupied with their own feuds, had shown a futile resentment in murderings, firings, and plunderings, but they had never risen to a concerted opposition. But now that America, the victim of a like intolerance, was successfully asserting her rights, and Lord North had given up being firm, the Irish were encouraged to raise a claim. Their requests were so reasonable that some small relief was granted, but North, as timid of his own countrymen as he had been tyrannical of others, was too much afraid of opposition in the great industrial cities of England to enter on a full programme of free trade. Burke was persuaded to be eloquent in their support and they found a sensible and energetic leader in Henry Grattan, who organized the resentment throughout the country as a Volunteer Arm. They were ready to wait at the doors of the Irish Parliament in 1779 when Grattan moved an amendment to the Address demanding free trade. The motion caused great agitation in England, but Lord North, finding few mistakes still left to him to make, did the right thing and in 1780 confirmed the free trade of Ireland by Act of Parliament.

The glass trade of both countries at once showed a reaction. Ireland had not been included in the duty of 1746 and there were no restrictions on weight which in England had encouraged " decorated glass," reduced size, limited style, restricted cutting, and increased prices, and in less than three years she had acquired a substantial export trade.

Nearly twenty years later in the hey-day of the manufacture the results of these two measures are stated thus : "At present we are able not only to supply our home consumption but to export very considerable quantities to America and elsewhere. Much of the glassware consumed in Ireland is imported, for our houses find the supply of the American market so much more lucrative and have so much of that trade that they think lightly of supplying the home consumption. The houses of this city (*i.e.* Dublin) which are in the American trade have generally orders for New York sufficient to occupy them entirely for two years. The principal

---

[1] For economic conditions in Ireland before 1780 see Lecky (W. E. H.), *History of Ireland.*

materials are imported from England, though we are able to undersell the British manufacturer."[1]

There was thus not only every promise to the new industry but every inducement to English glassmakers and glass-cutters to settle in a new country. English glass and Irish glass had always been and continued to be not two arts but one. Even before this time glassmaking in Ireland had only been a projection of English glass and Anglo-German ornament across the sea, distinct from English glassmaking only because it was two stages further from Bohemia than London, and one stage further than Bristol and Stourbridge. If we take London as the centre and the standard of English glassmaking in the 18th century there is ample evidence that Dublin, Belfast, Waterford were staffed by local workmen even less than Stourbridge or Bristol. Certainly both before and after 1780 they owed their technique and their style to Englishmen and in some degree even to Germans. Joseph Martin, the earliest English wheel-engraver of whom we have any knowledge,[2] came from London and was in 1735 " the only person employed by the managers of the glasshouse in Fleet Street (Dublin) in carving the said wares." In 1759 three Englishmen, T. S. Jeudwin, John Landon, and Henry Lunn, took over the Square Glasshouse in Abbey Street, Dublin, for the manufacture of window glass, and founded a new glasshouse for making flint glass. As they spent large sums on bringing artists from abroad it is likely that some at least of their workmen were Germans. For a short time they controlled the Ballycastle Glasshouse. It is probable that Charles Mulvany, who in 1785 founded one of the two most famous firms in Dublin, learnt his art from Jeudwin and Lunn, and in 1793 he took over a glasshouse in 1794 which Lunn had formerly occupied.[3] Again in 1764 we first hear of a family of four Williams', Richard, William, Thomas, and Isaac, who had lately come from Chepstow and founded one of the best-known glasshouses in Dublin and continued in business as late as 1829.[4] They appear to have superseded the previous firm, James Donelly & Co., who employed workmen from London, some of whom at least were probably Germans, for " any quantity or kind of flint or green glass, cut, flowered, or plain, as bespoke by James Donelly & Co., workmen from London."[5]

In 1766 the Chepstow firm, Dunbar Williams & Co., opened another

[1] Wallace (T.), *Essay on the manufactures in Ireland* (Dublin, 1798). There was also considerable export trade to the West Indies and the Continent. See extracts from Custom House Books cited by Westropp, pp. 144–55. In 1785 there were nine glasshouses " suddenly arisen " in Ireland, and the English manufacturers were being undersold ; see Sheffield (John, Lord), *Observations on the manufactures . . . of Ireland* (1785), where it is further remarked that before 1780 there had been no export of Irish glass.
[2] *Dublin Evening Post*, February, 1735 ; Westropp, p. 49.
[3] *Ibid.*, pp. 51–5. [4] *Ibid.*, p. 57. [5] *Ibid.*, p. 57.

factory in Fishamble Street, Dublin,[1] which was quite independent of the Williams' whose glasshouse was at Marlborough Street.[2] These two colonies of Chepstow must be connected with two changes in the title of the Chepstow firm. Before the departure of the Williams' (father and sons) in 1764 the style was Williams, Dunbar & Co. In 1765 another partner, Bradley, was taken in their room and the firm became Dunbar & Bradley. This style only lasted one year and in 1766 the name is simply Isaac Hays Dunbar.[3] There is no doubt that it was Bradley who set up in the glasshouse in Fishamble Street when he severed connection with I. H. Dunbar. The disintegration of the original firm within the space of two years was due, I suggest, to the business incapacity of the senior partner Dunbar ; after 1766 we hear nothing of the Chepstow glasshouse, and some time between 1766 and 1777 I. H. Dunbar also migrated to Ireland, but became insolvent in the latter year.[4] Finally Michael Dunbar, probably his son, formed another company in Ireland and some time between 1792 and 1795[5] acquired the glasshouse formerly occupied by Emanuel Quin & Co. in William Street, Newry. All these men worked in a Bristol tradition and they are a most convincing illustration of the colonization of Ireland by English glassmakers ; they were, too, the victims of the English Excise. Again in 1771 the proprietors of the Tyrone Collieries, who were, like the Penroses of Waterford and Thomas Burnell & Co. of Cork, capitalists and not craftsmen, ventured a glasshouse on their estate at Drumrea, where coal, sand, and fire clay were ready to hand, and brought over an English glassmaker, Benjamin Edwards of Bristol, to direct the manufacture.[6] There is no doubt that Edwards, like John Hill of whom we shall speak in a moment, brought over a complete team of glassmakers and glass-cutters. He did not long remain a hireling but in 1775 or 1776 he moved to Belfast and founded the Long Bridge Glasshouse of which the mark B. EDWARDS BELFAST is sometimes found in moulded lettering on the base of decanters ; in that manufacture his cutters were English.

In connection with his Bristol origin we may note that he made enamel glass which was certainly a speciality though not a monopoly of Bristol. By enamel glass he certainly meant the opaque white glass which we have already discussed.[7] The only other glasshouses in Ireland to make enamel glass were the Williams family at Dublin, and later the Gatchells of

[1] *Faulkner's Dublin Journal*, 14, vi, 1766, Buckley, *History*, p. 150 ; jellies, whips, wine-glasses, and decanters are mentioned.
[2] Westropp, p. 57.
[3] *Bristol Journal*, 22, xi, 1766, Buckley, *History*, p. 11.
[4] Buckley, *ibid.*, note 2.
[5] Westropp, p. 130.
[6] Westropp, pp. 99 and 101.
[7] I do not think Mr. Westropp can be right in suggesting (p. 201) that this means glass painted in enamel. Enamel glass was the ordinary 18th-century term for what

Waterford. If we couple this fact with their obvious Welsh nationality and the name of the firm, Williams Dunbar & Co., which worked the Chepstow Glasshouse (another colony of Bristol) there is little doubt that the Williams' also learned their technique at Bristol.

The infiltration of Englishmen into Ireland had thus been going on for some time. Between 1780 and 1786 it became a considerable immigration and included Germans as well as Englishmen. J. D. Ayckbowm was a London cut-glass maker[1] who had had an extensive custom in Ireland, travelled regularly there, and was well acquainted with both the restrictions and the opportunities of glassmaking in Ireland. He was precisely the type of glassmaker whom the Excise of 1777 hit hardest, and being only a denizen he had no reluctance to move his establishment. About 1783 when the boom in Irish glass was just beginning he came to Dublin and opened a warehouse and probably a glasshouse connected with it, continuing in business there until 1802. Of the same type as Ayckbowm is John Grahl, a German who came from the Saxon side of the Erzgebirge. Like Ayckbowm he had probably been working in London and came to Ireland as the result of the Excise of 1777. He was a particularly expert cutter and specialized in gilding cut-glass.

There is still another type of immigrant who went to Ireland during the decade 1780–90. The grant of free trade to Ireland in 1780 had reminded some Englishmen that Ireland existed and caused others, especially the sort who lived in Birmingham and Bristol, to wish that she did not. The economic relations between the two countries were thus very much disturbed. In 1785 the Government recognized the new conditions and eased itself by appointing a Commission to enquire into the commercial relations between the two countries. In the course of its

---

Dossie and modern usage calls white opaque glass. Edkins's " Amell " and Amatt's " Enamell " were certainly white opaque glass (Owen, p. 380 *et seq.*), and Waterford had a prescription for white " enamel " made with arsenic which from the ingredients and the size of the batch must mean a white opaque glass. Mr. Buckley states (p. 4) that " enamel glass " at Bristol included both white opaque glass and glasses with enamel-twist stems, but he does not refer to any authority for the latter ; but see p. 309.

[1] The London firm was styled Hermann and Dedereck Ayckbowm, but the name does not occur in London Directories after 1780 (Buckley, *History*, p. 139). J. D. Ayckbowm may have been a son of the London partners ; before his migration (*c.* 1783) he seems to have been " travelling " in Ireland (1774) on behalf of the London House (Westropp, p. 63), and no doubt established a personal connection which made it worth while to transfer the whole business as soon as there was free trade in Ireland. Probably he had at first (1783–99) only a cutter's business and a warehouse where he cut the glasses of the Irish factories, but about 1799 (*Dublin Ev. Post*, 4, i, 99, Westropp, p. 63) he opened a " new Venice glass and chrystal manufactory " which in 1802 was transferred to J. L. Rogers and Co. (*Dublin Gazette*, 4, iii, 02). The presence of an important German cutter in Dublin must have influenced very considerably the development of " Irish " cutting.

investigations this body came to the glass industry and thereupon called up for examination John Blades, who was then the most considerable English cut-glass maker in London, and after the death of Lazarus Jacobs received his appointment as glassmaker to George III.[1] In his interview with the Commission Blades stated that English glassmakers were continually going to and from Ireland and that the most important glassmaker at Stourbridge, John Hill, had recently collected the best team of workmen he could get in the county of Worcester and had gone to Waterford. The opportunities offered by Ireland and the low state of the English industry do not need further commentary. Hill is the Verzelini of Anglo-Irish glass and his migration the most important event in this last period. Having already his own business established he would need a very sure prospect to induce him to forsake it. The workmen whom he took with him included specialists in every stage of glassmaking from the mixing-room to the cutter's wheel and his transplantation to a country where economic conditions were more favourable is typical of the whole industry at that time.

He is without question the real founder of the celebrated Waterford factory, but he went to an assured position in the service of other men. In 1783, two brothers, George and William Penrose, who were not artists but rich merchants, perceiving that glass was likely to be a good thing in the new Ireland, established a glasshouse at Waterford, a port equally convenient for the American and for the English export trade on which the success of their venture would inevitably depend. They were very thorough in their methods and their initial outlay seems to have exceeded their estimate. Their warehouse was first opened on 1 October, 1783, and the following month they presented a petition to the Irish Parliament and succeeded in obtaining a Government grant. But they had spent nearly £10,000 on the fifty or so workmen whom they had brought from Stourbridge and on the erection of their factory, and in 1786 they again showed signs of distress and presented another petition. We do not know whether it was successful, but thereafter the manufacturers prospered exceedingly, supplied glass to George III and even in 1790 had become famous for the " elegance of the various articles in the warehouse."

The credit for the artistic achievement is entirely Hill's. When he entered the employ of the Penroses in 1783 he brought with him the prescriptions, and doubtless also the designs, that had been in use in his own factory. He was, however, an unfortunate man. He appears to have become unpopular among the Irish workmen who had been taken on for training by the Penroses ; and for some reason that does not appear he was unlucky enough to offend the wife of one of his employers ; and she out of pique or malice charged him with unseemly conduct towards her. The accusation distressed him so much that he could no longer

[1] Westropp, p. 71, Buckley, *History*, p. 139.

[266]

remain in Waterford. But during the three years of his stay (1783-6) he had become the friend of another Englishman, Jonathan Gatchell, a man of Somerset family and a Quaker, who was a clerk in the employ of the Penroses. On his departure Hill left a letter for his friend in which he protested his innocence and declared that " my mind is so hurt that I scarce know what I am writing."[1] He left also in token of his gratitude the recipes which had previously been known only to himself, as was the way with master glassmakers. He could not have done him a greater service. Now that their manager was fled the unskilful owners were in great difficulty, and the possession of the formula for mixing gave Jonathan a great handle on the firm and eventually the sole direction of it. But the story of Hill's flight is not merely of personal interest. The work of the firm for the next fifty years depended on the directions which John Hill had left behind him. Waterford glass had its greatest vogue under the Gatchell family but the tradition and the technique were derived from Stourbridge.

The foundation of glassmaking at Cork had a similar origin. The year before the Penroses founded the Waterford glasshouse a company was formed at Cork. The partners were Atwell Hayes, Thomas Burnett, and Francis Richard Rowe, and they also sought the support of the Government. Their petition was presented on the same day that the Penroses presented theirs and the methods of the two firms were the same. They sent an agent to England to enquire into the methods of glassmaking practised there, to arrange for the supply of English materials and to engage English workmen. Their outlay of £6000 was rewarded by " the most ample set of materials and implements and the most able artificers England could afford."[2]

It is clear from the foregoing account that Irish glass was never an independent and peculiar art but a complex of three English traditions. The Bristol tradition was continued at Dublin, Ballycastle, Drumrea, Newry, and Belfast. The Stourbridge tradition is represented at Waterford and probably also at Cork ; and there were German artists like Ayckbowm

---

[1] " It is impossible for me to express the feelings of my poor mind when I acquaint thee that I am obliged to leave this town and kingdom. My reason I need not tell thee, but I sincerely wish I had been made acquainted with the base ingratitude of the worst of villains (presumably one of the brothers Penrose) sooner, and probably then I might have remedied it, but now 'tis too late. For heaven's sake do not reproach me but put the best construction on my conduct. I wish it was in my power to pay thee and all my creditors but if ever fortune should put it in my power depend upon it I will satisfy every one. My mind is so hurt that I scarcely know what I write. I sincerely wish thee every success and am that the most miserable of mankind, Thine very sincerely J. Hill." It would appear that Hill, like Jonathan Gatchell, was a Quaker ; hence no doubt their friendship. The letter is in the possession of Mr. M. S. D. Westropp.

[2] Westropp, p. 115, quoting the petition of 1783.

and Grahl and one or two other names which appear to be of German origin. The interest of the Anglo-Irish period does not lie in futile attempts to distinguish this or that piece as the work of a particular factory. Such distinctions are rarely possible because all the Irish factories used one another's cullet and copied one another's designs. The real interest is in trying to trace the devolution of style of Irish glass from the English centres of glassmaking in which it had its origin.

Before, however, we come to the work of these several factories we may turn to the early history of the art and observe how even from its origins glassmaking in Ireland had been chiefly carried on by Englishmen, and passed generally through the same stages as in England.

§ 2. EARLY HISTORY

There is no need to suppose that in early times the practice of the craft in Ireland was much junior to the English manufacture; and the stages of development were roughly the same. As early as the 13th century we find the counterparts of the Chiddingfold glassmen working in Dublin. In the parish of St. Brigid, Dublin, William the Glassmaker received a grant of land for the purpose of making glass in 1258 and is thus almost contemporary with Laurence Vitrearius of Chiddingfold. There is little doubt that he was a Frenchman and he had perhaps worked in Sussex before he went to Ireland. The next name, William de Kemesye (Vitrarius), which occurs in 1309, is certainly French and contemporary with William le Verrir and Richard de Dunkshurst. Again in 1409 and 1434 we hear of Richard the Glazewright, in 1576 of William Cranch and William Hobelthorne, glaziers, and in 1579 of Richard Daioben, glazier. It is probable that most of these men had acquired their craft in Sussex, then the chief centre of glassmaking in England. Like the Schurterres and the Peytowes they were primarily glaziers, that is to say makers of window glass, but no doubt they also made rude vessels of the type which has been discovered in recent years at Chiddingfold.

There was, however, no serious enterprise until 1586 and the inception of vessel glassmaking in that year was the result of the stimulus provided by Carré, Briet, Becku the Lorrainers, and above all by Verzelini. In that year Captain Thomas Woodhouse, a retired army officer and a man of the same type as the later English monopolists, received a patent permitting him the sole right of making glass for glazing and drinking in Ireland for the space of eight years : " Her Majesty considering that the making of glass might prove commodious to both realms and that Woodhouse was the first that with any success had begun the art in Ireland is pleased to condescend to his petition and therefore orders that a grant be made to him of the privilege of making glass for glazing and drinking or otherwise, and to build convenient houses, for the term of eight years, the glass to be sold as cheepe or rather better cheepe than the similar glass in foreign parts."[1] To Captain Woodhouse, therefore, and not to Sir Jerome Bowes belongs the credit of establishing the first glassworks under royal patronage and native ownership. It may be noted that this patent was in itself a virtual infringement of Verzelini's monopoly[2] which technically extended to Ireland as well as to England, and it shows the general inconsistency of the monopoly system to which we have already referred in the case of Bowes and Mansell.

Woodhouse's enterprise does not seem to have been a success, for he only held his monopoly for two years. The failure was due partly to the inadequacy of the Irish market, but more probably to his own inexperience; for George Longe, a man astute in business and skilled in the art of glass, found it worth his while to pay Woodhouse £300 in purchase of the monopoly (1589).

The new monopolist may be claimed as the first practical British glassmaker. He was an Englishman, not an Irishman, and had learned his glassmaking in Sussex and in London. At the time of his purchase of the Irish monopoly he already owned four[3] out of the fifteen[4] or sixteen English glasshouses and he had sunk a capital of £500 in investigating the possibilities of the industry in Ireland, in seeking materials on the spot, and in the employment of a set of workmen in experiments, these during the two previous years. He had thus both wealth and enterprise and when Woodhouse did badly he saw an opening in the remote barbarian island. He might walk in upon Woodhouse's failure and extend his practice unembarrassed by so strong a competition as the Normandy men and the Lorrainers in plate glass and Verzelini in the finer drinking vessels; for Verzelini had now enjoyed his patent and his patronage for fourteen years. But " your Honor's poor Orator George Longe " had subtlety in his pleading as well as a sensible ambition. In 1589 the glass manufacture

[1] Abstract of Patent, Westropp, p. 21.

[2] The only difference is that Woodhouse's patent does not specify glasses " such as be accustomablie made in the towne of Murano." But the phrase " in foreign parts " must imply this.

[3] It is evident from his petition to Burghley that he undertook to limit the number of his English glasshouses to four, that he had spent his " tyme wholly in the trade, so hath no other Englishman," and that he was a man of considerable capital. *Petition of George Longe to Lord Burghley*, 3 Oct., 1589. Lansdowne MS. 59, Art. 75 ; cited by Hartshorne, pp. 401–3.

[4] Longe mentions fourteen, but these probably do not include Verzelini's glasshouse at Broad Street, nor his first glasshouse at the Crutched Friars if that was still working (*supra*, p. 75).

in England was already well established and the destruction of the woodlands was causing great wrath and anxiety. Now observe, says the Orator,
how in the ninth year of the Queen's reign certain strangers came to
England, neither subjects nor denizens, neither licensed nor forbidden, and
do (as it were by intrusion) continue the trade to the great prejudice of the
realm wasting timber for want of underwood. It will be a great advantage
to Her Majesty to grant the Irish petition, for she has had no custom from
English glass, whereas glass made in Ireland and transported by them
will yield Her Majesty great Custom. It will further advantage the country
that George Longe shall make glass in Ireland and that English glassmakers
shall be restricted ; for the woods in England (so important for the
ships[1]) will no longer be destroyed and the superfluous woods will be put
to better use than the harbouring of rebels and enemies. Many persons
will be set to work to cut wood, burn ashes, dig sand, and carry clay, and
" trade and civility will increase in that rude country by inhabiting those
great woods and the passage to and fro of ships for the transportation of
glass."

George Longe's petition was granted, and for at least eight years he
carried on a thriving business in both plate glass and coarse vessel glass
(*verres de fougère* probably showing Venetian influence) at a place called
Curryglas, on the edge of the great Drumfenning Woods in the county of
Cork.[2] When he next writes he gives the impression that his schemes had
succeeded as he wished, and if that is so I think Curryglas for " glazing "
may take rank beside Broad Street for " Venice drinking-glasses."

In the 17th century glassmaking had a very haphazard course. In
1608 we hear of an Adam Whitty of Arklow, County Wicklow, who received
a licence to make glass in the province of Leinster, and in 1618 a Venetian
glassmaker, the first we hear of in Ireland, thought it worth while to set
up a glasshouse, probably in the county of Waterford. A number of other
glasshouses all founded by Englishmen are known to have existed in Ireland
in the first half of the 17th century.[3]

Ireland did not enjoy the results of a monopoly system, and above all
she had no Mansell to give unity to the various enterprises in glassmaking
which have been recorded. The place of the English patentees was taken
by wealthy Irish landowners, like the Earl of Cork or Viscount Conway
and Kilulta, who were given to industrial schemes and found it profitable
or amusing to set up a glasshouse on their estates. One of these glasshouses

[1] Longe missed this argument ; see p. 89 *supra*.
[2] Petition dated 1597 " of George Longe who first brought glassmaking to Ireland "
preserved among MSS. of the Marquis of Salisbury and cited by Westropp, p. 23. Coarse
drinking-glass is expressly mentioned in this document. There is a place still called
Glasshouse a mile to the south of Curryglas.
[3] Boate (Gerard), *Ireland's Natural History* (London, 1652).

was founded, probably by the Earl of Cork, at Ballynegery (*i.e.* Bally-
nagerah) in the south of County Waterford about 1620. Some of the
accounts of this factory have been preserved,[1] and as they refer also to
" my ironworks " there is little doubt that they were owned by the Earl
of Cork, who is known to have had many industrial projects of this
kind.

This glasshouse is chiefly interesting because all the glassmakers
whose names are mentioned were certainly British and not Italian, *e.g.*
Davy, the glassmaker who appears to have been manager, and Hugh
Osborne, " founder, consore, or maker of the matter and metal of the
glass," and Darby the glassman. The factory made plate glass and also
vessel glass, probably *verre de fougère*, rather than *façon de Venise*, and seems
to have enjoyed an extensive custom over most of the south of Ireland.

Besides monopolists and landowners we have also the independent
Lorraine tradition. About 1623 Abraham Bigo, one of the Bigault family
whom we find also at Stourbridge, Bristol, and London, set up a furnace
for both window glass and drinking vessels at Birr, near Dublin. It would
appear that he, with his wife Hester and his sons Abraham and John, had
come to England some time after the four families of *gentilshommes*.
Abraham, probably soon after his arrival, set up a glasshouse in Purbeck
Island where there was a plentiful supply of fine white sand. Mansell also
had a glasshouse there and the date when we first hear of him at Birr (1623)
makes it probable that he fled to Ireland in order to escape Mansell's
domination.[2] Abraham Bigo seems to be the first of several Lorraine
glassmakers who settled in Ireland ; one of his " in-laws," Ananias Henzey,
whom we have already noticed, was making glass for Lord Conway about
fifty years later, and the Batchelor family of glassmakers,[3] who were
connected with some of the Lorrainers, are also found in Dublin.

The similarity of developments in Ireland to developments in England
appears again in 1638, when the industry was snubbed, but certainly not
suppressed,[4] by a proclamation which forbade the manufacture of glass in
Ireland after August, 1639. This measure may have been simply a bit of
vicarious oppression, but more probably it effected in Ireland what the
" Proclamation touching glasses " had effected in England in 1615. It is
important as showing that the Irish glass industry was about twenty-five

[1] In Marsh's Library, Dublin ; Westropp, p. 25, where the list of expenditures is
given.
[2] Mr. Westropp (p. 32) suggested that Bigo " failed " at Purbeck Island, and that
his failure was due to unsuccessful experiments with a lead flux. This is surely very
improbable in a glassmaker of the potash tradition at so early a date. Mansell was a
tyrant and the Lorrainers men of spirit.
[3] Buckley, *Glass Trade*, p. 53. The Batchelors were at Stourbridge in 1697 and at
Broseley in 1732 (Buckley, *History*, p. 14).
[4] Westropp, p. 32.

[271]

years behind England in its general development. Two years later (1641) the motive for the proclamation becomes apparent, for a Bill was passed which prohibited the felling of timber to provide fuel for the glass and iron industries. Thereafter there is little more foundation of country glasshouses and by the last quarter of the 17th century the industry had generally moved into the towns, where coal was more easily procured.

The history of glassmaking in Ireland after the invention of lead glass[1] (1676) and before the decade 1780–90 makes this quite clear. With the exception of one or two small and abortive factories[2] in the Irish counties Dublin alone had a continuous manufacture, and the later history of the art until 1780 is concerned entirely with the few Dublin flint glasshouses. There were besides a number of bottle glasshouses and plate-glass manufactories, but these do not require mention here.

The first Irish flint glasshouse in Dublin was worked by a Captain Philip Roche soon after 1690.[3] He was a man of good family, like many of the 17th-century owners, but after holding a commission from James II he had travelled widely in Europe and acquired a personal and practical knowledge of the art. When he returned to Ireland, being debarred from the services and professions by his political sympathies and his Roman Catholic religion, he was induced by his brother-in-law, an eminent tradesman of Dublin, to take over one of the glasshouses which already existed in the parish of St. Michan, Dublin, and became a professional glassmaker. He took as partners two brothers, Richard and Christopher Fitzsimons, who were men of the same class as himself. Richard Fitzsimons died in 1711 and Roche himself two years later, but the business was carried on continuously by the Fitzsimons family until 1755. At that time the head of the firm was Christopher Fitzsimons II, but he seems to have found business very bad, for in 1755 he petitioned the Irish Parliament

---

[1] In 1675 the King granted to be presented to the Lord-Lieutenant of Ireland a warrant for a patent of fourteen years' duration to Sir Philip Lloyd, Richard Hunt, and an Italian master glassmaker Odacio Formica " for their new invention of manufacturing of a particular sort of chrystalline glasses resembling rock crystal *which has never been exercised by any in that kingdom.*" This is the Irish counterpart of Ravenscroft's patent of 1673–4, and obviously the patentees wished to do in Ireland what Ravenscroft's patent prevented them from doing in England, to manufacture crystal glass with imported Italian pebbles as Ravenscroft had done *when he first took out his patent with Da Costa.* Cf. p. 131 *supra*, and see *S.P. Dom.* 29, v, 1675. I can find no evidence in the Irish State Papers that this project was ever put into effect.

[2] *E.g.* (1) the Gurteens Glasshouse near Waterford, first mentioned in 1729 and owned by John Head, 1731–40. It was mainly a bottle glasshouse. No glass was made at Waterford 1740–83. (2) The Ballycastle glasshouse, near collieries, founded 1754. Ballycastle coal was used by the Dublin glasshouses (Westropp, p. 133).

[3] This date is important. It shows how soon after 1681 the lead technique had found its way into the remoter provinces. Dublin glassmaking, until 1780 at any rate, was provincial to London, not " Irish."

for a grant. Irish industries generally were then very depressed, and it is probable that his petition failed. Five years later, at any rate, he had given up manufacturing glass altogether, and had become, like others of his kind, a glass merchant whose business consisted in importing glass from England. He is an excellent instance of the effects of the Excise Act of 1746. Roche had died a rich man and it is probable, though it cannot be proved, that the Roche glasshouse had at least some export trade early in the century; it was the loss of this which caused Christopher Fitzsimons to go into retailing.[1] The Roche-Fitzsimons glasshouse, generally known as the *Round Glasshouse*, was in St. Mary's Lane and advertised its wares very frequently until 1759. While it lasted it was a most enterprising and prosperous firm, and sold all the main types of glass which we find in English advertisements of the same period. The following is a list issued in 1752 : . . . "the newest-fashioned drinking-glasses, water-bottles, claret and Burgundy ditto, decanters, jugs, water-glasses[2] with and without feet and saucers, plain, ribbed, and diamond-moulded jelly-glasses of all sorts and sizes, sillybub-glasses, comfit- and sweetmeat-glasses for desserts,[3] salvers, glass plates for china dishes, toort (*i.e.* retort) covers, pine- and orange-glasses, bells and shades, hall lanthornes, glass branches (*i.e.* table chandeliers), etc., all in the newest-fashioned mounting now used in London."[4] All the patterns, glassmakers, and glass-engravers of this firm were brought from London and the proprietor claimed very justly that his was at that time (1752) the only (flint) glass manufacture in the country.[5] He prided himself on being in the latest mode in all that he did, and he brought London engravers who could execute " cut and flowered glasses . . . of any kind of pattern, viz. wine-glasses with a vine border, toasts *or any flourish whatsoever.*" The last phrase is a covert allusion to political engraving and makes it likely that a good many of the " Williamite " glasses were executed in this glasshouse. The commemoration of the Battle of the Boyne (1 July) and of William III's birthday (4 November) were regular festivals in Dublin,[6] for which special glasses were made, and it was just at the time of the Jacobite agitation that they became most enthusiastic. The date of the advertisement (1752) coincides fairly exactly with this, and Fitzsimons was then the only flint-glass manufacturer in Ireland.

[1] *Dublin Chronicle*, 11–13, ix, 1788. The failure is there ascribed to ill-health. Westropp, pp. 37 and 39–43.
[2] See Appendix IV.
[3] Proving the identity of sweetmeat glasses with the dessert glasses of the 18th-century advertisements. *Cf.* Lady Grisell Baillie's " cornered brim " sweetmeats (*Household Books*, p. 298).
[4] *Faulkner's Dublin Journal*, January, 1752, cited by Westropp, p. 43. *Cf.* p. 308 *init.*
[5] Westropp, *ibid.*
[6] See *Apollo*, III, 165 and 210.

T

After Roche's venture (*c.* 1690–7) we hear of no other flint-glass manufacture until 1734, when a glasshouse was established in *Fleet Street* for making " fine drinking-glasses, salvers, decanters, branches of several sorts " which were claimed later on (1737) to be " for beauty of metal and workmanship equal to those made in London." It was this firm who brought over Joseph Martin, and probably others of their workmen were also English. The ambition of this glasshouse, like the others, was to undersell the English imports and capture the Irish market, but after the Act of 1746 had prohibited the export of glass from Ireland the Fleet Street glasshouse found the home market insufficient and gradually succumbed. The owners, whose names are not known to us, held out an even shorter time than Christopher Fitzsimons, and as early as 1751 were occupied entirely with the retail of English goods.[1]

The next venture was in 1750 when Rupert Barter established a glasshouse on *Lazars Hill.* He was a man of different type from any of the others we have met. An oil-painter and a miniature artist rather than a glassmaker, he is comparable with Wolff, Schaper, and Schouman in Germany and with Michael Edkins and the Beilbys in England. It is not surprising, therefore, to find that his glass was peculiar, that he specialized chiefly in " bright green glass " and received an award of twenty pounds from the Dublin Society on account of its excellence. This green glass, in which he made chemists' bottles and decanters, was certainly not bottle glass, but dyed flint glass of the kind to which we have alluded in Chapter VI ; in England it is not uncommon even at the beginning of the 18th century, but this appears to be the first mention of its manufacture in Ireland.

With the exception of the glasshouses of Jeudwin Landon & Lunn in Abbey Street (1759), James Donelly & Co. in Marlborough Street (1764), the Williams family in Marlborough Street, and a second colony sent out from Chepstow[2] which had a glasshouse in Fishamble Street (1766), no other flint glasshouses of any importance were founded in Dublin before the Excise Act of 1777 and the Free Trade of 1780. After 1780 the more important Irish factories are known to us by marked specimens, as well as from literary sources, and although there are only one or two details of style which can be regarded as idiosyncrasies, it will be convenient to treat the several factories separately.

---

[1] *Dublin Journal*, October, 1734 and December, 1737 ; *Dublin Evening Post*, February, 1735, all cited by Westropp, p. 49.
[2] Probably managed or owned by Bradley, formerly of Dunbar and Bradley of Chepstow.

§ 3. THE NEW GLASSHOUSES (ENGLAND AND IRELAND)

A. WATERFORD

When John Hill fled from Waterford in 1786 his friend, Jonathan Gatchell, to whom he had bequeathed the secrets of the Stourbridge mixing-rooms, became indispensable to the brothers Penrose and the real controller of the Waterford glassworks. He and his family are worthy to be called a dynasty, and in the way they lived and thought they may be compared with the Titterys and the Hennezels and the other Protestant glassmakers, or with some of the potter dynasties of Staffordshire. Their character is spoken pretty clearly in the bundle of letters and account-books now in possession of Mr. Dudley Westropp. They were a shrewd, competent race, and subscribing daily to the three articles of their faith, the family, the business, and the mercy of God, they were raised to a wholesome mediocrity by the narrow discipline it afforded them. Their austere kindliness was a business asset as well as a family bond, but while it gave a decent habit to sale and purchase, it never led them into senti-mental politics; they respectfully informed their friends and the public that they gave no credit to customers. In their close pursuit of a competence they were for ever torn between a wariness of too great wealth and a cramped but very vivid appreciation of its indulgencies. They had to win their living from a hostile world and the qualities requisite in business were transformed into virtues and sanctioned by their religion. Method and industry, therefore, were at once a duty to themselves and one part of a plain contract with their Almighty; the other part of the contract was incumbent upon God, and in their balance-sheets they looked for its fulfilment. No one could ever mistake them for artists; they were not reckless and they had no imagination. Bristol glassmaking had a gay fancy and loved bright colours, but these things were outside the morality of Quakers; and in fact Waterford made very little coloured or painted glass.[1] Its art was a matter of procedure and its style is efficiency. For the Gatchells it was a purpose in life to keep their metal clear,[2] their shapes marketable, their cutting clean and exact,[3] and

---

[1] There is a prescription for enamel glass among the Gatchell papers; and it is likely that some little coloured glass was made at Waterford. But these types are not normal of Waterford. I have heard it stated several times that the factory only made coloured glass to special orders, but I am unable to quote any literary authority for this.

[2] There is evidence among the Gatchell papers that the Gatchells were at special pains to secure an absolutely clear white metal; cf. p. 17 supra.

[3] This was why the field of small diamonds and the miniature style of cutting generally became so characteristic of Waterford; see the designs reproduced by Westropp, Plates XIII and XIV (c. 1830), and the earlier decanters marked PENROSE WATERFORD, ibid., Plate XVIII.

those were in fact the qualities which made their business a success and the name of Waterford almost a synonym for English and Irish cut-glass. Cork glass is immeasurably better in design as its metal is technically inferior. But if at Waterford competence outran design, the Gatchells at least were in character with their age, and they have a distinguished affinity in Josiah Wedgwood.

The Gatchells were an English and not an Irish family, descended from a John Gatchell who had come over from Somersetshire at the end of the 17th century. They were not originally glassmakers and Jonathan Gatchell himself had been only a clerk when he first found an appointment in the Penrose firm. It was due partly to his good fortune, but partly also to his own energy that he acquired a complete knowledge of the technique and was able to take John Hill's place in 1786. In virtue of this knowledge he eventually succeeded to the sole conduct of the Waterford firm. George Penrose died in 1796, being succeeded by a third brother, Francis, but by 1799 both these men had disappeared from the business and a new company was formed. Jonathan Gatchell was now raised to the rank of partner on the score of his glassmanship and two capitalists, James Ramsey and Ambrose Barcroft, were introduced in place of the Penroses. The new firm under the style of *Ramsey, Gatchell and Barcroft* prospered exceedingly, built a new glasshouse and continued until 1810, when owing to the death of Ramsey and the extravagant habits of Barcroft the partnership was dissolved. Thus Jonathan Gatchell at last succeeded to the sole ownership and carried on the work alone till 1823. In that year a family company was formed for seven years and consisted of Jonathan, his brothers James and Samuel, and his son-in-law Joseph Walpole. This firm *Gatchells and Walpole* was to last for seven years (1823–30) and during its continuance Ireland suffered the first serious[1] excise on glass. In 1825 an Act of Parliament (6 George IV, c. 117) imposed a duty of two hundred and fifty shillings on every thousand pounds' weight of metal used for flint glass. This works out at twenty shillings a hundredweight, but as the English duty was by this time as much as ninety-eight shillings a hundredweight, the glasshouses in Ireland could still consider themselves very fortunate. In 1830 Gatchells and Walpole was dissolved and a Nehemiah Wright, a brother-in-law of Jonathan Gatchell's, was admitted into the firm, which then became *Gatchell Walpole and Company*. The same year, however, the other members of the Gatchell family ceased to take any active part in the business and Jonathan Wright, son of Nehemiah, became sole manager and virtually the proprietor. When *Gatchell Walpole and Company* was dissolved in 1835 George Gatchell took over the business and with a partner, George

[1] There had been a tax on bottles since 1797 at the rate of one farthing per quart bottle, and so on at the rate of one farthing for every additional pint or part of a pint (37 Geo. III, c. 28) ; but this, of course, did not affect the flint-glass industry.

Saunders, who had been one of the firm's Canadian clients, worked until 1848 under the style of *George Gatchell and Company*. In that year the partnership was dissolved and George Gatchell carried on alone till 1851. After that no more flint glass was made at Waterford.

In the whole of this history there are only two individuals of importance: Hill, who brought the art from England and first determined the style of the firm, and Jonathan Gatchell, who carried it on during his long regime of thirty-seven years (1786–1823). Only Jonathan among the Gatchells was directly in contact with the English tradition; he had ambition, technical knowledge, and business experience, and at his death the vigour and unity of the firm disappeared. The Excise which came two years after his death was a serious handicap and the frequent changes which we find in the personnel of the firm during its later history are themselves an indication that glassmaking no longer held their interest or contributed to their prosperity.[1] In 1835 there was an abatement in the duty and an increase in the firm's financial prosperity, but by that time those who worked in the glasshouse had lost touch with the old tradition, the cutting had grown petty and elaborate, and little was left of either beauty or sincerity. It is certain, therefore, that the best work of the glasshouse was confined to the years 1786–1823, when the original Stourbridge tradition was still effective, and though marked pieces of Waterford are very rare and almost exclusively of one form, and no other pieces whatever afford material for judgment, one may note one or two items which were the peculiarity, though hardly the monopoly of Waterford. Other types of vessel made at Waterford were made everywhere else also and of these we shall have something to say later. The metal of Waterford glass is extremely clear and white in colour and in this respect nearer than any other to realizing the general aim of the 18th-century glassmaker. There is evidence among the Gatchell papers that the firm were at special pains to secure a good, clear white metal. The dead horse of the "beautiful blue tint," first slain by Mr. Westropp, has now been flogged pretty often, but it shows such astonishing vitality that another blow may be excused. A dark bluish-black tint is a very common defect[2] in the 18th-century glass and especially so during the Anglo-Irish period (1780–1825), but it was entirely accidental and it occurred everywhere. It was probably the result of admitting too much black manganese—a substance generally used to clear other impurities, *e.g.* the green tint due to the presence of iron in the silica. The 18th-century treatises are unanimous in declaring the need for very great precision in its use; and even when the proportion was correct its effects were often unevenly distributed in the same pot of metal so that the lower

[1] There was a drop of more than 50 per cent in the gross profits after 1825. Westropp, p. 85.
[2] In some cases the darkening of the metal appears to be due to atmospheric action.

[277]

parts were darker than the rest. We have already discussed this question in the first chapter.

The Waterford decanters which bear the mark PENROSE WATERFORD in moulded lettering round the base have, I think, been considerably post-dated. They are usually placed *c.* 1820, but there are at least two grounds for assigning them to the period 1783–99. They are all of the round barrel-shape which was first introduced in England by Christopher Haedy in 1775 or a little earlier,[1] and in 1830 at the latest not only had the bodies of Waterford decanters become cylindrical with straight vertical sides,[2] but the cutting was very much more vulgar and elaborate than on any of the marked pieces. This last fact is clear from the patterns preserved among the Gatchell papers ; the cylindrical decanters designed by Samuel Miller[3] were *in use* in 1830, but they were probably introduced at least ten years earlier and they certainly mark a much later stage than any of the marked pieces. Moreover both the Penrose brothers were out of the business by 1799, and the style of the firm was then changed publicly to Ramsey, Gatchell and Barcroft. The later advertisements give no indication that Penrose was ever retained as the trade name of the firm, and it is incredible that so strong a personality as Jonathan Gatchell, whose whole career was spent in capturing the Waterford glassworks, should have retained another man's label twenty or even five years after it was obsolete. The marked decanters, therefore, must be assigned to the period of the Penrose ownership (1783–99) and with them they carry back into the 18th century some of the similar decanters which bear the marks of other Irish factories.

In this family of decanters we may note the following features :

1. Mushroom stoppers cut with radial flutes. On all these stoppers that I have seen the mushroom is divided from the part which is inserted in the neck by a rounded knop. This does not seem to occur on other marked decanters of the Irish factories.

2. There is a wide flat rim round the top of the neck.

3. Round the neck itself there are three triple rings quite plain.

4. Cutting. The important feature is a field of fine diamonds. This may occur in pendent semicircles round the middle of the barrel or in flat narrow arches which rest on small rectangular panels also of fine diamonds.

---

[1] They were advertised as " curious " by Haedy in the *Bath Chronicle*, 21 December, 1775 ; Buckley, *History*, p. 124.

[2] See Westropp, Plate X.

[3] Reproduced by Westropp, Plates X–XIV, from drawings which formerly belonged to Samuel Miller, foreman cutter of the Waterford glasshouse about 1830. The decanters have very broad heavy pillar flutes running up the entire body. Another common feature is the fan edge, commonly associated with a field of " prickly " diamonds. I am inclined to think that glass with both these features, made of a very white " slick " metal, are late Waterford work, *i.e.* after 1800.

5.   Marked decanters are also found with a single row of strawberry diamonds, with a circlet of arrow-heads above it.

6.   Round the base there are usually faint moulded flutings or several sets of cut splits resembling the tines of a sharp rake.

Beyond this it is impossible to go with any sense of assurance ; there is no proof that decanters which exhibit these features are Waterford or that those which do not are not.

B.   CORK

(a)   *Cork Glass Company*

There were two glasshouses in Cork which differ considerably in the dates of their foundation and therefore in their style, a fact which makes it absurd to call any pieces simply Cork.

The first glasshouse was in Hannover Street and was founded in the same year (1783) and in the same circumstances as the Waterford glasshouse, that is to say by local capitalists employing English workmen.   It had a very episodic career.   The original partners were Atwell Hayes, Thomas Burnett, and Francis Richard Rowe, who traded under the name of *Thomas Burnett and Glass House Company*.   About 1785 Rowe disappeared and two years later Burnett also.   For a short time the glasshouse was idle, but was refounded about 1788 by Atwell Hayes and Philip Allen, who carried on the work till 1793, when they were joined by a third partner, Hickman.   The work passed out of these hands about 1800 and in 1803 had been assumed by William Kellock, John Graham, and Joseph Sulkeld, who traded as Joseph Graham and Company.   Kellock retired a year later but the other partners carried on till 1810, when the factory was taken on by Smith White and Company.   In 1812 these last had become William Smith and Company, but there was considerable friction between William White and the other partners ; six years later the work ceased amid claims and squabblings.

The name Cork Glass Company which we find on decanters of this firm seems to have persisted despite the changes in personnel, and as the glasshouse ceased work altogether on several occasions, it is probable that there were secessions among the workmen themselves.   This lack of technical continuity is sufficient to account for the poor quality of many identified specimens.   The following features are found in the marked decanters of the Cork Glass Company:

1.   The mushroom stopper appears as in Waterford pieces, but it is often much flatter across the top and as far as I know never has the rounded knop noticed above.   A lozenge-shaped stopper with a check pattern is also found ; it is crudely moulded and irregular in shape, but intended to be circular.

2. The body sometimes approximates to the rounded barrel-shape of Waterford, but the C.G.C. decanters do not show the same uniformity in this respect. A squat mallet-shaped body with straight vertical sides and sloping shoulders is also found. Sometimes again there are taller decanters somewhat similar to those of Belfast or Bristol, in which the body tapers gracefully into a small neck. For Waterford and Belfast the general types are known ; Dublin is usually without much ornament ; and the more eccentric shapes *with* cutting can be put down to Cork with some assurance, but this only applies before *c.* 1825 ; after that there was a common jargon.

3. The three plain triple-rings already noticed are also found in C.G.C. decanters. Three rings cut in panels also occur. But the most characteristic ring is the feathered ring. This is a double ring with slight transverse markings ; the neck has sometimes two and sometimes three feathered rings.

4. The most typical device of all is the vesica. This is a diamond-shaped or oval compartment found in both cutting and engraving. The cut vesicas usually occur in a band round the middle of the body ; they often contain a star or a sun-burst and where they impinge on another they are parted by splits. Engraved vesicas are frequently hatched with a trellis pattern.

5. The base usually has a low border of faint vertical flutings, moulded.

The style of the Cork Glass Company is the most capricious of all the Irish glasshouses which can be said to have a style at all, and this is due probably to the coming and going of workmen which we have noticed. Of the devices the vesica is important because it sometimes enables one to identify pieces other than decanters which have no mark.

(b)   *Waterloo Company*

This glasshouse was founded several years before the Cork Glass Company ceased working and is first mentioned in 1815. Its founder was Daniel Foley, a dealer in glass. The wares he advertised illustrated the general tendency at this time. He made a speciality of toys and other fancy glass, *e.g.* musical instruments of glass, serpents, horns, trumpets, and even a pleasure-boat and a cot. The character bore resemblance to his wares, for he advertised that he employed more than a hundred workmen " from whose superior skill the most beautiful glass will shortly make its appearance to dazzle the eyes of the public " and at Christmas he was " to treat his men with a whole roasted ox and with everything adequate." In 1825 he took as partner Geoffrey O'Connell, who succeeded to the whole business when Foley retired in 1830. O'Connell carried on under great difficulties owing to the Excise and in 1835, when he became bankrupt, the Waterloo Glass Company ceased to be.

There is nothing very peculiar about the Waterloo decanters, for the glasshouse was founded when Waterford and the Cork Glass Company were already well known. And its style was almost entirely composite. It took from Waterford the round barrel-shaped body, the triple rings, and the mushroom stopper, and from the Cork Glass Company the vesica and splits. The only characteristic feature is a rope of looped and knotted ribbon-work clumsily engraved round the middle of the body.

(c)   *Ronaynes Glasshouse*

In 1818 two brothers, Edward and Richard Ronayne, started a manufactory known as the Terrace Glass Works, probably in the hope of gathering the custom of the Cork Glass Company, which had just come to an end. The Ronaynes used steam-power, which by this time had probably become general in the Irish glasshouses. The partnership was dissolved in 1838 and the whole business expired in 1841, being then the only glasshouse surviving in Cork. It is likely that marked specimens of Ronaynes glass exist but I have not seen any, and as the factory was founded so late it probably had little artistic merit.

C.   BELFAST

(a)   *Benjamin Edwards*

Benjamin Edwards, the Bristol glassmaker to whom we have already referred, seems to have migrated from Drumrea to Belfast shortly before 1781. His workmen were English and trained at Bristol, and the manufactory prospered so much that in 1787 he took several new apprentices and was able to reduce all his prices; this was probably because he eschewed dealers and did his own retailing. In 1800 he took his sons John and Hugh and his son-in-law William Ankatell into partnership, and the firm became Benjamin Edwards and Sons. Benjamin Edwards the elder died in 1812, and his son Benjamin, who succeeded him, carried on with indifferent success until 1826, when the business was bought by a company, Thomas Wright and Co. Both Benjamin Edwards, Junior and the Wright Company were ruined by the Irish Excise of 1825, and after 1829 we hear no more of this manufactory.

The most interesting fact about the decanters, B. EDWARDS, is the similarity to those of Bristol and the simple English taper decanters dating from *c.* 1770.

1. Of stoppers there are two main types, a lozenge-shaped stopper with a bevelled edge of the type seen in the pair of blue Bristol decanters

seen in *E.I.G.*, Plate II, and a round stopper with heavy fluted moulding round the edge instead of plain bevelling.

2.   The rim round the top of the neck is very narrow and scarcely projects at all ; it differs in this from Cork and Waterford.

3.   Edwards decanters usually have two plain triangular rings round the neck, *i.e.* rings with a bevelled edge.

4.   The body is pear-shaped and tapers gracefully into a tall neck.

5.   The shoulder is usually cut in flat vertical flutes—a feature which it shares only with Dublin ; less frequently there is a horizontal band of scale-pattern cutting.   Engraving is rare.

6.   The faint moulded fluting round the base is much shorter than in Cork and Waterford.

(b)   *Belfast Glassworks*

The later Belfast glasshouses were mainly derived from the Edwards firm, and probably preserved the same style.   As far as I know only Edwards's mark is found, but in case other marked pieces should come to light, one other factory may be mentioned.   In 1803 John Edwards withdrew from his father's firm and set up a glasshouse of his own on Peter's Hill. He did not succeed, and the glasshouse eventually passed (1806) into the hands of a company, Geddes, McDowell and Company.   It was generally known as the Belfast Glass Works and continued in various hands until 1850.   Flint glassmaking lasted longer in Belfast than anywhere else in Ireland except Dublin, and did not disappear entirely until 1868.

D.   DUBLIN

(a)   *Mulvany*, 1785–1835

After 1780 only one glasshouse of importance seems to have been founded in Dublin.   It was erected shortly before 1785 by an Irishman, Charles Mulvany, who had perhaps learned his glassmanship at Lunn's glasshouse in Abbey Street, and at a later date (1794) took over the manufacture at an address that had formerly been Lunn's.[1]   This first glasshouse was probably near the North Strand, and the date of its foundation coincides closely with the migration reported by John Blades in the same year.[2] In 1788 Mulvany was advertising the following articles : glass lustres, girandoles,[3] epergnes, lamps, decanters, hall and staircase bells,[4] goblets,

---

[1] Westropp, p. 54.

[2] *Supra*, p. 274.

[3] A word applied both to table candelabra and to brackets pierced into the wall of a room.   The word is derived from the Italian *girandola* (Lat. *girare*), a kind of firework like the Catherine wheel.

[4] *I.e.* globes for hanging oil lamps or candles.

bowls, fruit-dishes, butter-coolers, and like Edwards at Belfast he was his own retailer, his warehouse being in Capel Street. In 1793 he already had an export trade, and in 1801 his was the largest glass business in Ireland.[1] And in spite of some vicissitudes in the interim it still held the priority of the Irish glasshouses thirty-five years afterwards.[2] In 1801 Mulvany began to make window glass, and again about 1815 we find him making further extensions and building a new glasshouse. This last venture led him into bankruptcy (1818), but he made the most of that opportunity, and two years later he was able to build another glasshouse at Ringsend. In 1829 the Williams's glasshouse in Potter's Alley became vacant, and Mulvany transferred his business thither from Abbey Street. Soon afterwards he took a partner in E. S. Irwin, for he had now been in business for forty-five years, and he had to find a younger man to carry on the work when the time came for him to retire. In 1835 E. S. Irwin succeeded to the business outright, and with his brother Charles continued the glass manufacture till his own death in 1846. The Potter's Alley glasshouse subsequently passed into the hands of Thomas and Richard Pugh, the last of the Irish flint glassmakers.

(b) *Williams*, 1764–1829

The Williams' who founded a glasshouse at Marlborough Green shortly before 1764 were a family of Welshmen who had learned their art at Bristol or Chepstow. Irish trade was at that time in a state of depression, and Dublin had a society which sought, like the Society for the Encouragement of Arts and Manufactures in England, to stimulate industrial enterprise by monetary grants. In 1764 the Williams' received a premium of £1600, and it was doubtless this offer which enabled them to set up in business. Six years later the firm of Richard Williams and Co., if we can judge from the kind of business indicated by its advertisements, must have been fairly prosperous even on the restricted Irish market, and they certainly made most types of useful or decorated glass with which the London market was already familiar. In 1770 they advertised flowered glasses, that is to say glasses engraved on the wheel with floral designs, cut-glass, and enamelled glass; this last may mean either white opaque glasses or glasses flowered or otherwise decorated in enamel colours fired in a muffle. But we have as yet no means of identifying the style of these painted glasses, for only in the case of William and Mary Beilby of Newcastle-on-Tyne have we any evidence of signature or style. The Williams glass list of 1770 is moreover of great interest

[1] The advertisement cited in Westropp, p. 55 calls the business " confessedly the most extensive in Ireland."
[2] Westropp, p. 139.

because it throws several types of glass, notably rummers, to an earlier period than is usually assigned to them. The list includes beer- and cider-glasses, common wines and drammers (probably "tavern glasses" for spirits), rummers, decanters, water-glasses, and plates, epergnes and epergne saucers, cruets, castors, cans, jugs, salvers, jellies, sweetmeat glasses, salts, salt-linings, hall bells, globes, white and green phials, mustard and perfume bottles, and several other types of a purely utilitarian kind.[1] In 1773 Richard Williams and Co. opened a new warehouse on Lower Ormond Quay, and claimed, probably with justice, that they "had brought the manufacture to as great perfection as carried on abroad." Four years later, at any rate, the business had grown sufficiently to warrant the construction of a new glasshouse in Marlborough Street. When Ireland received full freedom of trade in 1780 the Williams' were the most successful manufacturers in Dublin, and the withdrawal of the ban on exports naturally gave a great impetus to their business. The prosperity of the firm increased, and between 1784 and 1794 the firm or various members of it were awarded three premiums for flint glass and two for glass unspecified. There seems little doubt that until it was outdistanced by Mulvany at the end of the 18th century the firm of Williams was the largest and most prosperous glass business in Dublin, and probably in Ireland, and to its success we must chiefly attribute the great increase in the export trade of Dublin glass which is apparent in the Custom House returns in the 1780's. In 1784, when these records begin, Dublin and Ireland generally had had about four years in which to develop the export trade which the Free Trade concession of 1780 allowed them. One of the last mentions of the firm appears to come in 1827, when we hear of the death of Thomas Williams, "proprietor (which seems to imply sole proprietor) of the glasshouse in Marlborough Street," and it may be presumed that the Excise of 1825, which imposed a duty of £12 10s. on every thousand pounds' weight of flint glass, is responsible for the demise of this firm two years later.[2]

(c) Chebsey, 1786–98

The success of the Williams' and of Mulvany provoked competition, and in 1786–7 a company was formed by Thomas and John Chebsey which took over an iron foundry near Ballybough Bridge, and converted it into a glasshouse. Their first advertisement occurs in 1787, and a year later they were exporting glass to Spain. They seem to have made a name for themselves fairly rapidly, for in 1788 they executed a set of lustres for St. Patrick's Hall to the order of the Lord-Lieutenant, and they

[1] Westropp, pp. 57–8 sq.
[2] Westropp, pp. 57 et seq.

received a number of premiums from the Dublin Society. The value of the glass they made increased from nearly £2000 in 1787 to £7000 in 1791, but dropped substantially during the next two years. The career of the company lasted only eleven years and ended with the death of Thomas Chebsey in 1798; John Chebsey and the other partners then dissolved partnership and gave up the glasshouse, John Chebsey joining the Newry glasshouse. I am not aware of any pieces which bear the name of Chebsey.

(d) Minor Factories and Dealers

Hermann and Dedereck Ayckbowm are a conspicuous instance of the contribution made by Germany to the development of English glass. They were already established in London in 1772[1] and they were specialists in cut-glass as well as manufacturers. They seem to have done considerable business in the English provinces, and in 1774 they had already established a connection in Ireland.[2] They were thus well acquainted with the state of the glass trade in that country, and when Ireland obtained Free Trade they were quick to take advantage of the boom in Irish glassmaking. A member of the family, John Dedereck Ayckbowm, who was probably a son of Dedereck Ayckbowm, was sent to Dublin to develop a branch business. His name first occurs in Dublin directories in 1783, and it may be inferred that he arrived in Ireland in that year, the same year in which John Hill went to Waterford.

He does not appear to have actually made glass, for his place of business is described as a warehouse, and it is probable that he was concerned with the retail trade. Since he came from a German firm and one which specialized in cutting glass, it is likely that he had a cutting-shop and decorated naked glass bought from Irish factories. Specimens of Irish glass of this period are often found, which were made for cutting but never cut (Plate CLVIII. a), and it is known that glass was frequently cut by specialists who had no connection with the factory where it was made. J. D. Ayckbowm would naturally be in touch with the styles of cutting which were then in vogue in London, and he and the London firm from which he came are a good instance of the manner in which German cutting paused in England to establish itself and then crossed the Irish Sea to the more favourable conditions in which it reached fruition.

Dublin desired always to follow the styles current in London, and it is likely that the dealers and retailers who sold glass there and were in touch with England did a good deal to determine the general character

---

[1] *Bath Chronicle*, 12, xi, 1772, Buckley, p. 127.
[2] *Limerick Chronicle*, 3, xi, 1774. "Ayckbourn & Co. Manufacturers from London are selling cut glass in Limerick for 10 days." Buckley, p. 128.

of the glasshouses which supplied them. Some of them even had their trade name inscribed on the glasses which they sold, and one occasionally meets the marks FRANCIS COLLINS DUBLIN and MARY CARTER & SON ; and since there is no trace of any glasshouse working under these names, Mr. Westropp is probably right in referring them to two of the Dublin retailers. A glass merchant of this type, James Donovan, was settled in Dublin as early as 1770, and a son of his was still at work in 1829. He had a glasshouse of his own at Ringsend, but his chief business, like that of Edkins at Bristol or Absalon at Great Yarmouth, was general decoration of china and pottery, as well as glass. There do not seem to be any specimens surviving which bear his name.

We may mention in conclusion two brothers, Thomas and Richard Pugh, the last of the Irish flint glassmakers. They did not set up in their own business in Dublin till 1852, but they are of some importance because their father had learnt his craft at Stourbridge and used it in the service of the Waterloo Company at Cork. The Pugh family are yet another instance of the migrants (probably Welshmen, Pugh=ap Hugh) who carried to Ireland the English art of glass.

E. NAILSEA AND SPON LANE

Nailsea was not a flint-glass factory, but it belongs to the same period as the Irish glasshouses, and since its foundation was probably due to the same causes, it may be suitably considered here. We have already seen how some of the English flint glassmakers fled to Ireland from the cumulative burdens imposed by the Excise Acts of 1745, 1777, and 1787. But the tax on the materials of bottle glass or green glass was very much less ; between 1745 and 1787 the flint-glass tax had risen from 9s. 4d. to 21s. 5½d., while the amounts for bottle glass were only 2s. 4d. and 4s. 0¼d. per hundredweight. The Nailsea factory was founded by a Bristol bottle-glass-maker in 1788, the year after the third Excise, and this date, as well as the earliest work of the factory, suggests that he hoped to evade the tax and compete with its victims by making some of the simpler domestic vessels in green glass instead of in flint. John Robert Lucas was the son of a Bristol bottle-maker, Robert Lucas, and had had a glasshouse at Wick, near Bristol. Five years after he went to Nailsea (1793) the firm was constituted with four partners, J. R. Lucas, William Chance, Edward Homer, and William Coathupe. Among these names that of William Chance is the most interesting because it was his son, Robert Lucas Chance, who in 1825 founded the famous glasshouse at Spon Lane, Birmingham, which is still in the hands of the Chance family. During the 19th century the title and personnel of the firm underwent frequent changes, through which it is not necessary to follow it, but the glasshouse remained in the families of the four original partners until in 1870 it was bought up by its own colony at Birmingham, which was now grown very prosperous. Nailsea finally ceased working in 1873.[1]

Nailsea is interesting for two reasons. For a few years it raised the rough practice of bottle-making to the dignity of an art, and its early wares, the jugs and flasks and bottles of black flecked with white and colours, have a casual comeliness which is not without its charm; it is difficult to say when the mottled glass ceased to be made, but one is inclined to think that it did not continue long into the 19th century. Glass which cannot be readily distinguished from it was made also at the Shropshire glasshouse of Wrockwardene; only the yellow mottling seems to distinguish it from the Nailsea types. The other type, *latticinio*, consists of two or more colours of glass blown together in a more or less regular stripe formation. There seems little doubt that at Nailsea it was introduced by French workmen who in the early days of the factory were regularly employed there. The French workmen were a distinct body in the village of Nailsea, and the houses where they lived are still called "French Row." There is no record of when the Frenchmen first came there, but there seems little doubt that most of the polychrome flasks and other *latticinio* pieces were made as late as the middle of the 19th century and at the much more important glasshouse of the Chances quite as much as at Nailsea. Some at least of the flasks are pretty things, but the earlier mottled wares originally made by the glassmakers in their own time[2] are certainly the most satisfactory from

[1] The later chronology of this factory may be briefly set forth thus:

1793. *Lucas, Chance, Homer and Coathupe* (J. R. Lucas, William Chance, Edward Homer, William Coathupe).

1807. Partnership renewed with capital of £60,000 and glasshouses at Stanton Drew and probably at Wick as well as at Nailsea.

1810. R. L. Chance, son of William Chance, manager of the Nailsea works.

1812. John Hartley of Dumbarton, one of the best-known glassmakers of his day, joined this firm.

1815. R. L. Chance went to London and sold his shares.

1821. The firm became *Lucas, Coathupe and Homer*: W. Chance sold his shares, Homer sold some of his also. J. E. Homer, son of Edward Homer, became a partner.

1827. Meanwhile R. L. Chance had bought the famous glasshouse at Spon Lane, Birmingham (1824) and in this year he induced John Hartley to join him.

1833. Death of John Hartley; the Spon Lane firm becomes *Chances and Hartleys* by the inclusion of Hartley's sons.

1836. The Hartleys went to Sunderland and the firm become *Chances Bros. and Co.*

Subsequent changes in the personnel at Nailsea are given by Gray (H. St. G.), "Nailsea Glass" in the *Connoisseur*, Vol. XXX, pp. 85 *sq.* (July, 1911), to which source I owe most of the foregoing information.

[2] Powell, *op. cit.*, p. 100.

an æsthetic standpoint, and include jugs, flasks, bottles, mugs, tumblers, and several other plain useful types reduced to an agreeable design. Mention must also be made of curious love tokens issued by Nailsea as well as by glasshouses at Bristol and on the Tyne, and doubtless also by Chance's and other Midland firms. There is a well-recognized tradition that they were chiefly made for sailors to leave behind with their wives at home when they went to sea. They are found in blue, black, and striped *latticinio* metal, and the first two or three are often painted in oil-colours, and very occasionally in enamel, with a ship at sea, and pious or amorous inscriptions in prose or verse. The tradition that they were used for smuggling spirits gains support from the fact that most of the rolling-pins are of fair size and have holes at each end. Among the later Nailsea-Chance products the striped flasks in two or more colours are certainly the most conspicuous, and they continued to be made until the middle of the 19th century.

The early work of the Nailsea factories has still the flavour of craftsmanship, but the wares of the factory as a whole, and certainly the whole of the later output both of Nailsea and Spon Lane, illustrate very well the two tendencies, industrialization and denationalization, which are most evident in the last stages of English glassmaking. The *latticinio* techniques which Nailsea owed to a degraded French tradition[1] were beloved of the merely ingenious glassmaker, and they appealed very readily to the taste of the 19th century. As far as our evidence goes, it was at Nailsea that they first established themselves[2] and if we are to assume that the early output at Spon Lane differed very slightly from that of the present factory, then Nailsea must be held very largely responsible for introducing into the Midlands the cheap technical trickeries which were exposed in all their monstrous vulgarity at the Great Exhibition of 1851. There were other influences at work besides the French. The marked influence of late Bohemian glass, especially cut-glass, on English style in the 19th century probably owes a good deal to the espionage of George Ensell, who returned to Stourbridge in 1788 with a very full knowledge of types and methods in Bohemia ; but it was probably from chemistry proper that the art of glass at this time received its most serious disservice.

The latter part of the 18th century had witnessed notable advances in chemical research which are chiefly associated with the names of Lavoisier (1743–94) and Priestley (1733–1804), and the chemistry of glass in particular had become a matter of interest to such men as Michael Faraday (1794–

---

[1] Gray, *op. cit.*, pp. 92–3.

[2] In the literal sense of a permanent French colony at Nailsea as distinct from itinerant French and Italian technicians. For the influence of late Bohemian glassmaking on English glass at the end of the 18th century and beginning of the 19th century *cf.* the notice of George Ensell's Travels in Bohemia given *supra*, p. 40.

1867). At the same time there came into being both in France and in England a type of working glassmaker who knew a great deal too much about the chemistry of his art, *e.g.* Bontemps and d'Artigues in France, Pellatt and Hartley in England; and several of the English and French manufacturers constituted themselves by correspondence a kind of learned society. Thus, when the master glassmakers became academic, the art of glass wandered out of the furnace-room and was soon hopelessly lost in the laboratory; that meant in effect that the glassmakers became more interested in materials and methods than in the objects they were making, and their effect on the sensibilities. The tendencies of which we have been speaking are summed up in the person of Apsley Pellatt. This man represents perhaps better than any other individual the change which reduced glassmaking from a technique to a technology, and with some brief notice of his significance this account may be fittingly brought to a close.

F. APSLEY PELLATT AND THE FALCON GLASSWORKS

Apsley Pellatt is in certain respects the Wedgwood of English glassmaking. Like Wedgwood he attained to great reputation in his own day, not only for his success in the practice of his business but also by his ventures into public life and politics, and like Wedgwood also he destroyed a handicraft to make an industry. It is perhaps only on that account that he requires mention here. Like Wedgwood he created enough that was new, or at least novel, to destroy the tradition which lay behind him, and his influence is not the less important because it has been partly destructive.

His father had a glass warehouse in Holborn and he himself was born in 1791. His father subsequently moved to St. Paul's Churchyard, and some years before he was thirty the son had started a glass manufactory in Falcon Street, Southwark. From the first he seems to have interested himself chiefly in the chemical and manipulative technique of glassmaking and he was on terms of professional intimacy with several of the more scientific French glassmakers. The invention for which he was chiefly notable was called Crystallo-Ceramie or glass incrustation, but he himself admits that the method was communicated to him by a foreigner residing abroad, probably by a Frenchman.[1]

The new technique is thus described by Pellatt in 1821[2]: "A patent has recently been taken out for ornamental incrustations called Crystallo-Ceramie which bids fair to form an era in the art of glassmaking. By the improved process ornaments of any description, arms, cyphers, portraits, and landscapes of any variety of colour may be introduced into the glass

---

[1] *Cf. Gentleman's Magazine*, 1821, i, 70. There is a group of crucifixes with "incrustation" which certainly belong to this period and seem to be French.

[2] Pellatt (A.), *Memoir on the origin . . . of glass manufactures* (London, 1821), pp. 30 *sq.*

U

so as to become perfectly imperishable. The substance of which they are composed is less fusible than glass, incapable of generating air and at the same time susceptible of contraction and expansion, as, in the course of manufacture, the glass becomes hot or cold. It may previously be formed into any device or figure by either moulding or modelling ; and it may be painted with metallic colours which are fixed by exposure to a melting heat. The ornaments are introduced into the body of the glass *white hot*, by which means the air is effectually excluded, the composition being actually incorporated with the glass. . . . Specimens of these incrustations have been exhibited not only in decanters and wine-glasses, but in lamps, girandoles, chimney ornaments, plates and smelling-bottles. Busts and statues on a small scale to support lamps or clocks and masks after the antique have been introduced with admirable effect." This was the most important lesson that Pellatt learnt from French glass technology, and it is not therefore surprising that his " incrusted " wares are often difficult to distinguish from contemporary French work. At so late a date the nature of the metal is a most uncertain guide ; and the national types which in spite of frequent imitations have yet kept their individuality throughout the 18th century were now merged in an international jargon. The portrait medallions themselves are often the most certain guide, and a good many of Pellatt's shapes as well as his style in cutting are sufficiently like the Anglo-Irish glass of the early 19th century to place their attribution beyond much doubt ; the jug in Plate CLXI is a good instance of this. It must be said for his incrusted wares that they at least show elegance and finish. Modern taste is out of sympathy with the blown damsels and the poised divinities which Wedgwood had let loose among the industrial arts, but such cheap Hellenism was still a fixed convention which Pellatt could not fail to observe ; and there is more reason to find fault with his attempt to combine two substances with such slight affinities as a heavy flint glass and fine white paste.

Pellatt's later inventions were entirely technological, and he devoted himself to studying the history of glassmaking, in which subject he acquired a considerable reputation. His two books, published in 1821 and 1849, are half trade circular and half history, and they show the Victorian industrialist tiresomely in love with his own dexterity. He did not die until 1863, but in middle and later life he was chiefly concerned with public works. He sat as Member for Southwark from 1852 to 1857, and was much preoccupied with Sunday observance and dissenters' disabilities.

§ 4. CONCLUSION

When a man or an art dies we are prone to seek out the causes of decease. English glassmaking as an individual art enjoyed a span of almost exactly a hundred and fifty years, and having had, even by comparison with the Near East or Venice, or Germany, a not inconsiderable achievement, it may be thought worthy of a short inquest. In its early days its excellence both as handiwork and as art won it a high reputation and a market. It was in a sense very natural that the Government under whose auspices it flourished should seek to benefit by its prosperity. Glassmaking survived the Excise of 1745–6 by changing its style and the later Excises of 1777, 1781, and 1787 partly by its migration to Ireland and partly also by reserving its art for a small repertory of highly wrought and very costly types. In Ireland the same types were being made but in much greater numbers, because until 1825 that country was entirely free from Excise duty ; the Excise when it did come did its disastrous work much more rapidly than in England. But so far as England itself was concerned, the period 1787–1825 witnessed incessant increases on the duty, which not only reduced the mere output by one-half, but gave to enterprise the colour of folly and robbed the industry of that sense of assurance which is the chief condition of artistic success. The detached critic of a later time is apt to be indignant with the legislative fools who destroyed a beautiful thing, but it has to be remembered that in the 18th century glass was just an ordinary industry which must pay for its existence and take its chance. England at that time was not self-conscious about her glassmaking : if she had been self-conscious she might perhaps have refrained from crippling it by taxation, but she would certainly have failed to make an art of it.

English glass in the time of its debility looked for stimulus to France and Germany. It began to copy the style of those countries, not eagerly and indeliberately as it had assimilated that of Venice and Germany a hundred years before, but in a spirit of commercial exploitation. Nailsea glasshouse and the Falcon Street glasshouse, the two instances in which full records have been preserved, were both aware of a certain inadequacy in their own work, and their adoption of French techniques gives them an historical interest entirely out of proportion to their artistic merit. They represent a tendency which was very general early in the 19th century and, during the 'forties and 'fifties, bore its miserable fruit at the Great Exhibition in a horrid medley of English metal and French ornament and German cutting and engraving devoid of art as it is of nationality.

The decline in the art of glass must be connected also with the process of change which is usually termed the Industrial Revolution. That phase has often been interpreted as an Act of God which descended on England early in the 19th century and suddenly transformed art into industry and beauty into ugliness. It may be well therefore to define as far as possible what these words imply in reference to English glassmaking. They do mean something, but they mean very much less than in certain other industrial arts of which textiles are the most notable example. Glassmaking is a very peculiar and a very limited technique, and it may be stated at once that the mechanical and scientific progress of the 19th century effected no general change in the principles of its manufacture. The increase in chemical knowledge and mechanical contrivance was certainly responsible for much improvement in the making of plate glass and glass used for scientific purposes,[1] but even in the 18th century these processes had always belonged to technology and not to art. The glassmaker only conditioned himself as artist when he used his metal as a medium for making something else. With this limitation the new influences may be divided into three main categories, (1) mechanical, (2) chemical, (3) economic.

There were only two mechanical innovations of much significance. Steam-power was already in regular use at Bristol and Stourbridge early in the 19th century[2] for turning the series of wheels used by the cutter and the engraver, but it can scarcely be held responsible for the deterioration in those arts. In the 18th century the glyptic processes had derived their power either from treadle machinery worked by the engraver himself, or from water-power. In Bohemia and Silesia, which were famous for their cut-glass long before England had even learnt the art, the series of wheels were often driven by water-power, and the conditions of work as far as the artist was concerned were much the same as if the motive power had been a steam-engine. In either case the condition of work is a set of perpetually revolving wheels each with its own workman, the art consists in the application to the wheel of the glass vessel; it has nothing to do with the force which keeps that wheel going. Even where the motion of the wheel is provided by a treadle the conditions are much the same; the only difference is that the workman is working with foot as well as with hand and eye, and can if he wishes vary the speed of his wheel. It has to be remembered that the design of the cutting was drawn beforehand and that, strictly speaking, the cutter was only a craftsman. Moreover the loss of design in the second quarter of the 19th century is as evident in the form of the vessel itself as in the composition of the cutting; the actual workmanship of cutting is as good as ever in some pieces of quite late date. But it was in the loss of design that the decline of the art really lay, and for the cause we must look, as we have already suggested, to psychology and not to mere technique.

A second device, that of " pressed glass," had been introduced from America before 1833.[3] It was in effect a species of moulding by which the same shape could be rapidly imparted to successive gatherings of metal, and it certainly encouraged mass production and abolished the care

[1] For a good account of these inventions and improvements v. Powell, op. cit., Chaps. VII–IX.
[2] See p. 45 supra.
[3] Powell, op. cit., p. 96.

which was formerly bestowed on individual pieces of work. But pressed glass in England never pretended to be anything but a cheap mode of reproduction and the glass which was most esteemed in the mid-Victorian period was usually made by the traditional methods.

The influence of chemical experiment in glassmaking was chiefly confined to the merely useful wares. In fine glassmaking its effect was to ensure much greater accuracy in determining the tone and texture of the metal, that is to say, it was concerned with a condition of the art, not with the art itself. In the 18th century the mixture of the batch depended on a rather haphazard empiricism ; every glasshouse had the lore of its elder workmen and adhered to the " way things have always been done," but the batch would be varied by a few shovelfuls with the hope of correcting peculiarities in the last pot or of seeing what would happen. As far as we can judge from the example of the Waterford factory and from the salesman's pride in a clear metal,[1] the ambition of the mixer was always to obtain an absolutely white and transparent glass, but the mixing was frequently so casual and the means of correcting impurities so uncertain that it is rare to find an 18th-century glass with the pure white metal which is technically satisfactory. Instead we find numerous tints of dark blue, black, light blue, pale green, and occasionally even mauve and purple. In the eyes of connoisseurs these accidents greatly enhance the beauty of a glass.

In the 19th century the purification of the silicate base became much more exact, and the properties and strength of the colouring ingredients could be chemically stated with much greater precision. The result was a much greater control of the materials, and technically a much more satisfactory metal. Moreover a perfectly fused metal could now be obtained without overcharging the glass with lead oxide, and the use of the higher oxides gave greater purity in the lead itself. English glassmaking lost a great deal by these improvements. The rich brilliance and the infinite variety of 18th-century metal have nothing to do with the art of glass but a great deal to do with its æsthetics. The older metal was more delightful to the eye. That is why, although we cannot attribute the decline in English glassmaking in any sense to chemical research, we may yet be very ready to deplore its consequences.

One of the evils attributed to the industrial revolution is known as mass production. It implies that in order to meet with a greatly increased demand, or even in order to create one, the manufacturer stereotypes his wares as far as organization and machinery will allow. Such a criticism is only applicable to English glassmakers in a very limited sense. In the

[1] A Dublin dealer in 1774 advertises " London and Newcastle glass . . . which by absence of all colour excels all other of England and Ireland." *Faulkner's Dublin Journal,* 15, xi, 1774 ; Buckley, p. 128.

second quarter of the 19th century certainly there seems to have been considerable increase in the use of moulding, and the fashioning of individual glasses by the workman at his " chair " to some extent gave place to more rapid methods of production. Moreover the number of glasshouses which exhibited their wares at the Exhibition of 1851 was still as high as seventynine ; there seems to have been some decrease in mere output between 1833 and 1851 ; and it is therefore difficult to suppose that the artistic failure of the later glass was due to an attempt to serve a larger market.

The real cause of the decline was the perpetual and exorbitant Excise. English glassmaking was subject to taxation for exactly one hundred years— 1746–1845, and during the latter part of that period the Excise officers became inquisitors as well as tax-gatherers. Their authority was as final and quite as damning as an actual State control. The glassmaker could not call his soul or his furnace or his blow-pipe his own; he must ask the Exciseman's permission to enter his own glasshouse, and plaster his walls with notices of forbidden things. The mixing and annealing were to be done behind locked doors and the glass blown under the eye of a sentry in a box; if he so much as thrust a blow-pipe into the pot he must be careful first to notify the Exciseman. The glassmaker paid with his profits for this benign supervision, and the State was annually the richer by half a million pounds. The Commission on Glass Industries of 1833 exposed the ignorance and pedantry of a Government department and the plight of its victims, but the duty on glass was not finally repealed until twelve years later. By that time the goose was outworn with parturition and the small gold eggs were scarcely worth the gathering. The repeal of the duty and the encouragement afforded by the Great Exhibition of 1851 gave a certain impetus to the industry, but by that time it was too late. The invigilation of the glasshouses had made glassmaking a public art. It had destroyed the confidence of the glassmaker and his artistic freedom, and robbed him of all furtive emulation. It is not too much to blame the publicity required by the Excise for the jargon of the 'thirties and 'forties in which the idioms of the several factories and the character of the art as a whole were gradually lost. During the middle of the century glasses, when they were expensive, were occasionally elegant, but generally speaking the industry had lost all interest in design. Certain revivalists of the Pre-Raphaelite persuasion attempted to introduce Art into the glasshouses ; that simply meant that a professional artist[1] made a design for a glass and had it executed, and the glassmakers cannot be held accountable for the results.

Glassmaking at the present day is a highly complicated technology, but industrialization has not really changed the conditions of work or the nature

---

[1] *E.g.* Philip Webb designed some table glass for William Homer in 1859 and in 1874 T. B. Jackson designed a complete set. Both were made at the Whitefriars glasshouse, and some specimens can be seen at the Victoria and Albert Museum.

of the art. In that fact lies the chief hope of any future art of glass. The recent work of the Czecho-Slovakian, Viennese, and Swedish glasshouses has given sufficient proof that fitness and beauty are still capable of unison and that good form in glass is not entirely a lost endeavour. In England glassmaking has suffered in the general depression of recent years, but there is no insuperable reason why she should not give a new direction to the old technique. Not the least obstacle to original design is the cult of the antique. The glasshouses themselves have a natural respect for their own traditions which leads them into a tedious repetition of dead themes ; and even their new forms too often are only fresh revivals. Their sterile conservatism is supported by the taste of the cultivated public. Sensitive people find themselves unsatisfied by the work of their own time, and they are too familiar with the art of the past to escape its influence. They begin to love that with which they are most familiar, and having gradually worked themselves into the taste of past epochs, they have no judgment left to build up a present taste for themselves. The public prejudice is fostered by the vested interests which gather round any human demand, and it is obviously to the advantage of those who have commerce in " antiques " that their customers should continue to live in any taste which their market can satisfy. Thus a contemporary taste is driven out and people make fashions of the works of art which are exposed for sale.

To hope for a new " will to form " in reference to the art of the glassmaker would sound perhaps like the merest idealism if there were no evidence that in other arts such a will were finding an effective expression. But the present century has witnessed in the arts of architecture and sculpture, as well as in painting and in poetry, a new insistence on formal values which during the 19th century were neglected altogether or smothered in narrative and sentiment. The movements known as Post-Impressionism and Cubism are usually described as modernist, but the name has a flavour of cheap novelty which does small justice to the service they have rendered to art. Modernism is an experimental restatement of principles which are evident in any art of the past which has won itself a permanent recognition. In the representational arts, that is to say, in the arts which have a recognizable content in human experience, there are two complements which are incapable of divorce. There is an emotional and sensitive content which is derived from experience and has issue in vitality, and there is a principle of order which is the fruit of an intellectual act. Representational art is apt to give predominance to a visual or emotional content, abstract art to a merely formal organization. All artistic achievement lies between these two extremes. The modernist movements collectively insist on pattern detached from all representational content, and in giving a practical statement to their principle they certainly have committed some extravagances. But this will to form, like that of any other epoch, had to be primitive before it could be prime ; it began by showing its teeth and it will bite off more life just so fast as it learns to chew.

The service of modernism to art is that it regards architecture as the normal art. On its creative side it regards not mood or sentiment, vitality or verisimilitude, but the construction of those materials, as the condition of artistic value, and in its criticism it looks first for the qualities of coherence which are apparent in a good building. It is in effect a reassertion of the sovereignty of the intellect in art, and that is largely why it resorts most readily to geometrical design ; for geometry itself is a construction which the mind puts upon the world, and because it fits, in a pragmatical sense, allows to remain there. The influence of geometrical design has not been confined to painting and sculpture, it has extended itself to architecture, the theatre, interior decoration, furniture, and it has produced a derivative popular art in the poster, the advertisement, and the shop window. But modernism is important not because it is geometrical, but because in an inchoate and uncertain way it possesses the architectonic on which all great art depends. Its geometry seems rather to be the first foothold of a new intellectual force—the " will to form " of the industrial society. That is why the geometrical artists of recent years may claim to be regarded as genuine primitives, as genuine in their mode of expression as the early Greek sculptors or the Italian primitives in theirs.

In England this new force in design has not yet penetrated the stale craftsmanship in which glassmaking is still hampered. The reason is partly that glassmaking is a highly traditional business and out of touch with the cultural movements of the time ; partly also that it has become too preoccupied with mere technology. But there is nothing in the *technique* of glass vessels or glass ornaments which prohibits all response to the last trend in design. There are certainly many who would deplore any movement towards geometrical design in glass, but until the new will to form is expressed in the glasshouse as well as in the studio, there can be little hope of a true revival of the art of glass. In Viennese, and in German and Swedish glassmaking, the new will has become effective, and it has produced a glass which is not only the best being made in Europe to-day, but the only glass which has definite affinities with contemporary painting and sculpture and can claim to belong to the 20th century. The work of such firms as Lobmeyrs at Vienna or the Orrefors firm in Sweden covers the whole field of blown glass, engraved glass, and cut-glass, and it is in the two last categories that it is perhaps most successful. This is not the place to consider their work, but two facts are important. They are successful because they do not rely on the glassmaker, but enlist, in much the same way that Wedgwood did, the services of artists who are in touch with recent tendencies in the other arts. And in the second place the work of both these factories exhibits a happy compromise of modernist design with a baroque convention in engraved ornament which on the Continent still survives from the 18th century. The last few illustrations in this book are specimens of this modern glass, blown, engraved, cut. They are not English—one wishes that they were—and they are not much concerned with the history of English glass, but as a challenge at least they are very relevant to its future.

APPENDICES

APPENDIX I

On Abjects, Orts, and Imitations

Glasses made in the manner of the 18th century may be divided into three main classes :

1. *Versions.* English glasses began to be cultivated as antiques about forty to fifty years ago. At that time 18th-century glasses could be purchased in taverns and rubbish shops for a few shillings and even for a few pence, and the nucleus of several of the best-known collections of the present day was being brought together by Hartshorne, Singer, and other Victorian collectors. Throughout the 19th century copies of old glasses, mainly the cut-glasses of the Anglo-Irish period, were being made in English glasshouses, but they were made without any consciousness of an antique market, even though at the end of the century a demand for 18th-century glasses had arisen. Versions properly so called are the last dregs of the original tradition and precede the canonization of old glass.

The 19th-century reproductions of Anglo-Irish cut-glass persisted side by side with the " prickly monstrosities "[1] of the Great Exhibitions (1851 and 1862), and they were the result of idle manufacture and an attempt to supply the more conservative taste. Cut-glass—and most of the reproductions were cut-glass—was unpopular in Victorian times after the Pre-Raphaelite movement became effective and the earliest collecting of glass because it was old had begun about twenty years later. The later versions of cut-glass (*c.* 1825–65) have all the characteristics of decadence. They are poorly designed and very much over-cut, the strawberry diamond being very common. At Stourbridge several varieties of the herring-bone pattern (Fig. 34, E) seem to have been a favourite motive, and these are still used very frequently on Stourbridge glass of the present day. But by far the best of the reproductions were the glasses made in Bohemia. The Bohemian glassmakers from the end of the Anglo-Irish period until the present day, have given repeated proof that they can make better Irish glass, technically always and very frequently artistically also, than was ever made in the Irish glasshouses. The deep bluish-black tone sometimes evident in late 18th-century cut-glass has been imitated with great success, and in glasses which are as remarkable for the precision of cutting as they are for the smooth perfection of the metal ; and only the most sentimental bias will deny the Irish glass of Bohemia a place beside the work of the Irish factories themselves. In the Bohemian and (*hodie*) Czecho-Slovakian glasses made in Irish fashion there is much more than technical adroitness ; in the cutting itself there is a fine sense of design, and form and cutting remember each other. In the first half of the 19th century English and Irish cut-glass was rather badly copied in France. This was probably due to the friendship of English and Irish glassmakers which followed Bontemps' residence in England. Whereas Czech metal is celluloid in appearance, the French is apt to have a sallow and faintly yellow look. The cutting is not sharp to the fingers and its design is loosely knit.

2. *Imitations.* The canonization of old English glass may be dated from 1897, when Hartshorne published his *Old English Glasses.* That book called the attention of connoisseurs to a branch of English industrial art which had hitherto been neglected, and the deliberate imitation of the 18th-century glasses followed very shortly. Most of these imitations were made, and still are made, without malice in response to " period cultivation," and since the recent war and the popular cult of the 18th century several of these revived forms have passed into the normal repertory of commercial glassmaking. But apart from these glasses, many of which are in " modern " metal, there are frequent attempts to imitate the metal as well as the form of the 18th century. Copies of this kind are made fairly extensively and on the ground of metal alone they are not always easy to

[1] The phrase is Mr. Bernard Rackham's.

APPENDIX I

distinguish from 18th-century specimens. Sometimes an accurate copy is made to measure from an old specimen, but in the numerous instances where the imitators commit themselves to rough approximation the result can usually be detected by errors in *proportion*, even though the general style of the glass is fairly plausible and the shapes of its parts properly conceived. Beauty of form in 18th-century glasses depends less on the shape of the parts than on their proportion to one another. An awareness of what is true to 18th-century proportion can only be acquired by study of numerous genuine specimens, but it is, on the whole, the surest guide to the detection of falsehoods. To consider the truth of a glass becomes ultimately an æsthetic judgment from the standpoint of 18th-century taste ; but it is the conclusion to the scientific business of detection, and not a substitute for it. Imitations in the glasshouse are made quite innocently and legitimately as a trade on the antique sentiment, but when once they go out into the world it is to be remembered that the name of most sensible dealers is *Caveat Emptor*.

3. *Fakes.* A fake is an imitation made in malice for the profit of the manufacturer and the delusion of " professional " collectors. The faker, therefore, has a much more skilled opponent than the period-fancier, and he must look very rigorously to his details and his chronology. The tendency of the faker is to kill as many birds as possible with one stone, to concentrate on the more impressive and expensive pieces. His delicate business is the first sale, and when he has crossed that barrier with one lucrative glass he is so much more in pocket with so little less of difficulty and danger. Smaller and more commonplace glasses are less worth his attention, but many imitations of these, originally made for the period-fancier, become fakes in the course of their career, and being simpler than the impressive piece are frequently more difficult to detect. " Big " fakes are usually copied from a well-known glass which is exhibited in a public collection, or has been published. Several fakes of the posset-pot in Plate LXXV. 3 were recently on the market. The metal was fairly plausible and the shape of the glass had been closely copied, but in several important details, *e.g.* the pincered ornament and the scalloping of the foot, the glass would not bear more than two minutes' inspection. Most fakers show lack of attention to detail and profound ignorance of the history of glass. A large posset-pot which recently came to my notice could not, if genuine, have been later than 1730, but bore the date 1750, and that in trailed figures which are always exceedingly rare. Anachronisms of a less flagrant sort are evident in the combination of one feature with another which is out of period with it.

Many glasses which from a collector's point of view are certainly " wrong," are certainly not fakes in the strict sense ; and on the whole these quite innocent " duds " seem to cause most trouble to collecting beginners. When a glass is in moot it will, I think, be considerable help to bear in mind the three degrees of falsehood to which it may belong, since the criteria of detection will vary in each case. There is a convention that an " antique " is more than one hundred years old, and in regard to glass it is not without point ; for as we have shown in the text, flint glass received its death-blow in 1825, and although the traditional reproductions continued for some time there was no original work (" prickly monstrosities " excepted) after that date.

Metal. No formula can be given to distinguish true and false, but the following notes may perhaps be helpful. 1. *Colour.* Modern metal is much *whiter* than 18th-century metal owing to the great advances made in the chemistry of glassmaking during the 19th century. There are certain exceptions to this rule, but generally speaking it is a sure guide. In imitations of " Georgian " glass made for the period-fancier modern metal is very frequently used and instances are quite easy to detect. But during recent years, and especially since the German war, the resources of chemical glassmaking have turned to the imitation of the deep blue-black tint evident in some English and Irish cut-glass. The Czecho-Slovakian (Bohemian) glasshouses have been especially successful in this respect, but the tint is usually too *uniform* and too deep to be convincing ; moreover, the metal is too smooth and refined and the cutting too precise. On the other hand, a white metal does occur not infrequently in genuine flint glass, and it was always the *aim* of 18th-century glassmakers. A very white metal is found in the best baluster-stemmed glasses of early 18th-century date, and in the small-diamond cut-glasses of Waterford; but even if these are placed beside a modern glass we can only distinguish the two by saying that the modern piece is still much whiter.

2. *Fusion.* The purpose of a solvent in glassmaking is to fuse the silicate and leave no trace in the finished glass. Modern metal[1] conforms perfectly to these conditions; it is smooth, white, clear; it is without waves, blotches, gatherings, striations; it is entirely unruffled. In 18th-century fusion there is no effortless grace, and 18th-century glasses are greatly over-fused. It was not merely a question of lavish precautions. The 18th-century glassmakers used their lead flux for its æsthetic as well as for its chemical effects; turning their faults to virtues. The lead is always eloquent in an 18th-century glass, making it specifically heavy, rich, and oily to the eye, soft and comparatively warm[2] in the fingers. These qualities are most evident during the Exuberance (p. 187), but all 18th-century glass, in contrast with modern, is conspicuous for them.

3. *Irregularities.* Certain defects resulting from imperfect fusion are a most helpful guarantee of antiquity.

(a) *Silicate specks*, i.e. small bits of silicate which have escaped solution. These appear white and are embedded in the metal, rather like minute fragments of white coral. They are commonest in incunabula.

(b) *Lead specks* either red, or more commonly black, also occur fairly frequently, especially during the Exuberance. I have seen late 17th-century glasses where these were two or three times the size of a pin-head, but often it is necessary to hold the glass up to the light or examine it under a magnifying glass.

(c) *Air-slips*, flat and round or oval in outline, are a not uncommon accident. I cannot recall any instance of their being imitated deliberately.

(d) *Air-bubbles* are very common in soda and potash glass, and are sometimes found in the cruder sorts of lead glass (*e.g.* Plate LXXXI. 1, 2).

(e) *Swirls.* Reckless twists in the grain of the metal, as of a sandy beach when the sea has gone down or a child playing with a paint-brush, are always a healthy sign.

(f) *Crizzling*, i.e. surface decay due to excessive use of salts for fusion, is naturally rare in lead glass and confined to incunabula (*e.g.* Plate XV). I have never seen faked crizzling.

(g) *Striations* and *undulations* on the surface are very common in all flint glass, but these have been imitated. Eighteenth-century metal is also apt to " gather."

(h) *Crackling*, i.e. small splits in the surface of the metal, is the result of too rapid annealing (see pp. 40–41) and commonest on curved surfaces. A very healthy sign.

Wear. A healthy glass shows signs of having been used, chiefly on its brim or foot. Wear usually takes the form of accumulated scratches, but the intact surface is often visible between the scratches. Where the foot-rim has a very sharp or narrow edge the scratchings are difficult to see, unless the glass has done heavy service; in which case they appear as a narrow line of abrasion. Where a wide surface is exposed to the table

---

[1] I allude here to the normal metal of modern English glass; but even when attempts are made to make 18th-century metal the "slickness" of modern metal usually intrudes upon the imitation in one respect or another.

[2] Lead glass is warmer than soda glass, and soda glass warmer than natural crystal, which is pure silicate and very cold. The cheeks or brow are more sensitive to the temperature of a glass than the fingers.

APPENDIX I

the wear is much more noticeable, but even here it should be possible to see the scratches. Purchasers should be wary of abraded bottoms where the scratches are lost in a rough surface ; for continuous abrasion may be procured by the use of emery. I have seen a border of faked abrasion quite half an inch wide, and also genuine glasses which have been artificially abraded to heighten the verisimilitude. Both rims and feet are liable to chipping, and chips are a blessing in disguise. It is not easy to calculate a chip in malice ; for if the chip becomes a crack the last state of the chipper is worse than the first. Most glasses gain more from this certificate of sincerity than they lose in complete beauty. Folded rims are less liable to chipping ; that was why they were folded.

Form. No tips can be offered for the detection of falsehood in shape. The forms current in the 17th and 18th centuries are known by acquaintance, not by description, and familiarity with what is actual in 18th-century glass is the only guide to what is possible. The collections in the Victoria and Albert Museum are now the largest public exhibition of English flint glass, and it should be possible for an observant student to derive from them a very fair idea of the main types of design in glass and the variations on them. The collection at the British Museum (Dept. of Ceramics) is not large, but it is especially valuable for late 17th- and early 18th-century glass, and it contains several specimens of the first importance. The collections at the Guildhall Museum and the London Museum are small, but not nearly so well known as they deserve to be ; they are largely composed of fragments which have been dug up during excavations in London, but these are well worth careful examination, if only because the attention is directed to detail when the æsthetic appeal is weakened. There are interesting fragments also at the Cuming Museum, Southwark. In provincial museums English glass is not well represented. Bristol Museum has a good exhibition of glass made in that city, but Bristol glass can be studied equally well in London. Among other provincial museums the exhibition at Saffron Walden (Essex) is much the best. There is a collection of locally made glass in the Warrington Museum. Cut-glass of the Anglo-Irish period is not well represented in public collections ; the Bles Loan at South Kensington is the only exception to this, and in the permanent collections of that museum there is a fairly representative series of the later cut-glasses. The National Museum of Ireland, at Dublin, has a notable collection of cut-glass, most of which was probably made in Irish glasshouses. A good knowledge of form may also be acquired from the transient accumulations on view at London dealers who concentrate on English glass. There are periodical sales of glass in several London auction-rooms, especially Messrs. Sotheby, Wilkinson and Hodge of Bond Street, and Messrs. Puttick and Simpson of Leicester Square ; but here there are perhaps as many opportunities for using knowledge as for acquiring it. It should be added in conclusion that the finest and most representative series of English glass are still in private collections, which taken together far surpass the public exhibitions. Illustrated articles on English glass appear from time to time in several London journals, *e.g. The Connoisseur, Apollo, Old Furniture* (all monthly), *Country Life* (weekly), and less frequently in the *Burlington Magazine* (monthly).[1] The industrial journal *Glass* sometimes publishes historical articles, and much interesting technical matter.

It is not, I think, possible to enumerate in so many words the specific errors of form committed by the faker. A general notion of 18th-century shapes may be gathered from the illustrations in this book, but little progress can be made without handling, as well as seeing, the glasses themselves. The types of error to be looked for are of two main kinds, anachronisms and false proportion. (1) Apart from metal a glass is an assemblage of items of style ; bowl curvature, stem thickness, various types of knop, the proportion of foot to stem and of stem to bowl, types of bowl, foot, and stem, folded rims, and the like.

[1] The notes contained in this paragraph are intended for strangers who may wish to study English glass in London.

The features include the parts of a glass, but many of them are details of workmanship or of proportion. Each of these features has a chronological range as an *original* contribution to style, and similarly every healthy glass has an evolutionary context ; sometimes fixable within five years. When a glass is in doubt it should be ascertained whether the several features are chronologically consistent with one another and with the whole. Considerations of this kind will almost invariably expose the casual copies made for the period-fancier, but when a doubtful glass is large or elaborate the chances are that it has been carefully made to measure ; here the enquiring eye will turn to the quality of the metal and to those minute details of workmanship which defeat or escape the cleverest of fakers. An artist's mistakes are part of his style and nothing is so difficult as to copy them. Asymmetry is a comfort to most collectors, as are glasses which were made in unequal pairs or " sagged " during annealing. The turn-up of a handle, the finish of a rim, the underside of a foot are like a horse's teeth and should be carefully examined ; in Edwardian days a good sharp pontil-mark was welcomed as a guarantee, but these are now copied with a most natural air, and taken by themselves will not bring you to a decision.

(2) There is, secondly, proportion. Most glasses have clearly defined parts and their beauty lies in the relationship of these parts to one another, a relationship which subsumes the parts and passes into rhythm. What is deemed proportionate varies from epoch to epoch. The 18th-century glassmakers had a quite definite, though quite indefinable, sense of proportion, and to think and feel one's way with that sense is better than a catalogue of tips at one's elbow. Some few 18th-century glasses, for example the drawn-stem and the taper decanter, are not " composed " like a baluster wine-glass or a stemmed bowl. They are brought off in a direct rhythm. But even a taper decanter has its inversely proportionate stopper,[1] and a flat foot will spoil the most graceful stem ever " drawn " (*cf*. Plate XCVI. 2). The system of proportions seems less complicated in a drawn-stem glass than in a heavy baluster ; that is why drawn-stems are among the most frequent fakes. But the proportion of drawn stems and " Kit-Cat " glasses is very subtly conceived. The foot, the tears, the thickness of the sides, and the solid part of the bowl are all remembered, and imitations, though easy and common, are not good, even as imitations.

Engraving. During the first half of the 19th century there was a good deal of poor engraving, much too bad to be anything but genuine. Some of this engraving follows the hop, vine, barley, and flower motives of the 18th century. Of a rather better type are the sporting, coaching, and hunting subjects which follow the sporting prints of the 'twenties and 'thirties.

Faked engraving is of two kinds. Faked glasses are themselves engraved, most frequently with historical subjects, for which there is a great demand. Of glasses made in the Stuart interest or in commemoration of William III, engraved with the Stuart rose and buds, the several mottoes and devices of the Jacobite Clubs, portraits of William III at the Boyne, of glasses commemorating the Bristol privateers, 18th-century celebrities, the opening of Sunderland Bridge (1796), Nelson's victories and death, and numerous other topical events—of all these fakes are legion. In many instances of this kind the engraving shows a bleak white, and is so badly done that it is difficult to think they were even intended to deceive ; they correspond to glasses made for the period-fancier. But I have seen very plausible specimens. In these inscriptions are the chief stumbling-block of the engravers. The antique sentiment turns them, hopelessly, to Gothic letter ; for the Gothic revival was only born when engraving on glass was nearly dead. Genuine engraving follows 18th-century typography fairly closely, and this is,

---

[1] For the adaptation of stopper design to the changing form of the decanter, see Plates CXXV–CXXVIII and Fig. 35. The stopper grew thinner with the body ; and when the latter became barrel-shaped the stopper turned into a disc or a mushroom.

APPENDIX I

of course, copied by the faker. But if faked specimens be examined under a magnifying glass it will be seen that the "channels" of the broad strokes (and this applies equally to the stems of flowers and plants) have small chips or breakages in their sides ; these occasionally occur in 18th-century engraving, but are much less common. One should also beware of lettering where the serifs (*e.g.* at the ends of the crossbar on a capital T) are segments of a circle rather than an incision. The faker is also apt to get his mood wrong. Eighteenth-century sentiment (the delicate shepherdess and the pierced heart) is pretty and playful, but as hard as nails. Victorian sentiment is a vulgar description of the most ordinary feelings ; and scenes or subjects of the latter sort are sometimes found on glasses which aspire to be 18th-century.

But the real serpent among fakers is he who takes an 18th-century plain glass and engraves it with a high-priced motto, emblem, or celebrity. Sometimes he works from a genuine engraved glass, but in some cases portraits are probably taken from contemporary (copper) engravings. Dean Swift, Admiral Byng, The Young Pretender, John Wesley, and Lord Nelson should be viewed with suspicion ; William III is always dangerous, being constantly revived in quite respectable glasshouses ; Charles II is impossible, though his coins are occasionally found enclosed in genuine flint glass. Engraving of old glasses is usually ambitious in this way ; the premium on flower subjects, and even on hunting, Chinese or other scenes is scarcely high enough to make fakes of them very common *on old glasses*. It should be added that the white appearance of new engraving can be toned down to some extent by the use of oil.

Cut-glass. Some old cutting shows irregularities in the design ; the lines or edges are not always straight, nor are the curves exactly the arc of a circle. But even during the 18th century cutting of great precision may be found (*e.g.* Plate CXXXIX), and the late cut-glass of Waterford is remarkable for its exactitude. In early 19th-century cut-glass which exhibits a field of small diamonds, the edges both of diamonds and, when it occurs, of scalloping are so sharp as to be almost dangerous ; " prickly diamonds " in this connection is a very apt term.

It is a comparatively easy matter to cut modern glass in the patterns of the 18th or early 19th century, and enormous quantities of faked Irish glass are now upon the market which are exceedingly difficult to detect. The larger pieces, fruit bowls, salad bowls, several kinds of covered bowl, pickle-jars, dishes, and especially chandeliers and lustres for chandeliers, are naturally the most profitable types. The cutting of such pieces may baffle anyone, and familiarity with 18th-century metal is the best means of detecting them. The notion that the best old glass is blue in tone has led to blue being greatly overdone. There are now far more blue pieces among modern glass than among old glass, and as far as it is possible to put the matter verbally, I should say that the tint is more uniform in modern imitations ; but even a highly trained eye may be deceived. The " Irish style " is one of several styles in contemporary Czecho-Slovakian cut-glass. Especial caution is required in the purchase of chandeliers. From the 18th century downwards these have been made in parts and frequently composed by dealers and others who purchase them from the glasshouse. A chandelier all of whose parts are old may have been recomposed several times in its history, and even in the 18th century household ladies had a hobby of altering the lustres on their chandeliers. Incomplete chandeliers are often made up with modern lustres, and fragments of old chandeliers may be recomposed to make a piece which may or may not be true to a " period " design. Absolutely pristine chandeliers are very scarce.

Ring. The tone of a glass when struck with the knuckles is sometimes a help in detecting imitations, but its value has been greatly over-estimated. Ring is only possible acoustically in certain shapes of glass, *i.e.* hollow and spacious vessels, such as bowls or big wine-glasses. Perfectly genuine dwarf wine-glasses of the middle of the 18th century give very little ring, and modern glasses of suitable shape and thickness of metal will ring as long and as deeply as an 18th-century specimen. But it remains true that many modern glasses, especially the imitations made for the period-fancier, give a dull, short leaden note which is very different from the long, vibrant wail of an 18th-century bowl or a healthy baluster. The variation of pitch and tone according to (1) the size, (2) the shape, and (3) the thickness of a glass vessel is an interesting question in acoustics to which the present writer cannot claim to have given much attention. It would appear, however, that the thickness of metal is responsible for a deep note, thin metal for a high one, and the shape and size of the glass for its duration. The ring of a big bowl, say eighteen inches in diameter, lasts longer than the ring of an ordinary goblet. Very thick glasses will not give a good ring unless they are correspondingly spacious. Any breach in the circuit, either by a flaw in the glass itself or by contact with a foreign body, will destroy the ring. Finally, the ring of a glass is the result of its anatomy and its health ; it has no necessary connection with its age.

Sagas and pedigrees. The knowledge that a glass has been continuously in private possession for thirty or forty years is proof that it is not a fake in the strict sense ; though it may still be a " version." Dealers in false glass will therefore be ready with some story of the origin of the glass which they wish to sell. For some types of glass proved ownership for fifteen years past is sufficient guarantee ; collectors may still look forward with interest to the first fake of a Ravenscroft glass.

A word may be said of " Jacobite " and " Jacobean," which are occasionally confused. A Jacobite glass is one associated with the Stuart attempts to regain the English throne (1715 and 1745). There is, for all practical purposes, no " Jacobean " glass. The term could only be applied in its present use, to glass made during the period of monopolies, but only one English glass is now known which can be definitely assigned to the first half of the 17th century. " Waterford " has become a trade name applied by many antique dealers to all cut-glass which either is or pretends to be more than a hundred years old. Glass is often described by the name of the monarch in whose reign it was made. Dynastic changes have contributed something to the evolution of English glass, but labelling glass by reigns is an irrelevant nomenclature ; the people, not the King, made glass. Description by decades, even though approximate, is more satisfactory.

APPENDIX II

Thomas Betts's Accounts

FROM BILLS IN THE POSSESSION OF MR. AMBROSE HEAL, PRINTED BY MR. FRANCIS BUCKLEY, IN " GLASS," VOL. V, P. 300 (JULY, 1928).

		£	s.	d.
1747.	2 Glasses fitted to Silvr	0	2	0
	1 Pr Neat Quarts Stopt and Hollod	0	7	6
	1 Pr Quarts Decanters Stopt and Cutt at Bottm	0	7	0
	1 Pr Pints ditto	0	4	6
	6 Half Moulded Egg End Beer Glasses to Patn	0	6	0
	12 Wormed Wines to Patn	0	6	0
	12 ditto, Olive Butten, Egg Bowles	0	7	6
	12 Water Tumrs to Patn	0	9	0
1752.	24 Wormed Egg Bowl Wine	0	14	0
	6 Small Dutch Shells	0	6	0
	6 Ditto with feet	0	6	0
	6 Cupps	0	9	0
	6 ditto	0	6	0
	1 Pr French Pattn Cutt Cruitts with Spire Stoprs	0	14	0
	1 Pr ditto	0	12	0
1753.	12 Wod Egg Bowl Wines	0	7	0
	6 ditto ditto Beers	0	7	0
	3 Pl Spanish Flutes	0	2	3
	1 Pr Cut Soy Cruits	0	6	0
	12 Wod Egg Bowl Wines	0	7	0
	2 ditto ditto Beers	0	2	4
1755.	1 P. Cutt Soy Cruits	0	5	0
	1 P. Neat Ice Champagne Quart Decanters	0	12	0
	2 Pr Waved Pints ditto	0	6	0
	1 Pr ditto Holld	0	4	0
	12 Large Water Glasses Holld.	1	4	0
	6 Carrafts Hold.	0	6	0
	6 ½ Pint Canns Hold.	0	6	0
	12 Wormed ½ Mo Egg Curs	0	15	0
	12 Wormed ½ Rib'd ditto Champagnes	0	10	6
	12 Wormed Short ditto	0	8	0
	36 C.S. ½ Mo Spanish Wine	1	1	0
	3 Cutt Cruits Stopt	0	15	9
	3 Soy ditto ditto	0	7	6
	12 Green ½ Mo Egg Champagne	0	12	0
1756.	4 Triangular Bottles Stopped	0	8	0
	2 Strong Ink Squares	0	3	0
1757.	16 Cut Wines	1	12	0
	18 Twd ½ Rib'd Wines	0	9	0
	4 Wod Flutes	0	4	0

		£	s.	d.
1757.	6 Water Glasses	0	4	0
	3 Cut Cruets	0	12	0
	1 Cup	0	1	0
	1 Pr Large Blue Vase Bottles	1	6	0
	1 Pr Less ditto ditto	1	1	0
	1 Pr Gilt Beakers	0	7	0
	48 Claretts	1	8	0
	6 Large Water Glasses Hold.	0	10	6
	6 Enamell'd Shank Flutes	0	6	0
	6 Large Tumblers Hold.	0	7	0
	6 Less Ditto	0	6	0
1758.	2 Cutt Squares Stopt	0	3	6
	2 Diad Egg Wines Cut Shanks	0	3	0
1761.	Cleaning Pr of Gerandoles	0	5	0
	A Cutt Saucer to Pattn	0	3	6
	A Starr to the Gerandoles	0	4	0

Betts was originally a glass-grinder and glass-polisher. As a cutter of fine glass he is first mentioned in 1738 when he had a shop at Charing Cross called the King's Arms Glass Shop. At first he employed a German cutter, one Andrew Pawl, but this man left him in 1744 and thereafter Betts had to learn the job himself. He died in 1767 and had a considerable reputation in the provinces. In his lists :

Quarts = quart decanters.
Stopt = with stoppers.
Half moulded ($\frac{1}{2}$ Mo) = moulded half-way up the bowl.
Egg bowles = egg-shaped bowls. Plate CXXVIII. 2.
Wormed wines = wine-glasses with air-twist stems.
Spire stoppers = cut or uncut stoppers of shape seen in Plate CXXV. 3.
Hollod, hold = with base ground smooth, *i.e.* the pontil-mark ground out.
Soy cruits = bottles for soy, a sauce made from beans (Chin. *shi* = salt beans, *yu* = oil).
Ice Champagne Quart decanters = decanters with pockets for ice, as in *Connoisseur*, Vol. LXXXIII, p. 275, Fig. V (*a*) and (*c*), May, 1929.
Spanish flutes = wine-glasses of " ale-glass " shape for Spanish wine. Pl. = plain. See p. 314.
Water-glasses. See p. 332.
Carrafts = water-bottles.
Green $\frac{1}{2}$ Mo Egg champagne = green glasses of the familiar type with ovate bowl and drawn stem.
Strong ink squares = square ink bottles.
Twd $\frac{1}{2}$ Rib'd wines = wine-glasses with externally wrythen stems and ribs running half-way up the bowl. (For wrythen stems see p. 211.) Twd = twisted.
Wormed flutes = wine-glasses with tall narrow bowls of " ale-glass " shape and air-twist stems.
Enamelled shank flutes = wine-glasses with tall narrow bowls of " ale-glass " shape and " white-twist " or " colour-twist " stems.
Cut squares stopt = square decanters with cut ornament and stoppers ; the shapes as in the familiar blue and green types.
Diad = cut in diamonds.

APPENDIX II

Diad egg wines cut shanks=wine-glass with ovate bowls cut in diamonds (Plate
   CXXVIII. 2) and cut stems (same illus.).
A starr to the Gerandoles, see Plate CXXXVIII. 2.
Olive butten=small-knopped stems.
Curs probably=custards, custard or jelly glasses.

   I do not know any glasses which can be identified as " Dutch Shells," nor which style
of cruet bottle is meant by "French Pattern cut cruits"; the cutting of the latter may
perhaps answer to the type found on Netherlandish and Spanish (La Granja de San
Ildefonso) cut decanters and bottles. Mr. W. W. Winkworth recently showed me an
English decanter of this type which had, like Betts's cruets, a spire stopper. I do not
think " French pattern " can refer to the common all-over flat diamonds found on mid-
18th-century cruet bottles (Plate CXXXVII. 1, 2). The body cutting of Plate CLI. 7
is a more probable identification.

APPENDIX III

List of Glasses and Chemicals from a MS. (Cardiff MS. 5·21) in the
National Library of Wales

March ye 3rd 1665.
Delivered for the use of ye worshipfull Sr Richard Wynne as foll

			£	s.	d.
		A parcell of glasses at	1	1	6
		sent more 6 beare venus glasses at	0	5	6
		6 beare venus glasses	0	6	6
		i dosen of venus wyne glasses at	0	10	0
		a deale box at	0	0	10
April	18	by Mr brygdalls for a whisling glass at	0	3	0
		a baskett at	0	0	4
		3 beare venus glasses	0	3	0
		a baskett	0	0	3
April		12 Leeches no 12	0	2	6
		½ds of the best Lemons	0	3	0
		3 orenges at	0	0	9
May	6	A purgeing bagge wth sena z4 etc	0	17	6
		boulter for the bagge	0	0	6
	22	by Mr Moore Dates i li	0	2	2
	23	4 King glasses at	0	4	0
		4 venus Tumblers at	0	3	4
		4 venus glasses more	0	3	6
		2 basketts	0	0	7
June	29	7 of the best Lemons	0	3	6
		A plaster against the wormes	0	2	4
		A baskett	0	0	3
July	12	by Mr Moore Carana	0	0	4
	16	9 King glasses at	0	9	0
		3 venus Tumblers at	0	2	3
		3 best wyne glasses	0	2	6
		Carana zii	0	0	9
June ye 18		by Aq. Cordiall frigd saxon li.ii	0	5	0
		Aq. cinamonii opt i li	0	4	0
		Aq. Coelestis ssli	0	5	0
		Confect de Hyacinth zi	0	4	0
	9	Confect Alkermes sine mosho zi	0	4	0
		Syr E. juces Lymoun lii	0	3	8
		Syr papaver erat lii	0	4	0
		Mana Calabrin zii	0	2	4
		Aqua dracontii lii	0	1	?
		Sp. vitrioli zi opt.	0	2	0
		5 duble bottles at	0	1	10
		A baskett	0	0	9
Aug.	1	Aq. mirabilis lii	0	3	8
		A bottle	0	0	4
		Aq. Cordiall frigd. Saxon li ii	0	5	0
		Aq. Cardui bened. li ii	0	2	0
		Aq. Thericall slillit lii	0	4	0
		Aq. Dracuntii li ii	0	2	8
		Confect de Hyacinth zii	0	8	0

[311]

APPENDIX III

			£	s.	d.
Aug.	1	3 qt. bottles & i pinte	0	1	10
		payd to the messenger for } Careing of these last things }	0	2	0
Aug.	28	Gallingall cubebs & Cardamomi	0	0	9
		Confect Alkermes sine mosho zi	0	4	0
		4 Trencher sacke glasses	0	2	8
		Carana	0	0	4

	£	s.	d.
this side	2	4	0
The other side	7	1	8
Sum due is	9	5	8

Venus=Venice; *i.e.* glasses of soda metal made *à la façon de Venise*.

Beare=beer.

Whisling glasses, glasses with a whistle attached for summoning the barmaid when the glass was empty.

King glasses, presumably glasses for drinking the royal toast; the Wynnes were a well-known Royalist family. But Mr. Francis Buckley ingeniously suggests glasses made at Kingswinford, Stourbridge; but at this date such an explanation does not seem very likely.

Trencher sacke glasses, either (1) glasses which stood by each guest's trencher at the dining-table, as in trencher salts, and distinguished from tavern glasses; or (2) glasses with wide flat bowls, perhaps the hemispherical bowl as in Pl. V. 1.

APPENDIX IV

Special Types

The development of style which has been traced in the preceding pages is here followed into some of the more important types of vessel or utensil. They are to some extent collectors' categories, but they are also the categories of the glassmakers who made them and the dealers by whom they were first sold. In them the general tendencies of form and ornament are modified by a particular function or a particular shape, and in that degree they require treatments of their own. In the notes which follow I make no pretence of covering every variant, but have tried to set out briefly the main stages in these minor histories.

1. CANDLESTICKS

1. The earliest type of candlestick which can be identified as English belongs to the end of the 17th century. It is clearly a version of the lacemakers' lamps and covered candlesticks which were being made in France of *verre de fougère* about the same time. The introduction of this type (Plate LIV) was probably due to Huguenot glassmakers. At the end of the 17th century candlesticks with *hollow stems* and a very high domed foot are occasionally found in lead glass ; they are clearly derived from a potash-glass original. Such pieces are probably " peasant art " ; until lead glass was " brought to perfection " candlesticks for refined use were made of other materials.

2. The earliest lead-glass candlesticks have heavy *knopped stems* solid all through. Their general range is 1681–1715. In form they are apt to follow contemporary candlesticks in brass or silver rather than stem forms in glass. The two pure balusters were the standard stem forms at this time, but they do not appear to have been used for candlesticks. That was because candlesticks usually had tall stems, and the pure balusters were essentially short-stem motives. Sometimes the glassmakers overcame the difficulty of height by superimposing a true baluster on an inverted baluster. But generally speaking the knopped candlesticks belong to the same stage as the pure balusters ; see Plates LVII, LVIII, LIX. *a.* The chief types of foot are a sloping dome (Plate LV. *b.* 3), a round dome (Plate LVIII. 3), and a square dome (Plate LIX. *a.* 2) ; terraced feet are not uncommon (Plate LIX. *b*).

3. About 1713–14 the influence of German shapes introduced the *shouldered or " Silesian " stem* for tapersticks and candlesticks. It is found in several varieties, *e.g.* with four, five, or more corners (bossed or plain) and stem flutes to correspond. It continued until it was superseded by cut stems about the middle of the 18th century. The shouldered stem is combined about 1715–30 with sockets ribbed vertically, and domed feet ribbed radially (Plate LV. *b.* 4) ; this use of ribbing is later than the plain types in candlesticks, as in jellies and sweetmeats. Two shouldered stems set inversely upon one another also occur.

4. *Filigree stems* were only made in small numbers, and for a short time, about 1740. Their vogue is much shorter than in wine-glasses. Cut stems are much more appropriate for lighting pieces because they amplify the light. Moreover, a candlestick is nearly all stem, and stems are a solid ground for cutting. Hence, the Excise of 1745 was cheated of a victim, and in this particular type cutting got a hold early and never let go. Of the filigree stems air twists are the more common ; enamel- or glass-twist candlesticks are fortunately rare.

5. *Cut-glass* candlesticks and tapersticks go back to the decade 1730–40. In 1742 the London glass dealer Jerom Johnson was advertising " diamond-cut and scalloped candlesticks " (*Daily Advertizer*, 21.xii.1742, Buckley, p. 120), and they were not described as new-fashioned. Cutting was used for all four parts of a candlestick—nozzle, socket, stem, foot.

APPENDIX IV

(a) Scalloping of the *nozzle* was certainly one of the earliest types of cutting ; you can scallop the edge even if the metal be thin and your skill not very great. It became very common from 1730–40 onwards. Jerom Johnson's scalloping probably refers both to nozzle and foot-rim.

(b) The *socket* sometimes had its surface cut in flat diamond facets, or in scale-pattern, both early motives (*cf.* Fig. 27). Jerom Johnson's " diamond cut " more probably refers to stems cut in diamond facets.

(c) The shouldered *stem* when adapted to cutting had flat vertical flutes, usually combined with flat diamond facets (Plate CV. 1), but it is not very common in cut-glass (*cf. E.I.G.*, Fig. 17, c). More usually we find a double-shouldered stem, better suited to the height of a candlestick (*c.* 1740), and a little later the cusped stem (Plate CXLIV. *b.* 4). This last corresponds with wine-glass stems with cut cusped stems (*c.* 1750–60), Plate CXVIII.

(d) Neither socket nor stem gave much chance for the later ingenuity of cut-glass design, and it is mainly by the elaborate cutting of the *feet* that the later candle-sticks of the Anglo-Irish period may be distinguished from those of date 1740–60. The rim was still scalloped or sliced, but the instep was cut too—in large relief diamonds plain or double cut, and in several curvilinear motives. Hence came a revival of the dome, which gave a fuller ground than the ordinary instep.

6. Other types of candlestick include the opaque white candlesticks made at Bristol, with or without a wrythen stem (Plate CXXXV. *b.* 2), and candlesticks whose stems resemble a classical column and date from the early days of classicism (Plate CXLIII. 1, 4). The latter are rare, and based on metalwork types. We may mention also a very common type made from about 1790 to 1820, with square foot and a short urn-shaped stem in which a degenerate classicism is apparent. Below the socket is often a scalloped tray with a fringe of pendent lustres or fingers. The design is ungainly. Both cut and moulded types are found.

2. " CHAMPAGNE " GLASSES

There is a lot of snobbery about champagne. It is a sentimental wine, and only acquired its regal status during the 19th century. In consequence of this there has been a tendency to give a prestige to well-made glasses by calling them champagnes. Champagne was first drunk in England after the Restoration. It is mentioned by Otway in 1678 in a phrase which suggests that it was not familiar (" powerful champaign as they call it "). In a line of Butler's *Hudibras*, which dates from the same year, it runs third to Bordeaux and Burgundy. Hartshorne held that its use was not at all common until the middle of the 18th century, and Mr. Simon cites wine-merchants' lists and dinner accounts which show that it was drunk in fair quantity in noble houses, but was generally too expensive even for the City of London. Several types of glass with hemispherical bowls were identified as champagnes by Hartshorne, but he quotes no authority, and I have never seen any contemporary evidence that these glasses were special to champagne. Hartshorne seems to have given the label to glasses which resembled the Victorian cham-pagne glasses, but these latter only came into vogue about 1830 ; Disraeli in a letter of 1832 mentions them as though he had not met them before (" a hemisphere of ground glass on a column of cut-glass "). It is clear from Thomas Betts's glass lists that special glasses *were* made for champagne, but none of his descriptions of them correspond with the types of glass identified as champagnes by Hartshorne and Mr. Grant Francis : wormed (" air-twist ") half-ribbed egg (-shaped) champagnes, wormed short egg (-shaped) champagnes, green half-moulded egg (-shaped) champagnes. The entry of " Spanish flutes " (1753) suggests that the tall well-made glasses of " ale-glass " shape, which Mr. Francis wants to call champagnes, were in fact used for Spanish wine (*cf.* p. 183,

SPECIAL TYPES

and Appendix II). Moreover, a good many of the so-called champagnes have not a "drinkable" rim; the rims flare outwards as in those intolerable 19th-century tea-cups from which you can scarcely drink with decency. In novels, I know, champagne is usually "sipped"; but there is not a little evidence that in the 18th century drinking was too whole-hearted, and glassmaking too sensible, for so precious a device. Glasses with "difficult" rims are dessert and sweetmeat glasses.

I shall mention here three types which are practicable wine-glasses, and which have been called champagnes, though there is no reason to think they were special to that or any other kind of wine.

1. *The hemispherical bowl* is taken directly from a well-known Venetian type and was among the designs ordered by Greene from Venice. In flint glass it cannot, I think, be dated earlier than 1700. It is usually combined with one of the simple balusters or a heavy knopped stem. I have seen one or two hemispherical bowls on shouldered stems, but most specimens are earlier than 1715. The bowl has sometimes gadrooned moulding round its lower part (Plate LXVII. a. 3).

2. *The double-ogee bowl*, of the open kind, may be seen in Plate LXXIII. a. 2, b. 2. While Venetian design was dominant in bowl form the line of the bowl was not broken, in "open" as well as in "closed" wine-glass bowls. I am inclined to think that the break in line which produced the open double-ogee was due to German influence quite as much as the incurvature of ordinary wine-glass bowls. It certainly dates from about 1715, and is most commonly associated with shouldered stems. The earliest double-ogee bowls have a plain surface, and are mounted on pre-shoulder knopped stems as well as on shouldered stems. The plain surface is *succeeded* by vertical ribbing of the bowl, and radial ribbing of the foot (as in Plate LXXI. 1); the greatest vogue of this variety lies about 1715, the same type of ribbing being found on other glasses of about that period. In the filigree period this bowl still survives, but is far from common; a good example may be seen in Francis, Plate XXV, 171. As soon as cutting became common the open double-ogee was affected in both its sides and its rim. Specimens which are fit for drinking practically disappear; on that ground alone it is probable that most of the open double-ogees are dessert-glass types, and not wine-glasses at all.

3. *Flutes.* This type is commonly called an ale-glass shape. The term flute is preferable, because (1) the shape is derived from the 17th-century flute, (2) flute was Thomas Betts's word (Appendix II), and (3) not all glasses of this shape are known to have been used for ale. Where flutes are engraved with hops and barley they may be presumed to be made for ale, but others are plain or engraved with vine motives. The well-made plain specimens which Mr. Francis would call champagnes were probably used for wine, and on the evidence of Betts's list (p. 308) it is likely that this was Spanish wine; Betts's "Spanish flutes" may be compared with a line of the poet Lovelace (1649), "Elles of Beer and Flutes of Canary." Flutes were made at the end of the 17th century with baluster or heavy knopped stems; with shouldered stems about 1715-30 (Plate LXXXVI. 2); with air-twist, enamel-twist, and cut stems (Plate CXIX. 2). The straight flute bowl begins in the 17th century. Heavy double-ogee flutes occur also about 1700 (Plate XLVIII. 3; they can be readily distinguished from the light double-ogee flutes of the Excise period.

3. CHANDELIERS

A chandelier may be defined as a branched support for holding a number of lights, suspended from above or standing on its own base, and made of wood, natural crystal, metal, or glass. The word was current throughout the 18th century. Ephraim Chambers (*Dict. of Arts*, ed. 1753, *s.v.* candlesticks) states that "larger and more stately candlesticks contrived for holding a great number of candles are called *branches* and *girandoles*, and when made of glass *lustres*." The word girandole, which seems to imply a revolving lighting piece (Ital. *girandola*, Lat. *girare*), probably refers to table chandeliers of the type illustrated in Plate CXLVI and in the trade-card of the Phœnix Glassworks at Bristol (Buckley, Plate LX). The term branch usually implies a bracket light fixed in a wall and has been referred to lighting pieces used in churches. The word lustre in the 18th century had two meanings, (1) glass drops, plain or cut, single or in festoons, and (2) entire lighting pieces. In the latter sense it included girandoles, branches, and candelabra. This last is a 19th-century word; the earliest use of it I have seen is in an advertisement in *The Times* in 1792 (Buckley, p. 101). Its meaning may be reasonably restricted to the later types of hanging chandelier, chiefly remarkable for festoons of glass drops and, later again, for fringes of fingers. Where terms have been used with so little precision in the past it is difficult to be exact, but it may be said that chandelier or lustre is the genus of which girandoles, branches, and candelabra are the species. Lustre and chandelier are used as synonyms in 1754 (*Liverpool Municipal Records*, ed. Picton II, 160).

Table chandeliers were derived from the ordinary table candlestick; they were suitable to more lights than one. Hanging chandeliers began as reproductions of the beautiful and costly chandeliers of rock crystal which had been in vogue in the 17th century. Lady Mary Wortley Montagu, writing in 1716, spoke of " large lustres of rock crystal." During the 18th century there are many references to crystal " chandeliers or lustres," but it is impossible to say whether these imply the natural or synthetic material. About 1750 we find allusions to glass chandeliers, but these were probably Venetian. There is no definite evidence that glass chandeliers were made in England before 1760. About that year the first glass chandelier was made by the Stourbridge firm of Bradley, Ensall and Co., but it was regarded as quite a curiosity, and was exhibited in the firm's glassworks in Brettle Lane for many years afterwards (*Glass Manuf. of Birmingham and Stourbridge*, p. 5, where the date is given as " about 1760 "). Cutting was well advanced in 1760 and it is likely that chandeliers were cut from their inception. If chandeliers were still curious in provincial glassmaking about 1760 they were probably normal in London; and a well-known firm of lighting specialists, Messrs. Perry and Co. of Grafton Street, now Messrs. Burt, Escelle, Perry and Co. of Wardour Street, began business in 1756 and have records going back to that date.

Between 1760 and 1780 progress was rapid both in design and cutting. That is a necessary inference, if you compare the " curiosity " of 1760 with Bosc d'Antic's high praise of English lustres in 1780 (cited on Plate CXL). Concerning the types in vogue in 1788 we are informed by designs for chandeliers ordered in that year from Messrs. Perry and Co. by Sir Roger Newdegate of Arbury Hall, Nuneaton. The correspondence connected with them proves that cut arms were going out of fashion in 1788; and that gives us 1790 as a good landmark. A comparison of the Perry designs with existing specimens suggests that the chandelier developed by three stages. These are denoted by an emphasis on one of the three parts of a chandelier—shaft, arms, and drops.

1. *The domination of the shaft.* Early table chandeliers seem to have been conceived as a super-candlestick, one that will hold many candles. The table chandelier begins with its shaft; it adds two, three, or four arms to support the lights; it links them together with strings of drops; and then it replaces the useful socket, in which the one candle had stood, by a decorative device, an acorn, a crescent, or a star. Hence, the early table chandeliers have little structure beyond what their use required. This gives them a grace and clarity of design which is often lacking in the more elaborate pieces made at the end of the 18th century. The same tendency may be observed in hanging chandeliers: the early examples have a dominant shaft and few branches; while drops are sparingly used. Mr. Winkworth's chandelier (Plate CXL) seems to belong to this phase, and may be contrasted with the obviously later specimen in Plate CXLVII. The domination of the shaft may be placed approximately 1760–75; the earlier and simpler specimens rarely

show the influence of Adam design (*e.g.* the urn summit which is sometimes found instead of star or crescent). At that time it is more likely that such pieces were made in London or Stourbridge than in the very few Dublin factories.

2. *The domination of the arms.* The arms are architecturally the link between shaft and lights, and about 1775–90 they control the design. Arms become so numerous and elaborate that the shaft is smothered. To this period belongs, I think, the elaborate cutting of the arms ; for they were the most obtrusive part, and therefore the most worth decoration. The disappearance of cut arms, mentioned in 1788, seems to show that another force, drops, was gaining the ascendant. When the branches are half smothered in festoons of drops and pendent drops, it is scarcely worth while cutting them. We thus reach the third phase :

3. *The domination of the drops.* During the last decade of the 18th century shaft and arms lost significance and became simply pegs for strings of drops. The chandelier, or as we may now call it the candelabra, is conceived as a solid ; some examples are designed after a classical vase form. Finally, during the Regency period the mass formation of drops gives way to a candelabra in which the principle of design is a set of cylinders enclosing one another or superimposed upon one another. The cylinders are composed of pendent fingers of glass. In both these last types the idea of a chandelier as built up of arms round a shaft has entirely disappeared.

I do not wish to press these phases too closely ; to some extent they overlap one another, but I think they summarize the development. Most of the chandeliers described as Irish belong to the second phase ; but Irish is a chronological rather than a local term. When the Irish factories were doing well in the 'eighties and 'nineties they probably made as much cut-glass as was made in England ; factory styles no doubt they had, but not a national style.

4. CREAM- AND MILK-JUGS

Cream was habitually taken in tea during the 18th century. The high ritual of tea-drinking was scarcely less elaborate than its Japanese counterpart The Tea Ceremony, and is pleasantly described in two poems, *Tea, A Poem* (London, 1745), and *Tea-drinking, a Poem* (Dublin, 1752). Both lay the tea-table in some detail, and in the second :

> Betty around attends with bended knee
> Each white arm fair the painted cup receives,
> Pours the rich cream or stirs the sweetened tea.

The tea-things were usually of " beau-complexioned porcelain." Glass never became fashionable for this purpose because " china " had tradition on its side, and glass is apt to crack if you pour in hot water too suddenly. Tea-things, moreover, being made in sets, glass cream-jugs and sugar-bowls were not common. There seem to be no cream-jugs which can be dated much before 1740, for it was only in the middle of the century that tea-drinking became a habit among the people. The earliest notice—in this case of milk-jugs—seems to be in 1763, when they were regularly made and decorated at Bristol (Owen, p. 381). From 1766 to 1785 " cream- and milk-ewers " were being sold by Christopher Haedy.

The following types may be enumerated :

1. *Tripod jugs* (Plate LXXXIV. *b.* 1) were analogous with a silver form and probably most frequent in the 1740's and 1750's. They are now scarce. Jugs of similar shape, but without feet, are fairly common.

2. *Waisted cream-jugs* is a convenient label for a group of cream-jugs which have a pronounced neck and swell into a bulb at the bottom. They vary considerably both in shape and material, but most of them date from the middle and latter part of the 18th century. The aristocrats of the series have a large flaring lip ; they are found in blue,

opaque white, and opalescent glass as well as in ordinary flint glass. They were decorated in gold and enamel colours by Absalon of Great Yarmouth ; and the milk-jugs in Edkins's accounts may well refer to larger jugs of the same shape. Both blue and flint-glass specimens are sometimes moulded diamond-fashion. The plebeians have small spouts, and are usually of a rough metal resembling bottle glass, but blown very thin and sometimes wrythen. Two or three specimens I have tested proved to be lead glass. The metal has not much virtue, but their innocent technique and their comeliness make them worth purchasing ; and they can be had for very little. They are often found in Yorkshire and the north, and may have been made at such factories as Catcliffe, Ferrybridge, and Rothwell.

3. There is another group of small jugs, with cylindrical neck and a shouldered body, which Mr. Buckley supposes to be rather later than the waisted types. This seems to me very likely ; several other vessels, *e.g.* decanters and cruet-bottles, have a conspicuous shoulder about 1760. This group also is found in white opaque, blue, and clear flint glass as well as in a coarse thin-blown metal which in one or two instances contains lead (Plate CL. 1, 2).

4. The boom in cut-glass at the end of the 18th century brought with it several new shapes, among them a globular jug form found both in large water-jugs and in small cream-jugs (Plates CLVII. 3 and CLVIII. *b*. 2). They have no feet and a very wide flaring lip. The design is usually good, especially in the squat specimens, and they illustrate very well the adaptation of cut design to formal design. The cut-glass jugs have a larger capacity than the other types mentioned here, and seem to have been used with dessert rather than at the tea-table. These milk-jugs have nothing peculiarly Irish about them. They were made in Ireland ; but they were made everywhere.

5. DECANTERS

The word decanter is derived from the Latin prefix *de*, and a root *kant*, which is common to both the romance and Teutonic languages, and means edge, rim, or corner. The word decant originally had an alchemical sense, to pour off a liquid from a precipitate, but in the second half of the 17th century it acquired a quite general sense of pouring off by tilting. This sense was *specially* applied to pouring out liquor from a bottle or decanter, brought on the table, into a drinking-glass. With the introduction of binning the word suffered a change of meaning. It was now applied to the pouring of wine from the common wine-bottle, in which the liquor was binned, into the polite decanter in which it was brought upon the table. This transition in meaning had already taken place when Johnson published his dictionary (1755). But the meaning of *decanter* was fixed thirty years before this as a vessel used for pouring wine or other liquor into drinking-glasses, and that meaning has never changed. Johnson and the later lexicographers who followed him went wrong on this point. See for authorities an article by the present writer in the *Connoisseur*, Vol. LXXXIII, pp. 196 and 271 (April–May, 1929), of which these notes are a summary.

The polite decanter of flint glass was a throw-off from the common wine-bottle. The earliest examples of the latter date from the second quarter of the 17th century, and their subsequent development proceeds by four stages.

1. *The shaft-and-globe*, about 1650. This is the most elementary of blown-glass forms, a long neck and a round body. In some of the later examples (about 1670) the body has almost straight beetling sides and a pronounced shoulder. The shortening of the neck leads to :

2. *The onion-bottle*, about 1690. This has a very low squat body and a very short neck, scarcely long enough for the hand to grip. The round sides of the body gradually

SPECIAL TYPES

become straighter and more upright, and at the same time the length of the neck increases. This brings us to :

3. *The slope-and-shoulder*, about 1715–50. This type has a higher body with almost straight sides sloping inwards and a marked shoulder at the top. The neck is about equal to the height of the body. The chronological tendency is for the sides to become more upright and the body taller (about 1735), giving an almost cylindrical bottle, but not yet made in a mould and often asymmetrical.

4. This form was fixed about 1750 by the introduction of moulding as the standard *cylinder bottle* which is still in use. The chief cause of the cylinder bottle was the introduction of binning ; a cylinder could be easily and economically binned and the swelling of the cork from contact with the wine prevented the ingress of air and made long storage possible.

All these four types are made of a coarse green or brownish-green potash glass, and all have a rim under the orifice below which the cork was tied.

The polite decanter was thrown off by the bottle in the third of the foregoing stages. Ravenscroft, it is true, had made bottles of flint glass (p. 127) which were no doubt used as decanters, but their form is peculiar (Plate X. 1) and they had no progeny. If we begin with the flint apologues of the slope-and-shoulder the evolution of decanter form develops thus :

1. *Slope-and-shoulder* (Plate LXI. 2). This is a very close copy of the corresponding wine-bottle. The bottom rises into a high dome and the string rim is retained. Stoppers were not made with them, since the orifice is not ground out. Some examples have handles. The slope-and-shoulder does not seem to have been ever cut or engraved. Range, 1710–30.

2. *The balloon decanter.* The decanter had no need to follow the wine-bottle when the latter was approximating a cylindrical shape ; decanters were not binned. At this point, therefore, the flint decanter broke with the bottle development and reverted to the most primitive of all glass forms, the shaft-and-globe. This departure is marked by two facts, the disappearance of the string rim, and the grinding out of the orifice for the stopper ; though some balloons lack both these features. Balloons were in the best fashion at the time of the '45 (Plate CXXV. 1), but these specimens lack the string rim and have the ground orifice. On that basis we may date the unground balloons with string rim 1725–35, the ground balloons without string rim 1735–50. At this stage we find commemorative engraving, but not, so far as I know, decorative engraving or cutting.

3. *The short shoulder.* The shoulder decanter with its two varieties the *short shoulder* and the *tall shoulder* are the normal types between 1750 and 1770. The short shoulder (Plate CXXV. 3) is the earliest type of decanter with cut decoration ; the latter is usually in the form of flat diamond facets, but a design based on the lunar slice is sometimes found (*Country Life*, Vol. LXIV, p. xcviii) ; necks are sometimes cut in flat flutes. The normal stopper for the short shoulder is the pyramid stopper—what Thomas Betts called " spire stoppers " (p. 308, *cf.* Plate CXXVII. *b* 1, and Fig. 35, A). Spire stoppers are plain when the body is plain, and cut when the body is cut ; the cutting consists of small diamonds slightly hollow. Short shoulders continued until about 1770, but after 1760 they begin to lose shoulder, and end up as a short taper.

4. *The tall shoulder* is what the slope-and-shoulder wine-bottles would have become if binning had not turned them into cylinders. It came into vogue about 1740–50. The earlier examples are undecorated and have a plain uncut spire stopper. Plate CXXV. 2 shows a well-known example with an equestrian portrait of William III, made for the Dublin festivals about 1750. About 1755 began the practice of engraving tall shoulders with labels of the liquor they contained ; in that year a Norwich dealer advertised " new-fashioned decanters with inscriptions engraven on them, Port, Claret, Mountain, etc. etc.,

APPENDIX IV

decorated with vine leaves, grapes, etc " (*Norwich Mercury*, 26 December, 1755). By 1764 decanters of this kind had become a commonplace and had the trade name of " label decanters " (*Aris' Birmingham Gazette*, 23 January, 1764). These last were cut as well as labelled ; and since, during the last thirty years of the century, " cut decanters " are mentioned fairly frequently, whereas " label decanters " do not seem to be mentioned at all, we must conclude that labelled decanters went out about 1770 ; this was to be expected, since the increase in cutting, especially all-over cutting, made an engraved label impossible. The decanters painted by William and Mary Beilby (Plates CXXX, CXXXI. 2, and pp. 226 *sq.*) are all of the shoulder type, some short and some tall.

5. *The taper decanter.* This is a refinement of the shouldered types, due almost certainly to the influence of Sir William Hamilton's collection of Greek pots, published in 1768. The shoulder disappears and the decanter takes on a slender elegance. An advertisement in 1768 of " newest-fashioned decanters," unspecified as engraved or cut, probably refers to the introduction of this shape ; since at that date it cannot refer to shouldered decanters or label decanters.

Tapers are seldom heavily or elaborately cut. The cutting consists of scale pattern or diamonds round the neck, comb-fluting round the base, and very light-cut festooning and stars which were scarcely more than polished engraving).

6. *The barrel decanter.* This is the most familiar of decanter forms and ranges from 1775 to 1825 or later. Its introduction is due to a well-known Anglo-German glass merchant, Christopher Haedy, who in 1775 advertised " curious barrel-shaped decanters cut on an entire new pattern " (*Bath Chronicle*, 21 December, 1775). The word " curious " here must refer to the shape, and marks the transition from the older decanter forms, which had been vertically conceived, to a new type which was horizontally conceived. Since Haedy was pre-eminently a maker and vendor of cut-glass, it is likely that the new shape was devised to take a heavier type of cutting, for which the tall shoulders and tapers had been grown too thin. It is at any rate the shape in which the heaviest cutting is found. At once it took root in England, and when Ireland won free trade the migrations carried it to Ireland, where it became the standard shape of the Cork and Waterford glasshouses (Plate CLIX. 1, 2). In pre-barrel shapes the cutter had stuck to the neck and the rim, or had preferred flat motives for all-over cutting. Now the body was often cut all over in relief, usually in a field of relief diamonds, or in curvilinear relief motives, while the horizontal tendency was emphasized by the rings which now encircle the neck for the first time, and by the use of horizontal stoppers (the mushroom stopper, Fig. 35, G). The barrel decanter held the field until the appearance of :—

7. *The cylinder decanter.* This was the last decanter form devised by the flint glassmakers before Victorianism set in. It was made in England as early as the 1790's, as we know from the Perry designs, and was freely made by Pellatt at the Falcon Glassworks, and in the third decade of the 19th century by the Gatchells at Waterford (Miller's designs). Its design was coarse and ungainly ; the sides were made very thick ; and the cutting shows every symptom of decadence (*cf.* p. 278). Flat flutes an inch wide, running the full height of the body, are very characteristic of it.

Stoppers follow the design of the decanter (Fig. 35). The earliest stopper type is the uncut spire stopper (Fig. 35, A) which is sometimes found with the early short shoulders and tall shoulders ; but more frequently it is cut in small, slightly hollow diamonds. It is succeeded by the flat vertical disc stopper (Fig. 35, B, C) ; this is most usual on the tall shoulders, short shoulders generally having the spire. The sides are sometimes cut, but more frequently the edge is notched. As the tall shoulder approximated the taper the round disc becomes correspondingly slim and lozenge-shaped (Fig. 35, E). The appearance of the barrel decanter brought in two new stoppers. The most familiar of these is the *mushroom* (Fig. 35, G). It is often cut, or later moulded, in radial ridges independently of the cut design on the body. The assimilation of stopper cutting to body cutting is a late feature, and does not occur before 1790. The second type of stopper which goes with the barrel is the *target stopper*. This is upright, not horizontal, and has a large boss in the middle with cut or moulded ridges round the edge. In early 19th-century decanters we often find a thin vertical disc stopper, not cut, but plain or lightly moulded ; it is often to be met with in decanters made by the Cork Glass Company and the Waterloo Company, of thin metal with ribbon-work engraving. The last stopper type is a tall *pinnacle*, solid and very heavy. This is found with the later types of cylindrical decanter, about 1825 and subsequently.

A word may be said in conclusion of *square decanters*. These were called " squares " in the 18th century, and are mentioned by Thomas Betts in 1758. They stand outside the general development of the decanter. Surviving specimens are confined to the second half of the 18th century. They were often made in blue and green glass of the type usually called Bristol, and had gilt labels, nearly always for spirits. Squares were already being cut in 1758 (Betts) ; the cutting probably consisted of a circuit of flat diamonds or scales round the top. Convex diamonds in the same position indicate a later stage, as does a band of convex diamonds round the body. The stoppers are of the type shown in Fig. 35, F. Squares were made well into the 19th century, but most of the good examples belong to the second half (not the last quarter) of the 18th century.

6. DESSERT AND SWEETMEAT GLASSES

Dessert glasses are the genus, sweetmeat glasses the species. " Dessert " in the 18th century was a quite general term including all the closing stages of a dinner, " sweets," fresh fruit, and preserved fruits or nuts. " Dessert glasses " were frequently advertised by 18th-century dealers and were no doubt of several distinct types. " Sweetmeats " in the 18th century meant what " sweets " mean to-day, in both senses of the latter word, (1) trifles, sundaes, zabaglione, iced creams, and the like, and (2) dry sweets, chocolates, bon-bons, " comfits," etc. These two varieties were distinguished as " wet sweetmeats " and " dry sweetmeats," and 18th-century cookery books abound in recipes for both kinds. Wet sweetmeats were sometimes served in glasses with lids (Lady Grisell Baillie's *Household Books*, 1727, p. 298). " Sweetmeat glasses " were quite frequently advertised by dealers in glass, and I am inclined to think that " sweetmeat glasses " imply wet sweetmeats. Glasses for dry sweetmeats were either " comfit glasses " or were included in the comprehensive term " desserts." Glasses for wet sweetmeats are naturally the more numerous. They were usually made with a fairly tall stem. The small sweetmeat glasses with short stems (*e.g.* Plate LVI. *a*. 2), or without stems at all (Plate XXIII. *b*. 1, 3), were probably for " dried sweetmeats " such as comfits or salted almonds.

Flint-glass sweetmeats may be arranged chronologically in the following groups :

1. A small bowl with folded rim and gadrooned base (Plate XXIII. *b*. 1) must be connected, on the score of form, workmanship, and metal, with the large marked bowls of Ravenscroft. Its size suggests that it was used for dry sweetmeats. A type of bowl closely similar to this is found mounted on a wrythen stem (Plate XXII. 1). Plates XXII. 1 and XXIII. *a*. 2 must also be included in the same series. All are of late 17th-century date, and several belong to the very beginning of lead glass. Small sweetmeat bowls on stems continued to be made early in the 18th century ; Col. Ratcliff's three bowls (Plate LXXXIII) are later descendants of the same family. The size and shape of Col. Ratcliff's glasses suggest that they, and the 17th-century glasses in the same series, were used for dry sweetmeats. Contemporary with the earlier group of these sweetmeats are a few straight-sided bowls which must have been used for wine (Plate XXII. 4). The use of a glass is easier for sweetmeats when its rim flares, easier for wine-drinking

Y

when its rim is upright. The date of these early wide-bowled wines is certainly about 1685, but I do not know why Mr. Francis calls them champagne glasses. At that date there is no evidence that champagne had a special shape of glass, and still less do we know what that shape was.

2. The second group includes glasses without stems or feet, or with very short stems. The reference in Nat Barry's list (1725), "glass saucers for holding sweetmeats," probably alludes to the former type ; examples of widely different shapes may be seen in Plates LXXXI. 4 and LXXXIV. *a*. 2.

Examples of sweetmeats ("dry") with very short stems may be seen in Plates LVI. *a*. 2 and LXXXIX. *a*. 3. Their shapes are very various and scarcely admit of classification, but the formation of the foot is the best clue to date.

3. We come now to sweetmeat glasses (" wet ") anterior in date to the appearance of the shouldered stem, ranging roughly from 1685 to 1710 or 1715. The stems are of baluster (Plate LXXIII. *a*. 1) or balustroid form (Plate LXVII. *a*. 1). The feet are frequently domed. The most usual shape of bowl is what I shall call the wide double-ogee (Plate LXVIII), but a squat bell-bowl (Plate LXVII. *b*. 3) also appears before the shouldered stem became general. In regard to ornament these bowls are of three types, (*a*) plain, (*b*) ribbed vertically, and (*c*) nipt or pearl-moulded. That seems to be the chronological order of their appearance. The flint glassmakers, having discovered a style of their own independent of *façon de Venise*, kept their surfaces plain for about ten years (1690–1700) ; then, having fixed their own manner they could afford to go in for surface ornament once more, first ribbing, and then pearl ornament. Sweetmeats with baluster or balustroid stems usually have plain bowls. Ribbed and pearled bowls overlap with the coming of the shouldered stem. Not all the early wet sweetmeats have lids ; where lids exist they are ribbed or pearled like the bowl. Feet also are plain, ribbed radially or pearled, following the bowl. Decoration by surface moulding probably went out of fashion about 1725 ; two years later cut sweetmeats had made their appearance. For the surface of sweetmeat glasses the following chronology may be suggested :

Plain	1685–1700
Ribbed	1700–1715
Pearled	1710–1730

If this sequence is checked by stem form a nearer determination may be reached.

4. Shouldered stems lasted until about 1740, but they are extremely rare after 1725 or 1730. Sweetmeat glasses were never quite captured by the filigree stems. It is not very easy to explain the comparative scarcity of filigree sweetmeats, but I am inclined to think it was due to the rapid progress of " scalloped " and " diamond-cut " sweetmeats which never gave filigree a chance. Such an explanation is at any rate consistent with the fact that sweetmeats were the type of vessel in which cutting first declared itself, while filigree was primarily an ornament for wine-glasses.

5. Lady Grisell Baillie was a Scotswoman with a genius for household management. She ruled her servants with the high discretion of an empress. In the standing orders which she issued to her butler she assumed that he was half-witted, and explained, to the nicest detail, the path of duty and decorum. Her dinners were thoughtfully and liberally conceived, her purchases careful and precise, her curiosity unbounded, and her eye final. All matters transacted in her house, what was eaten, what was drunk, things purchased, moneys paid, guests, visits, accidents, and improvements were noted in a book[1] which she kept for the purpose. It is a classic of feminine particularity, and invaluable to any historian of housekeeping. In the furnishings of a dinner-table she had the liveliest interest, and in other people's houses she noticed everything. Her house was in

---

[1] *Household Books*, printed by the Scottish History Society; see Bibliography.

SPECIAL TYPES

Scotland, but she came to London sometimes to follow fashion and observe her friends. She looked for novelties with the instinct of a provincial, but with the judgment of a woman of taste ; and so when she dined from home she took in the arrangements at a glance and noted them afterwards, with comment, in her household book. In 1727 she went to a dinner party in London where the arrangements impressed her greatly ; but what chiefly caught her eye were the " corner'd-brim " glasses in which the sweets were served (*Household Books*, p. 298).

Noted by that curious attention, they cannot have been new for very long. Lady Grisell's remarks upon them are the earliest evidence for cut sweetmeats. Her unmistakable phrase must refer to glasses with deeply scalloped rims like those of Plates CIV. 3 and CVIII. 2. It is worth note that Lady Grisell Baillie's remark is only five years earlier than the first advertisement of cut sweetmeats—a " chrystal cut sweetmeat glass " mentioned in 1732. It is quite consistent also with the earliest mention of cut flint glass in general (1719). There is, I think, no doubt that cut sweetmeats were made from the third decade until the end of the century, but they may be regarded as a curiosity until 1739, in which year we find Jerom Johnson advertising " scalloped dessert glasses." Until the end of the century they were probably luxury pieces made to special orders at a special price, and seem to have been in consequence independent of the state of the glass trade. Before 1740 at any rate cost was probably no object, and that is, I think, why these are the glasses in which the earliest experiments in cutting appear (see Plates CIII, CIV. 3, CV. 1, 3, CVII. 1, CVIII. 2). The Excise Act of 1745, with its restriction on bulk of metal, made less difference here than in the ordinary " lines " of wine-glass, in which the Excise did prove a serious hindrance to the development of cutting. Cut sweetmeats with cusped stems have been considerably post-dated ; the examples with large *relief* diamonds round bowl or foot or examples which are grossly over-cut are certainly late, but a good many other cusped glasses with flat or incised motives are certainly as early as 1750. Without pre-supposing any break in the development caused by the Excise it may be convenient to classify the characteristics of the earlier and later types. It may be remarked in doing so that the so-called " Irish " sweetmeats were a continuation of the development, and not a departure from it.

(*a*) *Early characteristics*. First of all come features which survive in cut sweetmeats from the days before cutting. The most notable of these is the shouldered stem which in Plates CIII and CIV. 3 is found with no attempt to cut it. Another survival and a certain mark of early date (before 1740) is the radial ribbing of the foot which, as noted above, was a usual accompaniment of the ribbed bowl (Plate CIII. 1). Heavy uncut stems of baluster or balustroid form (*e.g.* Plate CIV. 1) are also a mark of early date in cut sweet-meats whose bowls and feet are cut. As for the cutting itself the earliest designs are composed of simple motives which are easy to execute. These are sliced or incised motives rather than motives cut in relief. The following are the more important, because they proved more fertile in design : (1) scalloping, either a plain zigzag (or " cornered brim ") as in Plate CIV. 3, or an arch-and-point as in the rim of Plate CIII. 1 ; (2) foot-cutting, taking the form of slicing the instep in fan-shaped panels, or cutting the edge of the foot so that it makes a regular polygon instead of a circle (Plate CVIII. 2) ; (3) plain intrenched lines ; (4) lunar slices sometimes simply used as in Fig. 23, some-times elaborately combined (Plate CIV. 1), but very easy to execute ; (5) arched ridges (Plate CIII) ; (6) plain flat triangles (Plate CIV. 3) ; (7) stem diamonds, small and fairly square, long and narrow, or hooked at the top. Special mention must be made of the cusped stem, which is very common in cut sweetmeats. It was an adaptation of the knopped stems of *c.* 1740 to the needs of stem-cutting. It begins about 1740 but lasts until the end of the century. Beyond the fact that a diamond-cut cusp is earlier than a straight stem diamond cut, it is, by itself, not of much use for dating a glass.

[323]

APPENDIX IV

(b) *Late characteristics*. Most of the early motives recur during the last quarter of the century, but there is a greatly increased emphasis on relief cutting, especially large relief diamonds round the bowl and the instep. About 1770–80 these diamonds are usually plain, in shape a very flat pyramid, but later they are cross-cut and double-cut. The cutting of the bowl-rim in a trefoil repeat (Plate CVIII. 3) belongs to the last quarter of the century ; so do fields of small diamonds in deep relief (Plate CVII. 3). The cutting of foot-rims in symmetrical curves and points, as in the candlesticks of Plates CXLIII. 2, 3 and CXLIV. 1, is also a late feature, not earlier than 1760–70. In sweetmeats, however, as in other cut-glass, the style of the Anglo-Irish period is not a matter of new motives so much as a profusion in the use of old ones.

7. Fruit Baskets

The molten metal of glass may be trailed crosswise in ropes without much difficulty. In this way the Liège glassmakers at the beginning of the 18th century made fruit-baskets (*corbeilles ajourées*), dishes, and even sets of dessert plates. Examples may be seen in the Museum at Liège (*cf.* Pholien, Fig. 64). English baskets, which follow the Liège types fairly closely, may sometimes be met with. They are of lead glass and have a stand or saucer, usually circular but sometimes oval in shape, with a basket-work rim. Col. Ratcliff has a small but interesting collection of them (Plate XCIX. *b*). They have a pronounced waist and turn outwards into a flaring rim, but they have no feet or handles.

" Glass baskets with handles and feet for deserts " were being made in flint glass by the St. Mary Lane (Round) Glasshouse at Dublin in 1729 (*Faulkner's Dublin Journal*, November, 1729, cited by Westropp, p. 41), and the very particular description of them suggests that they were then a new fashion, at any rate in Dublin ; most of the other glasses in the same list (except salts, for which see below) are only mentioned by name. But the Dublin baskets cannot have been of the Liège type. They were more probably small baskets of the " shepherdess " type. These latter sometimes occur and were closely copied from small-handled baskets made *à la pince* at Liège (Pholien, Fig. 37). The word " dessert," as we have seen (p. 321), includes sweetmeats, and in point of size the handled baskets were suited to them.

Baskets without feet or handles like Col. Ratcliff's may be identified with " glass fruit-baskets " which were being sold in 1725. They are mentioned in one account book under that year (*Notes and Queries*, 5th series, 1875, p. 381) as having been bought at Bristol for one Thomas Pembrock, afterwards Mayor of Cork, whose agent Nat Barry bought four dozen of them at 6s. 6d. a dozen. Glassmaking was then well established in Bristol, and it is likely that the baskets were made there. Bristol may well have been the chief centre of this manufacture. It is certainly significant that they are first mentioned there, for Bristol was the point at which Netherlandish styles and techniques first found a foothold in England ; Bristol delft is the most notable example. Baskets are again mentioned in 1746. The last reference to them is 1758, when they were being sold in Liverpool ; and as " comfit glasses " are mentioned immediately after them in the list, the baskets would seem to be for fruit rather than for sweetmeats. Feet and handles are not mentioned (*Liverpool Chronicle*, 24 March, 1758, cited by Buckley, p. 149).

8. Jellies

According to Mr. Buckley (*History*, p. 110) the small round glasses called " mortars " by Hartshorne (p. 342) were the earliest type of jelly glass, and these seem to accord as well as the taller glasses, with feet (Plate XXXVI. *b*. 3), with the first mention of jelly glasses in Robert May's *The Accomplisht Cook* (1678), p. 204, where directions are given for serving jelly " in little round glasses four or five in a dish." This early type is a small straight-

SPECIAL TYPES

sided bowl (a frustum of a cone inverted) with a folded rim and no foot. Several other types of low bowl with or without a short stem were used for the same purpose. Robert May's " dish " seems to imply a low plate rather than the stemmed salvers of later date. *Cf.* p. 328.

Jellies in the 18th century were used not only for jelly but for custard, iced cream, and several other sweet confections, for which recipes may be found in 18th-century cookery books, *e.g.* the *Compleat Family Piece* (1741), Moxon's *English Housewifry*, and Mrs. Raffald's *English Housekeeper* (1769). Their development shows the following stages :

1. The earliest jellies, about 1681–1715, follow the wine-glass bowl, the standard shape being the rounded-funnel bowl with or without a cyst at the bottom (Plate LXIX. 4). They have no stem and are usually set directly on a domed or spreading foot with or without a folded rim. The earliest examples seem to be those with a gadrooned collar round the base (Plates XXXVI. *b.* 3, LXVI. 1) which probably date from about 1685. Sometimes the bowl and foot are divided by a squashed knop with air tears in it, such examples being rather later than the collar. In this first phase we find glasses with a pair of single handles and (Plate LXIX. 4) with double handles. Until 1710 at any rate the surface is plain ; moulded ornament belongs mainly to the next phase and consists of pearl moulding, diamond moulding, and vertical ribs.

2. The advent of German forms in the second decade of the 18th century (*supra*, p. 169) introduced jellies with incurved bowls (Plate LXIX. 5 and Buckley, Plate LV) and double-ogee bowls. These types remained in vogue for most of the century, but varied considerably. The later examples, after about 1750, can usually be detected by the design and technique of the foot. Joseph Highmore's picture, " Lady Danvers ill-treats Pamela " (Melbourne Art Gallery), painted about 1745, shows several of the incurved jellies on a stemmed salver.[1] The main varieties were bell bowls, trumpet bowls, ordinary waisted bowls, and double-ogees. On all these we find decorative moulding—pearl ornament, diamond ornament, and vertical ribbing on the bowls ; radial ribbing, and very occasionally pearl ornament, on the feet. The earliest literary allusion to diamond-moulded jelly glasses seems to be in 1752 in Ireland (Westropp, p. 20), but the larger and heavier diamond-moulded jellies can be shown by a comparison of detail to be contemporary with shouldered-stemmed candlesticks and knopped balusters which go back to the second decade.

3. In the middle of the 18th century jellies, like other glasses, became lighter and smaller, but they do not seem to have been very frequently engraved ; for an example, dating from about 1730–40, see Buckley, Plate LV. The two handles are succeeded by one about 1730, and after 1745 (Excise) there is a characteristic economy of metal in the omission of both ; no handles are shown in Highmore's picture. In the middle of the century there begin to appear glasses rather shorter and wider than the incurved jellies. They have wavy sides and are often diamond moulded. The rims also are sometimes tooled in a wavy line. These glasses are set very low on their feet without a knop at all, and the feet are not well made. In some instances they may be salts (see Buckley, Plate LVI, 1).

4. Cut-glass jellies from Germany are first mentioned in the *London Gazette* in 1709, but there is no reference to them which clearly implies English cutting until 1752 (Buckley, p. 121). The earliest type has a scalloped rim. It probably came into vogue some time before glasses of the third phase had gone out, perhaps as early as 1725. Feet also are sliced or scalloped. I have not seen flat diamonds or simple lunar slices on jellies, but in the Anglo-Irish period double-cut diamonds and heavy curvilinear cutting are found not infrequently.

---

[1] I owe this reference to Mr. H. Clifford Smith.

APPENDIX IV

Some glasses, now called sweetmeats, were used for the same confections as jellies. These were called "wet sweetmeats" by Lady Grisell Baillie in 1727 (*Household Books*, p. 298), and they had covers. They are included here among the sweetmeats.

9. LAMPS

Glass lamps were never very common in flint glass, but there is one interesting family which, from their affinity with the lacemakers' lamps, seem to owe their design to France, perhaps to Huguenot glassmakers who settled here. Some two dozen of this type were tested and about half proved to be lead glass (see Plate LX) ; the non-lead specimens are presumably French. One or two of the lead pieces have marked English features, *e.g.* the moulding of Plate LX. 1, or the pedestal foot of Plate LX. 3, of late 17th-century date. Others have knopped or plain stems and seem to be not later than *c.* 1750. Four, three, and two " spouts " are to be met with, but the larger number seem earlier.

Lamps of other kinds are even scarcer. In the Hamilton Clements collection there is a small lamp with a metal mount for the wick, dating apparently from the middle of the 18th century. Mention may be made also of a family of night-lights found with air-twist and enamel-twist stems ; they have a flat bulbous bowl.

Flint-glass lamps were being made by the St. Mary's Lane Glasshouse at Dublin in 1729 (*Faulkner's Dublin Journal*, November, 1729, cited by Westropp, p. 41). The advertisement referred to seems to be the earliest mention of them, but is quite consistent with the features mentioned here. Large cut-glass lamps were occasionally made during the third quarter of the 18th century ; they have square feet like other stemmed vessels of that period, but not the two or more spouts found in the earlier specimens.

10. RUMMERS

The word rummer is a corruption of the German *Römer*, a name which seems to have implied originally " Roman glasses." It has no connection with the spirit rum ; the later types of rummer, to which we shall come in a moment, were used for rum (among other liquors), and this is no doubt responsible for the popular derivation. The vessel *Römer* was originally peculiar to Germany and made of *Waldglas* in Silesia and Bohemia. It had a rounded bowl, narrower at both lip and base than in the middle, opening into a thick hollow stem or bucket covered with prunts (Plate XVI. 1). In the 17th century drinking vessels of this type passed beyond the confines of Germany. They were made at Venice and in the Netherlands, and they were ordered from Antonio Morelli by John Greene of London (1667–72). Rhenish wine was what carried the *Römer* into other countries ; it was a German glass for German wine. In England it is one of the few types of drinking-glass which can be regarded as in any way special to a particular kind of wine. " A rummer of Rhenish " was a stock phrase in the 17th century, but the rummer was used for other drinks as well, at any rate in England. Merret (pp. 225–6) speaks of " the Romer for Rhenish wine, for Sack, Claret, Beer, plain moulded coloured in whole or in part." It is clear that this is the same type of vessel mentioned by Dryden, Gayton, and other 17th-century writers as " rummer." In 1706 rummers were still used for " Rhenish and sugar," and in 1728 Chambers (*s.v.* Music) mentions a Dutchman " who could break Rummer-glasses with the tone of his voice " ; the explanatory " glasses " seems to suggest that rummers were less familiar than formerly. But the word rummer as a " large drinking-glass " or " a wide-brimmed drinking-glass," keeps its place in most of the English dictionaries down to the time of Johnson (1755)—Edward Phillips (1696), the *Glossographia Anglicana Nova* (1707), Kersey's *Dictionarium Anglo-Britannicum* (1715), Nathan Bailey's Etymological Dictionary (1721 and many later editions), and Defoe's Dictionary (1735). All these references must refer to the well-known rummer form palpably copied from the German *Römer* (see Plates XVI. 2, XXI. 3, XXXII. 3, XXXIX, XL. 1, 3, XLI).

SPECIAL TYPES

Rummers are not mentioned in Ravenscroft's price list (p. 127), but it is certain that they were being made in England and of lead glass soon after 1681 (Plate XVI). It is highly probable that they had been made in England of soda glass for the past fifty years ; in much the same way that German stoneware " greybeards " were copied at Fulham. Merret's remark, already quoted, suggests that they were made here in 1662, and Hartshorne (p. 188) thought the *Römer* shape had been introduced by Paul Vinion about 1630.

The history of the English rummer is a gradual divagation from its German prototype ; this may be watched in Plates XVI. 1, XVI. 2, XL. 3, XXXIX. 2, XXI. 3, XXXIX. 1, XL. 1, XXXII. 3, and XLI. 1, 2, 3, taken in that order. Chronology follows this change. The earliest examples are those which are closest to the German ; while in the later examples only the *Römer* bowl is left, and the hollow bucket has been replaced by the baluster or its derivatives. The following stages may be noted : (1) the bowl no longer opens into the bucket. (2) The prunts decrease in number or are omitted altogether. (3) The plain hollow stem becomes solid. These three stages are all very early, probably before 1690. (4) The rummer stem is altogether abandoned, and its place taken by a plain knop-and-baluster, a baluster, or a knopped stem. When this change has taken place, about 1690, the development follows that of the wine-glass stem.

The German *Römer* had been made of a potash glass which had naturally a pale greenish tinge. The earliest dyed green flint glass was made to imitate this characteristic of the *Römer*. The date of this innovation is not easy to fix precisely. There are a number of green English rummers which on stem form may be dated about 1740 or a little later (Plate C. *a.* 1–3 and *b.* 2). The remarkable glass illustrated in Plate LXII seems to command an earlier date. It has several characteristics of Mr. Wilfred Buckley's clear flint-glass rummer with Ravenscroft's mark ; its bowl is faintly ribbed, and its prunted and hollow stem is very close to the *Römer* prototype. I have been content to date it to the first quarter of the 18th century, as there is no definite evidence of green flint glass of earlier date. But if we find a green flint glass with a good example of the long r.f. bowl and a shouldered stem, which cannot be much later than 1715 (Plate C. *b.* 1), there seems no reason why green rummers should not have been made during the latter part of the 17th century.

Rummers which show their *Römer* ancestry do not seem to have been made in the second half of the 18th century, and so far their progress is quite simple. But between 1760 and 1770 we encounter a new type of glass which was also called rummer and persisted well into the 19th century ; Hardy speaks somewhere of " a row of ancient rummers with ground figures on their sides." I shall call these glasses Rummer B to distinguish them from the true rummer. Two questions arise concerning them, when they were introduced, and to what extent they were derived from Rummer A. At the end of the 18th and the beginning of the 19th century Rummer B was made in several varieties, which on the evidence of dated pieces we must regard as parallel forms and not as consequential ; such are rummers with ovate bowls (Plate CLIII. *a*), cylindrical bowls (*E.I.G.*, Fig. 60), ogee bowls, and one or two less common bowl shapes. The stems are short and plain, long and plain, or have a half-way button. The feet are square and domed or round and flat-footed. Rummer B has been discussed by Sir John Risley (see Bibliography). Of its variants it is clear that the ovate bowl with a short plain stem approximates most closely to Rummer A, and this is in fact the type of which we have the earliest-dated document—the Rebecca Creedey rummer in Sir John Risley's collection (Plate CLIII. *a.* 2). This glass is dated 1766 and cannot be much subsequent to the later apologues of Rummer A ; the gap can scarcely be more than ten years. The earliest advertisement of rummers by glassmakers or dealers dates from 1770 when the Williams' were making " rummers " at Dublin (Westropp, p. 57) ; these must, I think, be Rummer B not Rummer A, since rummers become a fairly frequent item in advertisements during the last thirty years of

APPENDIX IV

the 18th century. The descriptions of " rummer " given in the later editions of Johnson and other dictionaries based upon it are not sufficiently explicit to be helpful. The connection between Rummer A and Rummer B cannot be settled at present, but in anticipation of further evidence I would suggest, (a) that a new shape of glass was " invented " about 1760–70, probably by a London dealer, (b) that the new shape, with ovate bowl and short stem, was suggested by the older Rummer B, which was almost extinct, (c) and the " inventor " called his new glass by the old name, because Rummer A and Rummer B might serve the same purpose, and the public is shy of new names.

11. SALTS

The progress of glass salts during the 18th century is not easy to fix, and it is usually necessary to date form by ornament rather than to make the safer reference from form to ornament. The parallel forms in silver, which can be dated with certitude, are better evidence than the stages of design in cutting. I set out here the more important types in their chronological order, as far as it can be fixed by silver analogy or cut design.

1. The *trencher-salt* is interesting because it is not solid, but blown in two films of thin metal (Plate CLII. 4). This feature itself is sufficient warrant for placing them at the end of the 17th or early in the 18th century (cf. the silvered bowl in Plate LXXXIX. a. 1, where the blown technique is similar). When flint glass was struggling for social recognition the glassmakers were apt to copy silver, which had an older tradition and better prestige. The glass trencher, a good example of this, is derived from a silver trencher which goes back to 1680. Jackson (Fig. 78A) figures, both in section and in perspective, a silver trencher with hall-mark of 1710 and a double layer of silver, as in our glass example. Mr. H. R. P. Lomas has a glass trencher with its surface silvered. Of the two trenchers here illustrated one is plain (Plate CLII. 4), while the other has moulded vertical ribs comparable with sweetmeats (Plate CLII. 1). The plain one is certainly the earlier, probably by ten years (cf. p. 322). Trencher salts seem to have gone out about 1730 ; in 1729 there is an advertisement of " ground and polished salts " which must refer to cut-glass (Westropp, p. 41). Both the form and the thin metal of the trencher make it impossible that it should have been adapted to cut ornament.

2. *Straight-sided salts*. These are a small bowl without stem or foot, but with folded rim. The metal and workmanship place them early in the 18th century ; and during the 19th century they were used as salts. They may have been made as jelly glasses (cf. p. 324), but I think they were originally for salt. Hartshorne (p. 342) wished to call them " mortars," but chiefly to find an instance of Mansell's " mortars at 1/4 a dozen " (p. 434) ; he brought no evidence to support this identification and ignored the gap of nearly a century between Mansell's mortars and the probable date of these glasses. The one Hartshorne illustrated came from a set of four, a likely number for salts (two pairs). We know that salts without feet were being made in 1752 (Westropp, p. 43).

3. *Double-ogee salts*, with diamond moulding all over and a substantial spreading foot, seem to be the next shape. This bowl probably came in with the waisted German bowls about 1715. The double-ogee salt is the only type found with nipt or moulded all over its surface, and with cutting. On that ground it may be regarded as a link between the disappearance of " Venetian " ornament and the all-cut salts of the second half of the century. The " ground and polished salts " of 1729, obviously a novelty, were probably of this shape ; the foot and rim would admit of elementary cutting, the simple slices or scallops which were the earliest ventures of the English cutter, and are found quite often in double-ogee salts. Examples with moulded ornament belong to the first half of the century. Those which are cut only about the rims and feet almost certainly go back to 1725. Even specimens with very elaborately scalloped rims and rows of convex diamonds round the bowl seem to go back to 1750 (Plate CLII. 3) ; convex diamonds cut with

SPECIAL TYPES

cruciform grooves occur in a wafer-stick containing a coin of 1750 (Plate CXXXVIII). The double-ogee is the most likely shape for the "diamond-cut" salts of 1747 (Westropp, p. 143).

4. *Tripod salts* are directly copied from a silver form. The prototype came in about 1720 and lasted for about forty years; it occurs most frequently in the 'forties and 'fifties. In glass the tripod salt was not normally cut. Claw feet are quite common and the legs are often sealed to the bowl by lion-masks or strawberry prunts (see Plate LXXXIV. b. 2 and Buckley, Plate LIV).

5. *Round salts* with straight or slightly curved sides set on a knopped stem were quite frequently made during the second half of the 18th century. Their most characteristic feature is vertical string cutting (Plate CLII. 8).

6. *Boat-shaped salts.* During the last thirty years of the 18th century we discover a new type of salt-cellar which shows the influence of the Adam refinement. The boat-shaped salt shares its shape with large fruit bowls as seen in Plate CXLIV. *a.* The boat salt is usually, but not invariably, found with a square foot or a parallelogram foot. The underside of this foot is moulded in a high dome or left quite flat, but the high dome seems to be the earlier. The boat salt was almost always cut or intended to be cut (*cf.* Westropp, Plate XXVIIA, 1), and its peculiar form was responsible for one or two new types of cutting, *e.g.* prismatic loops under the " bows " and " stern " of the " boat " (Plate CLII. 7). The rims were more frequently cut in a dentil edge than scalloped roundly, but in the early (c. 1775) pieces we find the wavy edges and bevelled (" ground ") edges that had been common thirty years before. For the lower part of the bowl flutes were also used, and at the end of the century we find a circuit of relief diamonds round the bowl. It may be suggested that the boat salt with parallelogram foot is the type referred to as " curious cut salts " in an advertisement of glass sent from London to Dublin in 1773 (*Faulkner's Dublin Journal*, 9 December, 1773, Buckley, p. 128). The word " curious," which here as always indicates a new fashion, probably refers to the shape of the vessel. Mr. Buckley would explain it of a new style in cutting, and looks for a motive to which it may allude. But if that were so one would surely expect some such phrase as " curiously cut "; when an advertisement emphasizes the cutting we usually find some such phrase as " neat cut," or " fine cut." The date is quite suitable; the first notice of " square feet " occurs only two years later.

A variant of the boat salt had, like some of the large salad bowls, a rim turned over outwards and cut in small polygonal facets or latitudinal flutes. This shape is always called Irish, and I do not know of any evidence that it was made in England.

7. Early in the 19th century the form of the salt becomes very various. Late specimens, even if they are made in an older shape, can usually be distinguished by the elaboration of the relief cutting and the overcrowding of the ground. Large convex diamonds in a field, small nailheads in a field, hatched lozenges in relief, strawberry diamonds, and fine dentil-cutting or fan-cutting round the edge, are among the most frequent themes. Two characteristic shapes of this period are a round tubby bowl and a longer coracle-shaped salt. Both these are found in the very white metal, and with the small and very sharp-cut relief diamonds which are characteristic of late Waterford glass. Both these shapes are without stem or foot (see Plate CLII. 9 and Westropp, Plate XXVII, B, 2 and 4). Both tubs and coracles were quite generally made, not peculiar to Ireland.

12. Spirit and Cordial Glasses

The spirits drunk during the 18th century fall into two classes. To the first belong brandy, gin, rum, hollands, arrack, and whisky. Of these brandy, distilled from wine and imported from France, had greater dignity than the rest. Hollands was a corn spirit imported from the Netherlands. Rum was made by distilling sugar-cane and came

APPENDIX IV

chiefly from the English colonies in Jamaica and America, but rum, in the modern sense, only came into use when bonding became legal in 1742. Arrack also was made from sugar-cane, but was of Eastern origin and chiefly imported into England from India, Ceylon, and Java. The drinking of gin in England dates from 1713 when Parliament abolished the monopoly hitherto held by the Distillers' Company, and gave free permission to any who pleased to distill spirits for drinking purposes (12 Ann., c. 3). At once new companies were formed and great quantities of gin, exceedingly bad gin, were put upon the market. It was the cheapest consolation the people had known, and the poorer classes became gin addicts by the thousand. Until 1713 men had drunk wine and beer, and these were wholesome and noble drinks. England had been as sober as any wine-producing country ; but now appeared a " drink question " for the first time in English history. The slang of gin drinking, gin traps, gin livers, gin slinger, gin spinner, and a host of others were added to the language. The sinister word became a pointed aposiopesis, or hid itself in a dozen euphemisms. For Squire Western the 18th century was the age of port ; for the people it was the gin age. It had its own painter Hogarth, and above all, its own joke ; for you may interpret an age by its jokes. The gin joke, still greeted with feeble laughter in the music-halls, is as eloquent of the 18th century as the pox joke is eloquent of Elizabethan times. Between 1713 and 1736 the ravages of gin caused a corresponding outbreak of zeal. A prohibition movement was set on foot and " Madam Gineva "[1] was assailed by the tracts and pamphlets of officious virtue. The two parties, pro-gin and anti-gin, attacked one another with statistics and indignation. At length, in 1736, Parliament, scenting revenue in the fumes of the gin shops, passed the Gin Act and did something to stop gin drinking by making it too expensive. But the people squealed for their lost courage, and kept on squealing for seven years ; at the end of which time (1743) Parliament was induced to repeal the Act. Gin drinking continued as before.

The other class of spirits corresponds with the cocktails and liqueurs of the present day. Spirit cordials were made from the juice and stones of cherries, peaches, apricots, and other fruits, *e.g.* persico, ratafia, baum, spirits of clary, wormwood, citron peel, juniper berries, orange peel, lemon peel, mint, rosemary. Numerous recipes for these and similar drinks may be found in 18th-century books on domestic economy (see p. 325). " Cordial " was the general name for them, and in 1703 they cost two shillings a pint. Cordials were a fashionable rather than a popular drink, and consumed in private houses rather than in taverns.

Glasses of small capacity which were obviously intended for potent liquors, may be correspondingly divided into two groups. Tavern glasses for spirits vary too much for classification, but they are usually short in the stem and sometimes without stems at all. Their workmanship is inferior to that of table glass, and their design poor. Different shapes have been called nips, joeys, brandy-glasses, and gin-glasses, but while gin was the spirit drunk most often in taverns, the small short glasses were used for other spirits too, and there is no ground for differentiation. Glasses made with thick sides, which hold less than they appear to, must have been made for a colourless liquid ; they were part of the gin joke.

Glasses with tall stems and small bowls represent a more polite usage and are usually of fine workmanship and graceful design. Polite cordials fall into two main groups.

1. *Tall applied stems and short bowls*. The earliest specimens date from about 1720. Their stems are plain, with or without knops, and often have a thin ring round the upper part (Plate CII). The bowl is slightly waisted or trumpet-shaped. We may mention

---

[1] Gin is an abbreviation of Gineva, which is derived from Fr. *genièvre* = juniper berry. Gin was distilled from juniper berries. For the gin controversy which culminated in 1736, see *Elegy on the lamented death of Madam Gineva*, London, 1736, *The life of Mother Gin*, London, 1736, *A short history of the Gin Act* (n.d., about 1736–43), and other pamphlet literature.

SPECIAL TYPES

here a type of glass with a tall multiple knopped stem and a wide open bowl (Plate LXIII. 3, Bles, Plate LXVIII). Hartshorne (p. 321) was uncertain about them, and Mr. Bles describes them as cordials. Their proportions suggest that the form is of French origin (*cf.* Gerspach, Fig. 107A), and if that is so they are perhaps brandy cordials, but on the whole I think they are more likely to be "dry" sweetmeats. An interesting type of cordial has a tall stem and small ovate bowl with very thick sides. These often have engraving commemorating William III, and are probably a factory type of a Dublin glasshouse, and made for the Williamite festivals held in Dublin. The plain-stemmed variety belong to the second quarter of the 18th century. Rather similar cordials were engraved for the supporters of Charles Edward Stuart about 1745–50 (*cf.* Hartshorne, Plate LII ; and Francis, No. 343, where the hypothesis is quite justified, though the inference is extraordinary). With the appearance of filigree stems tall cordial glasses become much more varied in design, and much more common. The most frequent bowl types are the bucket bowl, the ovate bowl, the straight-sided bowl, the ogee-bowl, occasionally the double-ogee bowl, and a trumpet bowl passing into a drawn stem. The general range of these features is 1735–80, though individual glasses can be more closely dated. The later and more slender versions of the baluster do not occur in tall cordials, but some very handsome glasses have the cusped stem (Plate CXVIII). The straight stem cut in diamond facets is found 1750–80 (Plate CXVII. *b.* 3). The tall cordials were engraved only very rarely, for the obvious reason that there was not room. A substitute was found in a circlet of quiet fluting (moulded) round the lower part of the bowl; this greatly enhances the beauty of the glass. Dimpled moulding is found also.

2. *Flute-cordials.* This is a convenient term for a group of cordials with long and extremely narrow bowls and a drawn stem (*cf.* pp. 183, 314–15, 321 for the term flute). With the ale-glass these are descendants of the 17th-century flute. Flute-cordials (Plate CLIII. *b.* 1, 3) are commonly called ratafia glasses, after what seems to be a 19th-century tradition, but there is no ground for thinking they were special to ratafia rather than to persico or baum. Like the short-bowl cordials they often have faint moulded fluting round the base of the bowl. All types of filigree stem may be expected. The top of the bowl is sometimes engraved with a festooned or trellised border. The range of the flute-cordials is 1740–80.

13. STANDS AND SALVERS

These glasses usually consist of a circular plate or dish set on a short stem and foot which follow in their development the same parts of wine-glasses. Stands vary in size and use from a large sweetmeat type to "confectioners rounds." The salver was at first a Venetian shape made with a high hollow pedestal foot instead of a stem, and until the end of the 17th century flint-glass stands followed this model. Plate XXIII. *b.* 2 shows an example of very thin lead glass which cannot be much later than 1685 ; it has several affinities with the Ravenscroft-Bishopp group.

In early glass of lead the stems were apt to be still hollow as in *façon de Venise*. A stand which still has this feature may be seen in Plate LXXXIX. *a.* 2. When the stems became solid and very heavy we find salvers with simple balusters (both types), acorn stems, several types of heavy knopped stem (Plate LXIV). These range between 1690 and 1715.

After 1715 stands begin to show the shouldered stem, and this continued for about fifty years, much longer than in any other type of glass. A peculiarity of many of the stands with shouldered stems is a set of three collars just above the foot. Stands were used for serving jellies ; the jelly glasses stood in a circle round a tall sweetmeat glass, and are so depicted in a picture painted by Joseph Highmore about 1745 (see p. 325). When this practice began is not certain, for in the latter part of the 17th century jelly glasses were brought in on a plate (Robert May, *u.s.*). Revolving stands were also made. Mr. Buckley (p. 113) suggests that these are the "new-fashioned salvers" mentioned in an advertisement of 1772, and quotes Mr. Winkworth's cut stand as an example. I have seen, however, revolving stands which were not cut at all and had a shouldered stem ; these would seem to be earlier.

Cut-glass stands are far from common. The cutting of the plate of Mr. Winkworth's stand (Fig. 33) suggests an early date. It is entirely composed of the lunar slice, one of the most elementary motives in cutting and one of the earliest. The design is excellently conceived, and without the aid of relief cutting. A design of cut motives as such is rare enough, but especially rare in the last quarter of the century, when cutting is generally used without discretion. This stand may well be earlier than Mrs. Dickson's silver-mounted bowls, and like them and Mr. Winkworth's toilet bottles, and Mr. de la Hey's wafer-seal, shows English cutting at its best (Plates CXXXIX, CXXXIII. a, CXXXVIII. a, and Fig. 33). It may be noted that the Winkworth stand has not a stem, but reverts to a pedestal of the Venetian type.

14. WATER-GLASSES AND FINGER-BOWLS

The identification of the water-glass, frequently mentioned in 18th-century advertisements, is not easy, but its use is clear. Smollett in his *Travells* (1, v, 1766) declares that " I know of no custom more beastly than that of using water-glasses in which polite company spirt and squirt and spue the filthy scourings of their gums." Twiss in his *Tour in Ireland* (1776) remarks that " the filthy custom of using water-glasses after meals is as common [*sc.* in Ireland] as in England : no well-bred persons touch their victuals with their fingers, and such ablutions ought to be unnecessary." The poet Cowper writes to William Unwin in 1784, " Your mother begs that you will bring for her eight blue, deep blue, water-glasses." As for the shape of the water-glass it would seem to be similar to the finger-bowl. To this probability we may add one or two facts. It resembled a tumbler ; *Phil. Trans.*, LXXIII, 305 (1779) speaks of " a common tumbler or water-glass," and the passage from Smollett shows it was a glass you could drink from. Water-glasses " with feet " are mentioned in advertisements, and they were also made " in great variety." A water-glass is therefore a drinkable glass with or without feet, rather shorter, we may suppose, than a tumbler, but rather higher than the low finger-bowls of the early 19th century. It may be regarded as a precursor of the finger-bowl. The earliest mention of water-glasses is by Lady Grisell Baillie in 1695. After 1770 they are seldom mentioned in advertisements.

Their place seems to be taken by " finger glasses," " finger cups," and " finger basins," which do not appear in advertisements before 1779 (Buckley, p. 137). The coarse custom of rinsing the mouth and washing the hands was passing away, and now only fingers were dabbled. Hence the word water-glass and its crude associations were abandoned by dealers for a more elegant term with " finger " in it. The more refined usage brought with it a change of shape. Finger-glasses became wider and shallower ; in that sort of vessel it was easier to rinse your fingers, and you no longer drank from them. Hence the earlier finger-bowls are the tall and narrow kind (*cf.* Buckley, p. 108), closest in shape to a tumbler. Plain finger-bowls of deep and narrow cylindrical form and without ornament certainly go back to the middle of the 18th century. Examples with feet naturally differed from them in design ; Plate CIX shows several glasses " with feet " for which it is difficult to suggest any other use. An interesting water-glass of opaque white flint glass with gilt ornament and no foot appears in Plate CXXXV. a. 1.

The later and more open finger-bowls were made of clear flint glass, green glass, blue glass, amber glass, and amethyst glass. They are either straight-sided or round-sided. The former type is perhaps the earlier ; it often has cut or moulded flutes about the base. Most of the coloured specimens are of late 18th-century or early 19th-century date.

SPECIAL TYPES

15. Jokes and Gestures

Where the idea is fanciful the technique is usually elaborate. Glass toys were made as much for the glassmaker's fancy as for his customer's. The glassmakers made strange toys to "show off," and it is therefore a mistake to regard objects of this kind as necessarily "late." As early as 1702 an ingenious artist, no doubt Venetian or Flemish, "in the presence of all spectators maketh beasts, birds, fowls, images, figures of men and women which he bloweth of all colours of glass" (*Flying Post*, 3 March, 1702, Buckley, p. 143). " Curious glasses for ornament " were being made at the Falcon Glasshouse in London throughout the first half of the 18th century (Buckley, pp. 116 and 142), and between 1760 and 1785 glass toys were advertised by Bench of Warwick and by Imison and King of Manchester (*ibid.*). The region about Birmingham and Stourbridge, not Bristol, was the chief centre of the glass toy manufacture, as Mr. Buckley has shown.

Special kinds of toys were made for the glassmakers themselves to use in their public rituals. At Bristol the glassmakers were formed into a Company and marched through the streets on occasions of ceremony. In 1738 when the Prince and Princess of Wales visited their city " The Companies of the City made a magnificent appearance in their formalities, marching two by two preceding the Corporation and the Royal Guests. The Company of Glass-men went first dressed in white Holland shirts, on horseback, some with swords, others with crowns and sceptres in their hands, made of glass " (*Daily Post*, 14 November, 1738, Buckley, p. 145). The glassmakers of Newcastle-on-Tyne had the same close craftsmanship and the same eye for a splendid occasion. The following account is taken from the *Newcastle Courant* of 20 September, 1823, but it clearly refers to an old-established custom, and is probably true of the 18th century. " On Monday last the flint glassmakers employed in the houses on the Tyne and Wear walked in procession in this town. . . . The men all wore sashes and glass stars suspended from their necks by chains or drops of variegated colour, the great majority of them having glass feathers in their hats, and every individual carried a glass ornament in his hand. The men from six glasshouses composed the occasion." The rest of the proceedings are described in some detail, but an abstract will show the glass objects used.

South Shields. A flag (of silk), a large cut glass on pillars supported by two swords, a bugle, a windmill, a fort with several cannon, a violin and a bow.

Sunderland, Wear. A silk banner with the arms of Messrs. White and Young, a large cut vase and cover, two chandeliers with branches ornamented with coloured button drops, cut decanters, wines, a windmill at work, goblets with engraving of Burns's song " Willie brew'd," a Bible lying open with two verses of the Proverbs, a glass case containing a ship, the *Henry*, mounting twenty-four guns, three glass cases containing a Cossack, another a gentleman driving a gig with his dog following him, and the third a representation of His Infernal Majesty. . . . The cutters had a rose, thistle, and shamrock supporting the feather in their caps.

Durham. A flag (silk) with the Gateshead arms on one side, etc., a large Prussian lamp obscured, and a painted figure of Justice, 28 swords, a crown of gilded glass with 2 tassels, cut candlesticks mounted with spangles and icicles, a crown borne by a person wearing a glass hat with the motto " Industry and Unity," a representation in stained, painted, and engraved glass declaring the judgment of God in Eli's house.

The details of this interesting list show the French and German influence which has been mentioned above (pp. 287 *sq.*). Some of the objects, *e.g.* the candlesticks with " spangles " (=drops) and " icicles," are quite familiar. Some others are met with only rarely, *e.g.* swords and models of ships. Of the more unusual objects a few examples may still exist, probably in families descended from a glassmaker, but the present writer at any rate has never seen an Infernal Majesty or a gentleman in a gig. These amusements are an opportunity for dealers who work the north of England ; and for fakers too. The list

[333]

also exhibits the low Protestantism, or gospel of work with which glassmaking, like pottery, has been usually associated in England (*cf.* p. 275).

Some notes of other toys may be added. *Birds and beasts*, as blown by the prestidigitator of 1702, are not common, but one sometimes sees pigs with a multi-coloured core overlaid with clear glass, and very small animals of egg-shell glass. These date from the latter part of the 18th century or early 19th century, but there is no ground for thinking they were made exclusively at Bristol or Nailsea. *Boot-shaped glasses* of clear, blue, and white opaque glass were also made. There is a tradition that they were derision for John Stuart, third Earl of Bute (1714–92), a favourite of George III and a shuffling politician. He collided with John Wilkes, who attacked him in the *North Briton*, and he was suspected of a liaison with Augusta, Princess of Wales. The populace always disliked him and after Wilkes's trial in 1763 a jack-boot and a petticoat were burnt by the mob. This seems to be the origin of glass jack-boots, but they were made until the end of the 18th century, and for a friendlier purpose. Long curved *tobacco-pipes* of clear flint glass, clear potash glass, blue glass, and white opaque glass were made in the latter part of the 18th century, not for use but as curiosities, and perhaps for glassmakers' processions. *Trumpets* in clear glass and blue glass are found not infrequently. They date from the same period as the last and were made for use. Bristol glasshouses made them and at Newcastle-on-Tyne a salute was sounded on a glass trumpet when a new Mayor was elected. Surviving specimens are quite blowable by a skilled trumpeter. *Walking-sticks* were made of clear glass, and of clear glass enclosing a twist of coloured enamel. The technique is substantially the same as that of the colour-twist stems, and some examples in Mrs. Applewhaite Abbott's collection are certainly as early as 1740–50. I know of no reference to them in advertisements, but there is no reason for thinking that only Bristol made them. *Swords* were made for processions at Bristol and Newcastle ; an example at South Kensington appears, from the treatment of the haft, to date from about 1750. The manufacture of *paper-weights* of *millifiori* glass was certainly due to French influence. They may have been first introduced at Nailsea (p. 286) and been carried thence to Spon Lane ; Birmingham and Stourbridge were certainly the chief centre for them. They attained their greatest popularity at the time of the Great Exhibition (1851). A number of canes of coloured glass, sliced to show the section, were laid together in a pattern and then enclosed in a mass of clear glass. The resulting designs are sometimes not without merit, but both in design and technique the French examples are superior.

TERMINOLOGY

Here is added a list of the more important or obscure terms used in glass studies, sometimes best explained by a reference to the illustrations. The list includes, (1) technical terms used by glassmakers themselves (some of them obsolete), which should form the basis of any terminology of the subject, (2) traditional phrases used by collectors and dealers, and (3) a few terms which it has been necessary to coin. The latter have only been used where no apt term was available ; but " without names nothing can be established."

Acorn, a tooled motive in stems and less frequently in lid handles ; for example see Plate L. 3. Hence *acorn-stem*=a glass in whose stem this motive predominates.

Air-twist, (1) spiral threads of air in the stem (or occasionally the handle) of a glass, made by nicking a blob of molten metal and then pulling it out with a twisting motion :
(2) A wine-glass with stem thus made.

Angular knop, a flat horizontal knop with acute edge (see Plate LII. 1).

Annealing (mixed deriv. from *an-* priv. with old Eng. aelan=bake, and old Fr. *neeler* to enamel, from late Lat. *nigellare*), the gradual cooling of hot glass by a deliberate process. See *leer*.

Annular stem. For example see Plates LVIII, LXXXVIII. 3.

Arch-and-sprig, a repetitive motive in cutting, found mainly round the lower part of the bowls of wine-glasses. For example see Fig. 25.

Ball-knop, a large spherical knop. See Plate XCI.

Baluster, (1) a stem or shaft formation derived from the calyx tube of the wild pomegranate (Gr. βαλαύστιον). In glass there are two pure baluster forms, the true baluster, less common (*e.g.* Fig. 16, A), and the inverted baluster (*e.g.* Fig. 16, B).
(2) A glass whose stem consists solely of one of the pure balusters (*e.g.* Fig. 16, G, 1).
(3) A glass whose stem combines one of the pure balusters with other motives.
The term baluster is correctly used in each of these three references. It is also applied loosely to stems which resemble a baluster or seem to be a degraded form of it. Both the baluster forms are, however, so well defined and so important stylistically that this latter application is misleading.

Balustroid. B. stems are those which resemble one of the two pure balusters or seem to be a degraded form of it.

Barilla (also *borillo*), (1) a sodiferous plant growing in Spain.
(2) Refined soda prepared from it by burning and used by the Venetians. See p. 11.

Batch, the prepared materials mixed in due proportions and ready for founding in the glass pots.

Bell-bowl, one of the waisted bowl forms in wine-glasses due to German influence ; *e.g.* Plates LXXXVII. 5, CVI. 3.

Blowing-iron, an iron tube from two to five feet long. A mass of molten metal is gathered from the crucible on one end and blown out into a hollow vessel by the application of the lips at the other.

Bocca (Ital.), mouth or opening in the side of a glass furnace for access to the glass pots. Also a hole in the side of the tower for setting glasses in position for annealing.

Bocellas, see *nose-holes*.

Boy, the master glassmaker's third assistant, sometimes called the taker-in because he carries the finished glasses to the leer.

Bullet knop, a small round knop which breaks the line of the stem. Called by Betts an " olive button."

TERMINOLOGY

Caulker (Ital. *calcaria* ; Merret, *calcar*), the furnace in which the sand or other siliceous material was burnt before it was fit to become an ingredient in the batch.

Cavalet, the iron ring surrounding the circular opening (*occhio* or *lumella*) between the furnace proper and the upper compartment (or *tower*, *q.v.*) where the annealing of the finished articles began.   Merret, p. 243.

Cavillator, the central block of clay enclosed by the concentric rings which form the crown of the furnace.   The modern use of the word is different from Merret's use of *cava-let*, *q.v.*

Chair, (1) a wooden bench at which the gaffer or master glassmaker works when he is tooling a vessel (Fig. 8).   It has no back and flat arms projecting in front.   See Chap. I.

(2)   The group of glassmakers working under a single "master" at his chair.

Conciator (Lat. *concieo*), the man who mixes the frit and attends to the caulker.   Merret, p. 240.

Consore =*conciator*.

Courbeilles ajourées, Liège name for pincered basketwork bowls as in Plate XCIX. *b.*

Cristallo, see *crystal*.

Crown =cavalet, *q.v.*

Crucibles =glass pots, *q.v.*

Crystal   (1)   Natural rock-crystal.

(2)   Synthetic crystal, *i.e.* fine glass of all kinds.

(3)   Venetian *cristallo*, a special variety of glass made with Alpine marble quartz and Levantine vegetable soda, distinguished at Venice from *vetro commune* made with coarse alkali from unrefined vegetable ashes.

(4)   In the 18th and 19th centuries *crystal* was in France applied to English lead glass (flint glass), continental soda glass being *verre*.

Cullet (Fr. *collet*=collar), a jagged circuit of glass surrounding the end of the blowing-iron after the vessel has been detached from it.   This rough glass was broken off and collected.   Hence *cullet* was extended to broken glass generally, which was collected both inside and outside the glasshouse to assist the fusion of future batches.   Merret, p. 277.

Cusp, a point at which two branches of a curve meet and stop.   In *cusped stems* (*e.g.* Plate CVI. 3) the cusp is a survival of a half-way knop, modified by cutting.

Cyst, a protuberance at the base of a wine-glass bowl.   See for example Plate LII. 1 and 3.

Diamond, (1) engraving instrument.

(2) motives in cutting ; see Figs. 24–28, 32, 34, A, B, F.

Domed foot, of two kinds : (1) the *sloping dome*, Plate LVI. *b.* 3, and (2) the *square dome*, Plate LVI. *b.* 1.

Double-ogee bowl.   For examples see Plates XLIX, LXIII. 3, LXX, LXXI, XCIV, XCV. 2.

As a description this term is often meaningless, but the group of bowls to which it refers is well defined, and the term has the sanction of long usage and general recognition.

Drawn stem, the stem of a vessel (usually a drinking-glass) made by pulling out a gathering of metal at the base of the bowl.

Drop-knop stem, a wine-glass stem part of which is in the shape of a frustum of a cone ; *e.g.* Plates XLVIII. 2, XLIX. *a.* 1 and 3, *b.* 1, LI. 2.

Eye (Ital. *occhio* and *lumella*), the central or hottest part of a furnace ; used by Merret of an opening in a three-story furnace between the melting chamber and the annealing chamber (tower).

TERMINOLOGY

Flint glass, (1) glass in which the siliceous ingredient is derived from calcined flints.

(2) glass made with lead oxide as the flux and sand as the siliceous ingredient. So called because English glass subsequently fused with lead had formerly been made with a flint silicate.

Flute, (1) a tall drinking-glass for wine or ale, with long narrow bowl. See p. 315.

(2) a vertical groove or channel ; in glass it is used also of a long narrow flat panel.

Flux, alkaline or metallic substance included in the batch to fuse the silica. See p. 10.

Foot-maker, the second assistant of the master glassmaker, employed *inter alia* for making the feet of wine-glasses.

Found, the time taken between the placing of the frit in the crucibles and its fusion into molten metal.

Founder, see *mixer* and *founding*.

Founding (Fr. *fondre*), the melting of the frit.

Fraiches or *fraches* (Fr. *fraiche* = a cool meadow), iron pans in which the finished articles are stood during annealing. In the tunnel-leer they have wheels and follow one another in a chain from the hotter to the cooler end.

Frigger, an experimental or apprentice piece.

Frit (Ital. *fritta*), generally synonymous with *batch*, *q.v.* ; but Merret used " frit " also of partially fused materials kept ready for founding or for making up into special batches for enamels, coloured glass, etc. See Merret, p. 271.

Gadget, a spring clip attached to the puntee to hold the foot of a wine-glass and so avoid leaving a puntee-mark.

Gadroons, convex curves used with a decorative intention.

Glass-pots, large clay vessels about four to five feet high with an aperture in one side (Fig. 2) which hold the prepared materials or batch and stand in the furnace. They were originally open at the top ; covered pots were introduced when coal fuel became compulsory (1615).

Hemispherical bowl. For examples see Plates V. 1, LXXII. 1, LXVII. *a.* 3.

Herring-bone fringe, a motive in " miniature " cutting ; see Fig. 34, E.

Inset bowl, a bowl which is partly let into the top of the stem, not superimposed upon it. See p. 182 and Plate XLIV. 3.

Iron = *blowing-iron*, *q.v.*

Jockey, a small pot or crucible which can stand on top of a large pot in the furnace.

Journey (Fr. *journée*), the total time for melting and working a batch of ingredients.

Knop, a protuberance, hollow or solid, in the stem of a glass vessel. This term may be restricted to protuberances which break the line of the stem. For undulations in a stem *wavy knop* is perhaps the most convenient term.

Knop-and-baluster, type of stem composed of a ball knop above a simple inverted baluster, *e.g.* Plate XXXIII. 1.

Lead glass, (1) glass fused with an oxide of lead (litharge = protoxide of lead, minium = dioxide of lead).

(2) a glass paste made at Venice and especially suitable for taking colours ; lead was a considerable ingredient. Neri, Lib. IV, and Merret's notes, p. 315.

Leer (derivation doubtful), the structural apparatus for cooling molten or very hot glass gradually (annealing).

(1) In very primitive glassworks the vessels were annealed simply by placing

z

them in the topmost compartment of the melting furnace (the *tower*) and leaving them to cool *in situ* as best they might.

(2) In the English glasshouses of the 17th and doubtless also for most of the 18th century the leer had two parts, (*a*) the tower of the melting furnace where the cooling process began, and (*b*) the leer proper, a tunnel-shaped passage about five or six yards long running between the tower and a room called the Sarosel (*q.v.*). Along this passage the glasses were slowly drawn on trays, whence they were taken by the saroleman in the sarosel. Merret, pp. 243–4.

(3) Since the latter part of the 18th century the leer has been a separate structure, a tunnel with a furnace below it. The iron pans are fitted with wheels and move in a continuous chain from the hotter to the cooler end of the tunnel (*cf.* pp. 39–40).

Leer-pans, see *fraiches*.

Linnet-holes, holes in the side of the caulker or fritting furnace to admit the heat from the main melting furnace. Merret, p. 244.

Marver (Fr. *marbre*), a slab originally of marble but usually of iron, on which the paraison was rolled ; it is used alternately with blowing for determining the shape of simpler types of vessel.

Merese, a sharp-edged button between the bowl and stem of a wine-glass ; see Plate XLIII. *a.* 1.

Metal, the substance glass considered as a technical medium. The word is applied both to molten glass and to the hard glass of finished objects. Its use dates from the beginning of the 17th century.

Milchglas, German name for white opaque glass. See p. 24.

Mixer, the workman who mixes the raw materials and attends to the founding ; hence called by Merret the *founder*.

Multiple knops, equal knops repeated as in the stem of Plates LXIII. 3, XCIX. *a.* 2.

Mushroom knop, a protuberance, shaped like a mushroom, in the stem of a vessel, *e.g.* Plate XLIX. *b.* 3.

"*Nipt diamond waies.*" This ornament was executed by applying vertical ribs round the sides of a vessel at equal intervals and then pinching them together to form diamond-shaped reticulations ; see Fig. 7 (Ravenscroft).

Nose-holes (=*bocellas*), small holes in the side of the furnace for withdrawing a sample of metal for inspection.

Ogee-bowl. For examples see Plate CXX.

Olive button. See *bullet knop*.

Paraison (Fr. *paraison*, *paraisonner*, from *parer*), the mass of molten metal at the end of the blowing-iron.

Passago (Ital.), a kind of iron callipers for hollowing out or " branching " the bowl of a glass. Merret, p. 247.

Pâte de riz, French term for opaque white glass (see p. 24).

Pedestal foot, see Plate LXXV. 2.

Piling pots (Merret, p. 246) ; see *jockey*.

Pillar flutes, curved convex panels on the outside of a decanter or other vessel.

Porteglo (Ital.), a skimming ladle for removing the sandever from the surface of molten glass.

Potash glass, glass fused with unrefined vegetable ashes, called at Venice *vetro commune*, in Germany *Waldglas*, in France *verre de fougère*.

Procello, *procellas* (Ital.), iron calipers for widening the bowl.

TERMINOLOGY

Prunt, a seal or button of glass, plain or moulded, applied to the stem or bowl of a glass for ornament, or for improving the grip.

Puntee, ponte, pontil (Ital. *ponteglo*), a solid iron rod, fixed in the hot metal at one end of an article and revolved on the arms of the chair with the workman's left hand, while he tools or trims the article with his right. Vessels are transferred from the blowing-iron to the puntee during fabrication.

Puntee-mark, pontil-mark, the mark left on a glass when it has snapped off from the end of the puntee ; almost always found on the base or foot and sometimes polished subsequently.

Purlee ornament, either a moulded diaper resembling pearls or looped and applied threads (purled). For discussion of this point see p. 128.

Quatrefoil knop, a knop or hollow bulb made in four lobes, either upright (Plate X) or spiral (Plate XXXVII). See p. 176. *Quatrefoil stem,* a stem with knop of this kind.

Quocoli, pebbles of white marble from which the Venetians derived their silica. See p. 7.

Rocchetta, refined vegetable soda prepared from sea-border plants of the Eastern Mediterranean.

Roemer, Römer, a German drinking vessel copied and adapted in England ; for examples see Plates XVI, XXXIX, XLI. "The Romer for Rhenish wine, for Sack, Claret, Beer, plain moulded coloured in whole or in part." Merret, pp. 225-6.

Rounded-funnel bowl (r.f. bowl), a bowl type for wine-glasses and some few other vessels ; a long and fairly narrow bowl maintaining its convex curvature throughout. See for examples Plate XLIV. 1–2.

Rummer, (1) anglicized form of *Römer* current in the 17th and 18th centuries, and probably referring to glasses of type seen in Plate XLI.

(2) a distinct form of drinking-glass probably introduced about the middle of the 18th century and common about 1780–1830. Used for rum *inter alia ;* but probably both name and shape are survivals of the German *Römer.*

Sandever (an anglicization of Fr. *suint de verre* = glass sweat), scum which rises to the surface of the molten glass in the crucibles, owing to impure ingredients or wrong proportions.

Saroleman = shoreman, q.v.

"The sarole-men those who draw the fraches along the leer and take them thence." Merret, p. 244.

Sarosel, the room in which the shoreman or saroleman works.

Scallop, a bivalve mollusc whose shell is edged all round with small semicircular lobes. Hence *scalloping* in glass = the cutting of rims in a curved outline.

Serpent formation in stems and lid handles. See for examples Plates XIX, XXVIII, XXX.

Servitor, the first assistant of the master glassmaker.

Shank, the 18th-century word for the stem of a glass.

Shoreman, the workman who tends the leer and removes the finished articles from the pans. *Cf. saroleman* from which the word is derived.

Shouldered stem. See Plate LXXXV and p. 171.

Siege (Fr. *siège*), the bed of the furnace where the glass-pots stand during the founding of the metal.

Silesian stem = shouldered stem, *q.v.*

Skittle, a small pot (or crucible) in which are mixed colouring matters and enamels ; so called from its shape.

Soda glass, glass fused with pure prepared soda usually derived from Levantine *rocchetta* or Spanish *barilla,* both plants of the *kali* family.

TERMINOLOGY

Spiei, a hooked and pointed iron for extracting a specimen of molten glass from the glass-pots during the found. Merret, p. 241.

Stampirons, iron moulds closed by pressure of the foot. Merret, p. 247.

Stitches, stoke-holes. Merret, p. 242.

Straight-funnel bowl (s.f. bowl), a bowl shaped as the frustum of an inverted cone.

Stuck shank, a stem made from a separate piece of glass and then welded on to the base of the bowl.

Tale glass, glass from the bottom of the pot of metal.

Tarso, marble quartz used by the Venetians to provide a silica base.

Tear, a bubble of air enclosed in the metal of a glass, usually in knobs, stems, the bases of bowls, or other thick parts ; either irregular in shape and accidental or regular and intentional.

Tease-hole (Ital. *tizzonaio*), stoke-hole.

Teaser (Fr. *tiseur*), stoker.

Terraced foot, a foot tooled in concentric terraces. See p. 185 and for example Plate LII.

Thistle-bowl, one of the waisted bowl forms in wine-glasses due to German influence ; *e.g.* Plate LXXXVI. 3.

Tiseur, see *teaser*.

Tower, the uppermost chamber of the melting furnace where the annealing of finished articles was begun.

Trailed ornament, looped threads of glass applied on the surface of a glass vessel ; perhaps =*purlee*, *q.v.*

Trefoil repeat, a motive in rim-cutting, commonest about 1790. See Plate CVII. 3.

Triple-ring knop. For examples see Plates LXX. 1, XCVII. 2, CIII. 2.

Trumpet-bowl, one of the waisted bowl forms in wine-glasses due to German influence ; *e.g.* Plate LXXXVII.

Vermicular collar, a wavy rope of glass encircling a stem or neck. See p. 175 and Plates IX, XVI. 1.

Verre d'albâtre, French term for opaque white glass. See p. 24.

Verre de foug're. See *potash glass.*

Verres fresés (" pock-marked glasses "), glasses with pearled ornament moulded ; Netherlandish term.

Vetro commune. See *potash glass.*

Waldglas. See *potash glass.*

Wavy knop. See *knop.*

Weighing-room, the room at the end of the leer where the finished articles were weighed for the excise duty=Merret's *sarosel.*

Wing-bowl, a wine-glass bowl of which the lower part is pressed out in wings (*e.g.* Plate XXVII. 1).

Wing-stem, a 17th-century stem of which the upper part is pressed out in wings (*e.g.* Plate XXVI. 1).

Wormed glasses, glasses whose stems contain spiral twists of air, coloured glass, or enamel, an 18th-century trade word. (Thomas Betts's lists.)

Wrything, external twisting of stem or bowl. For examples see Plates XXII, LXV.

SELECT BIBLIOGRAPHY

IT is only possible here to offer a general guide to the contemporary *sources*. From the list which follows (§A below) works which contain only an occasional reference to glass or glassmakers have been omitted, as also literary works which contain allusions to glass. The best hunting-grounds in 17th and 18th-century literature may be classified as follows :—

A. MANUSCRIPT.

        Household accounts.
        Trade accounts.
        Letters.
        Legal documents, especially those in possession of the Glass Sellers Company.
        Parish Registers.

B. PRINTED.

        Newspaper advertisements.
        Documents printed in the Calendar of State Papers.
        Manuals of technique, including dictionaries of the arts.
        Works on local history, especially works on London and the early county histories.
        Works on domestic economy.
        Broadsides and pamphlets.
        Almanacks and trade guides.

I give below a list of the more important works which I have consulted ; Howell, Merret, Plot, Houghton, Dossie and Bosc d'Antic are the most useful. In the bibliography proper the letter (A) follows works which reprint 18th-century advertisements, while (M) indicates those which contain reprints or abstracts of MSS. Included in the list of sources are some modern and other works which do not deal specifically with glass but contain relevant matter.

There is no satisfactory *bibliography* of the art of glass in England. The hand list of books on the silicate industries issued by the Patent Office is the nearest approach to one, but its contents are largely technological and much valuable work has been done since it was published (1914). Hartshorne, Buckley, and in a lesser degree Powell, are the only books which approach the subject from the point of view of art-history. Hartshorne is now chiefly valuable for the excellent introductory notices on continental glassmaking, and the MS. and other sources printed in the Appendices. The text contains a great mass of information, but one cannot refer to it often without wishing that the author's skill in arranging and using his material had been equal to his industry in collecting it. Many of Hartshorne's conclusions have since been superseded and he was considerably handicapped by the collectors' categories, which beset so much writing on glass history. But in its day it was a remarkable book and a tribute to the solid methods of the Victorian antiquary. Mr. Buckley's great advance lies in the use of contemporary advertisements, but his excellent *History* only deals with the 18th century. Mr. Westropp's book also is limited in scope. Powell's *Glassmaking in England* has the advantage of being written by a practical glassmaker, but it contains no critical apparatus and is at times misleading.

Beyond these books the literature follows the interests of the antiquarian or the collector and little notice has been given to technique. The antiquarian literature consists largely of papers published in the proceedings of local societies, many of them very valuable, but difficult of access. The literature of collecting includes (*a*) handbooks for collectors, (*b*) several illustrated works dealing with particular private collections, and (*c*) magazine articles. The small handbooks are very indifferent ; Percival is much the best of them.

SELECT BIBLIOGRAPHY

The magazine literature varies very much, most of it being chatter. The following lists contain a selection of these three types, together with some of the more useful books on continental glass. The contacts between England and other countries are so frequent at all periods that these are indispensable.

A. PRINCIPAL SOURCES

ADVERTISEMENTS, trade notices, notices of bankruptcy, etc., mainly collected from 18th-century newspapers, and published by Mr. Francis Buckley in his *History of Old English Glass*, and his articles in the Transactions of the Society of Glass Technology ; *q.v.*

AGRICOLA (G.). De Re Metallica. Basle, 1556.

AMORETTI (C.) and SOAVE (F.). Scelti opuscoli sulle scienze. Vol. XI. Milan, 1788.

APPENDICES to Hartshorne's *Old English Glasses*. Deeds, letters, extracts, etc., mainly of 16th and 17th centuries.

BEWICK (T.). A Memoir of Thomas Bewick Written by Himself. London and Newcastle-on-Tyne, 1862.

BIRCH (T.). History of the Royal Society of London. 4 vols. London, 1756–7.

BLAND (A. E.), BROWN (P. A.), and TAWNEY (R. H.). Select documents illustrative of English history. London, 1914. [M.]

BOSC D'ANTIC (P.). Œuvres : contenant plusieurs mémoires sur l'art de la verrerie, sur la faiencerie, la poterie, l'art des forges, la mineralogie, l'électricité et sur la medicine. 2 vols. Paris, 1780.

BOYLE (R.). The Sceptical Chymist. Latin ed., London, 1668 ; English ed., Oxford, 1680.
—— Works of R. B. Abridged by T. Shaw. 3 vols. London, 1823.

BRISTOL. Bristol Guide. Bristol, 1815.

BRITISH MUSEUM. Sloane MS. 857. *Papers relating to the Glass Sellers.*
—— Tracts relating to Trade. B.M. 816. M. 12.

BUCKLE (H. T.). History of Civilization in England. 3 vols. Oxford (World's Classics edition).

Calendar of State Papers : Domestic, Venetian, Ireland.

CARY (J.). An Essay on the State of England in Relation to its Trade. Bristol [1695].
—— A Discourse on Trade. 2 ed. London, 1745.

CHAMBERS (E.). Cyclopedia. London, var. ed., 1728–88.

Dictionarium Polygraphicum. London, 1735.

Dictionary of Arts and Sciences. 4 vols. London, 1754.

Dictionary of National Biography. Articles on Sir Jerome Bowes, Sir Robert Mansell, Christopher Merret, John Houghton, Robert Plot, Sir Edward Zouche, William Lewis, Apsley Pellatt.

DOSSIE (R.). Handmaid to the Arts. 2 vols. London, 1 ed. 1758 ; 2 ed. 1764. Cited as " Dossie."

DUDLEY (D.). Metallum Martis. London, 1665.

ELLIS (SIR H.). Original Letters illustrative of English History. 3 vols. London, 1824. [M.]

ERACLIUS. De coloribus et artibus Romanorum. In MERRIFIELD (M. P.). Original Treatises . . . on the Arts of Painting, etc. London, 1849.

Glass Manufactures of Birmingham and Stourbridge. Birmingham (privately printed), 1851. Cited as " Glass Manufactures."

GLASS SELLERS COMPANY. Essays on the Glass Trade in England. London, 1883.

GLASS SELLERS COMPANY. MSS. including deeds and the Court Minutes of the Company.

SELECT BIBLIOGRAPHY

GRAZEBROOK (H. S.). Collections for a Genealogy of the Noble Families of Hennezel, etc. Stourbridge (privately printed), 1877. [M.]

Guildhall Tracts.

HAUDICQER DE BLANCOURT (F.). L'art de la verrerie. Paris, 1697. English ed., London, 1699.

HOUGHTON (J.). A Collection of Letters for the Improvement of Husbandry and Trade. London, 1681–3 and 1692–1703.

HOWELL (J.). Epistolæ Ho-Elianæ. . . . Familiar Letters Domestic and Forren. London, 1645. Edited by J. Jacobs, London, 1890.

HUGUENOT SOCIETY OF LONDON. Publications. Vol. IV, Registres des Baptismes, Mariages et Morts et Jeusnes de l'église Wollonne et des isles de Jersey, Guernsey, Serq, Origny, etc., établie à Southampton. Edited by H. M. Godfray. Lymington, 1910.

—— Vol. VIII, Letters of denization and acts of naturalization for aliens in England, 1509–1603. Edited by William Page. Lymington, 1893.

—— Vol. X, Returns of aliens dwelling in the City and Suburbs of London from the reign of Henry VIII to that of James I. Edited by R. E. G. Kirk and Ernest F. Kirk. Aberdeen, Part 1 (1523–71), 1900 ; Part 2 (1571–97), 1902.

JACKSON (C. J.). Illustrated History of English Plate. London, 1911. Cited as " Jackson."

Journals of the House of Commons.

KUNCKEL (J.). Ars Vitraria Experimentalis. Amsterdam and Dantzig, 1679.

LABARTE (J.). Histoire des arts industriels du Moyen Age à l'époque de la Renaissance. 4 vols. and album (2 vols.). Paris, 1864–6.

LEWIS (W.). Commercium Philosophico-technicum. London, 1763. Cited as " Com. Phil. Tech."

London Gazette.

LOYSEL (J. B.). Essai sur l'art de la verrerie. Paris, 1799–1800.

MARCASSUS DE PUYMAURIN (A. DE). Mémoires, pp. 78–92. De la acide fluorique, de son action sur la terre siliceuse et de l'application de cette propriété à la gravure sur verre. Paris, 1811.

MATTHESIUS (J.). Sarepta oder Bergpostil. Nuremberg, 1562.

MERRET (C.). The Art of Glass, 1662. See NERI (A.). L'arte Vetraria. Florence, 1612.

NASH (T.). Collections for the History of Worcestershire. 2 vols. London, 1781.

NERI (A.). L'arte Vetraria. Florence, 1612.

—— Translated with observations [by Christopher Merret]. London, 1662.

—— Antonii Neri Florentini de Arte Vetraria Libri VII et in eosdem Christopher Merretti M.D. et Societatis Regiae Socii Observationes et Notæ. Amsterdam, 1686.

NERI (A.), MERRET (C.), and KUNCKEL (J.). L'art de la verrerie de Neri, Merret et Kunckel. Paris, 1752.

OWEN (H.). Two Centuries of Ceramic Art in Bristol. London, 1873. [M.] Cited as " Owen."

PELLATT (A.). Glass Manufactures. London, 1821.

—— Memoir on the Origin of Glassmaking. London, 1845.

—— Curiosities of Glassmaking. London, 1849.

PLINIUS SECUNDUS (C.). Naturalis Historiæ libri XXXVII. Ed. L. Janus and C. Mayhoff. 6 vols. Leipzig (Teubner) 1870–98.

The more important *loci* for glass are :

General, XXXVI, 191–9.

Sand from River Belus, V, 75.

SELECT BIBLIOGRAPHY

Sidon, V, 76.
Wheel-cutting, XXXVI, 159, 193 ; VII, 198.
Nitrum, XXXI, 110.
Magnes lapis, XXXIV, 148.
Alabandicus lapis, XXXVI, 62.
Obsianum, XXXVI, 196.
Coloured glass, XXXV, 46.
Imitation of natural stones, XXXV, 48 ; XXXVI, 197 ; XXXVII, 83, 98, 112, 117, 128.   Flexible glass, XXXVI, 195.
Theatrical use of glass, XXXVI, 114, 189.

PLOT (R.). The Natural History of Oxfordshire. Oxford [1677].
—— The Natural History of Staffordshire. Oxford, 1686.
PORTER (G. R.). Treatise on the Origin . . . of the Manufacture of Porcelain and Glass. London, 1830.
POUNTNEY (W. J.). Old Bristol Potteries. Bristol, 1920.

RAMSEY (W.). History of the Worshipful Company of the Glass Sellers of London. London, 1898. [M.]
ROVENZON (J.). A Treatise of Metallica. London, 1613.

SALZMAN (L. F.). English Industries in the Middle Ages. Oxford, 1923.
SCHUERMANS (H.). Lettres sur la verrerie. Published in the Belgian *Bulletins de la Commission Royale sur l'Art et l'Archéologie*. Vols. XIX–XXXI. Brussels, 1883–91. Based on MS. Cited as " Schuermans."
SCOTTISH HISTORY SOCIETY. Publications, second series, Vol. I. BAILLIE (LADY GRISELL). The Household Books of Lady Grisell Baillie, 1692–1733. Edited by R. Scott-Moncrieff. Edinburgh, 1911. [M.]
SECRETS. Valuable Secrets in Arts and Trades. London, 1758.
SEYMOUR (R.). Survey of London and Westminster. London, 1735.
SIMON (A. L.). History of the Wine Trade in England. 3 vols. London, 1906–9.
—— Bottlescrew Days. London, 1926.
SOCIETY FOR THE ENCOURAGEMENT OF ARTS AND MANUFACTURES. Transactions, early numbers 1756—.
SPRAT (T.). History of the Royal Society of London for the Improving of Natural Knowledge. London, 1667.
STOW (J.). Survey of London. London, 1598.
—— The Chronicles of England. 1 ed. London, 1565.
—— Ditto, continued unto this present year of Christ, 1598. London, 1598.
—— A Survey of the Cities of London and Westminster . . . corrected . . . in the year 1720 by J. Strype. 2 vols. London, 1754–5.
STURTEVANT (S.). Metallica. London, 1612.

URE (A.). Dictionary of the Arts. London, 1853.

WALLACE (T.). Essay on the Manufactures in Ireland. Dublin, 1798.
WATTS (W. W.). Old English Silver. London, 1924.

YOUNG (A.). A Six Months' Tour through the North of England, containing an account of the present state of . . . Manufactures, etc. 4 vols. London, 1770–1.
—— A Tour in Ireland . . . made in the years 1776, 1777 and 1778, and brought down to the end of 1779. London, 1780.
YOUNG (S.). History of the Glass Sellers Company. London, 1913. [M.]

SELECT BIBLIOGRAPHY

B. Works on Glass—General

BUCKLEY (W.). European Glass. London, 1926. Cited as " W. Buckley."

DILLON (E.). Glass. London, 1907. [M.]

FOWLER (J.). On the process of decay in glass, and incidentally on the composition and texture of glass at different periods, and the history of its manufacture (1876). *Archæologia*, Vol. XLVI, p. 65 (1880).

GERSPACH (E.). L'art de la verrerie. Paris, 1885.

HARTSHORNE (A.). Old English Glasses. London, 1897. [M.] Cited as " Hartshorne."

HUDIG (F. W.). Das Glas. Vienna, 1925.

LONDON PATENT OFFICE. Subject List of Works on the Silicate Industries (Ceramics and Glass). London, 1914. Largely technological.

NESBITT (A.). Catalogue of the Collection of Glass formed by Felix Slade. London (privately printed), 1871.

—— Descriptive Catalogue of the Glass Vessels in the South Kensington Museum. London, 1878.

—— Glass. London, 1878. (South Kensington Museum Handbook).

PELIGOT (E. M.). Le verre, son histoire, sa fabrication. Paris, 1877.

SCHMIDT (R.). Das Glas. Berlin and Leipzig, 2 ed. 1922. Cited as " Schmidt."

WALLACE-DUNLOP (M. A.). Glass in the Old World. London [1884].

C. Works on Other than English and Irish Glass

AUGUST-MATIFEUX (C.). Les gentilhommes verriers de Mouchamps en Bas Poitou. *Annales de la Société Academique de Nantes.* Vol. XXXII. Nantes, 1861.

BEAUPRÉ (J. N.). Les gentilhommes verriers de Lorraine. 2 ed. Nancy, 1846.

BOUTILLIER (F.). La verrerie et les gentilhommes verriers de Nevers. Nevers, 1885.

BUCKLEY (W.). Diamond-engraved Glasses of the 16th Century. London, 1929.

CASTEELE (D. VAN DE). Lettre . . . sur l'ancienne verrerie Liègeoise. 2 ed. Liège, 1880.

CZIHAK (E. VON). Schlesischer Gläser . . . nebst einem beschreibenden Katalog der Gläsersammlung des Museums schlesischer Altertümer zu Breslau. Breslau, 1891. Cited as " Von Czihak."

FRIEDRICH (C.). Die altdeutscher Gläser. Beitrag zur Terminologie und Geschichte des Glases. Herausgegeben vom Bayerischen Gewerbemuseum in Nürnberg. Nuremberg, 1884.

HOUDOY (J.). Verrerie à la façon de Venise. Paris, 1873.

HUDIG (F. W.). Diamond-engraving. In BUCKLEY (W.). European Glass. London, 1926. Cited as " Hudig."

KISA (A.). Das Glas in Altertume. 3 vols. Leipzig, 1908.

LE VAILLANT DE LA FIEFFE (O.). Les verreries de la Normandie : les gentilhommes et artistes. Rouen, 1873.

PAZAUREK (G. E.). Gläser der Empire—und Biedermeierzeit. Leipzig, 1923.

PHOLIEN (F.). La verrerie au pays de Liège. Liège, 1900. Cited as " Pholien."

PINCHART (A.). Les fabriques de verres de Venise, d'Anvers et de Bruxelles au XVIᵉ et au XVIIᵉ siècle. In the Belgian *Bulletins des Commissions royales d'art et d'archéologie.* Vols. XXI, XXII. Brussels, 1882-3.

SELECT BIBLIOGRAPHY

RIAÑO (J. F.). The Industrial Arts in Spain. London, 1879 (South Kensington Museum Handbook).

SCHEBEK (E.). Böhmens Glasindustrie und Glashandel. Quellen zu ihrer Geschichte. Prague, 1878.

SCHMIDT (R.). Brandenburgische Gläser. Berlin, 1914.

—— Die Gläser der Sammlung Muhsam. Berlin, 1914.

—— Die Gläser der Sammlung Muhsam. Neue Folge. Berlin, 1922.

—— 100 Jahre österreichische Glaskunst. Vienna, 1924.

VENICE. LA GUIUNTA SPECIALE PER L'ESPOSIZIONE DI VENEZIA, 1873. Monographia della vetraria veneziana e muranese. Venice, 1874.

WETTERGREN (E.). Orreforsglas. Stockholm, 1921.

D. WORKS ON ENGLISH AND IRISH GLASS—GENERAL

BATE (P.). English Table Glass. London, 1905.

BLES (J.). Rare English Glasses of the 17th and 18th Centuries. London, 1926. Excellent illustrations with introductory notices. Cited as " Bles."

BUCKLEY (F.). History of Old English Glass. London, 1925. [A.] Cited as " Buckley " or " Buckley, *History*."

LEWIS (J. S.). Old Glass and How to Collect it. London, 1916.

PERCIVAL (M.). The Glass Collector. London, 1918.

POWELL (H. J.). Glassmaking in England. Cambridge, 1923. Cited as " Powell."

THORPE (W. A.). English and Irish Glass. London, 1927. Cited as " E.I.G."

WESTROPP (M. S. D.). Dublin Museum of Science and Art. General Guide to the Collections. Glass. Dublin, 1 ed. 1912 ; 2 ed. 1918.

—— Old Irish Glass. London, 1920. [A. and M.] Cited as " Westropp."

WILMER (D.). Early English Glass. London, 1910.

YOXALL (J. H.). Collecting Old Glass, English and Irish. London, 1916.

E. WORKS ON ENGLISH AND IRISH GLASS—SPECIAL

ADAMSON (C. E.). John Dagnia of South Shields, Glassmaker. Reprinted from the *Proceedings of the Society of Antiquaries of Newcastle-upon-Tyne*, Vol. VI, pp. 163–8. [Copy with MS. notes by J. C. Hodgson.] South Shields (privately printed), 1894.

BATE (P.). An Eighteenth-century Industry : Bristol Enamel Glass. *Magazine of Fine Arts*, VII, 151 (1905).

BOWLES (W. H.). History of the Vauxhall and Ratcliff Glasshouses and their Owners. London (privately printed), 1926. Cited as " Bowles."

BUCKLEY (F.). English Baluster-stemmed Glasses of the Seventeenth and Eighteenth Centuries. Edinburgh (privately printed), 1912.

—— Old London Drinking Glasses. Edinburgh (privately printed), 1913.

—— The Glass Trade in England in the 17th Century. London (privately printed), 1914. (MSS., etc.) Cited as " Buckley, *Glass Trade*."

—— The Taxation of English Glass in the Seventeenth Century. London (privately printed), 1914. (MSS., etc.) Cited as " Buckley, *Taxation*."

—— Old London Glasshouses. London (privately printed), 1915.

—— Development of English Cut-glass in the Eighteenth Century. *Burlington Magazine*, Vol. XLV, p. 299 (1924).

—— Note on the Glasshouses of the Leeds District. *Transactions of the Society of Glass Technology*, Vol. VIII, p. 268 (1924). [A.]

SELECT BIBLIOGRAPHY

Buckley (F.)   The Development of the Wine-glass in the 19th Century.   *Glass*, Vol. I, p. 441 (1924).
—— Cruet Bottles of the 18th Century.   *Glass*, Vol. I, p. 489 (1924).
—— Lancashire Glasshouses of the 18th Century.   *Glass*, Vol. I, p. 537 (1924).
—— Bottles [mainly medicine phials].   *Glass*, Vol. II, p. 618 (1925).
—— Early Glasshouses of Bristol.   *Transactions of the Society of Glass Technology*, Vol. IX, p. 36 (1925). [A.]
—— Glasshouses on the Wear in the Eighteenth Century.   *Transactions of the Society of Glass Technology*, Vol. IX, p. 105 (1925). [A.]
—— Nottingham Glasshouses.   *Transactions of the Society of Glass Technology*, Vol. X, p. 270 (1926). [A.]
—— Glasshouses on the Tyne in the Eighteenth Century.   *Transactions of the Society of Glass Technology*, Vol. X, p. 26 (1926). [A.]
—— Notes on the Glasshouses of Stourbridge 1700–1830.   *Transactions of the Society of Glass Technology*, Vol. XI, p. 106 (1927). [A.]
—— Glasshouses of Dudley and Worcester.   *Transactions of the Society of Glass Technology*, Vol. XI, p. 287 (1927). [A.]
—— Cassilari.   *Glass*, Vol. V, p. 103 (1928).
—— John Bellingham.   *Glass*, Vol. V, p. 150 (1928).
—— Sir Robert Mansell.   *Glass*, Vol. V, p. 199 (1928).
—— John Akerman [Glass Seller].   *Glass*, Vol. V, p. 247 (1928).
—— Thomas Betts.   *Glass*, Vol. V, p. 299 (1928).
—— The Duke of Buckingham.   *Glass*, Vol. V, p. 341 (1928).
—— Jerom Johnson.   *Glass*, Vol. V, p. 392 (1928).
—— Jackson.   *Glass*, Vol. V, p. 488 (1928).
—— Bowles.   *Glass*, Vol. V, p. 540 (1928).
—— Old Decanters.   *Country Life*, Vol. LXIV, No. 1664, p. xciv (8 Dec., 1928).
Buckley (W.).   Anglo-Dutch Glasses of the 18th Century.   *Old Furniture*, Vol. IV, p. 151 (1928).

Clark (G. T.).   Some Account of Sir Robert Mansel, Kt.   Dowlais (privately printed), 1883.

Clephan (J.).   The Manufacture of Glass in England.   The Rise of the Art on the Tyne. *Archæologia Æliana*, new series, Vol. VIII, p. 108 (1880).

Cope (E. E.).   Some Notes on the Warrington Glassworks.   *Connoisseur*, Vol. LXVII, p. 40 (1923).

Dawson (C.).   Old Sussex Glass.   *Antiquary*, Vol. XII, p. 8 (1905).

Francis (G. R.).   Jacobite Drinking Glasses.   Reprinted from the *British Numismatic Journal*, Vol. XVI, 1921–2.   London, 1925.
—— Old English Drinking Glasses.   London, 1926.   Cited as " Francis."

Gray (H. St. G.).   Notes on Nailsea Glass.   *Proceedings of the Somerset Archæological Society*, Vol. LII (2), p. 166.
—— Nailsea Glass.   *Connoisseur*, Vol. XXX, p. 85 (1911).
—— Notes on the Nailsea Glassworks.   *Connoisseur*, Vol. LXV, p. 127 (1923).
Gray (H. St. G.) and Lavington (M.).   Nailsea Glass in the Collection of Mr. J. Lane. *Connoisseur*, Vol. LVII, p. 67 (1920).

Halahan (Mrs. Brenda C.).   Chiddingfold Glass and its Makers in the Middle Ages. Paper read before the Newcomen Society, 21 April, 1925.
Hallen (A. W. C.).   Scottish Glass.   *Scottish Antiquary*, Vol. IV, p. 88 (1890), and Vol. V, p. 88 (1891).

Hewlett (S. G.).   Some Eighteenth-century Glass.   *Connoisseur*, Vol. LV, p. 81 (1919).

SELECT BIBLIOGRAPHY

HODGSON (J. C.). The family of Williams of Newcastle, Glass Manufacturers. *Proceedings of the Society of Antiquaries of Newcastle-upon-Tyne*, 3rd series, Vol. VII, p. 207.

HUGHES (G. B.). Old English Decanters and their Labels. *Old Furniture*, Vol. VI, p. 227 (1929).

HULME (E. W.). French Glassmakers in England. *Antiquary*, Vol. XXXIV, p. 142 (1898).

—— Old English Glasses. *Antiquary*, Vol. XXXIV, p. 112 (1898).

—— Note on Knole Glassmaking. *Antiquary*, Vol. XLI, p. 164 (1905).

—— On the Invention of English Flint Glass. Paper read before the Newcomen Society, 16 Dec., 1925.

KENWORTHY (J.). The early History of Stocksbridge and District, with an Account of some old Industries in Hunshelf and Waldershelf. Bolsterstone Glasshouse and its Place in the History of English Glassmaking. Deepcar, 1914.

LEEDS (E. T.). On the Dating of Glass Wine-bottles. *Antiquary*, Vol. L, p. 285 (1914).

LENNARD (T. B.). Glassmaking at Knole, Kent. *Antiquary*, Vol. XLI, p. 127 (1905).

McC. (J.). A rare Glass Tankard. *Connoisseur*, Vol. LXII, p. 165 (1922).

PRENTISS (E. L.). The Manufacture of Cut-glass. *Brush and Pencil*, Vol. XVI, p. 131 (1905).

PRICE (R.). Notes on the Evolution of the Wine-bottle. *Transactions of the Glasgow Archæological Society*, N.S., Vol. VI, Pt. 1, p. 116.

RACKHAM (B.). Three Elizabethan Glasses. *Burlington Magazine*, Vol. XXIV, p. 23 (1913).

—— Verzelini and his Followers. *Burlington Magazine*, Vol. XLVII, p. 182 (1925).

READ (H. E.). The Bles Collection of English Glass. *Burlington Magazine*, Vol. XLIII, p. 247 (1923).

—— Two Anglo-Venetian Glasses. *Burlington Magazine*, Vol. XLVIII, p. 277 (1926).

—— English Glasses in the Collection of Mr. John M. Bacon. *Connoisseur*, Vol. LXXVII, p. 201 (1926).

RISLEY (SIR J. S.). Old English Glasses with white spiral stems. *Burlington Magazine*, Vol. XXXIV, p. 219 (1919).

—— Sea Power under George III illustrated in contemporary Glass. *Burlington Magazine*, Vol. XXXV, p. 203 (1919).

—— Jacobite Wine-glasses. *Burlington Magazine*, Vol. XXXVI, p. 276 (1920).

—— Exhibition of Oxburgh and Berkley Glasses. *Burlington Magazine*, Vol. XXXVII, p. 51 (1920).

—— Georgian Electioneering Glasses. *Burlington Magazine*, Vol. XXXVII, p. 220 (1920).

—— Georgian Rummers. *Burlington Magazine*, Vol. XXXVIII, p. 271 (1921).

SALZMANN (L. F.). Sussex Glass. *Victoria County History of Sussex*, Vol. II, p. 254 (1907).

TAYLOR (MISS M. V.). Stourbridge Glass. *Victoria County History of Worcestershire*, Vol. II, pp. 278–82 (1906).

THORPE (W. A.). The Rees Price Collection of English Glass. *Apollo*, Vol. II, p. 25 (1925).

—— Jacobite Glasses in the Collection of Mr. C. Kirkby Mason. *Apollo*, Vol. III, p. 14 (1926).

—— Drinking Glasses Commemorative of William III. *Apollo*, Vol. III, pp. 165 and 210 (1926).

—— Anglo-Irish Glass. *Country Life*, Vol. LXI, p. xl (1927).

—— The Beilby Glasses. *Connoisseur*, Vol. LXXXI, p. 10 (1928).

SELECT BIBLIOGRAPHY

THORPE (W. A.). English Glass : some Specimens in the Collection of Lady Davy. *Country Life*, Vol. LXIV, p. iii (1928).
—— The Henry Brown Collection of English Glass. *Apollo*, Vol. VIII, pp. 141 and 208.
—— The Evolution of the Decanter. *Connoisseur*, Vol. LXXXIII, pp. 196 and 271 (1929).
TRAPNELL. Catalogue of the Trapnell Collection. London, n.d.
VARTY SMITH (J. C.). Concerning Old Pattern Books [of Ford's Glasshouse, Edinburgh]. *Queen*, 18 Sept., 1915.
WAY (H. W. L.). Glass Paper-weights. *Connoisseur*, Vol. LVIII, p. 222 (1920).
—— Apsley Pellatt's Glass Cameos in the Collection of Mrs. Applewhaite-Abbott. *Connoisseur*, Vol. LXII, p. 78 (1922).
—— Coloured Glass. *Connoisseur*, Vol. LXIV, p. 212 (1922).
WINKWORTH (W. W.). Seventeenth-century Glass in the Clements Collection. *Burlington Magazine*, Vol. XLIV, p. 289 (1924).
—— Cut-glass in the Collection of Robert Frank, Esq. *Old Furniture*, Vol. II, p. 188 (1927).
—— Moulded and Blown Glass in the Collection of Robert Frank, Esq. *Old Furniture*, Vol. III, p. 35 (1928).
WYLDE (C. H.). Mr. Charles Edward Jerningham's Collection of English Glasses. *Burlington Magazine*, Vol. IV, p. 131 (1904).
—— Drinking Vessels Painted in Enamel Colours. *Connoisseur*, Vol. X, p. 25 (1904).

F. WORKS MAINLY TECHNICAL

BONTEMPS (G.). Guide du verrier. Paris, 1868.
DUTHIE (A. L.). Decorative Glass Processes. London, 1907.
FLAMM (P.). Le verrier du XIXe siècle. Paris, 1863.
HENRIVAUX (M. J.). Le verre et le cristal. 2 vols. Paris, 1883.
HERMANN (F.). Painting on Glass and Porcelain and Enamel Painting. London, 1897.
KNOWLES (J. A.). Mediæval Processes of Glass Manufacture. *Glass*, July-September, 1927.
LOBMEYR (L.). Die Glasindustrie. Stuttgart, 1874.
MARSON (P.). Glass and Glass Manufacture. London [1918]. Cited as " Marson."
POWELL (H. J.). The Principles of Glassmaking. London, 1883.
STREHBLOW (H.). Der Schmuck des Glases. Leipzig, 1920.

INDEX TO VOLUMES I & II

The Arabic figures refer to page numbers in Volume I, and the Roman figures
to Plate numbers in Volume II

INDEX

INDEX

2 A

INDEX

Buckley, Francis, 83, 103, 153, 197, 212, 234, 240, 244
Buckley, Wilfred, 78, 82, 133, 136, 147
bugle, 333
Buré, Jan, 66
Burghley, Lord, 65, 79, 85
Burgundy, 64
Burke, 262
Burnell, Thomas, & Co., 264
Burnett, Thomas, 267, 279
Burnett, Thomas, and Glasshouse Company, 279
burning glasses, 211
Burroughs, 110
Butler's *Hudibras*, 314
butter-boats, CLVI
butter-coolers, 283
butter-dishes, 254, LXXV, CLX
butterflies, 241
Byng, Admiral, 306
Bywell, 228

C

Calabria, Jean de, 59
calcaria, 29
calcination, 8
calender, 212, XCV
callipers, 35
Camden, Wm., 57
candlesticks, 225, 246, 251, 255, 313, LIV, LV, LVI, LVII, LVIII, LIX, LXXXI, CXXXV, CXLIII, CLXI
canopies, XXVI, XXXIV, LXXVI, CXXXVIII, CXL, CXLI, CXLVII
Capel Street, 283
carbonic acid, 10
carnations, 241
Carré, Jean, 57, 61 *sq.*, 74, 268
Carter, George, 137
Carter, Mary, & Son, 286
Cary, John, 157, 158, 215
Casselari (Casiler, Cassilari), Domenico (Domenyck, Dominych), 64, 74, 75
Casselari, Josepo, 61, 62, 74
Castelli, family of, 73
casters, 284, CLIV
Catcliffe glasshouse, 70
Catherine of Braganza, VII
caulker, 29
Cavato, Thomaso, 62
Cecil, Lord, 62, 63, 85
celery glasses, CLX

cementation, 86
Central America, 86
" chair," 130, 164
Chambers, Ephraim, lexicographer, 14
champagne glasses, 308, 314, 322
champagne glasses, green half-moulded egg, 314
champagne glasses, Victorian, 314
Champney, Arthur, 137
Chance, R. L., 287
Chance, William, 286
Chances Bros. & Co., 287
Chances & Hartleys, 287
chandeliers, 251, 255, 315, 333, CXXXVIII, CXL, CXLVI, CXLVII, CLXIII
Charles I, 85, 110
Charles II, 13, 101, 107, 125, 155, 306, V, VI, VII
Charnock, T., 55, 58
Chartres, Bishop of, 63
Chatham, Earl of, 140
Chebsey, John, 284
Chebsey, Thomas, 284
Chelsea, 21, 100
Chelsea, 100
chemical improvements, 293
Chenaye des Bois, 59
Chenopodiaceæ, 11
Chenopodium, 11
Chepstow glasshouse, 263, 264, 265, 274, 283
Cherryburn, 228
Chesterfield, Lord, 100
Chevalier, John, 63, 64
Chichester, Bishop of, 65
Chiddingfold, 9, 12, 52 *sq.*
Chiddingfold, glass found at, 57
Chiddingfold shapes, 56
Chinese influence, 225, 227, 245, 251, 256, CXXI, CXXXIII, CXXXV, CXXXVI, CXL
Church, Prof., 27
cider glasses, 284
citron peel, 330
Civil War, the, 100, 106, 108
clarificants, 16
clary, 330
classicalism, 244, 252, 256 *sq.*, 290, 314, 317, 329, CXLIII, CXLV, CXLVI, CLII, CLIV, CLXI
classical ruins, 227, 245
Clavell, Sir William, 97, 98

INDEX

INDEX

INDEX

INDEX

facets, triangular, 249

façon de Venise, 14, 61, 63, 79, 80, 99, 100, 105, 106, 148, 152, 160, 165, 168, 174, 195, 210, 212, 331, VIII, XIX, XXX

façon de Venise, domestication of, 161

fakes, 302

Falcon Glasshouse, 333

Falcon Glassworks, 289 *sq.*, CLXI

Falcon Stairs, 139, 141

Fall, the, XXXVII, CI

false proportions, 304 *sq.*

fan moulding, CIII

fan panels, 257, 323

Faraday, Michael, 288

Farlonger, Lawrence, 64, 74

feet, claw, 329

feet, domed, 184, 209, 313, XLIX, LI, LII, LIII, LIV, LV, LVI, LVII, LVIII, LIX, LXVII, LXVIII, LXIX, LXX, LXXI, LXXII, LXXIII, LXXIV, LXXVI, LXXVII, C, CIII, CIV, CV, CVIII, CXIII, CXXXVIII, CXLII, CXLIII

feet, lion mask, LXXXIV

feet, parallelogram, 329, CLII

feet, pedestal, 184, 331, XXVI, XXXIV, XXXVI, LIV, LX, LXXV, LXXVIII, LXXXIX, CXLIX

feet, spreading, 184, 209

feet, square, 255, 314, 329, CXLIV, CXLVIII, CLII

feet, terraced, 185, 313, LII, LV, LVI, LVII, LIX, LXVII, LXVIII, LXXII, CXLIII, CXLV

fern, 12

Fernfold Wood, 63

Ferrara, 73

Ferri, family of, 60, 73

Ferrybridge glasshouse, 70, 143

festoons, 242, 250, CVIII, CLII, CLIV

"Ffrannce," 64

fialai, 73

Fiat, CXII, CXIII

filigree process, 37

filigree stems, 206

filigree work, 198, 212, 322

Filiolo, Vincencius, 74

fingers, 314

"finger basins," 332

"finger cups," 332

finger-fringe, CLXIII

"finger glasses," 332

Fire of London, 76

firing glasses, 227

Fishamble Street glasshouse, 264, 274

Fitzsimons, Christopher, 272, 273

Fitzsimons, Richard, 272

Flanders, 149

"Flanders glasses," 210

Fleet Street glasshouse, 274

fleurs-de-lys, 111

flint glass, 8, 27, 111, 116, 118, 122, 146, 151

flint glass, export of, 150

flints, 7–9, 80, 104, 109, 120, 122

"flintt sack," 111

Florence, 52

"flowered glass buttons," 240

"flowered glasses," 236, 239, 240, 241 *sq.*, 243, 246, 283, CXIV, CXXVI, CXXVII

flowers, 241

flute cordials, 331

flute-cutting, CV, CVI, CLI, CLIV, CLVII

flutes, 115, 308, 309, 315, IV, VI, XXI, XXXV, XXXVI, XLIV, XLVIII, LXXXVI, CXVII, CXIX, CLI

flutes, flat vertical, 249

flutes, pillared, 254, CLVI

flutes, rounded, 249

flutes, Spanish, 308, 314

flutes, stem, 257

fluting, 251, 254, CLI

fluting, comb, 251, CLVII

fluting, neck, 258

flux, 10, 48, 109, 186

Foley, Daniel, 280

Fontainebleau, 9

foot formation, 184, 209

"footmaker," 36, 164

Formica, Odacio, 131, 272

Forsett, Edward, 88, 89

fort, made of glass, 333

"founding," 30

France, 12, 24, 51, 56, 111, 175, 179

Francis, G. R., 172, 178, 205, 243, 322, CX

Frank, potter of Bristol, 222

Franklin, Joseph, 119

Frederica Sophia Wilhelmina, consort of William V of Orange, CI

Frederick, George Augustus, Prince of Wales, CXXIV, CXXX

French glassmaking in England, 51 *sq.*

INDEX

INDEX

INDEX

2 A*

INDEX

INDEX

INDEX

INDEX

INDEX

INDEX

INDEX

INDEX

INDEX

INDEX

A HISTORY of
ENGLISH AND IRISH
GLASS

A HISTORY *of* ENGLISH AND IRISH GLASS

by

W. A. THORPE
of The Victoria and Albert Museum

VOLUME TWO

HOLLAND PRESS

This facsimile edition was printed in 1969

Printed in Germany

LIST OF ILLUSTRATIONS TO VOLUME TWO

Descriptions of glasses and names of owners will be found on the Plates

[v]

LIST OF ILLUSTRATIONS

[vi]

LIST OF ILLUSTRATIONS

[vii]

LIST OF ILLUSTRATIONS

[viii]

[ix]

LIST OF ILLUSTRATIONS

LIST OF ILLUSTRATIONS

NOTE

IN the descriptions of the plates all glasses are English where the contrary is not stated. In the earlier descriptions "English" has been occasionally used of pieces which are of English workmanship and metal, though not in the normal English style. In the later descriptions "English" is used in contradistinction to Irish; if, on form, a piece of cut-glass is dateable after 1780 there is greater probability that it was made in Ireland; if on form it is earlier than 1780 the chances are that it is English. Before 1780 the very few Irish factories were provincial to London.

G.l. = glass of lead (flint-glass), *r.f.* = rounded funnel, *s.f.* = straight funnel. All clear glasses are glass of lead (flint-glass) where not described otherwise. The order of illustrations is in general chronological, but the photography of glasses in different collections has made it impossible to follow this arrangement in details.

PLATE I

Wilfred Buckley, Esq.   *Hamilton Clements, Esq.*

1. Goblet of soda-glass. The bowl diamond-engraved in line ; below the rim a hunting scene of a stag, a unicorn, and two hounds each separated by a tree ; below, a zone of foliated ornament broken by three panels containing respectively $\substack{\text{JOHN}\\\text{JONE}}$, DIER 1581, and the royal arms as borne by Queen Elizabeth ; round the base a border of gadroons. The stem a fluted bulb between two smaller bulbs. Flat foot with a gadrooned border round the stem. Anglo-Venetian, probably made in the Broad Street Glasshouse during its tenure by Giacomo Verzelini ; the engraving perhaps by Anthony de Lysle. Dated 1581. H. 8¼″.

                         See pp. 80 *sq. and Rackham* (B.) *in Burl. Mag., Oct.* 1913. *Probably a marriage glass for John and Joan Dyer, the names mis-spelt by a foreign engraver.*

2. Goblet, soda-glass. R.f. bowl diamond-engraved in line ; below a fringe of cresting the motto IN GOD IS AL MI TRUST in a border ; below, a zone of foliated ornament, broken by panels containing respectively a merchant's mark and the date 1583 ; round the base a border of gadroons. Moulded stem and folded foot. Anglo-Venetian, probably made in the Broad Street Glasshouse during its tenure by Giacomo Verzelini ; the engraving perhaps by Anthony de Lysle. H. 8¼″. See pp. 80 *sq.*

PLATE II

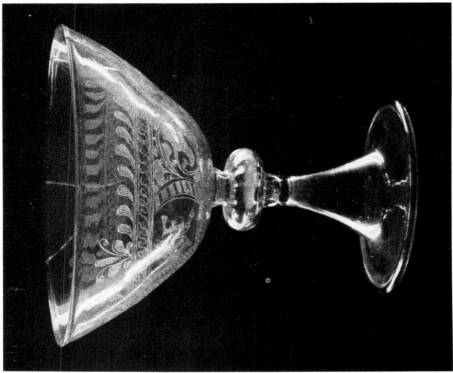

British Museum   *Wilfred Buckley, Esq.*

1. Goblet of soda-glass. Ovate bowl divided by two applied bands into three zones, and engraved with the diamond in line ; in the upper zone three panels reserved in a ground of foliated ornament and containing respectively the initials G S knotted together (twice) and the date 1586 ; in the middle zone the legend IN GOD IS AL MI TRUST within a crested border ; the lower zone gadrooned. Short moulded stem with ribbed and gilt knop. The foot engraved with a circuit of gadroons. Probably Anglo-Venetian and made in the Broad Street Glasshouse during its tenure by Giacomo Verzelini ; perhaps engraved by Anthony de Lysle. H. 5¾".

   For discussion see pp. 80–82.

2. Goblet, soda-glass, open bowl, diamond-engraved in line with a border of gadroons, and below it a zone of foliated ornament with the initials A F and the date 1580 in reserved panels ; flat foot with folded rim and pedestal supporting a hollow bulb stem. Probably Anglo-Venetian and made in the Broad Street Glasshouse during its tenure by Giacomo Verzelini ; perhaps engraved by Anthony de Lysle. H. 5⅛".

For discussion see pp. 80–82.

PLATE III

Musée de Cluny, Paris.

Goblet of soda-glass. The bowl is diamond-engraved on the inside and divided into three zones ; in the upper zone are hounds chasing a unicorn, each beast being divided from the next by a tree ; in the middle zone on a ground of foliated ornament are reserved three panels containing respectively (1) three fleurs-de-lys ; (2) the initials $\begin{smallmatrix} & A & \\ M & & M \\ & D\ C\ P & \end{smallmatrix}$ and (3) the date 1578 ; the lower zone is gadrooned. Fluted bulb stem.

The glass probably French and engraved in France to a French order, perhaps by Anthony de Lysle, before he came to England.

For discussion see p. 80, and for similar engraving see Pl. I 1.

PLATE IV

Victoria and Albert Museum.

1. Flute, soda-glass ; the bowl engraved with zones of formal ornament in diamond point, moulded urn-stem, folded foot. Possibly English, first half of 17th century. H. $8\frac{1}{2}''$.

2. Goblet, soda-glass, bell-bowl diamond-engraved with formal ornament and the legend BARBARA POTTERS 1602 in a border. Thin baluster above a moulded urn-stem, folded foot. Probably English, made in the Broad Street Glasshouse during its tenure (see p. 87) by Sir Jerome Bowes ; dated 1602. H. $8\frac{1}{8}''$.

3. Goblet, soda-glass, r.f. bowl with spiked gadrooning below a threaded circuit, moulded urn-stem. English, middle of 17th century. H. $6\frac{7}{8}''$. See p. 165.

PLATE V

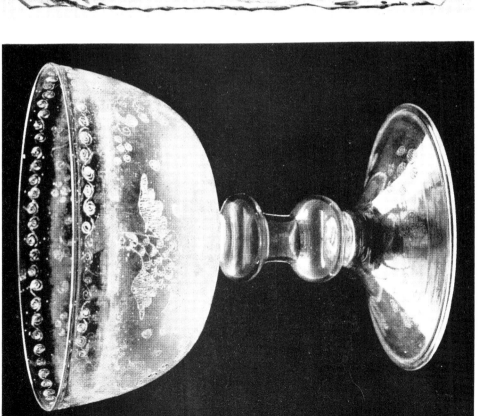

Col. R. F. Ratcliff.   *Victoria and Albert Museum.*

1. Goblet, soda-glass, hemispherical bowl, diamond-engraved in line with foliated ornament and a bird below a scrolled border ; hollow double-knopped stem, folded foot. *Façon de Venise*, probably English, 17th century. H. $5\frac{5}{8}''$.

2. Panel of potash-glass moulded with a portrait of Charles II. English, 1660–1685. $8\frac{1}{2}''$ by $6\frac{1}{4}''$.

PLATE VI

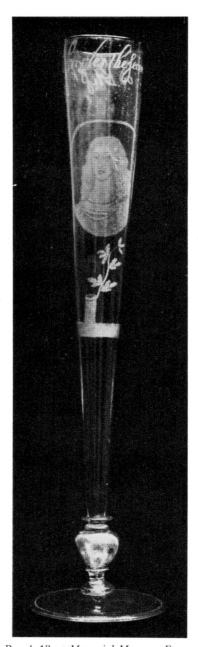

Royal Albert Memorial Museum, Exeter.

Flute of soda-glass. The bowl is diamond-engraved in line with the inscription *God Blefs King Charles the Second,* a bust of Charles II in a medallion, and a stump of an oak-tree. Short baluster stem. Made for the coronation of Charles II in 1660, probably in an English glasshouse worked by Italians and engraved by a Netherlandish hand. H. 17″.

PLATE VII

British Museum (given by Albert Hartshorne).   *Victoria and Albert Museum (Bles Loan).*

1. Rummer, soda-glass, the bowl diamond-engraved in line with four medallions containing figure subjects emblematic of the seasons, with vine-branches between; prunted bucket-stem inscribed with a diamond *August the 18th* 1663 and $\genfrac{}{}{0pt}{}{\text{H}}{\text{W}\quad\text{E}}$; pedestal foot engraved with a landscape containing a windmill. Probably English, dated 1663. H. 8¾".

> *Probably a marriage glass, the initials being for the names of the parties. This arrangement of initials is the normal English arrangement for marriage initials on glass and pottery. The glass may well have been made in an English glasshouse (? the Duke of Buckingham's at Greenwich) staffed by Venetians. The engraving is certainly by a foreign hand, and may be by a Netherlandish engraver working in England. The probability of an English origin is about the same for this glass and for the Royal Oak goblet. Illus. by Hartshorne, Pl. 28, and discussed by him p. 223.*

2. Goblet, thin soda-glass, decoration engraved in line with the diamond point. Portraits of Charles II and his bride Catherine of Braganza, the Royal Arms, and a representation of Charles II hiding in the Boscobel Oak with the legend ROYAL OAK. Made for the celebration of the King's marriage and dated 1663. H. 5⅝".

> *Probably by a company of Venetian glassmakers employed by the Duke of Buckingham in his glasshouse at Greenwich. For the attribution of this glass see p. 105.*

PLATE VIII

The late C. Kirkby Mason.

1. Goblet, not g.l., 17th century. *Façon de Venise*, possibly English. For the treatment of the knop *cf.* Pl. VII. 2. H. 6¾".

2. Lamp, not g.l., 17th century. This type is usually called French, but may well have been made in England by the Lorraine immigrants before the invention of lead glass. H. 10½".

3. Goblet, not g.l., 17th century. *Façon de Venise* English or Netherlandish. H. 8". *Cf.* W. Buckley, 15D. and Pl. XLVII. 3.

These pieces, whether actually English or not, illustrate the manner of the two traditions then at work in England.

PLATE IX

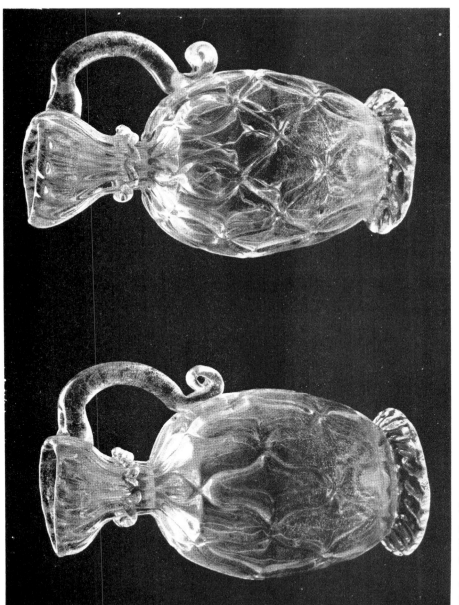

The late C. Kirkby Mason.

Pair of decanter jugs, "nipt diamond waies" all over; vermicular collar round the neck. For gadrooning of foot *cf.* Pl. X (1). Metal of one jug not g.l., both highly crizzled. Probably Ravenscroft's "particuler sort of Christalline Glass," about 1674. For treatment of handles *cf.* Pl. XIV (1), for metal Pl. X, and generally, pp. 134 *sq.* H. 8½".

PLATE X

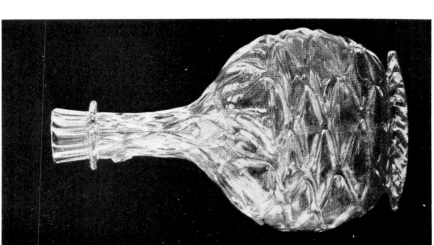

British Museum.

The late C. Kirkby Mason.

1. Decanter-bottle, g.l., highly crizzled, ornament "nipt diamond waies"; for gadrooning of foot *cf.* Pl. IX. Mark, a seal bearing a raven's head, moulded. Made by George Ravenscroft at Henley-on-Thames or the Savoy, 1676–1678 (*cf.* pp. 116 *sq.*). H. 8".

2. Jug, ribbed bowl and foot (*cf.* Pls. XV and XVI. 1), hollow quatrefoil knop above a flat collar; g.l. highly crizzled. Mark, a seal bearing a raven's head, moulded. Made by George Ravenscroft at Henley-on-Thames or the Savoy, 1676–1678 (*cf.* pp. 116 *sq.*). A Renaissance form which occurs not infrequently in Italian and other tin-enamelled earthenware (*e.g.* Rouen, Strasburg), and in Normandy glass (Gerspach, fig. 111). H. 9".

PLATE XI

The late C. Kirkby Mason.

1. Bowl (g.l.), gadrooned base. Mark, a seal bearing a raven's head. Made by George Ravenscroft at Henley-on-Thames or the Savoy, 1676–1678. *Cf.* pp. 116 *sq.* and Plates XII, XIII, XXIII. (b. 1). Diam. 8¾".

2 Bowl (g.l.), gadrooned base below a thread circuit. Probably by Hawly Bishopp ; about 1681 or a little later. *Cf.* Pl. XII and pp. 134 *sq.* Diam. 11⅞".

PLATE XII

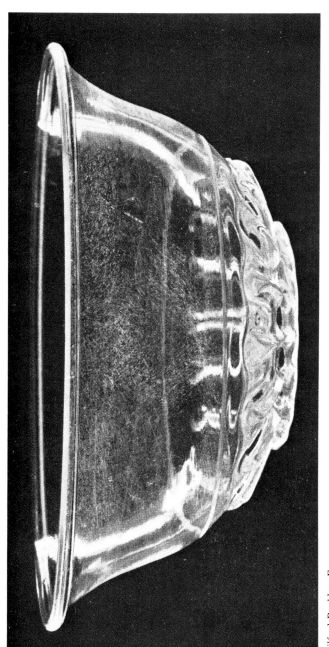

Wilfred Buckley, Esq.

Bowl, gadrooned base below a threaded circuit, g.l. somewhat crizzled. Mark, a seal bearing a raven's head, moulded. Made by George Ravenscroft at Henley-on-Thames or the Savoy, 1676–1678. *Cf.* Pl. XI (2) and pp. 116 *sq.* Diam. 9¼"

PLATE XIII

The late C. Kirkby Mason.

Bowl, trailed circuit and gadrooned base ; metal more leaded than Pl. XII. Probably by Hawly Bishopp, about 1685. Diam. $9\frac{3}{4}''$ *Cf.* pp. 134 *sq.* and Pls. XI, XII.

PLATE XIV

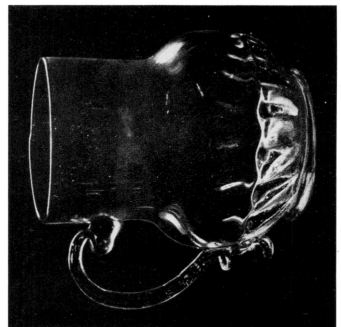

Victoria and Albert Museum.

H. Helliwell, Esq.

1. Beer-tankard, g.l., crizzled, gadrooned base; on the handle an applied seal moulded with a raven's head. Made by George Ravenscroft at Henley-on-Thames or the Savoy, 1676–1678. H. 3½″.

The shape occurs in Lambeth enamelled earthenware and in Fulham stoneware of the 17th century.

2. Beer-tankard, g.l., slightly crizzled, ribbed base. Perhaps made by Hawly Bishopp at the Savoy, about 1681 or a little later. *Cf.* No. 1 and pp. 116 sq. H. 4″.

PLATE XV

Wilfred Buckley, Esq.

Jug, as Pl. X (2), but more leaded and less crizzled. Probably made by Hawly Bishopp at the Savoy, about 1681 or a little later. *Cf.* pp. 116 *sq.* H. 10¾″.

PLATE XVI

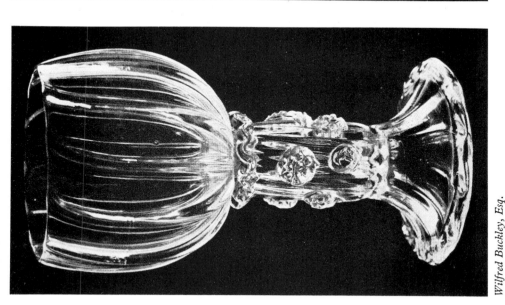

Wilfred Buckley, Esq.

A. O. Curle, Esq.

1. Rummer (after the German *Roemer*), g.l., slightly crizzled, the bowl ribbed vertically, hollow bucket-stem with prunts below a vermicular collar; for treatment of foot *cf.* Plate XV and p. 184. Mark, a seal bearing a raven's head, moulded. Made by George Ravenscroft at Henley-on-Thames or the Savoy, 1676-1678 (pp. 116 *sq.*). H. 6½″.

Cf. pp. 133, 169 *sq. For prunts cf. Pl.* XXXIX (2).

2. Rummer, g.l., slightly crizzled, hollow bucket stem divided from bowl and prunted, pedestal foot. About 1681-5, perhaps made in the glasshouse of Hawly Bishopp in the Savoy. H. 8⅞″.

Compare and contrast the Ravenscroft rummer ; for pedestal foot cf. Pls. XV and XXIII (b). There are specks of lead and undissolved silicate in the metal

PLATE XVII

British Museum.

1. Ewer, lead glass, gadrooned base ; pincered and pressed ornament on body and handle.   English, about 1685.   H. 4¹⁵⁄₁₆″.

For the gadrooned moulding cf. No. 2 and Pl. XI (1).
For a somewhat similar glass, but plain, see Pl. XXXV (3).

2. Posset-cup, not g.l., gadrooned base ;   plain spout with a moulded and applied seal—apparently showing a female figure shooting with a bow.   English, probably by the firm of John Bowles and William Lillington, about 1678–81.   H. 3″.

The agreement of these manufacturers with the Glass Sellers is dated 1 Apr., 1678 ; and it appears to have been the latter who insisted on a seal (Buckley, History, p. 27). Moreover it was unlikely that B. and L. made non-lead glass for very long after Ravenscroft's patent expired (May 1681) ; hence the date. Illus. by F. Buckley, op. cit. Pl. III A and discussed p. 29.

PLATE XVIII

Robert Alexander, Esq.

Covered jug, lead glass, double ogee neck with vermicular collar round
the base, the body encircled with spiked gadroons below two trailed circuits ; clipped handle and gadrooned cover. About 1685. H. 11¼″.

*Very similar to a covered jug in Mr. Mason's Collection, Pl. XX
(1), which has one trailed circuit and smooth gadroons.*

PLATE XIX

Saffron Walden Museum.

Posset-pot, heavy lead glass. Double-looped handles with pincered fringe and a circuit of prunts on a double thread above a gadrooned base, lid gadrooned above a circuit of prunts on a single thread, crown handle of serpentine work with pincered fringes. About 1685. H. 11½″.

> *The treatment is that of Netherlandish* façon de Venise *rather than of Venetian glass proper. For the shape cf. Pl. LXXV* (3), *for the crown handle Pl. XXVIII* (stem).

PLATE XX

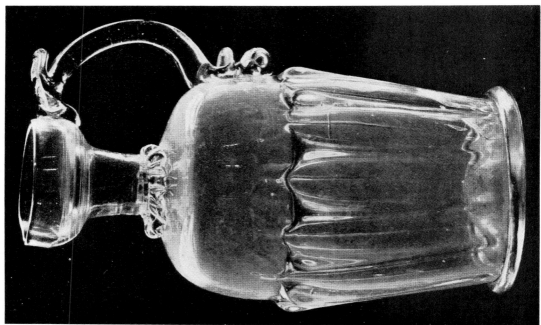

Victoria and Albert Museum (Rees Price Collection).

The late C. Kirkby Mason.

1. Jug, g.l., slightly crizzled ; vermicular collar round the base of the neck, trailed ornament round the shoulder, gadrooned base, clipped handle ; hollow-blown stopper with gadrooned ornament. About 1685. H. 11⅜″ (with stopper).

2. Jug, g.l., slightly crizzled ; vermicular collar round the base of the neck, gadrooning round the base, clipped handle ;

PLATE XXI

The late C. Kirkby Mason.

1. Wine-glass, long bucket bowl gadrooned at base, squat baluster stem, wrythen; folded foot. About 1681–1685. *Cf.* Pl. XXII (3).

2. Flute (ale-glass) solid quatrefoil knop, folded foot. About 1681–1685. H. 7″.

   For the early development of the flute in lead glass cf. Pls. XXXV (1), XXXVI (a 3); for the quatrefoil cf. Pls. X (2), XV, XXIV (3), XXVI (3), Figs. 19, 20 (Ravenscroft fragments).

3. Rummer, not g.l., gadrooned bowl, hollow stem with applied seal (device illegible), thin folded foot. About 1680. H. 4½″.

   Probably a contemporary imitation of Ravenscroft's earliest lead glasses which appear to have borne for a short time a seal, but not a seal with a raven's head; see p. 129. For small rummers (g.l.) of rather later date cf. Pl. XLI. This piece shows at what stage the devolution of the rummer had arrived before the use of lead glass.

Victoria and Albert Museum.

1. Sweetmeat glass, folded lip, gadrooned bowl, wrythen knopped stem, folded foot. H. 3½".

2. Sweetmeat glass, folded lip, gadrooned and trailed bowl, wrythen knopped stem, gadrooned foot with folded rim.   H. 4¾".

3. Drinking-glass, gadrooned bowl, knop and baluster stem, wrythen, folded foot. H. 5⅞". *Cf.* Pl. XXI (1).

4. Drinking-glass, gadrooned bowl, double-knopped wrythen stem, folded foot. H. 4⅛".   (*Bles Loan.*)

All about 1685.   *See pp.* 136 *and* 321.

PLATE XXII

PLATE XXIII

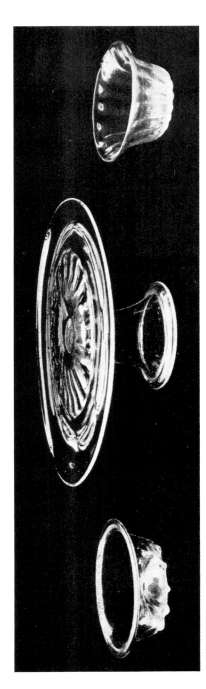

The late C. Kirkby Mason.

Sweetmeat glasses with gadrooned bowls.

1. Knop-and-baluster stem, wrythen. H. 2¾″. For stem *cf.* Pl. XXXVI (b 2), for gadrooning, Pl. XI (1). 2. Plain inverted baluster with collar above. H. 3¾″. For the wide bowl *cf.* Pl. XXII (2); for the stem, Fig. 16 B and Pl. XXIV (1) (stem) and Pl. XLIII (a 1) (stem). 3. As No. 1. H. 2¾″. 4. Trailed circuit above the gadrooning, wide baluster stem wrythen. H. 3″. For stem *cf.* Pl. XXI (1).
Refer this series to Pls. XI (1), XXIII (b 1), XXII (1), and thence to Pl. LXXXVIII.

The late C. Kirkby Mason.

1. Small bowl, thin g.l., gadrooned base. Probably made in the glasshouse of Hawly Bishopp. About 1681–1685. Diam. 4″. *Cf.* p. 136.
2. Stand, thin g.l., the underside decorated with gadrooning and a trailed circuit. About 1681–1685. Diam. 8½″. *For a similar stand in silver [(hall-mark, 1683) see Jackson, Pl. facing p. 256.*
3. Small bowl, ribbed. Late 17th century. Diam. 3½″.

PLATE XXIV

The late C. Kirkby Mason.

1. Sweetmeat glass, gadrooned bowl with flat rim, inverted baluster below a collar, folded foot. About 1685. H. 4⅛″. *Cf. Pl. XXIII (a 2); for the stem Fig. 16 B and Pls. XXIII (a 2), XLIII (a 1); for the bowl Pl. XXIII (b 1), and thence to Pl. XI (1).*

2. Ale-glass, funnel bowl, with wrything ending in a flammiform fringe; winged stem below a collar, folded foot. About 1690–1695. H. 5¾″. *Cf.* Pl. XXVI (1).

3. Wine-glass, s.f. bowl let into a quatrefoil stem, folded foot. 1681 or soon afterwards. H. 4¼″. *For bowl cf. Pl. XLIII (a 2), for the stem cf. Pls. XXXI, XXXII, XXI (2), X (2), and Figs. 19, 20 (Ravenscroft fragments).*

4. Sweetmeat-glass, gadrooned bowl, winged and knopped stem. About 1685–1690. H. 4¼″.

PLATE XXV

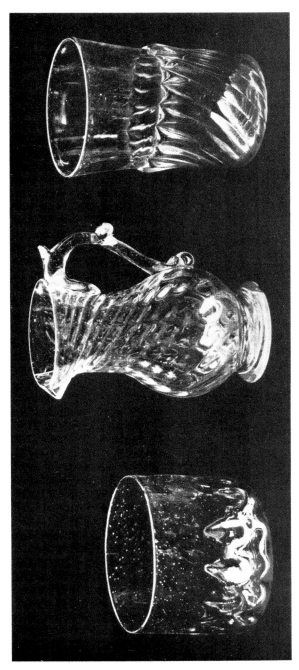

The late C. Kirkby Mason.

1. Brandy tumbler, not g.l., gadrooned base. ? English, second half of 17th century. H. 2". *Cf.* Fig. 16 M.

2. Cream-jug, g.l., wrythen body, clipped handle. English, late 17th century. H. 3½".
   Probably a provincial experiment in lead glass ; the metal is rough and full of small air particles due to imperfect fusion.

3. Tumbler, g.l., with a border of wrythen gadroons round the base. About 1685. H. 3"

PLATE **XXVI**

The late C. Kirkby Mason.

1. Wine-glass, r.f. bowl with spiked gadrooning, winged stem, folded foot. About 1685. H. 5½″.
   Cf. Pl. XXVII (1).

2. Posset-glass, bowl with spiked gadrooning below a trailed circuit let into canopied pedestal foot, reeded handles. About 1685. H. 6½″.
   For the canopy cf. Pl. XXXIV.

3. Sweetmeat glass, double bowls; the upper bowl "nipt diamond waies" about the base, the lower with gadrooned canopy; between them a hollow quatrefoil knop with collars above and below. About 1681–1685. H. 4⅜″.
   For the quatrefoil knop refer to Pl. XXI (2), *and thence to the Ravenscroft jug, Pl. X* (2).

PLATE XXVII

The late C. Kirkby Mason.

1. Wine-glass, winged bowl, short inverted baluster below a set of wings, folded foot. About 1685. H. 5¼".

2. Wine-glass, drawn double-ogee bowl with winged gadrooning above a winged collar, folded foot. About 1685. H. 6¾".

3. Wine-glass, double-ogee bowl, inverted baluster, folded foot. About 1690. H. 6⅜". Cf. Pl. XLVIII (1).

PLATE XXVIII

Hamilton Clements, Esq.

Covered goblet, light lead glass ; the bowl gadrooned at base below a thread circuit ; serpentine stem, wrythen, with pincered fringes.   About 1685.   H. 15″.

For the stem and handle cf. Pl. XXX.   Some attempt is still made to adhere to a thin glass in lead metal ; contrast especially Pl. XIX for a more exuberant use of lead metal, and see pp. 186–7.

PLATE XXIX

Wilfred Buckley, Esq.

Goblet, bucket-bowl gadrooned at base, stem composed of hollow ball-knop, wrythen knop and quatrefoil baluster ; between each a double collar and single collar at the base ; the ball knop containing a fourpenny-piece of 1680. London, about 1685. H. 11″.

Apparently from the same glasshouse as Pl. XXXI (2) but probably a little earlier.
? Bishopp's Savoy glasshouse. For bowl and gadrooning cf. Pl. XXVIII.

PLATE XXX

British Museum.   *Victoria and Albert Museum.*

1. Goblet of lead glass, r.f. bowl "nipt diamond waies," serpentine figure-of-8 stem and handle. The bowl engraved with a ship and an inscription in Dutch, signed *Jacob Sang fec* and dated 1757. The glass English, about 1690; the engraving Dutch as dated. H. 19½".

   Cf. Read (H. E.) in Burl. Mag., XLVIII 277 (1926), and for the engraver see Schmidt (R.), Das Glas, pp. 361 and 363. For the shape cf. Pl. XXXII (2).

2. Goblet (g.l.) r.f. bowl gadrooned, serpentine stem and serpentine handle. English, about 1681–1685. H. 15¾". *(Bles Loan).*

   Façon de Venise in lead glass. Cf. p. 152.

PLATE XXXI

British Museum.

1. Goblet, lead glass, r.f. bowl, wheel-engraved with the arms of William III and " nipt diamond waies " about the base ; the stem composed of two hollow quatrefoil bulbs with collars below each ; folded foot engraved with a wreath. English, about 1689–1690. H. 8$\frac{7}{10}$″. (*Slade Bequest.*)

> *Presumably made for the accession of William III. The engraving by a Dutch or German metic. For the stem cf. Pl. XXXII (2).*

2. Goblet, bucket bowl, gadrooned at base, wrythen ball-knop between two quatrefoil knops, all hollow. London, about 1685. H. 11″.

> *See Pl. XXIX for a similar glass, and for bowl and gadrooning cf. Pl. XXVIII. For a comparable goblet in silver, dated 1680, see Jackson, Eng. Plate, Fig. 262.*

PLATE XXXII

G. F. Berney, Esq.

1. Wine-glass, r.f. bowl with spiked gadrooning, winged stem below a collar; folded foot. About 1685. H. 5⅞".

For collar cf. Pl. XXI (2) and Fig. 16 B.

2. Goblet, r.f. bowl with base "nipt diamond waies," hollow quatrefoil knop above a double collar, folded foot. About 1681–1685. H. 6¼".

3. Rummer, gadrooned bowl, inverted baluster and knop, folded foot. About 1700. H. 5¼".

Cf. Pls. XXXIX–XLI and pp. 169 sq. and 326 sq.

PLATE XXXIII

Hamilton Clements, Esq.

1. Sweetmeat glass, gadrooned base, knop-and-baluster stem. About 1690. H. 5¼″.

A good instance of simplification, cf. p. 160 and Pl. XLIV (4). For other varieties of the knop-and-baluster see Pls. XXII (3) and XL (1).

2. Wine-glass, thin lead metal, drawn trumpet bowl, three collars and quatrefoil knop. About 1685. H. 5⅞″.

For bowl cf. Pl. XLV, for quatrefoil Pls. X (2), XXI (2).

PLATE **XXXIV**

Victoria and Albert Museum.

Punch-bowl, heavy lead glass, bowl decorated with a trailed circuit above a border of ornament " nipt diamond waies," the lid similarly decorated, crown handle of serpentine work with pincered fringes (p. 175), pedestal foot with tooled canopy. English, about 1690. H. 15½". (*Bles Loan.*)

Cf. Pls. XIX, XXVIII, XXX.

PLATE XXXV

Guildhall Museum.

1. Flute, g.l., wrythen bowl let into spiral quatrefoil stem, folded foot. English, 1681 or soon afterwards. H. 6¼″.
   For the form see p. 183; for the quatrefoil cf. Pls. XXXVII and XXXVIII (b 2) and p. 177.

2. Wine-glass, g.l., r.f. bowl, welded on a short inverted baluster. English, 1681 or soon afterwards. H. 5″. *Cf. Pl. XXXVII.*

3. Posset-glass, g.l., folded rim, gadrooned collar round the base, plain handles and spout. About 1685. H. 3⅞″.
   For the collar and the shape, cf. Pl. XXXVI (b 3); for the handles, Pl. XVII (2); and for the spout F. Buckley, Pl. 3A.

PLATE XXXVI

London Museum.

1. Stem of a rummer, g.l., hollow and prunted, vermicular collar, folded foot. English, *c*.1685. H. 2⅝″.
2. Stem of a rummer, g.l., as No. 1, but more prunts, pedestal foot. English, 1681, or soon afterwards.
   For these two fragments cf. Pls. XXI (3), XXXIX, XL, and pp. 169 and 326.
3. Fragment of a flute, g.l., bowl let into multifoil stem. English, *c*. 1685. H. 3″.
   Cf. Pl. XXXV (1) and p. 183.
4. Fragment of a wine-glass, g.l., r.f. bowl welded on quasi-baluster stem. English, 1681, or soon
   afterwards. H. 2⅞″. *For the join of bowl cf. Pl. XXXV (2).*
5. Fragment of wine-glass, not g.l., wide funnel bowl let into quatrefoil stem. English, c. 1670–
   1680. H. 2⅜″. *Cf. p. 161 for this fragment.*
   *No. 5 is probably contemporary with Ravenscroft's work or rather earlier. Nos. 1–4
   are early lead glass immediately following the expiry of his patent (May 1681).*

Henry Brown, Esq.   *London Museum.*   *The late C. Kirkby Mason.*

1. Fragment of a wine-glass dug up at Yeovil, the bowl with spiked gadrooning and let into a
   wrythen baluster. About 1685.
   For implications cf. Pls. XXIII (b 3) and XXVI (1).
2. Wine-glass, g.l., r.f. bowl with spiked gadrooning, knop-and-baluster stem wrythen, folded foot.
   About 1685. H. 6″. *For combination of wrything, spiked gadrooning and knop-and-baluster
   stem cf. No. 1 and Pl. XXII, and pp. 165 and 177.*
3. Jelly or posset glass, g.l., the bowl let into a gadrooned collar. Dug up in London. English,
   about 1685. H. 4½″. *Cf. Robert May's* The Accomplisht Cook (*London*, 1678), "*Serve jelly ...
   run into little round glasses four or five in a dish.*" *For the collar cf.
   Pl. XXXV (3).*

PLATE XXXVII

Mrs. W. D. Dickson.

Goblet, thin g.l., r.f. bowl, let into spiral quatrefoil stem, folded foot.   The bowl diamond-engraved in line with the Fall and the words *Adam & Eve*. English, probably Bristol, about 1685.   H. 6″.

For the engraving cf. Pl. CI (1); the treatment resembles the representations of the Fall on Bristol enamelled earthenware.

PLATE **XXXVIII**

Mrs. W. D. Dickson.

Early experiments in lead glass.

1. Wine-glass, g.l., r.f. bowl with winged gadrooning, knopped stem, folded foot. About 1685. H. 6¼″.
2. Wine-glass, g.l., r.f. bowl with moulded gadroons round the base, winged stem, folded foot. About 1685. H. 6⅜″. 3. Wine-glass, g.l., r.f. bowl gadrooned, folded foot. About 1700. H. 6¼″.
Flecks of lead are discernible in all these glasses, but the metal is not rich.

The late C. Kirkby Mason.

1. Wine-glass, r.f. bowl gadrooned, winged and knopped stem, folded foot. Probably provincial, about 1685. H. 5½″.
2. Wine-glass, r.f. bowl with painting in oil colours, let into spiral quatrefoil stem; folded foot. Probably Bristol, about 1685. H. 6″. *Cf. Pl. XXXVII for the attribution.*
3. Wine-glass, r.f. bowl gadrooned and let into stem, folded foot. Probably provincial. About 1685. H. 5½″. *For stems of Nos. 1 and 3 cf. Pl. XXXII (1) and p. 169.*

PLATE XXXIX

G. F. Berney, Esq.   *William Roscoe, Esq.*

1. Rummer, gadrooned bowl, stem composed of ball knop above an inverted baluster with smaller knop at base. About 1690. H. 12½″.

> *Cf. Pls. XVI (1, 2), XXXVI (a) and XL (3). This glass appears to be the latest of the series by reason of the development of the stem; Pl. XL (3) is the earliest on account of the vermicular collar (for which cf. Pl. IX).*

2. Rummer, after the German *Roemer*. Gadrooned bowl (V) divided from hollow prunted stem (G). Note mixture of styles and *cf.* p. 169 and Plates as above. About 1690. H. 9¾″.

PLATE XL

Hamilton Clements, Esq.

1. Rummer, gadrooned base, double knop and baluster stem. About 1690. H. 9¼".
   Roemer bowl (G), gadrooning (V), combined with an English solid stem. Cf. Pl. XXXIX and p. 169.
2. Ale-glass, wrythen funnel bowl, poor baluster stem, wrythen. Late 17th century. H. 5¼".
3. Rummer, gadrooned bowl, hollow bucket-stem with prunts, and round the top a vermicular collar. About 1685. H. 12¼".
   The Roemer stem retained but separated from the bowl.

PLATE XLI

The late C. Kirkby Mason.

1. Rummer, gadrooned bowl, knopped stem, cone foot with folded rim. Early 18th century. H. 4¾".
2. Rummer, gadrooned bowl, knopped stem wrythen, folded foot. Early 18th century. H. 4¾".
3. Rummer, ribbed bowl, knopped stem, cone foot with folded rim. First half of 18th century.

For derivation of these glasses cf. Pls. XXXIX, XL and p. 170.

PLATE XLII

Victoria and Albert Museum.
Posset-pot, heavy lead glass. About 1690. H. 9¾″. (*Bles Loan.*)

PLATE XLIII

Henry Brown, Esq.

The definition of English design.

1. Wine-glass, s.f. bowl, short inverted baluster with merese above, folded foot. About 1681–1685. H. 7¼″. *For this form, especially the angle of aperture of the bowl and the collar, cf. Greene's design, Fig. 16 B, C, G. Metal fairly light.*

2. Wine-glass, s.f. bowl, let into inverted baluster, folded foot. About 1685. H. 5⅞″. *Cf. Pl. XXIV* (3).

3. Wine-glass, s.f. bowl, let into inverted baluster, folded foot. About 1685. H. 7″.

For all three glasses cf. pp. 178 and 181.

J. M. Bacon, Esq.

The definition of English design.

1. Wine-glass, r.f. bowl, inverted baluster and knop, folded foot. About 1690. H. 6⅞″.

2. Wine-glass, s.f. bowl, inverted baluster, folded foot. About 1685. H. 7½″.

3. Wine-glass, s.f. bowl, angular knopped stem, folded foot. About 1690–1695. H. 7″.

PLATE XLIV

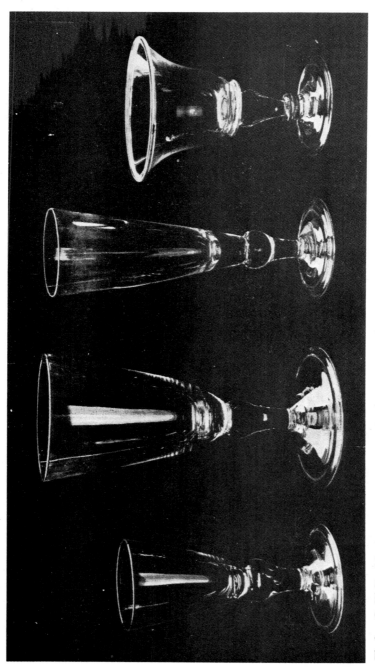

The late C. Kirkby Mason.

1. Wine-glass, r.f. bowl, inverted baluster, folded foot. About 1685–1690. H. 6¼".

2. Wine-glass, r.f. bowl, inverted baluster, folded foot. About 1685–1690. H. 8⅜". *See pp. 178 and 182.*

3. Flute (" ale-glass "), the bowl set in an inverted baluster, folded foot. About 1685. H. 8¼". *Cf. Pl. XXI* (2).

4. Sweetmeat glass, incurved bowl with flaring rim folded at the edge, inverted baluster below a collar; collar at the base of the baluster and folded foot. About 1685. H. 5⅞". *Cf. Pl. XXXIII* (1).

PLATE XLV

The late C. Kirkby Mason.

1, 2. Wine-glasses, soda metal, trumpet bowls, drawn stems, plain feet. Continental, probably Venetian, 17th century. H. 6½″, 7¼″.

3. Wine-glass, lead metal, trumpet bowl, drawn stem, folded foot. English, late 17th century; probably about 1685–1695. *Cf. Pl. XLVII for early specimens of the thick drawn stem. The origin of the drawn stem. Thin drawn stems were being made as late as c. 1730–1740, but the metal of No. 3 suggests an early date.* H. 6¾″.

PLATE **XLVI**

Henry Brown, Esq.

1. Goblet, trumpet bowl, heavy drawn stem, cone foot. About 1690–1700. H. 11½".
2. Goblet, square bucket-bowl, straight plain stem, folded foot. Early 18th century. H. 10⅜".
3. Goblet as No. 1, but with folded foot. About 1690–1700. H. 11".

For the thickening of the Venetian drawn stem refer from Pl. XLV to Pl. XLVII and thence to Nos. 1 and 3.

PLATE XLVII

The late C. Kirkby Mason.

1. Wine-glass, s.f. bowl engraved CHARELS AND MARY SCRIVEN 1709, with initials in diamond engraving below, folded foot. Dated 1709. H. 7⅛″.

   The earliest document known to me for this type of glass is dated 1696 in diamond point on the foot. The engraving probably by a Dutch or German metic; compare a glass in the coll. of Sir John Risley (Bles, Pl. 44 and Apollo III, 166) engraved SUCCESS TO WILᴹ & MARY (1688–1694).

2. Wine-glass, s.f. bowl, drawn stem ; folded foot. About 1700. H. 5½″. *In this and No. 3 the line of bowl and stem is almost straight.*

3. Wine-glass, s.f. bowl, drawn stem with solid ball knop at base, folded foot. About 1690–1700. H. 7⅛″.

   For the derivation cf. Pl. VIII (3) of which this is an adaptation in lead metal. Contrast this series with Pl. XLV.

PLATE XLVIII

Henry Brown, Esq.

1. Wine-glass, double-ogee bowl, short inverted baluster, folded foot. About 1690. H. 5⅞″.

Cf. Pl. XXVII (3).

2. Wine-glass, double-ogee bowl, drop-knop stem, folded foot. About 1695. H. 5¼″.

3. Flute, double-ogee bowl drawn into long inverted baluster with tears, domed foot. About 1700–1710. H. 6⅜″.

Cf. Pls. VI, XXI (2), XLIV (3) for earlier flutes.

PLATE XLIX

G. F. Berney, Esq.

1. Wine-glass, s.f. bowl, drop knop and ball knop, folded foot.   About 1700.   H. 8″.
   For shorter and earlier drop-knop stems cf. Pl. LI (1) and No. 3 here.
2. Wine-glass, bell bowl, double baluster, domed foot with folded rim.   About 1710–1715.   H. 8½″.
3. Wine-glass, double-ogee bowl, drop-knop stem, folded foot.   About 1695.   H. 7½″.

G. F. Berney, Esq.

1. Wine-glass, double-ogee bowl, drop knop above a straight stem, folded foot.   About 1705.   H. 7½″.
   See above for similar but shorter stems.   *Cf. Pl. XLVIII (3).*
2. Wine-glass, double-ogee bowl, angular knopped stem, domed foot with folded rim   About 1695–1700.   H. 8⅜″.
3. Wine-glass, thistle bowl, mushroom knop stem, folded foot.   About 1710.   H. 8″.
   For a rather earlier mushroom-knop glass see Pl. LI (3). For the beginnings of German influence (the thistle bowl) cf. p. 173.

PLATE **L**

Henry Brown, Esq.

The defined English style.

1. Wine-glass, r.f. bowl, inverted baluster, folded foot.   About 1690.   H. 8".
2. Wine-glass, r.f. bowl, heavy knopped stem, folded foot.   About 1700.   H. $9\frac{3}{8}$".
3. Wine-glass, r.f. bowl with cyst below, acorn stem, folded foot.   About 1700.   H. $8\frac{5}{8}$".
4. Wine-glass, s.f. bowl, angular knop above short (true) baluster, folded foot.   About 1695.   H. $7\frac{7}{8}$".

Cf. Pl. XLIV (2), and refer from Fig. 16 G to No. 1, 2, 3, and from Fig. 16, B, C, G, to Pl. XLIII (a), and thence to No. 4.   For lengthening of stem cf. p. 204.

PLATE LI

1. Goblet, r.f. bowl, heavy knopped stem, folded foot. About 1695. H. $11\frac{7}{8}''$.
2. Goblet, double-ogee bowl, drop-knop stem, sloping-dome foot with folded rim. About 1690. H. $11\frac{7}{8}''$.
3. Goblet, r.f. bowl, mushroom-knop stem, domed foot with folded rim. About 1705. H. $10\frac{1}{2}''$.
4. Goblet, r.f. bowl, heavy knopped stem, sloping-dome foot with folded rim. About 1710. H. $10\frac{3}{4}''$.

PLATE LII

G. F. Berney, Esq.

1. Wine-glass, small r.f. bowl with large cyst at base, angular knop above a true baluster, domed and terraced foot. About 1710. H. 5⅞″.

2. Wine-glass, r.f. bowl, cushion-knop with small knop at base, domed and terraced foot. About 1700. H. 7½″.

3. Wine-glass, small r.f. bowl with large cyst at base, angular acorn stem, domed and terraced foot. About 1710. H. 5¾″. *See p. 185.*

PLATE LIII

J. M. Bacon, Esq.

1. Goblet, s.f. bowl let into wide baluster stem (*cf. Pl. XXXVI* (b 1)), with knop, folded foot. About 1700. H. 9⅝″.
2. Goblet, bucket bowl, triple-ring knop and inverted baluster, sloping-dome foot with folded rim. About 1710. H. 10″.
3. Goblet, r.f. bowl with cyst below, cushion-knop stem, folded foot. About 1705. H. 9⅞″.

Lady Davy.

1. Wine-glass, trumpet bowl drawn into long baluster stem, folded foot. About 1715. H. 7½″.
2. Goblet, r.f. bowl, with cyst, inverted baluster and knop, domed foot with folded rim. About 1700–1705. H. 9″.
   For a similar stem which can be dated before 1707 *and probably to* 1702 *see Francis, Pl. XXXVI.*
3. Wine-glass, incurved bowl, double baluster, domed foot with folded rim. About 1705–1710. H. 7¾″.

PLATE LIV

Mrs. W. D. Dickson.

1. Candlestick, g.l., hollow knopped stem, high pedestal foot. About 1685. H. 10″.

> *Early experiment in lead glass, perhaps by French-men working in England. ? Stourbridge.*

2. Candlestick, g.l., hollow knopped stem, pedestal foot. About 1685. H. 8″.

> *The tendency to solidify hollow forms in lead glass is apparent in the upper part of the stem. For the nozzle cf. the later pieces illustrated in Pls. LV (b) and LVI (b).*

PLATE LV

The late C. Kirkby Mason.

1. Candlestick, g.l., plain socket, knopped stem, sloping domed foot with folded rim. Probably provincial, late 17th century. H. 5½″.
2. Goblet, lead glass, rummer bowl with an interior bulb containing a coin of 1680, pear-shaped balustroid stem, sloping domed foot with folded rim. Late 17th century. H. 6⅞″.
3. Posset-glass, lead metal, without ornament. About 1690. H. 5½″.
    Cf. Pl. XXXV (3) for an earlier, more ornate type ; and for the same tendency in large posset-pots refer from Pl. XIX to Pl. XLII.

Sir John S. Risley.

1. Candlestick, rimmed socket, true-baluster stem with knop above, high domed foot   About 1695. H. 7¾″.
2. Candlestick, as No. 1. About 1695. H. 8¹⁄₁₀″.   *Cf. Pl. LIV (2) (foot) for these two.*
3. Candlestick, plain socket, knopped stem, double-domed foot. About 1700. H. 8¾″.
4. Candlestick, rimmed socket, shouldered stem (G) with three collars above and knop below, domed foot with radial ribs. About 1715–1725. H. 7½″.

PLATE LVI

Hamilton Clements, Esq

1. Candlestick, double socket in tray. About 1690. H. 2¼″.
2. Sweetmeat glass, terraced bowl and foot, about 1690. H. 3⁵⁄₁₆″.

Hamilton Clements, Esq.

1. Candlestick; composite knopped stem including acorn, flat knop, squat baluster, and multiple-ring knop; square-dome foot, the rim terraced; about 1700–1710. H. 8¼″. *For acorn cf. Pl. LIX* (b).
2. Candlestick, g.l., hollow knopped stem, pedestal foot. About 1685. H. 10¼″.
   Early attempt to use the lead flux. Probably provincial, by a glassmaker of the potash tradition; perhaps an immigrant Lorrainer. Cf. Pl. LIV (1) and p. 313.
3. Candlestick, true baluster between knops, sloping domed foot. About 1690–1700. H. 9″.
   Early solidification of the tall-stem candlesticks with multiple knops.

PLATE LVII

Hamilton Clements, Esq.

1. Candlestick, heavy knopped stem with tears, domed and terraced foot. About 1695. H. 8¼".
   For the arched dome with terraces cf. Pl. LIX (b).

2. Candlestick, ball-knop below triple collars, flat dome foot with terraces. About 1695. H. 6½".

3. Candlestick ; ball-knop pearled above triple ring, square dome foot rising from terraced rim. About 1700. H. 9¼".

   The heavy knopped candlesticks are a stage earlier than similar stems in wine-glasses and contemporary with the simple balusters. This was probably due to the fact that wine-glasses had a prescribed tradition, whereas candlesticks of glass had not ; the simple baluster does not appear to have been used for candlesticks at all. Contrast Pl. LV (b 3) for composition of long stem, and see p. 313.

Plate LVIII

Victoria and Albert Museum   *William Roscoe, Esq.*

1. Taper-stick, multi-knopped stem with tray, domed and folded foot. About 1690–1700. H. 5¾". (*Rees Price Collection*).

2. Candlestick, multi-knopped stem with annulated knop below, domed foot with terraced rim. About 1700. H. 7". (*Rees Price Collection*).

3. Candlestick, ball-knop above annulated knop, domed foot. About 1695–1700. H. 6½".

See p. 313. *For annulated knop cf. Pl. LVII* (3).

PLATE LIX

G. F. Berney, Esq.

1. Candlestick, plain socket, annular stem with teared knop below, double-domed foot, the lower part
   terraced. About 1690. H. 4¾″. *For the annular stem cf. Pl. LVIII.*
2. Candlestick, plain socket, knopped and annular stem, domed foot with terraced rim. About
   1700–1705. H. 8″. *Cf. exx. below which are slightly later.*
3. Candlestick, plain socket, knopped stem, domed and terraced foot. About 1685–1690. H. 4¾″.

Col. R. F. Ratcliff.

Set of four candlesticks, plain sockets, stems composed of acorn knop, teared ball knop below two collars,
and annular knop; domed and terraced feet. About 1705. H. 9½″.
For the acorn cf. Pls. L (3), LII (3), LXXXV and p. 178.

PLATE LX

Robert Frank, Esq.

1. Lamp, g.l., four spouts, nipt decoration below a threaded circuit, pressed foot. About 1685. H. 3⅜".
2. Lamp, g.l., two spouts, gadrooned bowl, plain straight stem, folded foot. Early 18th century. H. 5¼".
3. Lamp, g.l., three spouts, pedestal foot, all undecorated. About 1690–1700. H. 4". *For plain surface cf. Pl. XLII.*

PLATE LXI

William Roscoe, Esq.

1. Goblet, r.f. bowl, inverted baluster stem, folded foot. About 1685–1690. H. 7″.

   An early tavern glass following in some degree the dining-table balusters (Pl. XLIV (1, 2)).

2. Handled decanter (g.l.), after the shape of the contemporary green glass wine-bottle. First quarter of 18th century. *Cf.* pp. 318 *sq.*
   H. 5⅞″.

PLATE LXII

Formerly in the possession of Wilfred Buckley, Esq.

Rummer, green flint glass, fluted stem with prunts below a collar, folded foot. First quarter of 18th century. H. 6⅝".

For derivation see Pl. XVI and for descendants Pl. C and pp. 215 and 327.

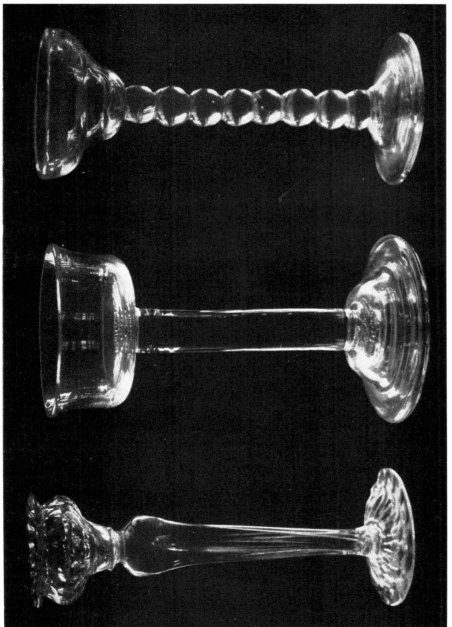

PLATE LXIII

Hamilton Clements, Esq.

1. Stemmed glass, probably for a toilet table, lead metal, double-ogee bowl with reticulated moulding and flaring rim, long shouldered stem, moulded foot. English, about 1720. H. 6¾″. *The stem is a French version of the German shouldered stem.*

   The form is French; cf. Gerspach, Fig. 104 (i).

2. Glass, probably a wine-glass, straight plain stem, domed foot. Early 18th century. H. 6½″.

3. Glass, probably a sweetmeat glass, squat double-ogee bowl, eight-knopped stem. Early 18th century. H. 6¾″. *French or Netherlandish type.*

PLATE LXIV

Victoria and Albert Museum.

1. Stemmed bowl, true baluster elongated, folded foot, slightly domed, crinkled rim. About 1725   H. 5¾".

2. Stand, acorn-knop stem. About 1700–1710. H. 3½".

3. Stemmed bowl, nipt in small diamonds, inverted baluster below triple-ring knop, domed foot also nipt in small diamonds and sunken for the stem, folded foot-rim. About 1710. H. 4½".

PLATE LXV

Henry Brown, Esq.

Ale-glasses.

1. Wrythen bowl, short inverted baluster, folded foot. Late 17th or early 18th century. H. 5¼″.
2. Wrythen bowl, plain winged stem below a collar, folded foot. Late 17th century. H. 5¾″.
3. Wrythen bowl with flammiform fringe in high relief, cross-hatched wings below a collar, folded foot. Late 17th century. H. 6⅞″.
4. Wrythen bowl, pinched stem below a collar, folded foot. Late 17th century. H. 5½″.
5. Wrythen bowl, pinched stem below a collar, folded foot. Late 17th century. H. 5″.

No. 3 seems to be derived from the flute ; for the collar and short stem see Pl. XXXII (1).

PLATE LXVI

J. M. Bacon, Esq.

Posset- or jelly-glasses.

1. Folded rim; bowl set in a gadrooned collar, for which *cf.* Pl. XXXVI (*b* 3). About 1685. H. 4⅛".
2. Folded rim, teared knop. Late 17th or early 18th century. H. 3¼". 3. Folded rim. Late 17th or early 18th century. H. 3¾".

Ale-glasses, with wrythen bowls and stems.

Nos. 4–8, late 17th century, Nos. 3 and 4 being the earlier. For the form derivation *cf.* Hartshorne, p. 51. No. 9, middle of 18th century. H. 4⅞", 4½", 4⅞", 4⅝", 5", 5".

PLATE LXVII

Henry Brown, Esq.

1. Sweetmeat glass, flat bell-bowl, ball knop with tears above an inverted baluster, domed foot with terraced rim. About 1700–1710. H. $5\frac{7}{8}''$.   *Cf. Pl. LIX (a 2) for terracing.*

2. Rummer, knopped stem, folded foot. About 1710. H. $7''$.

3. Wine-glass, hemispherical bowl gadrooned about the base, triple-ring knopped stem, sloping domed foot with folded rim. About 1705. H. $5\frac{5}{16}''$.   *For the bowl form see p. 183.*

G. F. Berney, Esq.

1. Sweetmeat glass, open double-ogee bowl moulded in vertical ribs, with flaring rim ; triple-ring knop on a straight stem ; domed foot moulded in ribs, with folded rim. About 1710. H. $6\frac{3}{4}''$.
     For the knop cf. Pl. LVIII.

2. Sweetmeat glass. Double-ogee bowl pearl-moulded, with flaring rim ; shouldered stem pearl-moulded, with two collars round the bottom ; domed foot pearl-moulded, with folded rim. About 1710–1720. H. $7''$.

3. Sweetmeat glass. Open bowl with flaring rim, inverted baluster stem with knop at bottom, domed foot with folded rim. About 1700. H. $7''$. *Cf. Pl. LXXIII (a 1) (earlier) and Pl. LXXI (1, 3) (later).*

PLATE LXVIII

G. F. Berney, Esq.

1. Covered sweetmeat glass, bowl and lid ribbed, triple ring handle rising into three knops, inverted baluster stem with knop below, domed foot ribbed radially, folded rim. About 1710. H. 9″. *For stem cf. Pl. LIII (b 2), for bowl Pl. LXXI (3), for handle Pl. LXXI (2).*

2. Posset-glass, double-ogee bowl, double-looped handles, short knopped stem, domed foot with terraced rim. About 1700. H. 7⅞″. *Cf. Pl. LXIX.*

3. Covered sweetmeat glass, bowl and lid "nipt diamond waies," inverted baluster, folded foot, flat baluster knob. About 1695–1700. H. 8¼″. *Cf. Pl. XLIV (3) for a slightly earlier stem of this type.*

PLATE **LXIX**

Henry Brown, Esq.

1. Jelly-glass, pearled bowl, double-loop handles, domed foot. About 1725. H. $4\frac{7}{16}''$.

2. Jelly-glass, pearled bowl, single handles. About 1725. H. $4\frac{1}{4}''$.

3. Jelly-glass, plain waisted bowl, double-loop handles. About 1700. H. $4\frac{1}{16}''$. *Cf.* Pl. XXVII (2) for the bowl shape.

4. Jelly-glass, plain r.f. bowl with flaring rim, double-loop handles, domed foot. About 1700–1710. H. $4''$.

5. Jelly-glass, plain waisted bowl, single handle, domed foot. About 1710–1720. H. $4\frac{5}{8}''$.

The plain bowls precede the moulded bowls as in sweetmeat glasses (Pl. LXVII (a 1), LXVII (b 3 and 1), LXXI (1 and 3).)

PLATE LXX

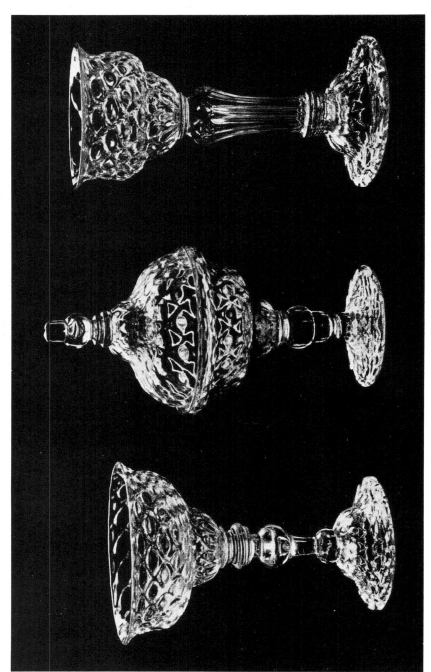

Hamilton Clements, Esq.

1. Sweetmeat glass "all over nipt diamond waies," double-ogee bowl, triple-ring knop and inverted baluster, domed foot also diamonded. About 1710. H. 6⅞".

2. Covered sweetmeat glass "all over nipt diamond waies," acorn knob and acorn stem. About 1700. H. 8¾".
   Note the appearance of the acorn, a pure English feature in a "Venetian" glass, cf. p. 178.

3. Sweetmeat glass, double-ogee bowl, "nipt diamond waies," shouldered stem with bosses (G) and collars at base, domed foot. About 1710–1715. H. 7⅞".

PLATE LXXI

The late C. Kirkby Mason.

1. Sweetmeat glass, ribbed double-ogee bowl, ball-knop and inverted baluster, domed foot with radial ribs. About 1710. H. 5⅜″.

2. Covered goblet, r.f. bowl, triple ring above an inverted baluster, domed foot with folded rim. About 1710. H. 11⅝″. *For covered goblets cf. p. 174.*

3. Sweetmeat glass, ribbed double-ogee bowl, ball-knop above a shouldered stem, domed foot with radial ribs. About 1710–1715. H. 6½″.

PLATE LXXII

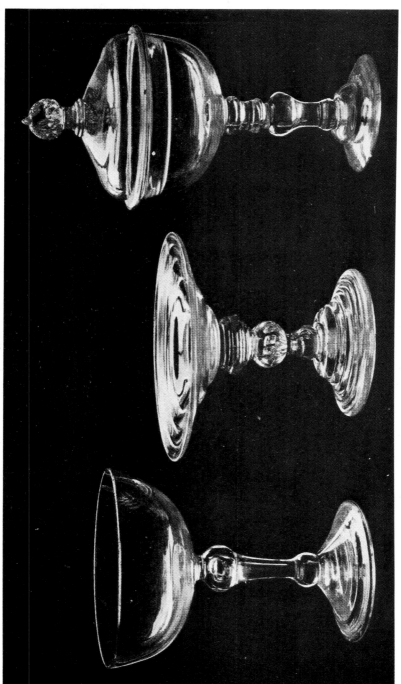

Hamilton Clements, Esq.

1. Wine-glass, hemispherical bowl (V), long inverted baluster and knop, conical foot. About 1710. H. 7½″.

2. Sweetmeat stand, bowl terraced on the underside, triple ring and ball-knop with tears, domed and terraced foot. About 1700. H. 9″. *For bowl and stem cf. foot and bowl of Pl. LVI (a 2), and for foot Pl. LVII (3); but the bulk of metal is less than in that glass.*

3. Covered bowl, inverted baluster below bobbin knop, small domed foot. About 1710. H. 10″.

PLATE LXXIII

G. F. Berney, Esq.

1. Wine- or sweetmeat glass, open bowl, inverted baluster stem below two collars, folded foot. **About 1690–1695. H. 4¾".**
2. Wine- or sweetmeat glass, open double-ogee bowl, knopped stem, domed foot with folded rim. About 1705. H. 5¾".
3. Sweetmeat glass, open bowl with ribs and flaring rim, shouldered stem, folded foot. About 1715. H. 5".

For the German stem cf. p. 171, and for early German influence contrast p. 170. For this series see pp. 183, 314 sq.

Hamilton Clements, Esq.

1. Wine- or sweetmeat glass, truncated funnel bowl, heavy knopped stem with tears, domed foot sunken for the stem. About 1705. H. 6".
2. Sweetmeat glass, double-ogee bowl, drop-knop stem, domed foot with folded rim. About 1705. H. 5".
3. Wine- or sweetmeat glass, truncated funnel bowl, slightly incurved, stem composed of **triple rings,** thin inverted baluster and four knops, folded foot. About 1720. H. 6¼".

PLATE **LXXIV**

Mrs. W. D. Dickson.

Covered sweetmeat glass, wrythen bowl, the lid moulded in radial panels, teared knob, triple-knopped stem, domed foot wrythen. Beginning of 18th century. H. $10\frac{1}{4}''$.

PLATE LXXV

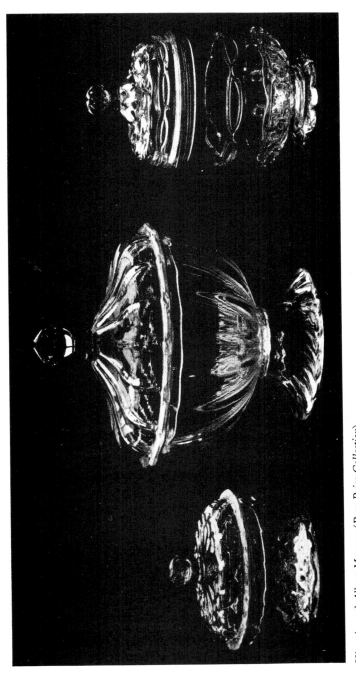

Victoria and Albert Museum (Rees Price Collection).

1. Butter-dish with pearl moulding and teared knob. Early 18th century. H. 4½".
2. Covered bowl, radial ribs and pedestal foot, showing Venetian influence; teared knob. Late 17th century. H. 9¾".
3. Posset-pot, bowl and lid both having a trailed circuit and border of nipt ornament; teared knob and foot tooled in scallops. Late 17th century. *Cf.* Pls. XIX and LXXVI (*b* 1). H. 7½".

For a parallel in silver (hall-mark 1695) see Jackson, Fig. 278.

PLATE LXXVI

Hamilton Clements, Esq.

1. Sweetmeat glass, double-ogee bowl with trellised edges, shouldered stem (G) with collar at base, sloping-dome foot with folded rim. About 1715. H. 10". *Cf. Pl. LXXVII* (1).
2. Punch-bowl, the base "nipt diamond waies" below a trailed circuit, quatrefoil knop, domed foot with canopy "nipt diamond waies" and folded rim; ladle gadrooned. About 1685. H. 10⅜".
Cf. generally Pl. XXXIV ; and for quatrefoil knop Pl. X (2).

Mrs. W. D. Dickson.

1. Posset-pot, the base and lid gadrooned, simple threading round the top, teared knob. About 1700. H. 6¼".
2. Sweetmeat bowl with basketwork rim. About 1710. H. 4".

PLATE LXXVII

Victoria and Albert Museum (Rees Price Collection).

1. Sweetmeat glass, double-ogee bowl, ribbed; trellised rim with prunts; shouldered and bossed stem with collars round the base; domed foot with radial ribs and folded rim. About 1715. H. 8½″.

2. Goblet, the bowl decorated with trailed circuit and ornament "nipt diamond waies." Hollow prunted knop containing coin of 1664. Late 17th century. H. 9½″.

PLATE LXXVIII

Victoria and Albert Museum.   *Rev. and Mrs. M. de la Hey.*

1. Tankard, threaded border round the rim, gadrooned base, pedestal foot, containing a threepenny-piece of 1710. Probably contemporary with the coin. H. 5".

2. Tankard, threaded border round the rim, base "nipt diamond waies," below a thread circuit, reeded handle. In the base a half-crown of 1746. Made to commemorate the defeat of the Stuart Rebellion, 1746. H. 7¼".

3. Tankard, threaded border round the rim, base "nipt diamond waies," reeded handle. Early 18th century. H. 4½".

No. 3 is of richer metal than the others,

PLATE LXXIX

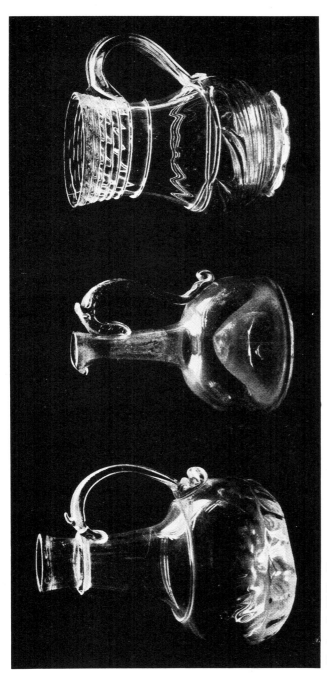

The late C. Kirkby Mason.

1. Decanter-bottle, lead glass, ringed neck, globular body with threaded circuit and gadrooned base; clipped handle. About 1690. H. 7¾".
   For threading cf. Pl. LXXVI (b 1), and for handle Pls. XVIII, XX. The shape follows the wine-bottle.

2. Decanter-jug, lead glass, clipped handle, domed bottom. English, early 18th century. H. 6½".
   Cf. Connoisseur, April 1929.

3. Tankard, soda glass, threaded border below the rim; wrythen base with flammiform fringe below a trailed circuit, foot pressed in scallops, reeded handle. Netherlandish, late 17th century. H. 6½".
   For flammiform fringe cf. Pl. LXV (3), for foot and trailing Pl. LXXV (3), for threading Pl. LXXX (1).

PLATE LXXX

Col. R. F. Ratcliff.

1. Tankard, barrel-shaped, with threaded ornament round the rim and base; reeded handle. Middle of 18th century. H. 5".

2. Wine-glass, trumpet bowl engraved with a border of baroque scrollwork and a portrait of William III in a medallion; above, a ribboned legend THE GLORIOUS & IMMORTALL MEMORY OF KING WILL iii, and below, a further inscription HE WAS BUT WORDS ARE WANTING TO SAY WHAT SAY ALL THATS GREAT & GOOD AND HE WAS THAT (*sic*); drawn stem with tear drop and folded foot. Probably Irish (Dublin), about 1720. H. 9½".

The engraving probably by a German.

3. Tankard, waisted, with decoration " nipt diamond waies "; reeded handle and foot rim. First half of 18th century. H. 5¼".

Cf. Pl. LXXVIII.

Plate LXXXI

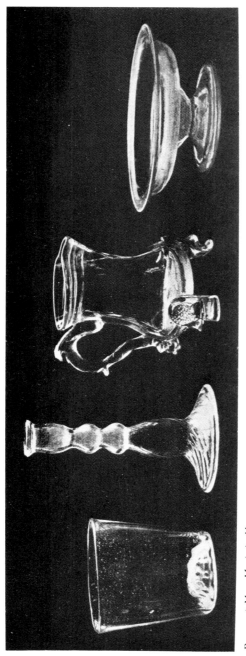

Rev. and Mrs. M. de la Hey.

1. Tumbler, g.l., probably an early attempt of a potash glasshouse to make lead glass. Late 17th or early 18th century. H. 2¾″.

2. Candlestick, g.l., hollow knopped stem, wrythen. Late 17th century (as No. 1, an experimental piece). H. 4¼″.

3. Cream-jug, clipped handle, prunted and pincered feet. About 1725. H. 3½″. *Cf.* Pl. LXXXIV (*b* 1) for a lion-mask jug of similar type. Refer back to Pl. XXV (2) for handle.

4. Sweetmeat bowl, flat double-ogee bowl, no stem, domed foot, with folded rim. Early 18th century. H. 1½″.

PLATE LXXXII

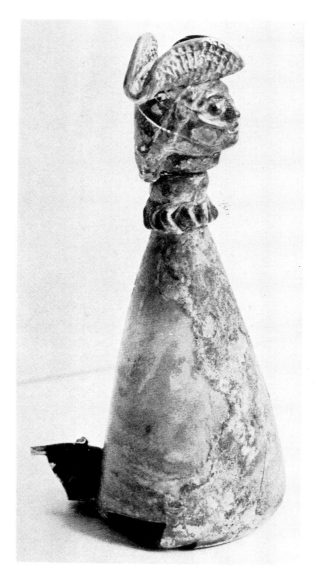

Guildhall Museum.

Bird-bath, g.l. blown and moulded, with man's head and a " hat of the Ramillie Cock," and collar below. Perhaps by T. Meyer, about 1705. H. 6".

Cf. F. Buckley, p. 143, *for an advertisement of Meyer's.*

PLATE LXXXIII

Col. R. F. Ratcliff.

Three sweetmeat glasses.

1. Gadrooned bowl with folded rim, straight indented stem, folded foot.   Early 18th century.   H. 3¼".
   The bowl is the " *mortar* " *shape ; see* p. 324

2. Gadrooned bowl, balustroid stem.   Early 18th century.   H. 2⅞".

3. Incurved bowl, the base gadrooned, flaring rim, straight air-twist stem.   About 1730.   H. 4".

PLATE LXXXIV

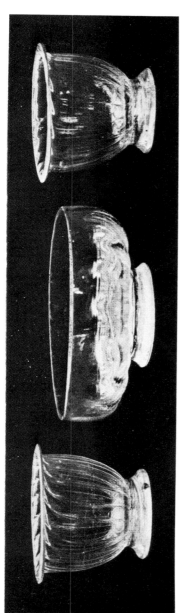

Saffron Walden Museum.

1, 3. Sweetmeat bowls (? salt cellars), lead glass, ribbed, flaring rim. Late 17th century. H. 2".

Similar bowls were ordered by Greene from Venice, but plain and without the rim. One of the plain kind is in V.A.M. The metal of these two is slightly crackled owing to faulty annealing. Cf. p. 39.

2. Sweetmeat dish, lead glass, gadrooned base. Late 17th century. H. 1½", diam. 4". *The metal crackled as above.*

Saffron Walden Museum.

1. Cream-jug, border of threads below the rim, lion-mask feet. About 1740. H. 3⅞". *This shape is copied from silver; cf. Jackson, Old English Plate, p. 985. Also a silver shape; Jackson, fig. 788–789.*

2. Tripod salt, bulbous body slightly ribbed, lion-mask feet. About 1740. H. 2", diam. 3".

3. Mug, undecorated. First half of 18th century. H. 3½".

PLATE LXXXV

Col. R. F. Ratcliff.

Covered goblet showing the first influence of German imported glasses on English style. German features not yet assimilated (contrast Pl. LXXXVII), but combined in a rather haphazard manner with Anglo-Venetian and pure English features. The glass may be analysed :—

        Anglo-Venetian : ornament " nipt diamond waies " on bowl and lid.

        German : bowl form, and shouldered stem with bosses and the *fact* of the lid.

        Independent English : Ball-knop and acorn-knob (Pl. LXX (2)).

        Netherlandish (probably) : wrything of ball-knop and of the acorn's cup.

About 1710.   H. 12½″.

PLATE LXXXVI

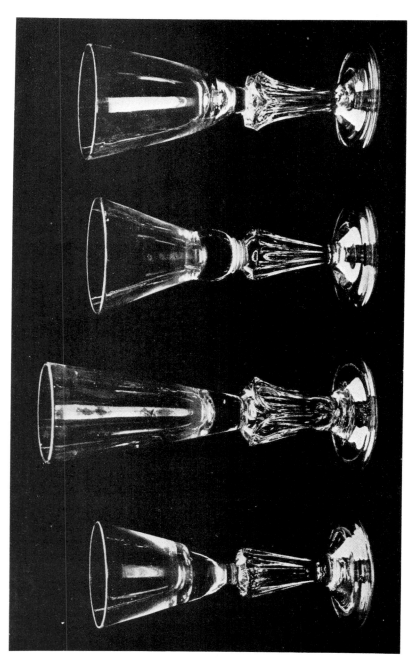

The late C. Kirkby Mason.

German influence assimilated.

1. Wine-glass, r.f. bowl (E), shouldered stem, folded foot. About 1710–1715. H. 6″.
2. Flute, four-shouldered stem (G), folded foot. About 1710. H. 7¼″.
3. Wine-glass, thistle bowl (G), shouldered stem (G), folded foot. About 1715. H. 6¼″.
4. Wine-glass, r.f. bowl, small knop above a four-shouldered stem with bosses, folded foot. About 1710. H. 6⅜″.

The earlier glasses are those in which the German stem is combined with the older English r.f. bowl of the Venetian tradition. The shouldered stem continues until c. 1740, but not in these combinations.

PLATE LXXXVII

J. M. Bacon, Esq.

German influence assimilated.

1. Wine-glass, trumpet bowl on shouldered and bossed stem with collars at the base, folded foot. About 1715–1720. H. 6½".
2. Wine-glass, thistle bowl on shouldered stem, folded foot. About 1715. H. 7".
3. Wine-glass, r.f. bowl, ball knop above a four-shouldered stem with domed top, folded foot. About 1715–1720. H. 7⅞".
4. Wine-glass, r.f. bowl, small knop above shouldered and bossed stem, about 1710–1715. H. 6⅞".
5. Wine-glass, bell-bowl, shouldered stem. About 1720. H. 6⅜".

Cf. Pl. LXXXVI.

PLATE LXXXVIII

Henry Brown, Esq.

1. Wine-glass, s.f. bowl, square knop moulded with the toast *GOD SAVE KING GEORG*, above a shouldered stem with bosses (G), folded foot. About 1714. H. 6¼″.

   A type used by the Hanoverian clubs early in the reign of George I. V. Apollo, Vol. III, pp. 165 et seq. A similar glass in the London Museum.

2. Wine-glass, s.f. bowl drawn into stem of three knops and a short baluster. About 1720–1730. H. 7½″. Cf. *Pl. LIII* (b 1) *and p. 180.*

3. Wine-glass, bell bowl, annular stem with knop at base, folded foot. About 1720. H. 6″.

   For the stem cf. Pl. LVIII and for the glass p. 173.

PLATE LXXXIX

1. Bowl, g.l., blown double, silvered and ribbed, pedestal foot ribbed. Late 17th century. H. 4".
   Perhaps a water-glass ; made in imitation of silver.
2. Stand, late 17th or early 18th century. H. 4¾".
3. Sweetmeat bowl, ribbed ; short knopped stem, domed and ribbed foot. Beginning of 18th century. H. 2⅞".

Lady Davy.

1. Wine-glass, g.l., r.f. bowl, short double-knopped stem, folded foot. Probably provincial, first half 18th century. H. 5⅜".
2. Wine- or cordial-glass, thin drawn stem with air-twist. About 1730–1740. H. 7¼".
   For the shape cf. Pl. XLV.
3. Wine-glass, funnel bowl drawn into a true baluster with cyst and a knop below ; domed and folded foot (" tulip glass "). Early 18th century. H. 5½".

PLATE XC

W. W. Winkworth, Esq.

Covered sweetmeat bowl engraved with vine-leaves and grapes; teared knob. Early 18th century, the engraving about 1740. H. 8¾".

Col. R. F. Ratcliff.

Covered sweetmeat bowl. The lid has an engraved border transitional between the formal baroque of German engraving and the later English naturalism, probably by a German working in England. Note also the combination of ball-knop with bossed and shouldered stem (German); teared knob and domed foot. About 1720. H. 10″.

PLATE XCII

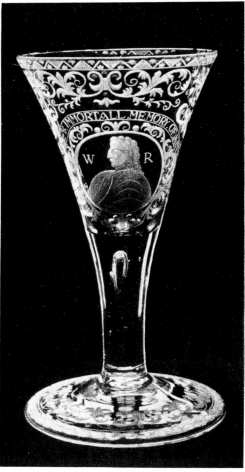

Mrs. W. D. Dickson.   *Hamilton Clements, Esq.*

1. Wine-glass, trumpet bowl and drawn stem with large tear-drops. Diamond-engraved with a vine branch coiled round the stem and spreading its leaves and grapes round the bowl; on one side an armorial shield surmounted by a pierced heart and containing the inscribed legend *Charming Miss Betty Phillips* over the signature *A. Jameson*, with the motto *OMNIA VINCIT AMOR* in a ribbon below; on the other side the arms of Jameson, surmounted by a three-masted ship, with the motto *VIVAS UT VIVAS* in a ribbon below. About 1720. H. 9¾".

> *The vine, shields, etc., done to order by a professional engraver, perhaps a silversmith, the legend added by the donor, no doubt a sailor.*

2. Wine-glass, trumpet bowl, engraved with baroque foliated scrollwork below a formal border and a portrait bust of William III flanked by the letters W. R. in a scrollwork medallion under the legend *THE GLORIOUS AND IMMORTAL MEMORY OF KING WILLIAM AND HIS QUEEN MARY*, drawn stem with large tear drop, and folded foot engraved with a foliated border. Probably Irish (Dublin), about 1720. H. 9⅞".

> *The engraving probably by a German.*   *Cf. Pl. LXXX (2).*

PLATE XCIII

Sir John S. Risley.   *Hamilton Clements, Esq.*

1. Goblet of lead glass, r.f. bowl with decoration stippled in diamond point by Frans Greenwood of
   Dordrecht and Rotterdam (b. 1680, d. 1762), heavy knopped stem, domed foot. The glass English
   (probably Newcastle-on-Tyne), about 1710–1720 ; the engraving about 1725. H. 11¼″.

   > *Dated works of Greenwood vary between 1722 and 1749, and the
   > form of the glass suggests an early date in this period. By reason
   > of its bulk it can scarcely be later than 1720 ; for glasses of
   > similar proportions but less bulk (i.e. later) cf. Pl. CXV (2).*

2. Goblet, r.f. bowl, diamond-engraved, acorn stem with knop. About 1710. H. 15¼″.

   > *The subject, Silenus riding on an ass, copied from a Dutch 17th-
   > century painting (? by Jordaens), probably by a dining amateur.*

PLATE XCIV

Henry Holford, Esq.   *William Roscoe, Esq.*

1. Wine-glass, s.f. bowl, engraved with a border of baroque scrollwork, balustroid stem, folded foot.
   About 1710–1720. H. 7½″.

   The engraving probably by a German metic. See p. 238.

2. Wine-glass, double-ogee bowl, acorn between two knops, domed foot; the bowl engraved with a
   baroque border, probably by a German metic. About 1710–1720. H. 6¾″.

   For the shape cf. Pl. XLVIII (1) and p. 172.

PLATE XCV

Col. R. F. Ratcliff.

1. Wine-glass, trumpet bowl, drawn air-twist stem; the rim engraved with a border of baroque scrollwork.   About 1720.   H. 8⅝″.

> *The engraving probably by a German metic.   For form and engraving cf. a green air-twist glass in the British Museum (F. Buckley, Pl. LVIII a).   In the same Museum is an English calender with* millifiori *base and a shaft with similar air-twist; it has a contemporary metal mount inscribed E. C., with the date 1716.   In both the calender and this glass the air-twist is primitive.*

2. Wine-glass, double-ogee bowl, drawn stem; the bowl engraved with a border of baroque scrolls and naturalistic flowers; the upper part of the stem with vine leaves.   About 1730.   H. 7½″.

> *In this glass may be observed three stages of engraving : (1) baroque scroll-work ; (2) naturalistic bouquets ; (3) vine motive.   The engraving is probably English ; pp. 238 sq.*

PLATE XCVI

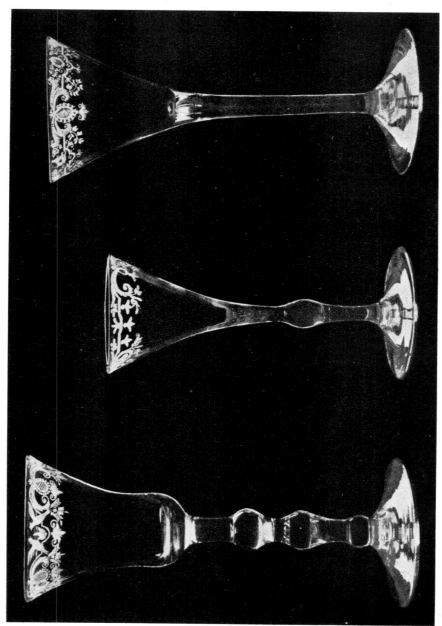

Henry Brown, Esq.

Anglo-German baroque engraving.

1. Wine-glass, bell bowl, knopped stem. The engraving probably by a German metic. *c.* 1725. H. 8″.
2. Wine-glass, trumpet bowl, drawn stem with wavy knop. The engraving probably by an English pupil or imitator. *c.* 1730. H. 6¼″.
3. Wine-glass, trumpet bowl, drawn stem. The engraving probably by a German metic. *c.* 1725. H. 7½″.

The metic engravers were probably free-lance workers and did not necessarily use new glasses. In some instances, such as No. 3, the glass may be some years earlier than the engraving. Cf. Pl. XLV for No. 3.

PLATE **XCVII**

The late C. Kirkby Mason.

1. Wine-glass, trumpet bowl and drawn stem with air-twist. Anglo-German engraving of formal foliage. About 1740. H. 6½". See p. 238 *sq.*

2. Wine-glass, with bell bowl, the stem composed of a thin baluster and triple-ring knop ("light baluster"). Foliated border showing early English attempt to copy German baroque engraving. About 1730. H. 6½". See p. 240.

3. Wine-glass, trumpet bowl drawn and let into double-knop air-twist stem. Foliated border engraved by an Englishman, probably unfinished. Domed foot. About 1730. H. 6½". See p. 240.

4. Wine-glass, bell bowl, wavy knop, and domed foot. English engraving of vine-leaves and grapes. About 1740. H. 6⅞".

PLATE XCVIII

G. F. Berney, Esq.

1. Wine-glass, r.f. bowl engraved with a border of birds and baroque scrollwork, double-knop stem with air twist.   About 1745.   H. 6⅛".
   The engraving probably by a German metic.
2. Wine-glass, bell bowl engraved with a foliated baroque border, straight stem with double-coil air twist.   About 1745.   H. 6⅞".
   The engraving probably by an Englishman.
3. Wine-glass, straight-sided bowl engraved with a border of naturalistic flowers, straight air-twist stem, domed foot.   About 1750.
   The engraving English.

PLATE XCIX

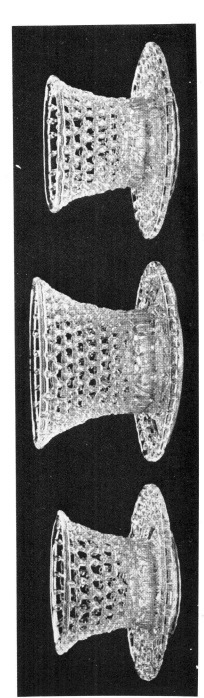

Victoria and Albert Museum.
1. Jug. First half of 18th century. H. 5″.   2. Linen-smoother. First quarter of 18th century. H. 5¼″.
3. Jam- or honey-pot. First half of 18th century. H. 5″.

Col. R. F. Ratcliff.
Fruit-baskets and stands (g.l.), twisted and pincered work. Probably about 1730 (p. 324). H. 5¼″, 6¼″, 5¼″.

PLATE C

G. F. Berney, Esq.

1. Rummer, deep green flint glass, gadrooned bowl, double-knopped stem with air-twist, domed foot. *c.* 1740. H. 6½″.
2. Rummer, pale green flint glass, gadrooned bowl, double-knopped stem wrythen, folded foot. *c.* 1730–40. H. 4¾″.
3. Rummer, deep green flint glass, plain bowl, wrythen stem. *c.* 1740. H. 6⅝″.
4. Rummer, the bowl of pale green flint glass, the stem composed of green glass with prunts and clear glass with white enamel twist, domed foot of green glass. *c.* 1750. H. 6¼″.   *Cf. Pl. XLI and p.* 327 *for these glasses.*

G. F. Berney, Esq.

1. Wine-glass, deep green flint glass, long r.f. bowl, shouldered stem with bosses, domed foot. *c.* 1710–20. H. 6″.
2. Rummer, green flint glass, solid knopped stem. First half of 18th century. H. 8⅛″.
3. Wine-glass, pale green metal, inverted baluster stem. Beginning of 18th century. H. 5⅞″.

PLATE CI

Rev. and Mrs. M. de la Hey.

1. Wine-glass, r.f. bowl diamond-engraved in line with a representation of the Fall and the initials
   I $\cdot$ E (with A above); shouldered stem, folded foot. English (probably Bristol), about 1710. H. 7¼″.

   > *Probably a marriage glass. For the shape cf. Pl. XXXVII which has an earlier version of the same subject. The treatment is comparable with that of Bristol enamelled earthenware ; as also is the lettering.*

2. Wine-glass, ogee bowl with diamond-stippled portraits of William V of Orange and his consort, Frederica Sophia Wilhelmina; probably executed by D. Wolff of Dordrecht and The Hague; fluted and notched stem. The glass English (probably Newcastle-on-Tyne), the engraving Dutch ; about 1790. H. 5⅝″.

   > *For the date cf. W. Buckley, Pl. 77 A, and Muhsam Catalogue (i), No. 52. If Wolff died at an early age in 1808 (Hudig, p. xxxi) this glass can scarcely be a marriage glass dating from 1767 when William V married Frederica Sophia. Wolff's dated glasses range between 1786 and 1796. The details of the engraving conform to Dr. Hudig's first type (i.e. glasses which are completely stippled and have no lines).*

3. Wine-glass, short funnel bowl engraved in Holland, with a drinking scene and the legend *ABSENTE-VRINDE* ; annulated knop above a long inverted baluster with a knop at the base ; domed foot. English (Newcastle-on-Tyne), about 1740. H. 7⅜″.

   > *For attribution see Connoisseur, LXXXI, 20–21, and W. Buckley in Old Furniture, July, 1927. For similar engraved subject probably by a Dutchman working in England, see Hartshorne, Pl. 46.*

PLATE CII

Dr. Tancred Borenius.

Pair of wine- or cordial-glasses, engraved with equestrian portrait (l.) of William III, and the inscription TO THE GLORIOUS MEMORY OF KING WILLIAM, BOYNE IST JULY 1690. Note straight funnel bowl and double collars on a plain stem. Probably Dublin, middle of 18th century. H. 6¼″.

PLATE CIII

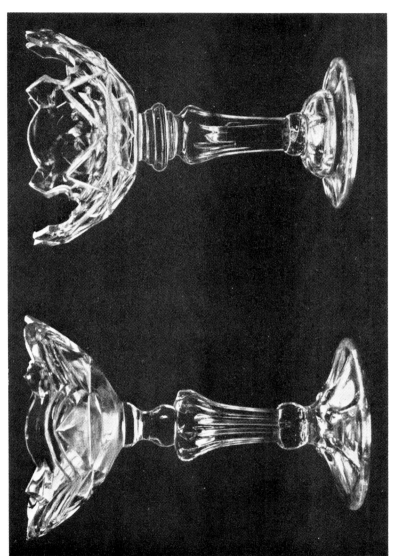

Rev. and Mrs. M. de la Hey.

The late C. Kirkby Mason.

1. Sweetmeat glass, bowl cut in triangles below double arches, scalloped rim, shouldered stem, fan-moulded foot. About 1730. H. 6⅜″.

2. Sweetmeat glass, deeply scalloped rim, shouldered stem with triple-ring knop, domed foot with fan moulding. About 1730. H. 6¼″.

PLATE CIV

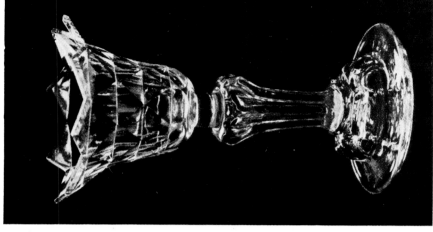

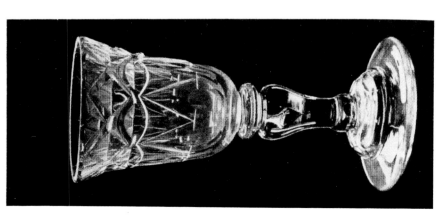

The late C. Kirkby Mason.

1. Sweetmeat glass, bell bowl cut raised diamonds, festoons and circuit of zig-zags, inverted baluster below a collar, domed foot. About 1730. H. 9″.

   For this early zig-zag motive in cutting cf. Pl. CIII (2). F. Buckley, Pl. XXII.

2. Goblet, r.f. bowl cut in flutes about the base and engraved with the initials T Y between crossed sprays, heavy knopped stem cut in small facets, folded foot. The glass and cutting about 1720; the engraving later. H. 10″.

   Cutting of German type, probably by a German metic.

3. Sweetmeat glass, bell bowl cut in flat triangular facets, rim cut in an angular scallops; small knop above a shouldered stem, domed foot ribbed radially. About 1720. H. 8″.

   For the combination of these two types of early cutting of Pl. CV (1), a glass with a shouldered stem cut. A "corner brimmed glass." (Lady Grisell Baillie, 1727).

Hamilton Clements, Esq.

PLATE CV

Col. R. F. Ratcliff.

1. Sweetmeat glass, scalloped rim, double ogee bowl, the upper part cut in flat arches, the lower in flat triangles (*cf.* Pl. CIV (3)); shouldered stem cut in flutes, foot moulded in radial ribs, foot-rim cut in scallops. About 1730. H. 5¾″.

> *For upper bowl cutting cf. Pl. CIII (1); for the lower bowl cutting, and for the foot moulding, Pl. CIV (3).*

2. Double sweetmeat glass, scalloped rims, the upper bowl cut in diamond panels of quadruple relief diamonds, the lower with a circuit of large relief diamonds. Straight stem cut in flutes and notches. About 1770. H. 8¾″.

3. Sweetmeat glass, cup bowl with scalloped rim and a circuit of double-grooved diamonds; shouldered stem, domed foot with radial ribs. About 1725. H. 7¾″. *Cf. Pl. CIII.*

PLATE CVI

Hamilton Clements, Esq.

Early cutting in wine-glasses.

1. Wine-glass, bell bowl cut in diamonds, straight stem cut in long diamond facets, foot cut in terraces and round the edge in flat slices, the edge of the foot cut and undercut alternately. About 1740. H. 7½″.

> *A heavy glass probably dating from before the Excise Act of 1745–1746 (p. 248), and showing the elaboration possible even so early, given a good bulk of metal.*

2. Wine-glass, small r.f. bowl cut in arches and diamonds, cusped stem cut in flutes, foot cut in radial fans. About 1750. H. 5⅞″.

> *Cutting adapted to a small light glass; probably subsequently to the Excise.*

3. Wine-glass, bell bowl engraved with double bouquets and cut in a circuit of double arches with lunar slices and facets below, cusped stem cut in long diamonds, domed foot cut with ellipses. About 1740–1750. H. 7½″.

> *For the circuit of lunar slices in zig-zag cf. Pl. CIV (1).*

PLATE CVII

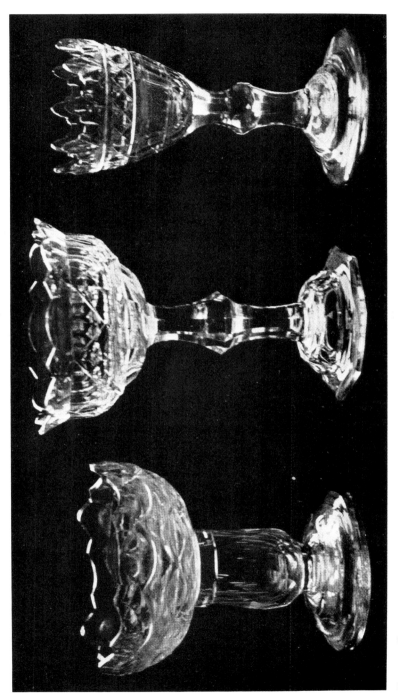

Hamuton Clements, Esq.

1. Sweetmeat glass, scalloped rim, the bowl cut in geometric patterns, the stem in hollow diamonds. About 1740. H. 7″.

Early type of cutting. Probably prior to 1746 ; for the bulk of the metal cf. Pl. CVI (1).

2. Sweetmeat glass, scalloped rim, bowl cut in geometrical pattern, cusped stem cut in vertical flutes, polygonal foot. About 1750. H. 8¼″.

3. Sweetmeat glass, rim cut in a trefoil repeat, bowl cut with a border of relief diamonds above flutes, cusped stem cut in flutes. English or Irish late 18th century. H. 7¾″.

Bands of relief diamonds appear to be a later development of cutting.

PLATE CVIII

Robert Frank, Esq.

1. Sweetmeat glass, the rim cut in a double scallop repeat, the bowl with stars above a circuit of festoons, cusped stem cut in small diamonds; octagonal foot, domed. English, third quarter of 18th century. H. 6⅛″.

2. Sweetmeat glass, open double-ogee bowl, the rim cut in sharp cusps, the body in geometric pattern, cusped stem cut in small diamonds; octagonal foot, domed. About 1740. H. 8¼″.

> *For rim cf. Pl. CIV (3); for the flat sliced cutting which preceded (in English glass) the elaborate diamond compositions developed in Ireland cf. Pl. CIV (1). Lady Grisell Baillie spoke of " corner-brimmed glasses for desserts" (1727).*

3. Sweetmeat glass, rim cut in a trefoil repeat, elaborately cut bowl with a circuit of relief diamonds above festoons, cusped stem fluted and notched, petalled foot. Irish, about 1800. H. 6⅝″.

> *Later elaboration of Irish cutting; cf. Pl. CVII (3).*

PLATE CIX

Sir John S. Risley.

1. Water-glass with foot, threaded border below the rim, base "nipt diamond waies" and containing a coin of George II (date indecipherable). About 1730–1740. H. 4⅝".
2. Water-glass with foot, threaded border below the rim, trailed circuit, base "nipt diamond waies." Early 18th century. H. 4¼".   *Cf. p. 332 and Pl. CXXXV (a 1)*

Dr. Tancred Borenius.

1. Water-glass with domed foot (p. 332 ; *cf.* Pl. CXXXV (a 1)), engraved with Jacobite rose and one bud. About 1750. H. 4½".
2. Tumbler engraved with portrait of Charles Edward Stuart flanked by rose and thistle. ? Newcastle-on-Tyne, about 1750. H. 4⅛".

PLATE CX

Mrs. W. D. Dickson.

Wine-glass, straight-sided bowl engraved with a portrait (r.) of Charles Edward Stuart in a wreath flanked by rose and thistle, and on the other side an oak-leaf; double-knopped air-twist stem. About 1750. H. 8¾″.

One of a series in which the portrait appears to be copied from a glass with similar portrait (but l.) in Mr. Bles's collection. Mr. Francis (Jacobite Drinking Glasses, p. 25) argues that the engraving of the r. series was done abroad, on the ground that the Star and Garter are misplaced, and suggests that the series was engraved about 1752, to be given to Stuart's supporters in exile. These r. series may well be copies and dating from after the '45, but the oak-leaf on this glass is of a type normally found on Jacobite glasses, which are certainly English-engraved, and the rest of the engraving is quite in character with it. A copyist engraver at (say) Newcastle might well be ignorant of the position of the Orders, and in reversing the portrait, omit the alteration of them. There does not seem to be sufficient reason for postulating an engraver working abroad.

PLATE CXI

Hamilton Clements, Esq.

1. Wine-glass, straight-sided bowl engraved with a full-face portrait of Charles Edward Stuart, two buds, a thistle, and the legend :

   Charles, ye Great, ye Brave, the Just and Good
   Britannias Prince, ye noblest of her Bld
   Thy Glorious feats ye world may Prm
   Britannias Glory and Brittans Shame ;

   air-twist stem. About 1750. H. 7⅝". Formerly at Oxburgh Hall.
2. Wine-glass, straight-sided bowl with portrait of Charles Edward Stuart in a medallion above the motto *Audentior ibo* (Virg. Aen. ix, 291),
   air-twist stem. About 1745–1750. H. 7⅞".
3. Wine-glass, ogee bowl, engraved with a full-faced portrait of Charles Edward Stuart in a medallion beneath the legend *CAROLUS.*
   flanked by rose-and-bud and thistle, stem with double air twist. About 1745–1750. H. 7⅞".
   *Hartshorne, pp. 361 and 372 ; formerly in possession of the Berkeley family of
   Caynham Court, Shropshire. For the portraits see Francis, Jacobite glasses, fig. 2.*

PLATE CXII

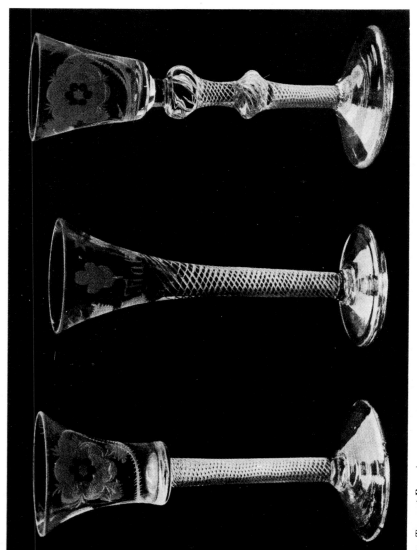

Dr. Tancred Borenius.

1. Wine-glass, trumpet bowl, engraved with the Jacobite rose and bud ; air-twist stem. About 1745–1750. H. 6".

2. Wine-glass, trumpet bowl engraved with emblems of the Cycle Club ; rose-and-bud star and oak-leaf and the motto *Fiat*. Drawn stem with air twist. About 1745–1750. H. 5¾".

3. Wine-glass, bucket bowl engraved with Jacobite rose and one bud ; double-knopped air-twist stem. About 1745–1750. H. 6".

PLATE CXIII

Hamilton Clements, Esq.

1. Wine-glass, trumpet bowl, drawn stem, with air twist ; the bowl engraved with rose and buds, oak-leaf, and the motto *Cujus est Cuique suum reddite*. About 1740–1745. H. 7″.

    A Cycle Club glass ; cf. Hartshorne, p. 363, for another with this motto. The motto taken from a medal ; cf. Medall. Illus. II, 312–313, *and Francis,* Jacobite Drinking Glasses, *pp. 15–16.*

2. Wine-glass, straight-sided bowl, air-twist stem, domed foot, the bowl engraved with a rose and two buds, star, and *Fiat*. About 1745–1749. H. 5 7⁄16″.

3. Wine-glass, trumpet bowl, air-twist stem, the bowl engraved with Jacobite emblems and the motto *Reddas Incolumem*. About 1750. H. 6½″.

PLATE CXIV

Rev. and Mrs. M. de la Hey.

1. Covered tankard, engraved with flowers, double-domed lid with air-tear knob, air-twist handle. About 1750. H. 6¼".

2. Drinking-glass, lead metal, hollow stem. English, 18th century. H. 6⅝".
   Probably a trick drinking-glass, the bulb making difficulties as with the " yard of ale."

PLATE CXV

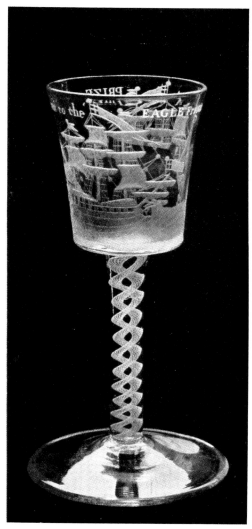

Henry Holford, Esq.   *W. W. Winkworth, Esq.*

1. Drinking-glass, square bucket bowl, slightly waisted, engraved with two ships at sea and the legend *Success to the* EAGLE *Frigate* and *A PRIZE*, straight stem with white enamel twist. Bristol, about 1757. H. 6¾".

> *The Eagle was a privateer operating from Bristol during the Seven Years War (1756–1763). Successive commanders, Dibden and Knill, are mentioned in 1757 (London Chronicle, 12 iv. 1757 and 28 vi. 1757).*

2. Wine-glass. Short r.f. bowl engraved with landscape by a German. Long knopped stem. Newcastle-on-Tyne, about 1730–1740. *Cf.* pp. 147, 151. H. 7⅜".

PLATE CXVI

Sir John S. Risley.

1. Covered goblet, the bowl engraved with a figure of Britannia and the legend *O FAIR BRITANNIA HAIL* within a wreath, cut stem and lid, foot engraved with a wreath. About 1760. H. 11⅝".

> *A German type of glass made for one of the patriotic societies which flourished during the Seven Years War (1756–1763) and later. Glasses with the same legend are occasionally met with. For the cutting of the stem cf. p. 251.*

2. Goblet, ogee-bowl engraved with a figure of Britannia in a medallion on a scrolled and trellised ground, white enamel-twist stem, foot engraved with a trellised border. About 1760. H. 7".

> *The engraving is German in character and probably by a German. Cf. Pl. CXV (1) for the historical context.*

PLATE CXVII

Henry Brown, Esq.

1. Wine-glass, ogee bowl cut round the base in flutes and scales, straight air-twist stem. *c.* 1750. H. 5¾".
2. Flute, the bowl cut in scales about the lower part, straight stem with twists of white enamel. *c.* 1755. H. 7¼".
3. Wine-glass, ogee bowl cut about the base in arch-and-sprig pattern, straight stem cut in notches. *c.* 1760. H. 5¾".

Henry Brown, Esq.

1. Wine-glass, ogee bowl with flat geometrical cutting, cusped stem cut in small diamonds, scalloped foot. *c.* 1750–1760. H. 6".
2. Wine-glass engraved with a crested border and cut in a lotus pattern; straight stem cut in small diamonds. Late 18th century. H. 5¾".
3. Cordial-glass, bowl engraved with a formal border, tall stem cut in oblong hooked panels. *c.* 1750–1760. H. 7¼".

PLATE CXVIII

Henry Brown, Esq.

1. Cordial-glass, ogee bowl engraved with a vine border and cut in flutes and sprigs round the base; knopped and cusped stem cut in facets and long diamonds; domed foot with lozenge cutting. About 1750–1760. H. 5⅝".

2. Wine-glass, small funnel bowl with arch-and sprig cutting round the base, cusped stem notched and facetted. About 1750–1760. H. 6¼".

3. Wine-glass, bell bowl engraved with a border of flowers and cut in arches about the base, cusped stem, petalled foot. About 1770. H. 6".

PLATE CXIX

Rev. and Mrs. M. de la Hey.

1. Wine-glass, ogee bowl, with engraved border below a flaring rim and arched cutting about the base, cusped stem cut in small diamonds. About 1760. H. 6⅛".

2. Flute, bowl cut with flutes to the rim, cusped stem cut in diamonds, foot cut in fan panels (Pre-Excise). About 1740. H. 8¼".

3. Wine-glass, r.f. bowl engraved *H : R* 1767 *BEATI NON NUMERANT HORAS* and cut in arches about the base, short stem cut in small diamonds. Dated 1767. H. 6".

4. Wine-glass, trumpet bowl cut in small diamonds about the base, fluted stem. About 1750. H. 7⅛".

5. Wine-glass, ogee bowl cut in arches about the base, the stem cut alternately in flutes and small diamonds, foot cut in fan panels. About 1760. H. 5⅝".

PLATE **CXX**

Henry Brown, Esq.

1. Wine-glass, ogee bowl with engraved decoration, straight stem with ridged cutting. English, late 18th century. H. 5¼″.
2. Wine-glass, ogee bowl engraved with a hunting scene, and cut in arch-and-sprig pattern round the base, straight stem cut in long diamonds. English, about 1760. H. 6⅛″.
3. Wine-glass, ogee bowl engraved with a ship and a castle on a hill, double twists of white enamel. About 1750–1760. H. 5½″.

Mrs. W. D. Dickson.

Three of a set of four wine-glasses engraved with scenes emblematic of the seasons, ogee bowls, double air-twist stems : *SPRING. SUMMER. WINTER.* About 1760. H. 7¼″.

PLATE CXXI

William Roscoe, Esq.

Four of a set of twelve wine-glasses, ogee bowls engraved with figures and landscapes in the Chinese manner ; stems cut in small diamonds. About 1760–1770. H. 5½".

PLATE CXXII

Mrs. W. D. Dickson.

Set of four wine-glasses, straight-sided bowls engraved with scenes, and cut about the base with arch-and-sprig repeat ; straight stems cut in small diamonds ; feet sliced in radial panels. About 1765. H. 6″.

G. F. Berney, Esq.

1. Wine-glass, s.s. bowl with oil-gilt decoration, enamel-twist stem. H. 7½″.

2. Ale-glass, s.s. bowl with oil-gilt decoration of hops and barley and gilt rim, enamel-twist stem. H. 8¼″.

3. Wine-glass, ogee bowl ; as No. 1, with gilt rim.

All third quarter of 18th century.

PLATE CXXIII

Hamilton Clements, Esq.

1. Firing-glass, with Masonic emblems painted in yellow enamel, the border in white, by William and Mary Beilby of Newcastle-on-Tyne. About 1765. H. 3⅛″.

2. Goblet, with landscape painted in enamel colours; by William and Mary Beilby of Newcastle-on-Tyne; air-twist stem. About 1765. H. 6⅞″.

3. Firing-glass, with Masonic emblems composing an armorial shield painted in colours by William and Mary Beilby of Newcastle-on-Tyne. About 1765. H. 3⅜″.

PLATE CXXIV

G. F. Berney, Esq.

Goblet, square bucket bowl painted in enamel colours by the Beilby family of Newcastle-on-Tyne ; on one side the Royal Arms and motto as borne by George III, supported by rococo scrollwork and festoons, on the other side the Feathers of the Prince of Wales below the signature *Beilby N Castle inv^t & pinx^t*. Straight stem with double twist of white enamel. Newcastle-on-Tyne, about 1762. H. $9\frac{1}{16}''$.

Probably made and painted to commemorate the birth of George III's eldest son, George Augustus Frederick, afterwards George IV (b. 12 Aug., 1762). Probably painted by William Beilby, with the assistance of Ralph, who was an heraldic engraver. See Connoisseur, *May 1928, pp.* 10 sq.

PLATE CXXV

The late C. Kirkby Mason.   *Victoria and Albert Museum.* (Bles Loan.)   *Victoria and Albert Museum.*

1. Decanter, lacking stopper ; globular body engraved with a portrait of Charles Edward Stuart in a medallion flanked by thistle and rose branches (the latter with one bud) ; above, the motto *AUDENTIOR IBO*, and on the other side a star. About 1745–1750. H. 9¼″.

2. Decanter, lacking stopper ; high shouldered body engraved on one side with a bouquet of flowers, on the other with an equestrian portrait of William III, with the Irish harp below, and above, the legend *THE IMMORTAL MEMORY OF THE GLORIOUS KING WILLIAM.* Irish (Dublin), about 1750. H. 12″.

3. Decanter, cut all over in diamond facets and round the neck in flutes ; pyramid stopper cut in diamonds. About 1755. H. 12″.

See pp. 318 sq. and for No. 3 cf. Pl. CXXVIII.

PLATE CXXVI

Rev. and Mrs. M. de la Hey.

1. Shouldered decanter with cut and engraved decoration. Neck cut in polygons, short flutes round base, disc stopper with lunar cutting. English, about 1755. H. 11¼".

2. Decanter, bulbous, neck with polished engraving, body moulded in diamonds, disc stopper cut in a cross. English, *c.* 1760. H. 10¾".

3. Shouldered decanter, cut and engraved; neck cut in polygons, body cut in plain zig-zag round the base and engraved with star festoons, scalloped stopper cut in four relief diamonds. English, *c.* 1755. H. 11¼". *For cutting cf. Pl. CXXVII* (b 1), *Fig. 23, and p.* 249.

PLATE CXXVII

Victoria and Albert Museum.

Two shouldered decanters, engraved with labels PORT and W. WINE. Disc stoppers cut in lunar scallops. English, about 1760. H. 11¼".

"*New fashioned decanters with inscriptions engraven on them, Port Claret Mountain, etc. etc., decorated with vine-leaves, grapes, etc.*" Norwich Mercury, 26 Dec., 1755.

S. D. Winkworth, Esq.   *W. W. Winkworth, Esq.*

1. Shouldered decanter, cut decoration, pyramid stopper. English, about 1760; for this earlier and simpler cutting see pp. 248 *sq.* H. 12½".

2. Shouldered decanter, engraved decoration, lozenge stopper cut in lunar scallops. English, about 1760. For naturalistic themes in engraving and the disappearance of German influence see pp. 241 *sq.*; for the stopper *cf.* Pl. CXXV (3); and for other examples of this type of decanter Pl. CXXVI. H. 11½".

PLATE CXXVIII

Rev. and Mrs. M. de la Hey.

1, 3. Pair of decanters, cut in flat diamonds, lozenge stoppers with hatched loop. English, about 1760. H. 9".
For cutting of this kind on an earlier decanter cf. Pl. CXXIV (3), and on other vessels, Pl. CIV (3); see also p. 250.

2. Wine-glass, the bowl similarly cut, cusped stem, cut in small diamonds. English, about 1760. H. 5".

Cf. F. Buckley, Pl. XXVII, A.1.

PLATE CXXIX

Col. R. F. Ratcliff.

1. Decanter, neck cut in facets, shouldered body crossed with cut ropework ; lozenge stopper bevelled to a ridge, with the edges straight-cut. About 1760. H. 11¾".

2. Punch decanter, shouldered body engraved with a floral panel containing the label ; cut pyramid stopper. About 1755–1760. H. 19".

3. Ship's decanter, four angular rings round the neck, target stopper. Late 18th century. H. 9½".

PLATE CXXX

Hamilton Clements, Esq. · *Wilfred Buckley, Esq.*

1. Decanter, lacking stopper, painted in enamel colours by the Beilbys of Newcastle-on-Tyne. Newcastle-on-Tyne, about 1762. H. 9″.

The Royal Arms as borne by George III ; cf. Pl. CXXIV for replica of this painting with the feathers of the Prince of Wales. Probably made for the birth of Frederick Prince of Wales, afterwards George IV (b. 12 Aug. 1762). For the shape and subsidiary painting cf. No. 2 and for the authorship see "The Beilby Glasses," Connoisseur, May 1928.

2. Decanter, lacking stopper, painted in white enamel by William and Mary Beilby, with butterfly-and-vine motive, and the label *MOUNTAIN* in a rococo panel. Newcastle-on-Tyne, about 1760–1765. H. 9″.

PLATE CXXXI

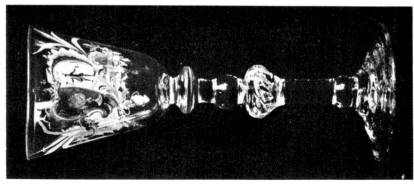

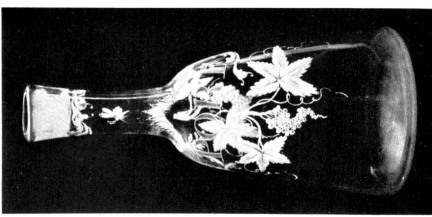

Wilfred Buckley, Esq.   *Sir John S. Risley.*

1, 3. Goblet, short funnel bowl, long knopped stem ; painted in enamel colours by William and Mary Beilby of Newcastle-on-Tyne and signed *Beilby pinxit*. Newcastle-on-Tyne, about 1770. H. 7½″.

See Connoisseur, *May* 1928.

2. Decanter, lacking stopper, shouldered type, labelled *PORT*, with decoration painted in white enamel by William and Mary Beilby at Newcastle-on-Tyne. Newcastle-on-Tyne, about 1765. H. 9½″. *Cf. Pl. CXXX* (2).

PLATE CXXXII

Henry Brown, Esq.

Three wine-glasses and a flute with decoration painted in white enamel by William and Mary Beilby of Newcastle-on-Tyne. Newcastle-on-Tyne, about 1770. H. 6$\frac{1}{16}$", 7", 5$\frac{3}{4}$", 6".

Cf. pp. 226 sq. and Connoisseur, *May 1928. There appear to be sets of Beilby glasses with the several subjects here shown.*

Mrs. W. D. Dickson.

Glasses made at Newcastle-on-Tyne and painted in white (1, 2, 4, 5) or coloured (3) enamels by William and Mary Beilby. About 1760–1778.

1. Ogee bowl with boating scene, air-twist stem. H. 5$\frac{3}{8}$".
2. Straight-sided bowl with pastoral scene. H. 6". *Cf. Pl. CXXIII (2).*
3. Short funnel bowl with gilt rim, two knops above an elongated inverted baluster, domed foot; pierced heart within a rococo panel. About 1760–1765.
   Probably a betrothal goblet. For the shape cf. Pl. CXXXI (1).
4. Straight-sided bowl with fishing scene, white enamel-twist stem. H. 6".
5. Ogee bowl with shooting scene, white enamel-twist stem. H. 5$\frac{3}{8}$".

Cf. pp. 226 sq. and Connoisseur, *May 1928.*

PLATE CXXXIII

S. D. Winkworth, Esq.

A set of three cut-glass toilet bottles from casket below.   About 1760.   H. 5″, 4⅝″, 5″.

> *The form shows Chinese influence.   The double zig-zag is among the earlier motives in cutting.*
> *Cf. Pl. CXLII and p. 249.*
>
> *Ladies' dressing-boxes and sweet-water bottles for "ladies' toilets" were advertised at Bath in 1766.*

S. D. Winkworth, Esq.

Casket of polished wood with panels of glass ; on a ground of light blue and dark blue mottled glass is superimposed a panel of clear glass with floral decoration in gold on the underside. About 1760. L. 10¾″, H. 7½″.

> *Fitted with the toilet bottles shown above, casket and bottles having been made for one another.*

PLATE CXXXIV

Victoria and Albert Museum.

1. Scent-bottle, blue glass painted in enamel colours; gold mounts. H. 2⅞″. (*Schreiber Collection.*)
2. Patch-box, blue glass painted in enamel colours; gold mounts. L. 2¼″.
3. Scent-bottle, blue glass cut in diamond facets and painted in enamel colours; gold mounts. H. 2⅞″.

All Bristol, about 1765. See p. 218.

PLATE CXXXV

(1 & 2) *H. R. P. Lomas, Esq.*   (3) *Victoria and Albert Museum.*

1. Water-glass (or finger-bowl), white opaque tin glass with oil-gilt decoration. Bristol, c. 1750. H. 4″.
   For similar shape cf. Pl. CIX (a 2) ; see also p. 332.
2. Water-glass (or finger-bowl), white opaque tin glass painted in enamel colours after the manner of Chinese porcelain of the *famille rose.* Bristol, about 1755. H. 2¾″.
   A similar glass appears in the Singer Catalogue.
3. Vase, white opaque tin glass with decoration painted in enamel colours in the manner of Chinese porcelain of the *famille rose.* Bristol, about 1755. H. 5¼″.

Victoria and Albert Museum.

1. Covered vase, white opaque tin glass painted in enamel colours with bouquets. Bristol, about 1755–1760. H. 10¼″. *Cf.* p. 225.
2. Candlestick, white opaque tin glass with nozzle of Battersea enamel, wrythen stem ; foot and socket painted in enamel colours probably by Michael Edkins. Bristol, about 1770. H. 9⅜″.
   For attribution cf. Frontispiece, a tea-caddy stated by his grandson to have been painted by Edkins and bearing on one side similar flower painting to that of the candlestick ; see p. 225.
3. Vase, white opaque tin glass with oil-gilt decoration. Bristol, about 1760. H. 8½″.

PLATE CXXXVI

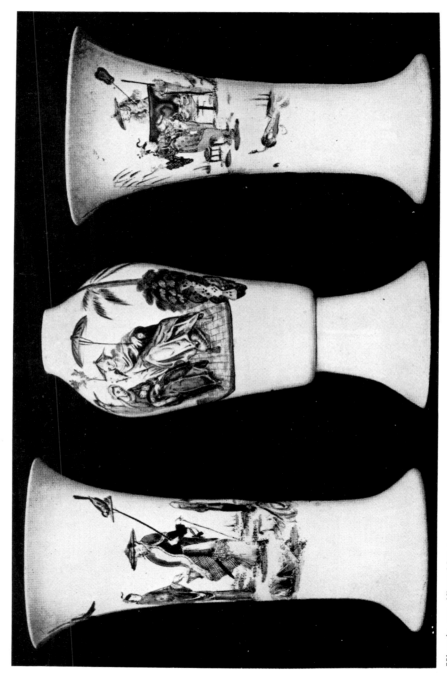

Victoria and Albert Museum.

Three vases, opaque white (tin) glass, painted in enamel colours with Chinese figures.   Bristol, about 1765.   H. 9″, 8¾″, 8″.   See pp. 225–6.

PLATE CXXXVII

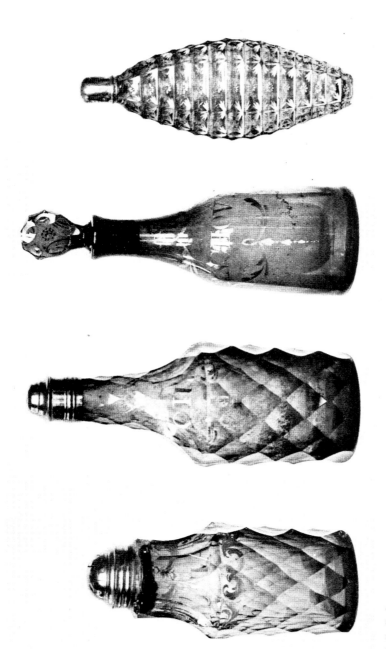

H. R. P. Lomas, Esq.

1. Mustard-bottle, blue flint glass cut in hollow diamonds and about the neck in flutes; on one side a panel of gilt rococo scrollwork containing the label. Perhaps Bristol, about 1750–1760. H. 4½".

2. Oil-bottle, as No. 1, with high mallet body and sloping neck. H. 5½".

3. Anchovy-bottle, blue flint glass, lozenge stopper cut in lunar slices, taper body slightly shouldered, gilt foliated panel containing the label. Perhaps Bristol, about 1770. H. 5½".

4. Scent-bottle, blue flint glass cut in horizontal flutes and gilt; gold cap. Perhaps Bristol, about 1770. H. 4¾".

Cf. p. 250, and for comparable silver cruet-bottle with hall-mark of 1752, see Jackson, Fig. 1096.

The colour is deeper than in Nos. 1 and 2. For a shape slightly later cf. E.I.G., Pl. II. For stopper cf. Pl. CXXVII (b 2) and Fig. 35.

PLATE CXXXVIII

Rev. and Mrs. M. de la Hey.

Wafer seal of cut-glass; the top cut in prisms, the ball cut in relief diamonds and containing a silver coin of 1750; the stem cut in hooked diamonds. English, 1750. H. 3⅞″.

By courtesy of Arthur Churchill, Esq.

Table chandelier, crescent and scalloped canopy with pendent lustres supported on a spear shaft, notched branches, plain domed foot. Probably English, *c.* 1770.

For absence of classical influence and of lustre strings contrast Pl. CXLI.

PLATE CXXXIX

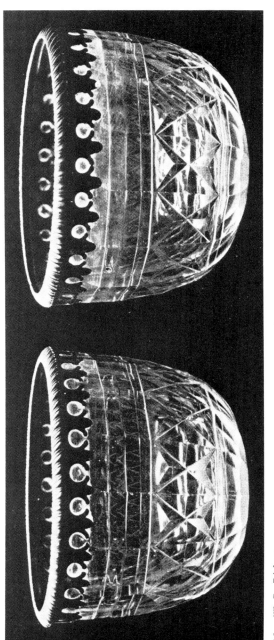

Mrs. W. D. Dickson.

Pair of bowls, cut-glass.   Below the rim a border of plain panels, round the middle a zone of large diamonds in relief, fluted base ;
silver mounts bearing the London hall-mark for 1771/72.   English, about 1771–1772.   H. 3¾″.

Apogee of English cutting.

PLATE CXL

S. D. Winkworth, Esq.

Chandelier, cut-glass ; notched urn body, three canopies cut in quadruple diamond panels and with lustres pendent from a scalloped edge, notched branches alternately supporting notched spear-shafts (themselves long and short alternately) and plain sockets for candles. English, about 1770. H. 3′ 1½″.

The canopies " Chinese."

The simplicity of the design and the absence of festooned lustres seem to indicate a date before 1780 ; in which case the chandelier is probably English. See p. 315 sq.

Cf. Bosc d'Antic, Œuvres, I, 159 (1780) : " Les Anglois ont une pâte de lustre de toute beauté. Les lustres qu'ils en font et dont il polissent supérieusement dont ils taillent et desposent avec le plus grand art toutes les pièces réfléchissent nécessairement les couleurs de l'arc en ciel ; l'emportent et pour le coup d'œil et pour leurs grands effets sur les lustres de cristal de roche. J'ai vu vendre de ces lustres jusqu'à deux cents louis d'or." The Irish florison did not begin till after 1780. For the meaning of lustre cf. Liverpool Municipal Records (1754), ed. Picton (1886), II, 160, " a glass lustre or chandelier."

PLATE CXLI

By courtesy of Arthur Churchill, Esq.

Epergne, urn-summit, scalloped canopy with pendent lustres, diamond-cut shaft, notched branches ; round the foot a circuit of relief diamonds. Probably English, about 1770–1780.

PLATE CXLII

S. D. Winkworth, Esq.

Cut-glass jug, scalloped rim, round the body a double circuit of zig-zags forming diamond panels, notched handle, domed foot cut in lozenges and scalloped foot-rim.   About 1770–1780.

Classical form with an early type of cutting.   For the notches of the handle cf. Pl. CXLI and p. 316.

PLATE CXLIII

Hamilton Clements, Esq.

1, 4. Pair of candlesticks, column stems moulded in flutes, domed feet with terraced rims. English, about 1770. H. 11″.

For the classicist influence cf. p. 255.

2, 3. Pair of candlesticks, cut-glass, nozzles scalloped, sockets cut in flat facets and stems in small flat diamonds, domed and scalloped feet cut in relief diamonds. English, about 1770. H. 14¼″.

PLATE CXLIV

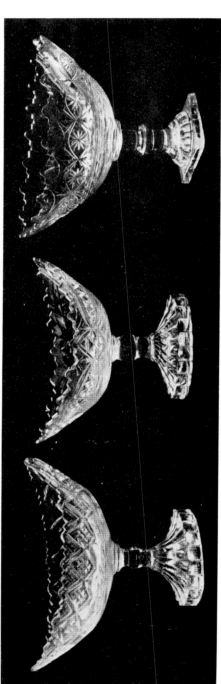

Robert Frank, Esq.

Three fruit-bowls, boat-shaped.   Probably Irish (Cork Glass Company), about 1790.   H. $10\frac{1}{2}''$, $9\frac{1}{2}''$, $9\frac{3}{4}''$.

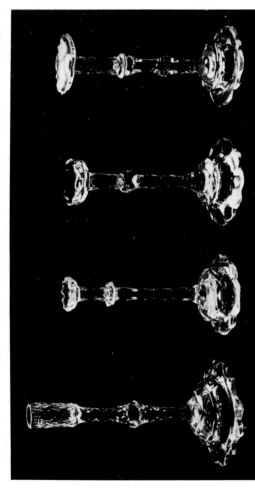

Robert Frank, Esq.

1. Taper-stick, diamond-cut socket, cusped stem cut in small diamonds, domed foot with geometrical cutting, scalloped rim.   *c. 1760–70.*   H. $7\frac{1}{2}''$.
2. Taper-stick, scalloped nozzle, cut socket with collar at the base, straight stem cut in small diamonds, domed foot with geometrical cutting, scalloped rim.   About 1770.   H. $6\frac{1}{8}''$.
3. Taper-stick, scalloped nozzle, cut socket, straight knopped stem cut in small diamonds, domed foot with the edge bevelled in fan-shaped panels and scalloped.   About 1770.   H. $6''$.
4. Taper-stick, scalloped nozzle, socket cut in flat diamonds, with a plain collar below, cusped stem cut in small diamonds, domed foot with scales round the shoulder and scalloped rim.   About 1760.   H. $6\frac{1}{4}''$.

PLATE CXLV

Robert Frank, Esq.

Jug, scalloped rim, the body cut with four rows of crossed diamonds in relief above a circuit of triple zig-zag; terraced foot. About 1780. H. $11\frac{5}{8}''$.

Classical form. For double-cut diamonds cf. Pl. CXLVIII, Fig. 28, and p. 253.

PLATE CXLVI

Mrs. W. D. Dickson.

Pair of table chandeliers of cut-glass, classical urn summit in a scalloped cup, notched spear-shaft supporting lustre chains, two notched branches supporting lustre chains ; the bases lined with blue glass gilt.
English or Irish, about 1780. H. 2′ 2″.

Notched branches went out of fashion shortly before 1788 ; *see p.* 252.

PLATE CXLVII

Cecil Davis, Esq.

Chandelier of cut-glass. Bouquet summit, scalloped canopy with pendent lustres, double balusters above a solid globe supported on double shaft ; two tiers of notched branches with lustres pendent from the lights, the upper tier supporting spear-shafts and stars ; basic canopy also with pendent lustres. English or Irish, about 1785.

For cut branches see pp. 252 and 316 ; and for an earlier chandelier of less elaborate design cf. Pl. CXL.

PLATE CXLVIII

Robert Frank, Esq.

Salad-bowl, the rim cut with quadruple relief diamonds within diamond panels, the bowl with a double circuit of lozenges ; square foot, domed. Irish, about 1785. H. 8½″.

PLATE CXLIX

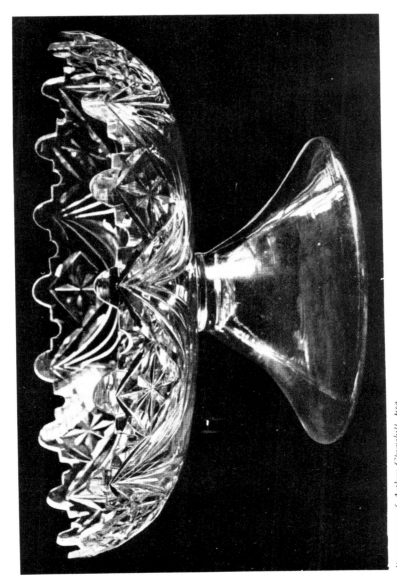

Fruit-bowl, with a circuit of large relief diamonds, double-cut, and crested rim; plain pedestal foot. Probably Irish (Cork Glass Company), about 1785.

PLATE CL

Rev. and Mrs. M. de la Hey.

(2–5) *Victoria and Albert Museum*

1. Jug, potash glass, shouldered body wrythen, folded rim. English, middle of 18th century. H. 4".

2. Jug, purple glass, shouldered body, wrythen, folded rim. English, middle of 18th century.

3. Jug, opalescent glass, pear-shaped body. English, late 18th century. H. 5".

4. Jug, pale blue potash glass, shouldered body, base moulded in flutes. English, first half of 18th century. H. 3½".

5. Jug, pale green flint glass, waisted body, wrythen; spreading foot. English, first half of 18th century. H. 4".

Jugs similar to Nos. 1 and 4 are usually "discovered" in the North of England; and they are scarcely fine enough to have travelled far from their original provenance.

PLATE CLI

(1–6) Rev. and Mrs. M. de la Hey.   *(7–9) Victoria and Albert Museum.*

1. Cruet-bottle, shouldered type, the body cut in zones of geometrical facets, the neck in flutes. Late 18th century. H. 5⅜″.

2. Cruet-bottle, shouldered type, the neck cut in flutes and cross-cut in ridges, the body in large diamonds. About 1740. H. 6½″. *Cf.* F. Buckley, Pl. XLI, 4.

3. Cruet-bottle, shouldered type, the neck cut in scales and flutes, the body in diamonds. About 1750. H. 6¼″.

4. Cruet-bottle, shouldered type, the neck cut in flutes and ridges, the body in a double lotus pattern. About 1800. H. 5⅞″.

5. Caster, the body cut in a zone of small relief diamonds above fluting ; round the neck two hatched rings. End of 18th century. H. 5¾″.

6. Cruet-bottle, urn type, cut in polygons, with flutes round the lower neck ; pared foot. About 1750. H. 4⅝″. *Cf.* F. Buckley, Pl. XLI, 2.

7. Cruet-bottle, mallet type, the neck cut in hexagons, the body with a circuit of lozenges above alternate stars and formal flowers. About 1730–1740. H. 7½″. F. Buckley, Pl. XLI, 1.

8. Caster, mallet type, the neck cut in scales, the body in flutes. About 1740. H. 7⅞″. F. Buckley, Pl. XLI, 3.

9. Vinegar-bottle, mallet type, the upper neck cut in flat diamonds, the lower neck in flutes, the body in a field of relief diamonds ; fluted pyramid stopper. About 1770. H. 6″. For shape *cf.* F. Buckley, Pl. XLII, 2.

PLATE CLII

Rev. and Mrs. M. de la Hey.

1. Trencher-salt, double blown and slightly ribbed on the outside. About 1715. H. 2⅜".
   For comparable pieces in silver also of double section, with hall-mark 1710, see Jackson, Fig. 784–5, and Watts (W. W.), Eng. Silver, 71 B (date 1723).

2. Salt, double-ogee bowl with pearl moulding above a knop. About 1740. H. 3".

3. Salt, double-ogee bowl cut in convex diamonds, scalloped rim; squashed knop with air-tears; foot-rim sliced. About 1750 or earlier. H. 3⅛".
   For relief diamonds cf. Pl. CXXXVIII (a).

4. Trencher-salt, double-blown, plain surface. About 1710. H. 2¼".
   See note to No. 1. Mr. H. R. P. Lomas has a pair of salts of this type silvered in imitation of the silver trencher salt. Plain surfaces are rather earlier than ribbing; for which cf. Pl. LXVII (b).

5. Boat-salt, cut in relief diamonds, scalloped rim, prismatic stem, parallelogram foot. English or Irish, late 18th c. H. 2⅞".

6. Salt, cut in festoons above a zig-zag, scalloped rim, cut-knop stem. English, about 1760–1770. H. 3½".

7. Boat-salt, cut in festoons at the ends with relief diamonds between, plain stem, parallelogram foot. English or Irish, about 1775–1790. H. 3⅜". Cf. Jackson, Fig. 793 (1781).

8. Salt, ogee bowl, cut in notched strands, square foot. English, about 1770–1780. H. 3½".

9. Salt-cellar without foot, rim cut in a trefoil repeat, below a diaper of simple relief diamonds. Probably Irish, late 18th century. H. 2 1/16".

PLATE CLIII

Sir John S. Risley.

1. Rummer, engraved with the arms of the Goldsmiths' Company, a crest above the initials *J.S.A.R.*, crossed heads of barley, the initials *S.W.* and the date 1790. H. 6".
2. Rummer, as christening mug, engraved with vine branch and round the rim the legend *Rebecca Creedey, Born April 23rd, 1766*. H. 5¾".
3. Rummer, engraved with Masonic emblems in a medallion flanked by crossed branches; on the other side the initials *B. S. K.* and the date 1795, above a wreath of flowers. H. 6".

See p. 327 and Burl. Mag., *June* 1921.

Mrs. W. D. Dickson.

1. Cordial-glass (" ratafia glass "), the bowl engraved with a floral border, white enamel-twist stem. About 1750–1760. H. 7¼".
2. Sweetmeat glass, double-ogee bowl with rim drawn out into a fringe; short stem with white enamel twist, foot moulded with radial ribs. About 1750. H. 4".
3. Cordial-glass (" ratafia glass "), the bowl moulded about the base in faint flutes, white enamel-twist stem. About 1750–1760. H. 8¼".

PLATE **CLIV**

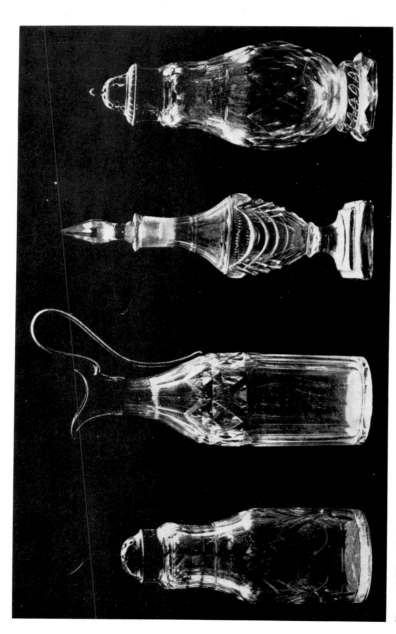

Rev. and Mrs. M. de la Hey.   (2) *Victoria and Albert Museum.*

1. Caster, cut in flutes round the neck and with a circuit of loops and zig-zag about the body. About 1765–1800. H. 5″.
2. Cruet-jug, taper-shaped, the neck and base fluted, round the middle a zone of quadruple relief diamonds. About 1770. H. 7″.
3. Vinegar-bottle, body of classical form cut with quadruple festoons, fluted neck and stem, square foot, fluted stopper. Late 18th century. H. 7″.
4. Caster, urn body cut in large flat diamonds above a squashed knop with air-tears, pared foot. About 1750. H. 5¾″.

PLATE CLV

Victoria and Albert Museum.

Portrait bust in moulded and cut glass of John Wesley. Probably Stourbridge area, about 1785. H. 6¼″.

For busts of John Wesley see an article by
Mrs. Katherine Esdaile, Times, 5. *iii.* 1928.

PLATE CLVI

S. D. Winkworth, Esq.

Two covered butter-boats with stands, cut decoration, mainly pillar-flutes, relief diamonds, and scalloping. English or Irish, about 1790.   H. 6½″, 7″.

For this later and more elaborate cutting see pp. 252, 254.

M. S. Dudley Westropp, Esq.

Bowl and stand with horizontal prismatic cutting.   Irish, about 1790.   H. 6″.

For the cutting see p. 254.

PLATE CLVII

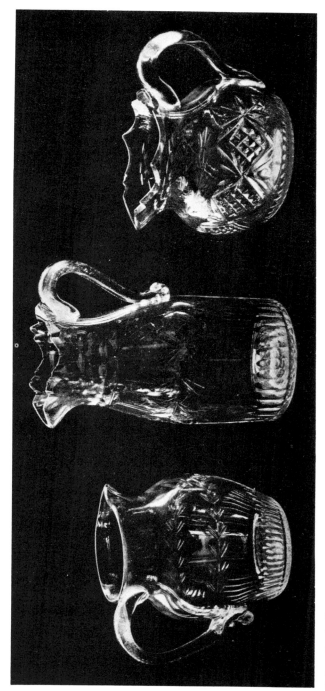

Robert Frank, Esq.

1. Jug, the body cut with a circuit of husk pattern, cut flutes round the base. English, about 1760–1770. H. 5⅞".

2. Jug, cut with lozenges round the neck, spiked circuit round the middle, and flutes round the base, scalloped rim. English or Irish, about 1770–1790. H. 8⅜".

3. Jug, cut with a circuit of panels containing relief diamonds with splits between. English or Irish, about 1790. H. 5⅞".

PLATE CLVIII

Robert Frank, Esq.

Fruit-bowl, jug, and salad-bowl, glass made for cutting but not cut. Fruit-bowl and jug English or Irish, salad-bowl probably Irish, all late 18th century. H. 7¼″, 8½″, 7″.

Henry Holford, Esq.

Three jugs with decoration cut, mainly in horizontal prisms. English, about 1800. H. 7½″, 3½″, 7½″.

PLATE CLIX

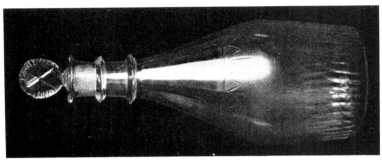

M. S. D. Westropp, Esq.

1. Decanter, barrel-shaped, round the neck three triple-rings, round the shoulder arches of small diamonds cut in relief, round the base moulded flutes; mushroom stopper. Mark, *PENROSE WATERFORD* in moulded letters on the bottom. Late 18th century. H. 9¾″. See p. 278.

2. Decanter, barrel-shaped, round the neck two double-notched rings, the middle engraved with a circuit of trellis and vesica with the letters W.O above, round the base moulded flutes; upright disc stopper with crossed-hatching. Mark, *WATERLOO CO CORK.* About 1820. H. 10½″. See p. 280.

3. Decanter, tapering barrel-shaped, the neck cut in flat flutes, comb fluting round the base; upright disc stopper with cut ornament. Probably Belfast, by B. Edwards. H. 10¾″.

PLATE CLX

Mrs. W. D. Dickson.

1. Salad-bowl and stand, cut in two fields of small relief diamonds, a zone of horizontal prisms between. Irish (probably Waterford), early 19th century. H. 7″.

2. Piggin, cut with a zone of relief diamonds on a fluted ground; dentil rim. Irish, about 1790. H. 4½″.

3. Celery-glass. Below a dentil rim a border of panels containing alternately strawberry diamonds and plain relief diamonds; below, a zone of horizontal prismatic cutting, and below it a diapered border of strawberry diamonds and transverse prismatic cutting; short stem and flat foot cut in radial grooves on the underside. Irish (probably Waterford), about 1820. H. 8″.

Mrs. W. D. Dickson.

1. Butter-dish, the sides cut with a circuit of large diamonds containing stars, fluted knop. Irish (perhaps Cork Glass Company), about 1785. H. 6″.

2. Sugar-bowl, a field of small relief diamonds below a fan rim. Irish (probably Waterford), first quarter of 19th century. H. 5¼″.

3. Butter-dish, the dish cut with a field of relief diamonds, the lid with a border of the same below horizontal prismatic cutting. Irish (probably Waterford), early 19th century. H. 5½″.

PLATE CLXI

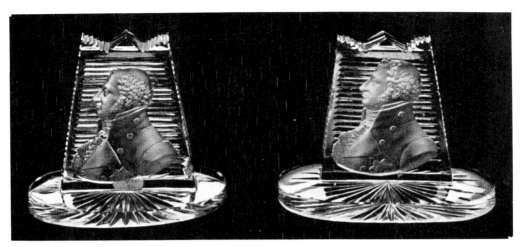

Mrs. Applewhaite Abbott.

Pair of cut-glass knife-rests, with incrusted cameo portrait of the Duke of York. Made by Apsley Pellatt at the Falcon Glassworks, Southwark, about 1820–30. H. 3⅝″, 3¾″. *For technique see pp. 289–90.*

Mrs. Applewhaite Abbott.

1. Scent-bottle, oval, with cut decoration mainly in small relief diamonds, and a classical female figure in cameo incrustation; ball-stopper. Made by Apsley Pellatt at the Falcon Glassworks, Southwark, about 1820. H. 8⅝″.

2. Candlestick with cut decoration in flutes and diamonds in relief; in the stem a classical female figure in cameo incrustation; about the tray a finger-fringe. Made by Apsley Pellatt, *c.* 1820. H. 11″.

3. Jug, with cut decoration mainly in horizontal and vertical prisms and in strawberry diamonds; in the side a group of *putti* in cameo incrustation; serrated rim and clipped handle. Made by Apsley Pellatt, about 1820. H. 7⅛″.

For incrustation see pp. 289–290, and for shape of No. 3 cf. Pl. CLVIII (a 2). This elaborate mode of cutting was well developed in 1810, a date borne by a marked piece of Pellatt's work.

PLATE CLXII

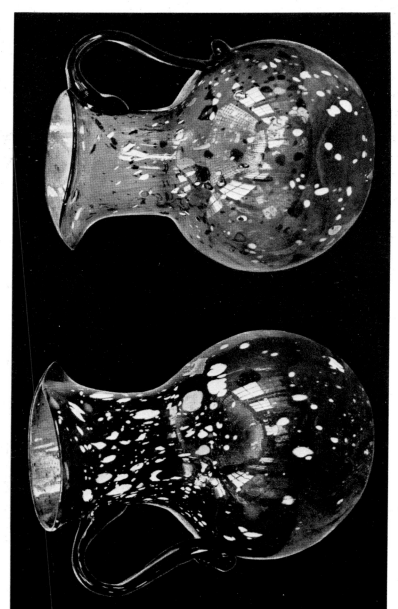

Mrs. Applewhaite Abbott.

Two jugs of greenish bottle-glass, mottled in colours. English (Nailsea type), about 1800. H. $10\frac{7}{8}''$, $10\frac{3}{8}''$.

PLATE CLXIII

The Worshipful Company of Ironmongers.

Chandelier of cut-glass, scalloped canopy fringed with pendent lustres, small urn stem cut in relief diamonds, plain uncut branches, festoons of lustre chainwork, lights encircled with a finger-fringe. English, presented to owners in 1804. H. 6′ 11″.

For the degeneration of the shaft and consequent development of festoon- and finger-work cf. back to Pl. CXLVII, CXL, and p. 315.

PLATE CLXIV

Mrs. Applewhaite Abbott.

Three vases, opaque white glass with decoration painted in enamel colours. English (Stourbridge or Birmingham), about 1830–1840. H. 7″, 10⅝″, 7″.

PLATE CLXV

By courtesy of the Orrefors Glass Company.
Tumbler with wheel-engraved decoration. By Edward Hald. Swedish (Orrefors), 20th century. H. 200 mm.

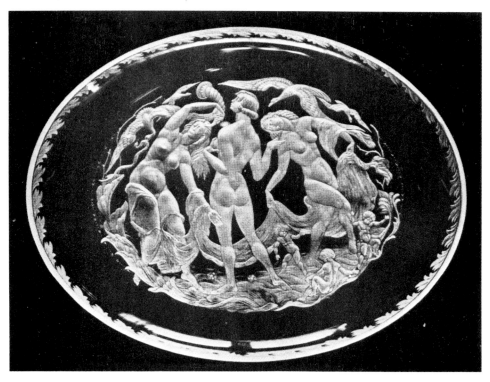

By courtesy of the Orrefors Glass Company.
Dish with wheel-engraved decoration. By Simon Gate. Swedish (Orrefors), 20th century. W. 260 mm.

PLATE CLXVI

By courtesy of Messrs. J. and L. Lobmeyr.

Beaker with design painted in black by Eva Rottenberg.   Viennese (Lobmeyr), 20th century.   H. 11·5 cm.

PLATE CLXVII

Group of wrestlers in blown and drawn glass. Viennese, 20th century. H. 6˝.

PLATE CLXVIII

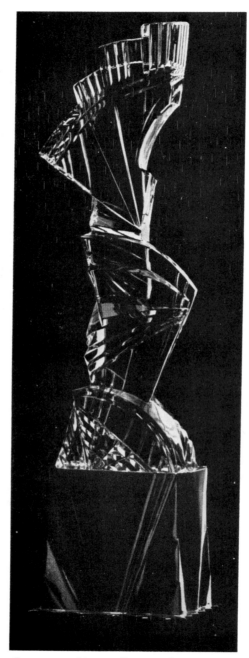

By courtesy of Messrs. J. and L. Lobmeyr.

Column of cut-glass. Viennese, 20th century. Designed by Otto Erich Wagner (School of Franz Czizek) and executed by J. and L. Lobmeyr of Vienna. H. 16¾".